Aging Matters

Aging Matters

An Introduction to Social Gerontology

Nancy R. Hooyman

University of Washington

Kevin Y. Kawamoto

H. Asuman Kiyak

PEARSON

Boston Columbus Indianapolis New York San Francisco Upper Saddle River
Amsterdam Cape Town Dubai London Madrid Milan Munich Paris Montréal Toronto
Delhi Mexico City São Paulo Sydney Hong Kong Seoul Singapore Taipei Tokyo

Editor in Chief: Ashley Dodge
Publisher: Nancy Roberts
Editorial Assistant: Molly White
Marketing Coordinator: Jessica Warren
Managing Editor: Denise Forlow
Program Manager: Mayda Bosco
Senior Operations Supervisor: Mary Fischer
Operations Specialist: Diane Peirano
Art Director: Jayne Conte
Cover Designer: Suzanne Behnke
Cover Image: Shutterstock: Monkey Business Images/Blend Images
Director of Digital Media: Brian Hyland
Digital Media Project Management: Learning Mate Solutions, Ltd. / Lynn Cohen
Digital Media Project Manager: Tina Gagliostro
Full-Service Project Management and Composition: Integra Software Services
Printer/Binder: Courier Corp.
Cover Printer: Courier Corp.
Text Font: 10/13 Adobe Caslon Pro

Credits and acknowledgments borrowed from other sources and reproduced, with permission, in this textbook appear on page 417.

Library of Congress Cataloging-in-Publication Data

Hooyman, Nancy R.
Aging matters : an introduction to social gerontology / Nancy Hooyman, H. Asuman Kiyak, Kevin Kawamoto.
pages cm
ISBN-13: 978-0-205-72764-3 (student edition : alk. paper)
ISBN-10: 0-205-72764-6 (student edition : alk. paper)
1. Gerontology. 2. Aging. 3. Older people—United States. I. Kiyak, H. Asuman, II. Kawamoto, Kevin. III. Title.
HQ1061.H5826 2015
305.26—dc23

2013031899

10 9 8 7 6 5 4 3 2 1

ISBN 10: 0-205-72764-6
ISBN 13: 978-0-205-72764-3

In dedication to students, faculty, practitioners and older adults committed to enhancing how we age across the life course—with special acknowledgment of our colleague and coauthor, Dr. Asuman Kiyak, who died before the completion of the book

—*NRH, KK*

With hope that my grandson Gus will inherit a world that supports active aging

—*NRH*

And to family and friends of all ages whose wisdom and love have enriched the world we all share.

—*KK*

Contents

3

Physical Well-Being: Physiological Changes and Health 60

4

Mental and Emotional Well-Being 100

Preface

Why This Introductory Text for Undergraduates?

Since 1987, Nancy R. Hooyman and H. Asuman Kiyak's textbook *Social Gerontology: A Multidisciplinary Perspective* has impacted thousands of students' learning about aging. It is always rewarding to hear from students and faculty in different colleges and universities nationally and internationally about how the textbook changed their knowledge and attitudes toward older adults, fostered the personal rewards that come from gaining insight into older people's lives, influenced career choices, or provided a comprehensive resource for future reference. It is deeply gratifying to have created a text that both undergraduate and graduate students find helpful and even inspiring, both personally and professionally. Indeed, it was that type of feedback that encouraged and motivated Drs. Hooyman and Kiyak to complete nine editions of *Social Gerontology: A Multidisciplinary Perspective*.

Along with the positive feedback, we would often hear comments such as "I would love to use your text but it is too dense, heavy, or long for my undergraduate class," "I wish you had a user-friendly undergraduate version of your text," or "When are you going to do an undergraduate version of your text?" Even though we knew that *Social Gerontology* was used by some instructors for upper-division courses, we consistently received feedback that it is not always appropriate for lower-division or community college courses. This book, *Aging Matters: An Introduction to Social Gerontology*, specifically responds to this criticism by attempting to meet the need for a user-friendly, readable, and evidence-based undergraduate social gerontology text. It also reflects our knowledge from teaching undergraduates—as well as research on changing attitudes toward aging—that exposing undergraduates, especially those in their early twenties, with content on aging and experiences with elders, can promote their positive attitudes, beliefs, and values about older adults. It may even influence them to consider a career working with older adults and their families.

Largely because of the visibility and influence of aging baby boomers, the issues of aging are increasingly attracting the attention of the media, politicians, businesses and industry, and the general public. Accordingly, a growing number of colleges and universities now offer coursework in gerontology. The goal of many of these courses is to prepare students to understand the process of aging and the diversity among older people, and to be able to work effectively with older adults and their families. These courses also attempt to enhance students' personal understanding of their own and others' aging. Frequently, students take such a course simply to meet a requirement, but they quickly learn how relevant the aging process is to their own or family members' lives.

We recognize that only a small proportion of students who read *Aging Matters* may pursue a specialized career in aging. But all of them are living in an increasingly older and more diverse society. Indeed, no matter what career path or work setting they choose, they will be interacting with older adults—even if they say that they don't ever want to "work with those older people." As citizens of our aging society and world, they need to see the connection between learning about the aging process and understanding their own behavior, the behavior of their parents, grandparents, neighbors, and work colleagues, and eventually the behavior of their clients, consumers, or patients across all work settings and fields.

Despite the increased visibility of more positive images of older adults, we live in an ageist society and many of us have internalized ageism. Undergraduates are not immune to holding negative views, myths and stereotypes about aging, and these need to be countered with factual information. Many undergraduates have not had positive opportunities to interact with older adults, particularly if their grandparents or great-grandparents were at a geographic distance when they were growing up. Given this likely context, we try to provide a balanced approach of both the gains and losses that often accompany the aging process. It is important for undergraduates to know that there are growing numbers of healthy active older adults and that a relatively small proportion of our society's elders is homebound or in skilled nursing homes. For example, we frequently remind the reader that we are all aging and that people can, to some extent, influence their own experience of aging. Our lifestyles during young adulthood can affect our health, cognitive and emotional well-being, and social lives in later years. We refer to recent research that demonstrates the role of individual choices and behaviors in whether we age in a healthy, active manner, or with multiple chronic diseases and without supportive social networks. But we also point to the necessity of policies, programs and communities to support aging in a healthy manner.

To help counter negative stereotypes, we emphasize that the majority of older adults continue to live in and be an integral part of their communities and contribute substantially to our cultural, family, and work lives. Recent research findings are presented on extending both years and quality of life by preventing or managing chronic diseases, enhancing active aging, and maintaining productivity (i.e., contributing to society in a wide range of ways) through both paid and unpaid activities. Examples of older adults' vital roles as family members as well as their civic engagement and volunteer activities, including cross-generational alliances related to solving social problems, are included.

But we also remind the reader that not all groups in our society, particularly those that are historically disadvantaged, low-income, or with limited education, have opportunities to experience healthy or active aging; instead, they face societal and economic barriers to productivity and civic engagement, to health promotion initiatives, even to having adequate food on the table. Therefore, we do not gloss over the very real problems of poor health, chronic illness, poverty, hunger, or inadequate housing that face many older adults—especially women, elders of color, immigrants, the oldest-old, and those living alone—and the social and health inequities and social structures that create such problems. *Aging Matters* includes numerous examples of how the economic and social well-being of older adults has been negatively affected by the worldwide recession while social and health services to support elders' well-being are cut nationwide and basic policies such as Medicare and Social Security are threatened. Growing numbers of older people must continue to be employed, or return to work, because of lost retirement income, the high cost of health care, unexpected rises in their housing costs, or even home foreclosures. Quite simply, students learn that aging matters as a social justice issue as well as a demographic challenge and that fundamental policy-level changes are needed to ensure well-being in old age.

Aims and Focus

Aging Matters is intended to be useful to a wide range of disciplines, including nursing, social work, sociology, psychology, health education, architecture, psychology, human services, and the allied health professions. Accordingly, we present the study of social gerontology from a multidisciplinary perspective. We illuminate the diversities of the aging experience related to the cultural, biological, physiological, emotional, cognitive, economic, and social aspects of aging so that students readily see how all these multiple facets interact to influence our social functioning and physical and mental well-being. We hope to convey that aging is a fascinating process (and subject to study), because these changes occur differently in each one of us. It is important for students to understand how changes within the aging individual, such as sensory modifications or issues of loss and grief, affect elders' daily interactions with social and physical environments. Through research evidence, case studies, personal illustrations, and timely excerpts from the media, we illustrate how dramatic increases in the numbers and proportion of older people in our population and worldwide have numerous implications for families, the neighborhood, and communities; the workplace; housing; health and social services; political processes; educational and recreational services; religious institutions; volunteerism; and the use of technology—and that these changes occur across multiple generations and the life course. Similarly, we emphasize that effectively addressing these complex changes requires a multidisciplinary approach.

Throughout this book, a unifying theme is the impact of these dynamic interactions between older people and their environments, including inequities based on age, gender, race, social class, and sexual orientation, on their quality of life and physical and mental well-being. But we also emphasize the remarkable resilience of older adults, many of whom have faced lifelong inequities. The differential effects that these changes have on three rapidly growing, but historically underserved, populations—women, LGBT adults, and elders of color—are frequently recognized, as well as the inner strength and resilience of these groups acknowledged. Culturally competent approaches to understand and respectfully meet the needs of an increasingly diverse older population are also identified.

We have tried to present up-to-date content, drawing upon current research, government reports, and Web sites. But because the field—and especially social, health, and long-term care policies and programs—changes so rapidly, some of the issues raised in this edition will inevitably be out of date by the time the text is published. And statistics on demography, diversity, and social-economic status will have undoubtedly altered because of the rapidly changing environmental context. Similarly, some Web site URLs may change over time. Given this, we encourage students to keep up with these changes by reading journals, periodicals, reports, and Web sites that report on recent research findings and policies related to aging and older adults.

Features and Organization of the Text

For those of you who have used Hooyman and Kiyak's *Social Gerontology*, *Aging Matters* is not simply a scaled-back version of the ninth edition. More than 20 educators nationwide reviewed the outline and provided us with insightful recommendations about how to write a text that fits for undergraduates. Here are just a few of the ways the two books differ.

- New content has been added likely to appeal to undergraduates: for example, the use of technology among older adults as well as by those who are planning communities, housing, and services to support aging in place in the community and age-friendly communities; expanded and updated content on LGBT aging and on older immigrants; and a concluding chapter on careers in aging.
- Chapters have been consolidated to reduce both their number and length.
- Although committed to ensuring that our content is evidence based and up-to-date, the number of citations is reduced to ensure readability and all citations occur at the end of the relevant paragraph.
- We have tried to use a writing style and tone that is user-friendly and to which undergraduates can easily relate.
- Each chapter includes boxed or highlighted content to help undergraduates relate to material that might otherwise seem quite distant or abstract to them and apply it to their lives. These include:
    - A list of learning objectives at the beginning of each chapter
    - Case studies or vignettes of older adults and highlights from current news stories about elders in order to bring to life many of the concepts discussed in these chapters
    - Points to Ponder for students to respond individually or in small groups to questions about the content
    - Reflection Breaks for students to think about issues privately or explore them with others
    - Easily readable and updated tables, charts, and graphs
    - An increased number and mix of color photos conveying positive and negative images of older adults
    - Discussion questions at the end of each chapter to promote a review of key concepts and critical thinking
    - A list of key terms defines key terms introduced in that chapter along with a comprehensive glossary at the end of the book

The book is designed to be completed in a semester, but readers can proceed at a faster or slower pace and select only the chapters most relevant to their focus of study.

Consistent with the multidisciplinary nature of gerontology, this book is organized in sections that first address demographic changes within the United States, other countries, and other cultures, and then the biological, psychological, and social aspects of aging. The Introduction briefly reviews the book's underlying themes, key terms, and research methods used to study aging and older people. Chapter 1 encompasses the changing demographics of the U.S. population, with attention to gender and racial differences in life expectancy and the increasing diversity of the older population by race, sexual orientation, age, and social class. Chapter 2 discusses the demographic characteristics and economic implications of aging globally and the distinctive challenges faced by older immigrants and refugees in the United States. Chapter 3 covers normal age-associated biological and physiological changes, including sensory functions, that affect older people's daily functioning as well as their risk of chronic diseases, disability, and accidents; how they cope with the most common chronic health conditions; and their use of health and long-term services and supports services, including models of chronic disease management, care transitions, and health promotion. It also addresses older adults' sexuality and intimacy, a topic that may alter many undergraduates' conceptions of older adults. Chapter 4 deals specifically with normal age-related changes in intelligence, learning, memory, and personality as well as increases in creativity and wisdom that often occur with age. It also reviews mental disorders faced by some older adults, such as depression and anxiety; the growing incidence of suicides and substance use; and the latest research on dementia, along with practices for supporting elders with such psychological disorders.

With this foundation in how physical and psychological changes affect the social aspects of aging, Chapters 5–8 focus on older adults' social well-being. Chapter 5 briefly discusses a range of social theories of aging that have shaped the types of research questions asked and, to some extent, how older adults are viewed in our society and how policies and programs are structured. These theories are also salient to understanding many of the issues faced by older adults in the context of family, friends, neighbors, and other multigenerational supports, current living arrangements, and community-based innovations in long-term care, productivity, and social/civic engagement in the later years, and the conditions under which people die. Chapter 6 addresses one of the primary components affecting how we age—informal social supports, including pets as a form of support. Whether we have friends, partners, neighbors, or children, oftentimes the intergenerational nature of these interactions affects our physical and mental well-being in old age. LGBT families are also specifically addressed. For older adults with chronic illness, disability, and increasing care needs, their social well-being is profoundly influenced by the availability of informal and formal caregivers. Chapter 7 addresses these caregivers who provide the majority of hands-on long-term personal care—family members, particularly adult children and partners, and direct care staff, and their need for supports for their vital roles, including a range of interventions. Issues of elder mistreatment by family members are acknowledged. Chapter 7 also recognizes the vital role that grandparents play as primary caregivers for their grandchildren and the distinctive challenges they face. Chapter 8 explores "productive" activities such as leisure, religious participation and spirituality, civic engagement, volunteerism and lifelong learning, and political activism that can be life enhancing and build upon older adults' strengths and resilience.

Chapter 9 discusses a subject—loss and grief—that touches the lives of all people. We include loss and grief as part of the social aspects of aging as they are profoundly social experiences that affect not only the person directly experiencing the loss but also the larger community. Loss is presented as broader than death. The loss of a home or a job, for example, can have a devastating effect on a person's life, especially as that person grows older and experiences a confluence of losses. As students read this chapter, they may be surprised to learn how many types of losses—in addition to the death of loved ones—we all experience across our life course. We also address issues salient to dying, including end-of-life care, advance care planning, and death with dignity.

The last section, Chapters 10–13, looks at the aging individual within the larger society. Chapter 10 covers retirement, employment/unemployment, economic status, poverty, and hunger, which are creating increasing challenges for growing numbers of older adults. It closes on a more optimistic note by briefly discussing changing conceptions of work and retirement that create new opportunities in old age. Chapter 11 examines where and how older adults live: different types of community-based living options as well as residential facilities, the use of technology to strengthen social connections and design age-friendly homes and communities to support aging in place, and the distinctive needs of homeless elders and older prisoners. Chapter 12 on technology, including increasing computer use by elders and universal design that help people age in place, is likely to change widely held images that older adults do not use such devices. Given the dramatically changing political arena, Chapter 13 on income maintenance, health, and long-term services and supports policies and programs—particularly Social Security, Medicare, and Medicaid—reflects contemporary debates related to federal and state budgets. It also reviews the Aging Network of basic services funded by the Older Americans Act and points to benefits for older adults funded by health care reform or the 2010 Patient Protection and Affordable Care Act (ACA). The last chapter, Chapter 14, on careers in aging, is particularly relevant to students wondering by the end of this book what kinds of jobs and careers they might find where they could work with older adults and their families. We hope that by the time they read Chapter 14 they will have realized that they will interact with older adults and their families in nearly every job setting.

We chose the title *Aging Matters* not only because the content relates to matters of aging, but also because we believe that the many topics and issues that we discuss in this book should *matter*—be of interest and concern—to people of all ages and from all walks of life. By the end of this book, students will realize that we are all affected in some way by an aging society and, perhaps more importantly, that we as individuals or in groups can contribute to creating a society where different generations live together with dignity, mutual support, and an appreciation for diversity. Such a society requires that citizens, health care providers, nonprofit organizations, businesses, governments, and other entities actively—and, in many cases, cooperatively—work toward meeting the needs of a growing and increasingly diverse older adult population.

Undergraduate students are at a pivotal stage of their lives as they consider potential career paths ahead of them, and we anticipate that this book will provide them with the knowledge, ideas, and critical questions to make informed decisions about next steps as well as planning for their own active aging. We also hope that a greater awareness of social gerontology and its multidisciplinary nature will inspire and motivate students to pursue meaningful interactions with older adults in their families, neighborhoods, communities, and workplaces. For all of us, aging matters.

Student and Teacher Resources

Pearson eText The eText that accompanies this textbook contains a variety of resources that will enhance your learning. Self-study quizzes, additional readings, or visual activities may be included as part of the virtual experience. Visit www.pearsonhighered.com to view digital options for this title.

Instructor's Resource Manual and Test Bank (0205826237) For each chapter in the text, this valuable resource provides learning objectives, chapter outline and summary, discussion questions and classroom activities, and additional resources. In addition, test questions in multiple choice, true/false, and short answer formats are available for each chapter; the answers are page-referenced to the text. The Instructor's Resource Manual and Test Bank is available to adopters at www.pearsonhighered.com.

MyTest (0205826210) This computerized software allows instructors to create their own personalized exams, to edit any or all of the existing test questions, and to add new questions. Other special features of this program include the random generation of test questions, the creation of alternative versions of the same test, scrambling question sequences, and test previews before printing. The MyTest is available to adopters at www.pearsonhighered.com.

PowerPoint™ Presentation (0205826229) These PowerPoint slides combine text and graphics for each chapter to help instructors convey sociological principles and examples in a clear and engaging way. In addition, Classroom Response System (CRS) In-Class Questions allow for instant, class-wide student responses to chapter-specific questions during lectures for teachers to gauge student comprehension. The PowerPoint Presentation is available to adopters at www.pearsonhighered.com.

This text is available in a variety of formats—digital and print. To learn more about our programs, pricing options, and customization, visit www.pearsonhighered.com.

Acknowledgments

We are grateful to the many people who have contributed significantly to the successful completion of *Aging Matters*, particularly to Brittany Barrett, a University of Washington undergraduate social work student, Varya Gracheva, Program Coordinator and Suzanne St.Peter, Gero-Ed Center Co-Director, both at the University of Washington, for their assistance with literature and Web site searches, art work, and updating references. Their willingness to do whatever tasks were necessary allowed us to concentrate on the big picture! We also thank our many colleagues around the United States who have given us valuable and candid feedback on the outline for this text. They include Laura Brown, State University of New York at Oswego; Brian Carpenter, Washington University; George Dicks, Edmonds Community College; Anna Hall, Delgado Community College; Cynthia Hancock, University of North Carolina at Charlotte; Erica Hunter, University at Albany, SUNY; Robert Johnson, University of Miami; Bruce LeBlanc, Black Hawk College; William Lugo, Eastern Connecticut State University; J. Meredith Martin, University of New Mexico; Jodi McKnight, Mid-Continent University; Julianne McMurtry, Mount St. Mary; Leah Moore, University of Central Florida; Jeanette Perlman, New York University, School of Continuing and Professional Studies; Catherine Solomon, Quinnipiac University; Alice Vestergaard, Ashford University; and Eldon L. Wegner, University of Hawaii at Manoa. We hope this new edition excites a new generation of students about seeking careers in working in some capacity with older adults and their families.

As you will learn in Chapter 14, our third author and beloved colleague Dr. H. Asuman Kiyak helped to conceptualize this text. Unfortunately, she died from cancer early in the writing process of *Aging Matters*. But her commitment to the importance of our writing an undergraduate introductory text and her enthusiasm about our approach have sustained us in our writing since her death.

Our families and good friends have been a mainstay of support throughout the preparation of this book, and we take this opportunity to express our gratitude to all of them.

An Introduction to Social Gerontology

Listen to the **Chapter Audio**

You are about to spend a quarter or a semester studying **social gerontology**, the multidisciplinary study of the biological, psychological, and social aspects of aging. You will learn why *aging matters*. Social gerontologists are interested, among other things, in how the social structure affects and is affected by the older population and the diversity of aging experiences. People who research, teach, and practice gerontology come from many different fields, including medicine, nursing, dentistry, social work, physical and occupational therapy, psychology, psychiatry, sociology, economics, political science, pharmacy, biology, architecture, urban planning, policy studies, and anthropology. We will also use the term **geriatrics**, a specialty within the health professions that is concerned with the prevention or management of diseases that may occur as individuals age.

We will begin every chapter by providing you with a list of major ideas or concepts to be covered it. In this Introduction, we discuss:

- Why aging matters: why we study social gerontology, and the kinds of perspectives we use to study it
- Key terminology in the field
- Research methods to study older adults and aging

Why Study Gerontology?

You have chosen an excellent time to study gerontology because as you are probably aware, the number of older adults in the United States and worldwide is growing rapidly and will continue to do so for several decades. You have undoubtedly heard or read about how the growth of the older population is influencing the lives of all of us, individuals as well as social institutions, such as the family, the workplace, health care and human services, religious organizations, and education. Because of gains in life expectancy (how long people are expected to live), our communities will be filled with many more older people than has been the case in past generations. You may already be observing these trends in aging in your own neighborhood or community. Or you may hear or read in the news media about the challenges facing Social Security and Medicare—two policies that benefit older adults and their families. Most certainly you have heard about health care reform (or Obamacare), but may not be aware of how it promotes older adults' well-being. Unfortunately, older adults' strengths and valuable contributions to areas such as politics, business, education, volunteer activities, and families are often not as visible in the popular media as they should be. As a whole, our society tends to view aging as a problem to be solved or even a crisis (you may have heard the term silver tsunami!), rather than recognizing the opportunities for all of us to live full lives as we age and the ways in which younger generations benefit from older ones.

Most of us tend to hold misconceptions of aging, to fear or deny it—or to focus on its negatives. This reflects what is called **ageism**, which refers to negative stereotypes about old age. As is true for sexism and racism, ageism attributes certain traits to all members of a group solely because of a characteristic they share—in this case, their age. In fact, ageism is one prejudice that we are all likely to encounter if we live long enough, regardless of our gender, race, ethnicity, social class, functional ability, or sexual orientation. A frequent result of ageism is discriminatory behavior against older persons. For example, some older workers may feel undervalued or even invisible in the workplace because of stereotypes about their abilities and productivity. Ageism is pervasive in our society—to see daily examples of it, just look at greeting cards that make fun of older adults or so-called antiaging ads that promote products to make us look as young and attractive as possible.

At this point in time, it is not possible to reverse the aging process, despite advertisements to the contrary. There is no such thing as anti-aging formulas that work. We only stop aging when we die, so if we are lucky enough to go on living, we are also fortunate enough to continue aging.

Another important point emphasized throughout this text is that people do not age in the same way. Although there are older individuals who need professional or personal care, far many more can influence their own experience of aging. Genetics plays a central role in our health status, but our lifestyles during youth and middle age also are critical in affecting our physical, emotional, and spiritual well-being at every stage in our life course. Having said this, it is important not to blame older individuals who have health problems that may be preventable. They may not have had the knowledge, financial resources, or supports earlier in their lives to make healthy lifestyle changes.

The goal for individuals at any age should not be to halt or reverse the aging process, but to age in a healthy manner, making good lifestyle choices as much as possible and nurturing supportive social networks that will serve them throughout their lives. You will read research in this book that helps you understand what you can do now to promote active aging and the positive aspects of your own aging.

In many ways, these are "the best of times" to grow old in our society, because of increasing attention given to aging by researchers, policy-makers, and funders. In recent years, the news media have been reporting a wide range of stories related to the aging of the baby boom generation—those people in the population born between 1946 and 1964. And many of these baby boomers are viewed as models of positive, resilient or active aging. However, the well-being of many people young and old has been negatively affected by the economic crises confronting our nation and the world. The high cost of living, limited affordable housing, and reduced income and retirement savings have hurt many older people. For example, many adults who were looking forward to retirement or had already retired now must continue their employment or return to work. At the same time, health care costs, living expenses, and home maintenance expenditures escalated. Moreover, the poverty rate among older adults increased slightly in 2010–2011, for the first time since the 1950s. It is important to keep in mind that poverty rates may differ for older adults from state to state and, depending on how poverty is measured, there may be many more poor elders than official statistics indicate. As people are living longer, there are societal concerns about the substantial costs needed to provide health care and long-term services and supports. So while aging has many positive aspects that we discuss throughout this book, we also balance that perspective with a realistic look at challenges that often accompany aging in contemporary society.

A Life Course and Strengths Perspective

The process of "growing old" should not be viewed as an inevitable march to dependency and increasingly poor physical or mental health. On the contrary, we can develop and sustain our internal and external resources to make the aging process an active and deliberate experience. Such resources that enable us to survive and even thrive in adversity are often described as **resiliency**. We build and strengthen our resilience throughout our lives, even in early childhood. People who have been able to overcome early hardships in their lives are often better able to cope with challenges later in life. You may know an adult who has faced numerous obstacles and losses throughout their lives, but nevertheless remains optimistic, positive, and eager to tackle new experiences. Remember that the next time you feel overwhelmed by life. Find healthy coping mechanisms that work for you—supportive social networks, exercise, meditation, yoga, creative expression, spirituality, psychological counseling, and so forth. Years down the road, these same coping approaches may enable you to deal with other, perhaps greater hardships.

Similarly, we view the study of aging from a **life course** and strengths perspective. This means that we understand older adulthood as part of a continuity of human development across the life span—from birth to old age. But it is not just a matter of individual development. Instead, a life course view takes account of historical, political, cultural, economic, and other societal circumstances that affect how we age. Throughout this book, we address how structural factors such as race, ethnicity, gender, education, social class, and sexual orientation affect the way in which we age across the life course. You will see that older women of color as a whole have a very different experience of aging than older Caucasian men, for example, because of having faced gender and racial discrimination throughout their lives, which increases the likelihood of their being poor in old age. In other words, as we age, we are affected not only by our current circumstances but also by our past experiences with both advantages and inequities.

From a **strengths perspective**, we view older adults as underutilized societal assets who have much to contribute to families, communities, and organizations. Even an elder faced with chronic illness and disability can still contribute to others through listening, offering emotional support, and sharing their wisdom. From the caregiver's side, helping to care for another human being can also strengthen core human values such as compassion, patience, and understanding as well as resilience. We encourage you to look beyond wrinkles, gray hair, or visible deficits to the strengths that most older adults have honed by living as long as they have. In doing so, you may learn a lot about how to live life fully and to age in active manner.

Reflection Break

A key concept in this chapter and throughout the book is resilience: the ability to survive difficulties in life through healthy coping mechanisms and the discovery of internal and external strengths, such as family, neighbors, or spirituality. Take a few moments to reflect on your own life, or the life of someone you know—it could be someone you know personally or have read or heard about through the media—who has faced tremendous obstacles and hardships but has managed to keep moving forward with optimism and an appreciation for life. What are some of the ways of building your resilience—your internal strength and your social supports? What are some of the strengths you have right now that you can depend on when things get difficult?

A Multidisciplinary Perspective

One of the goals of this book is to help you understand aging from a multidimensional and multidisciplinary perspective. This text is not geared to students going into any particular profession or field of study. Instead, it attempts to address the physiological, emotional, cognitive, cultural, economic, and social aspects of aging, all of which interact to influence our physical and mental well-being and social functioning throughout the life course. As you will see throughout, it is essential to understand the changes that occur within the aging individual, how these then influence their interactions with their social and physical environments, and how older persons and their family members are, in turn, affected by larger societal conditions, such as the economy and public policy.

For every generalization about the aging population, there are of course exceptions, given the tremendous diversity within this population. People age 65 and older vary greatly in their health status, productive activities, and family and social situations. Growing numbers are employed full- or part-time; most are retired. Most are relatively healthy; some are frail, suffering from chronic illnesses or dementia or homebound. Most still live—and want to remain—in a house or apartment as long as possible, but a small percentage are in retirement homes or skilled nursing facilities. Some receive comfortable incomes from pensions and investments, while others depend largely on Social Security and have little discretionary income. Most men over age 65 are married, whereas women are more likely to become widowed and live alone as they age. All of these characteristics of the heterogeneous older population–as well as others which will be addressed in the following chapters–affect the experience of aging. Indeed, the diversity of the aging experience is one of the reasons that studying older adults can be so fascinating. This book is also designed to provide a solid foundation of knowledge about aging that you can use as a way to better understand older family members, friends, and coworkers. Or this text may prepare you for more advanced study in the helping professions such as medicine, nursing, dentistry, pharmacy, physical or occupational therapy, social work, spiritual counseling, and others. As discussed more fully in Chapter 14, numerous jobs entail working with older adults in some capacity, even if that is not one's primary responsibility.

Key Terms

As with most other disciplines, the field of gerontology is constantly evolving, as is the recognition of language that makes sweeping generalizations or has negative connotations. Commonly used terms like "the elderly," "the aged," and "seniors" are frequently associated with negative images of the older population. For this reason, we have chosen the terms *older adults, older persons*, and *elders* throughout this textbook. The first two terms parallel those of younger persons/adults. The term elder, used widely among Native Americans and some Asian cultures, typically conveys respect and honor.

Another change in terminology is our use of the term *elders of color* or *people of color* rather than minorities to refer to four federally protected groups: African Americans, Latinos (including Mexican Americans/Chicanos, Puerto Ricans, Cubans, and Latin Americans), American Indians, and Asian/Pacific Islanders (APIs). These groups share the experience of collective discrimination and oppression by reason of their race. The terms *historically underserved, marginalized*, and *economically disadvantaged populations* are also used throughout the text to refer to these four groups.

We have chosen to use the word Latino in place of Hispanic wherever appropriate. This is because a growing number of scholars have suggested that Hispanic has been associated with colonialism and the conquest of Spanish-speaking people in the Americas. Except

Contrary to stereotypes of aging, elders enjoy doing many of the activities that people in younger generations do, such as playing or listening to music, as this African American couple are getting ready to do.

where dictated by publications, such as reports of the U.S. Census Bureau (where Hispanic is the standard term), we refer to older adults from Spanish-speaking origins as Latinos and Latinas.

How Do We Define Age?

Chronological aging is the definition of aging based on a person's years lived from birth. When we cite statistics about the older population in this book, we typically use a chronological marker of age 65 and older. This is how "older" is defined by the U.S. Census Bureau; additionally, for many years, it was the mandatory age of retirement, the age when a worker could receive full retirement benefits, and what our society typically considered as "turning" old. However, the age 60 is also frequently used to chronologically define "old"; for example, it is the age when a person can receive social services funded by the federal Administration on Aging. And in some traditional Asian cultures, one is considered old—and highly revered—at age 60. AARP—the largest membership organization of older adults in the United States—uses age 50 as its criteria for membership, although it may begin recruiting future members at an earlier age. And among some groups, such as the homeless and the chronically mentally ill, age 55 is considered old because they tend to face physical and health problems earlier in their lives. Globally, there may be other standards for defining an older person. In a country where life expectancy is much lower than in industrialized western nations, in many regions of Africa for example, people in their 40s may be considered old.

You probably have your own chronological definition when you consider someone to be old—or yourself to be old. And this definition may change as you age. The very concept of age is multidimensional, since people of the same chronological age could differ from each other biologically, physiologically, or psychologically.

The different chronological markers of "old age" illustrate its arbitrary nature. Throughout this book, you will see that chronological age is not necessarily related to

What Does "Old" Mean?

"Old age" may come earlier in some occupations than in others. For example, Brett Favre, quarterback for the Minnesota Vikings, threw for 33 touchdowns and 4,202 yards in 2009, leading his team to a 12–4 season and a trip to the Super Bowl. Sportswriters and fans were awed at his ability to play pro football at age 40. Despite multiple injuries and surgery, Favre returned for his 20th season in 2010, but after even more injuries, ended his football career because he was "too old." Sportswriters criticized Ken Griffey Jr. from the Seattle Mariners baseball team for being "too old" to make home runs. He retired at age 40 in the middle of the season. Fans were disappointed by this last year of play by a phenomenal athlete, who was chosen in the first-round draft pick of 1987 at age 17 and went on to make the fifth highest number of home runs in major league baseball. Or consider one of soccer's most talented players, Ronaldo, who announced his decision to retire in 2011 at age 34, saying he was not as fast as he had been in his youth and did not want to let down his team. His career spanned 18 years and made him the top goal scorer in World Cup history. These different perspectives by and about "aging" athletes makes us rethink what it means to be "old."

In contrast to athletes who are forced to retire because of age-associated physiological changes and injuries, politicians and intellectuals who are still productive at age 85 and older are often considered "sages" in their accomplishments. Until shortly before his death at age 92, Senator Robert Byrd of West Virginia—the longest-serving member of Congress—was participating in debates and casting votes in the Senate. Economist Paul Volcker, Chair of the Federal Reserve under Presidents Carter and Reagan, was appointed by President Barack Obama to chair the Economic Recovery Advisory Board in 2009 at age 83. He continues to speak out in favor of regulatory reform of U.S. banks. Can you think of other examples of how "old" varies with one's occupation?

a person's well-being, quality of life, or ability to function on a daily basis. You may know someone who exercises consistently and appears "physically young," but is chronologically old—or someone who is impaired and appears to be quite old in terms of their ability to carry out daily tasks, but is only in their 40s. Or you may remark that someone "looks younger (or older)" or "acts younger (or older)" than her or his age. This implies that the individual's biological or psychological or social age—which is not captured by the demographics of aging—does not seem consistent with their *chronological age.* These are critical distinctions in any discussion of the diversity of the aging experience:

- **Biological aging** or physiological changes reduce the efficiency of organ systems, such as the lungs, heart, and the circulatory system.
- **Psychological aging** encompasses alterations that occur in cognitive abilities (e.g., memory, learning, and intelligence), emotions and adaptive capacity, and personality.
- **Social aging** comprises an individual's changing roles and relationships with family, friends, and other informal supports, and both paid and unpaid productive roles such as work and volunteering.

So although you may hear the term "older adults" used as if describing a large and homogeneous category of people, remember they are actually more diverse than any other age group and becoming more so in the coming years. There is considerable truth to the statement that as we grow older, we become more unlike each other.

Cohort is another key term for understanding the wide variation of characteristics among the older population. **Birth cohort** is used to describe groups of people who were born at approximately the same time and therefore share many common life experiences. For example, cohorts now in their late 90s experienced the Great Depression and World War II, which profoundly shaped their lives. You or your parents may have known older people from the Depression-era cohort who saved everything and were frugal throughout their lives. Or someone who fought in World War II, often defined as the Greatest Generation, who benefited from the post-war boom in jobs and education, but perhaps never talked about horrific wartime experiences until late in life. The Great Depression and World War II generations also include large numbers of immigrants to the United States early in the twentieth century and many who have grown up in rural areas. Their average levels of education are lower than those of later cohorts, such as those growing up during the Vietnam War. Such cohort differences must be taken into account in any studies of older adults as well as policies and services to address their needs. Birth cohorts also influence the general population, as is the current situation with the aging of the baby boomers and how they are redefining aging, just as they redefined lifestyles earlier in their lives.

How Do We Study Older Adults?

As you read this text, you may find yourself wondering, how do we know what we know about older adults? Throughout, we draw upon a wide range of research from multiple disciplines. We next review some of the research methods that have been used to help us better understand older adults. Keep in mind, though, that this is a basic overview. Entire college courses are offered on research methods, and sometimes a single class may be devoted to just one method. What we offer here is meant to give you a sense of where our current knowledge about older adults comes from. Moreover, one of the many reasons that the field of gerontology, which is so complex and rapidly changing, is an exciting one is that there are constantly new research findings. Indeed, this means that sometimes recent research conclusions may appear to contradict earlier studies as well as many of your own beliefs about aging and the older population. So it is important for you to turn to up-to-date Web sites and recent publications for the latest research findings on any particular gerontological topic.

Research Methods

A major way of understanding how a person changes over time requires that a person be studied over a long period of time. This kind of research is known as a **longitudinal study**. It involves the measurement of the same person over a specified period of time, typically years. The Baltimore Longitudinal Study of Aging (BLSA) is the largest and longest-running such study, and we draw upon findings from the BLSA throughout this book.

Studying Older Adults for More Than Half a Century

The National Institute on Aging (NIA) conducts research to learn about the changes that take place as we age. One goal of NIA research is to help us understand medical problems that are common in older people. The NIA supports the Baltimore Longitudinal Study of Aging (BLSA), America's longest-running scientific study of human aging, begun in 1958. BLSA scientists are learning what happens as people age and how to sort out changes due to aging from those attributed to disease. More than 1,400 men and women are study volunteers, and range in age from their 20s to their 90s (http://www.blsa.nih.gov/).

The Kuakini Honolulu Heart Program, funded by the National Heart, Lung, and Blood Institute since 1965, is another example of a longitudinal design. This study followed 8,000 men of Japanese ancestry living on the island of Oahu in Hawaii. Researchers observed the participants' incidence of coronary heart disease and stroke over a period of decades. Findings have played a part in the U.S. government's recommended dietary guidelines, in the development of rehabilitation programs for heart attack victims, and in the discovery of "good cholesterol."

Although significant information can be gained from longitudinal studies, one major problem is that they are extremely expensive to conduct. You can imagine the time, energy, and expense involved in studying such a large group of people over such a long period of time. As is the case with many types of research, it also is not always clear how generalizable the findings are to the larger population. In other words, if the study participants do not reflect the larger population (in distribution by gender, age, ethnicity, educational attainment, income, health status, and so forth), are the findings from the study applicable to the general population?

Another type of study is referred to as **cross-sectional** and compares people of different chronological ages at the same measurement period. These studies are the most common in gerontology. Specifically, researchers compare a number of study participants of different ages on the same characteristics in order to determine age-related differences. Cross-sectional studies are frequently used because data can be readily gathered compared to other designs. An example would be a study comparing church attendance by American adults under age 65 with those 65 and older. The average differences among different age groups in each study might suggest the conclusions that people become more religious as they age. But the difference could also be explained by particular cultural and historical conditions (the birth cohort effect that we discussed above) that shaped each group of participants being studied. For example, a higher rate of church attendance among today's older adults than among younger adults probably reflects generational differences in attitudes toward attending church, as opposed to becoming more religious as we age. The major limitation of cross-sectional studies occurs when differences among younger and older respondents are erroneously attributed to growing old.

Sequential designs are another research method. Three types of sequential designs are (1) cohort-sequential, (2) time sequential, and (3) cross-sequential. A cohort-sequential design is an extension of the longitudinal design, whereby two or more cohorts or groups are followed for a period of time so that measurements are taken of different cohorts at the same ages but at different points in time. The time-sequential design is useful for distinguishing between age and time of measurement or historical factors. It can be used to determine if changes observed are due to aging or to historical factors. The researcher using this design would compare two or more cross-sectional samples at two or more measurement periods. The third technique is the cross-sequential design, which combines cross-sectional and longitudinal designs.

There are many other types of research methodologies that can be used to study and understand older adults. These may include observation in natural settings—for example, watching and documenting activities and interactions at a community center for older adults—or conducting in-depth interviews with older adults or their caregivers. U.S. Census data—along with other large databases such as the National Health and Retirement Study of more than 22,000 adults age 50 and older—are a primary source for research. Simple surveys—questionnaires—can be administered to groups of people to gather descriptive data. For example, you may want to find out from a group of 50 older adult participants at a senior center how many of them have a Facebook account and, among those who have one, how many visit their Facebook page once a week or more. In any type of research that you may do, you must consider ethical issues and be sure that you are taking account of factors such as confidentiality and safety of the participants.

Sampling, or how the participants for the study are selected, is a major challenge for researchers. If the sample is not representative, the results are of questionable external validity. In other words, the results cannot be used to make generalizations about the larger population. A representative sample means that each person in the sample was randomly selected from the larger population. However, comprehensive lists of older people are not readily available. Membership lists from organizations such as AARP tend to over represent those who are healthy, white, and financially secure. Studies in long-term care facilities tend to over represent those with chronic impairments. Because whites represent the vast majority of the population over age 65 today, it is not surprising that they are more readily available for research. But this is changing with the increasing racial and ethnic diversity of the older population and will necessitate culturally competent strategies to recruit elders from different cultural backgrounds to participate in research.

Reaching older persons of color through organizational lists can be especially difficult. More effective means of recruiting these groups involve the active participation of community leaders such as ministers and respected elders in churches or local community organizations attended by the population of interest. The problem of ensuring diverse samples of research participants is compounded if some elders of color mistrust research. Many African Americans, in particular, know about the unethical practices of the studies conducted in the early twentieth century where blacks were unknowingly exposed to illness as part of the study, and may be reluctant to participate in research today, despite significant improvements in the ethics of human research. Researchers must be sensitive to these issues when attempting to recruit elders of color into research projects. As another example, lesbian, gay, bisexual, and transgender (LGBT) older adults may be reluctant to disclose their sexual orientation to a researcher.

Such a disproportionate focus on whites and lack of data on historically underserved groups have slowed the development of gerontological theories that consider the impact of race, ethnicity, culture, and sexual orientation on the aging process. Yet, even as researchers and funding agencies emphasize the need to include more people of color in all types of research, multiple confounding factors must be considered. For example, Latino elders represent U.S.-born as well as immigrant populations who have come here from countries as diverse as Mexico, Cuba, and Argentina and speak different Spanish dialects. Therefore, any research that includes racial groups must distinguish among subgroups by language, place of birth, nationality, ethnicity, and religion, not just the broader categories of Latino, African American, and Asian. It is not necessary to include all possible subgroups of a particular racial population in a given study. However, it behooves the researcher to state clearly who is represented in order to assure appropriate generalizability of the findings.

As mentioned earlier, a comprehensive discussion of research methods can take up an entire semester. This relatively brief discussion should give you an idea of some ways that older adults have been studied—and some of the challenges of doing so. There are other ways, and we encourage you to do further investigation of research methods if this is a subject that interests you.

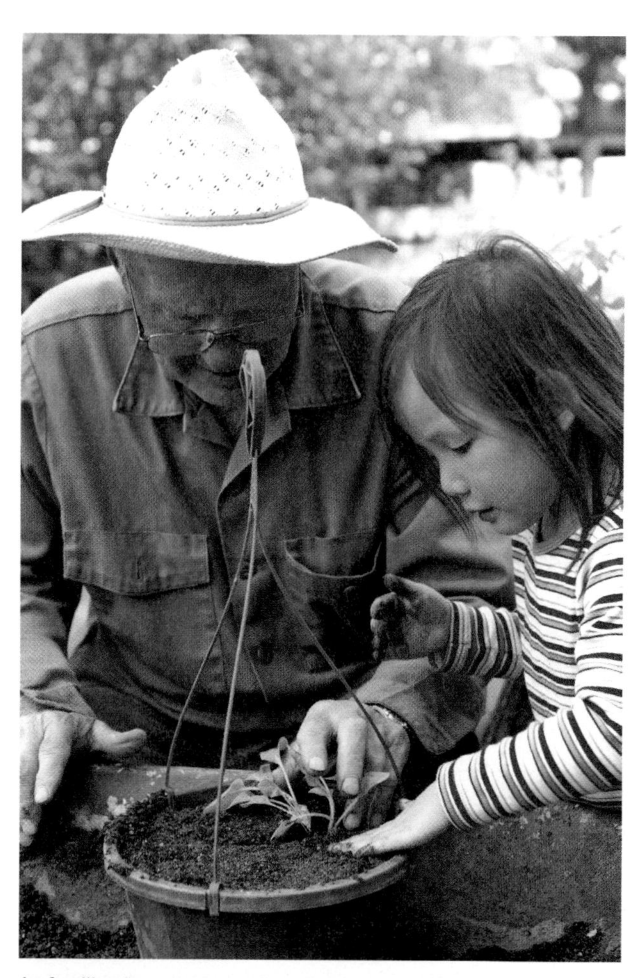

As families become more diverse, an emerging research area is interracial intergenerational relations.

summary

This text presents the study of social gerontology from a multidisciplinary perspective, with topics related to the biological, psychological, and social aspects of aging. It is geared toward students who may go into a wide range of fields where they will interact with older adults or who want to be informed about aging for personal reasons. Two key terms you will encounter in this text is gerontology, which is the study of aging, and geriatrics, which is a specialized medical field focused on the prevention and treatment of diseases related to aging.

Although many people would define age as the number of years a person is from birth (i.e., chronological age), this is only one way to define age. There is also biological, psychological, and social aging. This means that two individuals who are 65 years old in chronological age may have bodies whose organ systems (e.g., kidneys, liver, and heart) or learning and memory function vary differently from each other. These differences may be due to genetics, lifestyle choices, societal conditions, the cohort in which one was born—or all these factors. We can all make healthy choices throughout our lives to promote active aging, but there are many variables influencing how we age that we cannot control.

Research on older adults involves many different methods, each with its strengths and limitations. Some research helps us understand a group of individuals with particular characteristics, but whether those findings apply to a more heterogeneous group of older adults is not clear. More research on diverse groups of older adults using a wide range of methods is needed to continue our understanding of older adulthood and the diversity of aging experiences, including the factors that promote resilience and active aging.

key terms

ageism, p. 2
baby boom, p. 3
biological aging, p. 6
Birth cohort, p. 6
chronological aging, p. 5
cohort, p. 6
cross-sectional, p. 7
geriatrics, p. 2
life course, p. 3
longitudinal study, p. 6
psychological aging, p. 6
resiliency, p. 3
sequential designs, p. 7
social aging, p. 6
social gerontology, p. 2
strengths perspective, p. 3

review questions

1. How does the term geriatrics differ from gerontology?
2. What are some of the limitations of chronological age to describe an older adult?
3. How would you define biological, psychological, and social aging?
4. Define cohorts and give two examples of how cohort affects a person's experience of aging.
5. Briefly describe what the concept of resiliency means.
6. What are some limitations of cross-sectional research designs? What are some advantages of longitudinal research designs?

1 The Older Population in the United States

learning objectives

1.1 Demonstrate knowledge of changing demographics of the U.S. population, especially as related to aging.

1.2 Describe the increasing diversity among the older population and its social impact.

1.3 Discuss the need to plan and prepare for an aging population.

Listen to the **Chapter Audio**

You have probably heard of baby boomers—the cohort or group of people born between 1946 and 1964, a period starting just after the end of World War II and one of prosperity and growth for the United States. Perhaps your parents or grandparents are part of this cohort, which are groups of people born at approximately the same time span and therefore share many common life and historical experiences and characteristics. This generation was born and spent their youth in an affluent, economically booming era. They experienced upheaval during their high school and college years, including protests against the Vietnam War; rock "n" roll, drugs and the sexual revolution; and the Civil Rights and women's movements. Having come of age during the tumultuous period of the 1960s and early 1970s, baby boomers may be the first U.S. generation to experience a mixture of national pride and cynicism about the role of their country in the world. They are more highly educated, are healthier, have a higher percent of women in the labor force, are more likely to hold professional and managerial jobs, and are more diverse than prior cohorts. Of course, there are exceptions to these patterns, especially because some baby boomers have seen their incomes and retirement savings markedly decline during the Great Recession that began in 2008. Just as baby boomers redefined lifestyles when they were younger, they are now changing what it means to grow old in America. And a primary reason that we hear so much about this generation is that since January 2011, 10,000 baby boomers turn age 65 each day. Currently numbering 79 million, they are part of a phenomenon sometimes also referred to as the "senior boom" (Administration on Aging (AoA), 2012; Frey, 2010).

The baby boomers—or the young-old—tend to be healthier and more active than previous generations of older adults.

In this chapter, we will provide you with an overview of the older adult population in the United States. This includes:

- Changing demographics of the U.S. population
- Life expectancy and life span
- Rapid growth of the old-old and oldest-old
- Increasing diversity among the older population
- Trends for the future: Increased longevity in health or disease?

Changing Demographics of the U.S. Population

The senior boomers are changing the **demographics** of our country. By this we mean the characteristics of our population, such as its size, distribution of the very old and the very young, and geographic location. **Demographic trends** describe the changes in such characteristics over time. The long-range trend—and the focus of this book—is **population aging**, which refers to the sheer increase in the size of the population age 65 and older and a gain in the average age of a population. Population aging—fueled by baby boomers—is one of the most dramatic demographic changes in the United States and worldwide and is illustrated in Figure 1.1. Indeed, there is no historical precedent for population aging in any society around the world. It is the result of declines in birthrates and death rates, and differs from the **individual aging process**—or the physiological, psychological, and social changes of aging that we discuss throughout this book. We also consider other demographic characteristics such as race, ethnicity, gender, social class, education, sexual orientation, functional ability, and health status that impact the process of individual aging—sometimes more so than does chronological age.

- In 1900, people age 65 and older accounted for about 4 percent of the U.S. population—less than 1 in 25.
- By 2011, slightly more than 100 years later, they had grown to over 40 million, or almost 13.1 percent of the population. People over age 65 increased by almost 13 times during this period, compared with a threefold increase in the population under age 65.
- For the first time in history, by 2020, there will be more people age 65 and older than children under age 5.

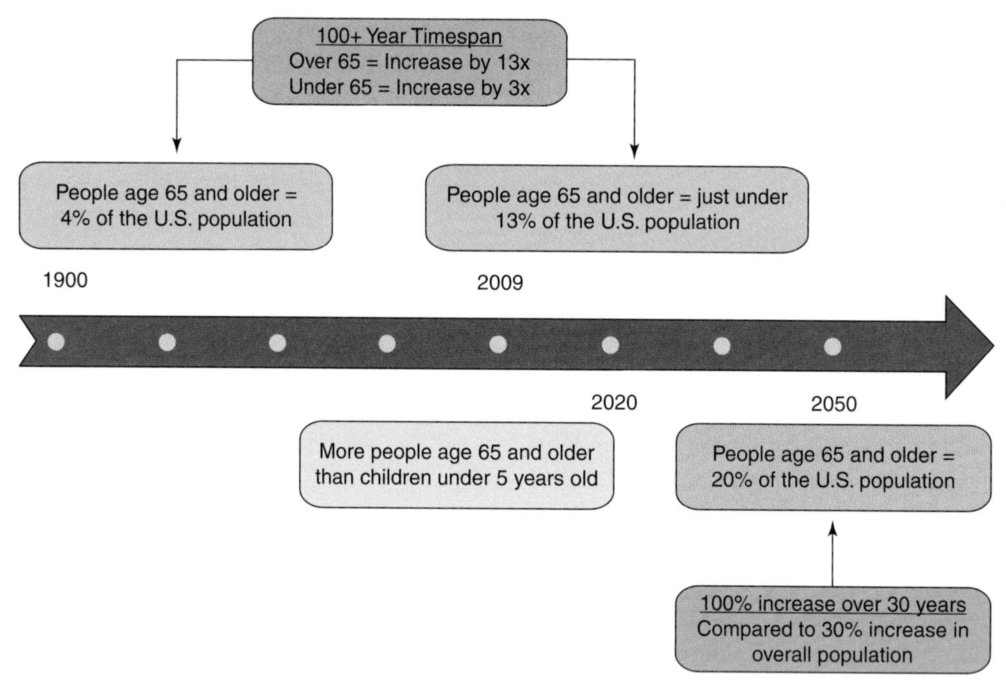

FIGURE 1.1 Population Aging, 1900–2050

Source: AoA 2012, "A Profile of Older Adults in America: 2011."

- By 2050, people age 65 and older may comprise nearly 87 million, more than twice their current number, or about 21 percent of the population. This represents a projected 147 percent increase since 2000, compared with a 49 percent growth in the overall population during the same time period (AoA, 2012; Howden & Meyer, 2011; U.S. Census Bureau News, 2011b).

points to ponder

Take a moment to reflect on what you know about the generation that came of age during the 1960s. Are your parents or perhaps your grandparents baby boomers? What have they told you about that time period? Were they engaged in any of the protests that burst onto the national scene? How did their experiences in the 1960s affect them in middle age and now in old age?

Changes in Life Expectancy

Why is the older population growing so rapidly? Chiefly because of increasing life expectancy—quite simply, people are living longer. Keep the term **life expectancy** (i.e., the average length of time one could expect to live if one were born in a particular year and if death rates were to remain constant) in mind as we refer to it throughout the book.

- In 1900, the average life expectancy at birth in the United States was 47 years.
- Today it is 30 years longer—slightly more than 78 years.
- It will be in the mid-eighties by 2050 (AoA, 2012; Federal Interagency Forum, 2012; U.S. Census Bureau News, 2011).

But population aging is also due to falling birthrates; when children are a smaller percent in the population, the average age of the population increases. In recent years, the birthrate in the U.S. has been declining. For teens ages 15–19 and for women in their early twenties, for example, the birthrate hit record lows in 2012 (Hamilton, Martin, & Ventura, 2013).

Look around your classroom. Four out of five of your classmates can expect to reach age 65, at which point there is a better than 50 percent chance for them to live past age 80. In fact, people who make it to age 65 today have an average life expectancy of an additional 19.2 years. This is a dramatic improvement from the early twentieth century, when it was 12.3 more years (Federal Interagency Forum, 2012).

The increase in life expectancy and the declining birthrate underlie an unusually rapid rise in the **median age** of the U.S. population—from 28 in 1970 to over 37 years currently. This means that half the population is older than 37 years and half younger. The median age will rise as even more Americans live into their eighties and nineties by 2030 (Howden & Meyer, 2011).

The world's oldest person changes often as verified record-holders die and are replaced by the next in line. For example, when Mr. Jiroemon Kimura, the world's oldest person—at the time—died in Japan in June 2013 at the age of 116, "the oldest person in the world" title passed on to another Japanese citizen, Ms. Misao Okawa, who was verified to be 115 years old. Sometimes individuals claim to be older than the person who is reported to be the oldest person in the world, but those claims cannot be independently verified (Hume, 2013).

points to **ponder**

You are learning about how people in the United States and many other parts of the world are living longer than they have in previous generations. In your opinion, is living a long life always a good thing? Or are there things that you would fear about living a long time? Try completing this statement: "I would like to live a long life—into my nineties or longer—if..." What are the personal and societal factors that would contribute to the quality of a long life?

It may surprise you to learn that the U.S. life expectancy lags behind that of 51 other countries. This is true despite the fact that U.S. medical expenditures, often for groundbreaking medical technology, are the highest in the world. Why do you think this might be the case? Factors such as better prenatal and early childhood services, more access to health care, and healthier foods in other countries contribute to their higher life expectancy rates at birth than those in the United States. Life expectancy in the United States is not rising as fast as it once was and is actually declining in the South. Increasing rates of poverty, obesity, heart disease, and diabetes along with past high rates of cigarette smoking may be contributing factors. Life expectancy may also be related to growing income inequality. When compared with 32 other developed countries, the United States has the third greatest disparity between its richest and poorest citizens. Only Singapore and Hong Kong have worse disparities (The Commonwealth Fund, 2011; Muennig & Glied, 2011).

Calculating Your Own Life Expectancy

You can calculate your own life expectancy online. You will see how important lifestyle factors, such as nutrition, exercise, and not smoking, are to how long you are likely to live. Developed by Dr. Thomas Perls, a highly regarded geriatrician who has studied centenarians, the Living to 100 Life Expectancy Calculator not only tells you how long you are likely to live, but it also offers personalized feedback from Dr. Perls on ways to live longer. Try Googling this life expectancy calculator or another one on the Web and plugging in your own numbers (Blow, 2011; Boyles, 2011; DyBunco, 2011).

Throughout this book, we will give numerous examples of lifestyle choices that can increase your chances of aging in a healthy manner. If you are a 20-year-old reading this, you will probably live well into your eighties, barring accidents or natural disasters. Consider what your life might be like then by completing the "When I am age 80" exercise on page 14.

Most gains in life expectancy have occurred in the younger ages, largely due to the eradication of many diseases that caused high infant and childhood mortality. Maternal, infant, and early childhood death rates have declined considerably, primarily because of improved sanitation, antibiotics, and advances in medicine. But the increase in life expectancy is also due to medical advances in middle and old age. A hundred years ago, adults generally died from acute diseases, particularly influenza and pneumonia. Few people survived long enough to need care for chronic or long-term conditions. Today, death from acute diseases is rare. The result is a growing number of people who survive to old age, but often with one or more **chronic diseases** that require long-term services and supports. For example, heart disease and cancer have become less fatal because of medical breakthroughs. Instead, they have become chronic illnesses, with many older adults who may keep on living for years with these "killer" conditions. Because of these shifts, health care providers refer to the need for chronic disease management rather than a cure. Indeed, medical advances such as stem cell therapy are likely to postpone deaths from heart disease and cancer even more. In the near term, however, gender and racial differences in life expectancy are likely to persist.

When I Am Age 80

What will your life be like at age 80?

Physical: Assume that you will get at least one major disease that runs in your family. You may already have some signs of that illness or disability now. Look at the members of your family, and extrapolate what physical problems you might have as well as physical advantages. Think about your five senses and which of them will have been impacted by aging and to what degree. Will you be able to communicate verbally or will you have to rely on nonverbal means of communication?

Social: What kind of a family and personal lifestyle will you have when you are older? What type of living situation will you be in? Will you have any hobbies? Where will you go when/if you go out? How will you get there and with whom (e.g., your spouse, partner, adult child, neighbor)?

Financial: What will your finances be like when you are older? Extrapolate from how you handle money *currently* in your life. Are you a saver or a spender? Will you have a retirement pension or will you have to rely entirely on Social Security?

Emotional/Mental: What kind of individual will you be? Research shows that our personalities do not change significantly as we age, but we become more like our "true selves" as a result of loss, change, stress, and illness. For example, if you now become irate fairly easily in traffic, what will you be like in the dining room of a group-living situation as you wait for your food to be served? How will you adapt to new technologies and social values? What will you do to keep your mind as sharp as possible?

Spiritual: How important will religion or spirituality be to you? Extrapolate from how important it is to you *now*. How will you practice your faith, or if you have none, what will be most important to you as you think about your own death?

Legacy: Since you are 80, you are thinking about what you will leave behind, in terms of both tangible items and intangible qualities about yourself. What will you be remembered for or what would you like to be remembered for?

Add in other things that you feel will be important to you at that age, or concerns that you will have that are not on the list. And then think about changes you might make in your life now to increase your chances of an active old age. What did you learn from this that may affect how you view older adults and aging?

Gender Differences in Life Expectancy

If you are at a social gathering of older adults, you may see more women in attendance than men—a sign men and women differ in how long they live:

- On average, females born today will live 5–6 years longer than men: 80.8 years compared to 75.7, respectively.
- Even at age 85, female life expectancy is an additional 6.8 years compared to 5.7 years for males (Federal Interagency Forum, 2012; U.S. Census Bureau, 2011).

No one fully understands why women live longer than men, but several different explanations are supported by research. Women's longer life expectancy may be due to a combination of biological factors, such as the genetic theory that the female's two X chromosomes make her physiologically more robust, and of lifestyle factors, such as women's greater likelihood of preventive health behaviors and their lower rates of smoking, substance abuse, and other high-risk behaviors across the life course. However, men who survive beyond age 85 are also likely to be "hardier"—to have fewer chronic illnesses or disabilities (AoA, 2012; Federal Interagency Forum, 2012).

As a result of these differences in life expectancy:

- Women represent 58 percent of the population age 65 and older, and nearly 70 percent of those over age 85. This means that there are approximately 135 women for every 100 men age 65 and older.
- Women at age 85 and over outnumber their male counterparts by five to two and among centenarians by three to one (AoA, 2012; Federal Interagency Forum, 2012; U.S. Census Bureau, 2011).

This pattern of increasing proportions of women relative to men after age 65 in 2010, 2030, and 2050 is shown in Figure 1.2 on page 15.

Racial Differences in Life Expectancy

Given their experiences of historical disadvantage across the life course, it is not surprising that elders of color in our country have a lower life expectancy than whites. For example, life expectancy at birth is approximately five years higher for white people than for African Americans.

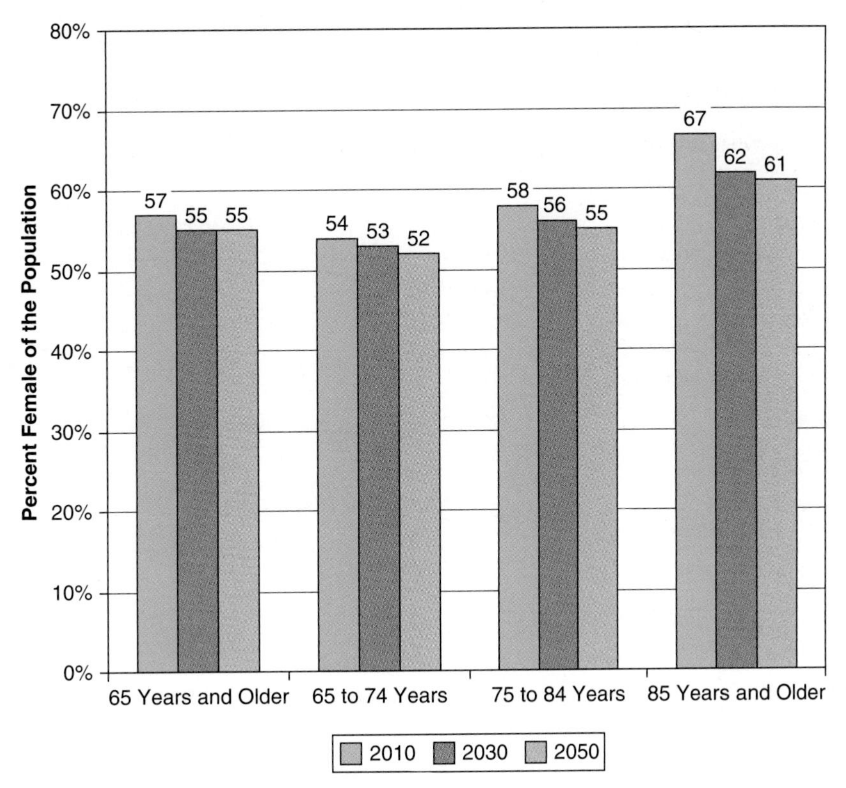

FIGURE 1.2 Percent Female for the Older Population by Age for the United States: 2010, 2030, and 2050

Source: U.S. Census Bureau, 2010, "The Next Four Decades: The Older Population in the U.S.: 2010–2050."

Figure 1.3 on p. 16 shows life expectancy at birth, by race and sex in the United States. One factor that underlies African Americans' shorter life expectancy is health care disparities—the current cohort of elders of color generally had unequal access to health care and preventive health services earlier in life. Consistent with the concept of the life course, inequities experienced as children and young adults in poverty, education, and health care are often intensified in old age, as reflected in lower life expectancy and more chronic illness. On the other hand, African Americans (especially men) who survive to age 75 tend to be the most robust of their cohort, so that their life expectancy after age 75 is longer than for whites. This is known as the **crossover effect** (Center for American Progress, 2010; Federal Interagency Forum, 2012; Sinn, 2011).

As is true with the total population of elders, women of color generally live longer than their male counterparts, with Asian American women living the longest. Among African Americans, the ratio of men to women age 65–75 is slightly lower than among other groups, because of higher death rates among African American men at every age. Tragically, some African American men do not live long enough to ever collect Social Security, because of their high rates of homicides and accidents in young and mid-adulthood and of chronic illness in their early sixties. Oldest-old women are the most rapidly growing group of African American elders, and they have the longest average remaining life expectancy.

In contrast, there are proportionately more Latino men to women over age 65 than among the white older population, even though Latina women live longer and outnumber men. The slight increase in proportion of men is due to the higher mortality rate of Latinas than white women at earlier ages, not to greater life expectancy among Latino men. Older Latino men marry or remarry more often than men in other groups of color: over 65 percent of older Latino males are married, but only 39 percent of older Latinas. Latinas more often remain widowed and live alone than their male counterparts. Nevertheless, the percentage of older Latinas living alone is lower than that of the general population, while the percentage living with other relatives is almost twice as high. This living arrangement points to the

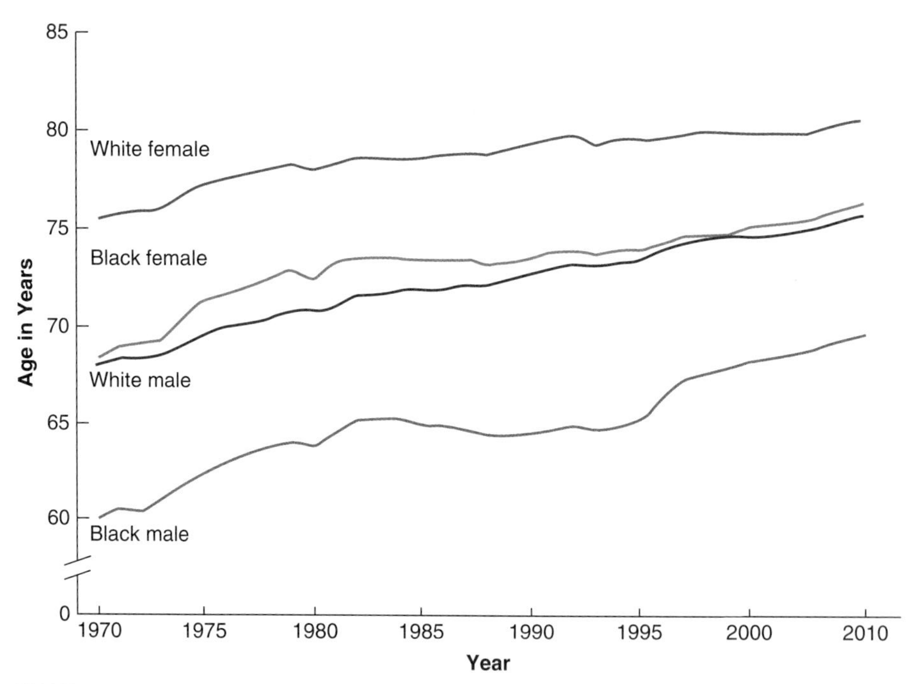

FIGURE 1.3 Life Expectancy at Birth, by Race and Sex: United States, 1970–2010

Source: U.S. National Center for Health Statistics, 2009.

importance of extended family among Latinos (CDC, 2011a; Russell, 2011).

Compared to other older adults of color and to white older persons, Asian-Pacific Islander (API) men outnumber their female counterparts until they reach age 75 and older. They also constitute a large percent of elders living alone. This pattern reflects the continuing influence of more API men than women immigrating in the early part of the twentieth century to the United States, and past restrictions on female immigration, rather than a higher life expectancy for men.

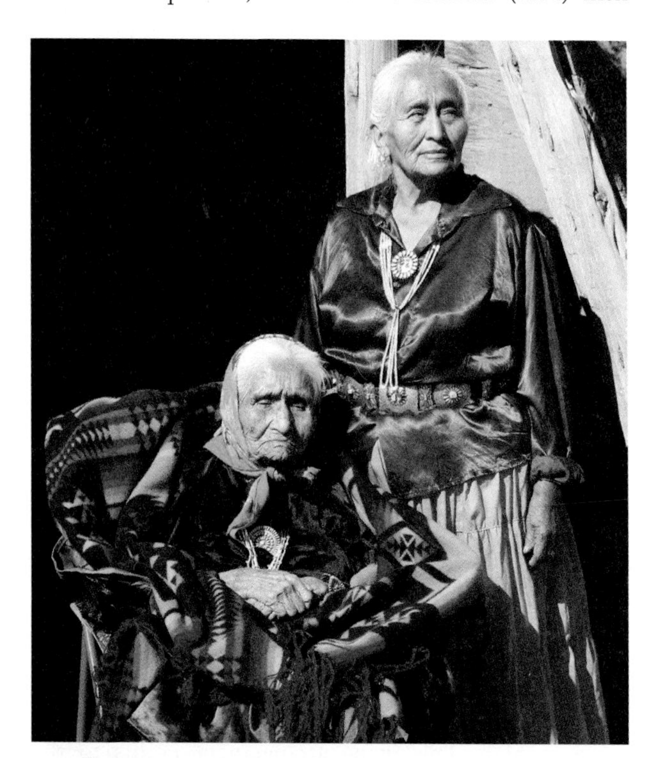

Women across racial and ethnic groups tend to live longer than men.

Maximum Life Span

Maximum life span is different from life expectancy; it is the length of years a given species could expect to live if all environmental hazards were eliminated. Many scientists posit that there is a "soft limit" to the human life span in the range of 85–90 years, unless there was some way to alter the basic biological process of aging—a conclusion that has not changed in the past 20 years. There appears to be a maximum biologically determined life span for human cells, so that even with the elimination of all diseases, we cannot expect to live much beyond 120 years—despite what you may hear in the media. For these reasons, more persons will expect to live longer in the future, but the maximum number of years they can

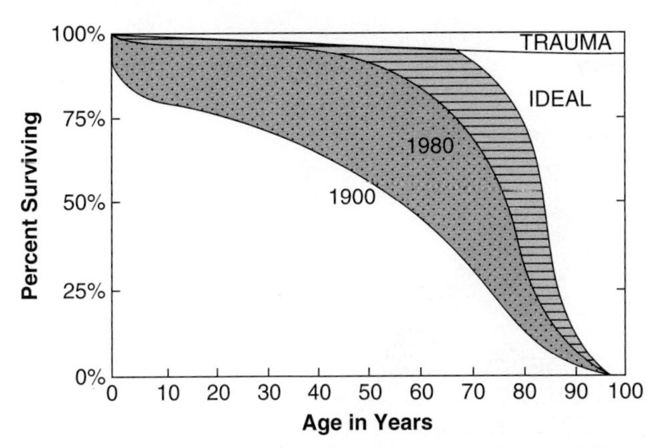

FIGURE 1.4 Ideal Rectangularization of the Survival Curve

Source: Fries, 1980

expect to live will not be increased dramatically, unless some extraordinary and unanticipated biological discoveries occur. The longest documented human life is of Jeanne Calment, a Frenchwoman who died at age 122 (Olshansky, 2010).

The ideal situation is one where all people would survive to the maximum life span, creating what is called a "rectangular survival curve" (shown in Figure 1.4). About 50 percent of all babies born after 2000 in developed countries are expected to reach age 85, more than two-thirds of the maximum life span of 120 years. We will not achieve the ideal survival curve until the diseases of middle and young-old age—including cancer, heart disease, diabetes, and kidney diseases, along with obesity—can be totally prevented or at least effectively managed as chronic conditions, which is a scenario far in the future (Kochanek, Xu, Murphy, Minino, & Kung, 2011; Pallarito, 2011).

Population Pyramids

Population pyramids visually capture the changing age distribution of the American population—the shift in the proportion of older adults in relation to younger persons.

- In 1900, when 4 percent of the U.S. population was age 65 and over, 40 percent was under age 17.
- By 2005, reduced birthrates in the 1970s and 1980s had resulted in a decrease of young persons as a percent of the total population.
- By 2030, the percentages of young and old persons are predicted to be similar, with those under age 17 forming 23.5 percent of the population, and older adults almost 20 percent.
- After 2030, the median age will be around 39 years, and the death rate will be greater than the birthrate because baby boomers will then be age 85 and older (U.S. Census Bureau, 2011).

Figure 1.5 on p. 18 contrasts the population pyramids for the years 2010, 2030, and 2050. The horizontal bars reflect birth cohorts and illustrate the importance of the baby boom generation in shaping the future population of the United States. By 2030, all of the baby boomers will have transitioned to the ranks of older adulthood.

Reaching the Maximum Life Span

Researchers worldwide are intrigued with Jeanne Calment for both her longevity and vitality. When younger, her life revolved around tennis, bicycling, swimming, roller-skating, piano, and opera. She took up fencing lessons at 85 and rode a bicycle until age 100. At age 121, she released two CDs, one in French and another in English, which featured Calment's reminiscing to a score of rap and other tunes. Researchers attribute her longevity to her extraordinary immunity to stress. But genes may also be a factor since both her parents were long-lived. She once said, "If you can't do anything about it, don't worry about it." Calment herself credited her longevity to an occasional glass of port wine, a diet rich in olive oil, and lots of laughter. She used to eat two pounds of chocolate per week until her doctor persuaded her to give up sweets at the age of 119. She quit smoking only at 119, largely due to pride rather than health—she was too blind to light up herself, and hated asking someone to do it for her. In later years, Calment lived mostly off the income from her apartment, which she sold cheaply to a lawyer when she was 90. The lawyer signed a contingency contract with Calment and agreed to pay a life annuity of 2,500 francs ($500) a month until she died and he became owner. He lost this gamble. When he died at age 77, his family was left still paying for the flat until Calment died several years later! How does one ferret out the role of genetics and lifestyle with someone like Jeanne Calment? Many researchers and others who have studied those who live to 100 years or more have attempted to figure this out as you will see in some of the studies reported below.

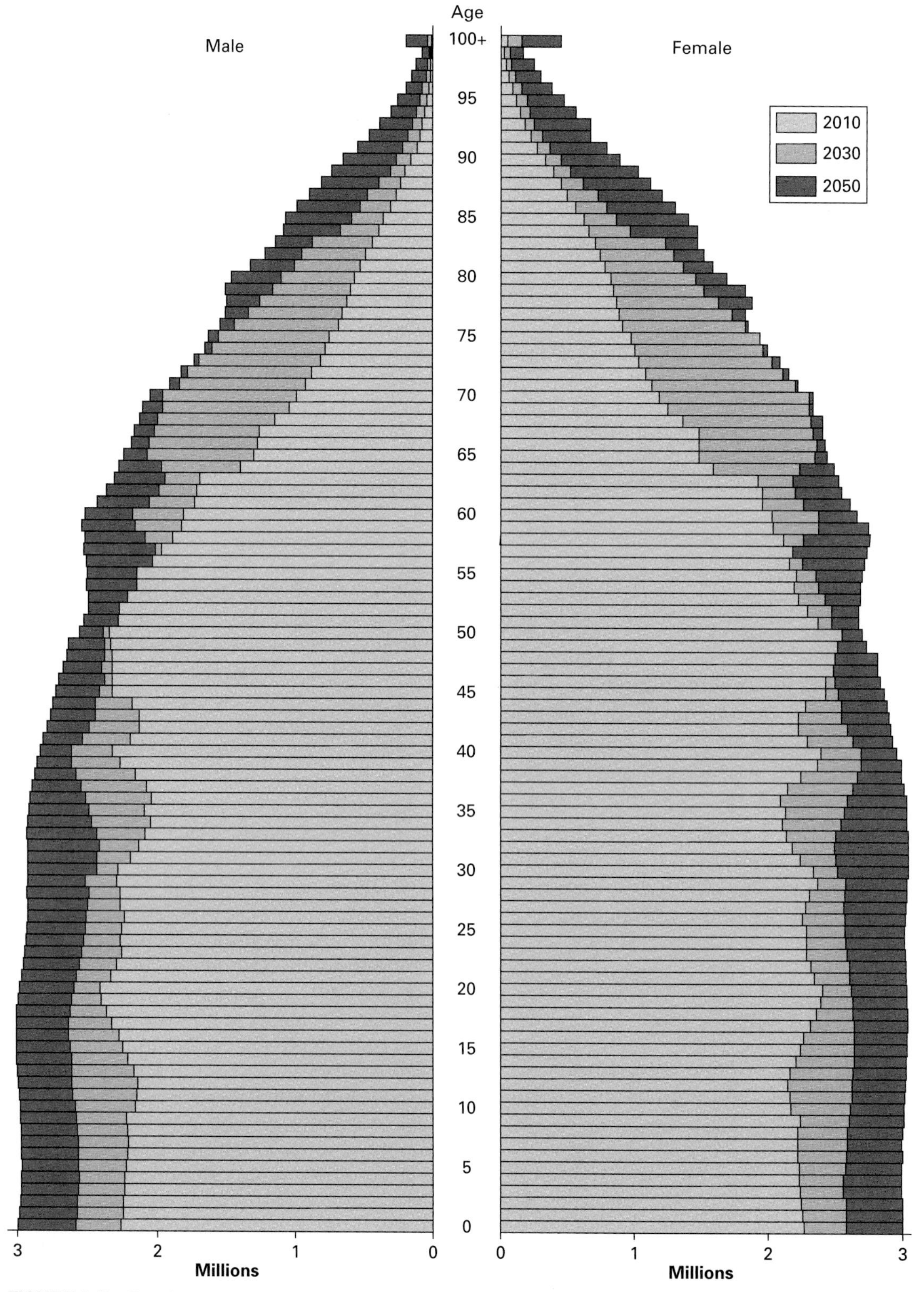

FIGURE 1.5 **Population Pyramids Changing Age and Sex Structure of the U.S. Population: 2010, 2030, and 2050**

Source: U.S. Census Bureau, 2010, "The Next Four Decades: The Older Population in the U.S.: 2010–2050."

Population pyramids that show the known and projected resident population of the United States during key points in time show a bulge in the area of the pyramid representing those residents born during the baby boom period. As years pass, that bulge moves higher up the pyramid—sometimes referred to as "the pig in a python phenomenon"—changing the shape of the pyramid into one that widens at the top. Declining birthrates and reduced death rates for older cohorts also contribute to this change in shape.

Support and Dependency Ratios

The changing age distribution in our population is also reflected in what is variously called the old-age support ratio or the "dependency ratio." You may have seen these terms in media coverage of the future of Social Security and Medicare. The **dependency ratio** refers to the number of people age 65 and older to every 100 people of traditional working ages (defined as 18–64). In 2010, this ratio was 22 people age 65 and older to every 100 people age 18–64. This will rise from 35 older adults in 2030 to 37 in 2050 for every 100 "working age" adults. The higher this ratio, the greater the potential burden of "dependent" older adults (Vincent & Velkoff, 2010).

Another way of measuring this burden is the **support ratio**. This indicates the relationship between the proportion of the population that is employed (defined as "productive" and able to support others) and the percentage that is not in the workforce (viewed as "dependent" or as "requiring support"). This ratio has decreased steadily in the past 100 years, which means that proportionately fewer employed persons support retired older persons today. In 1910, there were 10 employed people per retired older person; today there are fewer than 5 employed. It is projected that there will only be about three employed people per retired person by 2030 (Orr, 2010; Vincent & Velkoff, 2010).

Such changes fuel public perceptions about older adults as a "burden" on the younger population. However, the population under age 16—not older adults—will continue to be the largest "dependent" group. As more elders remain in the workforce longer, there will be fewer retired elders who require economic support from younger adults. What is unknown, however, is how the Great Recession that started in 2008 and the increasing numbers of unemployed adults will affect this ratio in the next 10–20 years. There are likely to be fewer employed persons of all ages to support those who are not employed. The rapid growth of the population age 85 and older also has numerous implications for public perceptions that older adults are a burden.

These trends are also captured in Figure 1.6 on p. 20.

What Causes Longevity? Genes or Behavior?

Journalist Dan Buettner has traveled to world regions where it is not unusual to find vigorous, active **centenarians**—those who live to age 100 and older. He labeled these "Blue Zones," places with large numbers of long-living residents who share healthy lifestyles, diets, engagement in their community, and a positive worldview. Yet these elders in different parts of the world—Okinawa, Sardinia, the northwestern region of Costa Rica, and Loma Linda, California—share genetic qualities and cultural norms that have tied the community together for hundreds of years. These Blue Zones are generally more remote, less stressful environments than typical communities. While some aspects of their lifestyles may be adopted—such as strong connections with family and friends, engaging in physical labor into advanced old age, walking and exercise, a low-calorie, plant-based diet, and a positive outlook—some are fundamental societal and genetic factors and cannot be replicated by those in other communities (Buettner, 2008).

The Rapid Growth of the Old-Old and Oldest-Old

Do you know anyone who is between the ages of 75 and 84? They fall into the **old-old** age group as defined by gerontologists. Or perhaps you have a grandparent or great-grandparent who are among the **oldest-old**—people age 85 and older. These categories represent an important demographic distinction, because it is the oldest-old who are growing most rapidly, even though the

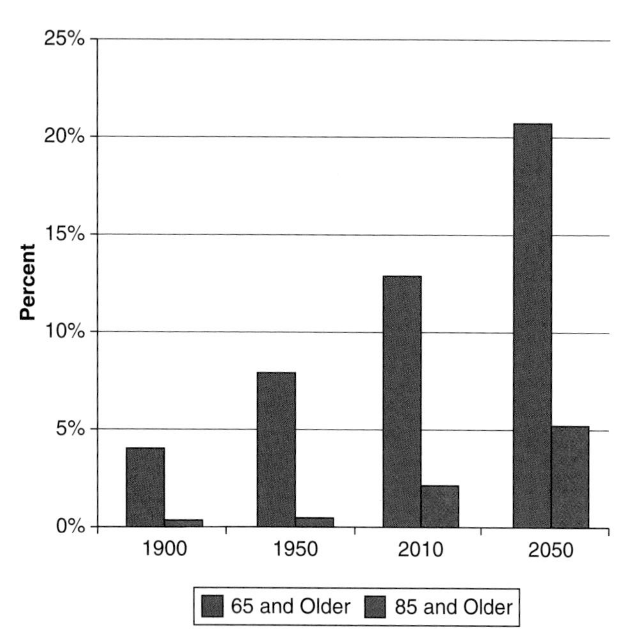

FIGURE 1.6 Population Age 65 and Over and Age 85 and Over: 1900, 1950, 2010, and Projected 2050

Source: www.aoa.gov, "Projected Future Growth of the Older Population"

young-old are over 50 percent of the older population in the United States. In other words, the older population itself is becoming even older, due largely to the success of modern medicine. The 65–74 age group (about 21 million) is approximately 10 times larger than in 1900, the 75–84 group (over 13 million) is 17 times larger, and the group age 85 and older (5.5 million) is 45 times larger! As you can see, the absolute numbers of the oldest-old are not higher than those of younger groups, but their rate of growth is much faster (AoA, 2012).

Demographers, people who study population, project that the oldest old will reach 19 million or 4 percent of the U.S. population by 2050. This projection of a nearly fourfold increase in numbers is primarily attributable to the aging of baby boomers, who will start to turn 85 after 2030. This surge is considered to be a significant demographic trend because of its impact on social institutions as well as individual lives. Indeed, the term "silver tsunami" is sometimes used to refer to the fact that the growth of the oldest-old has profound consequences for families, health and social services, long-term services and supports, retirement and workplace policies, political power, educational and recreational services, religious institutions, housing, and communities. In other words, population aging affects all of us throughout our lives (AoA, 2012; Vincent & Velkoff, 2010).

Who Are the Oldest-Old?

- About 66 percent are women.
- Nearly 76 percent are widowed women compared to about 38 percent of men who are widowers.
- About 55 percent of the men are married, compared to 15 percent of women.
- Fifteen percent are foreign-born. Many emigrated from European countries in the early 1900s, but later immigrants are more likely to have come from China, Japan, the Philippines, Vietnam, and Latin America, as you will see in Chapter 2.
- They have fewer years of education compared to those ages 65–74.
- Their average personal income is lower than the rest of the older population.
- A higher proportion lives below or near poverty compared to those age 65–69 years.
- They are disproportionately represented in hospitals and long-term care settings such as skilled nursing facilities (SNFs) and assisted living facilities (ALFs). This is due to the fact that they are more likely to have multiple health problems and may have outlived a spouse or partner to care for them (AoA, 2012; Federal Interagency Forum, 2012).

Although their functional health is generally more impaired than younger age groups, the majority rate their health as good or excellent; moreover, there is ample evidence from many health studies that future cohorts of the oldest-old will be healthier and more active than today's population. Such gains may be due in part to physical activity. As an example of the importance of exercise, consider the surprising findings in the box on p. 21 about healthy elders in two very different environments: New York City and rural North Dakota.

And there are multiple and growing examples of people age 90 and older who remain active both physically and socially. Consider Ida Keeling, a 95-year-old woman from New York City who set a world record after running 60 meters in 29.86 seconds. Or Olga Kotelko, who started training for track and field in her seventies, and at age 91

The Importance of Physical Activity

At first it seems counterintuitive that New Yorkers have among the highest life expectancy in the nation, given the pollution and risks inherent in a densely populated city. However, it may not be the quality of the physical environment so much as the opportunities and need to walk everywhere and the constant interactions with other people that keep many of the oldest-old in New York active, socially engaged, and among the healthiest in the nation. Although different in its population density and lifestyles, North Dakota also has a high proportion of oldest-old persons who are active in their communities; this has been attributed to genetic factors, lifelong patterns of physical activity such as farming, and continued activity after retirement (Harrop, 2010).

is a champion on the "master athlete" circuit (i.e., people over age 35 who compete in their age categories such as 50–55 or 90–95). She holds 23 world records in her age category, including the shot put (16.1 ft.), the long jump (5.8 ft.), and the 100-meter dash (23.95 seconds). Prior to that, her only physical activity was playing softball and she had to give up her position on the team to a 55-year-old. While Ms. Kotelko does not represent the "typical" oldest-old person, her advanced cardiovascular and lung function and amazing accomplishments demonstrate that advanced old age does not necessarily mean disability (CDC, 2011a; Grierson, 2010).

Centenarians and Super-Centenarians

Within the oldest-old population, people age 100 and older, known as **centenarians**, are also increasing dramatically. Consider these facts:

- In 2010, almost 72,000 Americans had reached this milestone of living to 100 years, a 72 percent increase from 1990 (37,000).
- One in 26 baby boomers can expect to live to be 100 by 2025, compared with only one in 500 in 2000.
- By 2050, 600,000–800,000 centenarians are likely to be alive (Federal Interagency Forum, 2012; U.S. Census Bureau, 2011).

Although this sounds like a large number, Japan will have even more centenarians within their smaller total population, or 627,000 (representing 1 percent of its total projected population in 2050), compared to the United States. Sizable numbers of centenarians will also populate Italy, Greece, Monaco, and Singapore. This demographic pattern also reflects the gains in life expectancy in these countries compared to the United States and aging of the baby boomer generation.

Contrary to what you might imagine, most centenarians are remarkably healthy, mentally alert, free of major disability, able to perform most daily activities, and engaged in their communities. They generally do not suffer from chronic illnesses associated with age, including hypertension, type 2 diabetes, cardiovascular diseases, or Alzheimer's disease. Some experience these conditions in the last few years of life; others escape them altogether. Since as many as 30 percent of centenarians have no memory problems, it may be that the genetic mutations most closely associated with Alzheimer's disease are not present in the oldest-old. Instead, environmental factors that emerge much later in life appear to cause dementia in centenarians. In studies of centenarians in New England, more than 90 percent of their research volunteers were healthy into their nineties. About half continued to live in the community on their own or with their families. Indeed, Dr. Mark Lachs, author of *Treat Me, Not My Age*, posits that there is an escape velocity—an age at which the risk of death and disability actually begins to fall! In other words, the older you get, the older you are likely to get (Kaye, 1997; Lachs, 2011; Perls, 2010; Samuelsson et al., 1997; Silver et al., 1998).

The New England Centenarian Study has looked at differences between participants in that study who are at age 100 and those who have reached age 110 or more, or **super-centenarians**. Just as they have shown that people who live to age 100 are generally physically and

points to **ponder**

Do you know any centenarians personally or have you read or heard stories about someone living beyond 100? Was this long-lived person an inspiration to you? If so, for what reasons? Or did you have negative perceptions of this person?

cognitively healthier than people who live to 85 or less, researchers in the New England study have found that super-centenarians have fewer chronic diseases and physical disabilities, and these diseases were first detected much later than in centenarians. Among the super-centenarians, only 34 percent have cardiovascular disease compared to 49 percent of those younger than 110; hypertension rates are 27 percent versus 43 percent. Interestingly, men at every age above 100 had better physical and cognitive health than women (Perls, 2010).

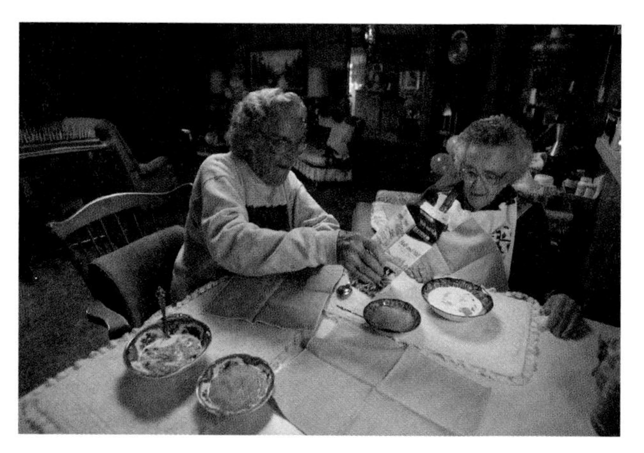

With increases in life expectancy, oldest-old adult children may live with centenarian parents, as in this photo of a 90-year-old daughter enjoying a meal with her 112-year-old mother.

points to ponder

Do you know an older person whom you would consider to be hardy? What are the characteristics that come to mind when you think of them? Does their hardiness seem consistent with what you consider to be their chronological age? What are your ideas about why they are hardy?

The Role of Genes Genetics plays an important role in predicting the likelihood that we will become centenarians. We can see this in the predominance of healthy 80-year-old adult children of centenarians. Consider the photo on this page of the 90-year-old daughter who is caring for her 112-year-old mother in the family home. The likelihood of a genetic advantage is also supported by the finding that male siblings of centenarians are 17 times more likely than the general population, and female siblings 8 times more likely, to survive to age 100. On the other hand, according to John Rowe, who served as director of the MacArthur Foundation Research on Successful Aging, only about one-third of aging is heritable, while the rest is acquired, which means we are partly responsible for our own old age (Christensen, 2001; Parker-Pope, 2005; Perls, Alpert, Wagner, Vijg, & Kruglyak, 1998; Poon et al., 2000; Willcox, Willcox, He, Curb, & Suzuki, 2006b).

Genetic factors also determine how well an older person copes with disease or other stressors in their lives. This is often referred to as their **hardiness**. The oldest-old are hardy because they have a higher threshold for disease and a lower risk of autoimmune diseases. They also show slower rates of disease progression than their peers who develop chronic diseases at younger ages and die earlier. For example, most of the 600 centenarians studied in Okinawa, Japan, had genetic patterns that placed them at lower risk of autoimmune diseases. There also appear to be gender differences in hardiness. As we noted earlier in this chapter, although women on average live longer than men, men who survive to age 90 represent the hardiest segment of their birth cohort. Between ages 65 and 89, women score higher on tests of cognitive function. After age 90, however, men perform far better on these tests. They also are more likely to remain robust and independent. This suggests that long-lived

Evidence for a Genetic Role in Becoming a Centenarian

It is not unusual for siblings to die at similar ages, suggesting a genetic factor in longevity. Twin sisters Kin Narita and Gin Kanie became national celebrities in Japan during the 1990s because they both lived to be over 100 while maintaining their sense of humor and a positive outlook on life. These sisters represented what younger generations strive to achieve, a long, happy life marked by continued learning and engagement with the world. At age 100, they sang a "granny rap" that brought them newfound wealth. They joked that they were saving money "to provide for our old age." The twins made their first trip abroad, to Taiwan, at the age of 102. They were famous by then. Kin died in 2000 at the age of 107; Gin in 2001 at age 108 (BBC News, 2001).

Aging Well as Centenarians and Oldest-Old

People who make it to age 100 and beyond provide us with inspiration and motivation to keep on going. In 2009, Emma Hendrickson became the oldest person (age 101) to compete in the U.S. Bowling Congress Women's Championships. Harriet Ames died the day after receiving her bachelor's degree at age 100. Monoel de Oliveira, one of Portugal's most prolific filmmakers, continues to direct highly regarded films. At age 101, his latest film, *The Strange Case of Angelica*, premiered at the Cannes Film Festival, shortly after his feature film *Eccentricities of a Blonde-Haired Girl* was released to great international acclaim. Closer to home, 107-year-old Dorothy Kuroiwa in Hawaii continued to live alone, enjoyed visits from her four children who were all in their seventies or eighties, and prepared most of her own meals. Or consider a remarkable woman among the oldest-old—Doris "Granny D" Haddock—who at age 88 began a walk 3,200 miles across America to promote campaign finance reform. When snows threatened to keep her from reaching Washington, DC on schedule, she skied the last 90 miles. At age 94, she became the Democratic nominee for one of New Hampshire's Senate seats (Arcayna, 2013; Park, 2010).

men have some reserve capacity or resiliency that allows them to bounce back from health problems earlier in life without long-term complications. This resilience also affects how they cope with or "shed" stress (Parker-Pope, 2005; Perls and Terry, 2003; Terry, Willcox, McCormick, & Perls, 2004).

The Role of the Environment As is true of all ages, environmental and lifestyle factors also play a role in living to be 100 or older. The lower rates of disease among centenarians in Okinawa were partially due to a low-calorie diet with a high intake of vitamins B6, B12, D, calcium, omega-3 fats, and high-fiber foods. The traditional Okinawa lifestyle includes high levels of physical activity, social integration at all ages, a deep spirituality, adaptability, and optimistic attitudes. In fact, Okinawans who move from the island and abandon their traditional diet and lifestyle experience higher mortality rates from diseases that are rare among lifelong Okinawans. In the New England Centenarian Study of 850 adults age 100 and older, researchers identified both behavioral and personality traits central to longevity, such as not smoking, optimism, humor, adaptability, willingness to try new things, being extroverted and easygoing, and staying lean (Bernstein et al., 2004; Perls, 2010; Snowdon, 2001; Willcox et al., 2006a, 2006b).

We now turn to four other important demographic trends—the growth of populations of color that will change the face of aging in the future; the increasing numbers of older adults who are "out of the closet" in terms of their sexual orientation; the geographic distribution of older adults; and the high school completion rate.

Increasing Diversity among the Older Population

As we noted in the Introduction to this book, the population age 65 and older is more heterogeneous than any other age group. As we will illustrate throughout this text, they vary greatly in their health and cognitive status, family and living situations, employment status, and incomes. All of these characteristics of the

A Long-Lived Family

In thinking about the interplay of genetics and lifestyle, consider the Hurlbut family in 2010. Among these long-lived siblings, three are over the age of 90, four in their eighties, and one is almost 80. Agnes, age 96, learned to drive at age 63 and only recently gave it up. She made Christmas dinner last year for everyone. Millie, age 93, reads a half dozen books every few weeks and exercises twice a week for an hour. James, age 91, has a new girlfriend and is an accomplished poet. Muriel at 89 writes poetry and sews quilts. Helen at age 88 sews intricate dolls complete with period costumes and drives to her volunteer job at a local hospital. Walter, 84, is an accomplished painter. Peter, age 80, taught himself to play the piano (he wrote all his children's wedding songs) and ice-skate after midlife. Peggy, the youngest at age 79, loves to cook and read and is determined to live as long as her siblings. They all love to watch *Jeopardy!* together and see who can call out the answers fastest. Their children and grandchildren try to learn from them how to keep active and reduce stress in their own busy lives (Park, 2010).

Centenarians' Zest for New Experiences

The obituary of a 108-year-old woman who died suddenly of congestive heart failure described her healthy lifestyle and enthusiasm for trying new activities. At age 103, she began to train as a shot-putter and participated in two Senior Games in Washington. She lifted a 6.5-pound shot and flung it 7 feet, a record for these Senior Games. Another obituary of a woman who died at 103 of a stroke noted that she celebrated her 100th birthday by taking her first hot-air balloon ride. To her it was no big deal, just something she wanted to do. Her daughter described her as "go, go, go, all the time. She liked to have fun" (Brown, 2009).

heterogeneous older population affect the experience of aging. But race/ethnicity and sexual orientation have profound differences on the individual process of aging.

Elders of Color

Today, slightly more than 20 percent of the population over age 65 is composed of persons of color, with African American elders the largest group, and American Indians the smallest. These groups include a smaller proportion of older people and a larger proportion of younger adults than the white population (7.2 percent are age 65 and older, compared with 15.7 percent among whites over age 65). Indeed, among Americans younger than age 65, almost 30 percent are persons of color. The difference results primarily from higher fertility and mortality rates among the younger nonwhite population and high rates of immigration of younger adults (AoA, 2012; Treas & Carreon, 2010).

This pattern is shifting, however. The proportion of older persons is predicted to increase at a higher rate for the nonwhite population than for non-Hispanic whites. Older adults of color will double their current proportion in the older U.S. population, from nearly 20 percent to about 40 percent of the older population in 2050. For those ages 85 and older, the increase will be from 15 percent in 2010 to 33 percent in 2050. You can see these patterns of growth for different groups and the proportion of elders in each population of color in Figure 1.7 (AoA, 2012; U.S. Census Bureau, 2010).

Much of this growth will result from populations with high immigration levels such as Latinos and Asians. A large percentage of children in these groups, unlike their parents and especially their grandparents, are expected to reach old age. Young Mexican immigrants, who have come

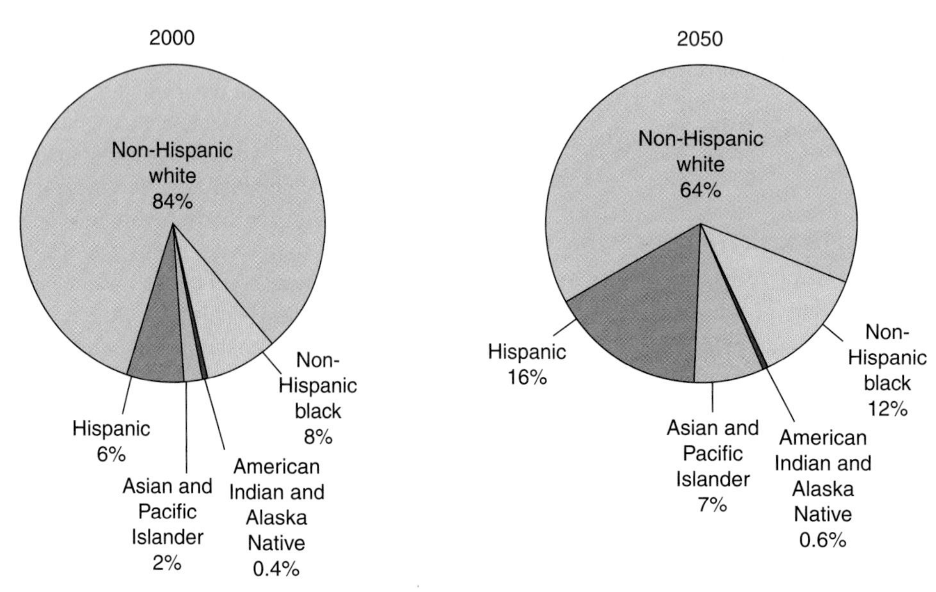

FIGURE 1.7 Projected Distribution of the Population Age 65 and Older by Race, 2000 and 2050

Source: www.aoa.gov, "Projections of Future Growth of the Older Population" (2012).

to the United States seeking jobs and education, will be old in 2050. Then, elders will make up nearly 16 percent of the Latino population, compared with fewer than 6 percent currently (AoA, 2012; Treas & Carreon, 2010).

Because many elders of color will have experienced inequities earlier in their lives, they may face more chronic illnesses and poverty in old age. On the other hand, they are likely to bring numerous strengths, such as strong social supports.

Lesbian, Gay, Bisexual, and Transgender (LGBT) Elders

The older population is also becoming more diverse in terms of those who identify as lesbian, gay, bisexual, and transgender (LGBT) adults. The general invisibility of being old is heightened for those who are old and LGBT—the most "invisible of an already invisible minority." Accordingly, it is difficult to know the size of this population because of limited existing empirical knowledge about them. This has occurred because gerontology research often fails to measure sexual orientation and gender identity, or does so incompletely, in population-based samples of older adults. Additionally, LGBT research frequently fails to include older adults. As a result of widespread social stigma, even when asked directly, research participants may underreport membership as a sexual minority. Accordingly, data on life expectancy of LGBT individuals are unavailable. Estimates of the percent of LGBT elders range from as low as 3 percent to as high as 18–20 percent. This translates into at least 2 million older lesbians and gay men, which will likely increase to over 6 million by the year 2030 (Fredriksen-Goldsen & Muraco, 2010; Gates, 2010; Institute of Medicine, 2011).

Because of the double stigma of being "twice hidden," some studies suggest that the aging experience is more difficult for LGBT adults, who may experience high rates of social isolation and mental distress; others indicate that lifelong marginalization and skills in managing a stigmatized status may stimulate adaptive strategies to the challenges of aging. What is clear is that LGBT elders have experienced disparities in access to health and long-term care due to legal and attitudinal obstacles. Many of these health care inequities result because they lack the legal protection of marriage, although some legal barriers have recently been removed. It is also important when you are interacting with older adults not to assume that they are heterosexual and to be aware of the discrimination that LGBT elders have undoubtedly experienced throughout their lives, which will affect their aging. For example, when interviewing an older adult, ask about their partner rather than their husband or wife (Barker, 2008; Blando, 2001; Fredriksen-Goldsen & Muraco, 2010; Fredriksen-Goldsen et al., 2011; Gabbay & Wahler, 2002; McFarland & Sanders, 2003; Thompson, 2006).

points to ponder

LGBT older adults are a part of the communities most of us live in. What do you think are some of the challenges that LGBT older adults experience in contemporary society compared to heterosexual elders? If you wanted to create an inclusive work or social environment for LGBT older adults, what kinds of things could you do?

Geographic Distribution

Although older adults live in every state and region of the United States, the map depicted in Figure 1.8 on p. 26 shows that they are not evenly distributed.

In 2011, 57 percent of all persons age 65 and older lived in 11 states that have the highest absolute number of older people. Not surprisingly, the highest numbers are in Florida. But what may surprise you is that many of these states are not ones with sunny retirement destinations that we traditionally associate with large numbers of retirees, but include West Virginia, Pennsylvania, Maine, New York, and Ohio. It is not just the absolute numbers that matter in terms of quality of life, but also the proportion of residents over age 65. Some states have a higher percentage than the national average, even though the absolute numbers may be smaller. For example, only 7 percent of the population of Alaska and 8.8 percent in Utah are age 65 and older, although both states report a tremendous increase in their older population in the past decade. Data on the geographic location and growth of older populations are important, because it affects the need for services and housing, and has implications for state and local government spending (AoA, 2012; U.S. Census Bureau, 2011).

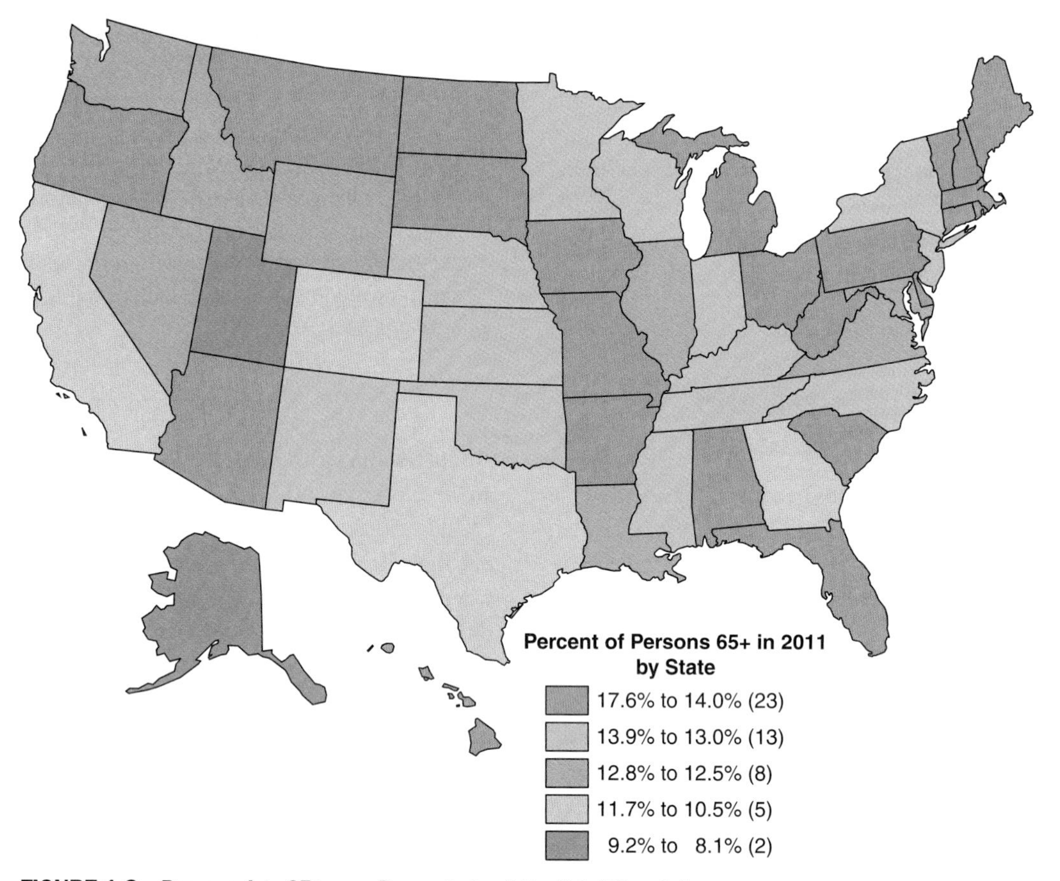

FIGURE 1.8 Persons Age 65+ as a Percentage of the Total Population

Source: www.aoa.gov, "A Profile of Older Americans: 2011" (2012)

In some cases (such as Florida), migration of retired persons to the state explains the increase, whereas in others (such as North Dakota or Maine), migration of younger persons out of the state (or out-migration), typically in search of employment, leaves a greater proportion of older people. In such instances, even though a state such as Pennsylvania may have a high percentage of elders, its growth rate of older adults is lower than in states with a lower proportion of older adults. Other states may simply reflect the generalized "graying of America." These regional differences are expected to continue in the future (Frey, 2010).

Contrary to the popular image of older adults' flocking to warm climates, older people typically do not relocate significant distances. The movement that occurs tends to be within the same region and state (such as within the same county) and similar types of environments. In a typical year, less than 6 percent of people age 65 and older move, usually within the same region, compared with nearly 17 percent of people younger than 65. Only about 21 percent of older movers leave the state when they relocate. The oldest-old are most likely to relocate, often into or near their children's homes, which is typically precipitated by widowhood, significant deterioration in their health, or disability (Frey, 2010).

points to ponder

What factors do you think might explain the higher percentages of older adults in states that do not necessarily have large absolute numbers of elders? What reasons do you think might explain these different population patterns across the states? What might these patterns mean for social and health services as well as for local and state governments?

Nearly 80 percent of older adults live in metropolitan areas.

- Among those, about 64 percent live in cities, with 36 percent in suburbs and smaller communities.
- Baby boomers, who tend to live in suburban areas, account for the graying of the suburbs.
- Despite their low distribution in rural communities, older adults make up 20 percent of rural and small town populations compared to 13 percent in the general population (AoA, 2012).

These geographic trends and their implications for living arrangements and community services are described further in Chapter 11.

Geographic Distribution among Elders of Color

We briefly discuss where elders of color live, since understanding their geographic distribution is relevant to the planning and delivery of social, health, and long-term services and supports. It is also important to learn about their national or tribal identity, particularly among immigrants, since service providers need to provide culturally appropriate care. While the African American population is distributed more evenly in the United States than other elders of color, those from other historically disadvantaged groups tend to be concentrated in the Northeast, Southwest, Florida, and California and, in the case of American Indians, along the Canadian border (AoA, 2012).

Patterns of and reasons for immigration also affect the need for services and other supports for elders. Recent Mexican immigrants—both documented and undocumented—have dramatically increased the size of this population in the United States, are the poorest group of Latina elders, and have fueled heated debates about whether and how to limit immigration from Mexico. In contrast to the early immigrants, who are now the oldest-old, the more recent Mexican immigrants are young. Their life course experiences will play a major role in the characteristics and needs of the Latino older population in the future. In contrast, Cubans, who were political refugees, created "Little Havana" in Miami, and represent the wealthiest and most educated of all Latino groups in the United States. Moreover, Puerto Rican elders, who are more likely to live in the east, are distinguished by their citizenship that provides full access to U.S. government services and their ability to travel freely to the United States, but they have not achieved the degree of economic success that Cubans have (Angel & Hogan, 2004; Matza, 2009).

Although some of you may think American Indians live mostly on reservations, this is not true for the majority today, young or old. About 60–70 percent live in urban areas. Among this highly diverse population, nearly 300 native languages are spoken, and cultural traditions vary widely. Despite the growing urbanization of American Indians, more elders live in rural areas than do other elders of color. Slightly less than 25 percent live on reservations or in Alaskan Native villages. Older American Indians rarely move as they age. For example, most urbanized American Indians prefer to age in place in the city rather than return to their reservations (Annie E. Casey Foundation, 2008; Ogunwole, 2002).

API elders, who are concentrated in three states—California, Hawaii, and New York—represent a wide range of cultural and language groups and have widely different immigration patterns that affect the lives of older family members.

- Asians include Burmese, Cambodian, Chinese, East Indian, Filipino, Indonesian, Japanese, Korean, Laotian, Malaysian, Polynesian, Thai, and Vietnamese people.
- Pacific Islanders encompass Fijian, Guamanian, Hawaiian, Micronesian, Samoan, and Tongan populations.

The first wave of Asian immigrants came from China and Japan in the late nineteenth and early twentieth centuries, often remaining isolated in large Western cities such as San Francisco and Los Angeles. In 1965, immigration

Reflection Break

Think about the community or state that you live in. From what you know about your community or state, where do you think you would like to live (or not live) if you were 65 years old or older? What would make some places better to live in than others? Are they closer to hospitals and health facilities? Is there better access to public transportation and shopping areas? What else? What makes a place more elder-friendly?

quotas based on race and nationality were repealed. This resulted in a rapid population growth of Southeast Asian immigrants. The process accelerated after 1975 when refugees from Vietnam, Cambodia, and Laos settled in many different communities throughout the United States.

In recent years, a wave of API elders have immigrated as parents and grandparents of younger immigrants, primarily from India, China, Korea, and Vietnam. As a result, between 1990 and 2000, the population of elders among Asian Americans increased by 78 percent, and the median age of this minority group is second only to whites. Although they only make up about 9 percent of the total older population, they are projected to increase rapidly by 2050. Today nearly 80 percent of Asian American elders in the United States are foreign-born and often linguistically isolated. About 60 percent do not speak English, which is higher than the percentage of Latino elders who speak only Spanish (AoA, 2012; Min, Moon, & Lubben, 2006; Wilmoth, 2012).

Never Too Old to Learn

When you discuss World War II in a history class, you primarily draw upon textbook knowledge, but not so with Nola Ochs, who received a college degree at age 95. In pursuit of a BA in History, she brings her personal memories to the history class—whether of the Civil Rights movement or the disco revolution. She began her college education in the 1970s after her husband died. But after completing 90 credits, daily demands, such as those from 13 grandchildren, got in the way. In 2009, she returned to complete the remaining credits and joined a graduating class that included one of her granddaughters. After graduating with her bachelor's degree, she pursued a graduate education and earned a master's degree in liberal studies with a history concentration (Park, 2009; Weber, 2010).

Educational and Economic Status

As you think of your older relatives, you may find that, in general, fewer completed high school or college than what you see among your cousins and other younger relatives. Nationally also this is true.

- In 1960, less than 20 percent of the older population had a high school degree.
- By 2010, slightly over 79 percent of the cohort age 65 and older had completed high school and slightly over 22 percent held a bachelor's degree or more. The greatest educational gains were among whites and Asian and Pacific Islanders, while the lowest were among Latinos (AoA, 2012).

Because of gender inequities in previous generations, only 15 percent of white women age 65 and older compared to 25 percent of white men have more than a high school education. Fortunately, future generations of older people will be better educated than their grandparents. More than 75 percent of baby boomers have at least a high school education. What do you think might be the implications of this shift in education for employment, political activism, and volunteerism among future generations of elders (Federal Interagency Forum, 2012)?

Differences in high school completion rates between whites and elders of color, shown in Figure 1.9, are striking and have numerous consequences for well-being in old age. The fact that so few Latinos and African Americans have a high school education is a result of historical patterns of discrimination in educational opportunities in the 1950s and 1960s. Nevertheless, the rate of high school completion is increasing among African Americans generally. Because of the high dropout rate among youth of color, however, it is unclear whether educational gains will continue for the current generation of teenagers and young adults (AoA, 2012).

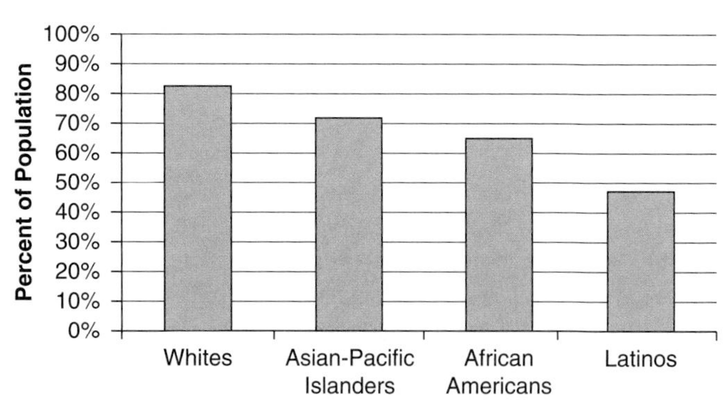

FIGURE 1.9 Educational Attainment of the Population Age 65 and Over: Selected Years, 1965–2008

Source: AoA, 2012

Since educational level is so closely associated with economic well-being, these racial differences often mean higher levels of poverty for persons of color across the life course and particularly in old age. What are some other implications of these gaps in educational attainment for achieving well-being by older adults of color? We will discuss older adults' economic well-being in detail in Chapter 10.

Longevity in Health or Disease? What Does the Future Hold?

With all the attention on baby boomers and their quest for longer, healthier lives, you are probably wondering if aging in the future will simply mean more years lived in good health. In fact, researchers and policy-makers have become more focused on the need to help people keep up their good health into their eighties and beyond. A strong argument was first put forth to support this idea over 30 years ago by Dr. James Fries. Fries suggested that more people will achieve the maximum life span in future years because of healthier lifestyles and better health care during their youth and middle years. Furthermore, he argued that future cohorts will experience a phenomenon he labeled **compression of morbidity** (i.e., lengthening the period of youthful vigor and experiencing only a few years of major illness in very old age). The concept of compressed morbidity, which some gerontologists refer to as the Longevity Dividend, implies that premature death is minimized because disease and functional decline are compressed into a brief period of 3–5 years before death. Until recently, it looked like compression of morbidity was in fact occurring; mortality rates among older adults had declined by about 1 percent per year and disability rates at about 2 percent per year. These healthier older adults of the future would therefore expect to die a "natural death," or death due to the natural wearing out of all organ systems, by age 100–120. Some elders would die of chronic diseases, but these conditions would not occur until later in life, requiring less medical attention in the middle years. More simply, treating disease can extend the period of old age but does not alter the biological process of aging (Butler, 2008; Fries, 1980, 1990, 2002; Olshansky, 2010).

Older adults who have had access to health care and been healthier throughout their lives are more likely to enjoy a healthy old age.

Unfortunately, a recent analysis of health trends in the United States revealed that the phenomenon of compression of morbidity has not continued. Although Americans continue to live longer, as described earlier in this chapter, the added years are more likely to be accompanied by disease and disability. Consider these alarming statistics:

- Between 1998 and 2008, the prevalence of many diseases among adults age 40 and older increased.
- In 1998, only 16 percent of men in their seventies complained that they had difficulty getting around on their own; this had increased to 25 percent by 2006 (Crimmins & Beltran-Sanchez, 2011).

You have probably heard of the striking increase in rates of diabetes, even among younger persons. Given all the additional health problems that diabetes can cause (e.g., vision loss, dental problems, amputation of limbs, disability), we can conclude—based on this one disease alone—that years of morbidity are actually increasing in the United States, not being compressed. Partly because of better diagnosis and treatment, there are more middle-aged and older adults who have many chronic diseases (the most common ones are described in Chapter 3). Thanks to regular checkups, medications, and other treatments to manage these conditions, people are surviving to advanced old age. The implication for future generations of elders is that they will experience a longer life, but these extra years will be filled with managing multiple chronic diseases, some of which may cause the person to be disabled. In many cases they will experience a longer **dependent life expectancy** and a shorter **active life expectancy**. Another way to describe this is that they will live longer but with chronic illness, and that the longest-lived will generally need to depend on others to help them with their daily activities, rather than living independent, healthy, and active lives (Crimmins & Beltran-Sanchez, 2011; Olshansky, 2010).

Not surprisingly, active life expectancy varies by gender, race, and social class:

- A 65-year-old woman today has almost 20 years remaining, 15.7 in active life expectancy, but 4 years in a dependent state.
- A 65-year-old man can look forward to living 16.2 more years, 2.5 years in a dependent state.
- The nonpoor experience 1–2.5 additional years of active life expectancy compared to the poor.
- The greatest gains in active life expectancy are experienced by non-Hispanic whites, followed by Latino men and women, and then African American women.
- African American men are likely to be disabled at 50 percent greater rates than white men and thus experience shorter active life expectancy (AoA, 2012; Rockeymoore & Lui, 2011).

Despite these trends, the adoption of healthier lifestyles by some adults, for example, physical exercise and maintaining a lean body weight—as well as advances in preventing heart disease, musculoskeletal problems, and stroke—may result in a longer active life expectancy for future generations. We discuss these patterns more in Chapter 3 (Schoeni, Freedman, & Martin, 2008).

points to ponder

Although you have just completed the first chapter in this textbook, you have probably also read or watched news stories over the years that pertain to older adults that influenced your view of old age. What do you remember about any of these stories? Did they help you view older adulthood as a positive time in a person's life or not? Why or why not?

summary

In this chapter, we demonstrated that a major reason for the growing interest in studying the aging process and the lives of older people is the dramatic increase in the population over age 65. In particular, there has been a steady growth in the oldest-old population, those over age 85. Even more interesting is the growth in the number of people who survive to age 100 and more. Many of these oldest-old and centenarians continue to live active, productive lives. These increasing survival rates reflect major achievements in disease prevention and health care since the start of the twentieth century. Improved methods of treating acute diseases like pneumonia in childhood and adulthood, particularly the advent of antibiotics, have helped to increase life expectancy at birth and at age 65. More recently, there has been increased attention given to learning about the aging process by studying centenarians. Those who live to be 100 and older may have a biological advantage over their peers who die at a younger age. Studies have found greater tolerance to stress and fewer chronic illnesses in centenarians.

In the United States, average life expectancy from birth has increased from 47 years in 1900 to 78.3 in 2010, with women continuing to outlive men. Yet, you have also seen in this chapter that people of color are now less likely to live a significant number of years beyond age 65 than their white counterparts. On the other hand, population projections anticipate a much higher rate of population growth for elders of color in the next 20 years. Because of the lower life expectancy of historically disadvantaged populations, there is increasing attention on reducing health and economic disparities from birth to old age (U.S. Census Bureau, 2011; Zarit & Pearlin, 2005).

The growth in the numbers and proportions of older people, especially the oldest-old, requires that both public and private policies affecting employment and retirement, health and long-term services and supports be modified to meet the needs and enhance the quality of life of those who are living longer. This will become a greater concern to society as people with low incomes and elders of color live into advanced old age with multiple, chronic diseases and disabilities. Fundamental issues need to be resolved about who will receive what resources and what roles will be played by informal (e.g., families) and formal sectors to care for the growing number of elders who may need assistance. Society must also address the increasing number of healthy, hardy elders who want to continue to be employed, participate in their communities as active volunteers and leaders, and live in their own homes as long as possible.

key terms

active life expectancy, p. 30
centenarians, p. 21
chronic diseases, p. 13
compression of morbidity, p. 29
crossover effect, p. 15
demographers, p. 20
demographic trends, p. 11
demographics, p. 11
dependency ratio, p. 19
dependent life expectancy, p. 30
hardiness, p. 22
individual aging process, p. 11
life expectancy, p. 12
maximum life span, p. 16
median age, p. 12
oldest-old, p. 19
old-old, p. 19
population aging, p. 11
super-centenarians, p. 21
support ratio, p. 19

review questions

1. What are three historical and cultural factors that have influenced the baby boom generation?
2. Discuss the differences between life expectancy, life span, longevity, and active life expectancy. How would you define each of these?
3. Describe the increasing diversity of the older population in the United States.
4. Identify characteristics that distinguish the oldest-old from the young-old.
5. Discuss factors that may explain the hardiness of people who are age 100 and older.
6. Identify steps that can be taken to avoid chronic illness in later years.
7. List the primary reasons that states like Pennsylvania and West Virginia have a high proportion of older people compared to the reasons for states like Florida and California.

media resources

Watch

- Success Across the Lifespan

View

- Aging and Elderly Slideshow
- The Elderly Population across the United States
- The Graying of U.S. Society

references

Administration on Aging (AoA). (2012). *A profile of older Americans: 2011*. Retrieved 2012 from http://www.aoa.gov/aoaroot/aging_statistics/Profile/index.aspx.

Angel, J., & Hogan, D. (2004). Population aging and diversity in a new era. In K. E. Whitfield (Ed.), *Closing the gap: Improving the health of minority elders in the new millennium*. Washington, DC: The Gerontological Society of America.

Annie E. Casey Foundation. (2010). *Urban Indian America*. Seattle, WA: National Urban Indian Family Coalition. Retrieved July 5, 2011, from http://www.unitedindians.org/documents/NUIFCURBINDIANAMERCA.pdf.

Arcayna, N. (2013, July 2). Youthful exuberance. *Honolulu Star-Advertiser*. Retrieved July 2, 2013, from http://www.staradvertiser.com/s?action=login&f=y&id=213926241.

BBC News. (2001). *Japan's oldest twin dies*. Retrieved August 1, 2011, from http://news.bbc.co.uk/2/hi/asia-pacific/1194040.stm.

Bernstein, A. M., Willcox, B. J., Tamaki, H., Kunishima, N., Suzuki, M., Willcox, D. C., et al. (2004). First autopsy study of Okinawan centenarians: Absence of many age-related diseases. *Journals of Gerontology: Medical Sciences, 59A*, 1195–1199.

Blando, J. A. (2001). Twice hidden: Older gay and lesbian couples, friends and intimacy. *Generations, 25*, 87–89.

Blow, C. M. (2011, February 19). Empire at the end of decadence. *New York Times*, p. A19.

Boyles, S. (2011). *U.S. smoking rates keep life expectancy down: Study shows high smoking rates in earlier decades affects life spans in U.S.* Retrieved January 30, 2011, from http://www.webmd.com/healthy-aging/news/20110125/us-smoking-rates-keep-life-expectancy-down.

Brown, C. (2009, April 16). She was not your average senior citizen. *Seattle Times*, p. B2.

Buettner, D. (2008). *The Blue Zones*. Washington, DC: National Geographic Society.

Butler, R. N. (2008). *The longevity revolution: The benefits and challenges of living a long life*. New York: Public Affairs.

Center for American Progress. (2010). *Racial health disparities by the numbers: We still have a long way to go on racial equality*. Retrieved July 4, 2011, from http://www.americanprogress.org/issues/2010/01/health_disparity_numbers.html/print.html.

Centers for Disease Control and Prevention. (2011a). *Fact sheet—CDC health disparities and inequalities report—U.S., 2011*. Retrieved July 4, 2011, from http://www.cdc.gov/minorityhealth/reports/CHDIR11/FactSheet.pdf.

Christensen, D. (2001). Making sense of centenarians: Genes and lifestyle help people live through a century. *Science News, 159*(10), 156–157.

Crimmins, E. M., & Beltran-Sanchez, H. (2011). Mortality and morbidity trends: Is there compression of morbidity? *Journals of Gerontology: Psychological Sciences, 66*, 75–86.

DyBunco, L. (2011). *Life expectancy falls in many parts of U.S. Why?* Retrieved June 16, 2011, from http://www.cbsnews.com/8301-504763_162-20071539-10391704.html#ixzz1Q4TdAdi7.

Federal Interagency Forum on Aging-Related Statistics. (2012). *Older Americans 2011: Key indicators of well-being*. Washington, DC: U.S. Government Printing Office.

Fredriksen-Goldsen, K. I., Kim, H., Emlet, C. A., Muraco, A., Erosheva, E., Hoy-Ellis, C. P., et al. (2011). *Executive summary: Disparities and resilience among lesbian, gay, bisexual, and transgender older adults*. Seattle, WA: University of Washington.

Fredriksen-Goldsen, K. I., & Muraco, A. (2010). Aging and sexual orientation: A 25-year review of the literature. *Research on Aging, 32*(3), 372–413.

Frey, W. H. (2010). Baby boomers and the new demographics of America's seniors. *Generations: Journal of the American Society on Aging, 30*(3), 28–37.

Fries, J. F. (1980). Aging, natural death, and the compression of morbidity. *New England Journal of Medicine, 303*, 130–135.

Fries, J. F. (1990). The compression of morbidity: Near or far? *Milbank Quarterly, 67*, 208–232.

Fries, J. F. (2002). Reducing disability in older age. *Journal of the American Medical Association, 288*, 3164–3166.

Gabbay, S., & Wahler, J. (2002). Lesbian aging: Review of a growing literature. *Journal of Gay and Lesbian Social Services, 14*, 1–21.

Gates, G. J. (2010). *Sexual minorities in the 2009 General Social Survey: Coming out and demographic characteristics*. Los Angeles, CA: The Williams Institute on Sexual Orientation, Law and Public Policy.

Grierson, B. (2010, November 28). The incredible flying nonagenarian. *New York Times*, Sunday Magazine.

Hamilton, B.E., Martin, J.A., & Ventura, S.J. (2013). *Births: Preliminary data for 2012* National Vital Statistics Reports, *62*, September 6, 2013. Retrieved September 18, 2013, from http://www.cdc.gov/nchs/data/nvsr/nvsr62/nvsr62_03.pdf.

Harrop, F. (2010, September 24). North Dakota and New York City: Where the good die old. *Seattle Times*.

Howden, L. M., & Meyer, J. A. (2011). Age and sex composition: 2010. *2010 Census Briefs*. U.S. Department of Commerce.

Hume, T. (2013). *World's oldest person dies, aged 116, just days after rival "supercentenarian."* Retrieved June 12, 2013, from http://www.cnn.com/2013/06/12/world/asia/worlds-oldest-person-dies/index.html.

Institute of Medicine. (2011). *The health of lesbian, gay, bisexual, and transgender people: Building a foundation for better understanding*. Washington, DC: The National Academies Press.

Kaye, J. A. (1997). Oldest-old healthy brain function. *Archives of Neurology, 54*, 1217–1221.

Kochanek, K. D., Xu, J., Murphy, S. L., Minino, A. M., & Kung, H. C. (2011). Deaths: Preliminary data for 2009. National Vital Statistics Report, 59, 1–69. Retrieved July 4, 2011, from http://www.cdc.gov/nchs/data/nvsr/nvsr59/nvsr59_04.

Lachs, M. (2011). *In old age, illness and dying can be postponed*. Retrieved June 27, 2011, from http://www.npr.org/2011/06/27/137064058/in-old-age-illness-and-dying-can-be-postponed.

McFarland, P. L., & Sanders, S. A. (2003). A pilot study about the needs of older gays and lesbians: What social workers need to know. *Journal of Gerontological Social Work, 40*, 67–80.

Min, J., Moon, A., & Lubben, J., (2006). Determinants of psychological distress over time among older Korean Americans and non-Hispanic white elders. Evidence from a two-wave study. *Aging and Mental Health, 9*, 210–222.

Muennig, P. A., & Glied, S. A. (2010, October 7). What changes in survival rates tell us about U.S. health care. *Health Affairs, 29*(11), 2105–2113.

Ogunwole, S. U. (2002). *American Indian and Alaska Native Population: 2000: Census Brief.* Retrieved July 6, 2011, from http://www.census.gov/prod/2002pubs/c2kbr01-15.pdf.

Olshansky, S. J. (2010). Aging, health and longevity in the 21st century. *Public Policy & Aging Report, 4*, 3–11.

Orr, A. (2010). *Americans work longer.* Washington, DC: Economic Policy Institute. Retrieved February 12, 2011, from http://www.epi.org/economic snapshots/entry/Americans work longer/.

Pallarito, K. (2011). *Life expectancy in U.S. trails top nations.* Retrieved July 4, 2011, from http://www.cnn.com/2011/HEALTH/06/15/life.expectancy.united.states/index.html.

Park, A. (2010, February 22). How to live to 100 years. *Time Magazine*, 56–66.

Park, C. (2009). *95-year-old woman becomes oldest college graduate.* Retrieved June 24, 2011, from http://www.associatedcontent.com/shared/print/shtml?content_type.

Parker-Pope, T. (2005, June 20). The secrets of successful aging: What science tells us about growing older—And staying healthy. *Wall Street Journal.* Retrieved January 12, 2013, from http://online.wsj.com/article/0,,SB111867751964458052,00.html.

Perls, T. T. (2010). Antiaging medicine: What should we tell our patients? *Aging Health, 6*(2), 149–154.

Perls, T. T., Alpert, L., Wagner, G. G., Vijg, J., & Kruglyak, L. (1998). Siblings of centenarians live longer. *Lancet, 351*, 1560–1565.

Perls, T. T., & Terry, D. F. (2003). Genetics of exceptional longevity. *Experimental Gerontology, 38*, 725–730.

Poon, L. W., Johnson, M. A., Davey, A., Dawson, D. V., Siegler, I. C., & Martin, P. (2000). Psychosocial predictors of survival among centenarians. In P. Martin, A. Rott, B. Hagberg, & K. Mongan (Eds.), *Centenarians.* New York: Springer Publishing.

Rockeymoore, M. M., & Lui, M. (2011). *Plan for a new future: The impact of Social Security reform on people of color.* Washington, DC: Commission to Modernize Social Security.

Russell, L. M. (2011). Reducing disparities in life expectancy: What factors matter? Paper presented at the Institute of Medicine Roundtable on Promotion of Health Equity and Elimination of Health Disparities.Retrieved July 4, 2011, from http://www.iom.edu/~/media/Files/Activity%20Files/SelectPops/HealthDisparities/2011-FEB-24/Commissioned%20Paper%20by%20Lesley%20Russell.pdf.

Samuelsson, S. M., Baur, B., Hagberg, B., Samuelsson, G., Norbeck, B., Brun, A., et al. (1997). The Swedish Centenarian Study: A multidisciplinary study of five consecutive cohorts at the age of 100. *International Journal of Aging and Human Development, 45*, 223–253.

Schoeni, R. V., Freedman, V. A., & Martin, L. G. (2008). Why is late-life disability declining? *Milbank Quarterly, 86*, 47–69.

Silver, M. H., Newell, K., Hyman, B., Growdon, J., Hedley, E. T., & Perls, T. (1998). Unraveling the mystery of cognitive changes in old age. *International Psychogeriatrics, 10*, 25–41.

Sinn, J. (2011). *Bridging the longevity gap: Sociologist seeks to increase life expectancy for African Americans, Hispanics.* Further findings, U of Texas, Austin. Retrieved July 4, 2011, from http://www.utexas.edu/opa/blogs/research/2011/05/25/bridging-the-longevity-gap-sociologists-seek-to-increase-life-expectancies-for-african-americans-hispanics/.

Snowdon, D. (2001). *Aging with grace. What the Nun Study teaches us about leading longer, healthier and more meaningful lives.* New York: Random House.

Terry, D. F., Willcox, M. A., McCormick, M. A., & Perls, T. T. (2004). Cardiovascular disease delay in centenarian offspring. *Journal of Gerontology: Medical Sciences, 59A*, 385–389.

The Commonwealth Fund. (2011). *Despite highest health spending, American's life expectancy continues to fall behind other countries.* Retrieved August 1, 2011, from http://www.commonwealthfund.org/Content/News/News-Releases/2010/Oct/Americans-Life-Expectancy.aspx?view=print&page=all.

Thompson, E. H. (2006). Being women, then lesbian, then old: Femininities, sexualities, and aging. Review essay. *The Gerontologist, 46*, 300–305.

Treas, J., & Carreon, D. (2010). Diversity and our common future: Race, ethnicity and the older American. *Generations,* 34, 38–44.

U.S. Census Bureau News. (2011a). *Births, deaths, marriages and divorces.* Statistical Abstract of the United States. Retrieved August 1, 2011, from http://www.census.gov/compendia/statab/2011/tables/11s0103.pdf.

U.S. Census Bureau News. (2011b). *Resident population projections by sex and age: 2010–2050.* Retrieved July 6, 2011, from http:///www.census.gov/population/www/projections/html.

U.S. Census Bureau News. (2011c). *Facts for features: Older Americans Month: May 2011.* Retrieved July 31, 2011, from http://www.census.gov/newsroom/releases/pdf/cb11-ff08_olderamericans.pdf.

Vincent, V., & Velkoff, V. (2010). *The next four decades: The older population in the United States: 2010 to 2050.* Washington, DC: U.S. Census Bureau, Current Population Reports.

Weber, G. (2010). A part of history. *Hayes Daily News.* Retrieved September 18, 2013, from http://www.hdnews.net/Story/nola051010.

Willcox, D. C., Willcox, B. J., Todoriki, H., Curb, J. D., & Suzuki, M. (2006a). Caloric restriction and human longevity: What can we learn from the Okinawans? *Biogerontology, 7*, 173–177.

Willcox, B. J., Willcox, D. C., He, Q., Curb, J. D., & Suzuki, M. (2006b). Siblings of Okinawan centenarians share lifelong mortality advantages. *Journal of Gerontology: Biological Sciences, 61A*, 345–354.

Wilmoth, J. (2012). A demographic profile of older immigrants in the United States. *Public Policy & Aging Report,* 22, 8–11.

Zarit, S. H., & Pearlin, L. I. (2005). Special issue on health inequalities across the life course. *Journal of Gerontology: Social Sciences, 60B, Special Issue II,* S5–S7.

2 Global Aging and Older Immigrants in the United States

learning objectives

2.1 Identify global trends in aging, including the countries that are aging faster than others and what can be learned from them.

2.2 Discuss how elders in different countries are affected by changing demographics, including migration of younger adults from rural to urban areas.

2.3 Recognize immigration patterns in the United States and the challenges that older immigrants and refugees may encounter in a new country and culture.

Listen to the Chapter Audio

Human populations are aging in countries all over the world—not just in the United States—and issues related to aging often traverse national borders in our increasingly global societies. Globalization affects every aspect of our lives—the clothes we wear might be made in Indonesia; we use Skype and Twitter to learn about events unfolding in the Middle East and other political "hot spots" around the world; and the voice on the other end of the line when you phone for technical support about your computer may be coming from India. We also are increasingly aware of the critical issues surrounding immigrants to the United States. Perhaps some of you are members of immigrant or refugee families, or have neighbors and friends who have immigrated to the United States. When we consider globalization issues, we tend to think of younger adults, because most immigrants are young, and they still represent the majority in **developing countries*** that most impact our global trade. But the proportion of older adults is growing worldwide. Moreover, older immigrants to the United States are increasing in numbers because younger immigrants are often followed by their parents or grandparents.

In this chapter, you will learn about the phenomenon of global aging and the lives of older immigrants and refugees living in the United States. This includes:

- The increasing population of older adults in industrialized countries other than the United States and in developing countries
- How demographic shifts affect employment, retirement, and family patterns in other countries
- How modernization has influenced elders' roles and intergenerational relationships in traditional societies
- Challenges faced by older immigrants and refugees in the United States

  (*Note that the term "developing countries" refers to countries with relatively lower material wealth compared with developed nations such as the United States, Japan, and Great Britain.)

Although we try to cover a number of different countries, we focus on a few in particular due to their distinctive relevance to the topic of global aging. As you review examples of aging globally, you may notice that this chapter refers to Japan quite a bit. The reason is that Japan is the world's fastest aging developed country, and many other countries can learn from Japan as their own population ages. Approximately one-quarter of Japan's population is 65 and older. It is the only country in the world with an aging population that large. By 2050, however, it is expected that 65 other countries will join Japan in having older adults that comprise such a large percentage of their population (United Nations Population Fund, 2012).

Global Trends in Aging

You learned in Chapter 1 that the U.S. population as a whole is aging and will continue to do so in the decades ahead. If you were ever thinking of moving to another country to avoid living around so many older people, think again. (And by the time you finish reading this book, we hope you won't be thinking that way!) This is because **population aging** is a global phenomenon, taking place in just about every country in every part of the world as older adults grow in both real numbers and in proportion to the larger population. We also refer to this phenomenon as **global aging**.

But before we begin, let's talk about world population in general. How many people currently live on the face of this earth? As of this writing, the total world population is over 7 billion. But by the time you read this book, this number may be out of date as the world population gets larger and larger by the minute. Two factors that contribute to larger world populations are declining death rates in Western industrialized countries and high birthrates in some developing countries. If you want to check what the world population is right at this moment, visit the U.S. Census Web site at www.census.gov, and search for the term "world population clock." It will not only give you an estimate of the world population today but also project what the population will be each month for up to a year from now. If you stare at a population clock that is updated in real time, the estimated population of the world increases before your eyes. To give you a sense of how the world population has been growing over the decades, consider this: The world population in 1950 was fewer than 3 billion people. By 2050, the world population will likely be more than 9 billion people (U.S. Census Bureau, International Data Base, June 2011).

So now that you know the estimated size of world population, here are some additional numbers to consider.

These have to do with the number of older adults in the world.

- In 2008, the number of people 65 years and older in the world was estimated to be 506 million, or about 7 percent of the total population.
- By 2040, that number is projected to increase to 1.3 billion people, or 14 percent of the world's population. At that time, about 76 percent of people 65 and older are likely to be in developing countries.
- In 2012, the number of people around the world age 60 and older was 810 million, up from 205 million in 1950.
- Each year, nearly 58 million people around the world turn age 60. That's about two persons every second.

These are a lot of numbers to think about, but here's the take-home message: As the world population increases, the number of older adults living in that world is also growing, both in real numbers and in proportion to the total population. And, as you learned in Chapter 1, the major reasons are more people living longer and declining birthrates (Kinsella & He, 2009; United Nations Population Fund, 2012).

Longevity Record-Setters

What do Besse Cooper, Dina Manfredini, Jiroemon Kimura, and Jeanne Calment have in common? They have all been listed as global record-holders for longevity. American Besse Cooper was 116 years old when she passed away on December 4, 2012. Dina Manfredini, a resident of Iowa who was born in Italy, then held the title for two weeks until she passed away on December 17, 2012, at the age of 115. Born on April 19, 1897, Japan's Jiroemon Kimura succeeded Manfredini as the oldest person in the world. The oldest known person in history is France's Jeanne Calment, who died in 1997 at the age of 122. Aside from their longevity, of course, each of these individuals has fascinating life stories. Manfredini, for example, was an Italian immigrant who moved to Iowa with her husband Riccardo in 1920. A mother of four, she worked at a food processing plant, helped make guns at a munitions factory during World War II, and cleaned houses until she was 90 years old. She once told an Iowa newspaper that she liked to work hard. According to the Guinness World Records, Japan's Kimura lived through three different centuries; experienced the advent of television, motorized vehicles, and the Internet; and was alive during the reigns or terms of multiple monarchs, emperors, and world leaders (Guinness World Records, 2012; Stump, 2012).

There was a time when Americans typically had much larger families than they do today. People also tended not to live long lives. This was before most of you were born. But you can ask your parents and grandparents about your own family history. Families would have had a lot of children around (although many of them died in infancy), and not a lot of very old people. This was generally the case on a worldwide basis as well. Consider these statistics:

- In 1950, there were 335 million children in the 0–4 age category, compared with 131 million people age 65 and older.
- In more recent times, there were 642 million children in the age category 0–4 and 523 million people 65 and older.
- Although the population of the world has increased overall, the ratio of very young to older adults has shifted as a whole. The United Nations Population Division predicts that the number of individuals in the 0–4 age category will decline in the next decade, and the number in the 65 and older category will continue to increase.
- Somewhere within that time frame, there will be more people 65 and older in the world than 0–4, signaling a reversal of past trends (Haub, 2011).

As you also saw in Chapter 1, the median age and proportion of older persons is even greater in some countries than in the United States. In fact, the increase in numbers of older adults has been especially evident in developing countries that have shifted from a primarily agricultural to an urbanized, industrial economy where access to modern health care is more widely available. Yet children under age 15 still represent 43 percent of the population of developing countries compared to 17 percent in developed countries. This means that these less developed regions of the world are experiencing population aging as they cope with providing jobs, education, and housing for the growing numbers of young people in their populations. These trends raise challenges for the health care systems and economic well-being of these countries. Indeed, given globalization, care for the most vulnerable segments—youngest and oldest—in these developing regions will increasingly become a concern for all countries (Cetron & Davies, 2010; United Nations, 2009a).

Another factor that affects global aging is life expectancy. Table 2.1 illustrates life expectancy at birth

TABLE 2.1 Life Expectancy at Birth, 2012 (United States and Other Select Developed Countries)

Country	Life Expectancy
Japan	83.91
Singapore	83.75
Australia	81.90
Italy	81.86
Canada	81.48
Sweden	81.18
Germany	80.19
United Kingdom	80.17
Portugal	78.70
United States	78.49

Source: Central Intelligence Agency, *World Factbook*, "Life Expectancy at Birth," https://www.cia.gov/library/publications/the-world-factbook/rankorder/2102rank.html.

for selected developed countries. Life expectancy affects a country's population aging, as well as its median age. As you learned in Chapter 1, it is a figure that changes over time due to a variety of factors, including better public health practices, advances in medical technology, and the availability of medicines to treat certain diseases. Life expectancy generally differs between men and women, and this difference can impact what a society of older adults looks like. For example, older Japanese women are outliving their husbands and will have to live alone, with family members or in supportive settings such as assisted living or skilled nursing facilities. These longevity gains mean that Japan's social and health care system needs to provide elder care services to its citizens for a longer period of time than in countries with shorter life expectancies (United Nations, 2007a).

Although there are many older adults in the United States, it does not lead the world in life expectancy at birth. This may be due to a number of factors, as discussed in Chapter 1, such as increasing rates of poverty, obesity, heart disease, and diabetes, along with past high rates of cigarette smoking.

Global Aging, Median Age, and Population Pyramids

Similar to projections for population aging in the United States that we discussed in Chapter 1, the global age distribution will change from a pyramid to more of a cylindrical form, as illustrated in Figure 2.1. What this graph is depicting is how many people in the world population belong to a particular age group (e.g., 50–59-year-olds). First, note that in 2025 (darker shading), there will be more people in every age category than there were in 2002. The greatest growth will be among people in their forties, fifties, and sixties, however.

Imagine you had a crystal ball and could look several decades into the future. Here is what you would probably see in terms of population aging. The most extreme societal aging will likely occur in Europe and industrialized Asian countries. By contrast, the developing world will remain comparatively young, creating a more pronounced **demographic divide** or dichotomy between the needs of young and old between developed and developing countries. But this will shift by 2050, when developing countries will have median ages as old as the developed countries are today (Hayutin, 2007a, 2007b).

The median age—the age at which half the population is younger and half is older—of these regions also varies but is increasing in all countries. An important point to remember is that a country's birthrate affects its median age. In general, if a country has a high birthrate, that will help keep the country's median age from rising as quickly

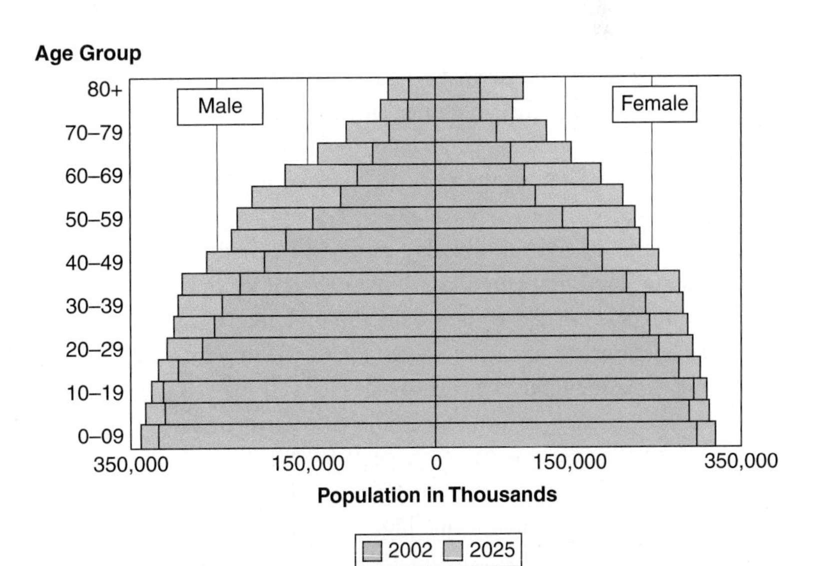

FIGURE 2.1 Global Population Pyramid in 2002 and 2025

Source: World Health Organization, *Active Ageing: A policy framework*. WHO, 2002.

TABLE 2.2 Median Ages around the World: Select Examples (2012 est.)

Country	Median Age
Japan	45.4
Germany	45.3
Italy	43.8
Switzerland	42
United States	37.1
Rwanda	18.8
Uganda	15.1

Source: Central Intelligence Agency, *World Factbook*, "Field Listing: Median Age," https://www.cia.gov/library/publications/the-world-factbook/fields/print_2177.html.

as a country that has a low birthrate. That's because a high birthrate adds to the number of people younger than the median age in a given country. Compare the median age of the countries in Table 2.2.

Note that the median age in Germany is about three times higher than that in Uganda. And not surprisingly, the median age in Rwanda is significantly lower than that in Switzerland, which means you will find many more older people in Switzerland than in Rwanda. You can find a complete and updated list of country profiles in the CIA's online *World Factbook*, including median ages for males and females separately.

Researchers who study global aging are particularly interested in following the demographic changes in countries such as Japan, Germany, and Italy in the coming decades because of their high median ages. How those countries respond and adapt to an aging population could pose lessons for the rest of the world. Compared to other developed countries, the United States will show a much smaller increase in median age due primarily to higher birthrates and more immigration. Moreover, many of the recent immigrants to the United States from Latin and Central American countries are young adults, which also contributes to keeping the U.S. median age relatively low.

The median age is also increasing in many parts of the world that you might not expect. In Africa, for example, with fertility rates three times higher than that of developed countries and high mortality rates, the median age will increase from 19 today to 27.4 in 2050. Similarly, Mexico's median age is also expected to increase significantly, from the current 26.3 to 38 by 2050, as illustrated in Figure 2.2, even though fertility rates in Mexico will remain high.

So far we have focused on the proportion or percentage of the population that older age groups represent. However, it is also important to consider the absolute numbers of older adults in a country. According to the state-run *China Daily*, there were 177.6 million people in China 60 years and older at the time of China's 2010 census, which represents 13.26 percent of the total population. That is almost 3 percent higher than the previous census in 2000. After 2013, the number of older adults is expected to exceed 200 million, and by 2050, to reach 437 million or 30 percent of the total population. Consider the fact that while it took France 115 years to double its population of elders, it will take China about 30 years to do so!

Accordingly, there will be far fewer people in China's working age group (ages 20–49) than those who will be retired and dependent on younger adults for their financial, health, and social assistance. This unparalleled increase in China's older adult population will impact pension systems, the availability of space in long-term care facilities, and the basic family structure—especially in rural areas, which many younger adults are leaving for better work opportunities in the city (He, 2011).

A major factor contributing to China's demographic shift is the country's decreasing fertility rate. This rate in 2010 was 1.56 (this means the average number of children a Chinese woman can expect to have in her lifetime is 1.56), a drop from 2.6 three decades earlier. The declining birthrate is largely a result of China's decades-long "one-child policy," created by the government to limit couples to one child, although there are exceptions, and the policy has been eased in recent years. But after decades of this policy, fewer children are being born while the

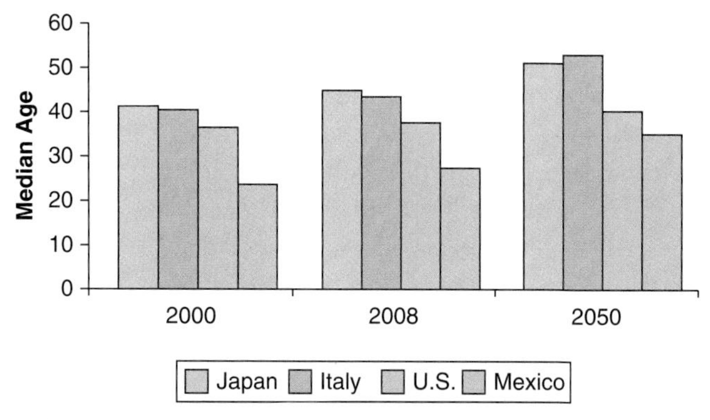

FIGURE 2.2 Median Age: 2000, 2008, and 2050

Source: United Nations, 2009.

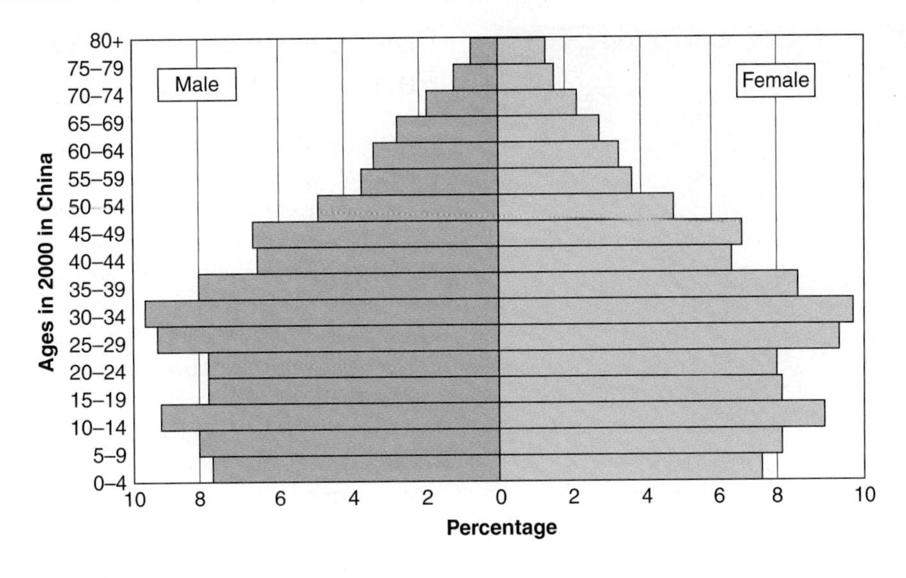

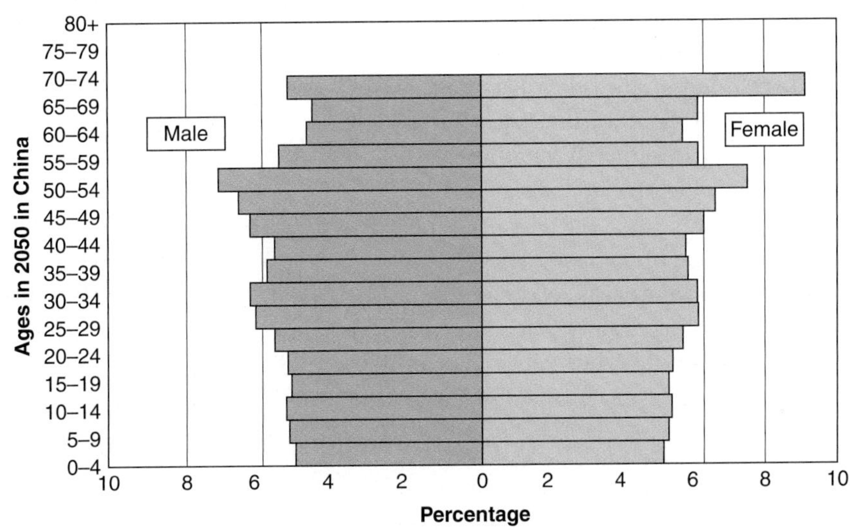

FIGURE 2.3 **Population Pyramids, China: 2000 and 2050**

Source: World Population Prospects: The 2004 Revision (2005).

number of older people in China is getting bigger, contributing to the so-called "4-2-1" phenomenon, in which an only child may be responsible for caring for two parents and four grandparents. For these reasons, a rectangular population structure will take shape, as seen in Figure 2.3. This phenomenon of a disproportionate number of older adults compared to younger persons will occur—albeit on a smaller scale—in other countries throughout the world as well (*Economist,* 2012; Kaneda, 2006; Population Reference Bureau, 2008a).

But not all countries will age similarly or as dramatically as China. Take, for example, a comparison of two countries in two very different regions of the world: Niger in Africa and the Netherlands in Northern Europe. Currently, both countries have about the same population. Niger has 16.9 million people and the Netherlands 16.8 million. However, the projected population for 2050 for Niger is 65.8 million people, whereas

points to ponder

Given the potential impact of a large proportion of an older population in smaller countries, what might be some of the societal and worldwide impacts of having half of China's 3 billion-plus population be over age 42 in less than 20 years?

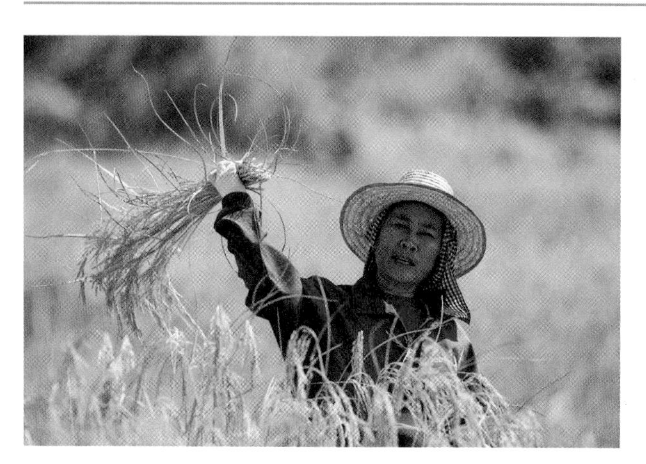

Older Asian woman cutting rice in her rural village.

it is 17.9 million people for the Netherlands. The fertility rate in Niger is much higher than in the Netherlands, and there are far fewer people age 65 and older in Niger than in the Netherlands (3 percent of the total population vs. 16 percent, respectively). In fact, the sub-Saharan countries of Africa will not only experience the largest population growth in the world but also the 10 countries with the highest fertility rates are all located in this region (Population Reference Bureau, 2013).

The following box illustrates one of the major issues facing China: the discrepancy between needed and available health care services for its booming older population. This discrepancy will not be unique to China but will be of concern to other countries where the older adult population may outgrow available health care services.

The challenge of caring for growing numbers of older adults has raised ethical and financial concerns for many countries in the developing and industrialized world, as well as for the children of aging parents. The problem is compounded in countries where many in the younger generation have immigrated to other countries or other regions within a country for work.

China's Elder Care Crisis

A recent article in the English-language *China Post* reported that the increase in China's aging population is putting pressure on the country's care system for frail elders. The country has only 2.5 million beds in nursing homes, but 8 million elders are estimated to be seeking this type of housing. The need for skilled nursing facilities for elders with dementia is acute. The Shanghai No. 3 Elderly Home is the first in China designed specifically for dementia patients. But China, like many countries, is using a 90-7-3 plan: 90 percent of elders will need to be cared for at home, 7 percent make occasional visits to a community center, and 3 percent will live in nursing homes. In addition to greater demands on families to provide care, the government estimates that 10 million nurses and other health specialists are needed to look after these elders, but to date only 220,000 are available in China. Even among this limited supply of care providers, 90 percent are estimated to be inadequately trained in long-term care and gerontology (Barboza, 2011).

Chinese Government: Visit Your Parents or Else ...

If news reports are accurate, China may be taking an unconventional approach by forcing adult children to visit their aging parents or risk being sued. At the end of 2012, various news organizations reported that China's national legislature would allow parents to sue their adult children for not visiting them often. A later law now requires that adult children visit or send greetings to parents. BBC News reported that China has a million people above the age of 80. It also reported that elder abuse and neglect are growing problems. As is happening in other regions of the world, employable Chinese workers are leaving rural areas to find jobs in the cities, often leaving their older relatives behind without support (BBC News Online, 2012).

What It Means To Be Old around the World

Who is considered an older adult in other parts of the world? There is no international standard for classifying someone as an older person, although the United Nations tends to use age 60. When you see this term or one of its variants used in research, you need to find out who would be included in this category. Outside the United States, someone may be categorized as an older adult based on whether he or she qualifies for pension benefits from the government; that age might be older or younger than age 65, which is the age that someone in the United States has typically been regarded as an older adult. In general, older adults are usually thought of as being around 60–65 if the age is tied to pension or retirement criteria. However, as you will read about in this section, the retirement age is a moving target in many countries, especially as governments around the world struggle with weak economies. Also complicating the situation is that in some countries, especially developing countries, there are no reliable birth records that can verify the ages of older people. You have also been learning that chronological age is not necessarily the same as biological aging, since some populations—especially those living in poverty—are physiologically old at age 50.

In developed countries, the number of older adults is expected to grow by more than 50 percent in the coming decades, rising from 264 million in 2009 to 416 million in 2050. The population age 65 and older formed 18 percent of Western and Southern European countries in 2008. As you have just learned in our discussion of life expectancy and median age, overall, Japan and Italy have the highest proportion of elders in the world (Population Reference Bureau, 2008a; United Nations, 2009b).

But keep your eyes on developing nations. Currently, 60 percent of older adults live in developing countries. The projected increase in the numbers and proportion of persons age 60 and older is higher for developing nations than for the more developed ones—increasing from 475 million in 2009 to 1.6 billion in 2050, when about 80 percent of the world's older adults will be living in developing countries. This is not surprising, considering that world population growth is taking place largely in developing countries and is likely to continue to do so (United Nations, 2009b).

As you learned earlier, one reason developing countries are aging rapidly is the reduction in fertility rates worldwide. In fact, for the 49 least developed countries, fertility rates are projected to drop from the current 4.39 children per woman to 2.41 by 2050. It is estimated that 120 countries will reach total fertility rates below replacement levels (i.e., 2.1 children per woman) by 2025,

Protestors in France demonstrate against government plans to overhaul the national pension system.

compared to 22 countries falling into this category in 1975 and 70 in 2000 (United Nations, 2009b).

As we noted earlier, low fertility rates combined with increased life expectancy in more developed countries have created a demographic divide. Such a dichotomy between the needs of young and old may result in conflicts over how to provide employment to both younger and older workers. One strategy is for national leaders to change retirement policies, as we have seen recently in many European countries, particularly Greece, Italy, and France. This can help lower deficits in spending by reducing the number of retirees who depend on government pensions (money paid by the government to retirees who paid into the retirement system during their working career), and by continuing the contributions of employed older adults to the economy. However, politicians who attempt to increase the retirement age in their countries have faced a barrage of angry citizens, as illustrated in the box on page 42 (Bloom & Canning, 2007).

In summary, the global demographic trends in aging can be summarized this way:

- The percentage of older people in the world population will dramatically increase over the next few decades, while the percentage of younger people will decrease.
- If you were to study the population at three different points in time—for example, 10, 20, and 30 years from now—you would find at each of those points a successively larger percentage of older people in the world population.
- More people age 65 and older will have to continue working in developed countries both to make ends meet due to diminished retirement investments and to reduce the burden on their country's economy.

Global Concerns about Elders' Human Rights

A Human Rights Day was established by the United Nations in 1950 to make people everywhere conscious of the importance of human rights and freedom. Over 60 years later—and with the globalization of aging—the UN General Assembly adopted a resolution establishing a working group to address protections for the rights of older people. This is the first meaningful step toward creating a Human Rights Instrument (a legally binding agreement) on the rights of older people. With such an instrument, governments would have an explicit legal framework that would enable them to ensure that older people's rights are realized in our increasingly aging societies.

Reactions in European Countries to Raising the Retirement Age

During the summer of 2010, students and union members rioted and looted in several French cities. Their reason: to protest a government plan to raise the retirement age from 60 to 62 (with eligibility for full state pensions raised from 65 to 67). Flights were canceled at French airports, as were intercity trains; there was a slowdown by truck drivers and dock workers as unionized employees protested the government's plan. Despite these inconveniences, 71 percent of French adults supported the strikers and their stance against increasing the retirement age. A similar plan by the government of Spain to raise the retirement age from 65 to 67 was also opposed by their labor unions. But the government held sway, and the increase in retirement age will become fully implemented by 2025.

In response to its declining population of young workers and increasing number of elders, Italy will also raise its retirement age. Currently government workers and men in the private sector can retire at age 65, while women in the private sector can do so at age 60. However, as in other countries, changes to Italy's retirement age will be implemented in 2015 in an attempt to curb government spending.

Keep in mind as you read about these changes in many of these countries that it is not just generous pensions and other benefits that have resulted in huge deficits but also inequitable tax policies that often favor the wealthy.

Baby Boomers in Japan Just as the baby boomers account for the huge bulge in the older population in the United States, this age cohort is changing Japanese society. Baby boomers in Japan account for almost 9 percent of the workforce, so their retirement will be a blow to Japan's economy at a time when the overall labor force is shrinking and fewer workers are available to pay into a pension system. Moreover, the decline of workers and young families will make it even harder for Japan to generate new wealth. Nevertheless, politicians and Japanese society in general have long resisted immigration as a way to increase the number of young workers contributing to the economic support of retirees. Reports by the United Nations and demographers project a need for 13–17 million new immigrants by 2050 in order to prevent the collapse of Japan's pension system. Yet in the past 25 years, only 1 million foreigners have been accepted as immigrants in this insular country (AARP, 2009; Bloom & Canning, 2007; Powell, 2010).

Although lacking an adequate elder care workforce, Japan has nevertheless been innovative in its approach to a rising older adult population. For example, the University of Tokyo has been working to turn the city of Kashiwa in Chiba Prefecture into a community geared toward the needs of an aging population. This small city will have home care services available 24 hours a day, housing complexes that incorporate workplaces, and other facilities designed with older adults in mind. Situated centrally in each of the new blocks will be a clinic capable of providing 24-hour in-home medical care and a center for home nursing visits and care, so residents with relatively minor illnesses will not have to go to a large hospital. The project emphasizes the maintenance of mental as well as physical health. Quite a few residents of the old housing blocks were found to confine themselves at home after retirement. So old five-story residential buildings where working families have lived for decades will be replaced with barrier-free 10–14-story condominium blocks equipped with elevators. There will be a community restaurant where residents can socialize and work. Takeout dishes will be available for older residents living alone and employed women. Many elders also hated commuting in crowded trains, wishing instead to work hours of their own choosing. With these residents in mind, a plan was drafted to create urban agriculture. Elders will also assist in child care, including after-school care for children (Yoshimura, 2010).

Japan's Aging Crisis

Japan is experiencing the most rapid rate of population aging in the world.

- In 1970, 7 percent of its population was 65 or older, but this increased to 22 percent in 2008. By 2050 they are expected to make up almost 40 percent of Japan's population.
- Even more striking is the prediction that 24 percent will be age 85 and older in 2030.
- By 2050, Japan is expected to have 1 million people age 100 and older.
- The fertility rate in 2012 was 1.41, up from its record-low of 1.26 in 2006 but below the replacement rate of 2.1.

This rise in the number of older adults along with reduced birthrates will eventually turn their population pyramid into an upside-down one, in less than 40 years.

Japan's Declining Immigrant Population

Japan has been very selective about allowing immigrants into the country. Between 1990 and the early 2000s, the government issued work visas to 366,000 Brazilians and other South Americans of Japanese descent. These guest workers made up the largest group of foreign blue-collar workers in Japan, employed by the industrial sector and performing jobs that native-born Japanese often prefer not to do. During the 2008 economic crisis, the government undertook an emergency program to offer South American guest workers $3,000 each for their airfare and $2,000 for each dependent to return to their home country. This offer was contingent on these immigrants agreeing not to return or apply for worker visas later. Despite its rising unemployment rate, Japan continues to have a shortage of staff to care for frail elders and has not made efforts to retrain its industrial workers for these types of jobs, or to bring guest workers from other countries to fill those positions (Tabuchi, 2009).

Economic Implications for Industrialized Countries

As you have seen, a number of countries in Europe—Italy and Germany in particular—are aging at a relatively rapid pace. Many gerontologists are interested in studying the shifting demographics of these rapidly aging societies because, like Japan, they may provide a glimpse into the future of other countries whose population is aging.

Before going any further, it should be noted that Europe is an extremely diverse region, although people sometimes refer to those countries as if they were a single entity. The European Union (EU), a multinational political and economic partnership that began after World War II, currently consists of 28 member states, but keep in mind that even the European Union does not represent all of Europe. Studying issues related to population aging in Europe can be a challenge because there are sometimes distinct variations from country to country—for example, different median ages and social structures. Comparing data from individual European countries can give you a sense of the wide diversity among European countries.

In an attempt to understand the older adult population in various European countries, a research project called SHARE—Survey of Health, Aging, and Retirement in Europe—has been collecting data since 2004 from a sample of individuals age 50 and older in 11 European countries. The project, centrally coordinated from the Mannheim Research Institute for the Economics of Aging in Germany, is collecting data on various topics (e.g., health, economics, and social support). SHARE has the potential to become a regional European longitudinal study. One of the findings from the research is that geriatric care needs improvement in all of the countries surveyed (Europa, 2008).

AARP International—www.aarpinternational.org—is another source of information about aging in 27 European countries. You can also find out a country's median age, health care expenditure, fertility rate, and other data.

Older Europeans in the Workforce

The proportion of older adults who continue to be employed in European Union countries declines precipitously with age. The working age population (ages 15–64) of EU member nations is expected to decline by an average of 7 percent between 2005 and 2030 compared to an increase in the population of elders by 52 percent. Of course, not all people choose to retire when they are eligible to do so. Some continue to work out of necessity or by choice (European Commission, 2005; United Nations, 2007b).

A concern for many European countries is the perception that older adults with pensions are benefiting more than younger generations. As you have learned, until recently state pension plans and early retirement incentives to avoid layoffs in the EU countries made it attractive for workers to retire in their fifties and early sixties. This allowed companies and governments to hire less expensive younger workers. But with the decline in the younger population and as middle-aged workers begin to retire, many companies are experiencing problems in replacing these skilled workers with new employees who have the necessary qualifications. EU countries project a decline in their 20–29-year-old population by 20 percent in the next two decades, coupled with an increase in the 50–64 age group by 25 percent. And as we saw earlier, the reliance of young retirees on public pensions

European Trends

Germany, Sweden, Belgium, Denmark, and Ireland all have relatively high median ages. A June 2011 Eurostat report, called *The Greying of the Baby Boomers*, suggested that over the next half-century, 31 European countries will experience population aging at unprecedented levels, but the magnitude, speed, and timing will likely vary. This phenomenon will lead to reverse population pyramids, with the majority of the population being comprised of older people (the top of the pyramid), and the minority of the population being comprised of younger people (the bottom of the pyramid). Immigration of younger people from outside Europe to these aging European countries could slow down population aging, but as in the United States, the policies and attitudes toward immigration are not without controversy and contention (Lanzieri, 2011).

for longer time periods has also contributed to the economic crises—and protests by pensioners—faced by some European countries (Von Nordheim, 2003).

In hindsight, it has become clear that the recession of 2008 was caused by a complex array of factors, including current tax policies and the collapse of major U.S. financial institutions. The recession has had severe consequences for many people around the world, especially the working class and older adults on fixed incomes who rely heavily on their pensions for basic necessities. The long-term effects of the global economic crisis may be even more pronounced as governments worldwide struggle to provide public benefits with dwindling public resources.

EU leaders have attempted to implement changes in pensions and social security systems to achieve a goal of having employees age 55–64 make up 50 percent of their workforce. Many developed countries are implementing incentives for—and removing barriers against—longer employment, such as improving the quality of working conditions for older workers. Through incentives, tax credits, training, attractive benefits, flexibility in scheduling, placement counseling, and other options, companies are offering older or retired workers an alternative to leaving the workforce so they will continue to contribute to the economy and the tax base of their country (United Nations, 2009b). Italy is another European country changing dramatically because of economic and demographic pressures. Many younger Italians are moving to other countries, often to find better paying jobs, but leaving older Italians behind. That puts more responsibility on an increasingly smaller population of younger adults who remain in Italy to provide care and funding for social services and pensions.

As we briefly discussed earlier, developed countries are also faced with whether or not to permit continued immigration of young workers as a way to address workforce needs. For example, more than 25 percent of all workers in Australia are immigrants as a result of liberal immigration policies. However, this is a controversial proposal for countries where immigrants often are not easily assimilated because of languages, religions, and cultures divergent from those of the host country. Resistance is strong in many Western European countries that do not define themselves as multicultural societies and fear losing their national identity. Some countries, such as France, have experienced tensions and even rioting over the treatment of foreign workers. In the United States, similar tensions have led some states to propose stringent laws to prevent immigration by uneducated workers. Resistance to immigrants meeting workforce needs is likely to intensify as long as there are growing unemployment rates due to the worldwide recession (Haub, 2007).

A Village of Italian Elders

In 2003, a BBC reporter visited a tiny village in southern Italy called Cersosimo. He profiled a 77-year-old woman who lived alone in the village. Her children were grown and had moved away. Two-thirds of the people who live in the village are over 65, and the younger people in the village are having fewer children. Classes in the local school had to be combined because there were so few students. The mayor offered a financial incentive to any family having a baby in the village, but that did not help much. One couple who had a child in the village said they would not have any more because it is too expensive. The 77-year-old woman said that what's needed is a long-term care facility. If funds can be raised, the unused portion of the school may be converted to one. This is an extreme case, but it illustrates what can happen when the population of older and younger people in a community is severely out of balance (Stephen Sackur (2003), http://news.bbc.co.uk/2/hi/programmes/from_our_own_correspondent/3117379.stm).

Reflection Break

Let's say you are at a social gathering, and someone you are talking to expresses interest in the gerontology class you are taking. That person says, "Tell me something about the global aging phenomenon. I vaguely know what that is, but I'd be interested in learning more details." How would you respond? If you can't come up with a thoughtful, well-organized response to this question, you may want to review the previous section and see if you can then do so. Here's a hint: You can begin by telling your questioner approximately how many people in the world are older adults, and then start talking about some prevailing patterns discussed earlier in regard to global aging. Also, mention what countries in the world are aging faster than others. What factors contribute to a rapidly aging population? What would be a way to slow that process down? Your listener will probably be very impressed by your knowledge of the global aging phenomenon!

Given what you have learned, you may be wondering which are the good countries to grow old in. Some researchers point to the Scandinavian countries—Denmark, Sweden, Norway, and Finland, for example. They are seen as having excellent so-called "cradle-to-grave" social programs, with their governments placing a priority on ensuring that their older adults have comprehensive elder care programs so they can live out their later years for as long as possible in their own homes. Home care services are available, and health care providers make house calls. Home visits by a nurse, for example, provide a sense of reassurance and an opportunity for regular health monitoring and education. One observer noted that the system helps where needed, but doesn't take over the elders' lives. These countries devote significantly more of their gross domestic product to long-term care compared to many other developed countries, but as one person noted: "It's not just about money, it's about a philosophy." These countries' approach to comprehensive elder care may have important lessons for other regions where the needs of an increasingly aging population loom on the horizon (Steed, 2008).

Many of the countries we have discussed thus far are modern, industrial societies, although they may have traditional villages and communities in their rural or outlying areas. The United States, Japan, China, and most of the countries in the European Union are tied into the global economic system, have technologically advanced industrial sectors, and can boast of urban centers that resemble big cities anywhere else in the world. Now we turn to examining a very different social setting, the traditional society.

Older Adults in Traditional Societies and the Impact of Modernization

As you may have noticed within your own ethnic or nationality group, the social position and experiences of older persons vary across cultures. You may have observed how older adults from different cultures in your neighborhood participate (or not) in the life of the community and of their extended family. By examining the different ways that other cultures address issues affecting their elders, we can learn more about the process of aging in our own society. The field of **comparative sociocultural gerontology** or an **anthropology of aging** has helped researchers differentiate what aspects of aging are universal or biological, and which factors are largely shaped by the sociocultural system (Infeld, 2002; Sokolovsky, 1997).

Such understanding of social and cultural differences can also suggest strategies for improving the social lives of older people in our ethnically diverse society. Within the constraints of this chapter, we can only glance at a few other cultures. For a more complete view, we urge you to turn to the available literature on the anthropology of aging, including the *Journal of Cross-Cultural Gerontology* and *International Journal of Ageing and Later Life*.

Differences in the status and roles of older adults are most distinctive between traditional societies and the modernized world, with its rapidly changing values, norms, and lifestyles. Prior to the industrial age, most of our communities could be characterized as traditional societies. As industrialization spread through various parts of the world, cosmopolitan urban centers began to emerge throughout the world, which attracted a wide mix of people in search of a new way of life. Traditional societies, however, did not disappear. They continue to exist today and are characterized by their preindustrial, often agrarian culture and multigenerational family units, long-standing norms and values, and tradition-based social structure. Elders, for example, may be afforded a more respected role in traditional societies and treated by younger members with deference. Although many of these societies experience an out-migration of their younger members who leave to pursue jobs or educational opportunities, these communities tend to be culturally homogeneous. Traditional societies have their strengths and positive attributes and should not be viewed as being primitive or inferior to modern societies. When people from traditional societies immigrate to a new country, they often bring valuable aspects of their home culture with them to their new homeland.

Definitions of old age—as well as the authority exercised by older people—have traditionally rested on the material and political resources controlled by them in traditional societies. These resources include

- time-honored skills and knowledge,
- security bestowed by property rights,
- civil and political power,
- information control, and
- contributions to the welfare of families and the larger society through services performed by older people, such as child care.

Older adults are afforded a special status—one of honor and respect—in many traditional societies across different cultures. They may hold positions of leadership and be consulted for their wise counsel. For example, they are offered the best pieces of food during meals and are served before younger members of the family. Children are taught from an early age to treasure the community's elders, and adult children and other community members step in as caregivers when their elders need their support.

In Asia, the concept of **filial piety** is a familiar one and a central part of many societies' ethical code of conduct, and illustrates the high status of elders in more traditional societies. Articulated by the Chinese philosopher Confucius, filial piety emphasizes the importance of being good and compassionate to one's elders and to honor one's ancestors. You will see examples of this concept in the discussion that follows. Even after an elder has died, his or her memory may be honored for generations through daily prayers and offerings at a home shrine or at a temple. Native American and Native Hawaiian cultures are well known for treasuring older members of the community. The Hawaiian word *kupuna*, which translates to "respected elder," connotes both affection and deep respect, and none of the negative associations that accompany the words "elderly" or "aged" in contemporary Western society. Contrast these traditional views and the treatment of older adults with ones you may find in more modern, urban societies, where popular culture appears largely youth oriented and older people may be overlooked, ridiculed, and even scorned.

Traditional systems of **social stratification** conferred respect and authority to older adults who controlled such resources or skills. Older people's social rank was generally determined by the balance between the cost of maintaining them and the contributions they made to the family unit and society as a whole. In some settings, older adults, such as the aged shaman of tribes and clans, have control over resources, knowledge, and traditions that younger members of society consider to be socially desirable or important. Elders in American Indian tribes and India also are afforded a special place in their traditional communities. Some East African societies assign politically powerful positions to men who reach a certain age. Pacific Islander grandparents play an important cultural role in transmitting cultural values to younger generations, often linking them with their ancestors, spiritual beliefs, and language. As age became a less important criterion for determining access to and control of traditional and political resources, older members of society lost some of their status and authority, however. We can see this process in many African countries, where rapid societal changes resulting from socio-demographic shifts, poverty, and the HIV/AIDS epidemic have placed unexpected burdens on older people to support younger generations.

With increasing migration of younger family members to urban centers, older adults in rural

Grandmother teaching traditional calligraphy to her granddaughter.

Africa cannot rely on their adult children to care for them. Instead, many provide a critical role as caregivers themselves to grandchildren left behind by parents who seek employment in distant cities. This responsibility has been compounded by the growing number of AIDS orphans, especially in sub-Saharan Africa. In most cases, they receive very little government support for their surrogate parenting. To make matters worse, most African countries provide little, if any, social security or pension benefits for their older citizens, assuming that the family will be the "safety net." Indeed, the role of grandparents as primary caregivers for grandchildren or great-grandchildren, because their adult children are unable or unwilling to provide care, is now a global phenomenon. When parents move to another community, often out of economic necessity, leaving children to be raised by grandparents, the living arrangement is sometimes referred to as a **skipped-generation household** in the United States. We will discuss these changing family patterns in Chapter 7 (United Nations, 2008).

We turn next to more examples of how modernization has had an impact on such traditional societies.

Modernization Theory

Many theories have been advanced to explain the declining status of older people in modern society. **Modernization theory**, one of these explanations, is defined as the transformation of a society from a relatively rural way of life toward an urban way, with highly differentiated institutions and individual roles. Additionally, modernized societies have a cosmopolitan outlook that emphasizes efficiency and progress (Cowgill, 1974, 1986).

Modernization theory can be a useful way to understand how societies change and the effect this change has on the lives of older people. All parts of the world are becoming increasingly urbanized, with 50 percent of the world's population now living in cities compared to 30 percent in 1950. Even in developing countries, urban populations are expected to double over the next 30 years. Moreover, the highest rates of urban growth are expected in the poorest parts of the world (United Nations State of World Population, 2011).

In the early stages of modernization, young people from rural areas are attracted to cities. Older parents and grandparents remain on the family farm or in rural villages. The resulting residential segregation of the generations has a dramatic impact on family interactions. The geographic and occupational mobility of the young, in turn, leads to greater social distance between generations, a reduced status of the old, and disruption of the tradition of family support for their elders (Hayutin, 2007b).

As another example, rapid urbanization has left almost 30 percent of old people in rural areas in India without their family nearby to care for them. Modern migration projects have resulted in more young people becoming educated and sometimes acting as if superior to their illiterate elders. Meanwhile, families who eke out a meager living in urban areas cannot assist their elders who live with them. In other Asian countries, such as Japan and South Korea, older people have benefited from improvements in health care, income, and long-term care services. Yet these gains often come at the cost of power, respect, and prestige that were accorded to previous generations of older adults (Silverman, Hecht, & McMillin, 2000).

Another change affecting the status of older adults is that communication and scientific technology create new jobs primarily for the young, with older workers more likely to remain in traditional occupations that become obsolete. The rapid development of high-tech industries today and the generational differences in the use of the Internet illustrate this phenomenon. Some older workers may feel marginalized and alienated if they are not able to contribute to a technologically skilled workforce, although growing numbers of older adults are becoming technologically savvy.

Modernization and Elders' Declining Social Status

According to modernization theory, older people lose political and social power, influence, and leadership as societies modernize. They also become less engaged in the life of their community. Younger and older generations tend to

points to ponder

Apply modernization theory to your community or one that you have studied, say in a history, sociology, or anthropology class. Are there examples you can think of where older people have lost their political and social power, influence, and leadership as a result of modernization?

South Korea's Efforts to Improve Care of Frail Elders

The government of South Korea has launched an effort to cope with its increasing population of older people, especially those with dementia. The population age 65 and older is projected to grow from 7 percent in 2000 to 14 percent in 2018 to 20 percent in 2026, a threefold increase over 26 years. The problem is exacerbated by the low birthrate of South Korea, with fewer young family members and workers to care for Korea's elders. The proportion of elders with dementia is also estimated to increase as more efforts are made to diagnose the condition early and to reduce its stigma. Care for elders with dementia is still largely provided by families, but there is also a trend toward more skilled nursing facilities. They have tripled since 2008, while adult day care and home care programs have increased fivefold in this same period. The Korean government is financing these new programs with a new long-term care insurance plan every Korean helps to finance through their national health insurance premiums. Government funds and public insurance are increasingly being spent on dementia care, the equivalent of 1 billion dollars in 2009. But this may not be enough as the number of frail elders grows and fewer young family members are available to be away from their jobs to care for their elders. The government is also financing programs to educate those whose work brings them into contact with many elders as "dementia supporters." Workers such as postal carriers and bus drivers are learning how to recognize dementia and to assist elders with this condition (Belluck, 2010).

become separated socially, morally, and intellectually. Youth is glorified as the embodiment of progress and achievement. This was evident during the protests in Cairo, Egypt, in early 2011, when young people took to the streets and used modern communication technologies such as Twitter and Facebook to reach out to the rest of the world, while older Egyptians tended to remain on the sidelines.

Taiwan is another country where modernization has eroded traditional family supports; young adults' support for multigenerational households has steadily declined. Similarly, adult children in China report feeling less obligated to help their parents if this conflicts with the demands of their job. Recall earlier discussions about challenges in China as its population ages. In such instances, it becomes vital for national and local governments to provide services such as public housing, health care, pension plans, and policies that support family care of elders. One example is the investment in long-term care facilities by the South Korean government, as illustrated in the box on this page (Hsu, Lew-Ting, & Wu, 2001; Zhan, 2004).

To summarize modernization theory, modernization over time contributes to the lower status of older adults through the following macro- (or societal)- level changes:

- urbanization
- communications technology
- health technology
- scientific technology used in economic production and distribution
- literacy and mass education

Some demographers have found that increases in the socioeconomic status of older persons or their adult children do not result in significant changes in traditional family structures and the value of family interdependence. In contrast, other demographers have suggested that the improved health and financial status of older populations and a trend toward individualism have resulted in more older adults choosing to live apart from their adult children. Others lose their family support system because their children move away. The box on page 49 about India illustrates what can happen when adult children immigrate to another country, leaving their aging parents behind with no one to care for them (Cameron, 2000; Kinsella & Velkoff, 2001).

In the early phases of rapid social change (illustrated by nations such as China and the Philippines), the occupational and educational status of older adults shows a decline, but later improves (exemplified by New Zealand, Canada, and the United States). Thus, as societies move beyond an initial state of rapid modernization, status differences between generations decrease and the relative standing of older people may rise. Societies in advanced stages of modernization may become more concerned about the older population's devalued status. Through public education, social policies, and the media, they then attempt to create more opportunities for, and positive images of, older people. Although there is still a long way to go, this has already been occurring to some degree in the United States, in part because of the aging of the baby boomers, who have the political clout and resources to change popular stereotypes of aging.

Long-Term Care in India

With many young Indians immigrating to Western countries, the population of India is growing older. This change in its population structure leaves many elders with no young family members to care for them, unlike their parents and grandparents who lived in multigenerational households and for whom long-term care was provided by younger generations. To make matters worse, India has a basic, limited social security system and few Indians have pensions. There are elders, abandoned by their adult children, who are forced to seek care in homes for the destitute. There is also a growing market for high-end nursing homes to accommodate older Indians whose children can pay for their care while they earn a living abroad.

Two men engaged in an intergenerational greeting.

Impact of Modernization on Respect and Care toward Elders in Asian Cultures

Depending on your cultural or ethnic background, you may have been raised to be respectful to elders. As we discussed previously, most societies have some norms of respect toward their elders, but considerable variability exists in practice. For example, the Confucian concept or value of filial piety may not be practiced uniformly by all Chinese families. Chinese society itself has changed, especially in recent years. Women have greater opportunities in the workplace, education, and their marriage prospects, which have an impact on traditional roles and relationships. The Chinese government's family planning policy encouraging one child per family has changed the structure of families and resulted in a disproportionate balance between the number of older adults and working age younger adults. Because male children have traditionally been favored by Chinese families, this policy has been criticized for contributing to a gender imbalance. The lower number of children and females in Chinese society can have serious implications for family caregiving and long-term care in general in the years ahead.

As discussed earlier, Japan is facing similar concerns due to the low birthrate and robust longevity in its population. The percentage of older retired parents living with their adult children in Japan has declined due to urbanization, industrialization, the growing number of employed women, and fewer adult children available to care for their aging parents. The number of households consisting of only an older couple has grown, and a greater percentage of urban elders live alone compared to their counterparts in rural areas. Middle-aged women (most often daughters and daughters-in-law) remain the primary caregivers to Japanese elders, as in most other countries. The Japanese concept of ***oya koko*** is based on the tradition of filial piety and understood to mean that adult children are obligated to take care of their parents when the time comes. Indeed, negligence toward one's parents is a source of great public shame. Moreover, the proportion of older parents living in multigenerational households is still higher than in any other industrialized nation. With the growing proportion of educated, professional women and newer cohorts influenced more by Western values than by Confucianism, many women do not want to leave their jobs to become caregivers to their parents or parents-in-law. Similar to their American counterparts, they increasingly are faced with juggling elder care, child care, and employment.

Given such demands, the Japanese government has responded by providing free basic medical services for all those 70 and older; establishing a public long-term care insurance system; and creating tax and other incentives for home care by families. More community-based long-term services and supports are needed in Japan, but this universal program appears to partially relieve the burden on Japanese families and hospitals, where most long-term care is provided today at a very high cost. Policy-makers in other developed countries are closely watching Japan's program as a possible model for day-to-day care of their oldest-old while still preserving adult children's responsibility for their parents' care. Recognizing the escalating costs of institutional care, Japanese policy-makers established an "Active Aging Society" framework by emphasizing prevention, such as exercise programs and nutritional counseling, and a community-wide care system (AARP, 2006; GSA, 2009; National Institute of Population and Social Security Research, 2006).

A strong belief in respect for parents also plays a dominant role in family attitudes and government policies regarding care for aging parents in South Korea. This is another country experiencing rapid aging, as we noted above, with a threefold increase in the number of people 65 and older in the past 25 years. At the same time, changing demographics today have placed a greater burden on women as caregivers, with average family size down to 3.0 and with 46 percent of all married women in Korea working outside the home. Nevertheless, more than 90 percent of young Koreans believe that adult children must care for their older parents. This reflects the traditional value of filial piety that you learned about earlier. As a result, 90 percent of older Koreans cite family as their primary source of support. Moreover, 65 percent of older people live with their adult children, even in urbanized areas like Seoul. As in most Asian countries, daughters-in-law are expected to provide most of the primary care for their aging parents-in-law. Such filial duties are performed within the framework of "serving" elders rather than "caring" for them. While this concept conveys a less egalitarian relationship, it places traditional parental obligations at the center of elder care. The government of South Korea promotes family-based caregiving by sponsoring a "Respect for Elders Day" and a "Respect for Elders Week," as well as prizes to honor outstanding examples of filial piety. These initiatives are intended to help reduce Koreans' expectations for long-term services and supports from the government (Lan, 2002; Levande, Herrick, & Sung, 2000; Sung, 2001).

U.N. Message for International Day of Older Persons (2012)

"On this International Day, I call on governments to do more to address the needs of older persons. The key interventions are well known: granting universal access to social services; increasing the number and worth of pension plans; and creating laws and policies that prevent age and gender discrimination in the workplace" Ban Ki-moon, Secretary-General, United Nations (Ban, 2012).

Other Asian countries where filial piety persists, despite changing work and family patterns, are Singapore, Thailand, and the Philippines, where the majority of parents age 60 and older live with their children. The importance of filial piety generally supersedes modern social and economic demands in these Asian countries. A more radical approach toward ensuring parent care occurred in Singapore when the government set up a special court where older persons can bring legal claims against their children for not providing assistance in their later years (Kinsella & Velkoff, 2001; Loong, 2009).

By 2050, Singapore's median age is expected to be similar to that of Japan and Italy. The state is preparing for its aging population through initiatives to encourage self-sufficiency. Government subsidies support public housing or purchase of a home for 90 percent of older Singaporeans. The Singaporean government has also invested in improvements to the country's infrastructure to allow people to age in place, by building barrier-free homes and expanding transportation options. A mandatory savings plan of risk-free bonds requires deposits throughout the working years and withdrawals only during retirement. In addition, the government controls health care costs for elders. Although the mandatory retirement age in Singapore is 62, employers can rehire workers for another three years. Singapore has also passed laws requiring adult children to care for their elders, or pay for them to receive long-term services and supports. Like Singapore, other countries are planning for the increased numbers of older retirees by encouraging more self-sufficiency and personal responsibility (Loong, 2009).

This overall pattern of rapid urban population growth globally is expected to continue through 2030. Urban growth at 4–6 percent per year in parts of Africa, Asia, and South America will accelerate the problem of isolated elders in rural areas and declines in intergenerational support as their children seek opportunities in urban centers (United Nations, 2005).

Immigrants to the United States

The United States continues to be the adopted homeland for millions of foreign-born residents, both young and old. Between 1990 and 2010, the number of foreign-born U.S. residents doubled from 20 million to 40 million, which was responsible for approximately one-third of the U.S. population growth. U.S.-born children and grandchildren of immigrants further contribute to an expanding population (Martin & Midgley, 2010).

In the past decade, the majority of legal immigrants came from Latin America (41 percent) and Asia (34 percent), with a much smaller number from Europe and Canada (15 percent). This is a dramatic change from the 1950–1959 time period, when almost half of legal U.S. immigrants came from Europe and Canada. Foreign-born residents age 65 and older have grown since 1990, from 2.7 million to 4.3 million in recent years. Every decade since then, the number of legal immigrants to the United States has increased. By 2050, the number of foreign-born elders in the United States may reach 16 million. The majority are concentrated in California, Florida, Illinois, New Jersey, New York, and Texas (Brown, 2009; Kandel, 2011; Martin & Midgley, 2010).

As you are probably well aware, immigration policy has given rise to much debate and varying points of view among Americans for more than a century. Arizona's tough immigration bill that was signed into law in 2010, for example, resulted in a legal challenge by the Justice Department against the State of Arizona. This struck down the most stringent and discriminatory parts of that bill. Despite these battles, more states are considering laws to limit immigration, even though immigration over the years has contributed to America's productivity and rich ethnic and cultural diversity.

Snapshot of Older Immigrants in the United States

- Foreign-born adults age 65 years or older comprise 11.9% of the total U.S. population 65 years and older.
- Among these immigrants, 43.9 percent are not naturalized U.S. citizens.
- The majority of this population immigrated before they were 65 and has lived in the United States for 30–40 years. In other words, they have grown old in the United States.
- So-called "later-life immigrants" (i.e., immigrants who come to the United States as older adults) represent a minority of immigrants.
- The majority of later-life immigrants are sponsored by their adult children.
- After a 1965 U.S. policy change making it easier for later-life immigrant family members to come to the United States, their numbers have steadily increased.
- Because of changes in the Immigration and Naturalization Act to give preferential entry for family members through the Family Reunification Act, the majority of older immigrants in recent years arrive as "immediate relatives of U.S. citizens."
- Nearly 75 percent of recent older immigrants are unable to speak English or have poor proficiency in the English language; this means they are more dependent on family members and others to help them when English language is needed for a range of everyday activities. In some instances, no one in the household speaks English.
- They are more likely than older native-born citizens to be living in a household with a grandchild.

(Borjas, 2007; Population Reference Bureau, 2008b; Wilmoth, 2012).

Elder mother and daughter enjoy spending time together.

Immigrant Elders' Changing Roles and Expectations

Adult children who precede their parents to the new country often encourage them to immigrate because they are concerned about providing care for their aging parents from a geographic distance, especially when other siblings are unavailable in the home country. In some cases, the assistance is mutually beneficial because the parents live with or near their adult children in order to help in family-owned businesses and as caregivers for grandchildren. In other cases, when elders immigrate for the sake of their children and grandchildren, their social and psychological well-being can be disrupted at a time when their own health may be declining.

Social isolation and depression often result. Depression rates run as high as 26 percent among immigrant elders. This may be linked to financial problems, lack of health insurance coverage, multiple chronic diseases, and grief over leaving their home and friends. In a study of older Chinese immigrants in Boston, elders with the most chronic diseases and worst self-ratings of health were the most depressed. Lacking economic and educational resources, older immigrants typically depend on younger generations for financial and social support.

points to **ponder**

Some cross-cultural researchers might want to clarify that filial piety is not an exclusively Asian concept or value but practiced to some degree in all cultures. Indeed, one of the Ten Commandments in the Judeo-Christian Bible says to "Honor your father and your mother..." Many Americans, even those who have no Asian background, honor and respect their elders and regard them as treasures, although perhaps they go about it in different ways. How do you feel about this? If your parents or grandparents needed care in the future, would you be the one to provide it? If you had your own home and a family, would you want your parents to live with you if they had serious care needs (or would you want to live with them so you could help with care needs)? What are some other ways you might provide for their needs if you did not think that living together was a good idea? Do you think filial piety is also a "Western" concept or value?

points to **ponder**

Imagine having to pack up and move to a new country in your sixties or seventies where you are unfamiliar with the customs, values, and often the language of the host culture. This move means that you must also leave behind your social relationships and all the places you have come to know like your local market or family doctor. What might you find to be the hardest changes? What and who would you miss? How do you think you would cope? This is how many immigrants to the United States may feel as they are adjusting to their new home.

This compounds their problems with acculturation to Western culture (Mui & Kang, 2006; Wilmoth, 2012).

Immigration to a Western country also alters elders' expectations of filial piety. A study of older Chinese and Korean immigrants in San Francisco examined their views on **biculturalism**, or the process of integrating two cultures into one's lifestyle. These elders described how their perspectives of family social support had changed as they became more peripheral to the nuclear families created by their adult children. They were more likely to live alone, relying on employment in poorly paid jobs, Social Security, and Supplemental Security Income (SSI). Their changing perceptions of filial piety were also evident in their recognition that they were no longer authority figures to their adult children and grandchildren. While this suggests what appears to be a successful adaptation to immigration, it highlights the loss of filial piety as Asian immigrant elders become more bicultural. It may also explain why some older Asians prefer to return to their home countries after immigrating to the United States and other Western countries (Wong, Yoo, & Stewart, 2006).

Language and cultural barriers often exacerbate elders' difficulties in accessing Western health care. Older immigrants who are not proficient in English must rely on their adult children to seek health or social services and manage the accompanying paperwork. When their adult child must accompany them to appointments in order to interpret for them, this represents an invasion of the elder's privacy. Most importantly, such dependence shifts the balance of power (Min, Moon, & Lubben, 2005; Mui & Kang, 2006; van der Geest, Mul, & Vermeulen, 2004; Wu, Tran, & Amjad, 2004).

Financial Dilemmas Facing Immigrant Elders

Financial self-sufficiency is an important determinant of an elder's social position in the family, whether they are immigrants or native-born Americans. As described in more detail in Chapter 10, in order to receive Social Security benefits, a worker must have been employed at least 10 years (or 40 quarters). For this reason, many older legal immigrants seek employment when they first enter the United States, remain employed for the mandatory 10 years, and then quit working. However, immigrants often face greater barriers to finding employment than native-born citizens due to linguistic, cultural, ethnic, educational factors or discrimination. Recognizing that less-educated immigrants are unlikely to have personal assets and to depend largely on employment income, it is not surprising that this group, whose members may have a high school education or less, is more likely to need to work than their college-educated counterparts (Borjas, 2007; Gerst & Burr, 2012).

The poverty rate for older noncitizens is approximately twice that of older U.S.-born Americans. Not surprisingly, they were more likely in the past to rely on Medicaid and SSI than U.S.-born elders. However, major policy changes took place in 1996 that severely limited noncitizen immigrants' access to these benefits. Euphemistically labeled "welfare reform," this change enacted by the U.S. Congress placed significant limits on noncitizen immigrants' eligibility for and access to public assistance benefits, including SSI and food stamps. These rules, aimed at reducing the federal government's expenditures, transferred decisions and responsibility for income maintenance programs to state and local governments (Gerst & Burr, 2012; Wilmoth, 2012).

The effects of this policy change have been to reduce income security for poor families and older immigrants who were not U.S. citizens when welfare reform was enacted. This problem affects some immigrant elders more than others, depending on the state where they reside. In states where budgetary and philosophical attitudes toward welfare programs are negative or funds increasingly tight, immigrants face lower benefits, restrictions on eligibility, and time limits. In states such as California, which has the largest number of noncitizen immigrants, the percentage of immigrant households receiving public assistance declined sharply, particularly given the magnitude of the recession in the state. The problem is worse for some elders who are eligible but have not applied for needed assistance because they think that they are ineligible or that they may be deported. Others who could be eligible for Medicaid and SSI by becoming citizens do not seek this status because they do not have the necessary English proficiency to pass the U.S. naturalization exam (Angel, 2003; Caro & Morris, 2004; Estes et al., 2006; Gerst & Burr, 2012; Gorospe, 2006; Nam & Jung, 2008).

In the current economic downturn, budget cuts in social and health programs are likely to reduce benefits for immigrants and older adults even more. According to the Center on Budget and Policy Priorities, 46 states plus the District of Columbia since 2008 have made cuts in all major areas of state services—K-12 education, higher education, health care, and services to older and disabled persons. The bottom line is that the lives of older immigrants in the United States are likely to become even harder in the next decade (Johnson, Oliff, & Williams, 2011).

Helping Isolated Older Immigrants

The "community ambassadors" program in Fremont, California, was started by city leaders. It helps older immigrants who move to the United States to live with their adult children and often move out when conflicts arise in cultural values and lifestyles. Those who continue to live with their children remain at home alone when the younger generation leaves for work or school, often feeling dependent and depressed because they cannot speak English to function independently. Community ambassadors are other immigrants from the same countries who help elders obtain medical and legal services, enroll them in government benefit programs, provide transportation, and otherwise fill gaps left by the elders' families (Shavelson, 2008).

Immigrant Elders in Multigenerational Households

Co-residence with adult children varies across nationality among immigrants. In an analysis of U.S. Census data, the living arrangements of Latino (mostly Cuban and Mexican), Asian (mostly from China or Southeast Asia), and non-Hispanic white (mostly from Europe) immigrants were compared. The highest rates of independent living were among white, Japanese, and Cuban immigrants. Living in another family member's home in multigenerational or an extended family arrangement was more common among other Asian groups and elders from Mexico. This was especially true for elders who were unmarried, had lower incomes, and had less than a college education, and those with a physical disability. As you will learn in Chapter 6, multigenerational and extended family living arrangements are growing, particularly in areas with many immigrant families or where the cost of living is high (Nasser, 2012; Wilmoth, 2001).

As noted earlier, living in a multigenerational or extended family may not always benefit the older immigrant, especially if their adult children live in a suburban community far from an ethnic enclave, such as Chinese and Southeast Asian neighborhoods in urban settings (think of the "Chinatowns" in many large American cities). You may look at these enclaves and wonder why anyone would want to live in such a crowded and often rundown area. Elders who choose to live in these enclaves lose their immediate access to family. But they gain the benefit of socializing with their peers and finding health and social service providers who speak their native language. Immigrant elders who opt to live in ethnic enclaves in the city may sacrifice the material comfort of life in the suburbs so that they can be closer to reminders of "home." For these older adults, their neighborhood takes on a meaning beyond physical safety and comfort and can serve to lessen their sense of displacement from their home country.

When immigrant elders need long-term care, traditional norms of filial piety generally play a dominant role in the decision by elders and their adult children about what services to use. Latino immigrants typically mobilize a wide network of extended family and friends to provide care in the community. Among families from Southeast Asia, regardless of religion (Sikh, Hindu, Muslim, or Christian), adult children who continue to hold values of respect toward elders are less likely to feel burdened by caring for an older parent than those without such a sense of obligation. Indeed, among some immigrant groups, placing an older family member in a skilled nursing home, even when they have acculturated to the United States, is viewed as a denial of one's obligations to one's parents. These values of providing care to frail elders at home can strengthen bonds in immigrant families. However, if adult children are already burdened by financial problems, job demands, and interpersonal conflicts with other family members, their parents' expectations of caring for them at home can cause considerable stress (Gelfand, 2003; Gupta & Pillai, 2002; Moon & Rhee, 2006).

Despite some traditional cultural discomfort about having nonfamily members care for aging parents and other loved ones, adult day health centers are an option that is gaining popularity among some older immigrants and their families. Older adults with cognitive or physical disabilities can attend such centers during the day but live at home with a family member or in another type of residential setting. Some are located in enclaves of older immigrants from Latin America or Southeast Asian countries or China, and reach out to these populations by hiring staff who are native speakers and by offering culturally appropriate programming and meals. One such example that has been replicated nationally is the adult day health program of the El Portal Latino Alzheimer's Project in Los Angeles that serves primarily Spanish-speaking elders. Another widely replicated model is OnLok, started in Chinatown in San Francisco in the 1970s. Other day health programs were started by leaders in these immigrant communities to serve vulnerable

Club Bamboo Serves Up Culturally Appropriate Food and Fellowship

The Asian Counseling and Referral Service (ACRS) in Seattle, WA, has been addressing the physical, mental, and social needs of the Asian immigrant population since 1973. Case workers there enhance the well-being of community elders by checking in regularly with clients to see how they and their caregivers are doing. To improve communication, case workers typically speak more than one language and often come from the ethnic community of their clients. The agency publicizes that a total of 30 different languages are spoken by its multicultural staff. The agency's food bank and congregate dining program provides culturally appropriate food that appeals to Asian palates (e.g., rice as a primary carbohydrate).

To encourage social interaction among clients, the agency has created a place for elders to gather for food and fitness. Called Club Bamboo, community elders can get nutritious meals at low cost, attend exercise classes, learn English, and more. It is run by a few staff members but many more volunteers, and the agency reports that more than 400 members are part of Club Bamboo. ACRS has other food programs aimed specifically at members of a specific Asian ethnic group (Young, 2013).

elders who live alone or are left home alone during the day while their adult children work and their grandchildren attend school.

If you are in a situation where you are working with older immigrants, it is important to recognize the challenges they face in adjusting to a new culture. Perhaps their younger, more Americanized family members brought them over thinking they would receive better care in the United States, but in reality the elder immigrant longs for life in the country of origin. Culturally competent programs such as Club Bamboo on p. 54 can help elders cope with such losses and enhance their well-being.

Additional Challenges Faced by Older Refugees

If older adults who voluntarily move to the United States have difficulty adjusting, imagine what an older refugee must experience when they are forced to leave their home country for reasons beyond their control. In the past 40 years, for example, waves of Indo-Chinese refugees have come to the United States from countries experiencing political strife, war, unrest, and other traumas. Some even suffer from posttraumatic stress, especially if they were forced to leave their country under duress. Property and other resources in their native lands that afforded them importance and power were generally stripped from them. Being in the United States has brought them a different life than the one they might have imagined for their later years. These older refugees do not have the ability to provide material goods, land, or other financial support, which has traditionally given them status. Accordingly, traditional power has been eroded as families have started new lives in the new culture and the balance of power has shifted to adult children.

As is the case for the older immigrant population in general, financial self-sufficiency is a major determinant of adjustment to life in the United States among older refugees, regardless of education, gender, and English proficiency. In a study of refugee elders from Cambodia, Vietnam, the Ukraine, and Jewish elders from the former Soviet Union, reports of loneliness and isolation were widespread. However, the majority of them were unaware of any social or health services that could help them adapt to their new situation. Refugees from countries in the midst of civil war often experience even greater mental health problems. Traumas such as torture, massacre of family and friends, and abrupt separation from family members can have long-lasting negative effects, even after escaping to the political safety of the United States (Morioka-Douglas, Sacks, & Yeo, 2004; Strumpf, Glicksman, Goldberg-Glen, Fox, & Logue, 2001).

Putting Yourself in Their Shoes

Just try to imagine what it must be like for an older immigrant to live in the United States. Let's say you are 60 years old. You love living in the United States, where you've always lived, but the cost of living is way too high and you did not save enough for retirement. Due to circumstances beyond your control, you are impoverished, living alone, and do not have a lot of family support. The Chinese government—now prosperous and a global superpower—has opened its borders to Americans age 60 and older who would like to immigrate there and live in modest retirement communities they have established for foreigners. The costs are relatively low there and you will receive health care for life. You don't really want to leave your home country, but it seems like the best thing to do. Some of your friends and relatives have already moved there. You decide to go.

When you arrive, you feel geographically, socially, and emotionally dislocated. They speak some English there, but most of the time you hear them speaking another language that you cannot understand. Only a minority of people look like you. You don't really feel like you fit in. You miss a lot of the things and places you enjoyed in the United States. People are nice to you most of the time, at least to your face, but you are having a hard time calling this place home. They have their own way of doing things, and you really feel like an outsider. You find groups of other Americans to hang out with, and often you all sit around and talk about what life was like back in the "old country." Some people point at you and accuse you of always sticking around other people like yourself. They refer to your retirement community as a ghetto.

You try to make the best of your circumstances, yet you feel sad that you may never go back to the United States to live. Some people there criticize you for not learning the native language and for clinging too much to artifacts and memories from the old country, like there's something wrong with that. They think you should be more grateful for the opportunities in your new homeland and to think of yourself as being Chinese, not American, since you're living in China now. They don't like some of your habits and customs and they call you names. You can't do much about it because you have little social and political power, being both poor and a foreigner. You hope things get better.

summary

Population aging is a global phenomenon that is occurring at different rates in developed as well as developing countries. This reflects the demographic transition from high-fertility rural societies to low-birthrate urban, industrialized societies. Developed countries have the largest proportions of elders, especially Japan and Western Europe. Life expectancy and the median age have increased dramatically in these countries in the past 20 years. However, the greatest absolute numbers (not percentage) of older people live in developing countries.

A key challenge associated with global aging, intensified by declining birthrates, is that fewer workers are available in most countries to support the increasing numbers of older people. China is already facing a crisis from its one-child-per-family policy that has resulted in fewer workers, daughters, and daughters-in-law to provide care for its burgeoning population of elders. Many developing countries, focused on the immediate needs of younger populations, have not yet established adequate public policies to address the growth of their older populations. In contrast, many industrialized countries, especially in the European Union, are attempting to implement new retirement policies in efforts to increase the number of older workers while reducing the burden on their state pension programs. Not surprisingly, these attempts to raise the retirement age are being met with resistance by many workers who had expected to retire with full benefits between age 55 and 64. However, many older adults around the world are realizing that they need to continue to be employed beyond age 65 because of the recent global economic crisis.

A basic principle governing the status of older adults is the need to achieve a balance between their contributions to society and the costs of supporting them. The process of modernization and technological development often conflicts with traditions of respectful obedience toward parents and ancestors. But the family continues to play an essential role in supporting its oldest members in most societies.

It is important for anthropologists, sociologists, economists, and others to direct their research to how the aging process and elders are viewed in different cultures and countries. It is also important to study how different economic, health, and social services are adapting to the growth of this population across the world and what the United States can learn from other countries.

Modern societies can also learn from traditional cultures about the valuable role that elders play in the community. It is easy to frame the global aging phenomenon as a looming financial crisis and a major social problem. While it does pose serious challenges to governments, societies, and families in the areas of long-term care and supports, health care, economic stability, and so forth, we should not characterize individual older adults as being problems. Rather, as future chapters will illustrate, they can contribute much to society as productive employees, volunteers, caregivers, mentors, companions, and friends. Even older adults with physical and mental impairments have much to teach us about patience, selfless giving, and compassionate ways to communicate and connect with other human beings. Our collective goal as global citizens should be to create and advocate for meaningful multigenerational communities in which older adults can live their lives with dignity wherever they happen to be in the world.

key terms

anthropology of aging, p. 45
biculturalism, p. 52
comparative sociocultural gerontology, p. 45
demographic divide, p. 37
developing countries, p. 35
filial piety, p. 46
global aging, p. 35
modernization theory, p. 47
oya koko, p. 49
population aging, p. 35
skipped-generation household, p. 47
social stratification, p. 46

review questions

1. Is population aging occurring in just a few developed countries like Japan, Italy, and the United States, or is it a phenomenon that is more widespread? Explain.
2. What two main factors contribute to population aging?
3. Name two countries where the proportion of older adults (e.g., 65 years and older) is among the highest in the world.
4. What kinds of families tend to live in multigenerational households? Consider ethnicity, culture, and economic factors when formulating your answer.
5. List three types of concerns that older immigrants generally have compared to native-born elders.
6. According to modernization theory, what challenges might older adults from traditional societies find after immigrating to a modern, urban society?
7. What would be an example of an organization that serves older adults from a culturally competent perspective?
8. What are the reasons that an elder might choose to live in an ethnic enclave like Chinatown in any major city rather than live with their adult children in a larger home in the suburbs?
9. Identify two reasons that younger adults often leave rural areas and their elder parents behind.
10. What problems might an elder refugee face if she does not have English-language proficiency or economic stability in a new country?

media resources

View

- The Odds of Surviving to the Age of Sixty-Five in Global Perspective
- Median Age at Death in Global Perspective

Read

- Fakhouri, Hani. Growing Old in an Arab American Family.
- Kim, Shin and Kwang Chung Kim. Intimacy at a Distance, Korean American Style: Invited Korean Elderly and Their Married Children.

references

AARP. (2006). Interview with Mr. Tatsuo Honda, Japan's National Institute of Population and Social Security Research. *AARP Global Aging Issues.* Retrieved April 23, 2009, from http://www.aarp.org/reserach/intl/globalaging/apr_06_newsmaker.html.

AARP. (2009). Interview with John Creighton Campbell, Professor Emeritus, University of Michigan. *AARP International.* Retrieved November 26, 2011, from http://www.aarpinternational.org/newsmakers/newsmakers_show.htm?doc_id=1060225.

Angel, J. L. (2003). Devolution and the social welfare of elderly immigrants: Who will bear the burden? *Public Administration Review, 63,* 79–89.

Ban, K.-M. (2012). Message for international day of older persons. *United Nations website. Ageing, Social Policy and Development Division.* Retrieved January 2013 from http://social.un.org/index/Ageing/InternationalDayofOlderPersons.aspx.

Barboza, D. (2011, February 13). Chinese revise approach to elder care. *Seattle Times,* p. A4.

BBC News Online. (2012, December 28). *China orders children to visit their elderly parents.* Retrieved January 2013 from http://www.bbc.co.uk/news/world-asia-china-20860264.

Belluck, P. (2010, November 26). In a land of aging, children counter Alzheimer's. *New York Times,* pp. A1, A12.

Bloom, D., & Canning, D. (2007). Demographic change, fiscal sustainability and macroeconomic performance. *Public Policy & Aging Report, 17,* 18–23.

Borjas, G. J. (2007). *Social security eligibility and the labor supply of elderly immigrants.* Paper presented at 9th annual Joint Conference for the Retirement Research Consortium.

Brown, P. L. (2009, August 30). Invisible immigrants, old and left with "nobody to talk to." *New York Times.* Retrieved from http://www.nytimes.com/2009/08/31/us/31elder.html?pagewanted=all.

Cameron, L. (2000). The residency decision of elderly Indonesians: A nested logit analysis. *Demography, 37,* 17–27.

Caro, F. G., & Morris, R. (2003). Devolution and aging policy. *Journal of Aging and Social Policy, 14,* 1.

Cetron, M. J., & Davies, O. (2010). Trends shaping tomorrow's world. *Futurist, 44*(3), 39–41.

Cowgill, D. (1974). Aging and modernization: A revision of the theory. In J. F. Gubrium (Ed.), *Late life communities and environmental policy.* Springfield, IL: Charles C. Thomas.

Cowgill, D. (1986). *Aging around the world.* Belmont, CA: Wadsworth.

Economist. (2012, April 21). China's Achille's heel. London: *The Economist Newspaper*, Ltd. Retrieved September 19, 2013, from http://www.economist.com/node/21553056.

Estes, C. L., Goldberg, S., Wellin, C., Linkins, K. W., Shostak, S., & Beard, R. L. (2006). Implications of welfare reform on the elderly: A case study of provider, advocate and consumer perspectives. *Journal of Aging & Social Policy, 18*, 41–63.

Europa. (2008). European elderly: How are they? Key findings from an EU-funded research database unveiled. Press release, November 28, 2008. http://europa.eu/rapid/pressReleasesAction.do?reference=IP/08/1837&format=HTML&aged=0&language=EN&guiLanguage=en.

European Commission. (2005). *Green paper on demographic change.* Brussels, EU.

Fishman, T. C. (2010). *Shock of gray: The aging of the world's population and how it pits young against old, child against parent, worker against boss, company against rival and nation against nation.* New York: Scribner.

Gelfand, D. E. (2003). *Aging and ethnicity: Knowledge and services* (2nd ed.). New York: Springer.

Gerontological Society of America. (2009, April 9). Tokyo running short on care facilities. *Gerontology News.*

Gerst, K., & Burr, J. A. (2012). Welfare program participation among older immigrants. *Public Policy & Aging Report, 22*, 12–16.

Gorospe, E. (2006). Elderly immigrants: Emerging challenge for the U.S. healthcare system. *Internet Journal of Healthcare Administration, 4*(1).

Guinness World Records. (2012, December 27). *Japan's Jiroemon Kimura confirmed as oldest man who ever lived at 115 years, 253 days.* Retrieved January 2013 from http://www.guinnessworldrecords.com/news/2012/12/japans-jiroemon-kimura-confirmed-as-oldest-living-person-at-115-years-253-days-46484/.

Gupta, R., & Pillai, V. K. (2002). Elder caregiving in South Asian families: Implications for social services. *Journal of Comparative Family Studies, 33*, 565–576.

Haub, C. (2007). Global aging and the demographic divide. *Public Policy & Aging Report, 17*(1), 3–6.

Haub, C. (2011). *World population aging: Clocks illustrate growth in population under age 5 and over age 65.* Retrieved July 2011 from http://www.prb.org/Articles/2011/agingpopulationclocks.aspx.

Hayutin, A. M. (2007a). Graying of the global population. *Public Policy & Aging Report, 17*, 12–17.

Hayutin, A. M. (2007b, March). *How population aging differs across countries: A briefing on global demographics.* Palo Alto, CA: Stanford Center on Longevity.

He, B. (2011). Aging population a challenge. *China Daily*, May 19. Retrieved September 19, 2013, from http://www.chinadaily.com.cn/bizchina/2011-05/19/content_12542054.htm.

Hsu, H. C., Lew-Ting, C. Y., & Wu, S. C. (2001). Age, period, and cohort effects on the attitude toward supporting parents in Taiwan. *The Gerontologist, 41*, 742–750.

Infeld, D. L. (Ed.). (2002). *Disciplinary approaches to aging: Anthropology of aging* (Vol. 4). New York: Routledge.

Johnson, N., Oliff, P., & Williams, E. (2011). *An update on state budget cuts.* Washington, DC: Center on Budget and Policy Priorities. Retrieved September 19, 2013, from http://www.cbpp.org/cms/?fa=view&id=1214.

Kandel, W. A. (2011, January 18). The U.S. foreign-born population: Trends and characteristics. *Congressional Research Service Report No. R41592.* Retrieved from www.crs.gov.

Kaneda, T. (2006). *China's concern over population aging and health.* Retrieved October 28, 2006, from http://www.prb.org.

Kinsella, K., & V. A. Velkoff. (2001). *An aging world: 2001.* Washington, DC: U.S. Government Printing Office, 95/01-1.

Kinsella, K., & He, W. (2009). *An aging world: 2008.* Washington, DC: U.S. Government Printing Office, 95/09-1.

Lan, P. C. (2002). Subcontracting filial piety. *Journal of Family Issues, 23*, 812–835.

Lanzieri, G. (2011). The greying of the baby boomers: A century-long view of ageing in the European populations. *Eurostat: Statistics in Focus* 23/2011.

Levande, D. I., Herrick, J. M., & Sung, K. T. (2000). Eldercare in the United States and South Korea. *Journal of Family Issues, 21*, 632–651.

Loong, L. H. (2009, Winter). Preparing for an aging population: The Singapore experience. *The Journal (AARP)*, 12–17.

Martin, P., & Midgley, E. (2010). *Population update bulletin: Immigration in America 2010.* Population Reference Bureau. Retrieved from http://www.prb.org/Publications/PopulationBulletins/2010/immigrationupdate1.aspx.

Min, J., Moon, A., & Lubben, J. E. (2005). Determinants of psychological distress over time among older Korean Americans and non-Hispanic white elders. *Journal of Mental Health and Aging, 9*, 210–222.

Moon, A., & Rhee, S. (2006). Immigrant and refugee elders. In B. Berkman & S. D'Ambruoso (Eds.), *Handbook of social work in health and aging.* New York: Oxford Press.

Morioka-Douglas, N., Sacks, T., & Yeo, G. (2004). Issues in caring for Afghan American elders: Insights from literature and a focus group. *Journal of Cross-Cultural Gerontology, 19*, 27–40.

Mui, A. C., & Kang, S. Y. (2006). Acculturation stress and depression among Asian immigrant elders. *Social Work, 51*, 243–250.

Nam, Y., & Jung, H. J. (2008). Welfare reform and older immigrants' food stamp program participation and food insecurity. *The Gerontologist, 48*, 42–50.

Nasser, E. N. (2012, October 25). More multigenerational households in immigrant areas. *USA Today.* Retrieved from http://www.usatoday.com/story/news/nation/2012/10/25/census-multigenerational-households/1653159/.

National Institute of Population and Social Security Research. (2006). *Housing with seniors: 1975–2010.* Retrieved October 15, 2006, from http://www.jinjapan.org/insight/html/focus10/page08.html.

Population Reference Bureau. (2008a). *World population data sheet.* Washington, DC: USAID.

Population Reference Bureau. (2008b). *World population highlights. Population Bulletin, 63.* Washington, DC: USAID.

Population Reference Bureau. (2013). *World population data sheet 2013.* Washington, DC: USAID.

Powell, J. (2010). The power of global aging. *Ageing International, 35,* 1–14.

Sackur, S. (2003). Ageing Europe is unprepared. *BBC News.* Retrieved January 2013 from http://news.bbc.co.uk/2/hi/programmes/from_our_own_correspondent/3117379.stm.

Shavelson, L. (2008). *Elderly immigrants flow into California.* National Public Radio program and transcript, March 17. Retrieved September 18, 2013, from http://www.npr.org/templates/story/story.php?storyId=88402850.

Silverman, P., Hecht, L., & McMillin, J. D. (2000). Modeling life satisfaction among the aged: A comparison of Chinese and Americans. *Journal of Cross-Cultural Gerontology, 15,* 289–305.

Sokolovsky, J. (Ed.). (1997). *The cultural context of aging* (3rd ed.). Westport, CT: Bergin and Garvey.

Steed, J. (2008, November 9). Elderly thrive in Denmark. *TheStar.com.* Retrieved from http://www.thestar.com/atkinsonseries/article/532841--elderly-thrive-in-denmark.

Strumpf, N. E., Glicksman, A., Goldberg-Glen, R. S., Fox, R. C., & Logue, E. H. (2001). Caregiver and elder experiences of Cambodian, Vietnamese, Soviet Jewish, and Ukrainian refugees. *International Journal of Aging and Human Development, 53,* 233–252.

Stump, S. (2012, December 7). Iowa woman, 115, becomes the world's oldest person. *Today News.* Retrieved January 2013 from http://todaynews.today.com/_news/2012/12/07/15753558-iowa-woman-115-becomes-the-worlds-oldest-living-person?lite.

Sung, K. T. (2001). Family support for the elderly in Korea: Continuity, change, future directions and cross-cultural concerns. *Journal of Aging & Social Policy, 12,* 65–77.

Tabuchi, H. (2009, April 26). Japan is paying immigrants to go home and not come back. *New York Times,* p. B1.

United Nations. (2005). *World Population Prospects* (Vol. II). Department of Economic and Social Affairs: Population Division.

United Nations. (2007a). *World Population Aging 2007.* Department of Economic and Social Affairs: Population Division.

United Nations. (2007b). *World Population Prospects* (Vol. IV). Department of Economic and Social Affairs: Population Division.

United Nations. (2009a). Opportunities and challenges for an aging world. *AARP United Nations Briefing Series.* Retrieved April 23, 2009, from www.aarpinternational.org/2008UNBriefingSeries.

United Nations (2009b). *World population to exceed 9 billion by 2050.* Retrieved February 6, 2012, from http://www.un.org/esa/population/publications/wpp2008/pressrelease.pdf.

United Nations Population Fund & HelpAge International. (2012). *Ageing in the twenty-first century: A celebration and a challenge.* New York: United Nations Population Fund.

United Nations State of World Population. (2011). *Linking population, poverty and development.* Retrieved August 1, 2011, from http://www.unfpa.org/pds/urbanization.htm.

U.S. Census Bureau. (2011, June). *International data base.* Retrieved January 12, 2013, from http://www.census.gov/population/international/data/idb/worldpopgraph.php.

Van der Geest, S., Mul, A., & Vermeulen, H. (2004). Linkages between migration and the care of frail older people: Observations from Greece, Ghana, and the Netherlands. *Ageing and Society, 24,* 431–450.

Von Nordheim, F. (2003). EU policies in support of member states' efforts to retain, reinforce and re-integrate older workers in employment. In H. Buck & B. Dworschak (Eds.), *Ageing and work in Europe.* Stuttgart, Germany: Federal Ministry of Education and Research.

Wilmoth, J. M. (2001). *Social integration of older immigrants in 21st century America.* Syracuse University Policy Brief No. 29. Syracuse, NY: Syracuse University Press.

Wilmoth, J. M. (2012). A demographic profile of older immigrants in the U.S. *Public Policy & Aging Report, 22,* 8–11.

Wong, S. T., Yoo, G. J. & Stewart, A. L. (2006). The changing meaning of family support among older Chinese and Korean immigrants. *Journal of Gerontology: Social Sciences, 61B,* S4–S9.

Wu, B., Tran, T. V., & Amjad, Q. A. (2004). Chronic illnesses and depression among Chinese immigrant elders. *Journal of Gerontological Social Work, 43,* 79–95.

Yoshimura (2010, April 2). University of Tokyo transforming Kashiwa into city for the elderly. *Japan Times.* Retrieved from search.japantimes.co.jp/cgi-bin/nn20100402f1.html.

Young, B. (2013, January 5). Club Bamboo serves Asian seniors food, fun and friends. *Seattle Times.* Retrieved from http://seattletimes.com/html/localnews/2020067604_needy06.html.

Zhan, H. J. (2004). Willingness and expectations: Intergenerational differences in attitudes toward filial responsibility in China. *Marriage and Family Review, 36,* 175–200.

3 Physical Well-Being: Physiological Changes and Health

learning objectives

3.1 Comprehend normal physiological changes associated with aging, including changes in organ and sensory systems.

3.2 Articulate a range of common chronic diseases often faced by older adults along with primary causes of death.

3.3 Identify health promotion programs and strategies to maintain optimum well-being in older adulthood.

Listen to the Chapter Audio

When you think of aging, you may immediately picture its visible physical features—graying hair, wrinkled skin, or a shuffling gait. You probably have little sense of internal physiological changes because of their invisibility. In this chapter, you will learn about some of these age-related biological and physiological alterations. You may know someone who is age 50 but appears to be much older and someone in their eighties who looks like they are in their sixties. This is because of individual differences in the rate and severity of physiological changes. There is so much variation in how we age, because of our genetic inheritance, nutrition and diet, physical activity, and environment. Fortunately, most normal changes in our organ systems do not imply disease but they may slow us down as we age.

Most of us fear that our health will decline as we age. We fear not only the pain and inconvenience of illness, but also how it affects our ability to perform daily tasks and remain at home. You will see that while many diseases are often deleterious, progressive, and long-term, they are not universal with age. Moreover, older adults with chronic illnesses may still enjoy satisfying active lives. Indeed, you will learn about modifications you can make now in your lives that will promote your physical well-being in old age.

To understand how older people differ from younger age groups, you will first learn about the normal changes in biological and physiological structures and then diseases that impair these systems and may affect elders' daily functioning. This chapter will cover:

- Theories of biological aging, including efforts to reverse or slow the aging process
- "Normal" aging—changes that are not disease related—in different organ systems and their impact on older people's functioning
- Definitions of health, functional ability, disability, frailty, and comorbidity
- Chronic diseases that occur most frequently
- Inequities by age, race, gender, sexual orientation, and social class that result in health disparities in old age
- Accidents and prevention of driving fatalities and falls
- Use of health services and prescription drugs
- Health promotion programs—exercise, nutrition, and an active socially engaged lifestyle—and their benefits

We turn first to normal biological changes that influence our physical well-being as we age.

Biological Theories of Aging

Biological aging, or **senescence**, is the normal process of alterations over time in the body and its organ systems that eventually affect our functioning but do not necessarily result in disease or death. Yet aging and disease are often linked in our minds, because declines in organ capacity and our immune system make us more vulnerable to illness, such as dementia, arthritis, and heart attacks that increase in incidence with age. However, a more accurate conception of the aging process is a gradual accumulation of irreversible functional losses to which the average person adapts—often in very creative ways.

One way of understanding variations in biological aging is to examine the major theories to explain cellular- and organ-level alterations, which can only be inferred from tests of physiological function. And scientific discoveries of the cause of a physiological process or disease can, in some instances, point to ways to prevent it.

Most biological theories of aging have one of two general orientations:

1. Aging occurs due to random genetic mutations and oxidative stress, or
2. Aging is a result of programmed senescence (Bengtson, Gans, Putney, & Silverstein, 2009).

We briefly discuss four primary theories of biological aging:

The **wear-and-tear theory** suggests that, like a machine, the organism simply wears out over time. This process is influenced by environmental stress, such as poverty and poor nutrition. Cells continually wear out, and existing cells cannot repair damaged components within themselves. This is particularly true in tissues located in the skeletal and heart muscles and throughout the nervous system, where declines in functional ability are greatest with age (Wilson, 1974).

The **cellular aging theory** posits that aging occurs as cells slow their number of replications. Aging is a preprogrammed process; that is, each species—insects, dogs, humans—has a biological clock that determines its maximum life span and the rate at which each organ system will deteriorate. Cells are apparently programmed to follow a biological clock and stop replicating after a fixed number of times (Dagarag, Evazyan, Rao, & Effros, 2004; Effros, 2009; Hayflick, 2000).

According to the **immunological theory**, aging is a function of the body's immune system becoming defective. The immune system serves as an important protective function early in life, but becomes less efficient in making the body resistant to pathogens and infections that attack and interfere with normal functioning. This process may be responsible for cardiovascular disease, Alzheimer's, cancer, diabetes, and inflammatory conditions that may have their origins in our immune system (Effros, 2001, 2009; Walford, 1969).

The **free radical theory** or oxidative stress model states that the progressive, irreversible accumulation of oxidative damage to cells explains loss of physiological functions as we age. This occurs when an organism cannot easily detoxify or repair the damage caused by free radicals. Although we all are exposed to oxidative damage from birth, the process accelerates in older adults, wears down the organism, and leaves them vulnerable to degenerative, age-related diseases such as some cancers, cardiovascular disease, Alzheimer's disease, and cataracts. Some researchers have proposed that ingesting antioxidants, such as vitamins E and C, and beta carotene can inhibit free radical damage and thus slow the aging process by delaying loss of immune function (Grune & Davies, 2001; Thavanati, Kanala, de Dios, & Garza, 2008).

Can Aging Be Reversed or Delayed?

When you hear about popular "antiaging therapies," remember that no scientific theory is fully able to explain what causes aging and death nor how to prevent this normal process. On the other hand, research on growth hormones and caloric restriction does suggest that aging may be slowed or perhaps one day reversible to some extent.

Genetic researchers have tested the effects of injecting growth hormones into aging animals and humans. They have found some startling discoveries—increased lean muscle mass and bone density and reduced fat levels, which led to increased activity and vigor. Although these effects are short-lived, it may not be long before a human growth hormone is marketed that can safely be administered, like daily doses of vitamins (Nair et al., 2006).

Caloric restriction (CR) through reducing the intake of fat, protein, or carbohydrates is found to extend the life of experimental animals without causing malnutrition. Total intake of calories must be reduced by 30–50 percent in order to increase life span by as much as 50 percent. The benefits of CR are greatest when initiated soon after birth, but even when mice were placed on such diets in early middle age, their average life span increased (Martini et al., 2008; You, Sonntag, Leng, & Carter, 2007).

The Baltimore Longitudinal Study, which you learned about in the Introduction, has examined the effects of feeding monkeys 30 percent less than their normal caloric intake. After 6 years, the monkeys showed higher activity levels, lower body temperature, less body fat, and lower fasting glucose and insulin levels. These results provide the first evidence in primates that CR may delay the aging process by slowing down metabolism, thereby reducing the number of free radicals and the growth of diseases. In the few human studies of CR, it has been associated with improved cardiovascular function and lower blood pressure, but much more research is needed (Colman, Beasley, Allison, & Weindruch,

Can Wine Extend How Long We Live?

Resveratrol, found in the skin of grapes and in red wine, has been offered as a partial explanation for the "French paradox," the puzzling fact that people in France enjoy a high-fat diet yet suffer less heart disease than Americans. Researchers have concluded that resveratrol activates a protein, which restores chromosomes in genes, protecting them against the effects of aging and extending the life span, even neutralizing the risks of diabetes from an unhealthy diet. Although viewed as a major landmark on the molecular genetics of aging, people should not think that red wine could reverse the effects of eating badly. In fact, a person would have to drink at least one hundred bottles of red wine a day or take megadoses of resveratrol supplements to reach the levels of the substance given to mice. Scientists caution against taking large doses of resveratrol nutritional supplements until more is known about its effects on human genes and a safe and effective form of this product is developed (Bauer et al., 2006; Oberdoerffer et al., 2008; Pearson et al., 2008).

points to ponder

How would you feel if your aging process could be reversed? What might happen to society if more people could achieve the maximum life span of 120 years? What are some of the ethical and resource allocation issues raised by scientific efforts to reverse or slow the aging process?

2008; Fontana et al., 2004; Holloszy & Fontana, 2007; Lefevre et al., 2009; Lane et al., 2002; Masoro, 2003; Mattison, Lane, Roth, & Ingram, 2003; Messaoudi et al., 2006; Miller, 2009; Roth, Ingram, & Lane, 2001).

Instead of reversing aging, some biologists are focused on **prolongevity**—extending the length of healthy life and eliminating some diseases associated with aging. This relates to the concept of a **healthy life span**—expanding the number of years we spend in good health. You learned in Chapter 1 about research on the role of genes in centenarians, which shows promise for identifying environmental and genetic determinants of healthy longevity and disease prevention (Bergman, Atzmon, Ye, MacCarthy, & Barzilai, 2007; Hayflick, 2004a, 2004b; Miller, 2009; Perls & Terry, 2003; Tatar, 2009).

"Normal" Physiological Changes with Age

As noted earlier, "normal" does not mean that everyone will experience these changes, or that there is a "right" way to age. It simply refers to general tendencies or patterns of physiological alterations that are observed in the majority of people as they age. As you will see throughout this book, the process of aging is complex and multidimensional, with significant decline in some physiological functions and minimal change in others. An additional complexity is that it is difficult to distinguish normal age-related changes in many human functions from those secondary to disease. Until the late 1950s, our knowledge about aging came largely from cross-sectional comparisons of young persons who tended to be healthy compared to older adults who often had chronic diseases. These comparisons led to the not-surprising conclusion that the organ systems of older persons function less efficiently than those of younger individuals. But older competitive athletes counter that conclusion, as shown by swimmer Diana Nyad.

Since the 1950s, longitudinal studies, most notably the Baltimore Longitudinal Study, have been undertaken with healthy younger and middle-aged persons to compare changes in various physiological parameters. Such studies have measured the **functional capacity** of various bodily systems—the performance ability and efficiency of the heart, lungs, kidneys, and other organs. We now turn to some of the major findings from such research.

Returning to Competitive Swimming after 31 Years

None of us can go back to relive periods where we think we could have done better. And no athlete, especially, can go back and capture that one moment he or she always dreamed of achieving. But Diana Nyad, who was a competitive swimmer in her twenties and swam the farthest open water swim in history, still had a goal—to become the first person to complete the 110-mile swim from Cuba to Florida without a shark cage. On September 2, 2013, 64-year-old Nyad achieved what many others considered to be impossible. The historic swim took her 53 grueling hours but the dream she had of doing it spanned decades. Nyad first attempted the swim in 1978 but was unsuccessful. She decided to take up the challenge again several decades later when she was in her sixties, which resulted in three more unsuccessful attempts to achieve her goal. She had found success in other areas of life—as a reporter and motivational speaker, for example—but this one dream continued to elude her. Despite her setbacks, she was intent on trying again. Training for the swim empowered her to believe that "you are never too old to follow your dreams" (Sloane, Hanna, & Ford, 2013).

Longtime athlete Diana Nyad continued to push her limits as a long-distance swimmer in her sixties. Despite numerous dangers, she successfully swam from Cuba to Florida at age 64.

Changes in Body Composition

We begin with typical changes—both visible and invisible—in body composition, skin, and hair that all of us will experience if we live long enough.

The proportion of our body weight contributed by water generally declines with age. Lean body mass in

points to ponder

In this chapter you are learning that people undergo a variety of physical changes as they get older. Think about your parents, grandparents, or great-grandparents. What kinds of physical alterations have you observed in them as they have gotten older? Or what kinds of physical changes have they complained about as they've gotten older? Did these changes they told you about influence your feelings about aging?

muscle tissue is lost, whereas the proportion of fat increases. Because the number of muscle fibers steadily decreases after age 50, muscle tissue loses its elasticity and flexibility and muscle mass declines. However, as illustrated by **master athletes**, a vigorous exercise program can prevent a significant loss of muscle tone (Rincon, Muzumdar, & Barzilai, 2006).

We tend to gain weight in our middle years, but after age 75, we generally consume fewer calories and lose weight. This is why we rarely see people in their eighties and nineties who are obese, but it is also rare for us to see older adults with excellent muscle tone.

Changes in the Skin and Hair

Changes in the skin's appearance and texture can have negative effects on how older people view themselves—and are perceived by others. The human skin is unique among that of all other mammals since it is exposed directly to the elements, with no protective fur or feathers to shield it from sunlight. In fact, ultraviolet light from the sun, which damages the elastic fibers beneath the skin's surface, is primarily responsible for the wrinkled, dried, and tougher texture of many older people's skin. This exposure also results in darker pigmentation known as **melanin** (which has been produced by the body to protect it from sun), and brownish age spots or liver spots on the face or hands. Compared to whites, many elders of color enjoy a skin rich in melanin and with fewer wrinkles (Ramirez & Schneider, 2003).

The process of cell replacement in the **epidermis**, the outermost layer of skin, is slowed with age. Additionally, the connective tissue that makes up the second layer of skin, the dermis, thins. These cellular changes result in reduced elasticity and fullness of our skin—it takes a longer time for skin to spring back into shape—and increased sagging and wrinkling. The loss of fat in the face can leave elders looking gaunt. Sweat glands generally deteriorate and the deepest, or subcutaneous, skin layers lose fat and water. In addition, the skin's blood circulation is diminished, which can damage the effectiveness of its temperature-regulating mechanism and make elders more sensitive to hot and cold temperatures. You may have noticed how some older adults frequently turn up the thermostat. It also takes them longer to adjust after being exposed to extreme temperatures. This leaves elders more vulnerable to **hypothermia** (low body temperature) and **hyperthermia** (heat stroke). Perhaps you have heard about older adults' dying during extremely cold winters or prolonged heat spells.

Our hair also alters in its appearance and texture as we age. Hair decreases in diameter, often resulting in fine, limp-looking hair. Gray or white hair results from pigment loss in the hair follicles and at the roots. However, some people never experience a loss of pigment production but live into an advanced old age with relatively dark hair.

points to ponder

You have a friend who is not an older adult yet but is concerned about the health and appearance of her skin as she ages. What information can you provide to her about skin health? What advice can you recommend about skin protection?

Organ Systems

It is important to learn about normal system changes, because they often affect older adults' sense of well-being and ability to carry out daily tasks.

Musculoskeletal and Kinesthetic Systems

Some of you may already be losing height and strength! We reach our maximum size, strength, and stamina at about age 25, after which our cells decrease steadily in number and size. After age 30, we lose on average 1/16th inch of height per year; some adults in their seventies or eighties have declined an average of three inches. Maximum strength at age 80 is 50 percent of that of a 25-year-old. But older persons who maintain an active physical fitness routine show much less decline.

Because of the loss of bone mineral density and strength in our trunk, arms, and legs, the spine becomes more curved, and disks in the vertebrae become compacted. This is why older people sometimes appear to be literally shrinking or are stoop-shouldered or hunched over. This condition, known as **kyphosis**, occurs because crush fractures of the spine cause the vertebrae to collapse (Frontera & Silver, 2008).

Shoulder width also decreases as a result of bone loss, weakened muscles, and loss of elasticity in the ligaments. This results in reduced range of motion or loss of upper body mobility, making it difficult for some elders to reach high cupboards or turn their heads to see cars behind them. You may hear older people talk about being stiff when they get out of bed in the morning. Such stiffness occurs because cartilage between the joints wears thin, and the fluid to lubricate them decreases.

The **kinesthetic system** lets us know our position in physical space. Because of age-related changes in the central nervous system—which controls the kinesthetic system—as well as muscle weakness and diminished vision, older people may be less able to judge the position of their bodies in physical space. These alterations in strength and motor functioning may result in greater cautiousness, such as an older person taking slow, shuffling, and deliberate steps. If elders lose both visual and surface cues of their position, they may experience postural sway or be unable to keep standing. You may have heard a seemingly healthy older adult complain of dizziness, vertigo, and "things spinning." These normal changes combined with slower reaction time, muscle weakness, and reduced visual acuity make it more likely that older people will fall and injure themselves (Nikolaus & Bach, 2003; Wolf et al., 2003).

Accommodating Changes in Kinesthetic and Motor Functioning

Mrs. Gutiérrez, age 83, lives alone and is determined to be as independent as possible. Her neighbors watch carefully, however, when she goes out to walk her small dog. She shuffles, moves very slowly, and often has to stop and grab hold of something to avoid falling. When her son visits, he shudders when she climbs on a stool to reach a can on the upper cabinet shelves. He has tried to make her home safer by moving the food to lower shelves, putting grab bars in the bathroom, removing throw rugs, clearing clutter from walking areas and installing better lighting.

points to **ponder**

What physical changes in your own body have you noticed taking place lately that may be related to aging? For example, do you wear glasses or contact lenses due to worsening eyesight? Do you have less stamina than when you were younger? Or maybe there are positive physical changes that have taken place, such as being a healthier weight now than when you were younger, due to increased exercise and better nutritional choices?

Respiratory System Almost every organ system shows about 1 percent decline per year after age 30 in functional or reserve capacity. Complex functions, such as **vital capacity** or maximum breathing capacity, which require coordination of the respiratory, nervous, and muscular systems, decrease most rapidly. Indeed, the maximum amount of oxygen that can be brought into the lungs with a deep breath declines by 50 percent for men between ages 25 and 70. Visualize a decrease from six quarts of air to three! You may see the effects of such changes when an older person has difficulty breathing after climbing up several flights of stairs. While this decline in vital capacity does not necessarily impair a person's daily functions, it may mean moving more slowly or resting on the stairway landing (Hornsby, 2001).

Of all organ systems, the respiratory system suffers the most punishment from environmental pollutants and infections. Cilia, hairlike structures in airways, are reduced in number and less effective in removing foreign matter, which then diminishes the amount of oxygen available. This change, combined with poor air quality and reduced muscle strength in the chest, makes elders more susceptible to chronic bronchitis, emphysema, and pneumonia.

Cardiovascular Changes Structural changes in the heart and blood vessels include a replacement of heart muscle with fat, a loss of elastic tissue, and an increase in collagen. These changes produce a loss of elasticity in the arteries, weakened vessel walls, and an abnormal swelling in veins that are under high pressure, particularly in the legs. In addition, the arterial and vessel walls become increasingly lined with fats, creating the condition of **atherosclerosis**, which makes it more difficult for blood to be pumped. This buildup of fats is made worse when our diet includes large quantities of saturated fats.

Blood pressure increases to some extent even in normal aging with no signs of cardiovascular disease. But extreme elevation of blood pressure is not normal. Instead, it is associated with unhealthy diet, obesity, and an inactive lifestyle, all of which have negative cumulative effects over the years.

These changes in the heart and lungs make them less efficient in utilizing oxygen. This, in turn, reduces an older person's capacity to maintain physical activity for long periods. Nevertheless, physical training can significantly reduce blood pressure and increase aerobic capacity. For example, physical training in older master athletes results in a greater volume of oxygen, more lean body weight, and greater reductions in cholesterol than is found in sedentary older persons—although these levels are worse than in younger athletes. But even those of us who exercise only moderately can experience some benefits. Aerobic capacity increases significantly among older persons after 24 weeks of low-intensity or high-intensity training (e.g., walking or jogging for 30 minutes). Such findings justify optimism that our physical health can be improved through lifestyle changes, even well into our eighties. But we can never eliminate normal physiological changes that may slow us down with age (Hayflick, 1996; Vincent, Braith, Feldman, Kallas, & Lowenthal, 2002).

Urinary System Our kidneys regulate our body's internal chemistry by filtering blood and urine through an extraordinary system of tubes and capillaries. Of all organ systems, **renal function**—defined by the rate at which blood is filtered through the kidneys—deteriorates most dramatically with age, irrespective of any diseases. The kidneys also lose their capacity to absorb glucose and their concentrating and diluting ability. This contributes to increased problems with dehydration and to a loss of salt in the blood that can affect an older person's tolerance of medications that are cleared by filtration.

Bladder capacity may be reduced by as much as 50 percent, and the sensation of needing to empty the bladder is delayed. As a result, **urinary incontinence** or leakage of urine is experienced by about 50 percent of older persons living in their own homes, and an even higher proportion of those in long-term care facilities. Incontinence can profoundly alter a person's social and living situations. It is often the "breaking point" in the family's ability to provide in-home care and precipitates skilled nursing home placement.

Incontinence sometimes results from a specific precipitating factor, such as medications, acute illness, or bladder or urinary tract infections, and can be treated with antibiotics if the cause is known. Other physical causes that physicians should assess are neurological changes associated with Parkinson's and dementia, prostate problems, anemia, diabetes, and various cancers.

Incontinence should not be assumed to be irreversible. Although some physicians prescribe medications, these often have unpleasant side effects. Noninvasive behavioral management techniques, such as restriction of fluid intake before bedtime, exercise, biofeedback, and systematic exercise of the pelvic muscle and Kegels to maintain sphincter muscle tone, are often just as effective. Indeed, eight out of 10 women who seek treatment for incontinence see an improvement or are cured, and their quality of life is enhanced. Support groups, such as those sponsored by the National Association for Incontinence, exist nationwide (HealthyWomen.org, 2013; Pringle-Specht, 2005).

Unfortunately, because of the taboo nature of incontinence, elders and their families are often unaware of methods to treat it. Many health care providers, in turn, do not ask about bladder problems. This widespread reluctance to acknowledge incontinence can have serious psychological and social implications—social isolation, falls, fractures, even admission to long-term care facilities. Consider Mrs. Red Horse in the box on the next page (Goode, Burgio, Richter, & Markland, 2010).

Gastrointestinal System Changes in the esophagus may include a decrease in the contraction of the muscles and more time for the cardiac sphincter (a valvelike structure that allows food to pass into the stomach) to open; quite simply, this means it takes more time for food to reach the stomach. The result may be a sensation

Learning from Master Athletes

The National Senior Games Association, committed to promoting healthy lifestyles through sports and fitness, involves thousands of participants in Senior Olympics. Older athletes defy expectations about inevitable physiological decline. For example, an 88-year-old shotput thrower claimed that his return to competitive track and field eliminated his migraine headaches. An 86-year-old who played guard for an NFL team in the 1930s broke records for his age group. Whether they have maintained their physical activity levels since youth or begun in middle or old age, older master athletes teach us about the effects of healthy lifestyles on normal physiological changes.

The Stigma of Incontinence

Mrs. Red Horse, age 75, who has mild dementia, has increasing problems with incontinence, especially since she began using diuretics for her high blood pressure. This has forced her to curtail social activities, even her afternoon tea breaks or trips to the grocery store, because she is afraid she won't be able to get to the bathroom in time. Her daughter is frustrated by her mother's lack of awareness about needing to go to the bathroom. But Mrs. Red Horse's mild dementia makes it hard for her to pay attention to signs that she needs to void (i.e., empty her bladder). And both of them are too embarrassed to talk with each other or her physician about the problem. Instead, Mrs. Red Horse hears her family whispering about the smell in her home and finds herself increasingly isolated.

of being full before having eaten a complete meal. This, in turn, may reduce the pleasure a person derives from eating and result in poor nutrition. This change explains why some older people eat small quantities at mealtimes, a behavior that worries their families.

Secretion of digestive juices in the stomach diminishes after age 50, which means that older people are more likely to experience chronic inflammation of the stomach lining and be at a greater risk for colon and stomach cancer. Because of this, elders who complain of heartburn or digestive problems should seek medical attention instead of relying on home remedies or over-the-counter medications.

Functional changes in the small intestine mean that the number of enzymes is reduced, and simple sugars are absorbed more slowly, resulting in diminished efficiency with age. Anatomical changes in the large intestine are associated with an increased incidence of chronic constipation, although behavioral factors, such as what we eat and how much we exercise, are probably more critical than physiological changes.

Endocrine System The endocrine system is made up of cells and tissues that produce hormones. An age-related change in the endocrine system is **menopause**, resulting in a reduced production of two important hormones in women—**estrogen** and progesterone. Many other hormones also decline with age. For instance, changes in insulin levels may affect an elder's ability to efficiently metabolize glucose in their diet, resulting in high blood sugar levels. It is unclear if the changes in hormone production are a cause or an effect of aging. Nevertheless, as you learned, some research to delay aging has focused on replacing hormones that decline with aging.

Immune System In the past, it was assumed that the aging process always results in deterioration of the immune system or immunodeficiency (i.e., an inadequate response to infections), increasing the older person's susceptibility to disease. Additionally, the altered immune function has been linked to age-related illnesses such as prostate and skin cancers and cardiovascular disease. Recent research contradicts this assumption, however. Studies of centenarians, for example, show highly effective immune responses when compared to some young-old persons. Nevertheless, the fact that most deaths in people age 80 and older are caused by infections points to failure of the immune system in those instances (Effros, 2001; Solana, 2003; Swain & Nikolich-Zugich, 2009).

Nervous System The brain is composed of billions of **neurons**, or nerve cells, which we lose as we age. You may be surprised to learn that neuronal loss begins at age 30. A moderate degree of neuronal loss does not create a major decline in brain function, however. In fact, contrary to popular belief, we can still function with fewer neurons, so their loss is not the primary reason for mild forgetfulness. Even in the case of dementia, severe loss of neurons may be less significant than changes in brain tissue, blood flow, and receptor organs.

Brain mass or weight is reduced with age, which is probably due to loss of fluids. But difficulties that we may experience in solving problems or remembering dates and names cannot be attributed to these slight alterations in the brain's size and appearance (Coffey et al., 1998).

However, neuronal loss, age-related changes in neurotransmitters, and reduced blood flow do slightly impair cognitive and motor function, resulting in a slower reaction time. This is a fairly widespread concern, even in middle age, when people begin to notice lagging reflexes and longer times to process information and react. Responding to a telephone or doorbell, crossing the street, or making decisions may take longer for older than younger people. Most elders adjust by creatively modifying their environment or personal habits, for example, leaving the house an hour before a nearby appointment, shopping in less crowded stores, and avoiding rush-hour driving. In sum, the brain has tremendous reserve capacity that takes over as normal age-associated losses begin.

Physiological Changes and Sexuality

A common myth is that age-related physiological changes detrimentally affect sexual functioning. Such misconceptions were shaped by early studies on sexuality, where questions about older adults' sexual behavior were rarely raised or addressed only the frequency of sexual intercourse. The subjective or qualitative aspects of sexuality in old age, including the sexual experience of LGBT individuals, were overlooked in these studies.

The frequency or the nature of sexual experience does not alter dramatically with age—for better or worse. Indeed, when sexual activity is broadly defined to encompass hugging, kissing, mutuality, loving, touching, and masturbation, it may be as or more satisfying than at younger ages. In their classic study, Masters and Johnson (1981) determined that few age-related physiological changes prevent continued sexual enjoyment and activity in old age. Another study from that time by Starr and Weiner (1981) revealed that older study participants rated sex as the same or better than when they were younger. Other research since then shows that older adults in their late fifties and beyond, into their eighties and nineties, can be, and many are, sexually active. More importantly, they enjoy a high degree of sexual satisfaction and excitement, enjoyment, and pleasure. When a partner is available, older people who remain sexually active do not change significantly in their frequency of sexual activities. But their experience may differ subjectively from earlier in life because of age-associated physiological changes (Bancroft, 2007; Lindau et al., 2007; Northrup, Schwartz, & Witte, 2013).

points to ponder

Is older adults' sexuality largely invisible to you? When you were growing up, how did you perceive your parents' and grandparents' sexuality? What were your sources of information about older adults and sexuality? Or did you hear about elders' sexuality mostly through jokes, the media, the Internet, or birthday greeting cards? If so, what did these images convey? How did they affect your understanding of sexuality and aging? Have your views changed?

Women and Age-Related Physiological Changes The major physiological changes affecting women's sexual function and enjoyment are due to reductions in estrogen and progesterone during menopause. Menopause is a period in a woman's life when the menstrual cycle gradually ceases because of the loss of reproductive ability.

Wide variability in symptoms and responses suggests that there is no inevitable "menopausal syndrome." But you may have heard your mother or grandmother complain about hot flashes or a sudden sensation of heat in the upper body, often accompanied by a drenching sweat. These occur when the nerves overrespond to decreases in hormone levels. This affects the hypothalamus (the part of the brain that regulates body temperature), causing the blood vessels to dilate or constrict. Blood then rushes to the skin surface, causing perspiration, flushing, and increased pulse rate and temperature. But hot flashes generally do not interfere with a woman's sexual functioning nor cause psychological difficulties. Nor is there a scientific explanation for why symptoms such as hot flashes occur in some women and not in others (NIA, 2012b).

Despite uncomfortable symptoms, such as the thinning of the vaginal walls, menopause does not physiologically impede full sexual activity. Generally, an older woman's sexual response cycle has all the dimensions as when she was younger, but it takes her longer to respond to sexual stimulation. In fact, some women, freed of worries about pregnancy, report greater sexual satisfaction. Older women's sexuality tends to be influenced more by sociocultural expectations than by physiological changes—by the limited number of available male partners for heterosexual women, stigma associated with lesbian relations for some older women, and societal definitions of older women as asexual and unattractive (Blonna & Levitan, 2000; Zeiss & Kasl-Godley, 2001).

Men and Age-Related Physiological Changes Relatively little attention has been given to men's hormonal rhythms compared to women's. There is, however, increasing evidence that **male menopause**, or **viropause**, occurs but at a more gradual rate. This is because the loss of testosterone (approximately 1 percent per year on average) is not as abrupt as the estrogen depletion for menopausal women. This loss of testosterone affects men's sexual response. These changes may include

- reduced muscle size and strength,
- decreased levels of calcium in the bones,

- declining immune system response, and
- fatigue, irritability, indecisiveness, depression, loss of self-confidence, listlessness, poor appetite, and problems of concentration (Lindau et al., 2007).

Although these physiological changes do not necessarily interfere with sexual performance nor reduce sexual enjoyment, they may alter the nature of the sexual response, as captured in Table 3.1. Yet most men as they age still find sexual activity to be sensual, pleasurable, and satisfying (Blonna & Levitan, 2000; DeLamater & Friedrich, 2002; Wierzalis, Barret, Pope, & Rankins, 2006).

Although not an inevitable consequence of aging, **erectile dysfunction** or **impotence** (i.e., an inability to get and sustain an erection) is the chief sexual problem for older men. This is caused by diseases, age-induced deterioration of the blood vessels, low testosterone levels, and excessive tobacco, drug, or alcohol use. Older men and their partners need to be informed of physiological reasons for impotence and that it is both common and treatable. In recent years, new ways to treat impotence have drawn increased attention. The marketing of a wide range of products, such as Viagra and Levitra, reflects, in part, drug companies' awareness of baby boomers' greater openness to talking about and wanting to experience sexual pleasure (NIA, 2013).

Health care professionals may reinforce perceptions that sexuality in old age is deviant. In one study, only 38 percent of men and 22 percent of women reported having discussed sex with a physician since turning age 50! Instead, health professionals should routinely ask about sexual enjoyment, determine whether there are obstacles and solutions to achieving a meaningful sexual relationship, and address issues such as sexually transmitted diseases and high-risk sexual behavior. Because of homophobia, older adult sexuality in the LGBT community involves a greater array of issues than in the heterosexual community. Historical taboos in regard to same-sex relationships have a negative impact on sexual expression for many LGBT elders (Connolly, Breckman, Callahan, Lachs, Ramsey-Klawsnik, & Solomon, 2012; Lachs, 2011).

TABLE 3.1 **Normal Physiological Changes in Women and Men**

Women	Men
Reduction in vaginal elasticity and lubrication	Response to sexual stimulation is slower
Thinning of vaginal walls	Erection may take longer to achieve and require more direct stimulation
Slower response to sexual stimulation	Erection is slower, less full, and disappears quickly after orgasm
Slower capacity for orgasm	Orgasm is experienced more rapidly, less intensely, and more spasmodically
Fewer and less intense orgasms	Length of time between orgasm and subsequent erections increases
Rapid return to pre-arousal state after orgasm	Occasional lack of orgasm during intercourse

Tips for Improving Sleep

- Increase physical exercise
- Increase exposure to natural daylight
- Drink less caffeine
- Avoid napping
- Improve the sleep environment (e.g., a quiet bedroom with heavy curtains or a sleep mask) (Ohayon et al., 2004)

Sleep Patterns

You may have older relatives complain that they can no longer sleep well. Indeed, this is the case for up to 40 percent of older people. As we age, it takes a longer time to fall asleep and we wake more frequently at night. Older adults also sleep more lightly, which means that they are easily awakened. When they compensate by taking more naps, their night sleep is further disrupted. Those who report sleep disturbances to their primary physician are often prescribed sleeping pills. Yet medications do not necessarily improve sleep patterns (Lesage & Scharf, 2007; Ohayon, Carskadon, Guilleminault, & Vitiello, 2004; Vitiello, Larsen, & Moe, 2004).

Sensory Functions

As we get older, we cannot see, hear, touch, taste, or smell as well as we did when we were younger. Some of you may already have noticed sensory changes. We reach our optimum capacities in our twenties, maintain this peak for a few years, and gradually experience a decline, with rapid rate of deterioration after middle age. But rates of sensory decline vary tremendously. Some older persons have better vision or hearing than 25-year-olds, which was probably true for them in their earlier years. There are also variations within older individuals. Hearing may show an early decline, while taste and touch change little until advanced old age. Over time, sensory decrements may affect an older person's social functions. Because these alterations are usually gradual, people adapt by using other senses or by modifying their behaviors (e.g., standing closer to an object to see it) and environments (seeking out quiet restaurants for conversations with friends).

Vision You may have older friends who had near perfect vision all their lives, but start to need reading glasses in their forties, or have difficulty reading street signs or detecting variations in color. Vision impairments increase markedly with age (about 14 percent of adults age 65 and older, 23 percent after age 85), and can cause problems with daily activities and even increase the risk of falls and fractures (Federal Interagency Forum, 2012; Stuen, 2006).

The cornea is usually the first part of the eye to change. Its smooth rounded surface thickens, becomes flatter, and may take on an irregular shape. The eye appears to lose its luster and is less translucent. In some cases, a fatty yellow ring may form around the cornea. But this has no impact on vision.

The pupils of the eyes become less sensitive to light levels and their opening is reduced to about two-thirds of its original size. These changes make it more difficult to see in darkness or to adjust to light level changes. In fact, older people may need three times more light than younger persons to function effectively. They may have difficulty making out images when there is poor light contrast such as driving at twilight or in foggy conditions. To cope, older people may avoid driving in rain, among fast-moving traffic, or at night when bright headlights create glare against surfaces.

Most elders experience **presbyopia**—a physiological change in the lens' shape and elasticity, which makes it difficult to see objects up close. You may know adults who hold their reading materials at arm's length or need bifocals and reading classes. These physiological changes also reduce **accommodative ability** or seeing clearly when shifting focus from near to far. This may result in caution and anxiety when driving or walking, or problems looking across a room, walking up or downstairs, or writing notes while looking up at a blackboard. When combined with the poor refraction of light through the cornea's uneven flattened surface, extreme sensitivity to glare often results. This creates difficulties in environments with a single source of light aimed at a shiny surface—such as streetlights on a rain-slicked highway, or a bright incandescent light shining on a linoleum floor.

Depth and distance perception also deteriorate rapidly after age 75, particularly in low-light situations and without orienting cues, such as stairs without color distinctions at the edges and pedestrian ramps or curb cuts with varying slopes. Narrower peripheral vision (the ability to see on either side without moving the eyes or the head and to be aware of approaching objects) may mean that older adults are startled when a car, bicycle, or other fast-moving object seems to appear suddenly out of nowhere. Or older drivers may not see cars approaching from the left or right at an intersection or in a passing situation.

With normal aging, the eye lens becomes more opaque and less light passes through. But some elders experience a more severe clouding of the lens that prevents enough light from entering to see. They have a disease known as **cataract**, a leading cause of vision loss experienced by nearly half of adults age 80 and older. Other symptoms are double vision,

Ever Wonder Why an Older Relative May Not Enjoy Eating Out?

Older people may feel frustrated when they go to a special restaurant for dinner, only to find that the tables are lit by candles. This makes it difficult to read the menu, to see the way to the table, and even to have eye contact with companions. Family and friends may be frustrated in such situations if they do not understand that the elder's complaints about the restaurant stem from vision changes, not from a lack of appreciation for their efforts. Some older people cope by avoiding restaurants altogether or going only during daylight hours. Restaurant owners can accommodate such changes by providing good lighting at each table and writing their menus in large, legible print against a white background. In response to baby boomers, some restaurants have begun to stock reading glasses to lend to customers!

Diagnosing Macular Degeneration

Mr. Lopez has noticed over the past 5 years that objects appear blurry when he looks directly at them but sharper as he glances more peripherally. After experiencing problems with driving, he finally went for an eye exam. The ophthalmologist diagnosed macular degeneration and was able to treat it with Visudyne. Mr. Lopez can now drive safely again.

problems with color discrimination (fading colors), and sensitivity to light, both nighttime and daylight.

If the lens becomes totally opaque, cataract surgery is recommended. This is the most frequent outpatient surgical procedure performed on older adults, carries relatively little risk, and improves their capacity to perform daily activities and the overall quality of life (Asbell et al., 2005; Robman & Taylor, 2005; Stuen, 2006).

Glaucoma, another eye disease, occurs when excess production of fluid occurs and causes pressure on the optic nerve. If caught early, it can be managed with a daily routine of eye drops. Because it is an insidious disease that progresses slowly, it may not be detected until its later stages; an individual's field of vision may become so narrowed so that they can focus only in the center, affecting safe mobility. More severe cases may require surgery or laser treatment to prevent blindness (Stuen, 2006).

Another eye disease is **macular degeneration**, or loss of acuity in the center of the visual field. It typically begins with a loss of detail vision; then central vision gradually becomes worse, making reading and driving impossible. When older persons compensate by using their remaining peripheral vision, they may appear to be looking at the shoulder of someone they are addressing while actually relying on peripheral vision to see a person's face. The incidence of macular degeneration grows even more dramatically with age than cataracts. Although it cannot be cured, treatments can slow retinal damage and improve central vision (Schultz et al., 2003; Stuen, 2006).

Even though most elders experience some vision loss, the good news is that a wide range of low-tech aids at minimal cost can enhance their vision—and their well-being. Here are few such aids:

- high-wattage light bulbs
- fluorescent lighting with color correction
- large-print labels for prescription bottles, spices, and cooking supplies
- large-print newspapers, books, calendars, phone books, clocks, and even playing cards
- magnifying glasses for situations where large-print substitutes are unavailable
- audiotapes of books
- needle threaders for sewing
- large numbers on phones and appliances
- large fonts on flat-screen computer monitors designed to reduce glare
- voice-activated computer software

Relatively modest changes can make home and work environments safer for elders with visual impairments. Here a few of them:

- Clearly mark edges and corners—stairs, walls, doorsills, curbs, and curb cuts—with texture or widely contrasting colors on opposite ends of the color spectrum, such as red and yellow, or green and orange, to aid depth perception.
- Use contrasting colors and light coding for ramps and other changes in elevation.
- Install nonslip and nonglossy floor coverings.
- Avoid glossy finish on walls or large windows at the end of a long, dark corridor that can cause glare.
- Increase the number of light sources and use dimmer switches to adjust lighting levels.
- Use indirect or task lighting (e.g., reading and countertop lamps).

Hearing Vision and hearing are perhaps our most critical links to the world—vision for negotiating the physical environment and hearing for communicating.

points to ponder

Consider how we rely on our hearing ability in everyday life: in conversations, localizing the sound of approaching vehicles as we drive or cross the street, and interpreting other people's emotions through their tone of voice. Imagine how you might function if these abilities gradually deteriorate. How might you adapt?

Practical Communication Strategies

Clara enjoys talking to her 89-year-old grandmother, Miss Helen. When she visits at her assisted living facility, they usually enjoy lunch in the dining room. Miss Helen uses a hearing aid. But Clara also uses some practical communication strategies to help enhance the conversation. Clara has learned that Miss Helen's left ear has more hearing capacity, so she sits next to her on her left side. When talking with Miss Helen, she looks directly at her and gives her an unobstructed view of her face and mouth. Without speaking more loudly or slowly than necessary, Clara does her best to pronounce words clearly and not talk too quickly or in a high pitch. If it appears Miss Helen does not fully comprehend something, Clara repeats it in a different way, focusing on the main points rather than a lot of extraneous details.

Clara's communication style comes across as natural and relaxed. Miss Helen says she has a much easier time hearing Clara than others. Understanding a person is more than just "hearing." A combination of effective strategies—and being attentive to nonverbal communication—can make a big difference between comprehension and confusion.

About 46 percent of older men and 31 percent of older women report trouble hearing, with rates increasing to nearly 60 percent among the oldest-old. **Presbycusis** or age-related hearing loss involves limited volume and range or distortion of sounds perceived. The greatest decline in hearing with age occurs in the cochlea, a snail-shaped circular structure in the inner ear. The vibration of hair cells in the cochlea affects our ability to detect and localize sounds, especially at lower volume and very high pitch or frequency. Changes in auditory thresholds can be detected by age 30, but the degeneration of hair cells and membranes in the cochlea is not observed until much later (Agrawal, Platz, & Niparko, 2008; Federal Interagency Forum, 2012).

The signs of hearing loss include the following:

- Difficulty distinguishing high-frequency consonants such as *z, s, sh, f, p, k, t,* and *g,* which negatively affects our comprehension
- Increasingly asking people to repeat what they said
- Raising the volume of the TV or radio or moving closer to it
- Withdrawing socially (Dalton, Cruickshanks, Klein, Wiley, & Nondahl, 2003; Strawbridge, Wallhagen, Shema, & Kaplan, 2000)

You may have experienced how hearing loss appears to be significantly affected by environmental causes. People exposed to high-volume and high-frequency noise throughout their lives (e.g., urban dwellers, construction and factory workers) experience more hearing decrements than do those from rural, low-noise environments. And hearing loss among people age 18–44 is increasing significantly. Future cohorts of elders are likely to have higher rates of hearing loss that was environmentally induced earlier in their lives—perhaps from listening to loud music on MP3 players in adolescence and young adulthood (Agarwal et al., 2008; Wingfield et al., 2007).

Older people who experience hearing declines can also reduce negative impacts by adopting the following strategies to change their behavior and social interactions:

- Raise the volume of TV, phones, and radios to make it easier to hear higher-frequency sounds and increase recognition of the consonants *p, t, k, b, d,* and *g* by 50–90 percent.
- Listen to music made by lower-pitched instruments, such as an organ.
- Seek out environments for visiting that dampen background noises.
- Use telephones with volume adjusters and lights that blink when the phone rings.
- Use a hearing aid (Kawamoto & Kiyak, 2014).

Older adults may have problems adjusting to hearing aids. Less expensive aids may merely raise the volume, particularly of background noises. Digital hearing aids have tiny computer chips that filter sounds to match each user's hearing loss profile without amplifying background noises. These newer designs are also less obtrusive and fit well inside the ear. However, they can cost about twice as much and are generally not covered by insurance.

Many older people resist a hearing aid because of its cost and social stigma. After President Clinton, in his

points to ponder

Imagine you have a loved one whose vision and hearing are deteriorating due to old age. What are some specific ways you can help this person have quality of life despite these physical limitations? What are some ways you can help this person modify his or her living environment for safety and comfort?

fifties, was fitted with a digital hearing aid in 1997, sales of hearing aids increased dramatically. But 6 years later, only 12 percent of older adults with hearing loss were using a hearing aid (Crews & Campbell, 2004). What other factors do you think would explain our reluctance to use hearing aids compared to wearing glasses?

Taste and Smell Although some older people may complain that food does not taste as good as it once did, these complaints are probably not due to age-associated changes. Slight losses of taste buds do not necessarily dull taste sensation, and there is tremendous variation within and across individuals. For example, some elders have more difficulty in discriminating between varying intensities of flavors—level of bitterness in coffee or the saltiness of food—but less so in terms of varied intensities in sweetness.

Appreciation of food also involves the sense of smell. And age-related declines for smell are greater than for taste. You may observe older adults who keep adding salt and sugar to food, often doing the exact opposite of what their doctor recommends. They also perceive airborne stimuli such as a flower's fragrance less intensely than younger persons. Using herbs and spices and color in food can sharpen older people's sensitivity to tastes and pleasant odors, improve the palatability of food, and ultimately help ensure adequate nutrition. Losing the ability to smell and taste is not just a matter of reduced enjoyment, but can foster risks such as unhealthy eating habits, social isolation, and not smelling dangers like smoke (Markovic et al., 2007).

Touch Touch sensitivity, especially in the fingertips, palms, and lower extremities, deteriorates slightly with age, due to changes in the skin and to age-related loss in the number of nerve endings. These changes affect performance of daily tasks that require sensitivity of the fingertips, such as selecting medications from a pillbox.

Pain perception is an important aspect of touch sensitivity. Older adults are less able to discriminate among levels of painful stimuli than younger persons, because nerve cells in the skin become less efficient with age. A dangerous effect is that elders sometimes experience more serious burns because they do not respond to a heated object until it is too late.

Tolerance for pain is a subjective experience. Some older adults increasingly complain about pain, while others attempt to minimize their pain by not reporting it. Or they may think that pain is "just something to live with." But underreporting, such as not reporting symptoms of a heart attack, can have serious negative effects.

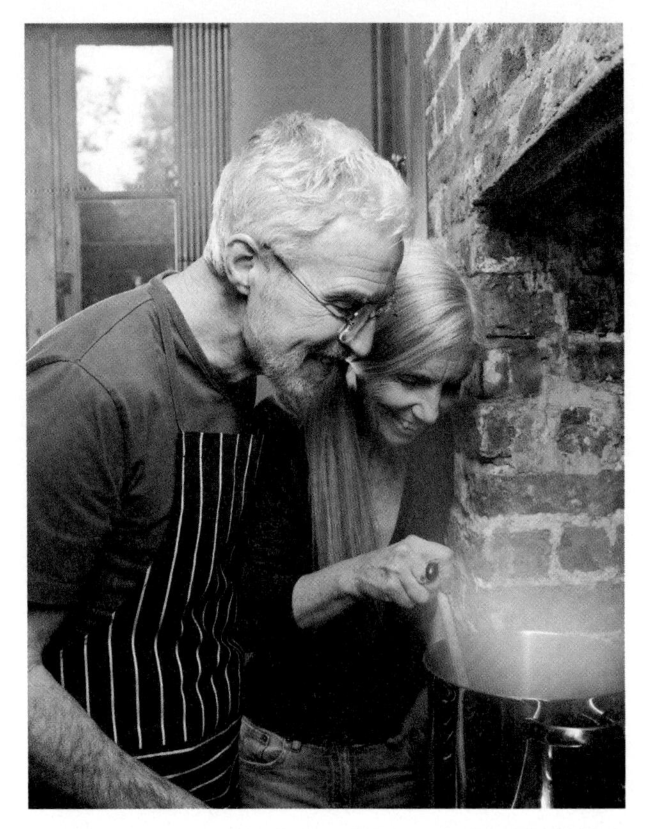

Cooking with spices can enhance olfactory and taste sensitivity.

As you have learned, most older adults adapt, oftentimes creatively, to these age-associated alterations in their physiological systems and consider themselves to be relatively healthy. We turn now to chronic diseases, which are not normal or inevitable, but do nevertheless increase in frequency with age.

Defining Health and Functional Ability

Our desire for good health, whatever our age, is nearly universal. But good health has different meanings depending upon our culture, age, and economic status. What does it mean to you to be in good health? As defined by the World Health Organization, **good health** is a state of physical, mental, and social well-being. This broad concept implies an integration of body, mind, and spirit—a perspective reflected in the growth of health promotion and wellness programs and alternative medicine. Social and health behaviors across the life course—such as diet, exercise, and engagement in the community, as well as the physical environment where we live, work, and obtain health care—all play a role in the development and progression of chronic diseases. For the majority of older adults, being able to do the things that they want at home and in the community is a primary component of **active aging** (Phelan, Anderson, LaCroix, & Larson, 2004).

A common perception is that being old means being in poor health. Yet about 40 percent of persons age 65 and older in community settings assess their health as excellent or very good compared to about 65 percent of younger adults. Elders who perceive themselves as reasonably healthy tend to be happier, more satisfied, more involved in social activities, and less lonely. These positive self-ratings of health decline, however, with age and among populations of color. Not surprisingly, those with severe disability rate their health the lowest. And elders who take multiple medications, experience chronic pain, and struggle with depression, low income, and ADL limitations report poorer health and lower quality of life and life satisfaction (Benyamini, Blumstein, Lusky, & Modan, 2003; Federal Interagency Forum, 2012; Health United States, 2010).

There are a number of terms central to understanding health and aging that you will encounter in research and lay discussion of older adults' physical well-being. **Health status** refers to the presence or absence of disease and the degree of disability in level of functioning. Older people's **functional ability** generally determines what they can do—or think they can do—and how healthy they are. It also indicates how much formal and informal assistance they need and has implications for where they can live. A person can have numerous illnesses, but still be able to function relatively independently on a daily basis—and still perceive themselves as healthy. **Activities of daily living (ADLs)** and **instrumental activities of daily living (IADLs)**, defined in the box on this page, are measures of functional ability and point to the level of care that an elder may need.

Other measures, such as lifting heavy objects, reaching above one's head, or walking two to three blocks, may be more closely linked to physiological capabilities than ADLs and IADLs, which may be influenced by social and cultural expectations and use of technology (Federal Interagency Forum, 2012).

Assessing Functional Ability

Activities of daily living (ADLs) summarize an individual's ability to perform basic personal care tasks on their own:

- Eating
- Bathing
- Dressing
- Using the toilet
- Getting in or out of a bed or chair
- Walking—the most common ADL limitation

Instrumental activities of daily living (IADLs) encompass a person's capacity to perform more complex activities:

- Maintaining the home
- Managing money
- Preparing meals
- Making a phone call
- Managing medications
- Shopping for groceries—the most common problem with IADLs

Disability is defined as impairments in the ability to complete daily tasks, which may mean that an older person requires assistance from other people or technology.

- Most elders are able to go about their daily routines without significant assistance.
- Around 40 percent of older people living in the community need help with one ADL and one IADL, although this rate increases with age.
- But only a small proportion need help with five or more ADLs and rely on family or paid caregivers for personal care; only 2 percent are homebound.

Remember that although disability increases with age, it is not inevitable, and disabling health changes occur at varied rates in each individual (AoA, 2012; CDC, 2011e; Federal Interagency Forum, 2012).

Frailty is another way of describing severe limitations in ADLs, such as unintended weight loss, difficulty walking up more than one flight of steps, slow walking speed, low physical activity levels, weak grip strength, and chronic exhaustion. This increases the risk of an older person becoming disabled, dependent and dying earlier than others of their age (Fried et al., 2001).

Chronic illnesses, defined as lasting more than three months, often require long-term management or care rather than a cure. These contrast with **acute illnesses**, which are short-term and more readily treated.

Comorbidity is the coexistence of two or more chronic illnesses.

Health disparities are inequalities in health, well-being, and mortality across the life course, which often reflect a lifetime of disadvantages in employment, finances, education, and access to health care.

A closely related term, **health care disparities**, refers to differences in access, quality, and use of health care services; these typically result in health disparities.

Quality of life encompasses an individual's functional health, relative independence in performing daily tasks, and satisfaction with their circumstances. Someone may have health problems as assessed by a doctor, but still be able to manage on a daily basis and perceive their quality of life as positive. Indeed, physicians tend to rate an older person's health more negatively than do the elders. This seeming paradox occurs because elders typically adjust their perceptions of their health in response to the aging process—or in comparison to less healthy peers.

points to ponder

Think about how you perceive your own health. How do you describe it to others? To what extent do you compare your health to others of your age, gender, race, or ethnicity? How does your ability to perform various daily activities influence your health perceptions? How does your health affect your overall quality of life?

Are Disability Rates Declining?

In 2006, the answer was yes. The proportion of older adults who reported problems with IADLs or ADLs had dropped significantly, and continued declines were predicted. It appeared that people were not only living longer, but were also more likely to manage their chronic diseases without frailty or disability. This decline among successive cohorts of elders was the result of factors such as improved medical treatment, more widespread use of assistive technologies, a growing emphasis on prevention, and rising education levels and gains in socioeconomic status (Manton, Gu, & Lowrimore, 2008).

But today, the answer is less clear cut, with some studies finding that after years of steady decline, disability rates among older adults have been rising since 2000. Other research suggests that while the decline in disability may have continued among those ages 85 and older, it ended or was reversed in the younger cohorts of older adults and that baby boomers will face higher disability rates (Crimmins & Beltran-Sanchez, 2010; Fuller-Thomson, Yu, Nuru-Jeter, Guralnik, & Minler, 2009; Martin, Schoeni, & Andreski, 2010).

Why would this reversal of a 20-year trend occur? A primary cause appears to be the doubling of obesity rates over the last three decades. Being overweight puts people at increased risk for several potentially disabling chronic diseases, such as heart disease and type II diabetes (CDC, 2010a; Federal Interagency Forum, 2012; NCHS, 2011b).

You may recall the term compression of morbidity from Chapter 1—the length of life without disease and loss of mobility. Nearly all of us would want to delay the age at which chronic illness and disabilities begin. But these recent data suggest that while people are living longer, many are also living sicker (Fries, 1980, 2003; National Health Interview Survey, 2012; NIH, 2011).

Chronic and Acute Diseases

While the risk of chronic disease increases with age, the incidence of **acute conditions** (or temporary) decreases. But when acute conditions occur, they are more debilitating and require more care. An older person who gets a cold, for example, faces a greater risk of pneumonia or bronchitis because of changes in organ systems that reduce resistance to stress and capacities to recuperate, and these risks are even greater when she/he has other chronic illnesses. For example, respiratory infection rates are similar in young and old, but hospitalization for influenza-associated respiratory problems and death from pneumonia and influenza occur much more frequently among older adults (Gerontological Society of America, 2013).

About 80 percent of older adults have one or more chronic disease, which has more severe consequences for elders' well-being than for younger adults. Some chronic conditions, like sinus infections and bronchitis, are hardly life threatening. However, the leading chronic illnesses tend to be more severe—hypertension, arthritis, heart disease, cancer, and diabetes—than those among younger people. Moreover, how we react to persons with chronic illness—such as assuming that they cannot manage or enjoy life—sometimes can limit them more than the actual physical condition. Of even greater concern is that older adults with multiple chronic illness (or comorbidity) have higher rates of hospitalization; more use of emergency room visits, home health care, clinician visits, and medications; and higher health care spending. Ultimately, the most negative consequence of a chronic disease is shortened life expectancy (AARP, 2011; National Council on Aging, 2010; NIA, 2011).

Multiple Chronic Illness: What Does Comorbidity Really Mean?

Mazie Piccolo, age 84, has so many health problems that it's hard to keep track. Congestive heart failure makes her short of breath and causes her legs to swell. An abnormal heart rhythm raises her risk for stroke. Arthritis in her knees makes getting around difficult, and she can no longer drive.

She also has osteoporosis, and has fallen several times in the past few years, once breaking her pelvis. On top of high cholesterol, high blood pressure, and gastric reflux, she has a history of depression, and it is sometimes hard for her to be motivated to care for her husband, who is even frailer than she is. Mazie should be taking 13 different prescribed medications—but this has been too expensive and confusing for her to manage. Other medications that might be advisable cause intolerable side effects, and the more drugs she takes, the greater the risk of dangerous drug interactions.

As a group, patients like Mrs. Piccolo fare poorly by any measure. They linger longer in hospitals, experience more serious preventable health complications, and die younger than patients with less complex medical profiles.

Yet complicated patients like Mrs. Piccolo are often treated as collections of malfunctioning body parts rather than as whole human beings. According to Dr. Mary E. Tinetti, a geriatrician, often no one is looking at the big picture or recognizing that what is best for a disease may not be best for the patient. And treating one disease in isolation can make another disease worse. Would Mrs. Piccolo get the most benefit from lowering her blood pressure or cholesterol level, being treated for osteoporosis, or taking a new medication for stroke prevention? Or is it more important to treat her depression so she can manage her overall health better, or improve her ability to physically get around and care for her husband?

Growing numbers of elders like Mrs. Piccolo are challenging our health care system that is more oriented to curing acute disease than effectively managing long-term illnesses (Carpenter, 2009).

Here are the reasons why many older adults are living longer, but with higher rates of chronic illness:

- Increased life expectancy: Quite simply, the longer we live, the more likely it is that we will have some type of chronic disease.
- High rates of unhealthy behaviors, particularly smoking and obesity.
- Treatment advances. Medications can now help control hypertension and cholesterol, allowing individuals with these risk factors for heart disease and stroke to live longer lives.
- Increased public awareness has meant that more people request testing and treatment. Illnesses that may have gone undetected in the past (or killed them earlier) now are diagnosed and treated (CDC, 2010; Federal Interagency Forum, 2012).

Health Disparities

Age is not the only factor that influences illness and disability. Gender, race, sexual orientation, social class, education, and lifestyle factors profoundly affect physical well-being and create health inequities. Poor people of all ages face a higher risk of health problems and disabilities. Accordingly, elders of color, who are more likely to be low-income, have higher rates of chronic illness—and, as a result, a greater incidence of hospitalization, longer hospital stays, and shorter life expectancy. It is not surprising that older persons of color with chronic conditions are less likely to describe their health as good or excellent than whites in every age group after age 65. These health disparities reflect, in part, the origins in early childhood of higher risk for illness. They are also due to discriminatory practices that disproportionately cause nonwhites to have lower incomes and inadequate nutrition across the life course. In addition, elders of color, because of past negative experiences with and distrust of services, may be less likely to utilize health care, especially for prevention. The box on page 77 illustrates how race intersects with gender, education, and class across the life course to increase the incidence of chronic illness in old age (Warner & Hayward, 2002; Whitfield & Hayward, 2003).

Primary Causes of Death in Old Age

There is a saying that "nobody ever died of old age." To a large extent, this is true. Older adults die from chronic diseases, although you may hear of instances where there

The Impact of Gender, Race, Education, and Class Inequities on Chronic Disease and Health Status

Gender Inequities

- Women experience more nonfatal chronic conditions—arthritis, incontinence, osteoarthritis, osteoporosis, and cataracts—than do men, which limit their functional ability, quality of life, and social interactions.
- Among women age 85 and older, 72 percent have disabilities and are more likely to require assistance than their male counterparts.
- Despite their higher rate of chronic disease, women are less likely to die from such conditions than are men and rate their health more positively than men.
- Women are also more likely to live in long-term care facilities.

Racial Inequities

- Most disabling chronic diseases occur earlier among African Americans, Latinos, and American Indians than among whites.
- African Americans and Native Americans are more likely to have diabetes but Latinos are most likely to die of diabetes.
- African American males have more difficulty performing ADLs and IADLs than whites.
- Older African Americans, American Indians, and Latinos are less likely to rate their health as excellent or very good than are whites or Asians.

Gender and Racial Inequities

- African American women are more likely to die of breast cancer than white women.
- Older women of color have the highest prevalence of comorbidities, functional limitations, and disability.

Class and Education Inequities

- Low-income and less well-educated older adults have higher rates of chronic diseases.
- High income is associated with positive self-assessments of health.
- Educational achievement moderates the effect of race on chronic disease and disability, especially among older women. For example, African American and white women with less than 8 years of school can expect more years of unhealthy life than their counterparts with more education. Education appears to benefit people into old age, perhaps by increasing their awareness of and access to preventive health services (AARP, 2011; AHA, 2011; CDC and National Center for Health Promotion, 2010b; Federal Interagency Forum, 2012; NCHS, 2009).

is no identifiable cause of death, suggesting that a person's body did just wear out.

- Two-thirds of deaths among older adults are due to heart disease, cancer, strokes, and diabetes. Over 80 percent of people who die of heart attacks are age 65 and older. You may be surprised to learn that more women than men die of heart disease each year, due to higher rates of hypertension, with the highest incidence among African American women. And more women die from heart disease than breast cancer. However, many women still think of heart disease as a man's illness and are unaware of symptoms.
- Health care disparities are also reflected in the fact that African American men age 55–64 are at the highest risk for death from heart disease and strokes, although the death rates decline after age 75. In contrast, Asian-Pacific Islanders have the lowest incidence of deaths due to heart disease (AHA, 2011; CDC, 2011b; Federal Interagency Forum, 2012; Women Heart, 2011).

points to **ponder**

What factors might explain higher death rates due to heart disease and stroke among persons of color? Access to quality health care across the life course, which allows early detection and management of these chronic conditions, is the primary variable for lower rates among whites. In the past, people of color have been less likely to have health insurance. When they do, they may encounter discriminatory attitudes or cultural insensitivity on the part of health care providers. Or they may not trust them. What other factors can you think of?

points to ponder

Think about older relatives or friends you know who have a chronic illness. How would you describe their health? Do they appear to be active and vibrant or frail? Then consider your own health. Do you have any chronic conditions? If so, how have these conditions affected your life and what you are able to do? How have you adapted to them?

Common Chronic Diseases

Next, we briefly discuss the most frequent chronic illnesses among older adults. As you will learn, these cannot be "cured." But knowing how to effectively manage a chronic disease is essential to maintaining quality of life. It is beyond the scope of this book to discuss each chronic disease in depth. But this section provides you with a foundational understanding of long-term illness—and points you to other resources that can help promote optimum health as we age.

Heart Disease and the Cardiovascular System

Coronary heart disease occurs when optimum blood flow to the heart is restricted because the cardiac vessels narrow. This may be caused by atherosclerosis, the accumulation of fatty deposits in the vessels, which can lead to a heart attack (a myocardial infarction). You just learned how heart disease is the primary cause of death, although death due to heart disease is declining; it is also a leading cause of serious long-term disability and limitations in ADLs (AHA, 2010; Federal Interagency Forum, 2012).

Heart attacks can be more difficult to diagnose in older than younger people, because their symptoms may differ or be confused with signs of other disorders, such as indigestion; in such instances, a heart attack may not be treated until it is too late. Symptoms also typically differ between men and women, which can result in deadly delays in seeking help (National Institute of Nursing Research, 2011).

Taking Warning Signs Seriously

Mrs. Carter, age 72, has a history of coronary heart disease, hypertension, depression, and tobacco use. She just recently moved to a new town to be closer to her daughter and does not yet have a regular physician who knows her heart history. Her daughter recently brought her to the emergency room because she had experienced shortness of breath and difficulty moving around her apartment. Since she was not feeling any chest pain, Mrs. Carter resisted going to the ER. The ER staff was not familiar with symptoms of heart attacks in older women and sent her back home. The next day, she had a heart attack.

points to ponder

People in industrialized nations have higher levels of atherosclerosis than those in developing countries, which may be due to differences in diet and lifestyle. However, this pattern is shifting with globalization, with the incidence of heart disease higher in India and China than in all developed countries combined. What are some of the factors that might explain this shift (Huffman, 2011)?

With the exception of a family history of heart disease, cardiovascular problems can be treated and, more importantly, prevented through lifestyle changes—diet, rest, exercise—and medications, such as those to control hypertension and cholesterol.

As you just learned, **hypertension** or high blood pressure is the major risk factor for heart disease, and is largely affected by lifestyle, although genetic factors also play a part. Adults 55–65 years face a lifetime risk of 90 percent of developing hypertension. Figure 3.1 contains some startling facts about hypertension and its incidence by age, gender, and race.

Elders may also experience **hypotension**, characterized by dizziness and faintness from exertion after a period of inactivity, and a risk factor for falls, typically due to low blood pressure. You may have observed an older person who appears to lose balance and sway when they stand up after sitting or lying down.

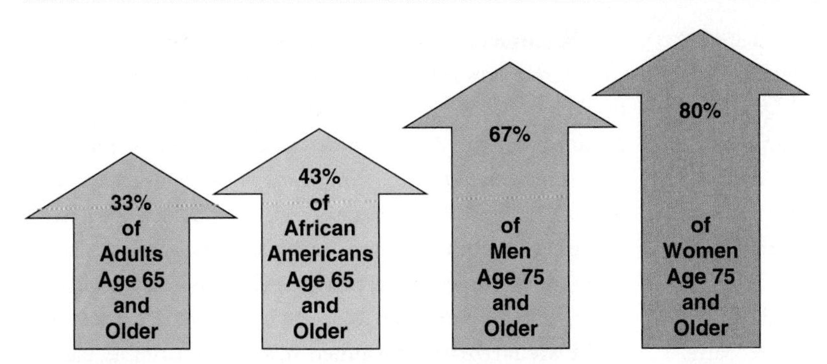

FIGURE 3.1 Hypertension and Its Incidence by Age, Gender, and Race, 2009–2010

Source: Nwankwo, Yoon, Burt, & Gu, 2013

Strokes and Other Cerebrovascular Problems

Heart problems and strokes are related. If blood cannot flow in sufficient amount to the brain, a stroke can occur. This impaired brain tissue circulation is called cerebrovascular disease. When a portion of the brain is completely denied blood, such as through a blood clot, a **cerebrovascular accident (CVA)**, or **stroke**, occurs. A stroke's severity depends on the particular areas as well as the total amount of brain tissue involved. Consider these facts:

- CVAs are the primary cause of disability for older adults and fourth leading cause of death.
- African American elders and men in general are at greatest risk of strokes but after age 75, women across all races are at highest risk.
- African American males are more likely to die of stroke than other groups (AHA, 2010; CDC, 2011b; Federal Interagency Forum, 2012).

Frequent blood pressure checks are essential since hypertension puts elders at risk for many other diseases.

The risk factors for strokes are similar to those for heart disease: increasing age, a sedentary lifestyle and unhealthy diet, as well as a low income and limited access to health care.

Regular sustained exercise and low-fat diets can lessen the risk of stroke by reducing fatty particles that clog the bloodstream. Over-the-counter drugs such as aspirin prevent blood clots and also reduce risk. Indeed, the death rate from strokes is dropping among older adults, because of these preventive measures and improved treatment (AHA, 2011).

Stroke survivors often require physical, occupational, and speech therapies and the recovery process can be slow and emotionally draining. Rehabilitation must also address mental health issues such as depression and anxiety, and support and respite for family caregivers. Recognition of this wider range of rehabilitation approaches has led to the creation of stroke support groups and Internet sites for both survivors and their families.

Cancer

Cancer is the second most common cause of death among elders. We typically associate the word cancer with "terminal," but people with cancer are now living longer, making cancer a chronic illness. Over 80 percent survive at least 5 years. This improvement in survival reflects earlier diagnosis and treatment. When elders feel surrounded by

Preventive Measures to Reduce Cardiovascular Disease Risk

- Control weight
- Engage in daily physical activity
- Manage diabetes
- Decrease salt, saturated fat, and processed carbohydrates
- Eat fruits rich in potassium (e.g., bananas, oranges) and vegetables rich in magnesium and foods high in calcium
- Replace animal fat with olive oil
- Avoid cigarette smoking and excessive alcohol intake (AHA, 2011)

peers with cancer, they may believe that cancer is inevitable if they live long enough. And they may be right, since almost 60 percent of all new cancers occur in older adults. The risk of cancer increases with age, until about age 90.

Diagnosing cancer in old age is often more difficult because of the presence of other illnesses and symptoms. Gender and racial differences also play out in the rates of different types of cancer. For example, older African American women experience higher rates of death from breast and cervical cancer than their white counterparts, primarily because of lower use of screenings to detect cancer in its early stage. Although future cohorts of older adults are more likely to take preventive measures, including cancer screening, the numbers of people with cancer will continue to increase simply because of the rapidly growing older population (ACS, 2010; CDC, 2011b; U.S. Cancer Statistics Working Group, 2010).

Causes of Osteoarthritis

- Heredity.
- Environmental or lifestyle factors:
  - Obesity
  - Occupational stresses, such as using a jack hammer
  - Wear and tear on joints, such as from kneeling in the garden or running long distances on pavement.
- Gender and race: Women and African Americans are most likely to be affected by arthritis.
- Age: Those age 85 and older report more ADL limitations, psychological distress, and joint pain (CDC, 2011a; Federal Interagency Forum, 2012).

Arthritis

Arthritis is the second most common chronic condition diagnosed in about 50 percent of older adults and a major cause of limited daily activity. Because its symptoms are closely identified with normal aging, older people may accept arthritis as inevitable. If so, they fail to seek treatment or learn strategies to reduce pain and support their daily functioning. Although many treatments are used to control arthritic symptoms, little is known about ways to postpone or eliminate arthritis (CDC, 2010).

Arthritis includes over 100 different conditions of inflammations and degenerative bone and joint changes. We discuss two of them here.

Rheumatoid arthritis, a chronic inflammation of the membranes lining joints and tendons, is characterized by pain, swelling, bone dislocation, and limited range of motion, and can cause severe crippling. This is not just a disease of the old, since symptoms commonly appear between 20 and 50 years of age. Treatment includes rest, exercise, use of anti-inflammatory agents, such as aspirin, and, in some cases, surgery to repair joints. Non-pharmacological treatments for pain, such as acupuncture, are also available.

Osteoarthritis, presumed to be an inevitable part of aging, is a gradual degeneration of the joints most subject to stress—those of the hands, knees, hips, and shoulders. Pain and disfigurement in the fingers are the symptoms, and osteoarthritis of the lower limbs can limit mobility and necessitate assistance with ADLs (CDC, 2011a).

Arthritis can have a highly limiting effect on elders' lives. Those with constant pain often develop the functional limitations classically associated with aging at much earlier ages, such as problems with climbing stairs or performing upper body tasks, as well as self-report poor health. The adage "use it or lose it" has special meaning to a person with arthritis. When someone tries to avoid pain by sitting still, the loss in the fluid that lubricates the surfaces and protects the muscles between the joints make movement even more painful and decreases mobility. Eventually, the muscles surrounding immobilized areas lose their flexibility, and affected joints freeze into rigid positions. This is why you may see an elder whose hands are so bent they cannot hold objects.

As you see with Mrs. Diaz, the pervasive, unpredictable nature of arthritic pain can result in social isolation and even depression. Elders need to be encouraged to

Living with Chronic Pain

Mrs. Diaz, age 84, lives alone and is experiencing severe pain from her osteoarthritis, especially in her leg and hip. She does not take pain management medication prescribed by her physician. Instead, she just takes aspirin and uses a heating pad. Her son thinks his mother is lonely and depressed—she tends to stay in bed most of the day and has lost interest in seeing friends from her beloved church. But he cannot convince her to do the doctor-recommended exercises to reduce the pain. Living on a fixed income, she is worried that she could not afford her doctor's recommendation for hip replacement surgery. Tired of being in pain all the time, she thinks about dying as a way to be free of pain.

Welcome to Fit & Strong!

Fit & Strong! is an award-winning, multicomponent, evidence-based physical activity program for older adults with osteoarthritis and has shown significant improvements in functional ability. It helps participants

- understand how physical activity can help them manage symptoms;
- learn safe stretching, balance, aerobic, and strengthening exercises; and
- sustain physical activity in their lives by a relatively modest goal of exercising three times/week for one hour.

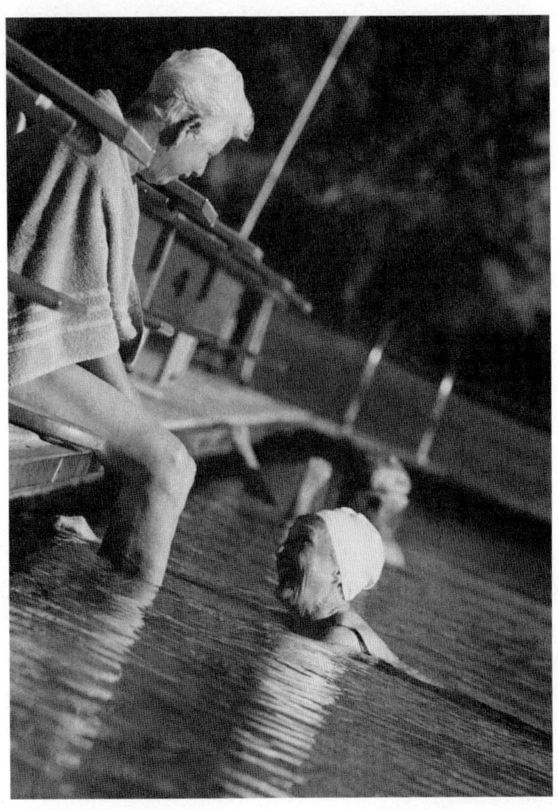

Regular swimming can relieve the pain of arthritis and build bone strength.

maintain physical activity. Tai Chi, aerobics, resistance training, and fitness walking all show promise in decreasing pain and stiffness. Additionally, the home environment may need to be modified so that a person with arthritis is able to keep up with daily activities (Rizzo, 2008).

Some progress has been made in minimizing inflammation and pain. But no technique can reverse or cure the disease. Because of the increasing prevalence of obesity, arthritis is expected to be more common among future cohorts of elders (Covinsky, Lindquist, Dunlop, & Yelin, 2009).

Osteoporosis or "Weak Bones"

You may have seen older adults who are hunched over, or noticed older relatives whose height is diminishing. These changes in physical stature are not normal aging, but probably due to a more dramatic bone loss called **osteoporosis**. Such increased brittleness of bones can result in diminished height, slumped posture, backache, and susceptibility to fractures, particularly of the vertebrae and thigh.

Osteoporosis is often a "silent disease," undiagnosed until a bone breaks. Many falls and associated hip fractures of old age actually represent a femoral neck that broke from bearing weight, causing the individual to fall: a person breaks their hip and then falls, rather than falls and breaks their hip. **Osteopenia** is a significant loss of calcium and reduced bone density but without the risk of fractures. Among older adults with osteoporosis and osteopenia, 80 percent are women, even though both men and women lose bone mass at similar rates after age 65. Additionally, Caucasian and Asian American women are more likely to develop these conditions than African American and Latina women (AARP, 2011; NIA, 2012).

Hip fractures are of great concern since about 24 percent of elders die within a year afterward. Moreover, they are often a turning point, when an older adult is no longer able to live in their own home. Even when death does not occur, falls can cause long-term disability and are responsible for more days of restricted activity than any other condition.

A striking prediction is that gains in life expectancy are expected to double the number of hip fractures within the next 50 years. This could affect some of you, since osteoporosis starts well before old age, perhaps as young as age 35. For women, reduced estrogen is the primary cause of increased bone loss in the first 5 years after menopause. You may have heard of **hormone replacement therapy (HRT)** to prevent further bone loss. For years, many women believed that taking estrogen was the best way to prevent osteoporosis. However, findings from the national Women's Health Initiative (WHI) in 2002 pointed to the increased risks of heart disease, breast cancer, and stroke from HRT. As a result, fewer women now take HRT, and do so at the lowest effective dose for the shortest time

Risk Factors for Osteoporosis and Hip Fractures

- Being a white woman: 50 percent of Caucasian women will have an osteoporosis-related fracture in their lifetime
- Age: the incidence of hip fractures is highest among the oldest-old
- Small stature and low body weight
- Loss of calcium and estrogen
- Sedentary lifestyle
- Cigarette smoking
- Excessive alcohol and caffeine consumption
- Long-term dieting
- Inadequate fluoride intake
- Genetic factors that determine bone density
- Family history of a hip fracture in a close relative

possible (Cawthon, 2011; International Osteoporosis Foundation, 2013; Nelson et al., 2006; WHI, 2002).

Increasing intake of calcium and vitamin D and weight-bearing exercise are the most effective ways to prevent or minimize osteoporosis. The National Institutes of Health (2012) recommends that women over age 50 consume approximately 1,200 mg of calcium daily. This is equivalent to five 8-ounce glasses of milk daily, far more than what most women drink. Older women who do not get enough fortified milk or exposure to sunshine should consult with their doctor about the appropriate dosage of calcium and vitamin D supplements. If you know an older relative who resists taking such supplements at least four days per week, point out to them that this amount has been found to reduce hip fractures by 29 percent (Margolis et al., 2008; NIH, 2012)!

Increased calcium may not prevent fractures after bone loss has occurred, however. A combination of aerobic and weight-bearing exercise and calcium may help in such instances. Vigorous walking on a daily basis for just 1 year has been found to minimize further bone loss in women with osteopenia and osteoporosis (NIH, 2011).

Chronic Obstructive Pulmonary Disease or Respiratory Problems

Chronic bronchitis, asthma, and emphysema are **chronic obstructive pulmonary diseases (COPDs)**, which damage lung tissue. They increase with age, develop slowly, and are progressive and debilitating, resulting in frequent hospitalizations, major lifestyle changes, and death. In fact, by age 90, most people are likely to have some signs of emphysema, with shortness of breath and prolonged and difficult exhalation. Simply getting through daily activities can be extremely exhausting.

Causes of COPD are both genetic and environmental. Three to four times as many men as women have these diseases; this is probably due a greater likelihood of smoking and exposure to airborne pollutants, particularly among cohorts age 85 and older; indeed, oldest-old men are three times more likely to die of COPD than their female counterparts. Treatment for COPD includes drugs, respiratory therapy, and avoidance of infections, smoking, and pollution (Ito & Barnes, 2009).

Diabetes

Compared with other systems of our body, the endocrine glands do not show predictable age-related changes, other than gradual slowing of functioning. However, insufficient insulin produced by the pancreas can lead to **diabetes**—characterized by above-normal amounts of sugar in the blood and urine, resulting from an inability to use carbohydrates.

The prevalence of diabetes has increased dramatically among all age groups. Among older adults living in the community, about one in four has diabetes. However, the greatest increase is among 30–39-year-olds, which has disturbing implications for future cohorts of elders. By 2050, diabetes is expected to increase threefold among today's middle-aged adults, who will then be 75 years or older; this predicted rise to over 30 percent of adults is due largely to increases in obesity (CDC, 2011d; Federal Interagency Forum, 2012).

The symptoms of diabetes typical in younger adults may not be present in older people. Instead, diabetes among elders is generally detected incidentally through eye exams, hospitalization, and testing for other disorders. Older people may experience fatigue, a sign of this disease, but attribute it to a slowing down mistakenly assumed to be normal aging. Type II diabetes, which develops in late life when the body gradually loses its ability to use and produce insulin, accounts for 90–95 percent of all diagnosed cases among older adults.

Primary risk factors are the following:

- age
- family history

- race/ethnicity: African Americans, Latinos, particularly Mexican Americans, and Asian and Pacific Islanders bear a disproportionate burden of diabetes
- health disparities, such as low income and unhealthy diets associated with high rates of obesity (AARP, 2011; CDC, 2011b,e; NIH, 2011)

Because the cumulative effect of high blood sugar levels can lead to severe complications, comorbidity is common among older diabetics. Look at the most frequent co-occurring health problems caused by diabetes:

- infections
- painful nerves in the feet, legs, and hands
- cognitive impairment
- skin problems and poor circulation in the feet, which can lead to amputation and impaired mobility
- depression, although the direction of causality is unclear
- kidney disease and failure
- blindness
- heart disease and stroke
- other limitations in ADL and IADLs. Older diabetics are two to three times more likely to report they cannot walk a quarter of a mile, climb stairs, do housework, or use a mobility aid
- dementia

Older diabetics have a life expectancy about 15 years less compared to those without the disease. As the seventh leading cause of death for older adults—and the fourth for African American women and Latina elders—most deaths are due to heart disease or stroke associated with the diabetes (ADA, 2009; CDC, 2011d; Golden et al., 2008; NIDDK, 2012).

Diabetes cannot be cured, but it can generally be managed—even without insulin—through a careful diet of reduced carbohydrates and calories and a strict exercise regimen. And better self-management decreases cardiovascular risk factors and complications such as kidney failure. Similarly, reducing fat intake and calories and increasing physical activity to moderate levels can reduce the risk (Palmer, 2009).

The Challenges of Managing Diabetes

Mr. Raha, age 77, has had diabetes for 4 years and is showing signs of mild dementia. He lives with his partner of 45 years in a small apartment. He has difficulty drawing up his own insulin due to osteoarthritis in his hands and fingers and occasionally gets confused about his insulin doses with his meals. His partner, who is still employed, is increasingly responsible for administering his insulin doses along with meal preparation, household chores, and financial management. He and his partner started walking at the local mall about six months ago and he has noticed an improvement in his energy as a result. He eats a diet appropriate for someone with diabetes but does like an occasional dessert. All in all, he is managing his diabetes, but his partner carries a heavy caregiving load.

points to ponder

Type II diabetes is a chronic illness that is increasing in American society. Assuming you do not have Type II diabetes now and that you want to avoid getting it later in life, what should you do to try to prevent its onset?

Problems with the Kidneys and Urinary Tract

Because the capacity of the kidneys to perform basic filtration tasks declines with age, the probability of urinary disease or infection increases. When the bladder is unable to empty completely, women often experience cystitis, an acute inflammatory state accompanied by pain and irritation.

Prostate cancer is another urinary system disorder. By the age 40, the risk of prostate cancer doubles every decade. The mortality rate among men age 65 and older is 100 times greater than for those under age 65, and African American men have the highest rate. But surgery is rarely advised for men over age 70 because the disease usually progresses slowly in this age group. Instead, hormonal therapy and frequent monitoring are recommended (Altekruse et al., 2010; CDC, 2011b; NCI, 2010).

Problems with the Intestinal System

Problems in digestion and continuing gastrointestinal distress are due to age-related slowing down of the digestive process along with unbalanced diets or limited fiber content. **Diverticulitis** is a common condition, especially for women, in which pouches (diverticula) in the intestines result from weakness of the intestinal wall; these sacs become inflamed and infected, leading to nausea, abdominal discomfort, bleeding, and changes in bowel function. This can usually be managed with a high-fiber diet and antibiotics (Jacobs, 2007).

Oral Diseases

Tooth decay and periodontal and gum diseases increase with age. Adults age 65 and older have lost on average 13 teeth. Strikingly, about 26 percent of them are **edentulous**—they have no natural teeth remaining. Edentulism increases with age to 33 percent of those age 85 and older, and among elders of color and those who are low-income, although rates have been declining overall since 1999. People with missing teeth who wear dentures tend to eat soft foods and avoid fresh fruits and vegetables, which can adversely affect their nutrition. Or they may simply stop wearing poor fitting dentures (American Dental Hygienists Association, 2010; Federal Interagency Forum, 2012).

You may be surprised to learn that oral health is associated with living longer. In the Baltimore Longitudinal Study, older adults with fewer than 20 teeth were more likely to die within a 15-year period compared with elders with more teeth. These higher death rates may also result from periodontal disease, which impairs the immune system, or poor nutrition caused by tooth loss. Newer cohorts of older people have better oral health than any preceding cohort; this change is due to historical differences in preventive dental care, such as the use of fluoride (Lamster, Northridge, & Takamura, 2008).

These patterns point to the importance of good dental care in old age. Unfortunately, older adults, especially elders of color and those who are low-income, are the lowest users of dental services. A primary reason is that Medicare does not reimburse dental care (American Dental Hygienists Association, 2010).

HIV (Human Immunodeficiency Virus) or AIDS (Acquired Immune Deficiency Syndrome)

It may surprise you to learn that about 25 percent of people with HIV/AIDS are age 50 and older (age 50 is considered "older" in CDC statistics on HIV/AIDS). This is largely due to unprotected sex and failing to learn about their partner's sexual and drug use; to blood transfusions before blood was tested for HIV; or to surgery in a developing country. Because of medical treatments, people with HIV/AIDS are living longer, and adults age 50 and older are predicted to account for 50 percent of all HIV/AIDS cases by 2015 (CDC, 2008).

As with many other illnesses, there are gender and racial differences in the incidence of HIV/AIDS.

- Men over age 50 are at far higher risk than women, but the number of new cases in older women is rising, due primarily to unprotected heterosexual sex.
- More than 50 percent of all cases are African Americans and Latinos age 50 and older.
- Rates are 12 times as high among blacks and 5 times as high among Latinos than among whites.
- Women of color, at greater risk than white women, form 70 percent of women with HIV/AIDS (CDC, 2008, 2011b; Nguyen & Holodniy, 2008).

You may be able to think of reasons why cases of HIV/AIDS often go undiagnosed in older adults. Here are a few:

- Older people are often unaware of their risk of infection and less willing to be tested for the virus.
- They may not seek medical attention in early disease stages because they assume symptoms—fatigue, lack of energy, general aches and pains, loss of appetite and weight, and short-term memory problems—are signs of normal aging or other chronic illnesses.

The High Costs of Lack of Knowledge of HIV/AIDS

Lois was a happily married woman until her husband of 32 years left her. After her divorce, she began dating Frank, a close family friend she had known for years. Because she was beyond childbearing years, she was not worried about pregnancy and never thought about using condoms. And because she knew Frank, it did not occur to her to ask about his sexual or drug history or if he had been tested for HIV. When she had a routine checkup at age 55, her blood tested positive for HIV. Frank had infected her. Lois will spend the rest of her life worrying that the virus might develop into AIDS, and that any cough, sneeze, rash, or flu could indicate AIDS and perhaps the beginning of the end of her life as she knew it.

- Because of ageist stereotypes that AIDS only affects younger populations and that older people are not sexually active, many physicians and HIV-testing programs do not routinely test older adults for HIV/AIDS or are uncomfortable discussing prevention.

The stigma of HIV/AIDS leads older adults to feel embarrassed and rejected so that they hide symptoms or a diagnosis from others and not seek services (Emlet, 2006). For all these reasons, it is essential to educate older adults about their risks and about prevention.

Although the rate of HIV/AIDS is growing among older adults, it is not a major cause of death due to antiretroviral drugs. It is now thought of as another chronic rather than terminal illness. However, older adults with HIV/AIDS are at high risk of social isolation and depression and less likely to seek out emotional support such as support groups (Jacquescoley, 2008; Poindexter & Emlet, 2006).

Accidents

Although mortality statistics suggest that older people are less likely than the young to die of accidents, these numbers mask the incidence of deaths due to accident-related injuries. For instance, if an older woman breaks her hip after falling on the stairs, she enters a hospital, is discharged to a skilled nursing facility, and soon after may die from pneumonia. Pneumonia is then listed as the cause of death, even though this was brought on by the accident. Indeed, the risk of death from physical injuries is four times greater for 80- than 20-year-olds. An area of concern to many families is driving accidents involving elders (U.S. Census Bureau, 2012).

points to ponder

What do you think—should older adults have to take additional or more frequent screening tests or meet different test requirements than younger drivers? Or does this reflect ageist assumptions or discrimination against older drivers?

Tragic Accident Attracts National Attention to Older Drivers

An 86-year-old driver mistakenly stepped on the accelerator instead of the brake, causing the deaths of 10 people and many injuries in a crowded market area. This unfortunate event raised questions about the need for mandatory tests and special license requirements along with restrictions on driving after a certain age.

Older Drivers

Almost 90 percent of people over age 65 still drive. Because accidents by older drivers are often visible in the media, you may be surprised to learn that while they form about 15 percent of licensed drivers, they cause only 7 percent of all accidents. Contrast this with youth under age 24 who account for 13 percent of drivers, but cause 43 percent of all accidents. This difference is because elders are less likely to speed or to drive while drunk.

Older people often view driving as key to maintaining their independence and active aging. Ask any family who had to convince an older relative that they can no longer safely drive, and they will attest to the resistance encountered, especially among men, to "giving up the car keys."

Let's look at statistics that capture why families "take away" the keys.

- Crash rates increase starting at age 70 and rise markedly after age 80.
- Even though most accidents by older drivers occur at low speeds, age-related declines in organ systems and brittle bones make them more vulnerable to injuries and death. Elders are 3 times more likely to die following a crash than are younger people.
- Drivers ages 75 and older have longer hospital stays, more complications, and greater need for rehabilitation services (Ackerman, Edwards, Ross, Ball, & Lundsman, 2008; CDC, 2011c; Loughran, 2010; SmartMotorist.com, 2013).

Three behavioral factors contribute to the high death rate:

- poor judgment in making left-hand turns,
- drifting within traffic lanes, and
- decreased ability to change behavior in response to an unexpected or rapidly changing situation.

Two Broken Hips, Two Different Outcomes

Katherine Aliminosa, 93, shattered her lower leg while getting snacks for her nieces. Susan Arnold, 87, broke her hip hanging a picture. After being moved to a skilled nursing unit of their retirement community, the two women began a recovery process that both hoped would return them to their previous lives. Both felt vulnerable and their world diminished. Both had led accomplished professional lives and been active in the community's independent living apartments. But neither could be confident about the future.

Upon entering the skilled nursing unit, Ms. Aliminosa was able to walk only in very small stretches. She was depressed, and feeling defeated, stating "It's made me very aware of my age, and that's hard to accept." But within a few months, she graduated to an independent living apartment and got around with a walker. She appeared robust and content.

Ms. Arnold, by contrast, was extremely angry about her broken hip, especially since it prevented a long planned vacation with her daughter. Even though she was 6 years younger, she faced the greatest long-term risks, because her body systems were weakened by a history of pulmonary disease and heavy lifelong smoking, which affected her recovery. Ms. Arnold never gained her strength. Her muscles atrophied from inactivity, and she developed pneumonia. She died within two months of her entry to the nursing facility (Adapted from Leland, *New York Times*, November 8, 2008, p. A1).

As you learned earlier in this chapter, these risk factors may, in turn, result from age-associated declines in vision or hearing, eye-hand coordination, reaction time, attention, and visual-spatial skills. Some older people cope with these age-associated changes by becoming more conservative in their driving. Others take refresher courses offered by AARP ("55 Alive Driver Safety Program") and the Automobile Association of America ("Safe Driving for Mature Operators"). Increasingly, insurance companies require drivers over age 80 to take courses and tests (CDC, 2011c).

Older adults can make other behavioral changes to increase their driving safety:

- Exercise regularly to increase strength and flexibility.
- Ask their doctor to review their medications that might affect their driving.
- Have eyes checked annually and wear glasses and corrective lenses.
- Drive during daylight and in good weather.
- Select familiar and safe routes with well-lit streets, intersections with left turn arrows, and easy parking.
- Avoid distractions in the car.
- Accept alternatives—riding with a friend or using public transit (CDC, 2011c).

Falls and Their Prevention

As you learned in our discussion of osteoporosis, falls are the leading cause of injuries and injury-related deaths and of about 95 percent of hip fractures for adults age 65 and older. When younger people fall, they tend to break their wrists catching themselves, but in older people, who have slower reactions and less upper-body strength, the weight more often falls on their hips. Falls often result in a downward cycle of health problems and negative social consequences. Elders who fall may become fearful of falling again and restrict their activities. Or they may become more rigid or overly cautious in walking, which increases the likelihood of falls. Their fears are grounded in reality, since 65 percent of those who fall do so again within six months. The majority of elders who experience fall-related fractures have not recovered their pre-fall functional level 1 year later. All these factors mean that the sequence of events after a fall is highly unpredictable, as illustrated on this page by two women Ms. Arnold and Ms. Aliminosa with very different outcomes (CDC, 2012).

These statistics capture how Ms. Arnold represents the more common pattern:

- Up to 30 percent of older adults in the community, and even more in long-term care settings, experience a fall in a given year.
- Older women are nearly three times more likely to fall than men.

points to **ponder**

Falls can have serious consequences for older adults. Let's say you are preparing an apartment that an older adult is going to be moving into soon. What are some of the things you can do to help make that apartment a safer living space and less likely for an older adult to fall in?

Risk Factors for Falls

Sarcopenia or atrophy of muscles, which weakens the upper body and arms, impairs balance, and causes difficulties in standing up and impairs gait

Inactivity and poor balance

Visual impairment

Fear of falling

Multiple diseases, particularly arthritis and cognitive impairment

Multiple medications that cause blood pressure to drop, or affect balance and the central nervous system

Hypotension

Environmental hazards—low lighting levels, slippery floors and other surfaces, loose area rugs, poorly demarcated stairs, unfamiliar environments

- Twenty percent of older hip-fracture patients die within a year.
- Twenty-five percent of such patients have to spend a year or more in a skilled nursing facility.

Despite fall prevention initiatives, fall-related deaths and hip fractures due to falls have increased since 1990 in contrast to declines in other health problems. The two boxes on this page summarize the risks as well as relatively modest changes to prevent falls (American Geriatrics Society, 2010; Hanlon, et al., 2009; International Osteoporosis Association, 2012).

Use of Physician Services

You might assume that the higher rate of chronic diseases would result in a striking growth in use of health care. It is true that adults age 65 and older average approximately seven visits to a doctor annually compared to 1.3 visits for younger adults. These data reflect older adults' greater use of their primary care physician for care of chronic illnesses. But it may surprise you to learn that only a small proportion of older adults are high users of all health care services. Low use, however, does not necessarily mean that all health needs are being met. For example, even with Medicare, low-income older adults report more unmet health needs while paying more out of pocket for health care compared to middle- or high-income elders (AoA, 2012; Federal Interagency Forum, 2012).

Our health care systems are not well suited to managing chronic diseases and most physicians are not trained to work with older patients. But there are many geriatricians who effectively meet older patients' needs and promote quality of life as illustrated on page 88.

Hospital Utilization

Older people on average have three times as many hospital days and for longer periods of time than younger populations. However, this may decline because more procedures are now performed in community-based settings. Additionally, health care reform, which you will learn about in Chapter 13, offers incentives to reduce hospital use and readmissions. In contrast, the use of emergency rooms, the most costly way to access health care, has been growing, particularly among low-income elders (AoA, 2012).

Medication Use

Older adults' increasing use of medications reflects the growth of pharmacotherapy in general for treating health. Elders with chronic illness take about eight or nine prescribed and over-the-counter medications per day. Too much or inappropriate usage is risky, because of age-associated physiological changes that prolong the effects

Falls Prevention

Remove loose rugs and substitute rugs with nonskid backing

Add lights in dimly lit areas and at top and bottom of stairs

Use nightlights

Clean up clutter

Put hand rails on both sides of stairs

Add "grab bars" near toilet and bath tub, and nonslip decals in tub or shower

Wear firm shoes that are not slippery; avoid loose slippers or socks

Engage in physical therapy and exercise to promote balance, stability, and postural control

Take medications to build bone density

Geriatricians Treating the Whole Person

Dr. R. Sean Morrison, a geriatrician at New York City's Mount Sinai Medical Center, starts with these questions: *Tell me about yourself. What do you like to do? What is your life like—your exercise habits, diet, use of alcohol and tobacco? What are things you would like to do that you cannot do anymore? What is important to you about your health now? Is your environment safe and convenient? What brings you here today?*

The exam is based on a patient's answers. With a healthy 75-year-old who plays tennis, the focus is preventive screening. But if a patient has several functional limitations, he addresses what can be restored or modified, such as reducing the risk of falls, streamlining medications, and modifying the home environment.

Dr. Chad Boult, Johns Hopkins University, explores four areas often missed if an exam just focuses on specific illness:

- Memory. *Are you having trouble with it? Is it O.K. if I check with a family member about this?*
- Risk of falls. To check balance, gait, and strength:
  - Meet a person in the waiting room, and watch how they stand up from a chair and walk to the exam room.
  - Throw a pen on the floor and ask a patient to pick it up.
  - Ask a person to sit in a chair and stand up three times as quickly as they can, without using the chair arms.
- Incontinence.
- Feet. Elders who cannot reach their feet to care for them may develop painful sores, leading to life-limiting problems (Adapted from Brody, 2009).

of some drugs in the body. Additionally, combinations of medications may cause adverse drug reactions, which can result in hospital admissions, falls, and cognitive impairments. Another problem is that elders who are worried about the costs of medications may cut them in half or take every other day, thereby minimizing benefits. Not surprisingly, medication misuse is often a reason for in-home help or a move to a long-term care facility. Older white women are the most likely to report using multiple medications, while Mexican Americans and Asians and Pacific Islanders are the least likely (Bartels, Blow, & Van Critters, 2006; CDC, 2010; Gu, Dillon, & Burt, 2010; Health United States, 2010).

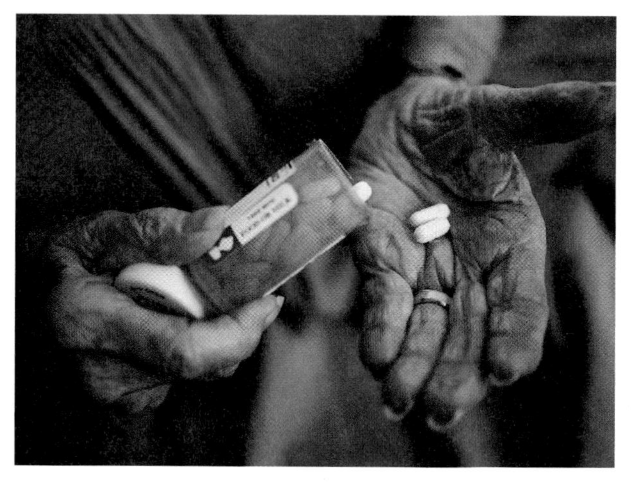

Older adults use more medications than other age groups.

Health Promotion

Health promotion is defined as health education and environmental changes to enhance an individual's ability to improve their well-being, not just manage their diseases. The "health enhancement" or "wellness" aspects of health promotion make it more than simply the prevention of chronic diseases and disability. In contrast to a biomedical model, where the physician is responsible to treat disease, health promotion emphasizes altering one's lifestyle practices such as diet and exercise, creating healthier environments, and changing cultural attitudes and expectations about health. This is because nearly 80 percent of chronic illnesses may be related to social, environmental, and behavioral factors, particularly poor exercise and nutrition. The good news is that health promotion activities decrease the risk of high blood pressure, heart attacks, strokes, diabetes, and certain cancers and lower rates of

Interventions to Prevent Medication Misuse

- Use of calendar blister packs compared to a standard bottle
- Home visit teaching sessions by health care providers
- Computer-based reminder systems
- Electronic monitoring instructions with pictorial icons

Lifestyle and Longevity

Arthur, age 97 and without any chronic illnesses, may be described as a "paragon of good living." He has never smoked, drinks a glass of wine occasionally, and has maintained his ideal body weight throughout adulthood—mostly by eating a diet rich in vegetables, fruit, and nuts and less saturated fats and combined carbohydrates. He walks two miles daily in his hilly neighborhood, and makes sure to get eight hours of sleep each night. Although he still grieves over the death of his wife of 60 years 5 years ago, Arthur's spiritual beliefs and strong family network of children, grandchildren, and great-grandchildren have all helped him cope with his loss. His lifestyle exemplifies the link between healthy habits and longevity.

hospitalizations, physician visits, and medications (*Healthy People 2020*, 2010; Peterson et al., 2009).

Healthy People 2020 provides 10-year national objectives for improving the health of all Americans. For three decades, it has established benchmarks and monitored progress to see the impact of prevention initiatives. These objectives are built on a growing scientific evidence of how specific health-promoting behaviors increase chances of living longer by as much as 10 years. Arthur in the above box has experienced some of these benefits.

Exercise as Central to Health Promotion

Regular moderate exercise may be the most effective health habit. But this is often an area where we have difficulty changing our behaviors. Up to 50 percent of physical changes in older people that are mistakenly attributed to aging may be due to being physically unfit. Physically inactive people age faster and look older than physically fit persons of the same age; this is due in part to **hypokinesia**, which is a disease of "disuse," or degeneration and functional loss of muscle and bone tissue.

The benefits of regular aerobic weight-bearing exercise such as brisk walking and strength training, even at moderate levels, are numerous, even for people with chronic illnesses. There are gains in

- healthy bones, muscles, and joints;
- lean muscle mass and strength;
- joint mobility, flexibility, and range of motion;
- HDL (good) cholesterol;
- metabolic rate; and
- balance.

And there are reductions in

- weight and body fat;
- arthritis and lower back pain;
- blood pressure;
- osteoporosis; and
- symptoms of anxiety and depression.

Benefits are greatest if people begin exercising in young or middle adulthood. Nevertheless, initiating regular exercise at any age, even after age 80, has benefits. Aerobic exercise needs to occur regularly, ideally at least 30 minutes daily. But even moderate walking can reduce the risk of heart disease or prevent hip fractures (CDC, 2013; Chipperfield, 2008; *Healthy People 2020*, 2010; NCOA, 2011; Peterson et al., 2009).

Strength training is successful even with 90-year-olds and even with residents in skilled nursing facilities. It improves muscle strength, walking speed, and stair-climbing ability. Some adults choose Tai Chi, yoga, or Pilates as a gentler form of exercise that strengthens muscles without injuring joints, reduces chronic pain, and improves flexibility, balance, and stability (CDC, 2013; NIH, 2011).

With benefits like these, how can anyone not exercise? Unfortunately, the majority of older adults do not. Only 25–35 percent of older people participate in regular physical activity (30 minutes or more at least five times per week), and only about 12 percent in strength training. Men are the most likely to exercise, whereas the oldest-old, women, Latinos, and African Americans are the least likely. Older adults' activity levels are so low that meeting the *Healthy People 2020* objectives will require significant behavioral changes among at least 60 percent of elders (CDC, 2013; *Healthy People 2020*, 2010; NCOA, 2011).

points to **ponder**

Identify healthy and unhealthy behaviors in your lifestyle. Have you ever tried to modify these? If so, what techniques worked for you? What were some of the obstacles? To what extent do you think that lifestyle changes when we are old can overcome the effects of poor health habits acquired earlier in life?

Some elders may be motivated to exercise but cannot afford to do so or face obstacles in their environments. They may live in communities that lack safe and affordable fitness opportunities (e.g., walking trails, low-cost gyms), lack support from friends and family to exercise, or feel embarrassed around younger people working out. Additionally, they may not have time because of caregiving or employment demands.

A number of strategies work to motivate physical activity. Perhaps you have used some of them in your own lives or can add to this list.

- Start slowly.
- Choose activities that make your heart beat faster.
- Set goals, including developing informal exercise contracts with others.
- Monitor yourself.
- Develop group or peer support (a walking group).
- Turn to peer telephone counseling for support (*Healthy People 2020*, 2010).

Nutrition

A healthy diet—no matter what our age—and even if we only make modest changes—has multiple benefits. For instance, a moderate reduction in saturated and trans fats can reduce cholesterol levels and the risk of heart disease. And most of us know how important vegetables and fruits are. U.S. Dietary Guidelines recommend about 2 cups of fruit and 2.5 cups of vegetables each day. In fact, *Healthy People 2020* recommends even higher intakes—seven to nine servings per day—for older adults. As one newspaper article touted, imagine a drug that could whittle your waistline, control blood pressure, protect your heart, strengthen your bones, cut the risk of stroke, and possibly help you sidestep cancer. And what if this drug was also easy to obtain, relatively inexpensive, and even tasted good? There's no pill with those benefits, but it is fruit and vegetables. Yet the number of elders eating healthy diets is far below the target of 50 percent set forth in *Healthy People 2020*. A primary barrier is the cost of fresh produce. Others are living alone or coping with other health issues, which detract from preparing healthy meals (*Healthy People 2020*, 2010; Squires, 2008).

Reflection Break

Do you know a family member or friend who does not seem to be getting much physical activity and sits at home for most of the day? Is there anything you can do that could safely add some physical activity to her or his life, perhaps just going shopping together or for a short walk outside? You might want to check with this person's health care provider to ensure that what you have in mind is safe, especially if the elder has serious health problems.

points to ponder

Reflect on your own eating habits on an average day. What kinds of fruits and vegetables are you eating? Are you eating two cups of fruit and two-and-a-half cups of vegetables a day, as recommended by U.S. Dietary Guidelines? If so, how are you doing that? If not, how can you increase your consumption of fruits and vegetables?

Programs That Work

The Administration on Aging funds evidence-based health promotion initiatives that have delayed the onset of diseases, reduced disability and health care costs, and extended life expectancy. Researchers have found these programs effectively empower older adults to take control of their health through increased self-efficacy and self-management. Here are a few examples:

- Physical activity—Enhance Fitness and Healthy Moves offer low-impact aerobic exercise, strength training, and stretching.
- Falls management—Matter of Balance addresses fear of falling, and Stepping On and Tai Chi build muscle strength and improve balance.
- Nutrition—Healthy Eating teaches the value of eating healthy foods.
- Stanford University Chronic Disease Self-Management helps people with chronic conditions change behaviors, improve health status, and reduce use of hospital services.

You can learn more about these and other effective programs at http://www.aoa.gov/AoA_Programs/HPW/Evidence_Based/index.aspx.

Some wellness programs, which emphasize the whole person, use the arts to engage older adults in healthy behaviors. One of these is Ruth's Table in San Francisco's low-income Mission District. It illustrates the benefits of the arts on physical and mental well-being and a way to build community.

Improving the Impact of Health Promotion Programs

Health promotion, particularly increased physical activity, can save individuals and society significant dollars otherwise used to treat disease. Yet only a small percentage of national health care funding is currently spent on prevention and wellness services. Fortunately, prevention is a cornerstone of the 2010 health care reform. Another encouraging sign is the increasing number of hospitals, health care clinics, universities, local governments, and corporations that sponsor health promotion programs. For example, some county governments offer insurance incentives for people who engage in healthy behaviors. And health promotion activities have been carried into senior centers, adult day health care, and assisted living, retirement, and skilled nursing facilities.

But we all know that we do not always act on information that would improve our health. The gap between health knowledge and health practices can be very wide. Think about the number of people who continue to smoke despite the empirical evidence linking smoking to lung cancer. In general, organized health promotion programs have difficulty recruiting more than 50 percent of the target population, even when focused on people with potentially deadly conditions, such as heart disease. Attrition ranges from 30 to 60 percent. In sum, sustaining health practices over time is difficult in the face of years of habit (Christ & Diwan, 2008; Federal Interagency Forum, 2012).

Finding the right exercise for an older adult's ability level can help motivate them.

Ruth's Table: Wellness and the Arts

A director of community programs for a low-income housing complex held focus groups with older adults to decide what to do with empty spaces on its first floor. Since the neighborhood was attracting "artsy" seniors, a decision was made to transform the space into an art-focused cultural center where older adults could learn through peer-led classes and share artistic talents. The kitchen became an exhibit space to host an artist-in-residence program. The dining hall was transformed into an art gallery hosting openings where local artists answer questions from community members. The arts center reached out to the larger community through Facebook and its Web site. Physical activities were also part of the offerings but combined with forming relationships. In a Tai Chi class, participants practice together, but then discuss issues and form new friendships after each class. An intergenerational modern dance program—Dance Generators—involves students from the University of San Francisco. Creating and sustaining community partnerships were a priority. Space was shared with the community music center, giving it a place to practice and older adults free music for listening and dancing (Gable, 2011).

Older people who are likely to participate in health promotion programs are those already oriented to prevention (i.e., regular users of physicians and dentists for checkups, nonsmokers) and those engaged in community activities generally. But what can be done to reach those who face barriers to participation? For example, is it realistic to expect a low-income grandmother caring for three grandchildren to have time or resources to join an exercise class? What might make her participation feasible? Here is a list of some strategies found to reduce barriers (Stepnick & Whitelaw, 2006).

Strategies to Increase Participation in Health Promotion Programs

- Take account of income, living arrangements, social supports, language and cultural values (e.g., offer free transportation, respite for caregivers, exercises and nutritional programs that fit with the elders' culture).
- Provide social support—exercise buddies and neighborhood walking.
- Sponsor intergenerational activities (e.g., healthy eating programs for grandparents and grandchildren).
- Design accessible community resources of outdoor paths or malls for walking.
- Offer written and oral materials in elders' native language.

- Expand outreach through senior centers, religious institutions, and doctor's offices.
- Increase the availability and affordability of fresh produce in local groceries.

Health promotion programs are sometimes criticized for their emphasis on individual responsibility for change. Encouraging older adults to exercise may be counterproductive if they live in cities with high levels of pollution or near industrial sites contaminated by toxic waste. Community- and organizational-level changes are essential that consider the roles of corporations, policy-makers, food manufacturers, and the mass media in creating unhealthy environments.

It is unclear if baby boomers will be healthier in old age. This cohort includes more informed, health-conscious consumers who will make more demands on the health care system. A significant proportion will continue their fitness activities. However, some baby boomers, particularly smokers and those who are obese, are likely to face multiple chronic diseases even as their life expectancy increases. Additionally, low-income boomers—and those who were moderate income but saw their resources diminished by the recession—may not have access to preventive services nor have the resources to adopt a healthy lifestyle, which will negatively affect their well-being.

Sustaining the Motivation to Change Health Behaviors

You have learned that motivating people to make and sustain changes in their health behaviors is a challenge. Allowing elders to set their own goals and providing peer support are often keys to success. One program, Enhance Wellness, focuses on motivation before teaching about healthy behaviors. A team of a nurse and social worker assesses an individual's strengths and risks, and develops a plan in which the participant, not the professional, chooses the behaviors they want to work on. As participants try out their individualized plan, a volunteer health mentor offers ongoing encouragement, feedback, and monitoring. Outcomes are reduced length of hospital stays, lowered medication use, diminished symptoms of mood disorders, and enhanced self-efficacy. The closely related Enhanced Fitness programs, offered in more than 200 sites nationwide, provide low-cost, evidence-based exercise programs of stretching, flexibility, balance, low-impact aerobics, and strength training that do not require expensive equipment or large space. Parks and Recreation department programs, such as walking groups, also offer accessible and low-cost exercise that build on peer support (Enhance Fitness, 2009).

summary

As shown by our review of physiological changes, the aging process is gradual, beginning in some organ systems as early as the twenties and thirties and progressing more rapidly after age 70 or 80, in others. Even with 50 percent deterioration in many organ systems, an individual can still function and experience quality of life, often by modifying their activities or their environments.

The rate of decline in various organs varies substantially, with the greatest deterioration in complex functions that require coordination among multiple systems, muscles, and nerves. Similarly, wide variations across individuals spring from differences in heredity or genes, diet, exercise, culture, and incomes. Many of the physiological declines that were assumed to be irreversible with normal aging are being reevaluated by researchers. Examples of master athletes who continue their competitive physical activities throughout life show that age-related declines are not always dramatic or inevitable. Even people who begin a regular exercise program late in life have enjoyed significant health benefits.

All of us experience some sensory loss with age, but intra- and interindividual differences are quite pronounced. Normal age-related declines in vision reduce the ability to respond to differing light levels, see in places with high levels of glare, discern color tones, and judge distances and depth. Peripheral vision and upward and downward gaze become somewhat narrowed with age. Elders have more diseases of the eye—glaucoma, cataracts, and macular degeneration; if not treated, blindness can result. Decline in auditory function generally starts earlier than visual problems and affects more people. Although hearing aids can frequently improve hearing, many older people feel uncomfortable and even stigmatized when using them. Hence, the solutions for communicating with hearing-impaired elders may lie mostly in changing the environment and communication strategies. Older people complain that food does not taste as good as it once did, yet changes in taste acuity with age are minimal.

Although older adults are at increased risk for chronic diseases, most rate their own health as satisfactory. Health status encompasses an individual's physical condition and functional ability. The majority of elders, however, are not limited in their daily activities by chronic conditions. The incidence and impact of such diseases varies with age-associated physiological changes, the individual's adaptive resources, and his or her gender, race, ethnicity, and income.

The leading causes of death among older persons are heart disease, cancer, stroke, and accidents. Diseases of the heart and blood vessels are the most prevalent. Because high blood pressure is a major risk for cardiovascular problems, preventive actions of weight control, dietary changes, appropriate exercise, and avoidance of cigarette smoking are essential. Cancers are the second most frequent cause of death, and the risk of cancer increases with age. Cerebrovascular accident, or stroke, is the third leading cause of death. Fortunately, mortality rates due to heart disease, stroke, and cancer are declining for older adults. This is because of preventive health care and early detection of cancer in the middle years. Similarly, accidents, particularly those associated with driving and falls, are often preventable.

Arthritis is a major cause of limited daily activity and, to some extent, affects most elders. Osteoporosis, or loss of bone mass and resultant increased brittleness, is most common among older women and may result in fractures. Physical exercise can help prevent fractures and falls as well as manage arthritis. Chronic respiratory problems, particularly emphysema, increase with age. Diabetes mellitus is a frequent problem and is particularly troubling because of comorbidity, including dementia. Diverticulitis and incontinence are commonly occurring problems of the intestinal track and urinary system.

Older people seek outpatient medical, dental, and mental health services at a slightly lower rate than their incidence of chronic illnesses would predict. The elimination or postponement of chronic diseases associated with old age and improvement of quality of life are major goals for wellness and health enhancement programs as well as biomedical researchers interested in delaying the aging process. Treatment methods are changing rapidly with the growth of medical technology and the increasing recognition given to environmental factors of stress, nutrition, and exercise in disease prevention. If health promotion efforts become more widely adopted, and if aging research progresses substantially, the chronic illnesses that you have learned about will be postponed, and disability or loss of functional status will decline among future cohorts. On the other hand, increases in obesity among younger populations may alter this optimistic prediction.

key terms

accommodative ability, p. 70
active aging, p. 74
activities of daily living (ADLs), p. 74
acute conditions, p. 75
acute illnesses, p. 74
atherosclerosis, p. 65
biological aging, p. 61
cataract, p. 70
cellular aging theory, p. 61
cerebrovascular accident (CVA), or stroke, p. 79
chronic illnesses, p. 74
chronic obstructive pulmonary diseases (COPDs), p. 82
comorbidity, p. 75
coronary heart disease, p. 78
diabetes, p. 82
disability, p. 74
diverticulitis, p. 83
edentulous, p. 84
epidermis, p. 64
erectile dysfunction, p. 69
estrogen, p. 67
frailty, p. 74
free radical theory, p. 62
functional ability, p. 74
functional capacity, p. 63
glaucoma, p. 71
good health, p. 73
health care disparities, p. 75
health disparities, p. 75
health promotion, p. 88
health status, p. 74
healthy life span, p. 63
hormone replacement therapy (HRT), p. 81
hypertension, p. 78
hyperthermia, p. 64
hypokinesia, p. 89
hypotension, p. 78
hypothermia, p. 64
immunological theory, p. 62
impotence, p. 69

instrumental activities of daily living (IADLs), p. 74
kinesthetic system, p. 65
kyphosis, p. 65
macular degeneration, p. 71
male menopause, p. 68
master athletes, p. 64
melanin, p. 64
menopause, p. 67
neurons, p. 67
osteoarthritis, p. 80
osteopenia, p. 81
osteoporosis, p. 81
presbycusis, p. 72
prolongevity, p. 63
quality of life, p. 75
renal function, p. 66
rheumatoid arthritis, p. 80
senescence, p. 61
urinary incontinence, p. 66
viropause, p. 68
vital capacity, p. 65
wear-and-tear theory, p. 61

review questions

1. Several biological theories of aging have emerged over the past 50 years. Pick three of these theories and summarize them.
2. Which organ systems tend to show the most age-related changes? Which show the least?
3. List three examples of "normal" age-associated changes in visual functioning and three examples of diseases that affect vision, which tend to increase with age.
4. Describe some communication tips and changes in the environment that professionals working with older people with hearing loss might use to improve communication.
5. What is the difference between acute and chronic disease? List the five most common chronic diseases that occur as we age. What lifestyle changes might make the most difference in reducing those chronic diseases?
6. What are the two most commonly used measures of functional ability? What are some of the reasons that there is a slight increase in disability rates among the baby boomers?
7. What are the primary causes of death in old age? Describe some differences in causes of death among populations of color.
8. What are some of the physiological changes that increase the risk of accidents among older drivers?
9. If you were developing a health promotion program for older adults, what activities would you be sure to include in the program? How might you increase the motivation of older adults to participate in such a program?

media resources

Watch

- U.S. Seniors Gym
- Physical Challenges of Living Longer

Read

- The Macarthur Foundation. Facts and Fictions about an Aging America.

references

AARP. (2011). *Chronic Care: A call to action for health reform.* Washington, DC: AARP Public Policy Institute. Retrieved from http://assets.aarp.org/rgcenter/health/beyond_50_hcr.pdf

Ackerman, M. L., Edwards, J. D., Ross, L. A., Ball, K. K., & Lundsman, M. (2008). Examination of cognitive and instrumental functional performance as indicators for driving cessation risk across 3 years. *The Gerontologist, 48,* 802–810.

Administration on Aging (AoA). (2012). *Profile of older Americans.* Washington, DC. Department of Health and Human Services.

Agrawal, Y., Platz, E. & Niparko, J. K. (2008). Prevalence of hearing loss and differences by demographic characteristics among U.S. adults. *Archives of Internal Medicine, 168,* 1522–1530.

Altekruse, S. F., Kosary, C. L., Krapcho, M., Neyman, N., Aminou, R., Waldron, W., Ruhl, J., et al., (Eds.). (2010). *SEER Cancer Statistics Review, 1975–2007.* National Cancer Institute. Retrieved from http://seer.cancer.gov/csr/1975_2007/

American Cancer Society (ACS). (2010). *Cancer facts, 2010.* Retrieved May 2, 2011, from http://www.cancer.org/

Research/CancerFactsFigures/CancerFactsFigures/cancer-facts-and-figures-2010

American Dental Hygienists' Association (ADHA). (2010). *Senior oral health*. Retrieved April 8, 2010, from http://www.adha.org/oralhealth/seniors.htm.

American Diabetes Association. (2009). *The Alzheimer's–Diabetes link*. Retrieved May 2009 from http://www.diabetes.org/diabetes-research/hottopics.jsp.

American Geriatrics Society (AGS). (2010). *AGS/BGS clinical practice guideline: Prevention of falls in older persons: Summary of recommendations*. Retrieved from http://www.americangeriatrics.org/health_care_professionals/clinical_practice/clinical_guidelines_recommendations/prevention_of_falls_summary_of_recommendations/.

American Heart Association. (2010). *Heart disease and stroke statistics—2010*. Retrieved May 2, 2011, from http://circ.ahajournals.org/cgi/content/full/121/7/e46#sec20.

American Heart Association. (2011). *Women, heart disease and stroke*. Retrieved April 27, 2011, from http://www.americanheart.org.

Asbell, P. A., Dualan, I., Mindel, J., Brooks, D., Ahmad, M., & Epstein, S. (2005). Age-related cataract. *Lancet, 365*, 599–609.

Bancroft, J. (2007). Sex and aging. *New England Journal of Medicine, 357*, 820–822.

Bartels, S., Blow, F., Van Citters, A., & Brockmann, L. (2006) Dual diagnosis among older adults: Co-occurring substance abuse and psychiatric illness. *Journal of Dual Diagnosis, 2*(3), 9–30.

Bauer, J., Pearson, K., Price, N., Jamieson, H., Lerin, C., Kalra, A., et al. (2006). Resveratrol improves health and survival of mice on a high-calorie diet. *Nature, 10*, 1038–1040.

Bengtson, V. L., Gans, D., Putney, N. M., & Silverstein, M. (Eds.). (2009). *Handbook of theories of aging* (2nd ed.). New York: Springer.

Benyamini, Y., Blumstein, T., Lusky, A., & Modan, B. (2003). Gender differences in the self-rated health-mortality association. *The Gerontologist, 43*, 396–405.

Bergman, A., Altzmon, G., Ye, K., MacCarthy, T., & Barzilai, N. (2007). Buffering mechanisms in aging: A systems approach toward uncovering the genetic component of aging. *PLoS Computational Biology, 3*, 170.

Blonna, R., & Levitan, J. (2000). *Healthy sexuality*. Englewood, CO: Morton Publishing.

Brody, J. (2009). New model of care is needed, experts say. *New York Times*. Retrieved from http://www.nytimes.com/2008/12/30/health/30bbox.html?_r=0.

Carpenter, S. (2009). Treating illness is one thing. What about a patient with many? *New York Times*. Retrieved from http://www.nytimes.com/2009/03/31/health/31sick.html?emc=eta1&pagewanted=print.

Cawthon, P. M. (2011). Gender differences in osteoporosis and fractures. *Clinical Orthopaedics and Related Research*, 469, 1900–1905.

Centers for Disease Control and Prevention (CDC). (2008). *HIV/AIDS among persons aged 50 and older: CDC HIV/AIDS facts*. Retrieved from http://www.cdc.gov/hiv/topics/over50/resources/factsheets/pdf/over50.pdf.

Centers for Disease Control and Prevention (CDC). (2013). *How much exercise do older adults need?* Retrieved September 17, 2013, from http://www.cdc.gov/physicalactivity/everyone/guidelines/adults.html.

Centers for Disease Control and Prevention (CDC). (2010a). Vital signs: State-specific obesity prevalence among adults—United States, 2009. *Morbidity and Mortality Weekly Release, 59* (Early Release), 1–5. Retrieved from http://www.cdc.gov/mmwr/pdf/wk/mm59e0803.pdf.

Centers for Disease Control and Health Promotion (CDC). (2010b). *REACH U.S.: Finding solutions to health disparities: At a glance, 2010*. Retrieved from http://www.cdc.gov/chronicdisease/resources/publications/AAG/reach.htm.

Centers for Disease Control and Prevention (CDC). (2011a). *Arthritis-related statistics*. Retrieved May 2, 2011, from http://www.cdc.gov/arthritis/data_statistics/arthritis_related_stats.htm.

Centers for Disease control and Prevention (CDC). (2011b). *Fast stats: Older persons' health*. Retrieved April 27, 2011, from http://www.cdc.gov/nchs/fastats/older_americans.htm.

Centers for Disease Control and Prevention (CDC). (2011c). *Injury prevention and control: Motor vehicle safety. Older adult drivers' data and statistics*. Retrieved from http://www.cdc.gov/Motorvehiclesafety/Older_Adult_Drivers/data.html.

Centers for Disease Control and Prevention (CDC). (2011d). *Number of Americans with diabetes rises to nearly 26 million*. Retrieved May 20, 2011, from http://www.cdc.gov/media/releases/2011/p0126_diabetes.html.

Centers for Disease Control and Prevention. (2011e). *QuickStats: Age-adjusted death rate from stroke, by all races, white or black race, and sex—United States, 1999–2008*. Retrieved May 1, 2011, from http://www.cdc.gov/mmwr/preview/mmwrhtml/mm6010a8.htm.

Centers for Disease Control and Prevention (CDC). (2012). *Falls among older adults: An overview*. Retrieved November 22, 2012, from http://www.cdc.gov/home_recreational safety.

Chipperfield, J. G. (2008). Everyday physical activity as a predictor of late-life mortality. *The Gerontologist, 48*, 349–357.

Christ, G., & Diwan, S. (2008). *Role of social work in managing chronic illness care*. In S. Diwan (Ed.), *Health Care and Older Adults Resource Review*. CSWE Gero-Ed Center, Master's Advanced Curriculum Project. Retrieved from www.gero-edcenter.org/mac

Coffey, C. E., Lucke, J. F., Saxton, J. A., Ratcliff, G., Unitas, L. J., Billig, B., et al. (1998). Sex differences in brain aging. *Archives of Neurology, 55*, 169–179.

Colman, R. J., Beasley, T. M., Allison, D. B., & Weindruch, R. (2008). Attenuation of sarcopenia by dietary restriction in rhesus monkeys. *Journal of Gerontology: Biological Sciences, 63A*, 556–559.

Connolly, M-T., Breckman, R., Callahan, J., Lachs, M., Ramsey-Klawsnick, H., & Solomon, J. (2012). The sexual revolution's last frontier: How silence about sex underlies health, well-being and safety in old age. *Generations, 36*, 43–54.

Crews, J. E., & Campbell, V. A. (2004). Vision impairment and hearing loss among community-dwelling older Americans: Implications for health and functioning. *American Journal of Public Health, 94,* 823–829.

Covinsky, K. E., Lindquist, K., Dunlop, D. D., & Yelin, E. (2009). Pain, functional limitations, and aging. *Journal of the American Geriatrics Society, 57,* 1556–1561.

Crimmins, E. M., & Beltrán-Sánchez, H. (2010). Mortality and morbidity trends: Is there compression of morbidity? *Journal of Gerontology: Social Sciences, 66B*(1), 75–86.

Dagarag, M. D., Evazyan, T., Rao, N., & Effros, R. B. (2004). Genetic manipulation of telomerase in HIV-specific CD8 & T cells. *Journal of Immunology, 2004,* 173, 6303–6311.

Dalton, D. S., Cruickshanks, K. J., Klein, B. E. K., Wiley, T. L., & Nondahl, D. M. (2003). The impact of hearing loss on quality of life in older adults. *The Gerontologist, 43,* 661–668.

DeLamater, J., & Friedrich, W. N. (2002). Promoting sexual health and responsible sexual behavior. *Journal of Sex Research, 39*(1), 10–14.

Effros, R. B. (2001). Immune system activity. In E. J. Masoro & S. N. Austad (Eds.). *Handbook of the biology of aging* (5th ed.). San Diego, CA: Academic Press.

Effros, R. B. (2009). The immunological theory of aging revisited. In V. L. Bengtson, D. Gans, N. M. Putney, & M. Silverstein (Eds.). *Handbook of theories of aging* (2nd ed.). New York: Springer.

Emlet, C. A. (2006). "You're awfully old to have this disease": Experiences of stigma and ageism in adults 50 years and older living with HIV/AIDS. *The Gerontologist, 46,* 781–790.

Enhance Fitness. (2011). *What is enhance fitness?* Retrieved September 2011 from www.projectenhance.org/enhance fitness_aspx.

Federal Interagency Forum on Aging-Related Statistics. (2012). *Older Americans 2011: Key indicators of well-being.* Washington, DC: U.S. Government Printing Office. Retrieved from http://www.agingstats.gov/agingstatsdotnet/Main_Site/Data/2010_Documents/Docs/OA_2010.pdf.

Fontana, L., Meyer, T. E., Klein, S., & Holloszy, J. O. (2004). Long-term calorie restriction is highly effective in reducing the risk for atherosclerosis in humans. *Proceedings of the National Academy of Sciences of the U.S.A., 101,* 6659–6663.

Fried, L.P., Tangen, C. M., Walston, J., Newman, A. B., Hirsch, C. Seeman T., et al., (2001). Frailty in older adults: Evidence for a phenotype. *Journals of Gerontology: Medical Sciences, 56A,* M146–M156.

Fries, J. F. (1980). Aging, natural death and the compression of morbidity. *New England Journal of Medicine, 303,* 130–135.

Fries, J. F. (2003). Measuring and monitoring success in compressing morbidity. *Annals of Internal Medicine, 139,* 455–459.

Frontera, W. R., & Silver, J. K. (Eds.) (2008). *Essentials of physical medicine and rehabilitation* (2nd ed.), pp. 259–265. Philadelphia: Saunders/Elsevier.

Fuller-Thomson, E., Yu, B., Nuru-Jeter, A., Guralnik, J. M., & Minkler, M. (2009). Basic ADL disability and functional limitation rates among older Americans from 2000–2005: The end of the decline? *Journals of Gerontology Series A: Biological Sciences and Medical Sciences, 64*(12), 1333–1336.

Gable, M. (January/February 2011). Affordable wellness: Creative providers bring wellness programs to affordable senior housing and community services. *LeadingAge Magazine, 1*(1), 16–29.

Gerontological Society on Aging. (2013). *What's hot in immunizations across the aging continuum—2013 update.* Washington, DC.

Golden, S. H., Lazo, M., Carnethon, M., Bertoni, A. G., Schriner, P. J., et al. (2008). Examining a bidirectional association between depressive symptoms and diabetes. *Journal of the American Medical Association, 299*(23), 2751–2759.

Goode, P. S., Burgio, K. L., Richter, H. E., & Markland, A. D. (2010). Incontinence in older women. *Journal of the American Medical Association, 303*(21), 2172–2181.

Grune, T., & Davies, K. J. A. (2001). Oxidative processes in aging. In E. J. Masaro & S. N. Austad (Eds.), *Handbook of the biology of aging* (5th ed.). San Diego, CA: Academic Press.

Gu, Q., Dillon, C. F., & Burt, V. L. (2010). Prescription drug use continues to increase: U.S. prescription drug data for 2007–2008. *NCHS Data Brief* (No. 42). Hyattsville, MD: National Center for Health Statistics.

Hanlon, J. T., Boudreau, R. M., Roumani, Y. F., Newman, A. B., Ruby, C. M., Wright, R. M., et al. (2009). Number and dosage of central nervous system medications on recurrent falls in community elders. *Journal of Gerontology: Medical Sciences, 64A,* M492–M498.

Harman, D. (1993). Free radical involvement in aging: Pathophysiology and therapeutic implications. *Drugs and Aging, 3,* 60–80.

Hayflick, L. (1996). *How and why we age.* New York: Ballantine Books.

Hayflick, L. (2000). The illusion of cell immortality. *British Journal of Cancer, 83,* 841–846.

Hayflick, L. (2004a). Anti-aging is an oxymoron. *Journal of Gerontology: Biological Sciences, 59A,* B573–B578.

Hayflick, L. (2004b). From here to immortality. *Public Policy & Aging Report, 14,* 1–7.

Health United States. (2010). Retrieved September 2011 from www://nchs/hus/older.htm.

Healthy People 2020. (2010). *Understanding and improving health.* U.S. Government Printing Office.

Holloszy, J. O., & Fontana, L. (2007). Caloric restriction in humans. *Experimental Gerontology, 42,* 709–712.

Hornsby, P. J. (2001). Cell proliferation in mammalian aging. In E. J. Masoro & S. N. Austad (Eds.). *Handbook of the biology of aging* (5th ed.). San Diego, CA: Academic Press.

Huffman, M. D., (2011). *Coronary heart disease in India: Center for chronic disease control.* Retrieved April 27, 2011, from http://sancd.org/uploads/pdf/factsheet_CHD.pdf.

HealthyWomen.org. (2013). *Incontinence.* Retrieved September 18, 2013, from http://www.healthywomen.org/condition/incontinence.

International Osteoporosis Foundation. (2012). *Capture the fracture report.* Retrieved September 17, 2013 from http://www.iofbonehealth.org/osteoporosis.

Ito, K., & Barnes, P. J. (2009). COPD as a disease of accelerated lung aging. *Chest, 135*(1), 173–180.

Jacquescoley, E. (2008). Behavioral prevention study gauges HIV/AIDS and depression in the older U.S. population. *AIDS Care, 20,* 1152–1153.

Jacobs, D. O. (2007). Diverticulitis. *New England Journal of Medicine, 357,* 2057–2066.

Kawamoto, K., & Kiyak, H. A. (2014). Sensory changes and communication in the practitioner–aged patient relationship. In P. Holm-Pedersen, A. Walls, & J. Ship (Eds.), *Textbook of Geriatric Dentistry,* 3rd ed. (In press).

Kirkland, J. L., & Peterson, C. (2009). Healthspan, translation, and new outcomes for animal studies of aging. *Journal of Gerontology: Biological Sciences, 64A,* 209–213.

Lachs, M. (2011, May 6th). *Exploring the sexual rights of older adults: Toward healthy sexuality and* freedom. Presentation at the colloquium, Exploring the Sexual Rights of Older Adults: Toward Healthy Sexuality and Freedom from Victimization in Later Life.

Lamster, I. B., Northridge, M. E., & Takamura, J. C. (2008). *Improving oral health for the elderly: An interdisciplinary approach.* New York: Springer.

Lane, M. A., Ingram, D. K., & Roth, G. S. (2002). The serious search for an anti-aging pill. *Scientific American, 287,* 36–41.

Lefevre, M., Redman, L. M., Heilbronn, L. K., Smith, J. V., Martin, C. K., Rood, J. C., et al. (2009). Caloric restriction alone and with exercise improves CVD risk in healthy non-obese individuals. *Atherosclerosis, 203,* 206–213.

Leland, J. (2008). Once just an aging sign, falls merit complex care. *New York Times.* Retrieved from http://www.nytimes.com/2008/11/08/us/08falls.html?ei=5070&emc=eta1&pagewanted=print.

Lesage, S., & Scharf, S. M. (2007). Beyond the usual suspects: Approaching sleep in elderly people. *Journal of Gerontology: Biological Sciences, 62A,* 53–54.

Lindau, S. T., Schumm, L. P., Laumann, E. O., Levinson, W., O'Muircheartaigh, C. A., & Waite, L. J. (2007, August). A study of sexuality and health among older adults in the United States. *New England Journal of Medicine, 357*(8), 762–774.

Loughran, D. S. (2010). 2025: A lot of older people on the roads: A risk to themselves. *New York Times.* Retrieved from http://www.nytimes.com/roomfordebate/2010/10/19/2020-a-lot-of-old-people-on-the-roads-32/older-drivers-a-risk-to-themselves.

Manton, K. G., Gu, X., & Lowrimore, G. R. (2008). Cohort changes in active life expectancy in the U.S. elderly populating: Experiences from the 1982–2004 national long-term care survey. *Journal of Gerontology: Social Sciences, 63B,* S269–S282.

Margolis, K. L., Ray, R. M., Van Horn, L., Manson, J. E., Allison, M. A., Black, H. R., Beresford, S. A., et al. (2008). Women's Health Initiative Investigators. Effect of calcium and vitamin D supplementation on blood pressure: The Women's Health Initiative Randomized Trial. *Hypertension, 52,* 847–855.

Markovic, K., Reulbach, U., Vassiliadu, A., Lunkenheimer, J., Lunkenheimer, B., Spannenberger, R., et al. (2007). Good news for elderly persons: Olfactory pleasure increases at later stages of the life span. *Journal of Gerontology: Medical Sciences, 62A,* 1287–1293.

Martin, L.G., Schoeni, R. F., & Andreski, P.M. (2010). Trends in health of older adults in the United States: Past, present and future. *Demography,* 47, 17–40.

Martini, C., Pallottini, V., DeMarinis, E., Marino, M., Cavallini, G., Donati, A., et al. (2008). Omega-3 as well as caloric restriction prevent the age-related modifications of cholesterol metabolism. *Mechanisms of Ageing and Development, 129,* 722–727.

Masoro, E. J. (2003). Caloric restriction, slowing aging, and extending life. *Science of aging knowledge environment, 8,* RE2.

Masters, W. H., & Johnson, V. (1981). Sex and the aging process. *Journal of the American Geriatrics Society, 29,* 385–390.

Mattison, J. A., Lane, M. A., Roth, G. S., & Ingram, D. K. (2003). Calorie restriction in rhesus monkeys. *Experimental Gerontology, 38,* 35–46.

Messaoudi, I., Warner, J., Fischer, M., Park, B., Hill, B., Mattison, J., et al. (2006). Delay of T cell senescence by caloric restriction in aged long-lived nonhuman primates. *Proceedings of the National Academy of Sciences of the U.S.A., 103,* 19448–19453.

Miller, R. A. (2009). "Dividends" from research on aging—Can biogerontologists, at long last, find something useful to do? *Journal of Gerontology: Biological Sciences, 64A,* 157–160.

Nair, K. S., Rizza, R. A., O'Brien, P., Dhatariay, K. K., Short, K. R., Nehra, A., et al. (2006). DHEA in elderly women and DHEA or testosterone in elderly men. *New England Journal of Medicine,* 355, 1647–1659.

National Cancer Institute. (2010). *Fact sheets: Prostate cancer; Surveillance epidemiology and end results.* Retrieved May 2, 2011, from http://seer.cancer.gov/statsfacts/html/prost.html.

National Center for Health Statistics (NCHS). (2009). *Beyond 20/20 WDS–Chronic conditions U.S. 1999–2007.* National Health Interview Survey. Retrieved May 2009 from http://205.207.175.HDI/Tableviewer.

National Center for Health Statistics (NCHS). (2011a). *Health, United States, 2010: With special feature on death and dying.* Hyattsville, MD. Retrieved from http://www.cdc.gov/nchs/data/hus/hus10.pdf#054.

National Center for Health Statistics (NCHS). (2011b). *NCHS data on obesity.* Retrieved from http://www.cdc.gov/nchs/data/factsheets/factsheet_obesity.pdf.

National Council on Aging. (2011). *Chronic disease.* Washington, DC: NCOA Center for Healthy Aging. Retrieved September 2011 from www.healthyagingprograms.org/content.asp?.

National Health Interview Survey. (2012). *Summary health statistics for U.S. adults*: 2010. Washington, DC: U.S. Department of Health and Human Services.

National Institute of Diabetes, Digestive and Kidney Disease (NIDDK). (2012). *National Diabetes Statistics*. Retrieved November 23, 2012, from http://diabetes.niddk.nih.gov/.

National Institutes of Health (NIH). (2011). *Disability in older adults* (Fact sheet). Retrieved May 19, 2011, from http://report.nih.gov/NIHfactsheets/ViewFactSheet.aspx?csid=37.

National Institute of Nursing Research. (2011). *Subtle and dangerous: Symptoms of heart disease in women*. Washington, DC: National Institutes of Health.

National Institutes of Health: Osteoporosis and Related Bone Disorders. (2012). *Calcium and vitamin D: Important at every age*. Retrieved November 24, 2012, from http://www.niams.nih.gov/Health-Infor/Bone.

National Institute on Aging (NIA). (2011a). *Supporting patients with chronic conditions*. Retrieved May 2, 2011, from http://www.nia.nih.gov/HealthInformation/Publications/ClinicianHB/06_chronic.htm.

National Institute on Aging (NIA). (2011b). *Exercise and physical activity: Getting fit for life*. Bethesda, MD: NIH/NIA.

National Institute on Aging (NIA). (2012a). *Hormones and menopause: Tips from the National Institute on Aging*. Bethesda, MD: NIH/NIA.

National Institute on Aging (NIA). (2012b). *Menopause*. Bethesda, MD: NIH/NIA.

National Institute on Aging (NIA). (2013). *Sexuality in later life: Age page*. Retrieved September 17, 2013, from http://www.nia.nih.gov/health/publication/sexuality-later-life.

Nelson, H. D., Vesco, K. K., Haney, E., Fu, R., Nedrow, A., Miller, J., et al. (2006). Nonhormonal therapies for menopausal hot flashes: Systematic review and meta-analysis. *Journal of the American Medical Association, 295*, 2057–2071.

Nguyen, N., & Holodniy, M. (2008). HIV infection in the elderly. *Clinical Interventions and Aging, 3*, 453–472.

Nikolaus, T., & Bach, M. (2003). Preventing falls in community-dwelling frail older people using a home intervention team (HIT): Results from the randomized Falls-HIT trial. *Journal of the American Geriatrics Society, 51*, 300–305.

Northrup, C. Schwartz, P., & Witte, J. (2013) *Sex at 50-plus: What's normal?* Retrieved September 17, 2013, from www.aarp.org/home-family/sex-intimacy/info-01-2013/seniors-having-sex-older-couples.html.

Nwankwo, T., Yoon, S. S., Burt, V., & Gu, Q. (2013) *Hypertension among adults in the United States*. Centers for Disease Control and Prevention. Retrieved from http://www.cdc.gov/nchs/data.htm.

Oberdoerffer, P., Michan, S., McVay, M., Mostoslavsky, R., Vann, J., Park, S. K., et al. (2008). SIRT1 redistribution on chromatin promotes genomic stability but alters gene expression during aging. *Cell, 135*, 907–918.

Ohayon, M. M., Carskadon, M. A., Guilleminault, C., & Vitiello, M. V. (2004). Meta-analysis of quantitative sleep parameters from childhood to old age in healthy individuals: Developing normative sleep values across the human lifespan. *Sleep, 27*, 1255–1273.

Palmer, S. (2009). Diabetes prevention: The best medicine. *Aging Well, 2*, 22–25.

Pearson, K. J., Baur, J. A., Lewis, K. N., Peshkin, L., Price, N. L., Labinsky, N., et al. (2008). Resveratrol delays age-related deterioration and mimics transcriptional aspects of dietary restriction without extending life span. *Cell Metabolism, 8*, 157–168.

Perls, T., & Terry, D. (2003). Understanding the determinants of exceptional longevity. *Annals of Internal Medicine,* 139, 445–449.

Peterson, M. J., Giuliani, C., Morey, M. C., Pieper, C. F., Evenson, K. R., Mercer, V., et al. (2009). Physical activity as a preventive factor for frailty. *Journal of Gerontology: Medical Sciences, 64A*, 61–68.

Phelan, E., Anderson, L., LaCroix, A., & Larson, A. (2004). Older adults' views of "successful aging": How do they compare with researchers' definitions? *Journal of the American Geriatrics Society, 53*, 211–216.

Poindexter, C., & Emlet, C. (2006). HIV-infected and HIV-affected older adults. In B. Berkman (Ed.), *Handbook of social work in health and aging*. New York: Oxford.

Pringle-Specht, J. K. (2005). Nine myths of incontinence in older adults. *American Journal of Nursing, 105*, 58–68.

Ramirez, R., & Schneider, J. (2003). Practical guide to sun protection. *Surgical Clinics of North America, 83*, 97–107.

Rincon, M., Muzumdar, R., & Barzilai, N. (2006). Aging, body fat, and carbohydrate metabolism. In E. J. Masoro & S. N. Austad (Eds.). *Handbook of the biology of aging* (6th ed.). Amsterdam: Elsevier/Academic Press.

Rizzo, V. (2008). *Chronic illness and aging: Osteoarthritis*. In S. Diwan (Ed.), *Health care and older adults resource review*. CSWE Gero-Ed Center, Master's Advanced Curriculum Project. Retrieved 2011 from www.gero-edcenter.org/mac.

Robman, L., & Taylor, H. (2005). External factors in the development of cataract. *Eye, 19*, 1074–1082.

Roth, G. S., Ingram, D. K., & Lane, M. A. (2001). Caloric restriction in primates and relevance to humans. *Annals of the New York Academy of Sciences, 298*, 305–315.

Schultz, D. W., Klein, M. L., Humbert, A. J., Luzier, C. W., Persun, V., et al. (2003). Analysis of the ARMD1 locus: Evidence that a mutation in *HEMICENTIN-1* is associated with age-related macular degeneration in a large family. *Human Molecular Genetics*. Retrieved February 2003 from http://hmg.oupjournals.org/content/abstract/ddg348v1.

Sloane, M., Hanna, J. Y Ford, d. (2013, September 3). *'Never, ever give up:' Diana Nyad completes historic Cuba-to-Florida swim*. Retrieved from http://www.cnn.com/2013/09/02/world/americas/diana-nyad-cuba-florida-swim/index.html.

Solana, R. (2003). *Immunosenescence in centenarians and the old-old*. Symposium presented at the International Association of Gerontology, Barcelona, July.

SmartMotorist.com. (2013). *Older drivers, elderly driving, seniors at the wheel*. Retrieved September 18, 2013 from http://www.smartmotorist.com/traffic-and-safety-guideline/older-drivers-elderly-driving-seniors-at-the-wheel.html.

Squires, S. (2008). To produce good health, bite into fruit and veggies. *Washington Post.* Retrieved from http://www.washingtonpost.com/wp-dyn/content/article/2008/06/20/AR2008062002600_pf.html.

Starr, B. D. & Wiener, M. B. (1981). *The Star-Weiner report on sex and sexuality in the mature years.* New York: Stein and Day.

Stepnick, L., & Whitelaw, N. A. (2006). *A new vision of aging: Helping older adults make healthier choices.* Washington, DC: Center for the Advancement of Health.

Strawbridge, W. J., Wallhagen, M. I., Shema, S. J., & Kaplan, G. A. (2000). Negative consequences of hearing impairment in old age: A longitudinal analysis. *The Gerontologist, 40,* 320–326.

Stuen, C. (2006). Older adults with age-related sensory loss. In B. Berkman (Ed.), *Handbook of social work in health and aging.* New York: Oxford.

Swain, S. L., & Nikolich-Zugich, J. (2009). Key research opportunities in immune system aging. *Journal of Gerontology: Biological Sciences, 64A,* 183–186.

Tatar, M. (2009). Can we develop genetically tractable models to assess healthspan (rather than life span) in animal models? *Journal of Gerontology: Biological Sciences, 64A,* 161–163.

Thavanati, P. K. R., Kanala, K. R., deDios, A. E., & Garza, J. M. C. (2008). Age-related correlation between antioxidant enzymes and DNA damage with smoking and body mass index. *Journal of Gerontology: Biological Sciences, 63A,* 360–364.

The American Geriatrics Society (AGS). (2010). *AGS/BGS clinical practice guideline: Prevention of falls in older persons.* Retrieved from http://www.americangeriatrics.org/health_care_professionals/clinical_practice/clinical_guidelines_recommendations/2010/.

U.S. Cancer Statistics Working Group.2010. *United States cancer statistics: 1999–2007 incidence and mortality Web-based report.* Atlanta: Centers for Disease Control and Prevention and National Cancer Institute.

U.S. Census Bureau (2012). *Motor vehicle accidents—Number and deaths 1990-2009.* Washington, DC: Statistical Abstract of the United States.

Vincent, K. R., Braith, R. W., Feldman, R. A., Kallas, H. E., & Lowenthal, D. T. (2002). Improved cardiorespiratory endurance following 6 months of resistance exercise in elderly men and women. *Archives of Internal Medicine, 162,* 673–678.

Vitiello, M. V., Larsen, L. H., & Moe, K. E. (2004). Age-related sleep change: Gender and estrogen effects on the subjective-objective sleep quality of healthy, noncomplaining men and women. *Journal of Psychosomatic Research, 56,* 503–510.

Walford, R. L. (1969). *The immunologic theory of aging.* Copenhagen: Munksgaard.

Warner, D. F., & Hayward, M. D. (2002). *Race disparities in men's mortality: The role of childhood social conditions in a process of cumulative disadvantage.* University of Pennsylvania, unpublished manuscript.

Whitfield, K. E., & Hayward, M. (2003). The landscape of health disparities among older adults. *Public Policy & Aging Report, 13,* 1–7.

Wierzalis, E., Barret, B., Pope, M., & Rankins, M. (2006). Gay men and aging: Sex and intimacy. In D. Kimmel, T. Rose, & S. David (Eds.), *Lesbian, gay, bisexual and transgender aging.* New York: Columbia University Press.

Wilson, D. L. (1974). The programmed theory of aging. In M. Rockstein, M. L. Sussman, & J. Chesky (Eds.), *Theoretical aspects of aging.* New York: Academic Press.

Wingfield, A., Panizzon, M., Grant, M. D., Toomey, R., Kremen, W. S., Franz, C. E., et al. (2007). A twin study of genetic contributions to hearing acuity in late middle age. *Journal of Gerontology: Medical Sciences, 62A,* 1294–1299.

Wolf, S. L., Barnhart, H. X., Kutner, N. G., McNeely, E., Coogler, C., Xu, T., et al. (2003). Reducing frailty and falls in older persons: An investigation of Tai Chi and computerized balance training. *Journal of the American Geriatrics Society, 51,* 1794–1803.

Women Heart. (2011). *Women and heart disease fact sheet.* Retrieved September 2011 from http://women heart.org/resources/cvdfactsheet.cfm

Women's Health Initiative (WHI). (2002). Risks and benefits of estrogen plus progestin in healthy postmenopausal women. *Journal of the American Medical Association, 288,* 321–333.

You, T., Sonntag, W. E., Leng, X., & Carter, C. S. (2007). Lifelong caloric restriction and interleukin-6 secretion from adipose tissue: Effects on physical performance decline in aged rats. *The Journals of Gerontology, Series A, Biological Sciences and Medical Sciences, 62*(10), 1082–1087.

Zeiss, A. M., & Kasl-Godley, J. (2001). Sexuality in older adults' relationships. *Generations, 25*(2), 18–25.

4 Mental and Emotional Well-Being

learning objectives

- 4.1 Understand cognitive functioning in older adulthood, including the relationship between aging and intelligence, learning, and memory.
- 4.2 Discuss different theories of personality as well as factors that promote resilient and positive aging.
- 4.3 Demonstrate knowledge of the different types of mental disorders among some older adults and risk factors and treatment for such diseases.

Listen to the **Chapter Audio**

Perhaps you have some classmates who have returned to college for a degree they started years ago—or for the sheer pleasure of learning. Have you noticed any differences between how these older adults learn compared to younger classmates? Or have you seen any differences in their personalities—the way they interact with others, how they express emotions, their self-concept, and their self-esteem—from your younger friends? Whether and how our personality and cognitive functioning—our ability to learn and retain information—change as we age is our focus here.

This chapter includes:

- The three major functions of how we think: intelligence, learning, and memory, and how they are affected by the aging process
- Ways that older adults can improve their learning and memory skills
- Wisdom and creativity in old age
- Different theories of personality that describe change or stability with aging
- Emotional expression, self-concept, and self-esteem as we age
- Concepts of successful, robust, positive, and resilient and active aging
- Major mental disorders in old age—depression, anxiety, and dementia

We turn first to cognitive functioning—intelligence, learning, and memory. How we think, learn, and remember is critical to our performance in every aspect of our lives. Researchers try to determine whether declines in cognitive functioning are due to age-related physiological changes or to diseases. Their findings are of interest to many middle-aged and older adults who fear memory loss. Their fears may be heightened by family members who are quick to label normal forgetfulness of sometimes trivial matters, such as not finding their car keys, as a sign of getting old—or even of Alzheimer's disease—when in fact we all may do this occasionally. When others start labeling memory lapses as a sign of cognitive decline or even dementia, elders are likely to become stressed and anxious, heightening any normal forgetfulness.

Aging and Cognitive Function

Intelligence is defined as the "theoretical limit of an individual's performance" (Jones, 1959, p. 700). While biological and genetic factors primarily affect this limit, environmental opportunities (e.g., challenging learning experiences) and constraints (e.g., the absence of books) also make a difference.

points to ponder

As you think about your own aging, which do you fear most—cognitive or physical decline? What are the reasons for your fears?

Perhaps you have heard someone say, "she's old, so she's just not as smart as she used to be." Many of us assume intelligence declines with age. It is true that some researchers have identified that older persons perform at a lower level than younger adults on intelligence tests. Yet others conclude that aging is not inevitably associated with diminishing intelligence. What is clear is that older people do not do as well as younger persons on standardized intelligence tests. But as you will see in our discussion, factors other than age, such as test anxiety, can explain such lower performance (Schaie, 1996).

Intelligence consists of three major sets of abilities: problem-solving, verbal skills, and social competence. Intelligence tests measure a subset of intellectual skills known as **primary mental abilities (PMAs)**. These include mathematical reasoning; the ability to generalize from specific facts to concepts; spatial relations; the capacity to retain and recall content from readings; and perceptual speed. People rarely decline in all five abilities (Cavanaugh & Blanchard-Fields, 2010).

These abilities comprise two different types of intelligence: fluid and crystallized.

Fluid intelligence or what is popularly called "native intelligence" encompasses skills such as abstract and mathematical reasoning, spatial relations,

points to ponder

Think of an older adult whom you consider "intellectually active." What kind of work does this person do? How would you describe their cognitive ability? What are the possible reasons why this person is still intellectually active?

and perceptual speed. These are biologically determined, independent of our experience or learning.

Crystallized intelligence is the knowledge and abilities—verbal meaning, social judgment, number skills, and verbal memory—that we acquire through education and experience (Cattell, 1963; Horn, 1970, 1982).

Intelligence and Aging

Most intelligence tests taken by older people show a **classic aging pattern** of scores: lower functioning on performance tests of skills such as perceptual speed (i.e., fluid intelligence), but stable scores on verbal scales (i.e., crystallized intelligence). This tendency to do worse on performance tasks may reflect both time constraints and age-related changes in sensory, perceptual, and psychomotor skills that have nothing to do with intelligence. For instance, slower reaction time and delays in receiving and transmitting messages through senses (e.g., poor hearing) may partially explain poorer performance on such tests. Speed of cognitive processing, such as time to perform simple math, also deteriorates with age. Nevertheless, it does appear that performance-related aspects of intellectual function decline somewhat independently of such psychomotor or sensory factors. But keep in mind that cognitive capability varies widely, even within an individual on different tests. And high test scorers earlier in life continue to do well even among the oldest-old (Bielak, Hultsch, Strauss, MacDonald, & Hunter, 2010; Hasher et al., 2002; Salthouse, 1996).

As another example that decline is not inevitable, the classic aging pattern suggests that our ability to recall stored verbal information and to use abstract reasoning (i.e., crystallized intelligence) tends to remain constant. In this case, an older person in your English class may do better than younger classmates because of their verbal skills and long-term familiarity with English literature. Declines in crystallized intelligence, where they exist, typically do not show up until advanced old age, or are results of disease-related cognitive impairment such as dementia. And recent studies in Denmark suggest that today's 90-year-olds are mentally sharper and scoring higher on cognitive function tests than their predecessors, which can be attributed in part to improved education levels (Hasher, Chung, May, & Foong, 2002; Szalavitz, 2013).

What Else Besides Age Affects Intelligence?

Multiple factors, which are not age related, affect intelligence. We encourage you to keep these in mind when you interact with older adults in learning situations. These include the following:

- A biological factor—some people are innately more intelligent.
- Anxiety about test performance.
- Education: Older adults with 12 or more years of education generally perform better than do those with 7 or fewer years.
- Occupation: Those in complex jobs that require verbal, thinking, and problem-solving skills show less decline on cognitive tests. Elders who use abstract and fluid skills in their jobs (e.g., architects and engineers) also perform better. Being "cognitively engaged" is a vital factor in intelligence.

points to ponder

Think about how the type of test can influence a person's peak performance, even for younger adults. If a group of 20-year-olds and a group of 70-year-olds took a timed test on mathematical calculations, the younger cohort would tend to get more answers correct. However, if the same two groups were given a test that asked them to figure out three meals for a family of four (two children and two adults) with a total weekly budget of $50—which group would tend to perform better on this test? What different abilities would be used on the two tests? What type of intelligence was used in each? What would you then conclude about intelligence and aging?

- Physical health: Older adults with diabetes, hypertension, and cardiovascular diseases tend to perform less well, especially on tests requiring psychomotor speed. Vision and hearing impairments are associated with poorer performance on tests of verbal meaning.
- Nutritional deficits, particularly low intake of certain vitamins, affect performance on visual, spatial, and abstraction tasks.
- Nearness to death. An apparent and rapid decline in cognitive function is found within 5 years of death.
- Cautiousness in recall situations that involve risk and uncertainty. Elders are more likely not to give an answer than to guess and risk being wrong, even when told it is acceptable to give wrong answers.
- Numerous problems measuring intelligence (Elias et al., 2004; Friedman et al., 2009; Gamaldo, Weatherbee, & Allaire, 2008; Hassing et al., 2004; Mackinnon, Christensen, Hofer, Korten, & Jorm, 2003; Murray et al., 2002; Rosnick, Small, Graves, & Mortimer, 2004; Schooler, Mulatu, & Oates, 2004; Waldstein, Giggey, Thayer, & Zonderman, 2005; Willis & Schaie, 2006; Yaffe et al., 2009).

The nature of the research design also affects findings about intelligence. You learned in the Introduction about cross-sectional research (e.g., people are tested or asked a series of questions just once). This is a problematic method in studies of intelligence because any identified age differences may reflect cohort or generational differences rather than actual age variations. Think about how changes over the past 100 years in our educational systems, higher levels of education among younger cohorts, and widespread access to technology have a greater impact on young adults than elders. Indeed, such cohort and historical factors may influence intelligence scores more than age per se (Schaie, 2005).

Even when longitudinal research designs (i.e., people are tested over time) are used, we may not get a clear picture of age differences. This is because older adults are more likely than younger persons to drop out of longitudinal studies. And those who drop out tend to have performed less well at baseline or their health status and functional abilities are worse than average. The results are then biased in favor of those who were superior performers at baseline and do not represent the wider older population (Schaie, 1996a, 2005).

How Communication Can Affect Older Adults' Performance

If you are ever in a position to administer a cognition test to an older adult, remember that the words you choose can affect the test-taker's anxiety level and self-esteem. Rather than saying, "We're going to find out if your memory is declining," you can reframe it by saying, "This test is going to help us learn what your strengths are." A positive tone of voice and attitudes, such as respect, sensitivity, and dignity, can assuage anxiety and affect performance.

Intellectual stimulation can help sustain higher-level cognitive skills.

How Aging Affects Learning and Memory

Learning and memory are cognitive processes that must be considered together, since learning occurs when we are able to retrieve information accurately from our memory.

Memory is the process of recalling information that was once stored; it also refers to a part of the brain that retains what has been learned throughout our lives. **Sensory memory** is the first step in receiving information from the long-term storage of memories via our touch, taste, or smell. For example, the aroma of freshly baked cookies often evokes memories of early childhood. Other examples of sensory memory are faces of people we know and landscapes we see or ocean waves we hear. When we rehearse information received from our senses, it is more likely to be passed into our memory (Pearlman & Storandt, 2004).

Our **working (primary) memory** is a temporary stage of holding, processing, and organizing information—not a specific storage area in the brain. It is called working

Intellectually Active Elders

Increasingly, older adults continue to participate in intellectually challenging jobs well beyond their sixties and seventies. Indeed, there is growing evidence that people who were engaged in reading, writing, and other mentally stimulating activities throughout their lives experience lower rates of cognitive decline. College campuses are full of senior faculty who retain emeritus status and continue to teach or conduct research into their eighties. Stanley Kunitz was appointed a Poet Laureate at age 95, and wrote poetry into his nineties. Dr. Hilary Koprowski, whose research in 1948 led to the adoption of the polio vaccine, continued to conduct medical research and was a linguist and an active music composer at age 93. But even someone who was not a "bookworm" early in life can boost their brain power later in life through reading and writing! Look around your campus or your neighborhood for examples of intellectually active elders (Dahl, 2013).

memory because it decides what information should be attended to or ignored. But if we are distracted while trying to retain even two to three bits of information for the 60 seconds needed to store it in short-term memory, we immediately forget it. We all experience situations where we hear a phone number or name, use it, and then forget it. In fact, older adults can typically recall seven, plus or minus two pieces, of information (e.g., digits, letters, or words) for only 60 seconds or less.

Receiving lots of new information at once makes it more difficult to retain it in our permanent **secondary**, or **long-term, memory**, which is where we keep everything we have learned throughout our lives. Unlike primary memory, it has an unlimited capacity.

Learning occurs when the new information or skills that we acquire through our sensory and primary memories become encoded or stored in secondary memory. Information must be rehearsed or "processed" actively in order to be retrieved later. For example, looking up a telephone number and immediately dialing it does not guarantee that we will learn the number. Only with considerable rehearsal, such as writing it down numerous times, is information from primary memory passed into secondary memory.

In summary, aging does not influence the storage capacity of memories. Instead, the process by which we rehearse or encode new information tends to decline in primary memory. This may also occur because **perceptual speed**—the time required to recognize and respond to a stimulus—deteriorates with aging. Such declines are a reason why older people do worse on memory tests, even when they have more time to complete them. The learning process is disrupted when an elder cannot retrieve information efficiently from secondary memory.

The **general slowing hypothesis** is closely related: It posits that aging causes a slowing of information processing in the nervous system. This results in older adults performing worse on complex tasks, although the extent of slowing varies with the task (Ratcliff, Spieler, & McKoon, 2000; Salthouse, 1996; Sülzenbrück, Hegele, Heuer, & Rinkenauer, 2010).

Additionally, aging may cause a decline in attentional resources or mental energy needed to organize newly acquired information in order to retain it in secondary memory. Older people tend to have more difficulty in holding information in their working memory while receiving new stimuli through sensory memory, and in ignoring irrelevant stimuli to complete working memory tasks. For example, if an older driver is trying to locate a street address that was just given to her, but is also listening to the radio, she is less likely to remember the address than would a younger person. This decline in attention

Secondary Memory and Aging

- Episodic memory of events (times, places, and associated emotions) declines the most after age 60. However, educated older adults and those given more practice opportunities do better on recalling such events.
- Semantic memory. The part of long-term memory dealing with words and their meanings shows the least decline with aging, because it is stimulated by concepts learned throughout one's life. Remember how older adults tend to do better in an English class than in math.
- Procedural memory—the memory of how to do certain actions and skills—is retained into advanced old age; people who have not ridden a bike in 50 years can get on and start pedaling. The poignancy of such procedural memories is captured by Julie Otsuka's memoir of her cognitively impaired mother who can remember how to turn cartwheels or rock a baby to sleep, but not how to use the new coffeemaker (Hoyer & Verhaeghen, 2006; Johnson, 2005; Otsuka, 2009; Siedlecki, Salthouse, & Berish, 2005).

may explain a busy person's saying, "I just cannot remember anything more right now!" (Bopp & Verhagen, 2005; Zacks, Hasher, & Li, 2000).

Tip-of-the-tongue states (TOTs) represent a specific type of difficulty in retrieval. We all experience situations when we know the name of a favorite restaurant, famous actor, or friend but cannot immediately recall it, that is, retrieve it from secondary memory. We search through our memory, drawing associations from similar names, or focusing on an image of the place or person. And we often experience a feeling of imminence—the sense that one can "almost" remember it or that it is on the "tip of one's tongue." When we experience a TOT, we may remember the word through spontaneous retrieval (i.e., letting a name pop into our primary memory later, when we are removed from the immediate pressure to remember it, such as recalling it when we are taking a shower or falling asleep). Additionally, we may use search strategies such as cues (e.g., listing similar names or going through the alphabet), or looking it up on our smartphone or in a Thesaurus (Schwartz, 2002).

Older people seem to rely on spontaneous recall more often than structured search strategies. This may be because as we age, we have a larger bank of names in our memory that makes it difficult to search for a specific word. Regardless of our age, we learn new names best when we are told we will be asked to recall them later and use visual associations to help process information about the name (e.g., facial features, a link between face and name) (Fraas et al., 2002; Reese & Cherry, 2004; Rendell, Castel, & Craik, 2005; Schwartz, 2002; Troyer, Hafliger, Cadieux, & Craik, 2006).

Playing a musical instrument in advanced old age is relatively easy for accomplished musicians who can draw upon procedural memory.

Improving Executive Function

In Experience Corps, older volunteers who were trained to help primary schoolchildren with reading and behavior management were compared with their counterparts who did not receive such training. After four to eight weeks, the trained elders scored higher on tests of executive function and memory compared to their baseline scores and a control group, who showed a decline at follow-up. These gains were attributed in part to the complex environment of schools, with their cognitive challenges and diverse stimuli that volunteers must master, and to the exercise of moving around the classrooms (Carlson et al., 2008).

Executive Function in Older Adults

Another important learning component is **executive function**: the ability to organize our learning and then efficiently use the information stored in our secondary memory to plan and make decisions and shift attention from one task to another. Normal aging is associated with only mild declines in executive function. But older adults with dementia and those who have experienced major changes in their environments, such as hospitalization, experience significant impairment in this ability. This decline also affects their ability to perform instrumental activities of daily living (IADLs), such as taking medications, which you learned about in Chapter 3 (Brooks, Weaver, & Scialfa, 2006; Ehlenbach et al., 2010; Gunstad et al., 2006; Insel et al., 2006).

Because executive function is so important, it is not surprising that numerous interventions to improve it, such as cognitive training, have been designed and tested. But it may surprise you that just six months of moderate levels of aerobic activity also improve executive function. Moreover, healthy diets of fresh produce, fish, and olive oil may protect against this decline. Even volunteering has benefits for executive function, as described in the box above (Erickson & Kramer, 2009; Feart, Samieri, & Barberger-Gateau, 2010; Li et al., 2010; Wolinsky et al., 2010).

Factors That Affect Learning in Old Age Attention is a critical first step in learning. Three of its components are central to people's ability to learn.

Selective attention is being able to select information relevant to a task while ignoring irrelevant data. You often have to use selective attention when listening to a lecturer who discusses multiple aspects of a concept secondary to the key information that you need to retain. **Vigilance,** or **sustained attention**, requires looking out for a specific stimulus over time. This is the type of attention that air traffic controllers must use when watching for blips on a screen. In such complex tasks, older people do worse than young adults. However, few differences between young and old are found when the task is simple or does not place significant demands on memory, or when participants have practiced that type of vigilance (Einstein, Earles, & Collins, 2002; Rogers & Fisk, 2001).

Attentional control refers to our ability to determine how much attention should be directed at specific stimuli and when to shift our focus to other stimuli. This is particularly important under conditions of divided attention. **Divided attention** tasks involve stimuli in the same sensory mode (e.g., listening to two channels of music simultaneously) or different sensory systems (e.g., listening to spoken words while reading a different set of words). Most of us attempt to multitask, such as speaking on the phone while cooking dinner, which can negatively affect our ability to learn and remember and reduce our efficiency.

Age differences with divided attention are inevitable. An older man who has practiced managing multiple tasks (e.g., an experienced cook who can prepare several dishes simultaneously) can shift his attention just as easily as his younger counterparts. However, if the task is highly complex or he is anxious, then his ability to perform tasks simultaneously is worse. For instance, divided attention can be a problem when driving and needing to attend to changes in traffic flow and speed (Hogan, 2003; Romoser & Fisher, 2009; Whiting, 2003).

Additionally, environmental and personal factors negatively affect elders' learning and memory. Here are just a few.

Physical conditions:

- An unfamiliar learning environment
- Poor lighting levels and small font size
- Low tone and volume of a test-giver's voice in an oral exam

Individual characteristics:

- Slowing of the central nervous system
- Verbal ability and educational level
- Previous experience with similar learning tasks
- Expectations about a task
- English as a second language

Strategies to Promote Older Adults' Learning Fortunately, numerous strategies can enhance learning, often by modifying environmental factors.

- Create supportive conditions for learning and test-taking. Expressions such as "These tasks can be hard for all of us" can reduce older people's anxieties about learning and retaining new information.
- Use positive feedback: "You are doing great."
- Pace the rate of information flow to allow opportunities to practice the new information (e.g., writing down or spelling aloud newly learned words).
- Allow self-pacing and extra time to reduce fatigue.
- Offer material perceived by the older learner to be relevant.
- Chunk or break long bits of information into smaller units—a process we all do with phone, Social Security, and pin numbers.

points to ponder

Think about your own learning abilities. Under what conditions do you learn best? To what extent is your learning affected by the physical environment, and your ability to devote selective attention and attentional control to a task? What other factors might affect your learning?

Age-Related Changes in Memory We retrieve information from our long-term memory through recall and recognition.

Recall is the process of searching through the vast store of information in our secondary memory, perhaps with a cue or a specific orienting question. There are two types:

Free recall—No aids are provided for retrieving information from secondary memory. For example, "List the capitals of each state"; "Describe how to repair a bicycle tire."

Cued recall—Hints are given to aid in the search, such as the first letter of a word. For instance, "The capital of New York begins with the letter 'A'; what is it?"

Not surprisingly, older people tend to do less well in tests of free recall but are aided significantly by cued recall. **Recognition** requires fewer searches because a stimulus in the environment triggers retrieval of that information, such as in multiple-choice tests. "Which of these three cities is the capital of New York?"

Here are some other examples of the challenges of recall as we age. Many events are firmly embedded in secondary memory because they are so important that subsequent experiences do not interfere with our recall of them years later. For example, we may readily recall events with great personal significance, such as the birth of a child or someone's death, or situations with profound impacts on world history, such as the bombing of Hiroshima or the 9/11 terrorist attacks. Perhaps you have asked an old friend "Do you remember the time when?" But you may not be able to determine whether their recall of distant situations is accurate because there may be no way to validate their memories.

Cues that helped an older person recall past events are generally less effective with recalling recent occasions because of "cue overload." That is, cues are so strongly associated with one's earlier life experiences that newer information becomes more difficult to retrieve. For example, older people may have difficulty memorizing new phone numbers because cues that helped them recall past numbers may cause them to confuse recent and old ones.

Another possibility is **disuse theory**—not using the information results in its loss. We can all identify with this situation; for example, if we have moved out of a community, we often forget many names and places associated with it.

Memory Retrieval or Loss?

Nearly all older adults worry about their memory, such as when they forget the most important item on their shopping list or their former college roommate's name. Rather than a slowing down of the brain, this often is lack of attention, perhaps intensified by poor sleep or medications. Doctors advise elders not to worry if they are occasionally slow to come up with a word they once knew. But if a previously familiar word means nothing on a repeated basis, then it's time to be formally evaluated by a doctor (Knox, 2011).

Older adults can remember names and faces of people in the past with whom they have had positive relationships.

Unless it is exercised, information can fade away. But this explanation does not account for the many facts—even trivia—that are deeply embedded in our memory store and can be retrieved after years of disuse, sometimes surprising us with what we suddenly remember. Participants at a 50th high school reunion who are trying hard to remember former close friends are grappling with the challenges of disuse!

Interference theory also helps to explain age-related problems with retrieval. Poor retrieval may be due to a combination of distraction during the learning stage and interference by new information with the material stored over many years that is being searched for in the retrieval stage.

Spatial memory—the ability to recall where objects are in relationship to each other in space—also declines with age. We use such memory when reading a map or finding our way back to our car parked in a large garage. When older people stand in front of a "You are here" map that is aligned 180 degrees away from their orientation, they take up to 50 percent more time and make 30 percent more errors than younger persons, because of increased problems with mental rotation of external images. However, when the map is aligned directly with the user, no age differences are observed (Das & Agarwal, 2000).

Reflection Break

Before moving on to the next section, let's test your memory. Without reviewing what was written prior to this point in the chapter, try answering the following three questions:

1. Today you still remember the lyrics to a song that was your favorite about 5 years ago and which, back then, you listened to over and over again. However, you

haven't thought about that song in a long time, until now. In what kind of memory—primary or secondary—did you store those lyrics?

2. You know how to type at a keyboard, but let's say you injure both of your hands and are not able to type for six months. Your brain has not been injured. Will you forget how to type when you can use your hands again? Explain your answer.
3. At a noisy family dinner, Grandpa can't remember the name of a neighbor's dog he occasionally encounters. It's on the tip of his tongue, so to speak, and after thinking about it for less than a minute, he remembers the dog's name. Is this a sign of dementia? What would be a better example of a memory problem in which Grandpa should be formally evaluated by a doctor?

If you weren't able to answer all these questions, it might be because you weren't paying close enough attention to the chapter content up to this point, or you were distracted when reading, or you might have test anxiety!

Remember these same factors may explain why an older adult forgets things.

Improving Cognitive Abilities

Cognitive retraining involves teaching older adults how to use techniques to keep their minds active, and maintain memory, problem-solving, and decision-making skills. It is based on the premise of maximizing one's remaining potential, a widely accepted concept in physical aging but only recently applied to cognitive aging. It also recognizes that age-related memory changes are not due to neuron loss per se, but rather affected by lifestyle factors. In other words, when we use our brains, this makes connections between neurons stronger and may even create new neurons. Cognitive retraining has even reversed declines in specific types of skills (e.g., reasoning ability) and improved older adults' ability to perform IADLs (Boron, Willis, & Schaie, 2007; Finch, 2007; Langbaum et al., 2009; Nyberg, 2005; Victoroff, 2002; Willis et al., 2006).

Playing Bridge to Keep the Mind Active

The *90+ Study*, conducted by researchers at USC and UC-Davis, has examined longitudinally more than 1,000 people age 90 and older without signs of dementia. Their behavioral, cognitive, and blood tests show that the oldest-old who spend several hours each day engrossed in mentally challenging activities such as puzzles and games are at reduced risk for developing dementia than their less-engaged peers. However, social connectedness is also an important component. Those who play contact bridge and other activities in a group are most successful in retaining high levels of cognitive functioning well into their nineties (Whittle et al., 2007).

points to ponder

While older adults may play bridge as a way to exercise their brains—and connect with others—what kinds of games do younger generations play to try to achieve similar effects? Do you think computer games would have similar beneficial effects to playing bridge?

An older learner's age and educational level influence the benefits from cognitive retraining. The young-old and those with a college degree or higher perform best on retraining tests. Moreover, older adults' mental status and physical health also affect their success in cognitive retraining. And practice tends to enhance learning and memory (Nyberg, 2005).

We turn next to a number of aids useful for cognitive retraining.

Memory Mediators **Mediators** are visual and verbal links between information to be encoded and information already in secondary memory. **Visual mediators**—in particular, the method of locations (or loci)—are useful for learning new words, names, or concepts. Each word is associated with a specific location in a familiar environment. For example, an individual is instructed to "walk through" each room of her own home mentally. As she does so, each item on a list is associated with a particular space along the way. Imaging is useful in everyday recall situations. We can remember what groceries to buy by visualizing using these items in preparing dinner. Or we use visual images to recall names (e.g., remembering the name "John Doe" by visualizing him as making dough). This type of exercise to strengthen memory in one task can help improve performance on other ones (Colcombe & Kramer, 2003).

Look, Snap, and Connect

The "look, snap and connect" technique is a practical method for retaining information efficiently in order to recall it later. Its components are as follows:

- ***Look:*** Actively focus on what you want to take in from the information, and record it through multiple senses.
- ***Snap:*** Create a mental snapshot or image of the object, person, or word(s) to be remembered; the more bizarre or unusual the image, the better it will be recalled (e.g., remember Mr. Brown's name by visualizing him covered with mud).
- ***Connect:*** Visualize a link to associate the images created through mental snapshots, thereby retaining the information through its connection with existing memories (e.g., remembering a grocery list by connecting items together, such as *flour* poured over *apples* that are swimming in a bowl of *milk*) (Small, 2002).

Verbal mediators or **mnemonics** are riddles, rhymes, and codes associated with new information. You may have learned such rhymes in elementary school: "*i* before *e* except after *c*" and "30 days hath September, April, June, and November ..." Some mnemonics are acquired through experience and our own efforts to devise ways to learn a new concept (e.g., you might make up a word "IntLeMe") to remember the three components of cognition—intelligence, learning, memory. Other verbal mediators are placing information into categories, associating the digits in a phone number with symbols or putting them into a mathematical formula (e.g., "the first digit is 4, the second and third are multiplied to produce the first").

External Cognitive Aids As a student, you may keep notes on your smartphone of what you need to do each day. Lists can also help older persons recall names, words, phone numbers, and daily chores. For example, a list organized by type of item (e.g., a grocery list that groups produce, meats, and dairy) can enhance memory. For elders with more severe problems of recall and recognition, charts listing daily or weekly routine can be posted throughout the house.

Other simple external cognitive aids for people of all ages are as follows:

- Associate specific behaviors as part of our daily routines. Link a new activity such as taking medications with routines that occur at a particular time each day: for example, take the first pill when you wake up, the second pill with lunch, and so on.
- Put "post-it" notes in visible spots, or post a small sign near the entry doorknob: "Keys, Stove Off, Lock Back Door, Water for Cat, Bus Pass."
- Use alarm clocks and kitchen timers to remind a person a stove is on.
- For those with serious memory problems, use a bracelet or necklace imprinted with their name, address, phone number, and relevant medical information.

Physical Exercise You learned earlier how exercise can improve executive function. An intervention to increase physical activity enhanced not only elders' physical performance, gait, speed, and balance, but also their scores on tests of working memory and psychomotor speed and their attention and decision-making skills. These cognitive benefits may occur because exercise improves blood flow to the brain and increases the efficiency of its neuronal networks (Colcombe & Kramer, 2003; Kramer, Erickson, & Colcombe, 2006; Williamson et al., 2009).

Do Chemical Aids Improve Memory? You may know someone who takes ginkgo biloba because they believe it will help their memory. But research has concluded that it does not help. Similarly, tests of Vitamin E and B12, lecithin, and folic acid have not demonstrated memory benefits. Instead, doses of these supplements high enough to show improved memory function can cause harmful side effects. And megadoses may even increase the likelihood of accidental deaths. Given such findings, caution must be exercised in taking any kind of supplement, even herbal, to improve memory (Bjelakovic, Nikolova, Gluud, Simonetti, & Gluud, 2007; DeKosky et al., 2008;

points to ponder

What are some of the techniques you draw upon to help you memorize newly learned concepts for a test? Are these the same methods you use to remember errands or what you need to do on the weekend? Can you expand the list of methods described above with your own methods for remembering? How might you apply some of these techniques to help an older person who is wanting to improve her memory?

Can Regular Aerobic Exercise Improve Brain Aging?

It's never too late to start an aerobic exercise program that can benefit not just our physical health but also our ability to remember. Participating in a relatively easy routine of walking 40 minutes three times a week over 1 year was found to increase the size of the brain in just 1 year. Just as with brain games, exercise helps to keep our brains at peak functioning. Specifically, the hippocampus, where we form memories and learn to navigate the environment around us, increased its volume with regular aerobic exercise. Imagine how much more benefit we can gain when aerobic activity is started earlier in life and continued into old age (Erickson & Kramer, 2009; Erickson et al., 2011).

van Dongen, van Rossum, Kessels, Sielhorst, & Knipscheld, 2003; Wilkins, Sheline, Roe, Binge, & Morris, 2006).

Remember if older people and their families are overly concerned with problems with retrieving information from secondary memory, they may become anxious and start to define themselves as forgetful or even as suffering from dementia. The most important aspect of memory enhancement across all ages may be the ability to relax and avoid feeling anxious or stressed during the learning stage (Verhaeghen, Geraerts, & Marcoen, 2000).

Wisdom and Creativity

Wisdom requires not only the experience, cognitive development, and self-knowledge that come with age, but also introspection, reflection, intuition, and empathy. These are qualities that we develop over many years and that can be integrated through our interactions. Younger people may have any one of these skills individually, but their integration requires more maturity. Wise individuals do not act impulsively; instead, they have the capacity for self-reflection and understanding the world in a deep manner, pulling together a wide array of information in making decisions and reflecting objectively on all viewpoints. Regardless of social class or education, an individual who has continued opportunities for growth can develop wisdom. But not all older people achieve wisdom (Baltes & Kunzmann, 2003; Baltes & Staudinger, 2000; Sternberg & Grigorenko, 2005).

Creativity refers to the ability to bring something new and valued into existence, such as applying unique solutions and coming up with original ideas or products. We generally think of creativity in terms of extraordinary products that have been created (e.g., public pieces of art by composers or painters). However, people who devise unique but smaller-scale products (e.g., an attractive garden, beautiful quilts, or a delicious meal) are also displaying creativity. As noted by the late Dr. Gene Cohen, a renowned geriatrician, "Creativity is like chocolate for the brain" (Gable, 2011, p. 18).

Creativity may increase with age as an individual becomes more self-confident, experienced, and free from social constraints—labeled as the "liberation phase" of psychological growth. Moreover, older adults with high physical and cognitive functioning use both hemispheres of the brain more equally than younger adults. This increased brain capacity, combined with feeling free from expectations of their younger years, allows older adults to express

Computer use has become widespread among older adults and can help with retrieval of information.

Improving Brainpower

The book *Brain Rules* lists 12 principles to enhance learning and memory for people of all ages. Here are some:

1. Physical exercise.
2. Seven to eight hours of sleep.
3. Reduce stress, which impairs our ability to learn.
4. Avoid multitasking because it distracts our attention, is inefficient, and causes mistakes.
5. Use emotional content rather than just plain text since the brain gets bored easily.
6. Vary content after a few minutes, since attention dwindles after about 10 minutes (Medina, 2008).

Creativity in Late Life

In *The Creative Age,* Dr. Cohen examines how creativity can expand with aging. Here are a few examples of scientists, artists, writers, and composers who produced their most innovative works in their later years.

- Sir Isaac Newton (1642–1727), the father of calculus, revised his book describing the three laws of motion at age 71 and again at age 84.
- The Renaissance painter Titian painted several masterpieces between age 78 and 83.
- Three early leaders of the women's rights movement started writing the six-volume *History of Women's Suffrage* in 1875. Elizabeth Cady Stanton was 72, Susan B. Anthony 67, and Matilda Gage 61 when the book was published.
- Grandma Moses, whose paintings hang in museums all over the world, began displaying her work at the age of 76. Even with her arthritic fingers, she continued painting until she died at 101.

their creativity in multiple ways. Indeed, Cohen argued that the term "senior moment" should refer to creative moments that increase with age, not to forgetfulness that we all experience (Cohen, 2000, 2005, 2009).

Creative activities may improve older people's physical health. People ages 65–103 who participated in a 2-year structured arts program had better physical health and fewer signs of depression, used fewer medications, reported less loneliness, and made fewer doctor visits than nonparticipants. Findings such as these motivate communities to support arts programs in senior centers and retirement housing (Baker, 2008; Cabeza, Anderson, Locantore, & McIntosh, 2002; Cohen et al., 2006).

Personality in the Later Years

To a large extent, our personalities—especially our temperament or how we react to people and situations—are relatively stable after age 30. **Personality** is a unique pattern of our innate and learned behaviors, thoughts, and emotions that influence how we interact with our environments. Essentially, it is all the qualities of who we are. An individual may be described in terms of personality traits, such as passive or aggressive, introverted or extroverted. Additionally, personality can be evaluated according to standards of behavior, for example, well-adjusted or maladapted, independent or dependent. Personality styles influence how we cope with age-associated changes that can affect our well-being.

Stage Theories of Personality

Most theories of personality emphasize developmental stages (or phases). These classical theories have significantly impacted how we think about old age and design programs for older adults. As we discuss these, keep in mind that these are not rigid, time-dependent stages with no room for individual or environmental differences. In fact, people do make choices regarding how they respond to common life changes. This then results in diverse expressions of personality during similar life stages such as retirement.

Erikson's Psychosocial Model of Personality

You may be familiar with Sigmund Freud's psychosexual stages of development that only addressed identity development through adolescence. Nevertheless, this work on earlier life phases shaped the **stage theories of personality** developed by Erikson who viewed personality as dynamic throughout the life cycle. In his model, we undergo eight stages of psychosocial development well into old age. At each stage, we experience a major task to be accomplished and a conflict to be resolved in order to proceed to the next phase. Moreover, each subsequent stage requires additional cognitive and emotional development—or what we think of as maturity. Indeed, standardized measures of personality demonstrate developmental growth in self-confidence, dependability, and identity as people age (Erikson, 1963, 1968, 1982, 1997; Erikson, Erikson, & Kivnick, 1986; Ryff, Kwan, & Singer, 2001).

Individuals in the last stage of life confront the task of **ego integrity versus despair**. This involves looking inward to integrate the experiences of earlier stages and to realize that one's life has meaning, whether or not it was "successful" in a traditional sense. Ego integrity means accepting the inevitability of death. Those who do not come to terms with their mortality may experience despair. Older people who achieve ego integrity feel a connectedness with younger generations and share their wisdom with them. **Generativity**, or the desire to help and mentor younger persons and to leave a legacy, can continue well into advanced old age, and may be the most critical component of achieving ego integrity (Cheng, 2009; James & Zarrett, 2006; Sheldon & Kasser, 2001).

But identity development is not a straightforward linear process. For example, some elders may achieve integrity of their intellectual and spiritual selves, but may not attain generativity. Nevertheless, because this process is dynamic, conflicts of an earlier stage can be resolved even as adults proceed through subsequent phases. **Life review**, a form of therapy that can help older adults attain ego integrity, is a process of sharing one's memories and experiences with others, whether orally or in writing. Life satisfaction, or the feeling that life is worth living, may also be achieved through life review (Cohen, 2005, 2009; Schachter, 2004).

points to ponder

Think about an older person you know who appears to have achieved the stage of ego integrity. What adjectives would you use to describe this individual? How would you portray your interactions with this person? Do they display behaviors that you consider generative? This might involve their giving advice or informal counseling, writing memoirs or letters, sharing oral traditions, assuming a leadership role in their community, or sponsoring a group of younger people for an event.

The stage theory of personality has been tested empirically. One such longitudinal study is the Grant Study of Harvard University Graduates involving a sample of men from the first stage of establishing a professional identity in their twenties and thirties to exploring their inner worlds in midlife—a major transition similar to Erikson's stage of ego integrity versus despair. Men who were emotionally stable and well adjusted in their fifties and sixties achieved higher levels of generativity, were less gender stereotyped in their interactions, and more nurturing and expressive as they aged (Vaillant, 1977, 1994, 2002).

Trait Theories of Personality

The Baltimore Longitudinal Study (BLS), which you learned about in Chapter 3, identified specific personality traits in the middle and later years. **Traits** are relatively stable

points to ponder

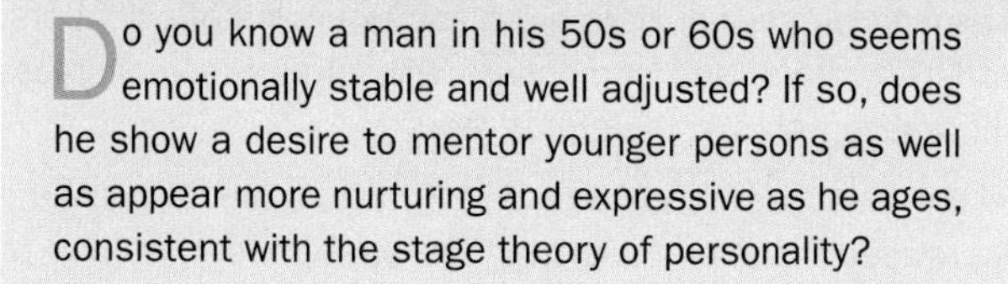

Do you know a man in his 50s or 60s who seems emotionally stable and well adjusted? If so, does he show a desire to mentor younger persons as well as appear more nurturing and expressive as he ages, consistent with the stage theory of personality?

dispositions, such as optimistic/pessimistic or extroverted/introverted, which distinguish us. Our personality traits do not change unless we make a conscious effort to do so, such as through therapeutic counseling. Costa and McCrae identified five core personality traits among BLS participants, which we all have to some degree: neuroticism, extraversion, openness to experience, agreeableness, and conscientiousness.

There seems to be some consistency between childhood and midlife on extraversion and conscientiousness. However, with aging, neuroticism generally declines, and agreeableness and conscientiousness increase and help us adapt to changes. This pattern may vary with positive or negative life events, cohort effects (later cohorts are more flexible and adaptable than earlier ones), and social and cultural values, such as gender expectations (Costa & McCrae, 1994, 1995; Hampson & Goldberg, 2006; McCrae & Terracciano, 2005; McCrae et al., 1999, 2000; McCrae et al., 2004; Terracciano, McCrae, & Costa, 2006).

Emotional Expression and Regulation

Our basic emotions—fear, anger, happiness, and shame—are hardwired, or part of our core personality. However, as we mature, our feelings often become more complex and expressed differently. For example, a young child often displays any emotion under any circumstance. By contrast, with socialization and a lifetime of experiences, older adults know how to regulate their emotional expression and anticipate others' responses. For example, they may maintain a positive emotional state by refocusing negative or angry feelings and concentrating on the good aspects of a situation. Such behavior can help them achieve and sustain meaningful interpersonal relationships. Indeed, older adults often comment that they let things "roll off their backs" more than they did when they were younger and focus on what is important in life, such as family and friends (Blanchard-Fields & Kalinauskas, 2009; Kliegel,

points to ponder

What messages did you receive from your family about the expression of emotions, such as anger or sadness? What messages does your culture convey about emotional expression? How do these affect how you interact with others? How do you think they might affect your own experience of aging?

Jager, & Phillips, 2007; Kryla-Lighthall & Mather, 2009; Kunzmann & Gruhn, 2005).

Similarly, a **positivity effect** has been found whereby elders are more likely to remember positive emotional content than negative. This suggests that as we age, our goals shift from gathering information and preparing for the future to regulating how we express our emotions and enjoying the present. This shift positively affects our well-being. On the other hand, elders tend to get more upset than younger persons about acts of injustice and suffering. A closely related concept is **socio-emotional selectivity theory (SST)**, which helps to explain an apparent paradox that elders' emotional well-being is often better than younger adults, despite losses faced. SST posits that when we are aware of our mortality and that our time is limited, we are more likely to pursue emotional satisfaction rather than focus on simply acquiring more information. Early familial and cultural expectations also influence emotional expression across the life course. Childhood messages about not sharing feelings, for example, can retain powerful meanings and need to be considered by providers' working with elders (Birditt, Fingerman, & Almeida, 2005; Carstensen, 2007a, 2007b; Carstensen, Mikels, & Mather, 2006; Charles, 2005; Charles & Carstensen, 2007; Philliips, Henry, Hosie & Milne, 2008).

Self-Concept and Self-Esteem

A major adjustment in old age is to redefine our **self-concept**—our cognitive image of the self. Our self-concept emerges from our interactions with our social environment, roles, and accomplishments. But in old age, previous roles are often lost and new roles assumed. And people confront negative stereotypes of aging. Then they have to confirm or revise these self-images. They do so either by

- assimilating new experiences or roles into their self-concept, such as community volunteer or grandparent, or
- accommodating or adjusting their self-concept to fit the new reality, such as letting go of trying to impress others with past accomplishments.

Not surprisingly, accommodation is more difficult and requires greater adaptive skills than assimilating changes (Whitbourne & Primula, 1996).

To the extent that a person's self-concept is defined independently of particular social roles, they can adapt more readily to loss of such roles. Even with declining health and loss of significant others, however, those who survive to advanced old age generally maintain some elements of their long-held identity (Diehl, Hastings, & Stanton, 2001; Maiden, Peterson, Caya, & Hayslip, 2003; Trzesniewski, Donellan, & Robins, 2003).

points to ponder

Many older persons continue to identify with roles they have lost. Think of those who continue to introduce themselves as a "doctor" long after retiring. How does a retired teacher identify himself after giving up the work that has been a central focus for the past 40 years? How does a woman whose self-concept is closely associated with her role as a wife express her identity after her husband dies?

Role losses can also negatively affect **self-esteem**, or how we feel about our identity relative to some ideal standard. Since self-esteem is based on an emotional assessment, it is more easily influenced by such external forces as widowhood, poverty, or declining health, others' reactions of respect or ostracism, and ageist stereotypes. Some older people talk about feeling invisible to others, which erodes their self-esteem or sense of the "ideal self." Not surprisingly, older people who are socially isolated, face stressful life events, or struggle with significant physical disabilities have the poorest self-esteem. In contrast, those who are actively engaged in a strong social network and participating in civic activities tend to experience a sense of personal competence. Moreover, those holding positive age stereotypes (e.g., have an optimistic view toward aging as a time of self-actualization and satisfaction) tend to be healthier and live longer (Levy, 2003; Ryff et al., 2001; Windsor, Anstey, & Rogers, 2008).

Role Loss and Its Impact on Self-Esteem

Think of an older woman whose primary role was as caregiver. If she becomes dependent on others for care, she is unwittingly robbed of this "ideal self," and her self-esteem may suffer. Or consider an older woman with a distinguished academic career who now feels ignored when she speaks in faculty meetings or walks into a room of younger colleagues. She must grapple with the loss of her ideal self as successful professional.

Maintaining an active lifestyle can enhance an older person's self-esteem and be central to successful aging.

Successful, Robust, Resilient, or Positive Aging

Researchers and clinicians are interested in ways to promote personality concepts such as successful, robust, or positive aging and resilience. Researchers know the most about **successful aging**, which is defined as a combination of physical health and functional ability, high cognitive functioning, and active involvement with society.

An older person who has aged "successfully" is characterized by

- a low risk of disease and disability, including depression;
- healthy lifestyle factors;
- actively using problem-solving, conceptualization, and language skills to foster mental stimulation;
- maintaining meaningful social contacts;
- exhibiting emotional optimism; and
- participating in activities that contribute to society (e.g., volunteering, paid or unpaid work) (Danner, Snowden, & Friesen, 2001; Rowe & Kahn, 1987, 1997, 1998).

This model is based on the MacArthur Studies of Successful Aging, a longitudinal study of adults age 70 and older, which identified the following predictors of successful aging:

- educational achievement
- involvement in strenuous physical activity
- **self-efficacy**—feeling competent to deal with new situations
- strong social supports

A closely aligned concept, **robust aging** considers exceptional functioning on measures of physical health, cognitive abilities, and emotional well-being. Robust elders are characterized by productive involvement, high physical functioning, and no cognitive impairment or depression. Even among the oldest-old, robust aging implies the ability to perform activities of daily living and actively participate in the broader community (Garfein & Herzog, 1995; Horgas, Wilms, & Baltes, 1998; Kryla-Lighthall & Mather, 2009).

You learned in the Introduction that **resilience** is the ability to endure and even thrive under difficult situations, turning adversity into a catalyst for growth and emotional well-being. Even people who have faced inequities all their lives or terrible tragedies—a child's death, a terrorist attack, or an earthquake—may be able to rebound from them. Our spiritual, family, cultural, and

points to ponder

Can you think of some problems or limitations of concept of successful aging? For example, how might it apply to low-income adults who may not have the resources to age successfully? Does it take account of the larger environment? How might anti-aging medicine misuse the concept? If you were an older woman on limited income, how might you react to being told you need to exercise more, buy healthy food and purchase new cosmetics so you can age successfully?

community capacities can protect against or moderate adversity, and enhance meaning and well-being in later life. For example, positive interpersonal relationships, strong cultural values, and a supportive community can promote a person's resilience even in the face of chronic health problems or lifelong inequities. Older adults who demonstrate this trait—by their optimism, hardiness, and avoidance of anxiety—can teach young people important survival skills (Kahn, 2003; Ryff & Singer, 2009; Ryff et al., 2001; Stix, 2011; Zarit, 2009).

Another closely related concept is **positive aging**. Men who aged "positively" in the Grant Study of Harvard Graduates, described above, were adaptable and proactive in coping with change and took life in stride. They were able to make new friends, accept the inevitability of death, and help and accept help from others. They also experienced a sense of meaning and contribution to society. These traits were expressed by a man whose closest friends and relatives had died: "Life is like a book filled with many chapters. When one chapter is finished, you must go on to the next" (Vaillant, 2002, p. 9).

In summary, the models of successful, positive, or resilient aging all draw upon evidence that personality influences how we age. Traits such as optimism, humor, adaptability to challenges, and a willingness to try new things—along with a sense of control, positive attitudes toward aging, and ability to "let go" of stress—all appear to be associated with well-being in old age. They also suggest that when we interact with older people, we can make a difference by reinforcing the more positive aspects of aging rather than slipping into ageist jokes or assumptions.

Resilience and Successful Aging

A 2012 study found that older adults who score high on resilience (e.g., the ability to adapt and persevere in the face of hardship) and do not suffer from depression also report high rates of "successful aging" or well-being, even in the face of declining physical and/or cognitive functioning. In fact, this pattern increased with age. It concluded that perfect physical health is neither necessary nor sufficient for successful aging. Clinical interventions to promote resilience and reduce depression may have effects on promoting successful aging as strong as that of reducing disability (Jeste et al., 2013).

For some elders, teaching young and old to dance is a sign of active and robust aging.

Mental Disorders among Older Persons

You have just learned how normal psychological development with aging includes relatively minor changes in intelligence, learning, and memory; overall stability in personality traits; and a progression through different developmental stages. The majority of older adults experience such changes without major disruptions in their behavior or mental health. In fact, older people have a lower prevalence of mental disorders than do younger age groups. Furthermore, most of these were chronic conditions across the life course, not due to aging per se (Institute of Medicine, 2012; Zarit, 2009).

Nevertheless, some people who showed no signs of psychological problems earlier in their lives may experience mental disorders for the first time in late life. For others, psychiatric disorders experienced in their younger years may reemerge. The stresses and losses of old age may compound any existing predisposition to psychological disorders. Moreover, mental disorders may be more difficult to diagnose among older people due to other illnesses, normal age-associated physiological changes, or impaired cognitive and sensory functions. Of concern, however, is that less than 25 percent of older adults who need mental health services ever receive adequate treatment. This is due in part to a shortage of geriatric mental health professionals and lower rates of reimbursement in the past for mental health services under Medicare and Medicaid (Garrido, Kane, Kaas, & Kane, 2011; Institute of Medicine, 2012).

Depression

Depression is the most frequently diagnosed mental disorder among older adults and is an indicator of general well-being, since people who report depressive symptoms often report higher rates of physical illness, greater functional disability, and higher utilization of health services (Federal Interagency Forum, 2012).

Estimates of the incidence of depression, as distinct from depressive symptoms, vary widely, in part because certain symptoms may be expressed differently in older adults. In 2010, 3–4.5 percent of community-living older adults had some type of depressive disorder.

Unipolar depression, the most common, includes the following:

- Minor or reactive depression occurs in response to a significant negative life event—life-threatening illness, disability, or death of a loved one. It tends to be short-term, but can nevertheless reduce quality of life. Symptoms include loneliness and loss of interest in the environment and social activities, neglect of self-care, changes in eating and sleeping patterns, and feelings of emptiness, anxiety, or panic for no apparent cause.
- Major depressive disorders persist beyond six months, are likely to have originated earlier in life, and are diagnosed in a very small percent of older adults living in the community. In contrast, nearly 50 percent of skilled nursing home residents suffer from major depressive episodes. While some symptoms, such as apathy and fatigue, are similar to minor depression, the primary difference is that symptoms are present most of the day, nearly every day for at least two weeks, and represent a major change from previous function. Other symptoms include feelings of self-blame, guilt, and worthlessness; agitation; significant weight change; poor concentration; and recurrent thoughts of death or suicide.

Bipolar depression—ranging from a depressed to a manic state—occurs in less than 0.1 percent of the older population in the community but increases among skilled nursing home residents (Adams & Moon, 2009; Hybels & Blazer, 2003; Institute of Medicine, 2012; Zalaquett & Stens, 2006).

It is important to remember that sadness, grief in response to loss, and temporary "blue" moods are normal. But persistent depression that interferes significantly with the ability to function is not.

Risk Factors for Depression Rates of depression are highest among certain groups: older women; the oldest-old; elders with serious chronic diseases or dementia, which may be due to factors such as social isolation and comorbidity; and those in hospitals or skilled nursing facilities (Health and Retirement Study, 2008; Marcantonio & Rabinowitz, 2003; Morrow-Howell et al., 2008).

We know less about depression among elders of color, in part because of problems with diagnosis and treatment or variation within racial groups. It is known that the prevalence of depression is generally higher for Chinese Americans than for Filipino and Vietnamese Americans. And rates are generally higher for older Asian Americans born in the United States than those born outside the country. Within the Latino population, the incidence of depression is higher for Cuban Americans and Puerto Ricans than for Mexican Americans. Another barrier to diagnosis is when some racial and ethnic groups view depression as a "personal weakness" or shameful. Some Asian American elders, for example, attach a stigma to mental illness—viewing depression as "thinking too much"—and are less likely to seek professional help and therefore to be diagnosed. Health professionals need to be attentive to structural barriers, cultural beliefs, and styles of coping with depression so they can accurately diagnose and treat it in elders of color (Adams & Roberts, 2010; Aranda, Lee, & Wilson, 2001; Das, Olfson, McCurtis, & Weissman, 2006; Institute of Medicine, 2012; Lawrence et al., 2006; Mills, Alea, & Cheong, 2004; Mui & Kang, 2006; Surgeon General, 2011).

Diagnosing Depression Grief may put an older person at risk of minor depression, but also make diagnosis difficult since symptoms of grief and depression overlap. Frank's situation (in box on next page) highlights some difficulties of diagnosing depression.

Risk Factors for Depression

- Being female
- Prior history of depression
- Being unmarried or living alone
- Comorbidity and difficulty performing ADLs
- Inadequate social supports
- Multiple role losses, including chronic financial strain (Barg et al., 2006; Gayman, Turner, & Cui, 2008; Mitchell & Subramaniam, 2005).

Is This Depression?

Frank, a 75-year-old African American, lost his wife, Sarah, of 40 years to a sudden heart attack 3 years ago. She was cooking dinner when she fell to the floor. Frank called 911 and tried to resuscitate Sarah, but the EMT said she died instantly.

Reserved his whole life, Frank didn't show much emotion at Sarah's funeral. He initially found comfort in his church and the close friends he played cards with. Although his four children and six grandchildren lived out of state, they kept in touch and visited as often as possible. While he put on a strong public exterior, Frank was devastated. He could not stop thinking about her and shake his despair. He blamed himself for not being able to save Sarah. Maybe he should have encouraged her to relax more, retire sooner, or go to the doctor when she complained of pain in her arms and chest. Yet he was ashamed of himself for still missing his wife and not being stronger. He lost interest in cooking and taking care of the house, but he did it anyway as if on autopilot. He felt empty and alone. He avoided his friends because he felt even lonelier with other couples.

Recently, Frank developed vision problems and painful nerve damage due to his diabetes, and had to stop driving. His house is a couple of miles from town—too far for him to walk. Since Frank does not like asking people for help with rides, he rarely goes out, spending most of his time dozing in front of the TV. He feels tired all the time and has trouble concentrating and sleeping at night. When his kids call, they worry about his flat affect and lack of energy. He has begun to have a couple of glasses of wine to help him sleep at night. Overall, Frank feels useless and stuck. Tears keep welling up in his eyes, and the recurring thought in his head is: "It just was not supposed to be this way."

Older adults may complain of vague aches, pains, and sleep disturbances that health care providers assume are "just part of aging," or are associated with medications that have a depressant effect on the central nervous system, or are other illnesses. Additionally, elders may hide symptoms from health care providers, fearful that memory problems caused by depression are a sign of dementia. On the other hand, some chronic illnesses, such as rheumatoid arthritis or Parkinson's disease, may be the cause of depressive symptoms and should be treated. All of these possibilities point to the importance of a thorough physical exam and tests to assess for depression. Since there are differences in how depression is exhibited by older people compared to the young, standardized rating scales have been developed for assessing its presence and severity in elders such as the Geriatric Depression Scale (GDS), Beck Depression Inventory (BDI), and the Hamilton Rating Scale for Depression (HAM-D) (Adams & Moon, 2008; Blazer, 2003; Dunlop et al., 2005).

Therapeutic Interventions If older adults do seek help for depressive symptoms, they typically turn to their primary care doctor. This stems in part from their reluctance to admit they need to see a mental health professional and from the fact that the number of geriatric mental health specialists is limited (Hasche, Morrow-Howell, & Proctor, 2010).

Pharmacological interventions—use of antidepressant medications—are the most common. Although antidepressants work well for some older persons, many cannot use them because of other medications or detrimental side effects. Fortunately, combinations of well-monitored medications and counseling have been found to be effective, even in the oldest-old, as illustrated by Mrs. Simon in the box below (Frazer, Christensen, & Griffiths, 2005; Gellis & McCracken, 2008; Reynolds et al., 2006).

Family members or professionals may assume that older people are "too old" for counseling. But they are just as likely as younger persons to benefit from therapy. Benefits are greatest from short-term, client-centered, and problem-solving directive therapy rather than nondirective psychoanalytical therapy. Brief descriptions of effective therapies are on the next page.

Can an Older Person Benefit from Therapy?

In the six months since the death of her husband of 52 years, Mrs. Simon has lost interest in all the activities that the two of them enjoyed together. Her weight loss, complaints of poor memory, and declines in energy have alarmed her adult children. They insisted she see her family physician, who prescribed an antidepressant. However, Mrs. Simon stopped taking these after two weeks because they made her dizzy and caused dry mouth. The physician spent time with her discussing the benefits from medications, but also arranged for Mrs. Simon to participate in cognitive-behavioral therapy with a geriatric mental health practitioner. After two months, Mrs. Simon has already seen the benefits of the combined therapies. She now attends a local senior center and has begun a regular exercise program of walking an hour every day and developing new friendships.

Evidence-based Therapy for Minor Depression

The Program to Encourage Active, Rewarding Lives for Seniors (PEARLS) is an innovative evidence-based therapy for older adults with minor depression. Using structured behavior therapy and positive event scheduling, it consists of six to eight in-home visits by a counselor over six to eight months. With their counselors, PEARLS clients develop and evaluate solutions to their depression. It has eliminated depression completely for about 33 percent of participants, reduced depressive symptoms by half in another 43 percent, and lowered hospitalization rates (www.cdc.gov/prc/prevention).

Reminiscence therapy can help work through difficult memories and process loss and grief (Bohlmeijer, Smit, & Cuijpers, 2003; Cully, LaVoie, & Gfeller, 2001; Zarit, 2009).

Cognitive-behavioral interventions (CBIs) use active, time-limited approaches to change negative thoughts and behaviors, such as self-monitoring and increased participation in pleasant events (Frazer, Christensen, & Griffiths, 2005; Zalaquett & Stens, 2006).

Problem-solving therapy, one type of cognitive-behavioral therapy, teaches goal-setting and effective coping techniques, and is found to be especially effective for elders of color. Motivational interviewing helps elders set short-term goals they feel they can achieve (Gellis & McCracken, 2008; Gellis, Mcginty, Horowitz, Bruce, & Misener, 2007; Institute of Medicine, 2012).

Suicide

Depression is the primary cause of **suicide** in older adults. We often hear about suicide among adolescents, but you may be surprised to learn that suicide rates among elders are about 50 percent higher than for younger groups or the population as a whole. Moreover, the actual suicide rate may be even higher than the statistics. This is because there are probably a significant number of indirect suicides that appear to be accidents or natural deaths (e.g., starvation or gas poisoning), and cases where suicide is not listed as the cause of death (Dombrovski et al., 2008; Fiske, Wetherell, & Gatz, 2009; NIMH, 2011).

The highest suicide rates are among white males who are widowed, age 85 and older, with recurrent major depression, chronic pain, cardiopulmonary diseases, and cancer, or who may abuse drugs and alcohol. Not surprisingly, rates are more than five times greater for widowers than for married men, perhaps due to loss of social roles and support. Suicide rates among American Indian males are the second highest. In contrast, African American, Latino, and Chinese American men are less likely to commit suicide, perhaps because of more extensive family supports, spiritual beliefs, and the centrality of religion in their lives. Although suicide rates peak for African Americans in young adulthood, they then decline significantly, with older blacks having the lowest suicide rate of all older adults (Gellis & McCracken, 2008; Institute of Medicine, 2012).

Older men are more likely to complete a suicide, often by shotguns, than younger men. Given this high completion rate, family members and health care providers need to take seriously signs of a contemplated suicide and seek professional help. It is striking that about 75 percent of older persons who commit suicide had seen a primary care physician in the preceding month, but their distress was not detected or adequately treated. Watching for subtle cues is important, because older people are less likely to threaten or announce their intentions of suicide than are young people (NIMH, 2011).

Anxiety

Anxiety disorders are almost as common in later life as depression. About 4.3 percent of older adults living in the community have symptoms of anxiety. Similar to depression, rates are higher among skilled nursing home residents,

Signs That an Older Adult May Consider Suicide

- A serious physical illness with severe pain
- The sudden death of a loved one
- A major loss of independence
- Financial instability
- Persistent depression
- Statements that indicate frustration with life and a desire to end it
- A sudden decision to give away one's most important possessions
- A general loss of interest in one's environment
- Isolation and feeling cut off from others

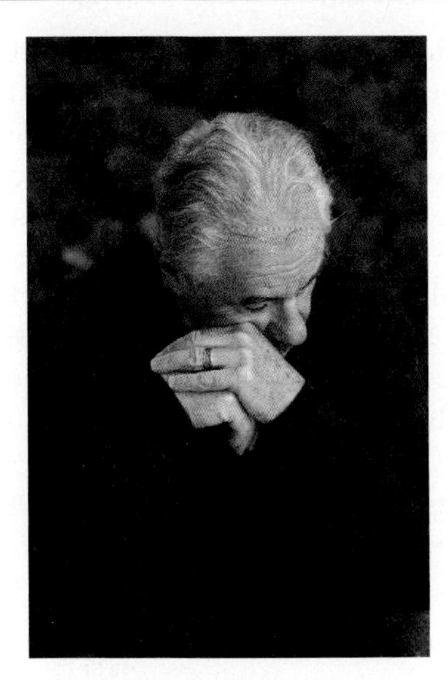

Untreated depression in older men is a risk factor for suicide.

and there are problems with diagnosis, since elders tend to minimize or underreport anxiety symptoms. Anxiety disorders are often masked by physical health complaints, symptoms with no known medical cause, behavior changes, symptoms of depression, and other medical conditions such as dementia. Because of this, health care providers must probe further when older patients complain of diffuse pain, fast or irregular heart rate, fatigue, sleep disturbance, and restlessness. Another complicating factor is that up to 25 percent of elders with anxiety also have major depression. In such instances, patients may respond poorly to depression treatment, and their medical conditions and disabilities may worsen. They may have more thoughts of suicide, become socially isolated, and experience less life satisfaction (Institute of Medicine, 2012; Jeste, Hays, & Steffens, 2006; O'Donnell & Kaszniak, 2011; Zarit, 2009).

Older people with anxiety can benefit from cognitive-behavioral therapy, relaxation training, psychosocial support, and, in some cases, medications. Learning more effective problem-solving skills and memory aids help reduce anxiety symptoms in older persons better than supportive counseling and medication (Gellis & McCracken, 2008; O'Donnell & Kaszniak, 2011).

Paranoia and Schizophrenia

Paranoia, defined as an irrational suspiciousness of other people, may result from social isolation, a sense of powerlessness, a steady decline in sensory abilities, memory loss, and problems with managing day-to-day activities.

It is important to distinguish actual threats from unfounded suspicions. Some suspicious attitudes represent accurate readings of elders' experiences. For example, an older person's children may in fact be trying to move her to a long-term care facility or a nurse's aide may be stealing from an older patient. Elders' perception of a threatening situation is reduced if they feel some control over their environment. Cognitive-behavioral therapy, in which an individual focuses on changing negative self-defeating misconceptions, may be useful in redirecting an individual's beliefs about causes of losses (e.g., recognizing that she misplaced her purse rather than believing that someone took it).

Schizophrenia is less prevalent than other mental disorders in old age; less than 1 percent of elders are diagnosed with schizophrenia. In general, older schizophrenics were first diagnosed in adolescence or middle age, but the severity of symptoms appears to decrease with age. Older schizophrenics are less likely to display thought disorders, loss of emotional expression, and problems with learning and abstraction that we see in young adults with this condition, and more likely to experience cognitive decline, depression, and social isolation (Harvey, 2005; Institute of Medicine, 2012).

Schizophrenics of any age, but especially older adults, need to have their medication regimens monitored and live in structured environments. However, many are unable to manage their medications or discontinue them because of adverse side effects. This often results in repeat hospitalizations and emergency room visits. Many older schizophrenics have lost contact with families and lack social supports. Fortunately, cognitive-behavioral treatment, social skills training, and health management techniques can improve an older schizophrenic's social functioning and independent living skills (Gilmer et al., 2009; Patterson et al., 2005; Van Citters, Pratt, Bartels, & Jeste, 2005).

Older Adults Who Are Chronically or Severely Mentally Ill

You may have seen an older person wandering on the streets who appears chronically mentally ill. The social disruption and years of treatment with psychotropic drugs have taken their toll; many chronically ill are physiologically old in their fifties and sixties and look much older

Confusion and loneliness may beleaguer homeless chronically ill elders without support systems.

than they are. When you see such persons on the streets, be sensitive to how they may have ended up there.

- They may have suffered mental or emotional disorders throughout life that impair their activities of daily living, self-direction, and social interactions. They are likely to have been in and out of hospitals and emergency rooms as their health has deteriorated.
- They may have survived major upheavals and social neglect, including substance abuse, and traumas such as war or interpersonal violence (Crane & Warnes, 2010; Sermons & Henry, 2010).

Chronically mentally ill elders' average life expectancy is estimated to be 25 years less than their healthy peers, often due to cardiovascular disease. Moreover, they may have trouble obtaining medical care because providers may attribute their physical symptoms to their psychiatric disorders. Health professionals need to perform a thorough exam to distinguish conditions caused by mental illness and to treat any systemic diseases. Unfortunately, the plight of chronically mentally ill elders—who are estimated to form 3–4.8 percent of the older population—has not been adequately addressed by mental health providers and advocates, typically because of limited funds (Institute of Medicine, 2012; O'Connell, 2005).

Dementia

Although we may think—or fear—that just about every older adult suffers from dementia, the majority do not. As you learned earlier, mild cognitive impairments do not necessarily signal a major loss, or mean that dementia is inevitable. However, over 3 million elders have problems with ADLs due to dementia, requiring help from family and eventually paid caregivers.

We tend to hear the most about Alzheimer's disease (AD). But **dementia** includes a variety of conditions caused by or associated with damage of brain tissue. What they have in common is a marked deterioration in cognitive function and problems with at least one of the following abilities:

- Speaking coherently or understanding language
- Recognizing or identifying objects
- Carrying out and comprehending tasks
- Recalling events in recent memory
- Paying attention
- Orientation to time, place, and person
- Understanding symbolic language (e.g., unable to interpret a proverb)
- Thinking abstractly and performing executive functions
- Showing good judgment

Although not every older adult will suffer from dementia, all types of dementia do increase with age. While about 11 percent of adults age 65 and older have AD, over 32 percent of those age 85 and older show AD symptoms, as shown in Figure 4.1. Indeed, every 68 seconds someone in the United States develops AD (Alzheimer's Association, 2013c; DeFries, McGuire, Andresen, Brumback, & Anderson, 2009).

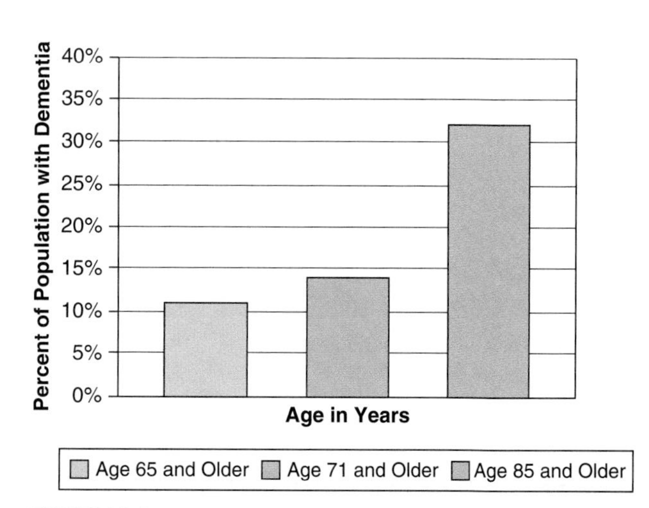

FIGURE 4.1 Increase of Dementia with Age

Source: Alzheimer's Association, 2013c

Reversible and Irreversible Causes of Dementia Some dementias are reversible and can be "cured." They are caused by reactions to medications, alcohol, hormonal or nutritional problems, infections, thyroid problems, depression, diabetes, or other diseases. **Irreversible dementias**, such as Alzheimer's or vascular dementia, have no discernible environmental cause and cannot yet be cured. It is essential that health care providers and families differentiate between reversible and irreversible causes to determine how best to respond.

Our focus here is on Alzheimer's disease (AD), because it accounts for 50–80 percent of all dementias (Alzheimer's Association, 2013a).

Alzheimer's Disease (AD) You probably have heard older adults worrying they have **Alzheimer's disease (AD)**, particularly whenever they forget something. Their fears are often grounded in some striking statistics, which may also explain why the general public is more aware of AD compared to other types of dementia.

- One out of eight Americans—approximately 5.2 million—have symptoms of AD.
- Another American developing AD will increase to one every 33 seconds in 2050, when 11–16 million of us will be diagnosed with AD. Moreover, rates worldwide are nearly doubling every 20 years to an estimated 65.7 million in 2030, and 115.4 million in 2050.
- AD, the sixth leading cause of death for older adults, is the only cause without a way to prevent, cure, or significantly slow its progression. As a result, deaths from AD are increasing, while deaths from other major diseases decline. One in three older adults dies with AD or another dementia (Anderson, Day, Beard, Reed, & Wu, 2009; Alzheimer's Association, 2013a; Alzheimer's Disease International, 2013).

points to ponder

If you had a history of some types of dementia in your family and you could afford a genetic test to predict the likelihood that you may develop this same condition 10–30 years later, would you want to be tested? How would you change your life, if at all, if you knew you were likely to develop dementia?

Early Onset AD: Missing One's Life

Ken, once a distinguished psychiatrist at a highly regarded medical school, was diagnosed with AD at age 47. For someone who has valued the life of the mind throughout his career, the loss of common words and the ability to communicate about his work can be especially poignant. At a phase in his life when he had planned to be at the peak of his career, he laments how he cannot understand a textbook that he authored when he was 35 or how his colleagues no longer ask his opinion, often avoiding him in the hallways at work. Although it is vitally important for him to keep meeting with his students and research team as long as possible, he realizes that he is no longer confident in his teaching and that conveying his ideas is really hard work. Sometimes, he can see his students and staff avoid his gaze when he misses a word or can't convey his thoughts. He misses being curious, creative, and independent, being part of what's happening, and most of all feeling wanted. He tells those who love him how much he misses his life.

Late-onset AD is most common, but there is also a rarer, early-onset form—familial AD—that appears in multiple generations of the same family, usually in early middle age. Although this represents only a small proportion of AD, it is of concern since the rate of decline among those with early-onset AD is faster and their lives and those of their families are often more severely affected. With about 5 percent of all cases occurring in persons younger than 65, the Alzheimer's Association now offers support groups for young children whose parents have been diagnosed with early AD (Alzheimer's Association, 2012).

Differentiating AD from Normal Age-Related Memory Changes Since the most common initial symptom is a gradual decline in short-term memory, many people assume they are showing signs of AD when they forget where they left their keys or parked the car. But as you learned from our discussion of cognitive changes, these types of forgetfulness are experienced by all age groups. Table 4-1 below highlights some major differences.

Potential Causes of and Risk Factors for Alzheimer's Disease There are numerous explanations of the causes of AD. Here are a few of them. There is no support for environmental causes, such as exposure to radiation, anesthesia, or aluminum. AD may be connected to inflammatory processes associated with aging that result

TABLE 4.1 Differentiating AD from Normal Age-Related Memory Changes

Normal Aging	Possible AD
Forgetting to set the alarm clock	Forgetting how to set the alarm clock
Forgetting someone's name and remembering it later	Forgetting a name and never remembering it, even when told repeatedly
Forgetting where you left your keys and finding them after searching	Forgetting places where you might find your keys
Losing things from time to time	Misplacing things and being unable to retrace steps to find them
Having to retrace steps to remember a task	Forgetting how you came to be at a particular location
Forgetting where you parked your car	Forgetting that you drove and parked car
Making occasional errors when balancing a checkbook	Inability to follow a plan or work with numbers
Sometimes having trouble finding the right word	Trouble following or joining a conversation; stopping in the middle of a conversation and having no idea how to continue
Forgetting which day it is and remembering it later	Losing track of the date or season

Source: Adapted from The Alzheimer's Association, 2014, Know the signs, from http://www.alz.org/alzheimers_disease_10_signs_of_alzheimers.asp

We All May Have a Little Bit of Alzheimer's

After 16 years of studying the brains of thousands of older people who showed no cognitive problems when they were alive, Dr. David Bennett, Rush University Medical Center, concludes that just as everybody has a little bit of heart disease after a certain age, many people have a little bit of Alzheimer's as diagnosed by their brain autopsies. But most people are able to tolerate this because of what is called cognitive reserve—extra brain capacity that compensates for whatever damage is occurring. Autopsies of centenarians show similar findings. The amount of cognitive reserve we have is in part due to our genes. Other factors also come into play. People who are able to tolerate such Alzheimer's-like brain damage tend to have a purpose in life, strong social networks, and stimulating activities. Rather than worrying about memory lapses, these researchers suggest that a better use of time would be to have an active social life and exercise (Knox, 2011).

in amyloid, a hard protein deposit, which when it clumps together builds up in toxic forms and damages nerve cell connections so that cells ultimately die. Other research points to chemical changes that result in age-related loss of dopamine, the brain chemical associated with pleasure. There is also research on genetic factors, and AD is more common among persons with Down syndrome. Strokes can accelerate the decline of cognitive function, and severe head injury during one's younger years may be a risk factor. Low estrogen levels may increase the risk of AD, and obesity is a risk factor for women, but not for men. And some research points to a positive correlation between recurring episodes of depression and risk for dementia. But what is most promising is the growing body of evidence related to the role of lifestyle factors (Brodaty, Withall, Altendorf, & Sachdev, 2007; DeCarli, 2006; Dotson, Beydoun, & Zonderman, 2010; Finch, 2007; Mrak & Griffin, 2004; Plassman et al., 2000).

The more intellectual activities pursued in middle age—learning a new language, taking challenging courses, or mastering a new skill—the lower a person's probability of AD, regardless of educational level, gender, and current age. Regular exercise—walking, swimming, weight training, and stretching—three or more times a week has numerous benefits, perhaps because it stimulates blood flow to the brain. The Swedish Twin Registry revealed that light exercise and participation in sports during middle age were associated with significantly lower rates of dementia in participants age 70 and older, even when twins were compared. In another study, participants with poor standing balance, slower walking speed, and weak handgrip were three times more likely to develop dementia than elders with good physical functioning (Andel et al., 2008; Etgen et al., 2010; Fitzpatrick et al., 2007; Friedland et al., 2000; Larson et al., 2006; Laurin, Verreault, Lindsay, Mactherson, & Rockwood, 2001; Liu-Ambrose et al., 2010; Podewils et al., 2005).

The Importance of a Thorough Diagnosis The most confirmatory diagnosis of Alzheimer's disease today can still be made only at autopsy, when the areas and nature of damaged brain tissue can be identified. However, psychological measures of cognitive functioning and a

Regular aerobic exercise may reduce the risk of AD.

Diagnosing Alzheimer's Disease

- A medical and nutritional history
- Laboratory tests, including tests for thyroid function
- In some cases, a CT (computerized tomography) scan, a PET (positron emission tomography) scan, or MRI (magnetic resonance imaging) to detect any tumors, strokes, or blood clots, and to test the response of specific areas of the brain
- Standardized tests of cognitive functioning, such as the Mini-Mental State Exam (MMSE), the Dementia Rating Scale (DRS), and the Blessed Dementia Index (Agronin, 2008; Alzheimer's Disease, 2013b; Folstein, Folstein, & McHugh, 1975)

thorough physical and neurological exam can provide clues to its existence in earlier stages, as noted in the box above. Or they may indicate that the observed changes in behavior or personality are due to a reversible condition. In fact, it is primarily by eliminating the possibility of other conditions that AD may be diagnosed. Another essential consideration when dementia is assessed is to provide support to families, since about 70 percent of all people with AD are cared for by relatives. A husband who had cared for his wife for 12 years poignantly states, "we have Alzheimer's."

The Nun Study

The Nun Study offers insights into the association between education, lifestyle, and cognitive and physical aging without the bias of socioeconomic status, diet, and health care that can occur with studies among the general population. Since the 678 members of the School Sisters of Notre Dame shared an adulthood of identical lifestyles, any differences among them are due mostly to their educational levels and intellectual and physical activities throughout their lives. By analyzing the autobiographies these nuns had written at age 22, researchers found an association between linguistic skills in youth and the risk of dementia 50–70 years later. Greater atrophy and more plaques and tangles were found in the brains of women whose writings during their youth had fewer complex ideas, a simpler vocabulary, fewer positive emotions expressed, and lower "idea density." Another surprising finding is many nuns at autopsy had the hallmarks of advanced AD in their brain samples, but they did not demonstrate any clinical symptoms of dementia before their death (Snowdon, 2001, 2003; Snowdon, Greiner, & Markesbery, 2000).

Fortunately, an increasing number of programs assess caregivers' needs for services as well as those of the person with AD (Sanders, Ott, Kellber, & Noonan, 2007).

Stages of Alzheimer's Disease Upon learning the diagnosis of AD, the person and their families often want to know exactly what lies ahead and how much time they have before they cannot remember anything. Unfortunately, there are no clear guidelines. Some research posits that AD proceeds through a series of stages, with symptoms becoming more prevalent and severe over time. But these stages are only approximations. Some persons with AD may show a rapid decline in memory, while their orientation to time, place, and people remains relatively intact. Others may experience mood and personality changes early, whereas still others maintain their pre-AD personality for years. Most people survive 4–8 years after a diagnosis, but a few live as long as 20 years. On average, 40 percent of a person's years with AD are spent in the most severe stage of the disease, which is the most stressful for caregivers—longer than any other stage (Alzheimer's Association, 2013b; Mayo Clinic, 2010; Xie, 2008).

A broad distinction is often made among early, middle, and advanced stages. Here are symptoms typical of these stages, but remember that variations exist.

Early stages (very mild decline):

- Difficulty in remembering new information—names, familiar words, or location of everyday objects
- Confusion as to time and place
- New problems with words in speaking or writing
- Misplacing things and losing the ability to retrace steps

The Experience of Dementia

A daughter captures the personhood of her father's dementia:

> His memory is blank; words float by him in a soup. He can't button a shirt or negotiate a toilet. Yet when I look at him—at his body, his face—I see ... him. Warm, enraged, rejecting, beseeching, profane, silly; much of his mind is gone, but his self is still there ... There may be no drug (yet) to cure Alzheimer's but relationships are always possible, as long as the person of sounder mind holds up his or her end (Levine, 2004).

- Difficulties with planning, organizing, and performing tasks and solving problems
- Decreased or poor judgment
- Changes in mood (symptoms of depression) and personality

Intermediate stages (moderate decline):

- Forgetfulness of recent events and of one's personal history, although a person may be able to describe vividly events from years ago
- Difficulty performing complex tasks—such as paying bills or planning dinner for guests
- Moodiness or withdrawal from social activities
- Inability to perform challenging mental arithmetic, such as counting backward from 100 by sevens
- Needing help with daily activities

Late stage (severe decline):

- Repeating same phrases and thoughts
- Losing awareness of recent experiences and surroundings
- Inability to recognize partners, children, and longtime friends
- Dramatically disrupted sleep patterns
- Major personality changes such as becoming more aggressive, suspicious, or delusional
- Needing help dressing, toileting, bathing
- Trouble controlling bladder or bowels
- Wandering or becoming lost
- Experiencing agitation—irritable behavior, pacing, and restlessness (Alzheimer's Association, 2013b; Snowdon, 2001)

Drug Therapy Only a few drugs have been approved for treating AD. Aricept and Namenda, the most widely used, have been found to slow the decline of memory loss and even to show modest improvements in cognition and daily behavior for up to 36 months. These medications also help to manage behavioral problems, such as agitation, delusions, aggressiveness, and wandering in the later stages. More recently, the Exelon Patch was found to improve ability to engage in reading, finding personal belongings, and keeping appointments. However, no drug reverses the destruction of brain tissue by plaques and tangles, and all of these must be used with caution, because of possible side effects. Some scientists now argue that drug treatment should start earlier when an individual shows the first symptoms of the disease. In fact, some researchers have tested drugs with young members of extended families with an inherited genetic mutation associated with dementia. Eventually these young people may be candidates for drugs that prevent the buildup of high levels of beta-amyloid and other abnormal proteins that are linked to dementia. A possible vaccine may eventually help the immune system produce antibodies against amyloid proteins and clear such deposits from the brain. Some people try vitamin supplements and anti-inflammatory drugs such as ibuprofen to prevent AD but results are mixed (NIA, 2011; Roan, 2010; Seltzer, 2006; Zandi et al., 2004).

Behavioral Treatment and Environmental Interventions Although no treatments can restore the cognitive loss resulting from Alzheimer's disease, there are benefits for symptom management by behavioral and exercise therapies and environmental modifications. For example, AD patients in a three-month exercise program had significantly fewer days of restricted activity, lower scores on a measure of depression, and less likelihood of nursing home placement up to 2 years later. These interventions appear to be most effective in the early to intermediate stages and slow the rate of deterioration (Teri et al., 2003).

The creation of dementia-friendly communities is a positive development in some areas, beginning in Great Britain, toward including and supporting persons with dementia and their families in a wide array of community activities to promote their autonomy and quality of life. These include accessible activities, such as visual arts, music and theater programs, and community cafes and easy-to-navigate environments. People with dementia are empowered to have aspirations and feel confident, knowing they can contribute and participate in activities that are meaningful to them. Fortunately, there are growing numbers of initiatives focused on the inclusion of people with AD in organizations and communities (Alzheimer's Society United Kingdom, 2013). Here are examples of other interventions for both the person with AD and their caregivers that can be implemented in home and long-term care settings.

Early to Moderate Stages of Dementia

- Maintain routines, written schedules of activities, simplified routes from room to room, and written directions for cooking, bathing, and taking medications.
- Encourage physical activity, which can help with sleep at night, and social interactions.
- Set up an orientation area in the home where the patient's critical items (e.g., wallet, keys, and glasses) can always be found.
- Put labels on doors and drawers.
- Keep in visible areas photos of family and close friends, with names clearly written on them.
- Keep grooming supplies (e.g., toothbrush, toothpaste, comb) visible and in a familiar sequence of use.
- Create a "memory box" with photos and mementos.
- Promote productive activities such as setting the table, folding laundry, and raking leaves.
- Use ID bracelets with alarms. The Alzheimer's Association offers the "safe return" program, which provides ID bracelets, maintains records, and assists emergency teams in locating a person with AD who is lost (Alzheimer's Association, 2013b; Riemersma-Van der lek et al., 2008).

Advanced Stages of Dementia

- Simplify daily routines but still encourage physical activity (e.g., walks in fenced-in yard).
- Try alternative means of communication (e.g., touch, music, sharing family photos).
- Maintain bright, even lighting throughout the day and at meals and avoid glare to prevent **sundowning**, a confused state when persons with AD become fatigued later in the day when natural light levels are lower.
- Turn to long-term services and supports that offer safety and social stimulation: adult day health care, adult family homes, and special memory units of long-term care facilities.

National Plan to Address Alzheimer's Disease

In 2012, President Obama announced a comprehensive plan to prevent and effectively treat Alzheimer's disease in the United States by 2025. This includes extensive research, clinical trials, public education, supports for caregivers, and training for health care providers with competencies to work effectively with persons with AD. The clock is ticking on not only finding a cure but perhaps more importantly improving the care.

Parkinson's Disease Although not a form of dementia, **Parkinson's disease** can display similar symptoms in its later stages. It is a neurodegenerative disorder that begins as a loss of muscle control and impaired balance and coordination, with tremors in the feet and hands. Speech can become impaired, muscles rigid, and the person moves slowly and with a shuffling gait. About 1 million adults have this condition, projected to double by 2040. It usually strikes people over age 60, although some people—such as the actor Michael J. Fox—are first diagnosed in their thirties (American Parkinson's Disease Association, 2012).

Some drugs and deep-brain stimulation help persons with Parkinson's. A promising research area is the possibility of implanting stem cells into the brain, which may revitalize damaged regions. Behavioral techniques such as meditation, biofeedback, and dietary modification are also recommended. The Parkinson's Association is a good source to learn about the latest treatments for this disease and techniques to improve mobility and safety, digestion and bladder problems, and communication, sleep, and mood changes (Lozano & Kalia, 2005).

Substance Use

Alcoholism and **drug abuse** are two other mental health conditions that practitioners need to screen for among older adults.

Alcoholism Only about 50 percent of older people drink alcohol. When they do, it is typically associated with socializing and occurs in moderation (i.e., less than once a week, and no more than two drinks each time). In fact, moderate alcohol consumption (averaging one glass per

When Social Drinking Becomes a Problem

Mrs. Cortez, a 73-year-old Mexican American, was diagnosed with type II diabetes several years ago. Although prescribed medication to regulate her blood sugar, she feels the medication and diabetes testing supplies are too expensive, even with her Medicare benefits. Instead, Mrs. Cortez prefers to use herbal remedies such as aloe vera and cactus to keep her blood sugar in check. Mrs. Cortez's five children have grown concerned that their mother is showing signs of increased physical decline, confusion, and poor memory. They are upset that their mother's once well-kept house is in disarray and that she is no longer concerned about her personal hygiene.

Mrs. Cortez's oldest daughter became alarmed when she was unable to reach her mother by phone one evening. The daughter called Mrs. Cortez's neighbor, who has a key to the house for emergencies. The neighbor found Mrs. Cortez on the floor and immediately called an ambulance. She was confused, uncharacteristically irritable and sweating, and her speech was slurred. When the neighbor bent down to check on Mrs. Cortez, she thought she noticed the smell of alcohol. But the neighbor, who has known her for 20 years, thought she must be mistaken because she has only seen Mrs. Cortez consume alcohol on special occasions such as baptisms or wedding receptions, and, even then, only a sip or two. The emergency medical personnel, aware of the gravity of Mrs. Cortez's condition, rushed her to the hospital. They also recognized the fruity smell on her breath but knew it could be due to either alcohol or a medical condition.

Mrs. Cortez was admitted to the hospital for a dangerous diabetic condition that can lead to coma or death due to excessively high blood sugar levels. Her blood alcohol level was 0.08. When interviewed by hospital staff, she denied any abuse of alcohol and medications, but did admit taking aloe vera. She told the social worker that she often felt lonely but did not want to bother her children busy with their jobs and families. The social worker discussed the ways Mrs. Cortez could attend to her diabetes, including ways consistent with her culture, and gently stressed the need for a diet appropriate for a diabetic and avoiding alcohol.

Mrs. Cortez felt badly that she had lied about her drinking. She had no idea that "a little alcohol" could be so harmful to her. Eventually, she told the social worker that she had become friends with a widow who frequently invites Mrs. Cortez for afternoon "tea," meaning drinks with vodka or rum and fruit juices. Mrs. Cortez said she never liked drinking alcohol, but these drinks are so good they don't even taste like alcohol. She says she feels better after drinking, and does not want to offend her new friend by refusing her hospitality. As the social worker talked with Mrs. Cortez and her children (with Mrs. Cortez's permission to do so), she noted that the disturbing behavior, memory problems, and poor hygiene seem to have developed since this friendship began.

day) may have some cardiovascular benefits (Balsa, Homer, Fleming, & French, 2008; Institute of Medicine, 2012).

Unhealthy drinking patterns are defined as four or more drinks in any single day during a typical month. However, it is difficult to get accurate statistics because of the stigma associated with alcoholism among today's older cohorts. Estimates of problem drinking vary greatly, from 3.8 to 4.2 percent. In general, alcoholism rates decline with age, although the number of drinks consumed as binge drinking may increase (Chan et al., 2007; Institute of Medicine, 2012; Merrick et al., 2008; SAMHSA, 2010).

Older men, particularly widowers and the never-married, are more likely to have alcohol problems than are older women. Women at greatest risk of alcohol abuse are smokers, not married, not religious, and lacking social support. Some studies find no differences of alcohol use by race, while others identify higher prevalence rates for African American and Native American elders. Although general population studies do not differentiate by sexual orientation, some research among LGBT populations has found that rates tend to be higher than for heterosexual older men (Bartels, Blow, Van Citters, & Brockmann, 2006; Cummings, Bride, & Rawlins-Shaw, 2006; Drabble, Trocki, & Midanik, 2005; Farkas & Drabble, 2008).

Some older alcoholics have had this problem since middle age, but increasing age may exacerbate the condition for two reasons:

1. The central nervous system, liver, and kidneys become less tolerant of alcohol because of age-associated physiological changes you learned about in Chapter 3. For this reason, a smaller dose of alcohol can be more deleterious for an older than a younger person. In fact, current thinking is that older people should consume about half the amount of alcohol acceptable for younger persons.
2. An individual who has been drinking heavily for many years has already irreversibly damaged the

central nervous system, liver, and kidneys, creating more problems than those due to normal aging alone. Chronic diseases common in older adults and the medications used to manage them can also exacerbate the effects of alcohol.

Regardless of the age of onset of problem drinking, older alcoholics tend to experience other co-occurring health problems. These include reduced bone density, sleep disorders, depression, dementia, and liver and gastrointestinal conditions. Alcohol can exacerbate depression, and depression can intensify alcohol use, creating a complex assessment process (Blow, Serras, & Barry, 2007; Institute of Medicine, 2012).

Findings are mixed about the benefits of age-specific treatment compared to age-integrated programs. What appears to be most important is to focus on older alcoholics' medical conditions because physical declines make them more vulnerable to alcohol's secondary effects. As with younger alcoholics, counseling and occupational and recreational therapy are important treatments.

Drug Abuse As you learned in Chapter 3, older persons use a disproportionately large number of prescription and over-the-counter drugs. They are more likely than the young to use tranquilizers, sedatives, and hypnotics, which have potentially dangerous side effects. They also are at risk of abusing aspirin, laxatives, and sleeping pills, often because of misinformation about the adverse effects of too high a dosage or too many pills. **Polypharmacy** refers to such use of multiple medications, or when more drugs are prescribed or taken than is clinically needed. It is not unusual to hear older persons state that they took more aspirin than

Medication Misuse Can Threaten Elders' Independence

Inability to manage their medications can be a threat to older people's remaining in their homes. Families often cannot be there to administer every medication, neighbors may help only intermittently, and home care workers are not allowed to dispense pills. Even assisted living facilities cannot provide the daily help needed with medications, unless the older adult pays an additional fee. Some elders use plastic pillboxes with the days of the week printed on each section or egg cartons or small cups that the family has labeled with instructions. However, these devices cannot help an older person remember the time of day for taking the medication and are ineffective for someone with dementia. Newer systems using digital technology that remind users when they must take their medications and dispense, the correct dose have been developed but may be too expensive for many elders.

Senior Stoners Turn to Pot as They Age

In her 88 years, Florence Siegel has learned how to relax: a glass of wine. A copy of the *New York Times*. Some classical music, preferably Bach. And every night, she lifts a pipe to her lips and smokes marijuana. Siegel walks with a cane and has arthritis in her back and legs. She finds marijuana has helped her sleep better than pills ever did. And she can't figure out why everyone her age isn't sharing a joint, too. "They're missing a lot of fun and a lot of relief," she said.

The use of the United States' most popular illicit drug is growing among retirees as the massive generation of baby boomers who came of age in the 1960s and 1970s grows older. For many boomers, marijuana never held the stigma it did for previous generations, and they tried it decades ago. Some have used it ever since, while others are revisiting the habit in retirement, either for recreation or to cope with pain. Older marijuana users often prefer to use the drug privately rather than in social settings. They say the quality of the drug has increased substantially since their youth, and they feel more comfortable using it. With recreational marijuana use now legal in some states, there may be even more boomers who turn to it.

Each night, 66-year-old Keith Stroup, the founder of an advocacy group to legalize marijuana, sits down to the evening news, pours himself a glass of wine, and rolls a joint. He's used the drug since he first went to college. "The kids are grown, they're out of school, you've got time on your hands and frankly it's a time when you can really enjoy marijuana," Stroup said. "Food tastes better, music sounds better, sex is more enjoyable." The drug is also credited with relieving glaucoma and macular degeneration. Patients in some states enjoy medical marijuana laws, but those elsewhere buy or grow the drug illegally to ease their conditions. Among them is Perry Parks, 67, a retired army pilot who suffered crippling pain from degenerative disk disease and arthritis. He found little success with prescription drugs. About 2 years ago he turned to marijuana, which he first had tried in college, and is now essentially pain-free (Adapted in 2011 from http://www.nbcnews.com/id/35519187/ns/health-aging/t/pot-use-among-seniors-goes-boomers-age/).

prescribed because they did not feel the recommended dosage was reducing the pain. Yet age-associated changes in body composition and renal and liver functions, combined with the use of multiple medications, make them more likely to experience adverse drug reactions. In general, older patients take too much or too little of a drug because of nonspecific or complicated instructions by the physician, or failure to read warning labels about side effects and interactions. In other instances, however, they deliberately do not comply, deciding that they no longer need a medication or that it is not working for them. Such noncompliance is a major cause of emergency room visits.

Assessing older patients for medication misuse is essential. The best approach often begins with a simple "brown bag review." In this technique, an older adult is asked to bring all medications, including over-the-counter ones, in their original containers, in a bag, for a health care provider to review. Fortunately, both health care providers and older people themselves are now more aware of the risks of polypharmacy, especially among those who seek naturopathic medicine and wellness approaches (Meadows, 2008; National Institute on Drug Abuse, 2011; Sambamoorthi, Shea, & Crystal, 2003).

Older persons do not abuse drugs to the extent that younger populations do, nor are they as likely to use illicit drugs such as heroin, cocaine, and marijuana. They also are far less likely to use hallucinogens, amphetamines, or mood-enhancing inhalants. However, the rate of drug abuse is predicted to increase by 50 percent between 2001 and 2020. As illustrated in the box on p. 127, these patterns reflect the aging of the baby boomers, whose illicit drug use throughout their lives is higher than those of earlier cohorts. Illicit drug use is greater among LGBT adults and Native Americans, African Americans, Puerto Ricans, and Mexicans than among white heterosexual populations. This has public health implications, given future projections of increased diversity of the older population (Cochran, Ackerman, Mays, & Ross, 2004; SAMHSA, 2010; Simoni-Wastila & Yang, 2006; Zarowitz, 2006).

summary

This chapter gave you an overview of cognitive functioning and personality in old age, both normal changes and those that are mental health disorders. The classic aging pattern is that fluid intelligence, which is biologically determined, shows the most declines with aging. But if older persons practice their fluid intelligence by using problem-solving skills, they will experience fewer declines. In contrast, aging does not appear to impair verbal or crystallized intelligence—the ability to remember word and symbol meanings.

Learning and memory are frequently examined together because tests of memory assess what a person has learned. According to the information-processing model, learning occurs when information reaches sensory memory and then is directed via one or more sensory stores to primary memory. It is in primary memory that information must be organized and processed if it is to be retained and passed into secondary memory, where information is permanently stored. Studies of recall and recognition show that aging does not dramatically affect the capacity of primary or secondary memory. But we do become less efficient in "reaching into" our secondary memory and retrieving material stored years ago. Tip-of-the-tongue states are an example of problems in remembering familiar names and words. Recognition tasks—giving a cue to associate with an item in secondary memory—are easier than pure recall for older people. Some types of memory, such as semantic and procedural memory, are retained into advanced old age.

There is growing evidence of some gains in cognitive abilities with age. Some older adults have the ability to select, optimize, and compensate for lost skills to adapt to their changing environment and enhance their learning and memory. Additionally, they utilize memory techniques, such as mediators and cognitive retraining, and engage in brain games and other activities to promote their memory. And aerobic exercise has been found to improve cognitive functioning.

Wisdom and creativity appear to be enhanced by changes in the aging brain. Contrary to early theories of personality, Erikson posited that personality continues to change and evolve into old age. According to his theory of psychosocial development, achieving generativity in the seventh stage is important for active aging. The eighth and last stage is characterized by resolving the conflict of ego integrity versus despair in dealing with one's legacy and impending death. Trait theories of personality are another approach; research has identified the five-factor model of personality. Another task for old age is to be able to redefine one's self-concept as prior roles are lost. The ability to negotiate these changes effectively appears to be related to self-esteem.

Successful, robust, or positive aging is defined as the ability to avoid disease and disability, function at a high cognitive level, remain engaged with others, and cope effectively with life events. Elders who remain physically, cognitively, and socially active, despite facing adversity, are characterized by resilience and their ability to draw upon internal and external strengths.

The prevalence of psychological disorders—abnormal changes in personality and behavior that may be caused or triggered by a genetic predisposition, environmental stress, and/or systemic diseases—in old age is difficult to determine, although estimates range from 5 to 45 percent of the older population. Depression, the most common mental disorder in late life, is difficult to diagnose. Both older adults and some health care providers may deny symptoms and accept "feeling blue" as normal aging, while others attribute it to other chronic illnesses. Reactive or minor depression that is secondary to major life changes is found most frequently in older persons, and responds well to environmental and psychosocial interventions. Antidepressant medications combined with short-term problem-solving and cognitive-behavioral therapies are effective treatments for major depression. Life review and reminiscence therapy are also often used. Depression is a risk factor for suicide in older people, particularly for white men over age 85 who have faced role losses.

Some studies have identified rates of anxiety disorders as high as or higher than depression, and both conditions are often co-occurring. Paranoia and schizophrenia are far less common, and typically develop earlier in life and are aggravated by chronic diseases.

Dementia, due to both reversible and irreversible conditions, results in major impairments of cognitive function, especially recall of recent events, comprehension, learning, attention, and orientation to time, place, and person. Thorough tests are needed to distinguish reversible dementias that can be treated from the irreversible dementias such as Alzheimer's disease, which can only be managed. The Nun Study and research on the cognitive benefits of exercise provide useful insights into early life experiences and activities that may prevent or delay the onset of dementia. The biological basis of Alzheimer's disease is receiving more research attention. Future treatments may involve medications that replace or prevent the loss of brain chemicals, as well as vaccines and even gene therapy.

Although cognitive functioning cannot be restored in irreversible dementias, older persons at the early stages often benefit from the newer medications, memory retraining, education, and counseling or psychotherapy to cope with changes. Environmental modifications that simplify tasks and aid in orienting the patient may slow the rate of deterioration and postpone placement in a long-term care facility. Support for family caregivers of persons with dementia is essential to help reduce the stress of dementia care.

Alcoholism and drug abuse are less common in older persons than in the young, although accurate estimates of prevalence are difficult to obtain. Physical health and cognitive function are significantly impaired in older alcoholics. Drug abuse in older persons often takes the form of inappropriate use or overuse of some prescription and over-the-counter drugs. Adverse reactions are more likely to occur because of age-related physiological changes. Rates of illicit drug use such as marijuana are projected to grow with the aging of baby boomers who often used drugs earlier in life.

key terms

alcoholism, p. 125
Alzheimer's disease (AD), p. 121
anxiety disorders, p. 118
attentional control, p. 106
classic aging pattern, p. 102
cognitive-behavioral interventions (CBIs), p. 118
cognitive retraining, p. 108
creativity, p. 110
crystallized intelligence, p. 102
dementia, p. 120
depression, p. 116
disuse theory, p. 107
divided attention, p. 106
drug abuse, p. 125
ego integrity versus despair, p. 111
executive function, p. 105
fluid intelligence, p. 101
general slowing hypothesis, p. 104
generativity, p. 111
intelligence, p. 101
interference theory, p. 107
irreversible dementias, p. 121
life review, p. 112
mediators, p. 108
memory, p. 103
paranoia, p. 119
Parkinson's disease, p. 125

perceptual speed, p. 104
personality, p. 111
polypharmacy, p. 127
positive aging, p. 115
positivity effect, p. 113
primary mental abilities (PMAs), p. 101
problem-solving therapy, p. 118
recall, p. 106
recognition, p. 107
reminiscence therapy, p. 118
resilience, p. 114
robust aging, p. 114
schizophrenia, p. 119
secondary or long-term, memory, p. 104
selective attention, p. 106
self-concept, p. 113
self-efficacy, p. 114
self-esteem, p. 113
sensory memory, p. 103
socio-emotional selectivity theory (SST), p. 113
spatial memory, p. 107
stage theories of personality, p. 111
successful aging, p. 114
suicide, p. 118
sun downing, p. 125
tip-of-the-tongue states (TOTs), p. 105
traits, p. 112
verbal mediators, or mnemonics, p. 109
vigilance, or sustained attention, p. 106
visual mediators, p. 108
working (primary) memory, p. 103

review questions

1. Define the classic aging pattern of intelligence. Identify three factors that can affect or explain this pattern of intelligence in old age.
2. List three factors other than level of intelligence (IQ) that could influence older people's performance on tests to assess their learning or intelligence.
3. Identify three factors that can affect tests of memory. Then list three strategies to improve our memory as we age.
4. Give three examples of how signs of dementia would differ from what is considered "normal" memory loss.
5. Self-concept and self-esteem are generally established early in life, but are modified through social roles and interactions and life experiences. Discuss some experiences of the later years that may negatively influence an older person's self-concept and self-esteem. What might be ways to boost older persons' self-concept and self-esteem?
6. Describe the elements of successful aging. How would you advise a baby boomer the best ways to prepare for a successful old age?
7. What are the two most common mood disorders faced by older people? What types of interventions have been found to be effective in treating these mood disorders?
8. What are two reasons that depression is often overlooked or misdiagnosed by health care providers?
9. List three causes of reversible dementia.
10. Discuss what is known about the causes of Alzheimer's disease. How does this research on causes affect the diagnosis and treatment of the disease?
11. Identify three factors that increase the stress for families caring for a loved one with Alzheimer's disease, especially compared to caregivers of relatives with illness other than dementia.
12. What interventions have been found to be most beneficial to older people with Alzheimer's disease and their family caregivers?
13. Describe why alcoholism is often more difficult to detect in older people than in younger adults.
14. What is the most common form of drug abuse among older people?
15. List three risk factors for suicide in old age. Why are some groups of older adults at greater risk of suicide than others?

media resources

View

- Health Care Costs for the Elderly and Disabled

Watch

- Attitudes toward the Provision of Long-Term Care
- Alzheimer's
- Alzheimer's and Dementia
- Ways We Live, Clip 2

references

Adams, K. B., & Moon, H. (2009). Subthreshold depression: Characteristics and risk factors among vulnerable elders. *Aging & Mental Health, 13*, 682–692.

Adams, K. B., & Roberts, A. R. (2010). Reported coping strategies and depressive symptoms among African American and white residents of congregate housing. *Journal of Gerontological Social Work, 53*(6), 473–394.

Agronin, M. E. (2008). *Alzheimer's disease and other dementias* (2nd ed.). Philadelphia, PA: Lippincott, Williams and Wilkins.

Alzheimer's Association. (2011). *Stages of Alzheimer's*. Retrieved August 6, 2011, from http://www.alz.org/alzheimer's_disease-stages_of_alzheimer's.asp.

Alzheimer's Association. (2013a). *Alzheimer's disease: Facts and figures*. Retrieved September 18, 2013, from http://www.alz.org/alzheimers_disease_facts_and_figures.asp.

Alzheimer's Association. (2013b). *What is Alzheimer's*. Retrieved September 18, 2013, from http://www.alz.org/alzheimers_disease_what_is_alzheimers.asp.

Alzheimer's Association. (2013c). *What is dementia?* Retrieved September 18, 2013, from http://www.alz.org/what-is-dementia.asp.

Alzheimer's Association United Kingdom. (2013). *Building dementia-friendly communities: A priority for everyone*. Retrieved September 20, 2013, from http://www.alzheimers.org/uk/dementifriendlycommunities.

Alzheimer's Disease International. (2013). *World Alzheimer's report 2013: A journey of caring*. Retrieved September 19, 2013, from http://www.alz.co.uk/research/world-report-2013.

American Parkinson's Disease Association. (2012). *Basic information about Parkinson's disease*. Retrieved November 23, 2012, from http://www.apdaparkinson.org/userND/AboutParkinson.asp.

Andel, R., Crowe, M., Pedersen, N. L., Fratiglioni, L., Johansson, B., & Gatz, M. (2008). Physical exercise at midlife and risk of dementia three decades later. *Journal of Gerontology: Medical Sciences, 63A*, 62–66.

Anderson, L. A., Day, K. L., Beard, R. L., Reed, P. S., & Wu, B. (2009). The public's perceptions about cognitive health and Alzheimer's disease among the U.S. population: A national review. *The Gerontologist, 49*(S1), S3–S11.

Aranda, M. P., Lee, P. J., & Wilson, S. (2001). Correlates of depression in older Latinos. *Home Health Care Services Quarterly, 20*(1), 1–20.

Baker, L. (2008). Studies suggest there's an art to getting older. *Washington Post*, March 11. Retrieved September 18, 2013, from http://articles.washingtonpost.com/2008-03-11/news/36910869_1_arts-group-arts-programs-arts-and-cultural-organizations.

Balsa, A. I., Homer, J. F., Fleming, M. F., & French, M. T. (2008). Alcohol consumption and health among elders. *The Gerontologist, 48*, 622–636.

Baltes, P. B., & Kunzmann, U. (2003). Wisdom. *Psychologist, 16*, 131–133.

Baltes, P. B., & Staudinger. U. M. (2000). Wisdom: A meta-heuristic to orchestrate mind and virtue toward excellence. *American Psychologist, 55*, 122–126.

Barg, F. K., Huss-Ashmore, R., Wittink, M. N., Murray, G. F., Bogner, H. R., & Gallo, J. J. (2006). A mixed methods approach to understand loneliness and depression in older adults. *Journal of Gerontology: Social Sciences, 61*(6), S329–S339.

Bartels, S., Blow, F., Van Citters, A., & Brockmann, L. (2006). Dual diagnosis among older adults: Co-occurring substance abuse and psychiatric illness. *Journal of Dual Diagnosis, 2*, 9–30.

Bielak, A. A. M., Hultsch, D. F., Strauss, E., MacDonald, S. W. S., & Hunter, M. A. (2010). Intraindividual variability is related to cognitive change in older adults: Evidence for within-person coupling. *Psychology and Aging, 25*(3), 575–586.

Bjelakovic, G., Nikolova, D., Gluud, L. L., Simonetti, R. G., & Gluud, C. (2007). Mortality in randomized trials of antioxidant supplements for primary and secondary prevention. *Journal of the American Medical Association, 297*, 842–857.

Blanchard-Fields, F., & Kalinauskas, A. (2009). Theoretical perspectives on social context, cognition and aging. In V. L. Bengtson, D. Gans, N. M. Putney, & M. Silverstein (Eds.), *Handbook of theories of aging* (2nd ed., ch. 15). New York: Springer.

Blazer, D. G. (2003). Depression in late life: Review and commentary. *Journal of Gerontology: Medical Sciences, 58A*, M249–M265.

Blow, F., Serras, A., & Barry, K. (2007). Late-life depression and alcoholism. *Current Psychiatry Reports, 1*, 14–19.

Bohlmeijer, E., Smit, F., & Cuijpers, P. (2003). Effects of reminiscence and life review on late-life depression: A meta-analysis. *International Journal of Geriatric Psychiatry, 18*, 1088–1094.

Bopp, K. L., & Verhaeghen, P. (2005). Aging and verbal memory span: A meta-analysis. *Journal of Gerontology: Psychological Sciences, 60B*, P223–P233.

Boron, J. B., Willis, S. L., & Schaie, K. W. (2007). Cognitive training gain as a predictor of mental status. *Journal of Gerontology: Psychological Sciences, 62B*, P45–P52.

Brodaty, H., Withall, A., Altendorf, A., & Sachdev, P. S. (2007). Rates of depression at 3 and 15 months post stroke and their relationship with cognition decline: The Sydney Stroke Study. *American Journal of Geriatric Psychiatry, 15*(6), 477–486.

Brooks, B. L., Weaver, L. E., & Scialfa, C. T. (2006). Does impaired executive functioning differentially impact verbal memory measure in older adults with suspected dementia? *Clinical Neuropsychologist, 20*, 230–242.

Cabeza, R., Anderson, N. D., Locantore, J. K., & McIntosh, A. R. (2002). Aging gracefully: Compensatory brain activity in high-performing older adults. *Neuroimage, 17*, 1394–1402.

Carlson, M. C., Saczynski, J. S., Rebok, G. W., Seeman, T., Glass, T. A., McGill, S., et al. (2008). Exploring the effects of an "everyday" activity program on executive function and memory in older adults: Experience Corps. *The Gerontologist, 48*, 793–801.

Carstensen, L. L. (2007a). Growing old or living long: A new perspective on the aging brain. *Public Policy & Aging Report, 17*, 13–17.

Carstensen, L. L. (2007b). Growing old or living longer: Take your pick. *Issues in Science and Technology, 23*, 41–50.

Carstensen, L. L., Mikels, J. A., & Mather, M. (2006). Aging and the intersection of cognition, motivation and emotion. In J. Birren & K. W. Schaie (Eds.), *Handbook of the psychology of aging* (6th ed.). San Diego, CA: Academic Press.

Cattell, R. B. (1963). Theory of fluid and crystallized intelligence: A critical experiment. *Journal of Educational Psychology, 54*, 1–22.

Cavanaugh, J. C., & Blanchard-Fields, F. (2010). *Adult development and aging* (6th ed.). Belmont, CA: Thomson Wadsworth.

Charles, S. T. (2005). Viewing injustice: Greater emotional heterogeneity with age. *Psychology and Aging, 20*, 159–164.

Charles, S. T., & Carstensen, L. L. (2007). Emotion regulation and aging. In J. J. Gross (Ed.), *Handbook of emotion regulation*. New York: Guilford Press.

Cheng, S.-T. (2009). Generativity in later life: Perceived respect from younger generations as a determinant of goal disengagement and psychological well-being. *Journals of Gerontology: Series B, 64B*(1), 45–54.

Cochran, S. D., Ackerman, D., Mays, V. M., & Ross, M. W. (2004). Prevalence of non-medical drug use and dependence among homosexually active men and women in the U.S. population. *Addiction, 99*, 989–998.

Cohen, G. D. (2000). *The creative age*. New York: Aron Books.

Cohen, G. D. (2005). *The mature mind: The positive power of the aging brain*. Cambridge, MA: Perseus Books.

Cohen, G. D. (2009). *Mirror, mirror on the wall: What is aging after all? Creative capacity and psychological growth in the second half of life. Positive brain and behavior changes that occur because of aging, not despite it.* Public Lecture, University of Washington, Seattle, WA, May 27.

Cohen, G. D., Perstein, S., Chapline, J., Kelly, J., Firth, K. M., & Simmens, S. (2006). The impact of professionally conducted cultural programs on the physical health, mental health, and social functioning of older adults. *The Gerontologist, 46*, 726–734.

Colcombe, S. J., & Kramer, A. F. (2003). Fitness effects on the cognitive function of older adults: A meta-analytic study. *Psychological Science, 14*, 125–130.

Costa, P. T., & McCrae, R. R. (1994). Stability and change in personality from adolescence through adulthood. In C. F. Halverson, G. A. Kohnstamm, & R. P. Martin (Eds.), *The developing structure of temperament and personality from infancy to adulthood*. Hillsdale, NJ: Erlbaum.

Costa, P. T., & McCrae, R. R. (1995). Solid ground in the wetlands of personality: A reply to Block. *Psychological Bulletin, 117*, 216–220.

Crane, M., & Warnes, A. M. (2010). Homelessness among older people and service responses. *Reviews in Clinical Gerontology, 20*, 354–363.

Cully, J. A., LaVoie, D., & Gfeller, J. D. (2001). Reminiscence, personality, and psychological functioning in older adults. *The Gerontologist, 41*, 89–95.

Cummings, S., Bride, B., & Rawlins-Shaw, A. (2006). Alcohol abuse treatment for older adults: A review of recent empirical research. *Journal of Evidence-Based Social Work, 1*, 77–99.

Dahl, M. (2013). Being a bookworm boosts your brainpower into old age. Retrieved September 18, 2013, from http://www.nbcnews.com/health/being-bookworm-boosts-your-brain-power-old-age-6C10532642.

Danner, D. D., Snowdon, D. A., & Friesen, W. V. (2001). Positive emotions in early life and longevity: Findings from the Nun Study. *Journal of Personality and Social Psychology, 80*, 804–813.

Das, A. K., & Agarwal, S. (2000). Effects of aging on memory for spatial location of objects. *Psyho-Lingua*, 30, 17–20.

Das, A. K., Olfson, M., McCurtis, H. L., & Weissman, M. M. (2006). Depression in African Americans: Breaking barriers to detection and treatment. *Journal of Family Practice, 55*, 30–43.

DeCarli, C. S. (2006). When two are worse than one: Stroke and Alzheimer disease. *Neurology, 67*, 1326–1328.

DeFries, E. L., McGuire, L. C., Andresen, E. M., Brumback, B. A., Anderson, L. A. (2009). Caregivers of older adults with cognitive impairment. *Preventing Chronic Disease, 6*(2), A46.

DeKosky, S. T., Williamson, J. D., Fitzpatrick, A. L., Kronmal, R. A., Ives, D. G., Saxton, J. A., et al. (2008). Ginkgo biloba for prevention of dementia: A randomized controlled trial. *Journal of the American Medical Association, 300*, 2253–2262.

Diehl, M., Hastings, C. T., & Stanton, J. M. (2001). Self-concept differentiation across the adult life span. *Psychology and Aging, 10*, 478–491.

Dombrovski, A. Y., Butters, M. A., Reynolds, C. F., Houck, P. R., Clark, L., Mazumdar, S., & Szanto, K. (2008). Cognitive performance in suicidal depressed elderly. *American Journal of Geriatric Psychiatry, 16*(2), 109–115.

Dotson, V. M., Beydoun, M. A., & Zonderman, A. B. (2010). Recurrent depressive symptoms and the incidence of dementia and mild cognitive impairment. *Neurology, 75*, 27–34.

Drabble, L., Trocki, K. F., & Madanik, L. T. (2005). Reports of alcohol consumption and alcohol-related problems among homosexual, bisexual and heterosexual respondents: Results from the 2000 National Alcohol Survey. *Journal of Studies on Alcohol, 66*, 111–120.

Dunlop, D. D., Manhiem, L., Song, J., Lyons, J. S., & Chang, R. W. (2005). Incidence of disability among preretirement adults. The impact of depression. *American Journal of Public Health, 95*, 2003–2008.

Ehlenbach, W. J., Hough, C. L., Crane, P. K., Haneuse, S. J. P. A., Carson, S. S., Curtis, J. R., & Larson, E. B. (2010). Association between acute care and critical illness hospitalization and cognitive function in older adults. *JAMA, 303*(8), 763–770.

Einstein, G. O., Earles, J. L., & Collins, H. M. (2002). Gaze aversion: Spared inhibition for visual distraction in older adults. *Journal of Gerontology: Psychological Sciences, 57B*, P65–P73.

Erikson, E. H. (1963). *Childhood and society* (2nd ed.). New York: Norton.

Erikson, E. H. (1968). *Identity, youth and crisis.* New York: Norton.

Erikson, E. H. (1982). *The life cycle completed: A review.* New York: Norton.

Erikson, E. H. (1997). *The life cycle completed: Extended version with new chapters on the ninth stage of development by Joan M. Erickson.* New York: Norton.

Erikson, E. H., Erikson, J. M., & Kivnick, H. Q. (1986). *Vital involvement in old age.* New York: Norton.

Erikson, K. I., & Kramer, A. F. (2009). Aerobic exercise effects on cognitive and neural plasticity in older adults. *British Journal of Sports Medicine, 43,* 22–24.

Erikson, K. I., Voss, M. W., Prakash, R. S., Basak, S., Szabo, A., Chaddock, L., et al. (2011). Exercise training increases size of hippocampus and improves memory. *Proceedings of the National Academy of Sciences of U.S.A., 108*(7), 3012–3022.

Etgen, T., Sander, D., Huntgeburth, U., Poppert, H., Förstl, H., & Bickel, H. (2010). Physical activity and incident cognitive impairment in elderly persons: The INVADE Study. *Archives of Internal Medicine, 170*(2), 186–193.

Farkas, K., & Drabble, L. (2008). Substance use and older adults resource review. In S. Diwan (Ed.), *Resource reviews.* Washington, DC: CSWE Gero-ed Center, Master's Advanced Curriculum Project. Retrieved August 2009, from http://depts.washington.edu/geroctr/mac/14sub.

Feart, C., Samieri, C., & Barberger-Gateau, P. (2010). Mediterranean diet and cognitive function in older adults. *Current Opinion in Clinical Nutrition and Metabolic Care, 13,* 14–18.

Finch, C. E. (2007). *The biology of human longevity.* San Diego, CA: Academic Press.

Fiske, A., Wetherell, J. L., & Gatz, M. (2009). Depression in older adults. *Annual Review of Clinical Psychology, 5,* 363–389.

Fitzpatrick, A. L., Buchanan, C. K., Nahin, R. L., DeKosky, S. T., Atkinson, H. H., Carlson, M. C., & Williamson, J. D. (2007). Associations of gait speed and other measures of physical function with cognition in a healthy cohort of elderly persons. *Journals of Gerontology: Series A, 62*(11), 1244–1251.

Folstein, M. F., Folstein, S. E., & McHugh, P. R. (1975). "Mini-Mental State": A practical method for grading the cognitive state of patients for the clinician. *Journal of Psychiatric Research, 12,* 189–198.

Fraas, M., Lockwood, J., Neils, S., Trunjas, J., Shidler, M., Krikorian, R., et al. (2002). "What's his name?" A comparison of elderly participants' and undergraduate students' misnamings. *Archives of Gerontology and Geriatrics, 34,* 155–165.

Frazer, C. J., Christensen, H., & Griffiths, K. M. (2005). Effectiveness of treatments for depression in older people. *Medical Journal of Australia, 182,* 627–632.

Friedland, R. P., Fritsch, T., Smyth, K., Koss, E., Lerner, A. J., Chen, C. H., et al. (2000). Participation in non-occupational activities in midlife is protective against the development of Alzheimer's disease: Results from a case-control study. *Neurology, 54,* Abstract #P05.076.

Friedman, D. B., Laditka, J. N., Hunter, R., Ivey, S. L., Wu, B., Laditka, S. B., Tseng, W., Corwin, S. J., Liu, R., & Mathews, A. E. (2009). Getting the message out about cognitive health: A cross-cultural comparison of older adults' media awareness and communication needs on how to maintain a healthy brain. *The Gerontologist, 49*(S1), S50–S60.

Gable, M. (2011). Affordable wellness: Creative providers bring wellness programs to affordable senior housing and community services. *LeadingAge Magazine, 1*(1) (January–February), 16–29.

Gamaldo, A. A., Weatherbee, S. R., & Allaire, J. C. (2008). Exploring the within-person coupling of blood pressure and cognition in elders. *Journal of Gerontology: Psychological Sciences, 63B,* P386–P389.

Garfein, A. J., & Herzog, A. R. (1995). Robust aging among the young-old, old-old, and oldest-old. *Journal of Gerontology, 50B,* S77–S87.

Garrido, M. M., Kane, R. L., Kaas, M., & Kane, R. A. (2011). Use of mental health care by community-dwelling older adults. *Journal of the American Geriatrics Society, 59,* 50–56.

Gayman, M. D., Turner, R. J., & Cui, M. (2008). Physical limitations and depressive symptoms: Exploring the nature of the association. *Journal of Gerontology: Social Sciences, 63B,* S219–S227.

Gellis, Z. D., & McCracken, S. G. (2008). Depressive disorders in older adults. In S. Diwan (Ed.), *Mental health.* Washington, DC. CSWE Gero-Ed Center. Master's Advanced Curriculum Project. Retrieved August 2009, from http://depts.washington.edu/geroctr/mac/14substance.html.

Gellis, Z. D., McGinty, J., Horowitz, A., Bruce, M., & Misener, E. (2007). Problem solving therapy for late life depression in home care elderly: A randomized controlled trial. *American Journal of Geriatric Psychiatry, 15*(11), 968–978.

Gunstad, J., Paul, R. H., Brickman, A. M., Cohen, R. A., Arns, M., Roe, D., et al. (2006). Patterns of cognitive performance in middle-aged and older adults. *Journal of Geriatric Psychiatry and Neurology, 19,* 59–64.

Hampson, S. E., & Goldberg, L. R. (2006). A first large cohort study of personality trait stability over the 40 years between elementary school and midlife. *Journal of Personality and Social Psychology, 91,* 763–779.

Harvey, P. D. (2005). *Schizophrenia in late life: Aging effects on symptoms and course of illness.* Washington, DC: American Psychological Association.

Hasche, L. K., Morrow-Howell, N., & Proctor, E. K. (2010). Quality of life outcomes for depressed and nondepressed older adults in community long-term care. *American Journal of Geriatric Psychiatry, 18*(6), 544–553.

Hasher, L., Chung, C., May, C. P., & Foong, N. (2002). Age, time of testing, and proactive interference. *Canadian Journal of Experimental Psychology, 56,* 200–207.

Hassing, L. B., Grant, M. D., Hofer, S. M., Pedersen, N. L., Nilsson, S. E., Berg, S., et al. (2004). Type 2 diabetes mellitus contributes to cognitive change in the oldest old. *Journal of the International Neuropsychological Society, 4,* 599–607.

Health and Retirement Study. (2008). *A longitudinal study of health, retirement, and aging*. Retrieved December 2009, from http://hrsonline.s.umich.edu.

Hogan, M. J. (2003). Divided attention in older but not younger adults is impaired by anxiety. *Experimental Aging Research, 29*, 111–136.

Horgas, A. L., Wilms, H. U., & Baltes, M. M. (1998). Daily life in very old age: Everyday activities as an expression of successful living. *The Gerontologist, 38*, 556–568.

Horn, J. L. (1970). Organization of data on life-span development of human abilities. In L. R. Goulet & P. B. Baltes (Eds.), *Life-span developmental psychology: Research and theory*. New York: Academic Press.

Horn, J. L. (1982). The aging of human abilities. In B. B. Wolman (Ed.), *Handbook of developmental psychology*. Upper Saddle River, NJ: Prentice-Hall.

Hoyer, W. J., & Verhaeghen, P. (2006). Memory aging. In J. E. Birren & K. W. Schaie (Eds.), *Handbook of the psychology of aging* (6th ed.). Burlington, MA: Elsevier/Academic Press.

Hybels, C., & Blazer, D. (2003). Epidemiology of late life mental disorders. *Clinical Geriatric Medicine, 19*, 663–696.

Insel, K., Morrow, D., Brewer, B., & Figueredo, A. (2006). Executive function, working memory, and medication adherence among older adults. *Journal of Gerontology: Psychological Sciences, 61B*, P102–P107.

James, J. B., & Zarrett, N. (2006). Ego integrity in the lives of older women. *Journal of Adult Development, 13*(2), 61–75.

Jeste, D. V., Savla, G. N., Thompson, W. K., Vahia, I. V., Glorioso, D. K., Martin, A. S., et al. (2013). Association between older age and more successful aging: Critical role of resilience and depression. *American Journal of Psychiatry in Advance, 170*, 188–196.

Jeste, N. D., Hays, J. C., & Steffens, D. C. (2006). Clinical correlates of anxious depression among elderly patients with depression. *Journal of Affective Disorders, 90*, 37–41.

Johnson, M. K. (2005). The relation between source memory and episodic memory: Comment on Siedleckie et al. *Psychology and Aging, 20*, 529–531.

Jones, H. E. (1959). Intelligence and problem-solving. In J. E. Birren (Ed.), *Handbook of aging and the individual: Psychological and biological aspects*. Chicago: University of Chicago Press.

Jones, R. N., Marcantonio, E. R., & Rabinowitz, T. (2003). Prevalence and correlates of recognized depression in U.S. nursing homes. *Journal of the American Geriatrics Society, 51*, 1404–1409.

Kahn, R. L. (2003). Successful aging: Intended and unintended consequences of a concept. In L. W. Poon, S. H. Gueldner, & B. M. Sprouse (Eds.), *Successful aging and adaptation with chronic diseases*. New York: Springer.

Kliegel, M., Jager, T., & Phillips, L. H. (2007). Emotional development across adulthood. *International Journal of Aging and Human Development, 64*, 217–244.

Knox, R. (2011). *Senior moments: A sign of worse to come*. Retrieved April 11, 2011, from http://www.npr.org/2011/04/11/135243606/sussing-out-senior-moments//.

Kramer, A. F., Erickson, K. I., & Colcombe, S. J. (2006). Exercise, cognition, and the aging brain. *Journal of Applied Physiology, 101*, 1237–1242.

Kryla-Lighthall, N., & Mather, M. (2009). The role of cognitive control in older adults' emotional well-being. In V. Bengtson, M. Silverstein, N. Putney, & D. Gans (Eds.), *Handbook on theories of aging* (pp. 323–344). New York: Springer Press.

Kunzmann, U., & Gruhn, D. (2005) Age differences in emotional reactivity: The sample case of sadness. *Psychology and Aging, 20*, 47–59.

Langbaum, J. B. S., Rebok, G. W., Bandeen-Roche, K., & Carlson, M. C. (2009). Predicting memory training response patterns: Results from ACTIVE. *Journal of Gerontology: Psychological Sciences, 64B*, P14–P23.

Larson, E. B., Wang, L., Bowen, J. D., McCormick, W. C., Teri, L., Crane, P., & Kukull, W. (2006). Exercise is associated with reduced risk for incident dementia among persons 65 years of age and older. *Annals of Internal Medicine, 144*, 73–81.

Laurin, D., Verreault, R., Lindsay, J., Mactherson, K., & Rockwood, K. (2001). Physical activity and risk of cognitive impairment and dementia in elderly persons. *Archives of Neurology, 58*, 498–504.

Lawrence, V., Murray, J., Banerjee, S., Turner, S., Sangha, K., Byng, R., et al. (2006). Concepts and causation of depression: A cross-cultural study of beliefs of older adults. *The Gerontologist*, 46, 23–32.

Levine, J. (2004). *Do you remember me? A father, a daughter, and a search for self*. New York: Free Press.

Levy, B. R. (2003). Mind matters: Cognitive and physical effects of aging self-stereotypes. *Journal of Gerontology: Psychological Sciences, 58*, 203–211.

Li, K. Z. H., Roudaia, E., Lussier, M., Bherer, L., Leroux, A., & McKinley, P. A. (2010). Benefits of cognitive dual-task training on balance performance in healthy older adults. *Journals of Gerontology, 65A*(12), 1344–1352.

Liu-Ambrose, T., Nagamatsu, L. S., Graf, P., Beattie, B. L., Ashe, M. C., & Handy, T. C. (2010). Resistance training and executive functions: A 12-month randomized controlled trial. *Archives of Internal Medicine, 170*(2), 170–178.

Lozano, A. M., & Kalia, S. K. (2005). New movement in Parkinson's. *Scientific American, 293*, 68–75.

Mackinnon, A., Christensen, H., Hofer, S. M., Korten, A. E., & Jorm, A. F. (2003). Use it and still lose it? The association between activity and cognitive performance established using latent growth curve techniques in a community sample. *Aging, Neuropsychology and Cognition, 10*, 215–229.

Maiden, R. J., Peterson, S. A., Caya, M., & Hayslip, B. (2003). Personality changes in the old-old. *Journal of Adult Development, 10*, 31–39.

Mayo Clinic. (2010). Alzheimer's disease: How the disease progresses. Retreived August 7, 2011, from http://www.mayoclinic.com/health/alzheimers-stages/AZ00041.

McCrae, R. R., Costa, P. T., deLima, M. P., Simoes, A., Ostendorf, F., Angleitner, A., et al. (1999). Age differences in personality across the adult life span: Parallels in five cultures. *Developmental Psychology, 35*, 466–477.

McCrae, R. R., Costa, P. T., Ostendorf, F., Angleitner, A., Hrebickova, M., & Avia, M. D., et al. (2000). Nature over nurture: Temperament, personality and life span development. *Journal of Personality and Social Psychology, 78*, 173–186.

McCrae, R. R., Costa, P. T., Hrebickova, M., Urbánek, T., Martin, T. A., Oryol, V. E., et al. (2004). Age differences in personality traits across cultures: Self-report and observer perspectives. *European Journal of Personality, 18*, 143–157.

McCrae, R. R., & Terracciano, A. (2005). Universal features of personality traits from the observer's perspective: Data from 50 cultures. *Journal of Personality and Social Psychology, 88*, 547–561.

Meadows, M. (2008). Medication use and older adults. *FDA Consumer Magazine*. Rockville, MD: Food and Drug Administration. Retrieved August 2008, from http://www.fda.gov/fdac/features/200/406olderadults.html.

Medina, J. (2008). *Brain rules*. Seattle, WA: Pear Press.

Merrick, E., Horgan, C., Hodgkin, D., Garnick, D., Houghton, S., Panas, L., et al. (2008). Unhealthy drinking patterns in older adults: Prevalence and associated characteristics. *Journal of the American Geriatrics Society, 56*, 214–223.

Mills, T. L., Alea, N., & Cheong, J. A. (2004). Differences in indicators of depressive symptoms among a community sample of African American and Caucasian older adults. *Community Mental Health Journal, 40*, 309–331.

Mitchell, A. J., & Subramaniam, H. (2005). Prognosis of depression in old age compared to middle age: A systematic review of comparative studies. *American Journal of Psychiatry, 162*, 1588–1601.

Morrow-Howell, N., Proctor, E., Choi, S., Lawrence, L., Brooks, A., Hasche, L., et al. (2008). Depression in public community long-term care: Implications for intervention development. *Journal of Behavioral Health Services and Research*, 37–51.

Mroczek, D. K., Spiro, A., & Griffin, P. W. (2006). Personality and aging. In J. E. Birren & K. W. Schaie (Eds.), *Handbook of the psychology of aging* (6th ed.). Burlington, MA: Elsevier/Academic Press.

Mui, A. C., & Kang, S. Y. (2006). Acculturation stress and depression among Asian immigrant elders. *Social Work, 51*, 243–250.

Murray, M. D., Lane, K. A., Gao, S., Evans, R. M., Unverzagt, F. W., Hall, K. S., et al. (2002). Preservation of cognitive function with antihypertensive medications. *Archives of Internal Medicine, 162*, 2090–2096.

National Institute of Mental Health. (2011). *Older adults: Depression and suicide fact sheet*. Retrieved April 5, 2011, from http://www.nimh.nih.gov/health/publciations/older-adults-depression-and-suicide-facts.

National Institute on Aging. (2011). *Alzheimer's disease medication fact sheet*. Washington, DC: Alzheimer's Disease Education and Referral Center. Retrieved November 25, 2011, from http://www.nia.nih.gov/Alzheimers/Publications/medicationsfs.htm.

Nyberg, L. (2005). Cognitive training in healthy aging: A cognitive neuroscience perspective. In R. Cabeza, L. Nyberg, & D. Park (Eds.), *Cognitive neuroscience of aging: Linking cognitive and cerebral aging*. New York: Oxford University Press.

O'Connell, J. J. (2005). *Premature mortality in homeless populations: A review of the literature*. Nashville, TN: National Health Care for the Homeless Council.

O'Donnell, R. M., & Kaszniak, A. W. (2011). Charting late-life affective disorders. *Generations, 35*, 46–56.

Otsuka, J. (2012). Diem Perdidi. In T. Perrotta (ed.), *Best American short stories* (pp. 152–162). New York: Houghton Mifflin Harcourt.

Patterson, T. L, Bucardo, J., McKibbin, C. L., Mausbach, B. T., Moore, D., Barrio, C., et al. (2005). Development and pilot testing of a new psychosocial intervention for older Latinos with chronic psychosis. *Schizophrenia Bulletin, 31*, 922–930.

Pearlman, A., & Storandt, M. (2004). Predictors of subjective memory in older adults. *Journal of Gerontology: Psychological Sciences, 59*, P4–P6.

Phillips, L. H., Henry, J. D., Hosie, J. A., & Milne, A. B. (2008). Effective regulation of the experience and expression of negative affect in old age. *Journal of Gerontology: Psychological Sciences, 63B*, P138–P145.

Plassman, B. L., Havlik, R. J., Steffens, D. C., Helms, M. J., Newman, T. N., Drosdick, D., et al. (2000). Documented head injury in early adulthood and risk of Alzheimer's disease and other dementias. *Neurology, 55*, 1158–1166.

Podewils, L. J., Guallar, E. L., Kuller, H., Fried, L. P., Lopez, O. L., & Carlson, M. (2005). Physical activity, APOE genotype, and dementia risk. *American Journal of Epidemiology, 161*, 639–651.

Ratcliff, R., Spieler, D., & McKoon, G. (2000). Explicitly modeling the effects of aging on response time. *Psychonomic Bulletin and Review, 7*, 1–25.

Reese, C. M., & Cherry, K. E. (2004). Practical memory concerns across the lifespan. *International Journal of Aging and Human Development, 59*, 237–255.

Rendell, P. G., Castel, A. D., & Craik, F. I. M. (2005). Memory for proper names in old age: A disproportional impairment? *Quarterly Journal of Experimental Psychology, 58*, 54–71.

Reynolds, C. F., Dew, M. A., Pollock, B. G., Mulsant, B. H., Franks, E., Miller, M. D., et al. (2006). Maintenance treatment of major depression in old age. *New England Journal of Medicine, 354*, 1130–1138.

Riemersma-Van der Lek, R. F., Swaab, D. F., Twist, J., Hol, E. M., Hoogendijk, W. J. G., & Van Someren, E. J. W. (2008). Effect of bright light and melatonin on cognitive and non-cognitive function in elderly residents of group care facilities. *JAMA, 299*(22), 2642–2655.

Riley, K. P., Snowdon, D. A., Desrosiers, M. F., & Markesbery, W. R. (2005). Early life linguistic ability, late in life cognitive function and neuropathology: Findings from the Nun Study. *Neurobiology of Aging, 26*, 341–347.

Roan, T. (2010, November 16). Alzheimer's disease vaccine is effective in mice. *Los Angeles Times*. Retrieved August 15, 2011, from http://articles.latimes.com/2010/nov/16/news/la-heb-alzheimers-20101116.

Rogers, W. A., & Fisk, A. D. (2001). Attention in cognitive aging research. In J. E. Birren & K. W. Schaie (Eds.), *Handbook of the psychology of aging* (5th ed.). San Diego, CA: Academic Press.

Romoser, M. R. E., & Fisher, D. L. (2009). The effect of active versus passive training strategies on improving older drivers' scanning in intersections. *Human Factors, 5*, 652–668.

Rosnick, C. B., Small, B. J., Graves, A. B., & Mortimer, J. A. (2004). The association between health and cognitive performance in a population-based study of older adults. *Aging Neuropsychology and Cognition, 11*, 89–99.

Rowe, J. W., & Kahn, R. L. (1987). Human aging: Usual and successful. *Science, 237*, 143–149.

Rowe, J. W., & Kahn, R. L. (1997). Successful aging. *The Gerontologist, 37*, 433–440.

Rowe, J. W., & Kahn, R. L. (1998). *Successful aging*. New York: Pantheon Books.

Ryff, C. D., & Singer, B. (2009). Understanding healthy aging: Key components and their integration. In V. L. Bengtson, M. Silverstein, N. M. Putney, & D. Gans (Eds.), *Handbook of theories of aging*. New York: Springer.

Ryff, C. D., Kwan, C. M. L., & Singer, B. H. (2001). Personality and aging: Flourishing agendas and future challenges. In J. E. Birren & K. W. Schaie (Eds.), *Handbook of the psychology of aging* (5th ed.). San Diego, CA: Academic Press.

Salthouse, T. A. (1996). The processing speed theory of adult age differences in cognition. *Psychological Review, 103*, 403–428.

Sambamoorthi, U., Shea, D., & Crystal, S. (2003). Total and out-of-pocket expenditures for prescription drugs among older persons. *The Gerontologist, 43*, 345–359.

SAMHSA (Substance Abuse and Mental Health Services Administration). (2010). *Results from the 2009 national survey on drug use and health: Volume I. Summary of national findings* (Office of Applied Studies, NSDUH Series H-38A, HHS Publication No. SMA 10-4856Findings). Rockville, MD: Substance Abuse and Mental Health Services Administration.

Sanders, S., Ott, C. L., Kelber, S. T., & Noonan, P. (2008). The experience of high levels of grief in caregivers with Alzheimer's disease and related dementia. *Death Studies, 32*, 495–523.

Schachter, E. P. (2004). Identity configurations: A new perspective on identity formation in contemporary society. *Journal of Personality, 72*(1), 167–200.

Schaie, K. W. (1996). Intellectual development in adulthood. In J. E. Birren & K. W. Schaie (Eds.), *Handbook of the psychology of aging* (4th ed.). San Diego, CA: Academic Press.

Schaie, K. W. (2005). *Developmental influences on adult intelligence: The Seattle Longitudinal Study*. New York: Oxford University Press.

Schooler, C., Mulatu, M. S., & Oates, G. (2004). Occupational self-direction in older workers: Findings and implications for individuals and society. *American Journal of Sociology, 110*, 161–197.

Schwartz, B. L. (2002). *Tip-of-the-tongue states*. Mahwah, NJ: Lawrence Erlbaum.

Seltzer, B. (2006). Cholinesterase inhibitors in the clinical management of Alzheimer's disease: Importance of early and persistent treatment. *Journal of International Medical Research, 34*, 339–347.

Sermons, M. W., & Henry, M. (2010). *Demographics of homelessness series: The rising elderly population*. Washington, DC: National Alliance to End Homelessness.

Sheldon, K. M., & Kasser, T. (2001). Getting older, getting better? Personal strivings and psychological maturity across the life span. *Developmental Psychology, 37*, 491–501.

Siedlecki, K. L., Salthouse, T. A., & Berish, D. E. (2005). Is there anything special about the aging of source memory? *Psychology and Aging, 20*, 19–32.

Simoni-Wastila, L., & Yang, H.-W. K. (2006). Psychoactive drug use in older adults. *American Journal of Geriatric Pharmacotherapy, 494*, 380–394.

Small, G. (2002). *The memory bible*. New York: Hyperion.

Snowdon, D. (2001). *Aging with grace: What the nun study teaches us about leading longer, healthier, and more meaningful lives*. New York: Bantam.

Snowdon, D. (2003). Healthy aging and dementia: Findings from the Nun Study. *Annals of Internal Medicine, 139*, 450–454.

Snowdon, D., Greiner, L. H., & Markesbery, W. R. (2000). Linguistic ability in early life and the neuropathology of Alzheimer's disease: Findings from the Nun Study. *Annals of New York Academy of Sciences, 80*, 804–813.

Sternberg, R., & Grigorenko, E. (2005). Intelligence and wisdom. In M. Johnson, *The Cambridge handbook of age and ageing* (pp. 209–215). New York: Cambridge University Press.

Stix, G. (2011). The neuroscience of true grit. *Scientific American, 304*(3), 29–33.

Sülzenbrück, S., Hegele, M., Heuer, H., & Rinkenauer, G. (2010). Generalized slowing is not that general in older adults: Evidence from a tracing task. *Occupational Ergonomics, 9*(2), 111–117.

Surgeon General. (2001). *Mental health: Culture, race, ethnicity supplement to "Mental health: Report of the surgeon general."* Retrieved 2001 from http://www.mentalhealth.org/cre.

Szalavitz, M. (2013). *Today's 90 year olds are mentally sharper than their predecessors*. Retrieved September 20, 2013, from http://healthland.time.com/2013/07/11/todays-90-year-olds-are-mentally-sharper-than-their-predecessors/#ixzz2YpD2W1Ii.

Teri, L., Gibbons, L. E., McCurry, S. M., Logsdon, R. G., Buchner, D. M., Barlow, W. E., et al. (2003). Exercise plus behavioral management in patients with Alzheimer disease. *Journal of the American Medical Association, 290*, 2015–2022.

Terracciano, A., McCrae, R. R., & Costa, P. T. (2006). Longitudinal trajectories in Guilford–Zimmerman Temperament Survey data: Results from the Baltimore Longitudinal Study of Aging. *Journal of Gerontology: Psychological Sciences, 61B*, P108–P116.

Troyer, A. K., Hafliger, A., Cadieux, M. J., & Craik, F. I. M. (2006). Name and face learning in older adults: Effects of level processing, self-generation, and intention to learn. *Journal of Gerontology: Psychological Sciences, 61B*, P67–P74.

Trzesniewski, K. H., Donellan, M. B., & Robins, R. W. (2003). Stability of self-esteem across the life span. *Journal of Personality and Social Psychology, 84*, 205–206.

Vaillant, G. E. (1977). *Adaptation to life*. Boston: Little, Brown.

Vaillant, G. E. (1994). Ego mechanisms of defense and personality psychopathology. *Journal of Abnormal Psychology, 103*, 44–50.

Vaillant, G. E. (2002). *Aging well*. Boston: Little, Brown.

Van Citters, A. D., Pratt, S. I., Bartels, S. J., & Jeste, D. V. (2005). Evidence-based review or pharmacologic and nonpharmacologic treatment for older adults with schizophrenia. *Psychiatric Clinics of North America, 28*, 913–939.

Van Dongen, M., van Rossum, E., Kessels, A., Sielhorst, H., & Knipscheld, P. G. (2003). Ginkgo for elderly people with dementia and age-associated memory impairment: A randomized clinical trial. *Journal of Clinical Epidemiology, 56*, 367–376.

Verhaeghen, P., Geraerts, N., & Marcoen, A. (2000). Memory complaints, coping and well-being in old age: A systematic approach. *The Gerontologist, 40*, 540–548.

Victoroff, J. (2002). *Saving your brain*. New York: Random House.

Waldstein, S. R., Giggey, P. P., Thayer, J. F., & Zonderman, A. B. (2005). Nonlinear relations of blood pressure to cognitive function. *Hypertension, 45*, 374–379.

Whitbourne, S. K., & Primula, L. A. (1996). Physical identity. In J. E. Birren (Ed.). *Encylopedia of Gerontology*. San Diego, CA: Academic Press.

Whittle, C., Corrada, M. M., Dick, M., Ziegler, R., Kahle-Wrobleski, K., Paganini-Hill, A., et al. (2007). Neuropsychological data in non-demented oldest-old: The 90+ Study. *Journal of Clinical & Experimental Neuropsychology, 29*(3), 290–299.

Wilkins, C. H., Sheline, Y. I., Roe, C. M., Birge, S. J., & Morris, J. C. (2006). Vitamin D deficiency is associated with low mood and worse cognitive performance in older adults. *American Journal of Geriatric Psychiatry, 14*(12), 1032–1040.

Williamson, J. D., Espeland, M., Kritchevsky, S. B., Newman, A. B., King, A. C., Pahor, M., et al. (2009). Changes in cognitive function in a randomized trial of physical activity. *Journal of Gerontology: Medical Sciences, 64A*, 688–694.

Willis, S. L., & Schaie, K. W. (2006). A co-constructionist view of the third age: The case of cognition. *Annual Review of Gerontology and Geriatrics, 26*, 131–151.

Willis, S. L., Tennstedt, S. L., Marsiske, M., Ball, K., Elias, J., Koepke, K. M., et al. (2006). Long-term effects of cognitive training on everyday functional outcomes in older adults. *JAMA, 296*(23), 2805–2814.

Windsor, T. D., Anstey, K. J., & Rodgers, B. (2008). Volunteering and psychological well-being among young-old adults: How much is too much? *The Gerontologist, 48*, 59–70.

Wolinsky, F. D., Vander Weg, M. W., Martin, R., Unverzagt, F. W., Willis, S. L., Marsiske, M., et al. (2010). Does cognitive training improve internal locus of control among older adults? *Journals of Gerontology: Series B, 65B*(5), 591–598.

Xie, J., Brayne, C., Mathews, F. E., & Medical Research Council Cognitive Function and Ageing Study Collaborators. (2008). Survival times in people with dementia. *British Medical Journal, 336*, 258.

Yaffe, K., Fiocco, A. J., Lindquist, K., Vittinghoff, E., Simonsick E. M., Newman, A., et al. Predictors of maintaining cognitive function in older adults: The Health ABC Study. *Neurology, 7*, 2029–2035.

Zacks, R. T., Hasher, L., & Li, K. Z. H. (2000). Human memory. In F. I. M. Craik & T. A. Salthouse (Eds.), *The handbook of aging and cognition* (2nd ed.). Mahwah, NJ: Erlbaum.

Zalaquett, C., & Stens, A. (2006). Psychosocial treatments for major depression and dysthymia in older adults. *Journal of Counseling and Development, 84*, 192–201.

Zandi, P. P., Anthony, J. C., Khachaturian, A. S., Stone, S. V., Gustafson, D., Tschantz, J. T., et al. (2004). Reduced risk of Alzheimer's disease in users of antioxidant vitamin supplements. *Archives of Neurology, 61*, 82–88.

Zarit, S. H. (2009). A good old age: Theories of mental health and aging. In V. L. Bengtson, M. Silverstein, N. M. Putney, & D. Gans (Eds.), *Handbook of theories of aging*. New York: Springer.

Zarowitz, B. (2006). Medication overuse and misuse. *Geriatric Nursing, 27*, 204–205.

5 Social Theories of Aging

learning objectives

5.1 Discuss the primary social theories of aging with a focus on those most salient to today's older population.

5.2 Identify the strengths and weaknesses of these theories.

5.3 Articulate key components of a strength-based life course perspective of aging.

Listen to the **Chapter Audio**

Social theories of aging help us to understand and explain changes in social relationships and systems that occur in late adulthood. They also provide the basis for examining the primary dimensions of older people's social environments that you will learn about in subsequent chapters: family, friends, caregivers, and other informal social supports; housing and community options; emerging roles and activities related to leisure, spirituality, and civic engagement. Social theories of aging are less well developed than biological explanatory frameworks. But as you will see from the different time periods of theoretical development, they are evolving rapidly. To some extent, all social gerontological theories tackle the question of what is the optimal way for people to age and are relevant to our focus on active aging throughout this book. They also serve as a guide for further inquiry and suggest possible practice and policy interventions in the aging process.

In this chapter, we will first briefly discuss the importance of social theories. We then review some of the theories that have had the greatest influence on the field of social gerontology, even though there are many theories other than these. This chapter includes:

- The early social gerontological theories were concerned with how individuals adapt to age-related changes in roles.
- Later theories recognized the diverse and dynamic nature of the aging experience and how social structures affect the aging experience.
- The most recent social theoretical perspectives, which are less quantitative and place greater emphasis on the meaning of people's lived experiences, are described as taking a "qualitative leap" over the earlier theories that focused on adaptation to age-related changes.

These later theoretical approaches explicitly articulate how older people's experiences, along with their social environments, vary by race, ethnicity, social class, functional ability, gender, and sexual orientation. They also represent a paradigm shift away from primarily quantitative approaches that attempt to study the objective facts of aging and toward an emphasis on the highly subjective nature of the aging experience or what it means to be old.

The Importance of Social Theories of Aging

All of us develop ways to explain and interpret the world around us, based on our experiences. Because of the pervasiveness of ageism in our society, some of our generalizations and assumptions may reflect negative age-based stereotypes. We may see an older woman walking cautiously across the street and assume that she is in poor health. But if we were to talk with her, we would learn that she is walking home from her power fitness class where she and her classmates celebrated her 80th birthday by doing 80 push-ups. And she has been cautious about crossing the street all her life, ever since a car nearly hit her when she was five years old! Or we may see an older man in worn clothing sitting on a park bench reading the newspaper; we may assume that he is low-income, lonely, and lacking friends. But his experience of aging may be entirely different. He is a retired college professor who loves to read the paper, always dresses casually, and has an active social life—he just likes reading the paper outside where he can see children playing!

You learned in prior chapters how chronological age is a poor predictor of social, physical, and cognitive abilities. Yet most of us, even gerontological scholars, may make positive or negative assumptions about someone simply on the basis of their apparent chronological age. Some of our stereotypes may be the result of unconscious theorizing about the meaning of growing old. For example, we may view aging as primarily a process of decline and withdrawal from society. This often occurs because we are surrounded by depictions of old age, particularly in the media, as something to be avoided, a disease to be dealt with by medical interventions or a problem to be addressed by cutting age-based policies. Having internalized such images, older adults may even shun the label "old," reserving it for those with obvious physical or mental decline. Perhaps you have heard an older person say: "I don't want to go to a senior center and hang out with those old people."

We may also hold negative views of aging because the biomedical study of aging, with its emphasis on disease and decline, dominated the disciplinary development of gerontology until recently. The growth of "antiaging medicine" in recent years, for example, represents a paradigm shift in how scientists and clinicians view the aging process. By

Checking Out Some of Our Informal Theories

A good way for you to check out some of your assumptions about optimal aging is to interview some older adults. You can even do such interviews informally when you are visiting older relatives or neighbors. Or more formally where you set up an interview time and secure the older adults' permission to interview them. Start out with some general questions, such as "Tell me about what your life is like now," or "How do you enjoy spending your time?" Once the elder is comfortable, you can move onto more specific questions about their health, daily functioning, living arrangements, or family. Be cautious not to impose your own assumptions or values about what the older person's life should be like.

supporting research and treatments to keep people looking "young," it supports the view that the physical changes with aging are the most visible—and the most feared.

In contrast to our personal observations about age changes, the scientific approach to theory development is a systematic attempt to explain why and how an age-associated change or event occurs. Theory-building—the cumulative development of explaining and understanding observations and findings—represents the core of the foundation of scientific inquiry and knowledge. By using scientific methods, researchers seek to understand phenomena in a manner that is reliable and valid across observations, and then to account for what they have observed in the context of previous knowledge in the field.

Scientists never entirely prove or disprove a theory. Instead, through both quantitative and qualitative research, they gather evidence that may strengthen their confidence in the theory, or move them closer to rejecting the theory by demonstrating that parts of it are not supported. Scientific theories not only lead to the accumulation of knowledge—they also point to unanswered questions for further research and suggest directions for practical interventions.

When you hear the term theory, you may immediately think of something abstract, hard to grasp, perhaps even ephemeral—but instead, a good theory is practical and can be applied. For example, some biological theories are useful in guiding people's health behaviors and lifestyle choices as well as the design of health services and policies, as you learned in our discussion of age-associated physiological changes in Chapter 3. But if the theory is inadequate in helping us to understand aging, then the resulting research, intervention, or public policy may fail by not achieving its intended goals (Bengtson, Gans, Putney, & Silverstein, 2009).

Many social gerontological theories have been formulated only since the 1950s and 1960s, and some have not been adequately tested. One reason for the relatively recent development of social theories is that early social gerontological research tended to be applied rather than theoretical. In other words, it attempted to solve problems facing older people—or help them adjust to problems that could not be solved—rather than to explain social phenomena. Researchers were understandably concerned with what were defined as the problems of aging—retirement, ill health, or poverty—and with identifying solutions to them. In fact, the term "theory" was largely absent from the early social gerontological literature. Moreover, "growing old" was itself defined as a problem as the aging person encountered difficulties of adjusting to the loss of roles in later life. Early perspectives on roles and activities later came to be called theories—specifically, role, activity, and disengagement theories.

As we review some of the major theories, take note of the time period in which they were developed. You will notice a shift from a focus on the objective and measurable problems of old age to more attention to the interactive processes that affect aging and the subjective meanings and personal experiences of age-related changes. You will also see more attention given to structural factors in recent years, such as social class, race, gender and sexual orientation, rather than only individual processes of aging. And keep in mind as we discuss these broad theoretical explanations of the psychosocial aspects of aging, there are always exceptions. You will undoubtedly think of older adults whom you know who do not display any of the characteristics posited by a particular theory.

points to ponder

What does theory offer or provide in any field of study? Can you think of ways that theory can help you better understand the aging process?

Social Gerontological Theory before 1961: Role and Activity

The early theories emphasized the consequences of role loss with age and how an individual's personal characteristics—their personality, intellectual ability, or health—affected adjustment to these changes. Role and activity theories not only postulated how individual behavior changes with aging, but also implied how it should change. These early classic theories are described here because of their significant influence on the field. It is important to note, however, that some of these theories are no longer used by gerontologists to understand behavior as people age, nor are they supported by empirical evidence (Powell, 2006).

Role Theory

Role theory was one of the earliest attempts to explain how individuals adjust to aging. In fact, this theory has endured partly because of its self-evident nature. It is one that people can readily relate to and understand. This is because we all play a variety of social roles across the life course, such as student, mother, wife, daughter, worker, volunteer, and grandmother (Cottrell, 1942).

points to **ponder**

Take a minute to make a list of all the roles you play: daughter, son, child, parent, friend, cousin, student, employee, employer. How have these changed as you matured? Now make a list of the roles you imagine yourself playing when you are old.

Such roles identify and describe us as social beings. They are typically organized sequentially, so that each role is associated with a certain age or stage of life. As we saw in Chapter 4, they are the basis of our self-concept and self-esteem—how we think and feel about ourselves. Losing any of these roles through job loss, retirement, widowhood, or other reasons can affect our well-being and opportunities to enjoy active aging.

Age Norms: What Do You View as Age-Appropriate Behavior?

A 79-year-old widow who starts dating a younger man may be told by family members that she should "act her age." Her behavior is viewed as not age appropriate. But this would not be a problem if she were in her thirties and dating a man in his forties.

In most societies, especially Western ones, chronological age is used to sort out a wide range of norms, expectations, and roles. They do so by

- determining who is eligible for various positions,
- evaluating the suitability of different roles, and
- shaping our expectations of how people should behave in social situations.

Some roles have a reasonable biological basis related to age (e.g., the role of mother). But many can be filled by individuals of a wider age range—the role of volunteer, neighbor, employee, or even student. Age alters not only the roles anticipated of people, but also the manner in which they are expected to play them. For example, a family's expectations of their 32-year-old mother are quite different from those of the same woman at age 82. How well individuals adjust to aging is assumed to depend on how well they accept their "typical" role changes that may occur during the later years.

Age norms serve to open up or close off the roles that people of a given chronological age can play. Age norms are assumptions that we all make about age-related capacities and limitations—beliefs that a person of a given age can and ought to do certain things.

Norms may be formally expressed through social policies and laws—mandatory retirement policies that have been mostly eliminated in the United States but still exist for some jobs, such as airline pilot. Typically, however, norms operate informally and subtly. For example, even though employers cannot legally refuse to hire an older woman because of her age, they can suggest that the job requires long hours and intensive training that "might be too much for her."

Individuals also hold norms about the appropriateness of their own behavior at any particular age. We all have social clocks that we have internalized in our heads. We often have expectations or age norms about what is an appropriate time line to assume certain roles. Many people

points to **ponder**

Within a five-year age range, how would you respond to the following questions *for most people, for your parents, and for yourself*? If your responses differ across these three groups, reflect upon why there are disparities. What does this tell you about how you view aging?

	For Most People	For Your Parents	For Yourself
Best age for a man to marry	______	______	______
Best age for a woman to marry	______	______	______
When most people should become grandparents	______	______	______
When most men should be settled into a career	______	______	______
When most women should be settled into a career	______	______	______
When most people should retire	______	______	______
When a man accomplishes the most	______	______	______
When a woman accomplishes the most	______	______	______

in American society, for example, have held age-normative expectations about the appropriate age at which to graduate from high school, start working, marry, have a family, reach the peak of their career, and retire. These expectations have been markedly shifting among baby boomers and their children, however. Age norms are changing, with the recession disrupting employment and retirement plans, more persons marrying later or choosing not to marry at all, more entering second or third careers in middle age, and more adult children facing difficulties in establishing their independence from their parents (Hagestad & Neugarten, 1985).

Every society conveys age norms through socialization. This refers to a lifelong process by which individuals learn to perform new roles, adjust to changing roles, relinquish old ones, learn a "social clock" of what is age appropriate, and thereby become integrated into society. You have been socialized to certain roles, such as son or daughter, since you were an infant. Older adults become socialized to gaining new roles, such as grandparent or volunteer. But they must also learn to deal with role losses, such as the loss of the spouse or partner role as a result of widowhood or divorce, or of the worker/breadwinner role due to retirement or unemployment. Even giving up the role of driver is often difficult, especially for men among the oldest-old for whom driving and owning a car were viewed as signs of success and protector of family. Some of the role losses that we may experience as we age erode a person's sense of identity and self-esteem. But most older adults are remarkably resilient and find ways to manage losses associated with role changes.

Older people may also experience role discontinuity; what they learned at one age may be useless or conflict with role expectations at a later age. For example, learning to be highly productive and competitive in the workplace may be antithetical to adjusting to more ambiguous and undefined roles in retirement or the slower pace necessitated by mobility difficulties. Nevertheless, older adults

Role Loss: Giving Up the Car Keys

A major role loss for many older people, especially older men, is that of driver. As you saw in Chapter 4's discussion of vision changes, families often worry about an older relative's driving, especially at night and if he or she has had a minor accident or some near-collisions. Yet some older drivers refuse to stop driving, blaming close calls on other drivers, poor brakes, or road conditions. A driver may deny the problem and resist giving up the keys, because the loss of the driver role carries negative consequences: loss of independence, identity, personal satisfaction, the ability to carry out daily tasks, and the sense of personal power and control. For many older people, giving up their ability to drive—to go where they want when they want—is a major role transition and symbolizes loss of autonomy. Any efforts to convince an older driver to relinquish the car keys must take account of what such loss of the driver role subjectively means to that individual.

Resilience in the Face of Role Loss

Eileen Allen, age 92, has macular degeneration. She is also very deaf and has severe arthritis that necessitates her using a walker. All these changes have affected her ability to do the three things she most loves in life—reading, writing, and walking. But she considers these to be challenges rather than handicaps. She began adapting to various physical difficulties in her early sixties, when her knees became arthritic. It was then that she learned to swim and began to focus on what she could do rather than what she couldn't. She realized that she could keep on learning—and, even more importantly, that she is the one who determines her perspective. She describes adaptations she's made to enrich her life: teaching herself to be more humorous and to be a better listener. Memorizing poetry when loss of vision meant she could no longer read. Walking three miles around the lake located across from her retirement center—with her walker. She believes that recognizing and accepting help when we need it frees us to put our remaining resources to good use. Happiness, she says, is a balance between looking inward and relating to others. She is choosing the final pieces to complete the picture—ones that show an old woman reinventing herself as many times as it takes to stay engaged and in love with life. And she frequently states, "I like my life" (Allen & Starbuck, 2009).

often display considerable flexibility in creating or substituting roles in the face of major life transitions.

In other words, the many role changes that occur with age are not necessarily experienced as losses. As another example, exiting from the employee role may also bring a sense of freedom and relief—and a new role of retiree,volunteer or hiker or even a new career direction, or what gerontologists now refer to as an encore career.

Unfortunately, some older people still lack desirable role options. Low-income older adults, especially women and elders of color, typically do not have the resources and even the time to attempt to move into new roles of volunteer or retiree or to emulate younger, physically fit older adults. An older African American grandmother who is the primary caregiver for her grandchildren and receives only $800 a month in Social Security benefits is unlikely to be able to pay a gym fee, buy organic food, or spend time volunteering.

Another barrier to moving into new roles is that until relatively recently, few positive role models existed for most elders. For years, older adults seen in the media and in the public realm were typically portrayed as frail, forgetful,

Many older men find a sense of pride and usefulness in filling the role of driver, which makes it difficult for them to "give up the keys."

ill, even incompetent; more recently, baby boomers are featured as youthful in appearance and behavior, looking as if they were trying to do everything possible to deny old age. Fortunately, the overall improved health of the older population and greater acceptance by growing numbers of older persons of some inevitable changes of age, such as wrinkles and gray hair, have fostered more positive options characterized by role gains than in the past. Even though numerous other theories have been advanced in recent years, role theory is still a useful perspective for understanding losses and transitions in old age and is applied in strategies to promote active aging. Nevertheless, the opportunities for all older adults to try out new roles that provide meaning and satisfaction remain limited compared to the multiple role gains available for younger adults.

points to ponder

We encourage you to develop a critical eye about role models for older adults portrayed in the media. Flip through a popular magazine, noting how older adults are portrayed in ads and news stories. What roles do older people play in the media? Are there differences between magazines aimed at younger versus older audiences (e.g., *Wired* vs. *Time*)? Are the roles mostly positive or negative images? Exceptional or realistic? To what extent is diversity portrayed in terms of race/ethnicity, gender, age, social class, sexual orientation, or disability? Or are the images of older people mostly homogeneous? Reflect on how these images fit with or contradict your own perspectives on others' aging as well as your own.

Activity Theory

Activity theory also tries to answer the question of how individuals adjust to age-related changes such as retirement, chronic illness, and role loss. It defines aging as a social problem that can be addressed by trying to retain the status, roles, and behaviors similar to those of earlier life stages. In sum, by remaining active!

From this theoretical perspective, people who age "successfully" are able to maintain in the later years whatever roles, relationships, and status they enjoyed in middle age. The Kansas City Studies of Adult Life in the 1960s posited that well-adjusted older persons replace past roles with age-appropriate productive roles in voluntary, faith-based, and leisure associations. It was assumed that the more active the older person, the greater his or her life satisfaction, self-concept, and adjustment. Accordingly, some age-based policies and programs, such as senior centers and community dining, were often designed as ways to develop new roles and activities and to encourage social integration (Havighurst, 1963, 1968).

To a large extent, activity theory is consistent with the value placed by our society on paid work, individual responsibility, and productivity. Losing any of these characteristics is viewed as evidence of decline. Many older people have themselves internalized this perspective and believe that keeping active helps them to maintain life satisfaction, as illustrated by Bob and Rose in the vignettes on this page.

A limitation of activity theory is that it does not take account of how personality, social class, gender, race, and lifestyle—particularly disparities in health and economic status—may be more salient than age in whether activity is associated with life satisfaction, health, and well-being. In fact, the value placed by older people on being active will vary with these other factors in their life experiences, not just with their age. And not all older adults seek or benefit from activity. For example, some elders who are contemplative and focused inward may experience a high level of life satisfaction without engaging in numerous activities.

Even though there are limitations to applying activity theory, you will undoubtedly see its influence as you read about various programs and policies to keep older adults active. A challenge to activity theory was formulated in 1961 as disengagement theory; this shifted attention away from the individual to the larger social system as an explanation for successful adjustment to aging.

points to ponder

Consider older adults who enjoy the solitude of reading, meditation, yoga, spirituality, or just sitting and reflecting. We often view such contemplative elders as wise, less materialistic, and experiencing greater meaning and purpose than younger adults who are preoccupied with earning money, consumerism, or getting ahead socially. How do you view such internal activities? What goes through your mind when you see an older adult practicing yoga or meditating?

Keeping Active

Bob lives in the Pacific Northwest. He retired at age 62 after 30 years of work as a manager in an aerospace company. He and his wife of 40 years carefully saved money so that they could be very active in their retirement. They spend their winters as "snowbirds," traveling in their mobile home to the Sun Belt in November and returning to the Northwest in April. Now, at age 69, they have spent seven years in the same community in Arizona, where they have a network of good friends from many parts of the United States, who are also retired. They golf, play tennis, volunteer at a nearby school, and belong to several community clubs. In the summer, they usually take one extended trip to the Olympic Mountains to hike and fish. They enjoy good health and believe that keeping active is the key to their zest for life.

Rose was a nurse for 30 years. In her career in direct patient care and teaching, she held positions of authority. She has always liked learning new things. When she retired, she was concerned about finding ways to keep active. Now 74, she is very active in her church and directs the adult education program. She has participated in the national travel program for older adults *Roads Scholars* four times and has traveled to Asia and Europe. She has taken two trips with her teenage grandchildren as well. She has completed several photography classes at a community college and loves showing her travel photos to others. For her, staying active means always to learn and expand her knowledge. She consistently looks forward to new intellectual challenges.

The Next Stage of Theory Development: Disengagement and Continuity Theory

We turn next to two theories that are quite different from role and activity theories and contrast with the model of active aging that we present throughout the book. One of these viewed aging as a time of withdrawal from activities characteristic of earlier life phases, which is a perspective no longer widely utilized, and the other posited that our behaviors and values in old age represent a continuation of lifelong patterns.

Disengagement Theory

Disengagement theory was seen as the first comprehensive and multidisciplinary theory advanced in social gerontology. Quite simply, it means to withdraw or separate from past roles and activities. Cumming and Henry, in their classic work *Growing Old* (1961), argued that aging cannot be understood separate from the characteristics of the social system in which it is experienced. All societies need orderly ways to transfer power from older to younger generations, and to prepare for the disruption entailed by the death of its oldest members. Therefore, the social system deals with the problem of aging, or "slowing down," by institutionalizing mechanisms of disengagement or separation from society. The primary mechanism for disengagement is retirement, where older adults withdraw from their paid occupational roles. But older adults as well as society are presumed to benefit from their decreased activity levels, more passive roles, less frequent social interaction, and a focus on their inner lives.

Disengagement is viewed as inevitable and adaptive, allowing older people to maintain a sense of self-worth while adjusting to the loss of prior roles by withdrawing from social responsibilities. This may include giving up the role of homeowner, employee, and civic leader, and ultimately preparing for death. Since disengagement is presumed to have positive consequences for society and the individual, this theory challenges assumptions that older people must be actively engaged in order to be well adjusted. In contrast to activity theory, it views old age as a separate and distinct period of life, not as an extension of middle age.

Given the growing emphasis on active aging, you can probably think of reasons why disengagement theory is now widely discounted by most gerontologists. It has generally not been supported by later empirical research, and is not seen as an "ideal" adaptation to aging. It also fails to account for variability in individual preferences, personality, culture, and opportunities within the aging population. As an example of cultural differences, elders in American Indian and Asian cultures frequently move into new roles of prestige and power rather than withdrawal.

Likewise, it cannot be assumed that older people's withdrawal from useful roles is necessarily good for

Disengagement and Adaptation

Even though disengagement theory is no longer widely used, you may know people who seem to thrive on withdrawing from past roles. Inga and John are older people who fit this description. As you read about them, think about how the larger society may benefit from such disengagement.

- Inga was an administrative assistant to a highly successful businessman. She never married and had only a few good friends. When she retired at age 62, she took a creative writing class, something she had dreamed of all her life but had not had the time to pursue. At 75, she is very content to sit in her rent-controlled apartment, which overlooks a park. She has lived there for 15 years. She finds much inspiration in watching life pass before her in the park. Writing poetry and short stories gives her an outlet for her thoughts. She feels that her writing has developed greater depth as she has achieved wisdom and contemplated the meaning of her life. She rarely feels lonely because she has lived alone all her adult life.
- John worked for 40 years on an assembly line at an auto factory. He believed that it was a good job that supported his family well, but he put in many overtime hours in this physically demanding job and had little time for leisure. Now 70, he sits in the chair in his living room, watches TV, and reads the paper. This has been his pattern since his retirement 5 years ago. Occasionally, he and his wife of 45 years will go out to dinner but he has no desire to volunteer or travel. John is glad not to have to go to the "rat race" of work every day and is content with his quiet life.

society. For example, policies to encourage retirement have resulted in the loss of older workers' skills, knowledge, and mentoring in the workplace. They have also meant that retired older adults rely on Social Security for longer periods of time—an unexpected outcome that now fuels debates about the future of Social Security.

In contrast to disengagement theory, growing numbers of older people remain employed, healthy, and politically and socially active and engaged. As demonstrated by the MacArthur Studies of successful aging described in Chapter 4, successful aging is more likely to be achieved by people who remain socially involved and integrated, even if they are "slowing down" in other aspects of their lives. But being active does not necessarily mean being busy, a social butterfly, or "on the go" every minute. What makes a difference in terms of life satisfaction is being socially connected with others, even if that is just one good friend or a partner (Bengtson et al., 2009).

Even though disengagement theory has been discounted, it nevertheless had a profound impact on the field and influenced how some people view the aging process.

Continuity Theory

Continuity theory challenges both activity and disengagement theories, but is still focused on how individuals adapt to aging. According to **continuity theory**, individuals tend to maintain a consistent pattern of behavior as they age; they substitute similar types of roles for lost ones and keep typical ways of adapting to the environment. In other words, people do not change dramatically as they age, and their personalities remain similar throughout their adult lives, unless they are faced with major illness, such as dementia, or other highly disruptive life events, such as Hurricane Sandy, which dislocated older adults from their lifelong homes. Older adults tend to be most satisfied if their current activities or lifestyles are consistent with their lifetime experiences.

Continuity theory essentially posits that, with age, we become more of what we already were when younger. Central personality characteristics become more pronounced, and core values more salient with age. For example, people who have always been passive or withdrawn are unlikely to become socially active or volunteer upon retirement. Think about the example given at the start of this chapter of an active older woman cautiously crossing the street who has been cautious her whole life. In contrast, people who were involved in many organizations, sports, or religious groups in middle age are likely to continue these activities, or to substitute new ones for those that are lost with retirement or relocation. As noted earlier, there are always exceptions to generalizations such as these. But for the most part, continuity theory suggests that people age successfully and "normally" if they maintain a personality into old age similar to their younger selves. Reflect for a moment about what continuity theory suggests about your own aging and what you may be like at age 75.

Continuity theory has some face validity because it seems reasonable. You can probably think of older people who have shown such consistency in their personality, core values, and lifestyle. However, it is difficult to test empirically, because how an individual reacts to aging involves many different biological and psychological changes that you learned about in Chapters 3 and 4; it is not just the continuation of lifelong patterns. By focusing on the individual, continuity theory also overlooks the role of external social, economic, historical, and political factors that influence the aging process. In other words, losing one's job and home because of the recession may have more impact on how one experiences aging than does one's personality and earlier life patterns. It is also important not to interpret continuity theory as justifying

Continuity and Adaptation

At age 80, Rabbi Green, who has taught rabbinical students for 40 years, still makes the trip from his suburban home into the city to work with students one day per week. He speaks with considerable excitement about his reciprocal relationships with his students, how much he learns from them, and how he enjoys mentoring. When students talk about their relationship with him, it becomes clear how much they value him as a mentor. Being a teacher is who he is now, and who he has always been. He insists that he will continue to work with students until he dies.

Mary, 70, was always the "cookie jar" mother to her children and their friends. She was there to offer goodies and a listening ear. Although her children and their friends now live far away, a new generation of children has moved into the neighborhood in the small town where she lives. She has become acquainted with many of them and their parents as they stop to talk with her while she works in her garden. Many of the children stop by for a cookie and a glass of milk after school. She is fondly called the "cookie jar grandma." The children say that, along with giving them cookies, she always takes time to listen to them.

Reflection Break

Let's think about the idea that people learn to be old in response to the way they are treated, which actually has wide-ranging implications for the way we behave toward not only elders but people of any age. If we subscribe to this perspective, then we believe that each of us plays a role in other people's self-perception, and by extension their quality of life, and conversely that other people play a role in the way we perceive our own reality. For example, if we repeatedly tell one child, Mark, that he is so interesting to listen to and that he has tremendous potential as a public speaker, he may begin to perceive himself as someone who is a talented oral communicator. However, if we tell Cindy that everything she says is ridiculous and that her voice is annoying to listen to, she may begin to see herself as not having anything intelligent to say and be embarrassed about speaking, leading to her remaining silent when she has something she would like to say publicly. These kinds of negative self-perceptions, influenced by others, can magnify over time and help or hinder a person's personal and professional success throughout the life course. Now let's bring the focus back to older adults. Consider how what we think about older adults and what we say to them or how we treat them. What kinds of adjectives (e.g., sweetie, cutie), voice tone (e.g., condescending or more neutral), and even inflection (e.g., questioning as if the person does not understand) do you use when you interact with an older person? How is that going to affect the way they think about themselves? How can their self-perceptions affect their quality of life or sense of potential? And, finally, what if that older person were you?

a "live and let live" approach to addressing problems facing older people or to assume that older people cannot change. We turn now to more recent theories that explicitly address the larger societal context that affects how we all age (Bengtson et al., 2009).

Newer Social Theoretical Perspectives

Activity, disengagement, and continuity theories have often been framed as directly challenging one another, even though they differ only in the extent to which they focus on individual behavior or social structure. During this early period of theory development, the factors found to be associated with optimal aging were, for the most part, individual ones—keeping active, withdrawing, or "settling" into old age. By not providing a link between the aging individual and the larger society, none of these early theories fully explains active aging, nor adequately addresses the social structure or the cultural and historical contexts in which the aging process occurs. Moreover, they failed to take account of how social structural variables, such as social class, race, ethnicity, gender, and sexual orientation, affect the aging process by limiting opportunities for active aging among some groups of older adults who have experienced disadvantage across their lifetimes.

A number of alternative theoretical viewpoints have emerged since the 1960s. Each of these has attempted to explain "the facts" of aging better than another, oftentimes by taking account of the larger environment or structural factors that influence our options, roles, and status as we age. We discuss five of them here: age stratification theory, social exchange theory, the life course theoretical perspective, the political economy theory of aging, and social constructionism. As you read through these, you will see growing attention to how social structures, particularly inequities across the life course, affect the aging experience. You will also learn how structural factors affect the types of policies and programs developed to address older adults' needs.

Age Stratification Theory

Age stratification theory, a perspective that explicitly takes account of how cohort and historical time period affect aging, challenges the focus on individual adjustment inherent in activity and disengagement theories. Just as societies are stratified in terms of social class, gender, and race, every society divides people into categories or strata according to age—"young," "middle-aged," "young-old," and "oldest-old." Remember the concept of age cohort discussed in the Introduction and the differentiation of oldest-old from young-old in Chapter 1. The cohort effect results in shared experiences among individuals born in a particular time period (e.g., young college graduates during the recession have had more difficulty finding jobs than earlier cohorts). Age stratification is defined by different age cohorts. This means that an individual's experiences with aging, and therefore their roles and their life satisfaction, vary with their position in the age structure. For example, a young-old adult who is still employed exhibits different behaviors and attitudes as a result of their position in the age structure than an oldest-old person.

Age stratification theory also considers a structured time component in which cohorts pass through an age-graded system of expectations and rewards. It recognizes that the members of one stratum differ from each other in both their stage of life (young, middle-aged, or old) and the historical periods (World War II, the Great Depression, the Vietnam War) they have experienced. Both the individual's life stage and the historical context explain differences in how people behave, think, and, in turn, contribute to society.

Figure 5.1 captures some of the famous people who symbolize particular cohorts. You may be able to think of others for each of these cohorts.

People within the same cohort share a common historical and environmental past, present, and future. They have been exposed to similar events and changes, and therefore come to see the world in comparable ways. The oldest-old today—who were children and young adults during the Depression—have generally valued economic self-sufficiency and "saving for a rainy day," compared to their children and grandchildren, who experienced periods of economic prosperity during early adulthood and grew up oriented toward consumerism. As a result, they may be reluctant to spend money on services that might improve their quality of life or may even resist putting their money in banks. By contrast, millennials, many of whom are in their late twenties or early thirties, are the most educated generation but are now facing unanticipated difficulties during the recession finding jobs and becoming financially independent from their parents—behaviors that are far different from what they were socialized to expect as children of high-achieving boomer parents! Such cohort differences may sometimes be visible in intergenerational conflicts or difficulties communicating within families.

Intergenerational Conflict and Age Stratification

Edna is a 90-year-old retired teacher who grew up during the Great Depression, and was a young bride during World War II. These two major historical events have shaped her life, because she learned to make do with whatever resources were available to her. As a result, she has always been frugal with her spending, to the point of saving a large nest egg to pass on to her grandchildren when she dies. However, she is often critical about the way her grandchildren seem to spend every penny they earn. Even worse, they use credit cards freely and don't worry about carrying debt. She has expressed her concerns to her daughter, telling her that these young people have not learned to save for a rainy day. Her daughter listens patiently but does not agree with what she considers her mother's penny-pinching ways. And her grandchildren try to explain to her that being in debt is a good way to build up credit for when they need a loan. She responds that she and her husband never took out a loan for anything, but always paid in cash.

Because of their particular relationship to historical events, people in the old-age stratum today are very different from older persons in the past or in the future, and they experience the aging process differently. This also means that cohorts collectively influence age stratification as they age. When there is a lack of fit in terms of available roles, cohort members may challenge the existing patterns of age stratification. As we noted in Chapter 1, baby boomers will alter the age stratification system as they grow old, given their sheer size, generally higher education and income levels, greater diversity, and how they have redefined lifestyles throughout their lives. Although they are heterogeneous—there are always exceptions to trends about baby boomers—they are bringing entirely different expectations to the aging process than prior cohorts.

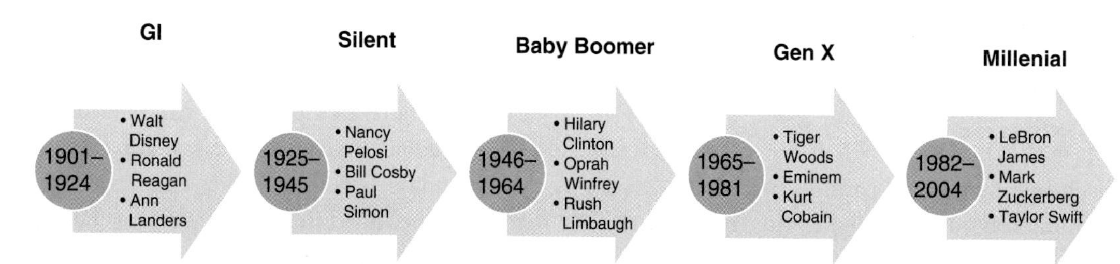

FIGURE 5.1 Some of the Famous People who Symbolize Particular Cohorts

Here are some examples of how the baby boomers who are retiring today differ as a whole from the cohort that retired in the 1950s. They tend to

- believe they should have lifestyle options and the freedom to choose living environments and services that are responsive, flexible, readily accessible, culturally appropriate, and often run by boomers;
- reject notions of "seniors," dependence, disability, and frailty, and place more emphasis on remaining productive, engaged, and pursuing new careers, paid or unpaid;
- view retirement and leisure more positively, although they may have fewer financial resources for retirement than they had anticipated because of the recession;
- be technologically savvy;
- be physically active and healthier, although growing numbers of baby boomers and younger cohorts are obese and many of them have abused drugs and alcohol since young adulthood;
- be more likely to challenge restrictions on their roles through age discrimination lawsuits, legislative action, and political organization and advocacy;
- live long enough to become great-grandparents;
- be more planful and proactive about the dying process and end-of-life choices and quality of care.

These variations, in turn, will affect the experiences and expectations of future cohorts as they age. In other words, as each successive cohort moves through the age strata, they alter conditions to such a degree that later groups never encounter the world in exactly the same way, and therefore they age differently.

Age stratification theory also encompasses the concept of **structural lag**. Such lag occurs when social structures cannot keep pace with population changes. For example, although life expectancy has increased, most workplaces, neighborhoods, communities, religious institutions, and voluntary associations are inadequately designed or prepared to build on older adults' strengths and contributions. Instead, they are more likely to see older adults as a problem and design programs that may segregate generations. In contrast, an age-integrated society would compensate for structural lag by developing policies—such as extended time off for education across the life course or new career options in old age—to bring social structures into balance with individuals' lives. As another example of reducing structural lag, age-friendly communities would enhance quality of life for all ages through the use of technology, intergenerational interactions, and physical modifications to make the environment accessible to all. In other words, our society would be elder-friendly in ways that would benefit all age groups. You will learn more about new options in retirement in Chapter 8 and about innovative age-friendly communities in Chapter 11 (Riley, Kahn, & Foner, 1994; Riley & Loscocco, 1994; Riley & Riley, 1994).

Social Exchange Theory

Social exchange theory also challenges activity and disengagement theories. By drawing upon an economic model of the cost–benefits of social participation, it attempts to answer why social interaction and activity often decrease with age. In contrast to the earlier theories, however, it takes account of structured exchanges of resources across generations.

Social exchange theory posits that withdrawal and social isolation result from an unequal exchange process of "investments and returns" between older persons and other members of society. In other words, if an older person perceives that their contributions are no longer valued by others (e.g., seen as benefiting themselves or others), they may begin to withdraw from participating in social activities, such as volunteering, and experience lower life satisfaction (e.g., costs or negative returns on their contributions). To some extent, this is adaptive behavior on their part—they adjust to a new less active role rather than actively seeking to influence their environment (Dowd, 1980).

However, older adults generally seek to maintain reciprocity and to be active agents in the management of their lives. They typically offer resources, especially financial ones, to younger generations for as long as possible, allowing them to exert some power in their relationships. Perhaps you have had older relatives who have given you financial support for college, travel, or a home mortgage. In most instances, being able to provide such assistance to others is a source of satisfaction—as well as a potential source of control—for your older relatives.

But at some point, because of changes in roles, illness, or relocation, elders may have fewer economic and material resources to exchange and their status may decline. However, this decline is not inevitable, since older individuals often have nonmaterial assets, such as respect, approval, love, wisdom, and time to give to other generations—even though these are not valued as much in our society as material resources are. Even when an older adult needs a family member to provide care for them, they may

Foster Grandparent Programs: Intergenerational Exchange

Ten-year-old Ann lives with her mother and older brother in a public housing high-rise apartment. Her mother has to work two jobs in order to make ends meet. This means that Ann is often left at home alone after school. Through the Foster Grandparent Program administered by the local senior services and available in Ann's school, Ann has someone to call after school if she is lonely or needs help with homework. And twice a week, her foster grandmother comes to visit her, taking her on neighborhood outings, making clothes for her favorite doll, buying a special treat, or tutoring her. Ann benefits from her foster grandmother's attention and love. And her foster grandmother, a widow in her mid-seventies, feels a sense of satisfaction, accomplishment, and responsibility in her relationship with Ann. She looks forward to her time with Ann and speaks with pride to her friends about Ann's achievements as if she were her real granddaughter. Most of all, the young girl and the older woman love each other—an emotional component of exchange relationships that may be even more salient to quality of life than economic exchanges.

still reciprocate by sharing their life experiences or mentoring and giving advice. Similarly, social policies and services can serve to increase opportunities for elders to contribute less tangible resources. For example, intergenerational programs recognize the knowledge, skills, time, and caring that older adults can share with youth and how both generations benefit from interactions. Exchange theory is also relevant to debates about intergenerational transfers through policies such as Social Security at a societal level, which you will learn about in Chapter 13 (Lynott & Lynott, 1996; Silverstein, Conroy, Wang, Giarusso, & Bengtson, 2002).

Life Course Perspective

The life course approach is not necessarily a theory but rather a framework for thinking about the differences that result from being born in a specific cohort and having access to particular opportunities (Elder, 1994, 1998). You learned about the concept of the life course in the Introduction to this book. We discuss it again here because we use the life course framework to aging throughout this book and because it is consistent with other theories that take account of the larger societal context.

As noted in the Introduction, the **life course perspective** attempts to bridge structural or societal level and individual psychological level factors that affect human development. As we discussed above, aging and its meaning are shaped by

- the structural influences of cohort, historical time period, culture, and location, and
- individual developmental factors such as the age-related stages defined by psychological and social experiences; for example, the sequence of life events, social relationships, and the capacity to make choices.

Moreover, human development cannot be solely equated with steady incremental growth. Instead, the life course for most people encompasses both gains and losses in roles and functions, often at the same time, as well as structured advantages and inequities. In addition, patterns of development are not the same in all individuals, as reflected by the considerable heterogeneity of life transitions among older adults.

In the life course framework, the cohort is the fundamental unit of social organization; as you just learned in our discussion of age stratification theory, the cohort affects human development and access to opportunities throughout life. This means that future cohorts of elders, such as Generations X and Y, with their instant electronic communications, will adapt to their own aging in the context of different patterns of social ties (e.g., via Facebook, tweets, and blogs) than previous cohorts, who relied more on face-to-face communication. But this does not mean that current cohorts of older adults cannot also adjust to using Facebook or iPhones for some communication, as you will learn in Chapter 12.

As another example, the concept of cohort is critical to understanding the different experiences of lesbian, gay, bisexual, and transgender (LGBT) persons, according to the historical period in which they first self-identified as gay. For example, those who were born before the Stonewall riots in 1969, which were the catalyst for gay liberation, had very different experiences in terms of being open about their sexual identity compared to many younger LGBT persons, who have benefited from the changes brought about by those protests and who now have the right to marry in a growing number of states.

The life course perspective also can provide a critical analysis of how caregiving for older relatives is now a standardized and "on-time" part of the life trajectory for the majority of adult children because of increased life expectancy among their parents' generation. Additionally,

Baby boomers who are LGBT may be more open about their sexual identity and will participate in events such as Gay Pride marches.

such caregiving roles across the life course affect well-being in old age. Because of care responsibilities, for example, women have limited opportunities to accumulate savings across their lives. This results in lower Social Security and pension income and higher rates of poverty than men in old age. In other words, inequities experienced by women earlier in their lives are often exacerbated in old age.

The life course perspective takes account of the role of individual decisions that affect one's future, along with the accumulation of risks and resources. In other words, it provides a framework for how both advantages and inequities persist throughout a person's life. Disadvantage increases exposure to risk, but advantage magnifies exposure to opportunity. For example, dropping out of high school or graduating as valedictorian has lifelong consequences on economic and social well-being. Last, it considers the intergenerational transmission of inequality and how childhood conditions structure the life course through both demographic and developmental processes. Those who are born poor have fewer educational and economic opportunities to try to overcome and reverse patterns of poverty and are more likely to be poor across the life course (Ferraro, Shippee, & Schafer, 2009; George, 2007).

Political Economy Theory of Aging

The focus of exchange theory on power and opportunity structures and the life course perspective on long-term inequities are reflected in the development of the **political economy of aging**. Indeed, you will see elements of these two theoretical approaches throughout our discussion of political economy. Political economy theorists reject the earlier activity and disengagement models of aging. They view social class as the primary determinant of older people's position and life satisfaction, with groups in power trying to sustain their own interests by maintaining class inequities. This fits with the adage that we often hear or say: "The rich get richer, and the poor get poorer." In fact, this adage has been even truer during the worldwide economic crisis, whereby income inequality has increased, particularly among older adults.

According to this theory, socioeconomic and political constraints, such as power and control of resources—not individual factors—shape the experience of aging and age inequities in society. These inequities that result in social stratification may include not just age and social class, but also race, ethnicity, gender, sexual orientation, and functional ability. These structured inequalities then result in **cumulative disadvantages** in old age. This term means that structural disparities experienced by people earlier in life are intensified in old age. The concept of cumulative disadvantage is captured in the box on p. 152 about older women of color (Estes, 2004; Estes & Associates, 2001).

Political economy theory posits that structural factors are institutionalized and reinforced by public policy, and serve to limit the opportunities and choices of later life. Political economists do not view aging or older adults as the problem causing the federal deficit or rising health care costs. Rather, they posit that the major problems faced by older people are socially constructed and therefore could be changed through political action and policy if those

Life Course Advantage: Opportunity in Old Age

James is a 72-year-old civil engineer who retired from the Army Corps of Engineers at age 66. But his expertise in designing large bridges has resulted in a second career as a consultant to state and federal projects, where he is asked to assess the safety of bridges and to evaluate them after natural disasters. He is doing so well in his consulting job that he withdraws only the minimum savings from his pension benefits. He enjoys the respect and friendship of his new colleagues as well as the opportunities to use his professional skills in this second career. The chance to still feel useful is more important to him than what he gets paid to consult.

A Political Economy Perspective on Older Women of Color

Discrimination during their younger years and lack of opportunity throughout life have placed today's cohort of older African American women at an economic disadvantage. Because of racial and gender discrimination in education and employment throughout the life course, many did not have access to good jobs with retirement and health benefits. Instead, they were often employed in poorly paid service positions. As a result, today many subsist on minimum Social Security benefits as their only source of income. Because they cannot afford supplemental health insurance, their health care options are structurally limited to providers who will accept Medicare and Medicaid. And because of past encounters with institutionalized racism, they may be wary of other age-based services through the Older Americans Act. Subsisting on a limited income and often busy caring for grandchildren, admonishments from care providers to exercise and volunteer do not take into account the demands that these women face daily just to get by.

with power were willing to allocate more resources to their solution. Accordingly, policies that focus on personal responsibility are critiqued for socializing elders to adapt to their devalued status and to hold themselves responsible, rather than altering the structural inequities that limit choices and result in poverty and age-segregated living situations in old age (Estes, 2004; Harrington, Wolf, & Himes, 2005; Walker, 2009).

Social Constructionism

Social constructionism shares some of the characteristics of political economy theory; this theory posits that aging is defined as a problem more by culture and society than by biology and bodily changes. From this theoretical perspective, the negative ways in which age is socially constructed has numerous consequences for social policy, employer practices, public perception of elders, and how they are treated by others (Estes, 2001; Kail, Quadagno, & Keene, 2009).

An example of the social construction of aging is how Medicaid, the federally funded health insurance for low-income persons, is disproportionately allocated toward skilled nursing home care rather than toward what most elders prefer—home care and support by families and other informal cargivers. Accordingly, the majority of public funds for health care go toward medical care for acute illnesses, not psychosocial and personal care services for managing long-term chronic diseases in ways to enhance elders' psychological and social well-being. Another illustration is how the general public tends to think of old age as a homogeneous physical condition, overlooking the tremendous diversity that exists across at least one-third of our lifetimes. By contrast, no one refers to childhood or adolescence solely as a physical condition (Cruikshank, 2013).

Social constructionists contend that we need to deconstruct the concept old; by this they mean we need to "unpack" how one's socially structured position or location—gender, race/ethnicity, social class, sexual orientation, and functional ability—creates lifelong disparities that shape the experiences of old age. This also suggests that gerontological practitioners should focus on eliminating structural barriers that can impair elders' strengths, resilience, and capacities to overcome adversity. For instance, new types of intergenerational living supports should be designed so older people can continue to thrive in the community (Bengtson et al., 2009).

Social constructionism differs from political economy, because it gives greater recognition to the importance of our interpersonal interactions in shaping the aging experience. Throughout this book, you will see examples of how what is considered to be old is socially constructed and varies with the economic, cultural, historical, and societal contexts. This means that we need to understand how individuals—whether professionals or laypersons—draw on age-related explanations and justifications in the ways that they relate to and interact with elders. Individual behavior then produces a "reality," which in turn structures individuals' lives as they age. In other words, the realities of age and age-related concepts are socially constructed through our interpersonal interactions. Accordingly, social reality

points to ponder

Of the theories you have just read about, which ones seem most helpful in understanding aging and older adults? Which ones do you find less helpful or outdated? Which ones are most consistent with your own view of aging?

A Social Constructionist Perspective on Skilled Nursing facilities

Skilled nursing facilities have traditionally been based on a hierarchical medical model in which professional health care providers believe that they know what is "best" for frail older residents. The medicalization of such facilities has meant that they are often viewed as places to die, not to live. Rules and regulations tend to be oriented to efficiencies and staff needs, not those of residents. When to get up and go to bed, when to eat meals, and when to have baths are all typically determined by administrative staff and licensing requirements. In addition, staff members are assigned particular tasks (such as the medication nurse or the bathing aide), without taking into account the residents' needs or preferences.

In contrast, recent efforts to transform nursing home organizational culture have encompassed resident-directed care. In this model, residents choose when to get up, when to eat breakfast, and the timing of all other daily activities. Past assumptions, and even licensing requirements, are questioned, and creative approaches to regulations implemented. Services are decentralized and task-focused roles eliminated so that staff can work with the same residents over time and build relationships. While the traditional nursing home has tended to be a microcosm of how our society has viewed elders, these new options typically put older adults in central decision-making roles, thus representing how socially constructed roles and positions can change.

and the meaning of being old shift over time, reflecting the differing life situations and social roles that occur as we age (Cruikshank, 2013).

Put quite simply, we learn to be old in response to the way we are treated by others. And when we encounter ageism, we often internalize it and question our own worth. For example, labeling older people as dependent, asexual, frail, or marginal is defined through social interactions by health care providers, family members, and society in general. It is no wonder that many older people—especially older women—start to feel invisible and think of themselves as useless or a bother to others. When adult children treat their aging parents as if they are incompetent or too old to live on their own, their parents may then unnecessarily limit their social activities and friendships that they previously had enjoyed.

The box above illustrates how the traditional structure of many skilled nursing facilities has resulted in residents who were often listless, bored, and, in some cases, declining more than they would in their own homes. But structures can be changed, and many long-term care facilities are making environmental modifications that allow residents to experience more choices and control. This is called the culture change movement and is discussed more fully in Chapter 11, where you will learn about different residential living options.

Recent Developments in Social Gerontological Theory

We turn now to the most recent phase of theoretical development, which is described as a qualitative leap in gerontological thought occurring since the 1980s. Both of these theories may seem a little hard to "wrap your heads around." We hope that the examples we have given make them less abstract. These theories are important to understand because they have a significant impact on both research and ongoing theory development today (Bengtson et al., 2009).

Social Phenomenology

Social phenomenology, the primary theory of this group, markedly contrasts with the quantitative approach of earlier theories. It may be a hard concept to grasp or even say. But put simply, it focuses on understanding the meanings that people give to their social lives in the context of everyday living rather than on the explanation of the "facts" of aging. Moreover, phenomenological theorists take issue with the presumed "facts of aging," and question the nature of age, how it is described, and whose interests are served by thinking of aging in particular ways (Longino & Powell, 2009; Powell, 2006).

Proponents of this theory claim that the data or facts of aging cannot be separated from researchers' own perceptions about time, space, and self—or from those of the individuals being studied. This is because we all actively participate in our everyday lives, creating and maintaining social meanings for ourselves and those around us. These meanings then influence what we each call "reality."

None of us, including researchers, directly or objectively "sees" a fixed reality. For example, researchers using a social phenomenology theory might use the qualitative technique of participant observer, perhaps taking on the position of nursing assistant, to learn about the social world of skilled nursing facilities, or working in a shelter to learn about the everyday lives of homeless elders. In this capacity, they would listen carefully to residents' stories to discern the subjective meanings of quality of care and quality of life for them—meanings that cannot be uncovered by predefined measurement scales or survey questions. As you can imagine, quantitative researchers may view phenomenological theories as impossible to test and closer to assumptions about meanings than propositions that can be proved or disproved (Bengtson et al., 2009; Longino & Powell, 2009).

For phenomenologists, it is the assumptions and interpretations of the purported facts that are critical in understanding older adults and the aging process. For example, this theoretical perspective might attempt to understand how policy-makers interpret the fact of the growth of the older population when debating whether to increase or decrease Medicare or Social Security benefits. If they perceive the aging population to be economically homogeneous, then policy solutions will not differentiate elders who have achieved a comfortable retirement from those who have experienced a lifetime of disadvantage and now poverty in old age. The resulting policy decisions might continue to perpetuate how women and elders of color typically receive lower Social Security benefits compared to those of higher-income older adults. Similarly, if they perceive the growth of the older population as a fiscal crisis, they will be quick to suggest major changes to these policies in order to reduce costs.

Recently evolving theoretical perspectives, called social constructivism, critical gerontology, and postmodernism, are other types of phenomenological approaches to knowledge development. While we will not discuss these here, it is important to remember that all of these theories take account of how individuals experience and make meaning of the aging process. Similarly, they posit that all forms of meaning and presumed "knowledge" are not to be taken for granted. There is no such thing as "objective" truth or reality. Truth is variable, depending

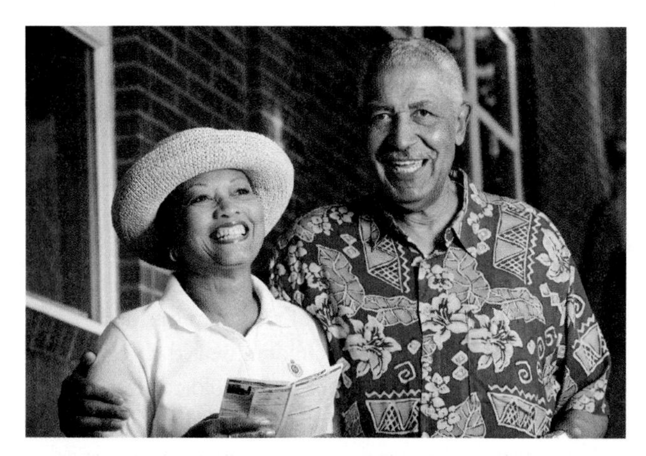

From a social phenomenology perspective, the facts and figures related to aging are not as important as interpretations and subjective experiences of aging.

The Reality of "Old" from a Social Phenomenology Perspective

Martha and James both illustrate the importance of others seeking to understand the experience of what it means to grow old, not taking actions based on the presumed "facts."

At age 86, Martha enjoys a brisk, daily 30-minute walk around the park near her home. She manages her household on her own, participates in exercise classes at the local senior center, and enrolls in one history class each semester at the local community college. The young people she meets at the park and in her college classes are always amazed at her vigor and intellectual curiosity. They often express surprise that she can do all she does "at her age" and ask her about her "secret to aging well." Martha tells them they need to expand their view of aging, discard their ageist stereotypes of growing older as an illness, and stop viewing active older people like herself as "exceptional." She views herself as a healthy adult, just as capable at age 86 as she was at 45. But many of these young adults rely on the negative images of aging that they have seen on TV or in popular magazines.

James is an 80-year-old retired dentist who was diagnosed with dementia five years ago and now lives in a skilled nursing facility. His personal funds ran out long ago, so his care is covered by Medicaid. His family visits him regularly and tries to contribute as much as possible to his financial needs. But they marginalize him by referring to him in the third person to staff and focusing on his dependence and losses, rather than on his remaining strengths. As a result, he increasingly doubts his capabilities and has even stopped going to the dining area or to any social events. His social world is constrained by how others have defined him.

A Feminist Theoretical Approach to Retirement and Economic Well-Being

Feminist gerontologists move beyond a traditional approach that documents that women have lower retirement benefits to ask *why* this exists and *why* it is viewed as "natural." Conventional gerontology may frame studies of women's retirement in terms of individual financial responsibility, while a feminist perspective questions what social and economic structures and policies make it difficult for women to accumulate savings despite decades of employment. For example, the lack of public and private pensions for a lifelong career as homemaker and caregiver leaves many older women economically vulnerable. Feminists also point to society's failure to consider caregiving as a serious and legitimate role that should be valued economically. An example of this is that in our society, family leave policies, with the exception of a few state policies, are unpaid (Cruikshank, 2013; Hooyman, Brown, Raye, & Richardson, 2002; Kail et al., 2009).

on the situation and circumstances, given the uniqueness and diversity of the aging experience (Bass, 2009; Powell, 2006).

Feminist Gerontology

Phenomenology has influenced other contemporary social gerontology theories, especially **feminist gerontology**. Feminist theorists have added a gender dimension to the political economy and life course perspectives regarding how institutionalized mechanisms disadvantage women across the life course by limiting their labor market opportunities. From a feminist theoretical perspective, gender-based inequities and the oppression of women across the life course differentially structure men and women's experiences of aging.

Feminist gerontologists are also critical of "mainstream" feminist theories that typically have focused on younger women. Their attention to issues such as employment equity or "breaking the glass ceiling" is important but not as relevant to women who are already old. Proponents of feminist gerontological theories contend that the current theories of aging are also insufficient, because they do not include gender relations as central to the aging experience. Simply adding women to research samples, models, and theories derived from men's experience is inadequate. This is because such approaches still consider gender an individual attribute, and men are viewed as the implicit standard for assessing women's lives. Instead, feminist theorists contend that gender should be a primary consideration in attempts to understand aging, particularly since women form the majority of the older population.

Because gender is institutionalized by processes by which people assume "masculine" and "feminine" to be natural, men and women experience aging differently. An example of this difference is how women are implicitly assumed to be the primary family caregivers. This is because in most cultures they are presumed to be the "natural nurturers." The gender identities that emerge in social interactions across the life course, particularly for the current cohort of older adults, generally serve to benefit men and disadvantage women. Feminist theorists examine women's caregiving, retirement, health, and poverty across the life course in terms of women's differential access to power in the paid labor force, in child rearing, and in unpaid housework throughout their lives, and how such power differences may negatively affect their well-being in old age. We will more fully examine such gender inequities in caregiving and employment in Chapters 7

A Feminist Theoretical Perspective on Caregiving

Maria grew up with the expectation that she would marry, have children, and take care of her family. She fulfilled this expectation, raising four children, caring for her husband when he suffered a heart attack in his early sixties, and later caring for both her mother and her mother-in-law. She never held a full-time job outside the home. Instead, she occasionally worked part-time in temporary positions in order to supplement her husband's income. When he died at age 65, she was left with only his Social Security income. All her years of caregiving work, which had contributed to her family's well-being and to the economy, were not compensated in any way. She feels that she is being penalized for following the "rules" expected of her as a woman throughout her life. If her caregiving work were valued by our society and viewed as legitimate, Social Security would be altered to provide benefits for such in-home care. This would mean that family caregivers such as Maria would receive Social Security benefits in their own right in old age.

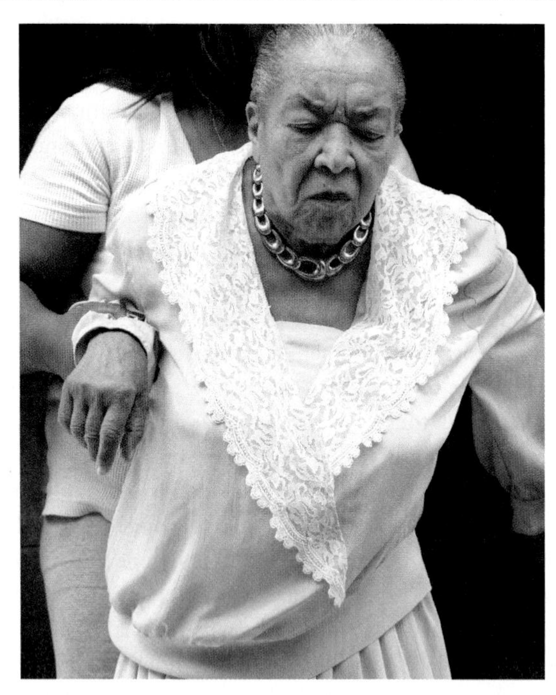

Women are often assumed to be natural caregivers, but gender inequities in informal caregiving can have long-term negative consequences for them.

and 10 (Bengtson et al., 2009; Calasanti, 2009; Calasanti & Slevin, 2006; Cruikshank, 2013).

Similarly, feminists contend that the consequences of caregiving should not be evaluated on the basis of individual characteristics such as burden. The real problem for women caregivers is public policies that fail to support their care work and thus perpetuate gender inequities. Feminists argue that unpaid caring by families must be changed to be more equitable and humane for both the givers and the recipients of care. They draw explicit linkages to practice and policy changes, such as paying family caregivers a modest stipend and legislating paid family leave (Calasanti, 2009).

The Interconnections of Gender, Race, and Sexual Orientation

Feminist theorists take account of the intersections of gender with race, social class, sexual orientation, and disability, and how these are embedded in social institutions, resulting in multiple and diverse experiences of old age. Gender inequities earlier in life underlie the fact that more older women than men are poor. But when intersections with race are examined, both African American men and women have higher poverty rates than white women. And older African American women, after a lifetime of inequities based on gender and race, are among the poorest groups in our society. The intersections of gender with sexual orientation, and how these affect both men's and women's well-being, are also analyzed by feminist theorists (Acker, 2008; Calasanti, 2004, 2009).

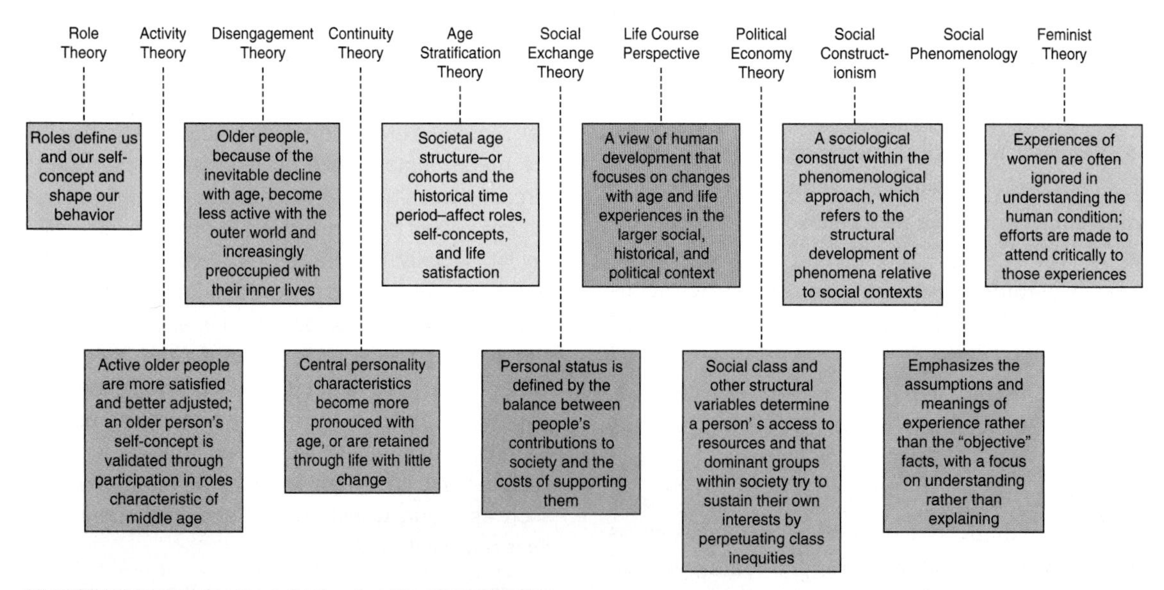

FIGURE 5.2 Major Social Theories Chronologically

summary

This review of social gerontological theories has highlighted the multiplicity of lenses through which we understand the aging process, which are summarized in Figure 5.2. Although we have emphasized explicit theoretical perspectives to build, revise, and interpret how and why phenomena occur, it is apparent that no single theory can explain all aging phenomena. Instead, these theories—or conceptual frameworks—vary widely in their emphasis on individual versus societal adjustment to age-related changes; their attention to social structure, power, economic conditions, and life course inequities; the methodologies utilized; and their reflective nature on the meaning of the aging experience. As noted early in the chapter, they represent different times or historical periods in the development of social theories. Some, such as disengagement theory, have been largely rejected by empirical data, while others, such as social phenomenology and feminist theory, are evolving and capturing the attention of a new generation of gerontological scholars. Other earlier perspectives, such as social exchange, still influence research questions as well as social policy and practice. As a whole, these theoretical perspectives point to new ways of seeing and new modes of analyzing aging phenomena by laying the groundwork for future research directions.

As the social, economic, and political conditions affecting older people change, new theoretical perspectives across a wide range of disciplines must develop or former ones must be revised through the gathering of information from diverse cultures, contexts, and circumstances. Most of the recent theories discussed in this chapter—social exchange, political economy of aging, life course perspective, social phenomenology, and feminist theory—reflect the changing nature of social theories of aging. These theories focus on the interaction between individual change with aging and structural demands and expectations of each cohort of elders. Given the increasing heterogeneity of the aging process, interdisciplinary research and theory-building are essential. Such research must take into account both individual and macro-level changes. It must encompass the role of gender, race, class, sexual orientation, and functional ability, and allow for the dynamic nature and meaning of the aging experience. In the next chapter, we turn to the social context and relationships addressed by many of the social theories of aging, beginning with the vital role of social supports in old age.

key terms

activity theory, p. 144
age norms, p. 141
age stratification theory, p. 147
continuity theory, p. 146
cumulative disadvantage, p. 151
disengagement theory, p. 145
feminist gerontology, p. 155
life course perspective, p. 150
political economy of aging, p. 151
role theory, p. 141
social constructionism, p. 152
social exchange theory, p. 149
social phenomenology, p. 153
structural lag, p. 149

review questions

1. How would you describe the difference between age norms and age roles?
2. Which of the early theories of aging lacks empirical evidence to support it?
3. What theory suggests that as we age, we tend to become more of who we already were?
4. Which of the theories has probably influenced the view that older adults should keep "busy" in retirement?

5. Cohort is a central concept to two of the theories described in this chapter. What are those theories?
6. Describe ways that the life course perspective differs from a focus on individual life span development.
7. What theories would you draw upon to explain the fact that African American women over age 75 are the poorest group in our society?
8. Which theories posit that individuals construct their own meanings of "reality"?

media resources

Watch

- Ways We Live, Clip I

View

- Social Interactions and Everyday Experiences

Read

- Newman, Katherine. Men and Women: Together and Apart in Later Years.

references

Acker, J. (2008). Feminist theory's unfinished business: Comment on Andersen. *Gender and Society, 22*, 120–125.

Allen, K. E., & Starbuck, J. R. (2009). *I like being old: A guide to making the most of aging*. Retrieved from Iuniverse.com.

Bass, S. A. (2009). Toward an integrative theory of social gerontology. In V. L. Bengtson, D. Gans, N. M. Putney, & M. Silverstein, M. (Eds.), *Handbook of theories of aging* (2nd ed.). New York: Springer.

Bengtson, V. L., Gans, D., Putney, N. M., & Silverstein, M. (Eds.). (2009). *Handbook of theories of aging* (2nd ed.). New York: Springer.

Calasanti, T. M. (2004). Feminist gerontology and old men. *Journal of Gerontology: Social Sciences, 59*, S305–S314.

Calasanti, T. M. (2009). *Handbook of theories of aging* (2nd ed.). New York: Springer.

Calasanti, T. M., & Slevin, K. (Eds.). (2006). *Age matters: Re-aligning feminist thinking*. New York: Routledge.

Cottrell, L. (1942). The adjustment of the individual to his age and sex roles. *American Sociological Review, 7*, 617–620.

Cruikshank, M. (2013). *Learning to be old.* Lanham, MD: Rowman & Littlefield.

Cumming, E., & Henry, W. E. (1961). *Growing old.* New York: Basic Books.

Dowd, J. J. (1980). *Stratification among the aged.* Monterey, CA: Brooks Cole.

Elder, G. H., Jr. (1994). Time, human agency and social change: Perspectives on the life course. *Social Psychology Quarterly, 57*, 4–15.

Elder, G. H., Jr. (1998). The life course and human development. In R. M. Lerner (vol. ed.), *Handbook of child psychology: Vol 1. Theoretical models of human development* (5th ed.). New York: Wiley.

Estes, C. L. (2001). From gender to the political economy of ageing. *European Journal of Social Quality, 2*, 28–46.

Estes, C. L. (2004). Social Security privatization and older women: A feminist political economy perspective. *Journal of Aging Studies, 18*, 9–26.

Estes, C. L., & Associates. (2001). *Social policy and aging: A critical perspective.* Thousand Oaks, CA: Sage.

Ferraro, K. F., Shippee, T. P., & Schafer, M. H. (2009). Cumulative inequality theory for research on aging and the life course. In V. L. Bengtson, D. Gans, N. M. Putney, & M. Silverstein (Eds.), *Handbook of theories of aging* (2nd ed.). New York: Springer.

George, L. K. (2007). Age structures, aging, and the life course. In J. M. Wilmoth & K. F. Ferraro (Eds.), *Gerontology: Perspectives and issues* (3rd ed.). New York: Springer.

Hagestad, G., & Neugarten, B. (1985). Age and the life course. In R. H. Binstock & E. Shanas (Eds.), *Handbook of aging and the social sciences* (2nd ed.). New York: Van Nostrand.

Harrington, M., Wolf, D. A., & Himes, C. L. (2005). Linking benefits to marital status: Race and Social Security in the U.S. *Feminist Economics, 11*, 145–162.

Havighurst, R. J. (1963). Successful aging. In R. Williams, C. Tibbits, & W. Donahue (Eds.), *Processes of aging* (Vol. 1). New York: Atherton Press.

Havighurst, R. J. (1968). Personality and patterns of aging. *The Gerontologist, 38*, 20–23.

Hooyman, N. R., Brown, C., Raye, R., & Richardson, V. (2002). Feminist gerontology and the life course: Policy, research and teaching issues. *Gerontology and Geriatrics Education, 22*, 3–26.

Kail, B. L., Quadagno, J., & Keene, J. R. (2009). The political economy perspective of aging. In V. L. Bengtson, D. Gans,

N. M. Putney, & M. Silverstein (Eds.), *Handbook of theories of aging* (2nd ed.). New York: Springer.

Longino, C. F., & Powell, J. L. (2009). Toward a phenomenology of aging. In V. L. Bengtson, D. Gans, N. M. Putney, & M. Silverstein (Eds.), *Handbook of theories of aging* (2nd ed.). New York: Springer.

Lynott, R. J., & Lynott, P. P. (1996). Tracing the course of theoretical development in the sociology of aging. *The Gerontologist, 36*, 749–760.

Powell, J. L. (2006). *Social theory and aging.* Lanham, MD: Rowman and Littlefield.

Riley, M. W., Kahn, R. L., & Foner, A. (Eds.). (1994). *Age and structural lag: Society's failure to provide meaningful opportunities in work, family and leisure.* New York: John Wiley.

Riley, M. W., & Loscocco, K. A. (1994). The changing structure of work opportunities: Toward an age-integrated society. In R. P. Abeles, H. C. Gift, & M. G. Ory (Eds.), *Aging and quality of life.* New York: Springer.

Riley, M. W., & Riley, J. W. (1994). Age integration and the lives of older people. *The Gerontologist, 34*, 110–115.

Silverstein, M., Conroy, S. J., Wang, H., Giarusso, R., & Bengtson, V. L., (2002). Reciprocity in parent–child relations over the life course. *Journal of Gerontology: Social Sciences, 57B*, S3–S13.

Walker, A. (2009). Aging and social policy: Theorizing the social. In V. L. Bengtson, D. Gans, N. M. Putney, & M. Silverstein (Eds.), *Handbook of theories of aging* (2nd ed.). New York: Springer.

6 Family, Friends, and Other Informal Supports

learning objectives

6.1 Articulate the difference between family/informal supports and formal supports and why informal supports are essential for elder care.

6.2 Discuss the variety of family/informal supports that exist in communities.

6.3 Demonstrate knowledge of LGBT relationships and how changing family structures contribute to expanding models of family/informal supports.

Listen to the Chapter Audio

Whether you're a young college student, middle-aged person, or an older adult, the presence of friends, family members, and other supportive people can enhance your life in both good and bad times. Imagine having to face something difficult in your life without anyone to share your fears and concerns with. Conversely, picture yourself having great news about an accomplishment and having no one to tell—a partner, relative, or a good friend—who would genuinely share in your happiness and excitement. The relationships that we form over the course of our life help to ensure that people are there when we need them, and that we are there when they need us. But those people often change over time. Some relationships end and new ones begin. Loved ones die and new members are born or adopted into our families. And as we get older, our social roles and relationships may change even more—as you learned in our discussion of role theory in Chapter 5.

This chapter focuses on informal social support systems that are vital to our well-being across the life course, but particularly in old age. It includes the following:

- Changing family structures, including the growth of multigenerational (three- or four-generation) families
- Older partners as social support, including lesbian, gay, bisexual, and transgender (LGBT families)
- Other types of family supports: adult children, siblings, grandparents, and great grandparents
- Friends, neighbors, and acquaintances
- Programs to strengthen social supports, including intergenerational projects
- Pets as social support

In Chapter 7, we address the vital support role played by informal caregivers to adults with chronic illness or disability.

We All Need Informal Social Support

The need for **social support**—informational, emotional, or instrumental assistance from your social networks—will continue for the rest of your life, regardless of your age. As social beings, we need to feel connected to others and experience a sense of belonging to a group or community at every stage in the life course. Our necessity for support may increase as we live longer. Doctors, nurses, social workers, physical therapists, nurses' aides, and other health care workers can provide formal support—that is, professional services that we either pay for or in some instances are funded by local, state, and federal governments. But most often, elders requiring assistance depend on informal support from family members, friends, neighbors, community volunteers, and even acquaintances. This includes assistance with caregiving, friendly visits, rides to appointments, shopping and other errands, and many other life-enhancing activities. Many elders are able to live safely and meaningfully in the community largely because of such informal supports. These also enable them to engage with the larger environment and continue the social interaction they enjoy and need in order to thrive emotionally, socially, and intellectually.

In our discussion of informal supports, it is important to remember that we are all interdependent. Despite the American value placed on independence, none of us, no matter what our age, is ever totally independent. Instead, each generation across the life course contributes to the other, through families and other informal supports.

The Benefits of Social Supports

A common myth is that older adults are lonely and isolated from family and friends. Contrary to this misperception, even older people who may appear socially isolated generally have some informal networks. Families, friends, neighbors, and even acquaintances, such as postal carriers and grocery clerks, can be powerful antidotes to some of the physical challenges of growing old.

Older adults—like many of us—first turn to informal supports before seeking formal assistance, such as social services. These may be face to face or at a distance through phone or the Internet. It isn't the practical support of relationships that make the most difference. Rather a person's assessment of the adequacy and availability of social exchanges (the giving and receiving of support) and the anticipation of support may be more important than the number and frequency of informal interactions. The extent of perceived control or self-efficacy (which means an individual's belief that he or she can succeed in a particular situation) may also increase the likelihood that social supports will benefit older adults' physical and emotional well-being. Even centenarians who may have outlived friends and family probably have a history of strong social relationships. In sum, as you learned in Chapter 4, people who are resilient and age well—or "successfully"—tend to have robust and meaningful social networks (Antonucci, Birditt, & Akiyama, 2009; Fiori, Antonucci, & Akiyama, 2008; Lyyra & Heikkinen, 2006; Moren-Cross & Lin, 2006).

Older adults who have strong social supports tend to fare better on a number of measures of well-being than those who do not. Specifically, they show

- improved health status, increased morale and self-confidence, reduced depression and anxiety;
- reduced risk of disability and even death;
- increased feelings of personal control, autonomy, and sense of being competent, including when dealing with stressful situations;
- improved cognitive abilities—learning and memory;
- diminished negative effects of adverse and stressful life events, such as retirement, illness, giving up one's longtime home, or widowhood and bereavement (Blazer, 2006; Krause, 2006; Lyyra & Heikkinen, 2006; Parker-Pope, 2005; Uchino, 2004).

Do Social Supports Change as We Age?

Although some older adults experience a decline in friendship and other informal relationships with age, many elders deal primarily with changes in the composition of their networks (e.g., less contact with couples or younger people), or in the roles people play (e.g., turning to a grandchild for help with yard work or transportation). Nevertheless, the oldest-old may watch their informal supports shrink as their peers become ill or die. But many older adults who choose to live relatively independently in their own homes can benefit from having younger friends or neighbors who can help when they may need assistance. That support may come in the form of a phone call or visit, a social outing, a trip to the grocery store, weeding the garden, or just keeping an eye out for an older neighbor.

Consistent with social exchange theory discussed in Chapter 5, most older adults try to maintain **reciprocal exchanges**—that means being able to help others who assist them. Some elders actually expand and diversify their networks by helping others through clubs, religious institutions, or volunteering, as you will learn about in Chapter 8. But even frail elders who require personal care from their families may still contribute through financial assistance or childcare. Other elders may cook, bake, or make crafts for those in their informal networks. The meaningful role of helping others also has numerous benefits for the helper—increased self-esteem, sense of purpose, life satisfaction, and physical and mental well-being. Indeed, maintaining such reciprocal exchanges is seen as vital to active aging (Kawachi & Berkman, 2001; Keyes, 2002; Morrow-Howell, Sherraden, Hinterlong, & Rozario, 2001; Uchino, 2004).

Even older adults who live alone can maintain reciprocal exchanges with family, friends, and neighbors

points to ponder

Most of us have people to turn to when we need assistance with a specific task or need advice or emotional reassurance. Think about your own life. How would you characterize your informal support network? Who are the most important people in this network? By contrast, have you ever felt that you had no one to turn to for a particular problem, and if so, how did that feel? There are probably people in your life that need or will need your support. What kind of assistance can you provide to a family member, neighbor, friend, or community member?

points to ponder

Given the benefits of informal social supports for our well-being in old age, what are some of the steps that you could take in your own life to ensure that you will have strong social networks in old age? What kinds of social relationships would you hope to have when you are older—with colleagues at work, family, neighbors, friends, younger adults, or your age peers?

to help counter loneliness, as illustrated by Beverly in the following box.

You will see throughout this chapter that the majority of older adults do not live alone. But some do. The percent of older adults who live alone increased from about 6 percent in 1900 to about 29 percent today; about 37 percent of women age 65 and older live alone compared to 19 percent of older men. Not surprisingly, the proportion living alone increases with advanced age. Among women age 75 and over, for example, almost half live alone. And those who live alone are more likely to be living in poverty than those living with a spouse or partner. But be careful not to assume that an older person living alone is socially isolated. There is a distinction between living alone and being lonely. As you just saw with Beverly, an adult of any age may live alone, by either choice or circumstances, and still have an active social life and effective support network (AoA, 2012; Pew Research Center, 2010b).

Nevertheless, being lonely is a challenge for many adults as they age. A 2010 AARP survey of over 3,000 adults age 45 and older found 35 percent were chronically lonely compared with 20 percent in a similar sample 10 years earlier. Surprisingly, those suffering the most were not the oldest-old, but adults in their forties and fifties. This rise in loneliness among the middle-aged and young-old may be another effect of the recession along with increased rates of divorce and separation. It is of concern since chronic loneliness and social isolation can take a physical and emotional toll, and may precipitate or worsen chronic health conditions. One recent study indicated that social isolation is a risk factor for death, just as smoking and alcohol consumption are, and that it may actually exceed other risk factors such as physical inactivity and obesity. Based on an analysis of 148 other studies involving more than 300,000 older adults—this is called a meta-analysis—researchers found that those with stronger social relationships had a higher likelihood of survival. Given this finding, they recommended

Living in Her Own Home—With Informal Support

Beverly Wong is an 82-year-old widow who lives alone in a small house that she owns and does not want to sell, even though some people close to her have urged her to move into an assisted living facility. Beverly no longer drives, and until recently had no problem taking the bus to wherever she needed to go. Because Beverly is not as steady on her feet these days, she has become less confident about using public transportation and has been staying at home more. She has fallen twice while walking outside alone.

Beverly's son is employed full-time during the workweek. On weekends he takes Beverly to the store and on other errands. Beverly has a niece who stops by twice a week to deliver some prepared food and spend about an hour visiting and helping with light household chores. The niece receives a modest compensation from Beverly's son, but this is not the niece's primary motivation for helping out. The arrangement is mutually beneficial. Beverly shares stories with her niece about their family history, which the niece appreciates hearing, and carefully listens to the niece talk about her problems with her boyfriend.

Other family members, neighbors, and friends also help out—and coordinate their efforts with each other. Her next-door neighbors check in on her daily and help with tasks such as mowing her lawn or bringing her the paper. Another neighbor brings her fresh fruit and vegetables from his garden. A longtime friend phones her daily just to chat and see how she is doing. A member of her church occasionally brings her a freshly baked pie. Even the postal carrier makes sure she is picking up her mail. In turn, Beverly keeps her eye on neighborhood children as they play outside on the street and is the unofficial block watch captain since she is home while most neighbors are working. She even does mending for a neighbor who is a single mother with young children. With a variety of informal "safety nets" in place, Beverly—despite her limitations in her ability to perform certain tasks—feels comfortable continuing to live alone in her own home—and, in turn, enjoys feeling valued for what she can contribute to the neighborhood she loves.

points to ponder

Imagine that you are living in an apartment in an urban neighborhood composed primarily of residents who have lived there most of their adult lives. Your next-door neighbor, who is 75 and low-income, lives alone. She was recently released from a rehab facility after falling and breaking her hip. What kinds of things could you and the other neighbors do to assist her as she recovers at home? How would you respond if she refuses offers of assistance?

that social isolation be added to the list of risk factors for mortality (AARP, 2010; Edmondson, 2010; Holt-Lunstad, Smith, & Layton, 2010; Pew Research Center, 2010a).

What Factors Affect Our Social Relationships?

You have just learned how social relationships—or lack of them—can affect a person's physical and mental health. Conversely, a person's health status may affect his or her social relationships. A process of social selection may occur whereby healthy people are more likely to have supportive social relationships precisely because they are healthy. Poor health may hinder them from initiating or sustaining social contacts. In some cases, negative interactions, such as conflict with one's neighbors or disappointment that one's children are not helping, can have adverse effects on health. As you may know from your own relationships with family or friends, close relationships have both positive and negative features (Jeon, Jang, Rhee, Kawachi, & Cho, 2007; Krause, 2004, 2006).

Gender, race, and social class may also affect the type and extent of informal social support needed. As you have learned, women outlive men and are more likely to be widowed, divorced, and living alone than their male counterparts. But as a whole, they have stronger friendship networks, as illustrated by Nan in the following box. Indeed, women's strong and supportive friendships are seen across different racial groups, cultures, and socioeconomic status (Antonucci et al., 2009).

Hanging out and teaching each other how to use text messaging can foster social support.

I Get By With A Little Help From My Friends

After 40 years of marriage, Nan was devastated by her husband's decision to divorce her. Her children lived across the country and she had no close relatives in the town where they had raised their family. Nan turned to two women whom she had confided in for more than 30 years as they shared child rearing and the ups and downs of their marriages. These other women, both divorced, provided emotional support as Nan grieved the loss of her marriage and a life of economic security. They helped her find a good divorce attorney and financial advisor, who in turn helped her obtain an adequate settlement from her husband. Most importantly, they were available 24/7 to assist her coping with this unexpected phase in her life, giving her more strength than her children or other relatives could have done. The three women had a history of supporting one another that Nan could draw on without feeling dependent or criticized.

The Centrality of Family Supports

The family is older adults' most important source of informal support and encompasses a diverse array of relationships—spouses/partners, adult children, parents, grandparents, and siblings. Ninety-four percent of older adults have other family members, and approximately 80 percent have children. The vast majority live in a household with other family members—a partner, child, grandchild, niece, or sibling, although these rates vary by gender, race, and culture. For example, white women and African American women are more likely to live alone than men and older Asian American and Latina women (AoA, 2012; Federal Interagency Forum, 2012).

Over 70 percent of older men live in a family setting, typically with a spouse or partner, compared to about 40 percent of women. This gender-based pattern reflects the fact that women are more likely to outlive their spouses. But widows are nearly three times as likely as older widowed men to live with children, siblings, or other relatives. Moreover, widows are more likely to live with a child than are divorced, single, or married women (Federal Interagency Forum, 2012).

points to **ponder**

Students in the helping professions often say that they don't want to work with older adults—they want to work with families. But nearly all families include at least one older member! In fact, effective counseling, health care, and other interventions with families need to take account of the total cross-generational family system.

Even though the majority of older adults have at least one child living close by whom they see regularly, most typically do not want to live with their children, often not wanting to be a "burden" on them. Nevertheless, some parents may feel pressured to move in with their children because of declining health, loss of a caregiver or partner, desire for companionship, and limited income. Shared households may also reflect adult children moving back into the family home, typically for financial reasons or following a divorce. Such arrangements—referred to as "boomerang children"—may strain family relationships and income. Adult children may also move in with a parent to provide assistance as the parent's care needs increase (Calasanti & Kiecolt, 2007; Davidson, 2006; Pew Research Center, 2010b).

For women and elders of color who are more likely to be low-income and struggling economically, informal supports can be particularly vital to their well-being. In such instances, social networks can play a buffering or protective role. Compared to their white counterparts, for example, more African American, Asian American, and Latina elders—especially women—live with a family member other than their spouse. They have larger extended families, more households shared with adult children and grandchildren, and greater levels of social support from their kin-like networks where caregiving flows in both directions than Caucasians do (Angel & Angel, 2006; Federal Interagency Forum, 2012).

Multigenerational relationships can be mutually supportive and enriching.

Families Are Changing

Think of people you know who may or may not live together in the same house and are not related biologically, but who care for each other and perhaps assist one another in a way that family members usually do. Even though these people are not necessarily related to each other by blood or marriage, they may identify themselves as family and share a bond that is stronger and more meaningful than with their own biological relatives.

Family structures have altered dramatically over the decades. Although there have always been diverse family types, the predominant view of family until recently has been the traditional nuclear family. Now we know that other types of families—often called nontraditional—are becoming more prevalent as social attitudes and behaviors shift over time. Indeed, family structures will continue to change as more states officially recognize same-sex marriages and civil unions.

A number of social trends underlie the increasing diversity of family structures:

- More couples living together but choosing not to marry
- More couples choosing not to have children
- A decline in the percent of children in the total population
- More unmarried couples raising children
- More single women having children without a male partner to help raise them
- More gay and lesbian couples raising children
- More mothers of young children working outside the home
- More interracial marriages (Pew Research Center, 2010a; Yen, 2011)

To take account of these changing structures, we define family in this textbook by its interactional quality, not necessarily by members' living together or by blood ties. Kinship is a matter of social definition. We can see this in

Does the Family We See in TV or Movies Really Exist?

Historically, television programs and other popular media often presented a view of families that was not complete or inclusive, and which reinforced the popular yet increasingly distorted public perception of a "normal" family. The traditional "television family" with two heterosexual parents—or later a single parent in a heterosexual relationship—and two or more children living in the same household was a common portrayal of the family unit. But many other variations exist outside the television world.

Occasionally, some television programs have shown successful nontraditional living situations. The NBC comedy *The Golden Girls*, for example, was about four older women living together, which functioned as a kind of family. You may also be familiar with the television shows *Modern Family, Brothers and Sisters*, and *Parenthood*, which have also dealt with the intricacies of family relationships. Other shows in recent years have featured gay and lesbian characters in family-like situations without playing off demeaning stereotypes. Consider the success of the 2010 movie *The Kids Are All Right* as a portrayal of LGBT families coping with daily issues similar to heterosexual families. Another change in the entertainment world is a greater openness among gay and lesbian show business personalities to reveal their sexual identity without the same level of fear that existed in previous eras when entertainers often hid their sexual identity to avoid losing work and fans.

some families of color, where **fictive kin** provide the kind of love and support that caring family members typically provide. This may include "play relatives," godparents, and friends who assume central roles in raising children. Or an increasing number of grandparents are the primary caregivers to grandchildren. Among LGBT individuals, chosen or "friendship" families are growing. Gerontological practitioners and policy-makers must be sensitive to the ways in which elders and their support systems define family in order to work effectively and respectfully with all members.

The Growth of the Multigenerational Family

Another shift in family structure is the growing number of **multigenerational families** defined by at least two adult generations and one other generation older or younger (grandchild, adult child, and parent). Multigenerational families, often sharing households, have always been prevalent in other cultures. In the United States, multigenerational family households have typically been more common among populations of color. African American, Latinos, and Asians are more likely to live in three- or even four-generational households than whites (see Figure 6.1). In many such families, the oldest generation is the bearer of family history and culture and assists with socializing the younger generation. For example, among Polynesian

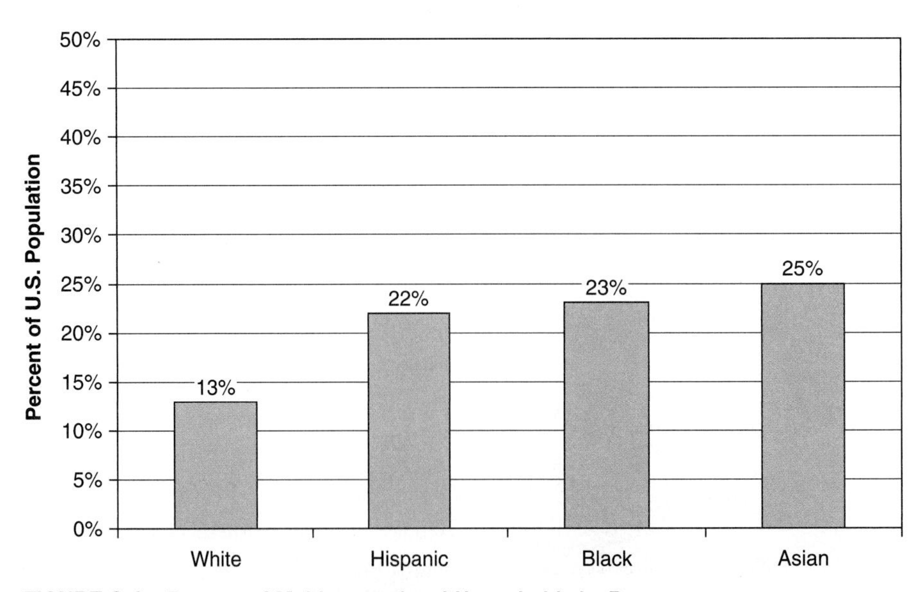

FIGURE 6.1 Percent of Multigenerational Households by Race

Source: Pew Research Center, 2010b.

families in Hawaii or Alaska natives, grandparents often play central roles in protecting their grandchildren from getting involved in crime and substance use by transmitting traditional cultural values. In Silicon Valley in California, thc avcragc Vietnamese family typically includes adult children, both for economic reasons but primarily as a way to share culture, including cooking traditional food (Bengtson & Putney, 2006; Blieszner, 2006; Joyner & Schneider, 2011; Swift, 2009; Vakalahi, Toafa, & Moala, 2008).

What has shifted since 1980 is the dramatic growth of multigenerational families in the United States across racial and ethnic groups and social class. The percent of Americans living in multigenerational households had declined from 1940 to 1980 to about 12 percent of the population. But from 1980 to 2000, such households increased by 39 percent. As a result, 16 percent of the total population—or about 6.6 million U.S. households—now encompass three or more generations. The growth of multigenerational families means that some parents and children now share five decades of life, siblings perhaps eight decades, and the grandparent–grandchild bond lasts three or more decades (Pew Research Center, 2010b).

If we look at intergenerational relations—two generations—49 million people live in such households. Many of these intergenerational arrangements are grandparent/grandchild or **skipped-generation households**, in which a parent is not present in the household. The percent of children under 18 who live in a household that included a grandparent has increased dramatically. Of the 7.8 million children who lived in households with a grandparent present in 2012, 4 percent were being raised solely by grandparents. Alternatively about 6 million grandparents have grandchildren under age 18 living with them (Generations United, 2012; Pew Research Center, 2010b; U.S. Census Bureau, 2010).

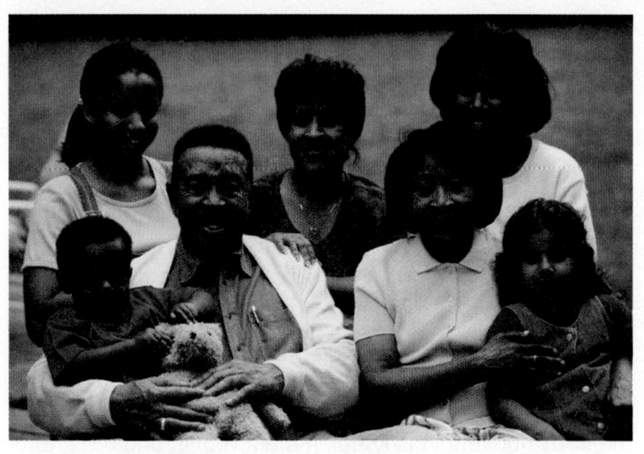

Family gatherings help maintain multigenerational ties.

Note the growth of multigenerational households over a period of 10 years as depicted in Figure 6.2, but particularly note the years 2008–2010. That two-year period saw a faster growth than any previous time since 2000.

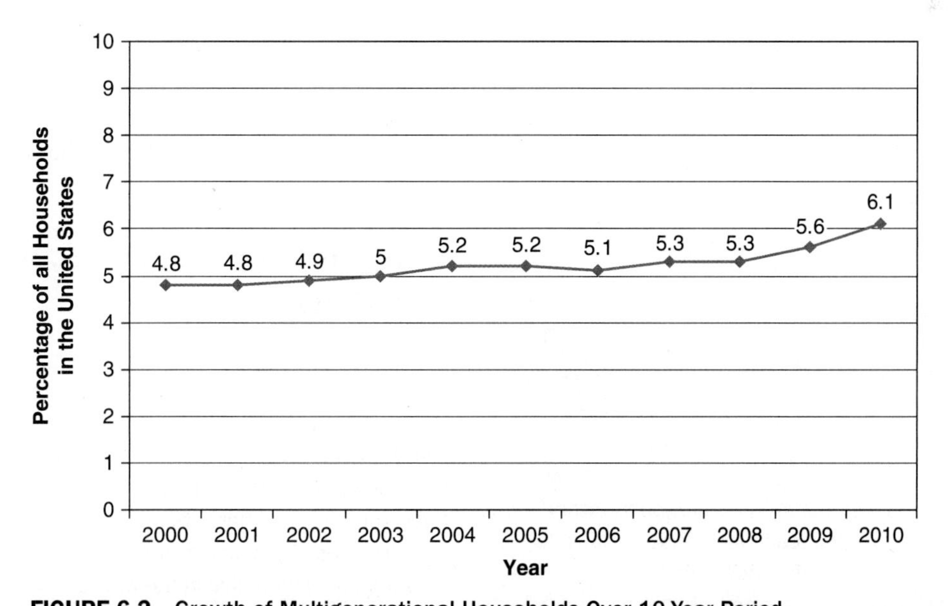

FIGURE 6.2 **Growth of Multigenerational Households Over 10-Year Period**

Source: AARP Public Policy Institute Fact Sheet, April 2011 http://assets.aarp.org/rgcenter/ppi/econ-sec/fs221-housing.pdf

A Four-Generation Family Living Together

When Sarah's parents divorced, she, her mom, and her brother all moved into her grandparents' home. When her great-grandfather got sick, her great-grandparents joined the household. Despite annoyances of different tastes in food, sharing only two bathrooms, and limited privacy, all generations perceive more benefits than disadvantages. The single mom has gained financial and emotional support, the grandchildren share their problems with their grandfather, the great-grandparents think the lively household is keeping them young, and the grandparents enjoy the laughter and chaos of their large home being filled.

Why is there an increase in multigenerational family households? In addition to people living longer, the rising percent of immigrants in the U.S. population are more likely to live in multigenerational families, as you learned in Chapter 2. But a primary factor is economic. High unemployment, rising home foreclosures, and lack of affordable housing have led to a growth in multigenerational households. Tough economic times contribute to the growing numbers of people looking to combine generations into single households, where expenses and responsibilities can be spread among more people. Real estate agents state that more buyers are showing interest in homes that could accommodate more than one generation, and builders are designing homes within homes or converting garages into apartments (Gittelsohn, 2011; Gonyea, 2013; Joyner & Schneider, 2011).

This trend toward shared households created by economic pressures has especially affected elders and young adults. Twenty percent of adults age 25–34—and 20 percent of adults age 65 and older—now live in multigenerational family households, frequently for financial reasons. This can be a good thing because parents, grandparents, great-grandparents, and even great-great-grandparents may all be a part of the family system at the same time and able to support one another. Although there can be many reciprocal benefits, there can also be tensions as generations negotiate roles, physical space, extended caregiving responsibilities, and interpersonal conflicts that are inherent in living together (Joyner & Schneider, 2011; Pew Research Center, 2010b).

points to ponder

Can you think of families where there are at least three generations living in the same house? How do these different generations help each other? What contributions does each generation make to the family and what benefits does each generation receive? Have you observed any of these generations in conflict with each other?

Older Partners as Social Support

Whether older people are married or have a partner can make a big difference in terms of the extent of their social support. Of all family members, spouses and partners are most likely to serve as confidants or close friends, offer emotional support, and guard against loneliness (Walker & Luszcz, 2009).

Older Adults and Marriage

Consider the older members of your extended family. Are most of them married, widowed, or divorced? Do you perceive any differences in marital arrangements by gender and age? Here is what is known about older adults' marital status.

- More than 58 percent are married and live with a spouse. Marriage rates are highest among Asian and Pacific Islanders, then whites, followed by Latinos and African Americans.

Living Together out of Economic Necessity

Four generations of women came together out of economic necessity, due to the high cost of housing in the San Francisco Bay Area. Lynn was diagnosed in her forties with Parkinson's and was no longer able to either care for her daughter or afford to pay her mortgage. She moved back into her mother's home, later joined by her great-grandmother. By pooling resources across generations, they are still able to live in the Bay Area and to help support one another with life's challenges (Swift, 2009).

Reflection Break

Analyzing Your Family Structure

Take a few moments now and try analyzing your own family. In your interactions with friends and relatives, you probably notice that people are part of a number of different types of family structures. Some people come from large families, and others from small ones. Some individuals live alone. Use the following questions to analyze the family that you are a part of, if you are currently part of a family. If not, analyze a family that you were once a part of.

- How many generations characterize your family?
- What are the ages of the oldest and youngest members of your family?
- Sketch your family tree as much as you can. Do you have any multigenerational households among your relatives?
- Ask the oldest family members how the structure of your family has changed since they were young.

- 45 percent of women and 72 percent of men age 65 and older are married and living with a spouse (see Figure 6.3).
- About 14 percent of women and 12 percent of men are divorced or separated—over twice as many as in 1980.
- Only 15 percent of women and 60 percent of men age 85 and older are married.
- LGBT older adults are less likely to be partnered (or married in states that allow same-sex marriage) (AoA, 2012; Federal Interagency Forum, 2012; Fredriksen-Goldsen et al., 2011).

Whether or not an older person is married or part of an intimate partnership affects his or her socioeconomic status, physical and psychological well-being, and the nature of care that is readily available in case of illness. Supportive intimate partnerships are found to promote effective coping with age-associated physical changes as well as to buffer stresses that might impair health. As a whole, people who are married enjoy numerous benefits: lower mortality, better physical and mental health, greater life satisfaction, and higher functional ability compared to unmarried cohabitating couples and widowed, divorced, and never-married people. And men tend to experience more benefits than women. This does not mean that all married older people are happier or better off than unmarried people, however. We all may be able to think of exceptions to these generalities. Moreover, it could also be the case that people who are healthier are more likely to get married in the first place (Manzoli, Villari, Pirone, & Boccia, 2007; Pienta, Hayward, & Jenkins, 2000; Prior & Hayes, 2003; Sarason & Sarason, 2009; Scafato et al., 2008; Simon, 2002; Thoits, 2011).

Older married persons can also be a source of comfort to each other when their children leave home for college or a job, creating a metaphorical **empty nest**. Those children may have provided many years of fulfillment to the couple, as well as the occasional challenges, and kept their parents' lives busy and exciting. Without children in the house, couples support each other as they find other ways to fill their lives—perhaps going on trips together, working on hobbies, or discovering new activities they never had time to pursue before.

Most studies that look at the connection between marital status and health have not included same-sex partners, largely because LGBT elders have not had the legal option of marriage until recently. Nevertheless, the research that has been done suggests that LGBT elders who are in committed relationships tend to be less lonely and enjoy better physical and mental health than their

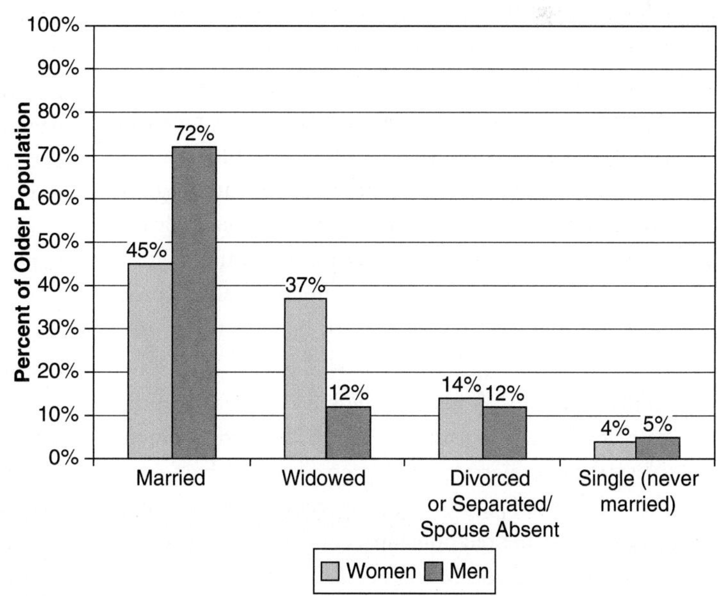

FIGURE 6.3 Older Adults, Marital Status

Source: AoA, 2012, "A Profile of Older Americans, 2011."

Older spouses and partners can be a vital source of love and support to each other, especially after children leave the home.

single peers regardless of sexual orientation. Overall, being in a committed relationship is a vital source of social support in old age, whether one is in a same-sex or heterosexual relationship (Cruikshank, 2013; Heaphy, 2007; Russell & Taylor, 2009; Wienke & Hill, 2009).

Marital Satisfaction The physical and emotional health benefits from having a spouse or partner are related to the quality of their relationship. Marital quality tends to vary by gender, life stage, and, to some extent, race and culture. Here are some of the patterns that occur:

- Men consistently experience increased levels of marital satisfaction over time compared to women, although this gender difference appears to be narrowing.
- Marital satisfaction is high among those recently married, lower among those in the child-rearing period—especially in middle age—and higher in the later stages, when children typically leave home and household division of labor may equalize with age. In later stages, couples often become more similar in their attitudes, beliefs, roles, and behaviors.
- Older African American women typically indicate lower marital satisfaction than white women. Nevertheless, marriage still promotes well-being for African American women, especially those in economically stable relationships, compared to those living alone (Calasanti & Kiecolt, 2007; Gibb, Fergusson, & Horwood, 2011; Scafato et al., 2008; Umberson & Williams, 2005; Umberson, Williams, Powers, Liu, & Needham, 2006).

Overall, research on marital satisfaction suggests that adequate communication, equality in gender roles, and joint decision-making all contribute to a happy marriage. A mutually supportive relationship can make a big difference in life satisfaction for older adults. As partners move though different roles and stages of their life such as retirement, post-parenthood, illness, or disability, they face the strain of modifying previous roles and adapting to new ones. Older partners' ability to adapt to new roles depends, in large part, on their prior flexibility and satisfaction in their marital relationship.

Divorce in Old Age Strains in partner relationships may be heightened by the fact that only recently have we seen such long-lived ones. Because of increased life expectancy, adults are likely to live together longer than the average married couple did in the past. This pattern of long-term marriages and lower divorce rates for adults over age 65 is declining, however, and more elders in future cohorts will be divorced and single. Consider this statistic illustrating this shift: Just one in five marriages of late-life couples is predicted to survive 50 years, while four or five will likely end in divorce or widowhood. This is because baby boomers have experienced a decline in first marriage rates and an increase in never-marrying rates, later age of first marriage, and increases in divorce and separation. Many boomers will enter old age as single after experiencing multiple relationships and divorces. In addition to emotional distress, people who consider divorce later in life face concerns about aging alone, economic hardship, and difficulties making new friendships. The desire for a happier life, however, may outweigh those concerns, especially as people are living longer and the realization sets in that an unhappy relationship may last a long time. How these shifts in marital patterns will affect well-being as the baby boomers age is unclear (Wu & Schimmele, 2007; Zhang, 2006).

Remarriage and Other Late-Life Romantic Relationships Separation, divorce, or the death of a spouse does not have to be the end of an older adult's romantic life, as reflected in the box on p. 171. Sometimes older people will decide to live together without getting married or, conversely, live apart in separate homes but continue to enjoy an intimate relationship with each other. Not combining households may be due to financial reasons (e.g., protecting an inheritance for their children) or just a lifestyle choice. As is the case across the life course, there are advantages and disadvantages to remarriage and other

Love at the Senior Center

Alma, 91, and Harold, 85, both recently widowed, met in an exercise class at their local senior center. Harold immediately "fell for" Alma, but she had no interest in a close relationship. She had been happily married for 65 years, had raised a family, and was content to live alone. But Harold persisted, asking her for a date. Alma, who had not dated in over 70 years, called her children about what to do. They encouraged her to do whatever made her happy. She went—and they now spend several nights a week at each other's apartments. They have no plans to marry, but are deeply committed to one another. As Alma admits with tears in her eyes, "I never thought I could love again after my husband died. But I was wrong. I love him deeply."

late-life romantic arrangements. A number of different factors come into play—socioeconomic status, gender, whether one is divorced or widowed, a desire for companionship, and health status—in affecting whether older people are likely or desire to remarry. For example, women have fewer options to remarry because they generally outlive their male peers, and men often marry women younger than themselves.

Dating in Old Age Older people who are single due to divorce, widowhood, and other reasons go on dates just as younger people who are single do. As is true among younger couples, they are motivated by the desire for companionship and intimacy. Since being single in later life is common, the stigma of looking for a new partner is diminishing, although women still face more barriers than men. In fact, baby boomers, accustomed to dating services, personal ads, and Club Med singles vacations, are redefining dating and turning to creative ways to finding a partner. Today there are Web sites specifically for older adults looking to pair up with others in their age cohort. Aware of the higher rate of divorce among remarried partners, older singles are often more interested in companionship—someone to do things with—than in marriage, especially when their children may be critical of potential partners or they fear needing to care for an older partner with health problems.

Never-Married Older People

Approximately 4 percent of the older population has never married. This number will likely grow since adults in younger age groups increasingly report being not married. The majority of never-married older persons typically develop reciprocal relationships with other kin, especially siblings, and with friends and neighbors and may not feel lonely or isolated. A single woman, for instance, may have been a "second mom" to a niece or nephew, who is then available to help with care if needed. While living alone in old age is often interpreted as a risk factor, it may not negatively affect health, emotional well-being, and social networks, particularly when an older person is long accustomed to living on his or her own and has other forms of informal support. Families and health care providers often assume that co-residence is desirable, but simply living with others tells little about the quality of relationships and life satisfaction. It may be that mental and physical well-being is most negatively affected when loss of a partner occurs later in life, rather than representing a lifelong pattern (AoA, 2012; Connidis, 2001).

As another example of well-being among those who have lived alone most of their adult lives, never-married adults who have had lifelong employment tend to enjoy greater financial security in old age. In addition, they may be more socially active and resourceful, with more diversity in their social networks—especially more interactions with younger persons, friends, neighbors, and siblings—than their married counterparts. This pattern of greater social and economic resilience tends to differentiate never-married women from their married, divorced, or widowed counterparts. Compared with widowed peers, they generally are more satisfied with their lives and self-reliant. When they do need others' assistance, they are more likely to turn to siblings, friends, neighbors, and paid helpers than are their married peers (Pinquart, 2003).

Childless Older Adults

Although most elders have living children, approximately 20 percent of those age 85 and older are childless. These oldest-old lack the natural support system of children and grandchildren and may have smaller social networks as result. Nevertheless, they may have extensive networks, be self-sufficient, and have more income and savings than older adults who are parents. Some childless unmarried elders, particularly women, develop "sisterly" non-kin relations and may be quite satisfied with their lives. Yet they may not want these friendships to be a source of care, fearing the change from voluntary mutuality into dependency. As a result, when they are faced with health problems and need for support with daily tasks, childless elders turn first to their partners/spouses (if available), then to siblings, then to nieces and nephews, and last to friends (Connidis, 2011; Dykstra, 2006; Dykstra & Hagestad, 2007; Dykstra & Wagner, 2007; Plotnick, 2009).

It is not surprising that unmarried childless elders with limited informal support systems tend to utilize formal social services and are placed in skilled nursing facilities more often than are married childless persons. Childless women—but not men—are more likely to enter long-term care facilities than those with children, and nursing home rates of admission decline with the number of children. On the other hand, simply having children does not guarantee adequate care in old age or satisfaction with the parenting role. Indeed, when adult children have problems or do not get along with their aging parents, this takes a toll on older parents' well-being. In addition, it is important to differentiate lifelong childlessness from outliving one's children, which may result in unresolved grief for years (Connidis, 2011; Koropeckyj-Cox & Call, 2007; Rothrauff & Cooney, 2008; Umberson, Pudrovska, & Reczek, 2010).

The growing number of childless and unmarried younger adults may affect the proportion of older people who will seek formal supports and develop alternative living arrangements, such as cohousing, in the future. Because of this trend of declining birth rates, there will be fewer elders with grandchildren. For example, the percentage of women age 60–64 that never experience grandparenthood will grow from the current 13 percent to over 20 percent by 2020. On the other hand, single and partnered childless adults may forge stronger friendship ties in the absence of obligations to raise children. We can learn a great deal from gay and lesbian communities about the family-like relationships that thrive when people come together in networks of mutual support (Connidis, 2011; Plotnick, 2009; Umberson et al., 2010).

points to ponder

In the future, there will be more people growing old without children as an informal support system. Given what you have been learning about the importance of social supports, what would you recommend to someone without children about how to build caring networks in old age?

Lesbian, Gay, Bisexual, and Transgender (LGBT) Partners

A major social trend that differs sharply from previous generations is the greater openness related to sexual identity. If you have older relatives who watched television during the 1950s to 1970s, it is unlikely that they saw LGBT characters or even any mention of them. They were a relatively invisible part of society. When they were talked about, the conversation might have taken on a disapproving, hushed, or shameful tone.

Although there are still lingering prejudices and stereotypes that may inhibit those who identify as LGBT from "coming out," the climate today is more tolerant than it was in previous generations. We can see this in changes in pop culture (e.g., more openly LGBT characters in non-deviant roles on television programs), the U.S. military's repeal of the "Don't Ask, Don't Tell" policy in 2010, President Obama's support of gay marriage along with greater public support for marriage equality, the Supreme Court's decision to strike down the Defense of Marriage Act, and consumer protections in the Affordable Care Act that extend to LGBT persons. A number of states have passed laws providing legal recognition to same-sex marriages, civil unions, or domestic partnerships.

At the federal level, the Internal Revenue Service (IRS) recognizes the marriage of same-sex spouses if the

LGBT elders can be a source of support to each other—as friends, caregivers, and partners.

marriage was validly entered into in a jurisdiction whose laws authorize such marriages, even if the couple now lives in a jurisdiction that does not recognize the validity of same-sex marriages. In 2013, the Social Security Administration posted a notice on its Web site saying that it was beginning to process some retirement spouse claims for same-sex couples and that payments would be made if the claims were justified. The U.S. Supreme Court's striking down of the Defense of Marriage Act left intact the states' rights to ban same-sex marriages. But many believe it was a historic Civil Rights decision because it, in effect, extended federal benefits to same-sex spouses in valid marriages, a move whose consequences will be felt for years to come. Also, by declining to decide a case regarding same-sex marriages in California, the most populous state in the nation, the Court effectively allowed same-sex marriages in that state whose citizens have been debating this issue for years (Internal Revenue Service, 2013; Liptak, 2013; Social Security Administration, 2013).

At one time, most gerontological family research focused on heterosexual couples and relationships. However, our overall knowledge about older LGBT elders is now growing. Today we are learning more about LGBT older adults in long-term committed relationships, raising children, taking care of each other and older relatives, and actively engaged in their local communities. Although gerontological family research has expanded to include LGBT individuals, there are still obstacles to acquiring accurate data about LGBT individuals and families. Participants in past surveys may have been reluctant to identify as LGBT because of the fear of discrimination and potential alienation from family and peers. Even though the 2010 Census did not ask about sexual orientation or gender identity, it was the first census to report counts of both same-sex partners and same-sex spouses.

In addition to the 2010 Census, two national surveys have greatly advanced what we know about LGBT elders and their informal supports. A 2009 National Survey of Sexual Health and Behavior found that 5.6 percent of adults identify as LGB. The first national project funded by the National Institutes of Health, Caring and Aging with Pride, found that 2 percent of adults age 50 and older self-identify as LGB, based on state-level population-based information. Indeed, the inclusion of LGBT elders through an expanded definition of minority populations in the report of the 2005 White House Conference on Aging and the 2011 first White House LGBT Conference on Aging are tangible federal recognitions of their needs (Fredriksen-Goldsen et al., 2011; Gates, 2011; Williams Institute, 2012).

A 2012 Gallup poll based on 120,000 interviews, the largest population-based survey of LGBT Americans ever conducted, found that 3.4 percent of adults surveyed identified as LGBT, and 1.9 percent of respondents who identified as LGBT were 65 or over. These numbers differ from other studies' findings and may again reflect the difficulty of attaining accurate statistics on a marginalized population that may still fear prejudice and ostracism. Perhaps more important than the specific numbers, however, are these more general findings from the Gallup poll:

- Women are more likely to identify as LGBT than are men.
- Younger Americans are more likely to identify as LGBT.
- Those in domestic partnerships, or never-married singles, are more likely to be LGBT.
- Non-white individuals are more likely to identify as LGBT (Gates & Newport, 2012).

These findings will have implications for future cohorts of LGBT older adults.

What We Now Know about Older LGBT Families Families headed by LGBT adults are as diverse as families headed by heterosexual adults.

- More than 25 percent of same-sex partners include a partner age 55 or older, and more than 10 percent a partner over age 65. The proportion may be higher, however, because these relationships may have been hidden over the years. Although many gays and lesbians are part of a live-in couple at any one point in time, as older adults they are more likely to live alone (55–66 percent), and less likely to be living with life partners and to have children than their heterosexual counterparts. In the Caring and Aging with Pride study, over 50 percent of respondents experienced loneliness.
- Since the majority of the current cohort of LGBT elders are childless, they often create a surrogate family through a strong mixed-age network of friends and significant others; these networks either complement or replace support within their family of origin and provide care for one another as they age.
- LGBT elders, especially lesbians, tend to have well-developed mutually helpful **social networks of choice** composed of friends, members of their

family of origin or **family of choice**, and the larger community. Moreover, they are building innovative housing arrangements and empowering communities, such as cooperatives or cohousing for LGBT adults as they age.

- Although LGBT partners may still face discrimination, families are more accepting of LGBT partners today than in the past. Moreover, LGBT-friendly advocacy groups, such as Parents and Friends of Lesbians and Gays, support families in the process of coming to terms with a relative's sexual orientation (Bennett & Gates, 2004; Fredriksen-Goldsen et al., 2011; Heaphy, 2007; Hecht, 2004; Hostetler, 2004; Kurdek, 2005; Lambert, 2005).

Effects of Race, Class, and Cohort with Sexual Identity Some studies suggest that the aging experience of gays and lesbians is qualitatively different, in part because of a double stigma of age and sexual orientation. Transgender elders, who are transitioning to the other sex in late life, face distinctive challenges, especially since few states have laws that forbid gender-based discrimination. Additionally, lifelong marginalization because of sexual orientation may stimulate adaptive strategies to meet the challenges of aging. In a 2006 MetLife national survey, about 40 percent of respondents believed that negotiating nonheterosexual identities and coping with homophobia throughout their lives facilitated their preparation for aging through greater resilience or better support networks. A 2010 MetLife national survey reinforced this perspective, with three out of four respondents saying that being LGBT has helped them prepare for aging, although half say their sexual orientation or gender identity makes aging more difficult. However, in contrast to a comparison group drawn from the general population, more LGBT boomers say they expect to be treated with dignity and respect at the end life. Researchers suggested that LGBT boomers have more experience demanding respect when it is not forthcoming. Respondents in the Caring and Aging with Pride study also displayed resilience qualities, with 81 percent stating that they feel positive about belonging to their LBG communities. A successful transition to one stigmatized status—being LGBT—may contribute to resilience and competence in moving to another stigmatized status—being old—thereby buffering other normative age changes such as friends and family moving away or dying. Experiencing greater blurring of gender-role definitions, gays and lesbians tend to be more egalitarian in their relationships. Overall, older LGBT individuals, especially among the boomers, generally emphasize positive aspects about aging, experience self-acceptance and high self-esteem, and have satisfying long-term relationships. However, this is not meant to be "making lemonade out of lemons"! Our society still has lots of work to do to ensure the full rights of LGBT elders (Butler, 2006; Cook-Daniels, 2007; Cruikshank, 2013; Fredriksen-Goldsen et al., 2011; Heaphy, 2007; Hostetler, 2004; MetLife, 2006, 2010).

More research is needed on the interconnections across race, ethnicity, culture, age, social class, and cohort with sexual orientation, which produce distinctive and diverse experiences of growing old. The 2010 Census found that same-sex couples are more likely than heterosexual couples to be interracial or interethnic. Moreover, couples that include an ethnic or racial minority are more likely to be raising children. Although this does not infer anything about LGBT older adults, it does support findings that LGBT relationships often involve ethnic and racial diversity. As one example of the influence of race, age, and cohort, older African American gay men in one study reported experiencing higher levels of ageism than older white gay men and higher levels of perceived racism than younger African American gay men. But despite such racism and ageism, older African American gay men did not experience significantly higher mental distress than older white gay men or younger black gay men. Indeed in the 2006 MetLife survey, Latino and African American respondents were more likely than the sample as a whole to agree their LGBT identities helped them approach midlife and anticipate a relatively positive transition to old age. In contrast, some studies suggest that coming out to family is even more difficult for elders of color and for working-class men (David & Knight, 2008; MetLife, 2006).

Age and cohort perhaps most profoundly affect LGBT individuals' aging experience. Older LGBT individuals share concerns similar to other elders—health, income, caregiving, living arrangements—but what is unique is that they have lived the majority of their lives through historical periods actively hostile and oppressive toward homosexuality. Some LGBT elders, especially those in their seventies and eighties, remain concerned with "passing" or being "invisible" in a heterosexual society, since being "out" was far riskier for them than for current cohorts (Cruikshank, 2013).

Consider these examples of cohort effect and life course experiences on LGBT relationships:

- Generally today's LGBT elders belong to the pre-liberation era; they did not benefit from the NYC 1969 Stonewall riots, which was a watershed for gay pride.
- They also lived through historical periods where homosexuality was a reason to be placed in an institution for the mentally ill. For example, until 1973, homosexuality was classified as a mental illness by the American Psychiatric Association and was not removed from the *Diagnostic and Statistical Manual of Mental Disorders* (DSM) until 1986.
- Unlike their younger counterparts, older LGBT persons are less likely to have benefited from antidiscrimination laws and supports for same-sex partners (Rosenfeld, 2003).

Because of these cohort effects, those who "come out" in middle age or late adulthood are likely to have a very different experience from those who did so in their youth. For instance, they risk rejection from their children and other family members at a time when they really need familial support. They may also encounter heterosexist attitudes and practices from health care providers and long-term care settings. They may even face ageism among younger LGBT persons and feel excluded from the primarily youth-oriented gay community (Barker, 2004; Butler, 2006; Porche & Purvin, 2008).

Barriers to Supports for LGBT Elders In addition to heterosexism and ageism, LGBT adults face disparities and legal and policy barriers that can affect their well-being in old age. The Caring and Aging with Pride study identified higher rates of disability and mental distress compared to heterosexual older adults. Moreover, LGBT elders faced inequities in accessing health care, with one in 10 of study participants having been denied health care or provided with inferior care and 15 percent fearful of accessing health care outside the LGBT community. Although friendship networks often offer assistance, their ability to do so for long periods of time may be limited, especially if decision-making is required for the elder receiving care. When a domestic partner is hospitalized or relocates to a skilled nursing facility, if a durable power of attorney for health care is not in place, blood relatives can control visitation, treatment options, and discharge planning in jurisdictions that do not legally recognize these rights even for married or registered same-sex couples. This means that long-term partners can be excluded from decision-making and rights to an inheritance. For years, LGBT partners have faced challenges when it came to visiting their loved ones, making decisions about their health care if their partners are incapacitated, and rights to an inheritance. Government policies for equal treatment are advancing, however. In April 2010, President Barack Obama's Presidential Memorandum on Hospital Visitation specifically referenced LGBT individuals who are not allowed to be at the hospital bedside of their partners with whom they may have spent decades of their life. In response, the Health and Human Services Secretary Kathleen

LGBT Elder-Friendly Organizations

SAGE (Services & Advocacy for Gay, Lesbian, Bisexual & Transgender Elders) is the oldest and most influential national organization, providing services, advocating at a policy level, and training services providers, and it has extensive resources at www.sageusa.org. New Leaf Outreach to Elders, Open House in San Francisco, Older Lesbians Organizing for Change, and the National Association of Gay Gerontologists are other support and advocacy organizations working on behalf of older LGBT individuals. Moreover, the Administration on Aging funded the first National Resource Center on LGBT Aging in 2010, which is housed in SAGE in New York City. The center provides training, technical assistance, and educational resources to aging-related service providers, LGBT organizations, and LGBT older adults.

Protecting the Rights of LGBT Elders

A number of national organizations, such as Lambda Legal, have made protection of LGBT and HIV-positive elders' rights one of its priorities. Some of the issues being addressed by Lambda Legal include

- discrimination by staff and residents at senior centers;
- denial of housing;
- denial of the ability for same-sex couples to share a room in an assisted living facility or nursing home;
- disrespect of gender identity including while incapacitated or at death;
- denial of equal Social Security benefits and survivor benefits as compared to their heterosexual counterparts (http://www.lambdalegal.org/issues/seniors/).

points to ponder

Imagine being a gay or lesbian elder who attends an adult day health or senior center daily. Because of fear of ostracism, you need to respond to every question without mentioning a lifelong partner—either a partner at home or your grief over a partner's death. And imagine maintaining that silence day after day, perhaps year after year. This is what life is like for many older LGBT adults.

Sebelius announced new rules specifying that hospitals that participate in Medicare and Medicaid must respect the right of all patients to choose who they want to visit them (Fredriksen-Goldsen et al., 2011; McFarland & Sanders, 2003; Muraco & Fredriksen-Goldsen, 2011; U.S. Department of Health and Human Services, 2011).

Working with LGBT Elders In the Caring and Aging with Pride study, 21 percent of LGBT older adults had not revealed their sexual orientation to their primary physician, which can interfere with adequate diagnosis and prevention. This and other challenges faced by LGBT elders point to an important lesson for health and social service providers: not to assume that all clients are heterosexual. As a beginning point, it is important to use the words partner or committed relationship rather than spouse or marriage. Assessments, psychosocial histories, and care planning practices must recognize that older LGBT individuals may have distinctive needs resulting from a lifetime of dealing with stigma and discrimination that may deter them from seeking services. In addition, LGBT elders who are concerned with maintaining privacy may be uncomfortable with allowing formal caregivers, such as home health aides, into their homes. Finally, health care professionals need to be aware of the significance of identity cohort membership or the historical period when LGBT individuals first identified as such, since this has profound implications for later life experiences (Cook-Daniels, 1997; Fredriksen-Goldsen et al., 2011; Neville & Henrickson, 2008; Zodikoff, 2006).

Staff members committed to enhancing the quality of life of elders in long-term care settings also need to advocate for non-homophobic policies and practices that allow LGBT partners to be together and to participate in critical end-of-life decisions. Some LGBT elders in long-term facilities have "gone back into the closet" out of fear that staff or residents will be uncomfortable with their sexual identity. Fortunately, such needs are being recognized by more service providers, and agency culture in some long-term care residences is being changed to be more inclusive of LGBT elders, often through staff training. For example, the Boulder County's Aging Services in Colorado developed Project Visibility to create an aging services community that is informed of, sensitive to, and supportive of LGBT elders. Additionally, some communities now have independent living, assisted living and skilled nursing facilities specifically for LGBT elders (Hecht, 2004; Project Visibility, 2011; Turnbull, 2013).

Sexuality, Intimacy, and Emotional Support

In Chapter 3, you learned about the normal physiological changes that may influence sexuality and sexual satisfaction as we age. Here we focus on some of the psychosocial factors that may affect older adults' sexuality and intimacy—in both heterosexual and same-sex relationships. Intimate bonds are a vital source of emotional support, no matter what one's age.

If you watch a lot of television or go to the movies, you probably do not see many older people in roles where they are expressing their sexuality. There are some exceptions, but what you mainly see are younger people in romantic leads and situations. Ageism contributes to the distorted view that older people are unattractive, asexual, and lacking the energy or capacity for sexual activity. The reality is that sexuality is a part of our lives well into older adulthood. Older adult sexuality is often misunderstood and in some cases even ignored, denied, or ridiculed. Residents in a long-term care facility, for example, may inhibit their sexuality if they feel that staff and other

points to ponder

What are your images of older adults' sexuality? What has influenced the images you hold—your personal experiences, movies, the print media? How would you respond to a friend who starts laughing at the idea of older adults as romantic partners?

residents will negatively judge them. This is unfortunate because for many older adults, regardless of where they live, sexual activity enhances their lives. Mark Lachs, a geriatric physician and author of *Treat Me: Not My Age*, maintains "despite the stereotypes and bad jokes, intimacy is alive and well in our aging population. And it is time to get comfortable with it … If we have learned nothing else from the past half-century of personal freedom and experimentation, it is that we are profoundly sexual beings. The details may change with age, but our basic physical and psychological needs do not" (Lachs, 2010, p. C1).

Those who work with older adults can play a vital role in enabling older adults to realize sexual intimacy or deep companionship, if that is what they wish, in an appropriate and respectful setting. This may involve providing couples in long-term residences with privacy and the dignity to allow their late-life romance to blossom to its potential. Some long-term facilities even encourage healthy romantic relationships among residents, while remaining attentive to issues of cognitive impairment and consent.

On the other hand, not all older adults desire to have sexual physical contact; that choice should be respected as well. Others prefer intimacy or physical contact of a nonsexual manner: deep love, attachment, and friendship are all cherished aspects of life, vital to an older person's well-being, quality of life, and meaningful aging. Physical touch—for example, holding hands or hugging—when it is mutually desired can be highly satisfying not only for elders but for people of all ages. Appropriate physical touch conveys genuine human warmth and affection.

What We Know about Older Adults and Sexuality

As you learned in Chapter 3, early sexuality studies—Kinsey, Hite, Janus, and National Health and Social Life Survey—included only a small percentage of older adults, if at all. Studies were also limited by defining sexual activity as heterosexual intercourse and making conclusions based on responses from people who—as a historical group or cohort—may have been influenced by more conservative values about sexuality and who lacked racial and socioeconomic diversity.

You also learned in Chapter 3 that sexuality is much broader than sexual intercourse, encompassing expression of feelings—love, loyalty, passion, esteem, and affirmation of one's body and its functioning—as well as intimacy, the freedom to express and respond to human closeness. All of these supportive functions can benefit both physical and mental well-being.

Figure 6.4 illustrates the findings of a 2010 AARP study on sex, romance, and relationships of 1,670 adults 45 years and older (Fisher, 2010).

As the baby boom generation, which ushered in the sexual revolution during the 1960s, enters the ranks of older adulthood, it is expected that they will be more comfortable

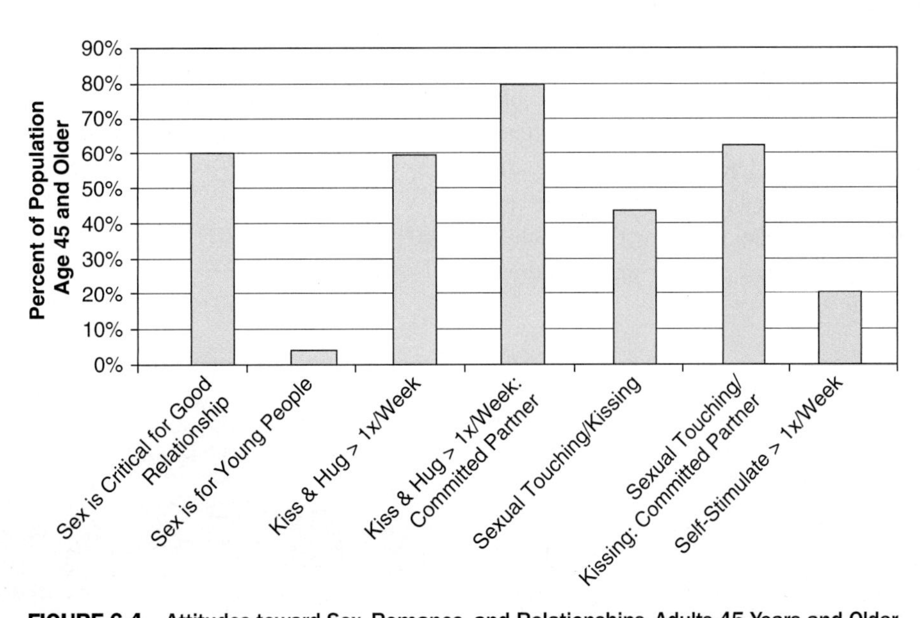

FIGURE 6.4 Attitudes toward Sex, Romance, and Relationships, Adults 45 Years and Older

Source: Fisher, 2010.

Never Too Old for Love

Esther and Harry had been lifelong friends. After their first spouses died, they reconnected at with each other in the retirement home where they both now live. Married to each other when Esther was 89, Harry 87, they are deeply in love. They are comfortable with showing their affection publicly, holding hands and hugging frequently, and fully enjoying each other's company, especially when talking about what they love—family, travel to warm places, football, and each other. They traveled around the world together when they were in their early nineties. They value as a gift each day they have together.

and open in expressing their sexuality in a variety of forms. As the children and grandchildren of baby boomers well know, there is nothing "dirty" about the sexual feelings that we experience from adolescence on. The bottom line is that elders should be able to make their own decisions about sexual expression, and families and health care providers can play a role in making that happen by understanding that the desire for sexual intimacy is normal and a vital source of social support throughout a person's life course.

Other Types of Family Supports

We have focused thus far on the partner relationship in old age—and how well-being may vary among those who are members of multigenerational households, childless, divorced, remarried, or living with a partner of the same sex. We turn now to other family relationships with adult children, siblings, and grandchildren or great-grandchildren, which affect well-being.

Relationships with Adult Children

After spouses/partners, adult children are the most important source of informal support and social interaction for older adults. Typically, the flow of support is not unidirectional from adult child to older parent, but rather is reciprocal. As you learned earlier, the vast majority of older people prefer to maintain their sense of independence and not to live with their children. But the majority see their adult children at least once a week. The quality of these cross-generational relationships—especially whether older parents feel valued and respected—is vital to their well-being and their taking actions that benefit younger family members. Most intergenerational relationships inherently involve some conflict, with parents concerned about their children's lifestyle, or children being frustrated by their parents' resistance to accepting help. Nevertheless, most families report affection, mutual support, and sharing of resources across generations. As long as the oldest generation is healthy, most resources flow to younger generations. However, this shifts when the older adult needs help with daily activities, as you will learn in Chapter 7 (Cheng, 2009; Fingerman et al., 2011).

When parents and adult children do not see each other often, it is often because the adult child lives far away. Older parents who live closer to their children have more contact and feel greater affection for them, and are more involved with grandchildren. It should be noted, however, that geographic separation does not necessarily weaken socio-emotional bonds. Indeed, the Internet, Skype, social networks, and cell phones have made it easier for those separated by geographic distance to still experience a close relationship.

Although a relatively small proportion of elders live with their adult children, the likelihood of living together increases with advancing age, extent of functional disability, and declining income. It is also more common for those who are widowed, separated, and divorced and among some elders of color. When older parents do live with their children, they usually choose to live with the one who has the greatest potential to provide emotional support, typically a daughter (American Community Survey, 2007; Blieszner, 2006; Connidis & Kiecolt, 2007).

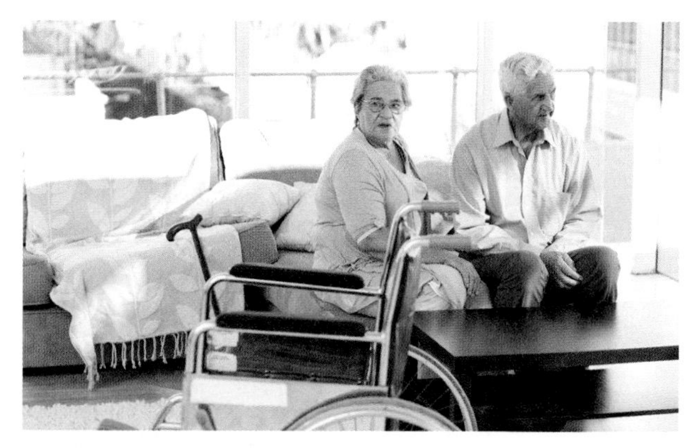

Relationships with family members continue to be important to elders in long-term care facilities.

104 Years Together

As an example of the long-lived nature of sibling relationships, consider the Delaney sisters, Sarah and Bessie. When Sarah died at 104, 107-year-old Bessie admitted that letting go of her sister was the hardest thing she had ever done. She had to learn that she was a separate human being for the first time in her life. One way she did this was coauthoring a second book at age 107! Although their bonds were particularly long and deep, many siblings, especially sisters, are extremely close, particularly as they age (Delaney & Hearth, 1997).

Sibling Relationships

Sibling relationships carry a distinctive importance, because they have the longest duration of any human relationship—and are ones that we do not choose. Because most siblings are within 10 years of age, we are likely to share a relationship for more years than any other family relationship. Even at age 80, most people still have a sibling alive. And while friendships may come and go, sibling relationships are permanent and provide deep roots to the past (Cicirelli, 1995; Cress & Peterson, 2010).

Siblings who get along, especially those who are close in age, have someone to talk to who understands the family dynamics that "outsiders" may lack knowledge and insight about. Remember what you learned in Chapter 4 about the importance of reminiscence or life review, which often occurs among siblings. Older adults with siblings report higher life satisfaction and morale, and lower rates of depression. In times of illness or crisis, siblings are shown to provide emotional and psychological support to each other. This exchange of support is common between siblings who live far away as well as those who live nearby (Cicirelli, 1995; Connidis & Campbell, 1995; Eriksen & Gerstel, 2002).

Of course, not all sibling relationships are positive. Dysfunctional or problematic relationships between siblings can be a source of distress at any age. Siblings sometimes grow apart once they start their families or pursue their careers. However, siblings often come back together in old age around significant life events such as death, divorce, birth of grandchildren, relocation, retirement, and illness. Earlier rivalries or conflicts are often put aside in a desire to share this rediscovered emotionally close relationship. And sometimes just knowing that a sibling is there, even if we do not turn to them, can be a critical source of emotional support (Cress & Peterson, 2010; Eriksen & Gerstel, 2002).

The increasing rate of divorce and remarriage will undoubtedly affect sibling relationships. The growth in **blended families**—those structured through remarriage—will result in more half-siblings and step-siblings. For divorced older people who do not remarry, interactions with siblings may become more important than when they were married. The sibling relationship is also important to LGBT elders, presuming their siblings have accepted their sexual orientation (Connidis, 2001).

Grandparenthood and Great-Grandparenthood

If you are a college undergraduate, it is likely that you have at least one living grandparent. The grandparent–grandchild relationship can be a source of informal social support for both generations. Although we address grandparents as primary caregivers in the next chapter, we discuss grandparents in this chapter as well since they can be significant in the lives of family members, regardless of whether they are caregivers or recipients of care.

The number of grandparents in the United States has hit a record high and is growing. More older people today are experiencing the role of grandparenthood and, increasingly, of great-grandparenthood, although they have proportionately fewer grandchildren than preceding generations. The transition to grandparenthood typically occurs in middle age, not old age. You may be surprised to learn that the average age of grandparents is 50 years! But

Grandparents and grandchildren can be a source of joy and comfort to each other.

grandparents vary in age from their late thirties to over 100 years old, and grandchildren can range from newborns to retirees. This also means that more adults are reaching the stage of great grandparent—or even great-great grandparent—and creating four and five generations. Contary to stereotypical images of grandma in a rocking chair, most grandparents are employed, engaged in their communities and sharing resources with their grandchildren (Grandparents.com, 2011; Hills, 2008; MetLife, 2011; Reitzes & Mutran, 2004a).

Since this phase of life can encompass more than 40 years, it is not surprising that multiple grandparenting roles and meanings exist. Early research found the grandparent role to be peripheral and not a primary source of identity, meaning, or satisfaction for older adults. More recent studies conclude that grandparents generally derive great emotional satisfaction, sense of purpose, and feeling valued from interacting with their grandchildren and observing their development and activities. They want to have an influence on their grandchildren, typically to encourage moral standards, religious beliefs and values, integrity, and a commitment to succeed, and to leave a legacy of contributing to future generations—a pattern consistent with the concept of generativity discussed in Chapter 4. As you may have experienced, grandparents often have the freedom to spoil their grandchldren or, freed from other responsibilities, to try to be a better grandparent than they were as a parent (Hebblethwaite & Norris, 2011; Lumby, 2010; Theiele & Whelan, 2008; Winefield, 2010).

Consistent with role theory, grandparenthood provides opportunities for older adults to experience a sense of meaning, morale, and positive role identity, to relive their lives through their grandchildren, and to indulge them with unconditional love. Grandparents and grandchildren often enjoy a special relationship, qualitatively different from the parent–child relationship. This can often be seen in the pride that grandparents display when announcing the birth of a new grandchild, or when sharing stories about grandchildren's accomplishments. In some instances, grandparents provide the acceptance and affection that are not always forthcoming from a child's own parents, and grandchildren may value this special relationship throughout their lives. Overall, grandparent identity tends to be associated with life satisfaction and psychological well-being. Additionally, grandparents' involvement with their grandchildren is compatible with the concept of active aging that you have learned about throughout this book (Drew & Silverstein, 2004; Mueller & Elder, 2003; Neugarten, 1964; Neugarten & Weinstein, 1964; Reitzes & Mutran, 2004a, 2004b; Soliz & Harwood, 2006).

A number of factors influence the extent of grandparent–grandchildren interaction and roles. You learned earlier about how multigenerational households are becoming more common with 7 percent of children living in grandparent-headed households. About 80 percent of grandparents not living with grandchildren nevertheless see a grandchild at least monthly, and nearly 50 percent do so weekly. For grandparents who are at a geographic distance, this does not markedly affect the quality of their emotional bonds with their grandchildren. They may still experience what is called **intimacy at a distance**. Parents primarily determine the degree of interaction when grandchildren are young. Family size also affects these cross-generational bonds. Grandparents with many children and grandchildren tend to be less invested in any particular grandchild. But with declining birth rates resulting in fewer grandchildren, grandparents increasingly have more time and resources to invest in grandkids (Bengtson & Putney, 2006; Goyer, 2010; MetLife, 2011; Monserud, 2008; Umberson et al., 2010).

Culture and race also influence grandparenting roles and responsibilities. Some studies point to greater interactions among populations of color through an extended kin network and more grandparent responsibility for child rearing; for instance, grandparents often play an authoritative parental role in African American extended families. In Asian immigrant families, grandparents who offer child care while their adult children work may help foster the family's economic success and derive a sense of meaning from this contribution to the family. Mexican American families tend to have strong grandparent–grandchild ties, with the oldest generations often providing financial

points to **ponder**

What type of relationship have you had with your grandparents—or even great-grandparents? Were they actively involved in your life or at a geographic or psychological distance? Did you have strong emotional bonds with them? How would you describe the impact that they had on your life? And how did the nature of your relationship affect how you view old age?

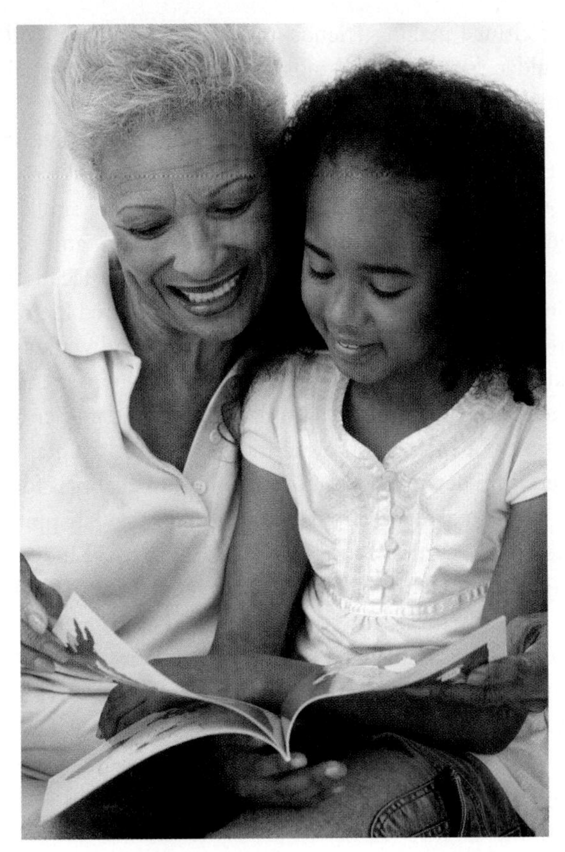

Older family members may have more time to spend with their younger relatives.

to travel more during retirement than past cohorts. Baby boomers with the financial resources, however, often take their grandchildren on trips, with some travel sites specializing in grandparent–grandchild trips (MetLife, 2011).

Approximately 50 percent of all persons marrying today will face divorce—which will profoundly affect the meaning of the grandparenthood experience. The fact that over 30 percent of children live in one-parent families or with neither parent also affects the nature of grandchild–grandparent relationships. The tie between grandchildren and their grandparents is typically mediated by the grandchildren's parents, but divorce and resulting custody arrangements disrupt these links and may require renegotiating existing bonds. The grandparents whose adult child is awarded custody have more contact, frequently because the parents require more help with child care and finances. And grandmothers generally maintain more contact with their grandchildren than do grandfathers after an adult child's divorce. In some instances, controveries regarding grandparents' rights for visitation erupt, with state laws generally favoring the parents' wishes regarding contact with grandparents.

These issues become even more complex when stepfamilies are involved. Based on marriage and divorce patterns during the 1990s, it is estimated that by 2030 the population age 70–85 may have one step-grandchild for every 1.7 biological grandchildren. From a grandparent's

assistance to young generations. The relationships of immigrant grandparents with their grandchildren are sometimes negatively affected by the pressures of acculturation, with the younger generations sometimes rejecting the grandparents' values and lifestyles. Less is known about the role of secondary kin of extended families—cousins, aunts, uncles, nieces, and nephews in helping to raise younger family members (Chadiha et al., 2005; MetLife, 2011; Saxena & Sanders, 2009; Youngkyeong, 2008).

Age also affects the types of grandparent–grandchild interactions and grandparents' satisfaction with the role. Younger grandparents, especially grandmothers, generally have more frequent and informal contact through child care and shared recreational activities, while older grandparents—particulary those with with higher incomes—may have a more formal and distant relationship but help out with their grandchild's educational, medical, or living expenses. But you may see exceptions to these patterns among your own extended family. These age differences may shift, however, as baby boom grandparents remain employed longer or choose

The Internet As A Tool For Intergenerational Communication

Grandparents at a geographic distance who have the financial means and are computer savvy are discovering that they can stay in touch with their grandchildren of any age through Web-based video-calling technologies such as Skype. This real-time video interaction provides a different kind of communication experience than exchanging photographs or e-mails over the Internet. Instead, grandparents can participate in "tea parties," sing favorite songs, make faces together, or read stories to their grandchildren even when geographically separated. For some grandparents, they feel like they are actually interacting face to face with the younger generation and thus need to travel less to have that experience. For others, the illusion of proximity makes them ache for the real thing. How such Internet-based interaction will affect long-term grandparent/grandchild relationships is unknown (Harmon, 2008).

Grandparenting and Legal Issues

Laura and David's son was killed in an auto accident. He left behind two girls, ages 3 and 5, and their biological mother, who was his girlfriend, but who had left the relationship after the birth of the second child. David and Laura had always been close to their grandchildren and involved in their care. After their son's death, his girlfriend returned to assume responsibility for the girls. In her grief and anger, the girlfriend claimed the paternal grandparents had no legal right to visit the girls and refused to allow contact. She later married, and her new husband felt even more strongly that Laura and David should not be allowed to visit the girls. The grandparents took their case to court, but the court ruled in favor of the mother.

perspective, the growing pattern of divorce–remarriage means sharing grandchildren with their newly acquired relatives under conditions in which grandchildren will be scarcer because of declining birthrates. Grandchildren, in turn, may find themselves with eight or more grandparents. Kinship systems are further complicated by the fact that, with the increased divorce rate occurring after 20 or more years of marriage, grandparents may no longer be married to one another. Just imagine, a grandchild may have step-grandparents, ex-step-grandparents, parents of a cohabitating partner of a parent, or LGBT grandparents. Groups such as the Foundation for Grandparenting and the National Committee of Grandparents for Children's Rights play important roles in disseminating up-to-date resources to grandparents regarding the complexities created by divorce in either generation and by step-grandparenting (Copen & Silverstein, 2004; Ehrenberg & Smith, 2003; Ganong & Coleman, 2006; U.S. Census Bureau, 2011).

We turn now to the vital role of other informal supports—friends and neighbors—in older adults' lives.

Friends and Neighbors as Social Supports

It is difficult to overestimate the role that friends and neighbors play in older adults' lives, especially those who live alone or whose family members are unable to visit often. As we noted at the start of this chapter, we never outgrow the need for friendship and to remain socially connected. And these bonds are vital to our physical and mental well-being. It is particularly important for elders to continue making friends at different age levels so that as older friends die or move away, there are others that remain connected.

Despite the benefits of cross-generational friendship networks, both men and women tend to select friends from among their social peers—those who are similar in age, gender, marital status, sexual orientation, and social class. Age homogeneity plays a strong role in facilitating friendships in later life, in part because of shared life transitions, reduced interactions with children and work associates, and possibly the equality of friendship interactions. The extent of reciprocity, intimacy, and quality rather than quantity of interaction are critical factors in maintaining friendship networks. Moreover, friendship quality is found to be related to psychological well-being and happiness (Adams, Blieszner, & de Vries, 2000; Hogan, Linden, & Najarian, 2002; Shaw, Krause, Liang, & Bennett, 2007).

Friends are critical for intimacy and exchange of confidences, especially when compared to relatives other than marital partners and after major role transitions such as widowhood or retirement. For example, an older widow generally prefers help from confidantes because relatives may reinforce her loss of identity as wife, be overly protective, or, alternatively, minimize her loss. To the extent that friendships are reciprocal and satisfy social and instrumental needs, they can compensate for the absence of a partner and help mitigate loneliness (Stevens, Camille, Martina, & Westerhof, 2006).

Gender differences in informal supports are more pronounced than life course differences. Women generally have

Friendships among Older Women

Five women had gone to high school together, married their high school sweethearts, and remained in the same Midwestern town, raising their children, volunteering, and working part-time. They met occasionally to play bridge, helped watch each other's children, and shared in the joys and sadness of family life. Within an eight-year time period, all became widows. They began to meet more often than when their husbands were alive—joining each other for meals, shopping trips, and bridge. When one of the women, Marge, suffered a stroke, the other four became her primary caregivers—bringing her food, accompanying her to the doctor, visiting with her daily, and helping to clean her home. This friendship network greatly relieved the caregiving burden for Marge's daughter.

more emotionally intimate, diverse, and intensive friendships than men. For many men, their wives are their only confidants, a circumstance that may make widowhood or divorce more difficult for them. In contrast, women tend to satisfy their needs for intimacy throughout their lives by establishing close female friendships and therefore are less emotionally dependent on the marital relationship. The resilience of some older women, in fact, may be rooted in their ability to form close reciprocal friendships as captured in the box about lifelong women friends (Blieszner, 2006; Moen, Erickson, & Dempster-McClain, 2000; Stevens et al., 2006).

Although friends are vital resources, their helping efforts usually do not approach those of family members in duration or intensity, and do not fully compensate for the loss of a partner or children. Even the best of friendships may involve negative interactions, such as unwanted advice or assistance. Friendships may also become strained if the relationship is not reciprocal and one side makes excessive demands for assistance. Nevertheless, since friendships are so central to well-being, professionals need to encourage older adults to sustain these relationships or assist them with building new ones. A thorough psychosocial assessment by a health care provider, for example, would include questions about an older person's networks of friends and neighbors (Hogan et al., 2002; Litwin, 2003).

As you have also learned, neighbors can be vital to older adults' well-being. In communities where neighbors feel a sense of responsibility for one another, older adults may thrive and feel secure. Checking in briefly with an older neighbor, spending time with an elder for longer visits, or offering a ride to do errands can help elders feel more connected to the community, even if they cannot get out as much. As you will learn in Chapter 11, the majority of older adults want to remain in their own homes and neighborhoods as long as possible. A number of age-friendly neighborhood initiatives, such as the village concept where neighbors exchange services with one another, build on neighbors' desire for social connection and helping each other out, no matter what age.

Programs to Strengthen or Build Neighborhood and Community Supports National and local initiatives that aim to strengthen existing community ties or to create new ones can promote supportive environments for elders. Network-building initiatives aim to strengthen existing ties, often through **natural helpers**—nonfamily members that others can turn to because of their concern, interest, and understanding. Perhaps you were a natural helper in your school—or know someone who others always turn to. Such natural helpers provide emotional support, assist with problem-solving, offer concrete services, and act as advocates. Neighbors often perform natural helping roles, and may strengthen these activities through organized block programs and block watches.

Even people in service positions, often referred to as **gatekeepers**, can fulfill natural helping functions, because of the visibility of their positions and the regularity of their routine interactions with elders. For example, mail carriers can be trained to observe whether an older person is taking in the mail each day. This can help maintain the elder's security and help build on routine everyday interactions. Pharmacists, ministers, bus drivers, local merchants, beauticians, and housing managers are frequently in situations to offer companionship, advice, and referrals. In high-crime areas, local businesses and restaurants may have a safe house decal in their windows, indicating where neighborhood residents of all ages can go in times of danger or medical emergencies.

Religious or faith-based institutions may also serve to strengthen and build personal networks, in some cases creating a surrogate family for older people. Members of religious institutions can help with transportation, friendly visiting, housework, home repair, and meal preparation, as well as offer psychological support. At the same time, older members may take on leadership and teaching roles within the church, synagogue, or mosque, thereby enhancing their sense of belonging and self-worth. In many private and public programs, volunteers are commonly used to develop new networks or expand existing ones for older persons. For example, older volunteers deliver meals on wheels, offer peer counseling and information and assistance, and serve as friendly visitors to other older adults. You will learn more about the social support benefits of religious participation and volunteerism in Chapter 8.

Neighborhood and community-building is another approach to strengthening a community's self-help and problem-solving capabilities. Increasingly, boomers are creating their own communities and support systems, sometimes called Circles of Caring or care teams, to meet their emotional, spiritual, and physical needs as they age. A group called Fiercely Independent Seniors in a rural area of Washington State meets weekly; members reciprocate by assisting each other with tasks and regularly checking up on each other. "Time Banks" are growing in popularity among many communities, even in large cities like New York and San Francisco. These allow people of different ages and with varied skills essentially to barter services. A retired English teacher may do some tutoring for a child, for example, and use the credit she earns to get computer help from another volunteer. A young adult may offer to walk an older person's dog and trim their trees in exchange for a home-cooked meal. A software has even been developed to facilitate the exchange of such resources within neighborhoods. The idea is to promote a mix of ages, one where older residents do not need to move from their home if their health fails or where younger adults can benefit from elders' skills. It is not surprising that the cohort who engaged in consciousness-raising during the 1960s is fostering movements identified as "conscious aging," or "aging your way." Such approaches are consistent with findings that those who provide peer support may benefit as much as its recipients and are central to active aging. You will learn more about these approaches, including the village model to support aging in place, in Chapter 11 (King, 2006; Neergaard, 2011; Trenshaw, 2004).

Community building may also involve advocacy through lobbying and legislative activities. Such initiatives aim to build upon the strengths and resources of local communities, including within communities of color. Many of these include an intergenerational component. The Tenderloin Project, which has existed for over 40 years in a low-income area of single-room occupancy units in San Francisco, is a model of neighborhood development. Nearby residents acted cross-generationally on the immediate problem of safety, crime and victimization of older people and then dealt with community-wide issues such as nutrition, child care, and economic revitalization. In the process, weekly support groups were formed, social support systems strengthened, arts and cultural events sponsored, and an urban farmers market thrived. Neighborhood-based intergenerational helping networks connect the formal service system to provide personal care services to frail elders. Targeted senior center activities often promote community-based support and advocacy that extends outside the center itself. And many healthy aging initiatives that seek to create age-friendly communities include a neighborhood and advocacy component. For example, a Food Dollars Program in low-income neighborhoods in Boston helps older adults prepare healthy meals on a tight budget but also to empower elders to advocate for changes to reduce hunger and poverty. And Age-Friendly New York City through its Aging Improvement Districts uses a community development approach to mobilize low-income communities of color for changes in neighborhood housing and services (Bookman, Leutz, & Bercaw, 2012; Finkelstein & Roher, 2012; Kehoe, Aday, & Farney, 2006; Schieman & Meersman, 2004).

Intergenerational Programs The practice of separating older adults, even those in residential care settings, from the rest of society is gradually losing traction as we learn more about the benefits of encouraging people of all ages to interact socially. **Intergenerational programs** that link older people with schoolchildren, high-risk youth, children with special needs, and young families are a rapidly growing type of mutual help. This can also be extended to address cross-generational neighborhood and community problems, such as safety and the environment (Moody, 2008).

The most common type of intergenerational programming involves older adults serving children and youth. For example, after-school telephone support, pen pal projects, tutoring, and assistance at day care programs are provided through Retired Senior Volunteer Programs (RSVP). The Foster Grandparents Program offers tutoring and mentoring, generally to low-income youth. The Computer Pals Program fosters youth and elder e-mail partnerships, with adolescents often teaching computer skills to older adults. Big Brothers and Big Sisters in some communities now pairs

A Planned Cross-Generational Community

Hope Meadows, located on what was once military housing in a rural area of Illinois, is an example of an innovative residential community housing three generations that are often marginalized in our society: "hard to place" children in the public child welfare system, foster families who have agreed to adopt at least three special needs kids, and retirees who seek new avenues for meaning in their lives. Older adults serve as honorary grandparents, volunteer at least six hours a week to support the kids or their foster parents, and in return receive reduced rent. Hope seniors serve as mentors, tutors, and grandparents for the children as well as companions and support for their parents so that all three generations benefit from caring mutual support. Hope Meadows has become a national model of a supportive cross-generational community and is being replicated in other cities (Eheart, Hopping, Power, Mitchell, & Racine, 2009).

older adults (the "bigs") as mentors with youth. Residential facilities for high-risk youth sometimes involve older adults as mentors and surrogate grandparents. There are even intergenerational schools within retirement communities, which encourage lifelong learning and involve older adults as both mentors and students. Some programs involve elders and youth in social action projects that seek to improve society through environmental activism, gardening, music, and art. Elders can also assist young families with parenting skills, literacy training, social support, and job hunting, and in creating supportive communities for foster and adoptive families or other families with high-risk children. But help can flow both ways. Adolescents, even those who are marginalized, can assist older neighbors with yard work, home maintenance, and friendly visiting. Shared housing communities or cohousing living arrangements, which you will read about in Chapter 11, also encourage intergenerational contact and assistance. In these settings—which often look to outsiders like they are townhouse or condo developments—families and singles live independently but come together occasionally for shared meals, community meetings, gardening, or home repair (Butts & Lent, 2009).

Other residential settings that are designed specifically for older adults such as assisted living facilities and nursing homes may have on-site preschools or elementary schools so that residents can see the children playing and entertaining during their occasional visits. In such instances, it is important to respect the needs of both elders and children; for example, some older adults may not want to interact daily with children and may resent an environment that is too child-centered. Careful planning is necessary to ensure that interactions are age and developmentally appropriate, and allow elders to have choice and decision-making control (Hayes, 2003; Salari, 2002).

Participants in some intergenerational programs have experienced significant health benefits as well as increased social interaction. This was the case in an intergenerational school in a skilled nursing facility, where elders served as reading mentors and computer pals in the classroom, and students volunteered in the facility, each generation valuing their shared educational experiences. In light of growing evidence that such interaction is vital to active aging, it would be desirable if intergenerational projects could grow in the future (Butts & Lent, 2009; Whitehouse, Fallcreek, & Whitehouse, 2005).

Such growth would be consistent with President Obama's emphasis on community service by all age groups, and the expansion of AmeriCorps for Seniors.

An Intergenerational Gran Pal Project

A second-grade public school teacher involves his class in visiting regularly with their "Gran Pals" in a nearby skilled nursing care facility. In preparation for their visits, he first has them participate in a simulation of what it feels like to be "old and frail" by wearing glasses with Vaseline on the lens, being pushed in a wheelchair, wearing gloves while opening a bottle, learning to speak clearly and directly to someone while wearing earplugs, and so on. Such simulations are frequently created for undergraduate students, but this program involves 6- and 7-year-olds, who then write and talk about what they experience when their usual activities are restricted. Each visit to the skilled care facility begins with the teacher talking with the children about what they might experience, and is then followed by the children's writing and discussing what they learned. The teacher is motivated not only by the social benefits for the older residents, but also by the recognition that by the time his second graders enter the job market, 20 percent of the population will be older adults.

Practitioners in schools, senior centers, long-term care facilities, and other community-based settings can play pivotal roles in fostering cross-generational exchanges that benefit both young and old. On the other hand, because public funding tends to be based on age, ongoing fiscal support for intergenerational projects is limited, and many depend solely on volunteers. Nearly everyone will agree that intergenerational programs are a good idea, but neither the government nor private funders in the past have provided adequate support. The Association of Gerontology in Higher Education, Generations United, and Generations Together are national groups that promote intergenerational policy and practice.

The Unconditional Love of Pets

If you've ever had a pet, you know that animals can be an important source of companionship, happiness, and affection, as well as a responsibility that requires continuous attention. Many older adults talk to and confide in their pets, and believe that animals are sensitive to their moods and feelings. Having a pet to feed, groom, or walk can provide structure, a sense of purpose, and an anchor in days that might otherwise lack meaning, and may even serve to reduce depression. Pets, with their unconditional

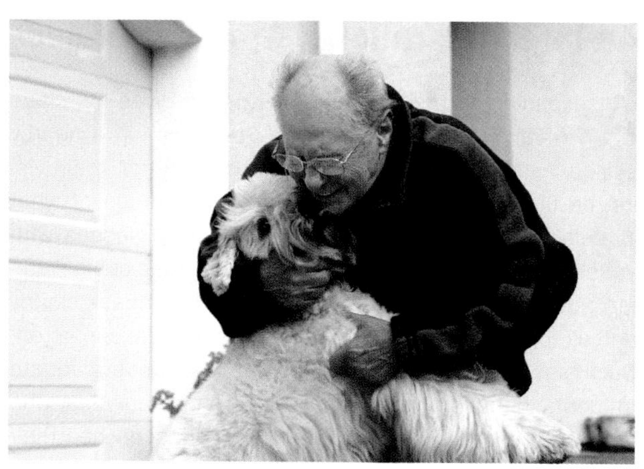

Animal companions can bring joy, purpose, and friendship later in life.

love, may compensate for lack of family members in the home, but simply owning a pet does not appear to reduce elders' loneliness. In some studies, pet owners score higher than their peers without pets on measures of happiness, self-confidence, morale, self-care, alertness, responsiveness, dependability, and sense of control. These benefits may be partially explained by the fact that pet owners are more likely to be younger, physically active, and married or living with someone. On the other hand, one of the few longitudinal studies on the benefits of pet ownership found that people who continuously owned a pet were healthier than those who had never had one or who had ceased owning a pet. The mobility benefits from walking a dog and preventing further health deterioration have also been highlighted (Baun, Johnson, & McCabe, 2006; Connell, Janevic, Solway, & McLaughlin 2007; Johnson, Meadows, Haubner, & Sevedge, 2003; Nunnelee, 2007; Watt & Pachana, 2007).

The perceived benefits of pets have led to an increase in pet-facilitated programs and "house pets" for older adults in long-term care settings, as well as loan-a-pet or pet day care programs for elders in their own homes. A study of pets in skilled nursing homes identified significant benefits, particularly in terms of reduced depressive symptoms and improved perceptions of quality of life. Pet visitation with residents has been found to improve health, self-concept, life satisfaction, and mental functioning (Coleman et al., 2002; Columbo, Buono, Smania, Raviola, & De Leo, 2006).

However, a pet—real or robotic—should not be viewed as a substitute for human relationships. Some cases of self-neglect involve homes filled with pets, but lacking food, hygiene, and other social interaction for the elder. Additionally, a strong bond with a pet can result in an intense sense of grief when the pet dies or is lost. This can have devastating effects on an elder's well-being. Pet ownership can be costly and labor intensive. On balance, however, the benefits of enhanced well-being and quality of life seem to outweigh the costs. In recognition of these benefits, the National Institutes of Health's definition of complementary/alternative medicine (CAM) includes human–animal interaction as pet ownership, animal-assisted activity (e.g., pet visitation), or animal-assisted therapy (structured sessions with treatment goals) (Banks & Banks, 2002; Johnson et al., 2003; Saito, Okada, Ueji, Kikuchi, & Kano, 2001).

summary

Informal networks are vital to older adults' physical and mental well-being. Among these, the family is the most important source of support. Families include spouses/partners, adult children, parents, grandparents, and siblings, as well as people who may not be related to us biologically but who love and care for us—and vice versa—as loving family members do. Our definition of family is broader today than it was several generations ago, and we will continue to see more diverse and complex family structures and living arrangements in the future.

Providers need to be sensitive to the wide variation of family forms that can be supportive environments, including grandparents as caregivers, LGBT partners, mothers who have delayed childbearing and are simultaneously caring for a toddler and an older parent, widowed, divorced, childless, or never-married older adults with extensive friendship networks, and elders of color with fictive kin networks. Additionally, friends and neighbors are vital sources of support for all age groups, and particularly for older adults who live alone.

Another shift is the dramatic growth in multigenerational families. Health and human service providers in schools, community clinics, public child welfare, hospitals, and mental health centers, regardless of their area of expertise, will increasingly encounter three-, four-, and even five-generation families.

All of these changes highlight the need for gerontological practitioners in a wide range of settings to gain skills in assessing and intervening with families, not only with the older person. Given the complexity of family forms, professionals will be challenged to think outside traditional age-based silos and models of service delivery, and develop new ways to utilize older adults as a civic resource.

Some older adults are also finding support and companionship from their peers as they date, discover romance, and even marry or remarry late in life. Contrary to popular stereotypes, many older adults do desire intimacy and find enjoyment in various forms of sexual expression. Deep friendships can also be a source of comfort and support in one's later years.

Creating more opportunities for reciprocal intergenerational relationships is a good way for older and younger people to enhance each other's lives and learn to value each other's contributions to society. Situating assisted living communities near preschools or elementary schools, for example, enables greater interaction between the generations.

It seems inevitable that information and communication technologies will increasingly play a role in helping older adults remain connected and engaged, although they should not be a complete substitute for face-to-face human interaction. Older generations who use social media may actually learn much more about their younger family members than they would through the occasional and brief phone call or letter.

To close, the majority of older persons continue to play a variety of social roles—partner, parent, grandparent, friend, and neighbor—and to derive feelings of satisfaction and self-worth from these interactions. The good news about the changing structure of families is that there are many more options, places, and relationships for elders to receive and give informal support. It could be in a traditional family environment, or it could be in an innovative living arrangement that several decades ago would not have been socially acceptable. Elders today and in the future will benefit from informal supports that come from a widening array of interpersonal relationships, including pets.

key terms

blended families, p. 179
empty nest, p. 169
family of choice, p. 174
fictive kin, p. 166
gatekeepers, p. 183
intergenerational programs, p. 184
intimacy at a distance, p. 180
multigenerational families, p. 166
natural helpers, p. 183
neighborhood and community-building, p. 183
reciprocal exchanges, p. 162
skipped-generation households, p. 167
social networks of choice, p. 173
social support, p. 161

review questions

1. What are the ways that informal support systems often change as people age? Discuss the benefits of informal supports for physical and mental well-being in old age.
2. The Beatles had a famous song with the line "I get by with a little help from my friends." Identify at least three ways that friendship networks can enhance well-being in old age.
3. We often have an image that older adults live alone, are lonely, and are socially isolated. Cite evidence from the readings that is contrary to this image.
4. List three challenges in accessing health and long-term care that LGBT elders may face compared to their heterosexual peers.
5. What are some of the reasons that different studies and polls have varied findings regarding the number of LGBT elders in the total population?
6. What are three of the ways that contemporary families are changing? Identify the primary reasons that there has been an increase in multigenerational families in the past decade.

7. Discuss how living arrangements, such as whether one is living alone or with family or caring for grandchildren, may vary among older adults of color.
8. What are two of the reasons why sibling relationships can be a powerful source of social support in old age?
9. If you were training staff in a long-term care facility, such as a skilled nursing home, to respect older residents' privacy, what would you tell them about older adults' sexuality and desire for intimacy? Be sure to include the needs of LGBT elders in your response.
10. What are some of the ways that the grandparenting role benefits both the grandparent and grandchild?
11. What are some of the pros and cons of pet ownership for older adults?

media resources

View

- Aging Stereotypes

Read

- Index of Family Relations
- Bengston, Vern. Beyond the Nuclear Family: The Increasing Importance of Multigenerational Bonds.
- Montgomery, Rhonda J.V., and Mary McGlinn Daywyler. Women and Men in the Caregiving Role.

references

AARP. (2010). *Loneliness among older adults: A national survey of adults 45+*. Retrieved December 1, 2011, from http://www.aarp.org/personal-growth/transitions/info-09-2010/loneliness_2010.html.

Adams, R. G., Blieszner, R., & de Vries, B. (2000). Definitions of friendship in the third age: Age, gender, and study location effects. *Journal of Aging Studies, 14*, 117–133.

Administration on Aging (AoA). (2012). *Profile of Older Americans: 2011*. Washington, DC: Department of Social and Health Services, Administration on Aging.

American Community Survey. (2007). *The marriage measures guide of state-level statistics*. Retrieved November 2009, from http://aspa.hhs.gov/hsp/07/marriagemeasures.html.

Angel, R., & Angel, J. (2006). Diversity & aging in the United States. In R. Binstock & L. K. George (Eds.), *Handbook of aging and the social sciences* (6th ed.). New York: Academic Press.

Antonucci, T., Birditt, K., & Akiyama, H. (2009). Convoys of social relations: An interdisciplinary approach. In V. B. Bengtson, D. Gans, N. M. Putney, & M. Silverstein (Eds.), *Handbook of theories of aging* (2nd ed.). New York: Springer.

Banks, M. R., & Banks, W. A. (2002). The effects of animal-assisted therapy on loneliness in an elderly population in long-term care facilities. *Journals of Gerontology, 57A*, M428–M432.

Barker, J. (2004). Lesbian aging: An agenda for social research. In G. Herdt & B. deVries (Eds.), *Lesbian and gay aging: Research and future directions*. New York: Springer.

Baun, M., Johnson, R., & McCabe, B. (2006). Human–animal interaction and successful aging. In A. Fine (Ed.), *Handbook on animal-assisted therapy* (2nd ed., pp. 287–302). San Diego, CA: Academic Press.

Bengtson, V. C., & Putney, N. M. (2006). Future "conflicts" across generations and cohorts. In J. Vincent, C. Phillipson, & M. Downs (Eds.), *The futures of old age*. London: Sage.

Bennett, L., & Gates, G. (2004). *The cost of marriage inequality to gay, lesbian and bisexual seniors*. Washington, DC: Human Rights Campaign.

Blazer, D. (2006, November 18). *"How do you feel about ...?" Self-perceptions of health and health outcomes in late life.* Kleemeier Award lecture delivered at Annual Meeting of the Gerontological Society of America Dallas, Texas.

Blieszner, R. A. (2006). Lifetime of caring: Dimensions and dynamics in late-life close relationships. *Personal Relationships, 13*, 1–18.

Bookman, A., Leutz, W., & Bercaw, L. E. (2012, November 15). *Reducing food and economic insecurity among elders: Assessing community-based models for change*. Presented at the Annual Meetings of the Gerontological Society of America, San Diego, CA.

Butler, S. (2006). Older gays, lesbians, bisexuals and transgender persons. In B. Berkman (Ed.), *Handbook of social work in health and aging*. New York: Oxford University Press.

Butts, D. M., & Lent, J. P. (2009). Better together: Generational reciprocity in the real world. In R. Hudson (Ed.), *Boomer bust? The boomers and their future* (Vol. 2). Westport, CT: Praeger.

Calasanti, T., & Kiecolt, K. J. (2007). Diversity among late-life couples. *Generations, 31*, 10–17.

Chadiha, L. A., Miller-Cribbs, J. E., Rafferty, J., Adams, P., Pierce, R., & Kommidi, S. (2005). Urban and rural African American female caregivers' family reunion participation. *Marriage and Family Review, 37*, 129–146.

Cheng, S.-T. (2009). Generativity in later life: Perceived respect from younger generations as a determinant of goal disengagement and psychological well-being. *Journal of Gerontology: Psychological-Social Sciences, 64B*, 45–54.

Cicirelli, V. G. (1995). *Sibling relationships across the life span*. New York: Plenum Press.

Coleman, M. T., Looney, S., O'Brien, J., Ziegler, C. Pastorino, C. A., & Tumer, C. (2002). The "Eden Alternative." Findings after one year of implementation. *Journal of Gerontology: Medicine, 57A*, M419–M421.

Columbo, G., Buono, M., Smania, K., Raviola, R., & De Leo, D. (2006). Pet therapy and institutionalized elderly: A study on 144 cognitively unimpaired subjects. *Archives of Gerontology and Geriatrics, 42*(2), 207–216.

Connell, C. M., Janevic, M. R., Solway, E., & McLaughlin, S. J. (2007). Are pets a source of support or added burden for married couples facing dementia? *Journal of Applied Gerontology, 26*(5), 472–485.

Connidis, I. A. (2001). *Family ties and aging*. Thousand Oaks, CA: Sage.

Connidis, I. A. (2006). Intimate relationships: Learning from later life experience. In T. Calsanti & K. Slevin (Eds.), *Age matters*. New York: Routledge.

Connidis, I. A. (2011). Interview: Single and childless: New ways of growing old. *Aging Horizons Bulletin*. Retrieved July 15, 2011, from http://aginghorizons.com/2011/01/interview-single-and-childless-new-ways-of-growing-old/.

Connidis, I. A., & Campbell, L. D. (1995). Closeness, confiding and contact among siblings in middle and late adulthood. *Journal of Family Issues, 16*, 722–745.

Cook-Daniels, L. (1997). Lesbian, gay male, bisexual and transgendered elders: Elder abuse and neglect issues. *Journal of Elder Abuse and Neglect, 9*, 35–49.

Cook-Daniels, L. (2007). Planning for late life: Transgender people. *Age Concern*. Retrieved November 2009, from http://www.ace.org/uk.

Copen, C., & Silverstein, M. (2004). Predictors of grandparent–grandchild closeness after parental divorce. *The Gerontologist, 44*, 91–92.

Cress, K., & Peterson, K.C. (2010). *Mom loves you best: Forging and forgiving sibling relationships*. Far Hills, NJ: New Horizon Press.

Cruikshank, M. (2013). *Learning to be old: Gender, culture and aging*. New York: Rowman & Littlefield.

David, S., & Knight, B. G. (2008). Stress and coping among gay men: Age and ethnic differences. *Psychology and Aging, 23*, 62–69.

Davidson, K. (2006). Flying solo in old age: Widowed and divorced men and women in later life. In J. Vincent, C. Phillipson, & M. Downs (Eds.), *The futures of old age*. London: Sage.

Davies, C., & Williams, D. (2002). *Grandparent study*. Washington, DC: American Association of Retired Persons.

Delaney, S., & Hearth, A. H. (1997). *On my own at 107: Reflections on life without Bessie*. San Francisco, CA: HarperCollins.

Drew, L., & Silverstein, M. (2004). Intergenerational role investments of great-grandparents: Consequences for psychological well-being. *Ageing & Society, 24*, 95–111.

Dykstra, P. A. (2006). Off the beaten track: Childlessness and social integration in late life. *Research on Aging, 28*(6), 749–767.

Dykstra, P. A., & Hagestad, G. O. (2007). Childlessness and parenthood in two centuries: Different roads, different maps? *Journal of Family Issues*, 28, 1518–1533.

Dykstra, P. A., & Wagner, M. (2007). Pathways to childlessness and late-life outcomes. *Journal of Family Issues, 28*, 1487–1517.

Edmondson, B. (2010). All the lonely people. *Magazine*, 55, 58, 84.

Eheart, B. K., Hopping, D., Power, M. B., Mitchell, E. T., & Racine, D (2009). *Generations of Hope communities*. White Paper Series. Champaign, IL: Generations of Hope Development Corporation.

Eheart, B. K., Power, M. B., & Hopping, D. E. (2003). Intergenerational programming for foster-adoptive families: Creating community at Hope Meadows. *Intergenerational Relationships, 1*, 17–28.

Ehrenberg, M., & Smith, S. (2003). Grandmother–grandchild contacts before and after an adult daughter's divorce. *Journal of Divorce and Remarriage, 39*, 27.

Eriksen, S., & Gerstel, N. (2002). A labor of love or labor itself: Care work among adult brothers and sisters. *Journal of Family Issues, 23*, 836–856.

Federal Interagency Forum on Aging-Related Statistics. (2012). *Older Americans 2011: Key indicators of well-being*. Washington, DC: Federal Interagency Forum on Aging.

Finkelstein, R., & Roher, S. (2012, November 15). *Aging improvement districts: Empowerment through inclusion*. Presented at the Annual Meetings of the Gerontological Society of America, San Diego, CA.

Fingerman, K. L., Pitzer, L. M., Chan, W., Birditt, K., Franks, M. M., & Zarit, S. Z. (2011). Who gets what and why? Help middle-aged adults provide to parents and grown children. *Journals of Gerontology: Psychological Sciences, 66B*, 87–98.

Fisher, L. L. (2010). *Sex, romance, and relationships: AARP survey of midlife and older adults*. Washington, DC: AARP. Retrieved from http://assets.aarp.org/rgcenter/general/srr_09.pdf.

Fiori, K. L., Antonucci, T. C., & Akiyama, H. (2008). Profiles of social relationships among older adults: A cross-cultural approach. *Ageing and Society, 28*, 203–231.

Fredriksen-Goldsen, K. I., Kim, H.-J., Emlet, C. A., Muraco, A., Erosheva, E. A., Hoy-Ellis, C. P., Goldsen, J., & Petry, H. (2011). *The aging and health report: Disparities and resilience among lesbian, gay, bisexual, and transgender older adults*. Seattle, WA: Institute for Multigenerational Health, University of Washington.

Gates, G. J., & Newport, F. (2012). Special report: 3.4% of U.S. adults identify as LGBT. *Gallup Politics*. Retrieved January 2013 from http://www.gallup.com/poll/158066/special-report-adults-identify-lgbt.aspx.

Ganong, L., & Coleman, M. (2006). Patterns of exchange and intergenerational responsibilities after divorce and remarriage. *Journal of Aging Studies, 20*, 265.

Gates, G. J. (2011). *How many people are lesbian, gay, bisexual, and transgender?* The Williams Institute, University of

California—Los Angeles. Retrieved July 2011, from http://www.law.ucla.edu/williamsinstitute/home.html.

Generations United. (2012). *Grandfamilies statistics.* Retrieved January 1, 2013, from http://www.gu.org/OURWORK/Grandfamilies/GrandfamiliesStatistics.aspx.

Gibb, S. J., Fergusson, D. M., & Horwood, L. J. (2011). Relationship duration and mental health outcomes: Findings from a 30-year longitudinal study. *British Journal of Psychiatry, 198*, 24–30.

Gittelsohn, J., (2011, November 26). Home sweet 3-generation home emerges. *Seattle Times*, A1, A6.

Gonyea, J., (2013). Changing family demographics, multigenerational bonds, and care for the oldest-old. *Public Policy & Aging Report, 23*, 11–15.

Goyer, A (2010). *More grandparents raising grandkids. New census data shows an increase in children being raised by extended family members.* Washington, DC: AARP. Retrieved January 15, 2013, from http://www.aarp.org/relationships/grandparenting/info-12-2010/more_grandparents_raising_grandchildren.html.

Grandparents.com. (2011). *Surprising facts about grandparents.* Retrieved July 16, 2011, from http://www.grandparents.com/gp/content/opinions/from-the-editors/article/surprising-facts-about-grandparents.html.

Harmon, A. (2008, November 28). Grandparents stay in touch via webcams. *Seattle Times.* Retrieved September 21, 2013, from http://seattletimes.com/html/nationworld/2008444549_webcam28.html.

Hayes, C. (2003). An observational study in developing an intergenerational shared site program: Challenges and insights. *Journal of Intergenerational Relations, 1*, 113–132.

Heaphy, B. (2007). Sexualities, gender and ageing: Resources and social change. *Current Sociology, 55*, 193–201.

Hecht, R. (2004, May–June). No straight answers. *AARP the Magazine.* Retrieved November 29, 2006, from www.aarpmagazine.org/people/Articles/.

Hebblethwaite, S., & Norris, J. (2011). Expressions of generativity through family leisure: Experiences of grandparents and adult grandchildren. *Family Relations, 60*(1), 121–133.

Hills, W. E. (2008). Grandparenting roles in the evolving American family. In D. Wiseman (Ed.), *The American family: Understanding its changing dynamics and place in society* (pp. 65–78). Springfield, IL: Charles C. Thomas.

Hogan, B., Linden, W., & Najarian, B. (2002). Social support interventions: Do they work? *Clinical Psychology Review, 22*, 381–440.

Holt-Lunstad, J., Smith, T. B., Layton, J. B. (2010). Social relationships and mortality risk: A meta-analytic review. *PLoS Medicine Journal.* Retrieved July 15, 2011, from http://www.plosmedicine.org/home.action.

Hostetler, A. J. (2004). Supportive housing for LGBT elders. *Generations, 29*, 64–69.

Internal Revenue Service. (2013). *Answers to frequently asked questions for individuals of the same sex who are married under state law.* Washington, DC: Internal Revenue Service. Retrieved September 23, 2013, from http://www.irs.gov/uac/Answers-to-Frequently-Asked-Questions-for-Same-Sex-Married-Couples

Jeon, G. S., Jang, S. N., Rhee, S. J. Kawachi, I., & Cho, S. I. (2007). Gender differences in correlates among elder Korean. *Journal of Gerontology: Social Sciences, 62B*, S323–S329.

Johnson, R., Meadows, R., Haubner, J., & Sevedge, K. (2003). Human–animal interaction: A complementary/alternative medical intervention for cancer patients. *American Behavioral Scientist, 47*, 55–69.

Joyner, T., & Schneider, D. (2011). Georgia sees an increase in multigenerational households. *The Atlanta Journal Constitution.* Retrieved September 21, 2013, from http://www.ajc.com/news/news/local/georgia-sees-an-increase-in-multigenerational-hous/nQJrG/.

Kawachi, I., & Berkman, L. F. (2001). Social ties and mental health. *Journal of Urban Health: Bulletin of the New York Academy of Medicine, 78*, 458–467.

Kehoe, G., Aday, R., & Farney, L. (2006). Impact of senior center friendships on aging women who live alone. *Journal of Women and Aging, 18*, 56–74.

Keyes, C. L. (2002). The exchange of emotional support with age and its relationship with emotional well-being by age. *Journals of Gerontology: Psychological Sciences, 57B*, 518–525.

King, M. (2006). Elderly seek to grow old together, form new support groups. *Seattle Times*, May 1, pp. A1, A11.

Koropeckyj-Cox, T., & Call, R. A. (2007). Characteristics of older childless persons and parents: Cross-national comparisons. *Journal of Family Issues, 28*, 1382–1414.

Krause, N. (2004). Stressors in highly valued roles, meaning in life and the physical health status of older adults. *Journals of Gerontology, 59B*, S87–S117.

Krause, N. (2006). Social relationships in late life. In R. Binstock & L. George (Eds.), *Handbook of aging and the social sciences* (6th ed.). New York: Academic Press.

Kurdek, L. A. (2005). What do we know about gay and lesbian couples? *Current Directions in Psychological Science, 14*, 251.

Lachs, M. (2010, November 13–14). Desire in the twilight of life. *Wall Street Journal*, C1–C2.

Lambda Legal. *Seniors.* Retrieved November 30, 2011, from http://lambdalegal.org/issues/seniors.

Lambert, S. (2005). Lesbian and gay families: What we know and where to go from here. *Family Journal: Counseling and Therapy for Couples and Families, 13*, 43–51.

Liptak, A. (2013, June 26). Supreme Court bolsters gay marriage with two major rulings. *New York Times.* Retrieved September 23, 2013, from http://www.nytimes.com/2013/06/27/us/politics/supreme-court-gay-marriage.html?pagewanted=all&_r=1&.

Litwin, H. (2003). The association of disability, sociodemographic background, and social network type in later life. *Journal of Aging and Health, 15*, 391–408.

Lumby, J. (2010). Grandparents and grandchildren: A grand connection. *International Journal of Evidence-Based Healthcare, 8*(1), 28–31.

Lyyra, T. M., & Heikkinen, R. L. (2006). Perceived social support and mortality in older people. *Journals of Gerontology, 61B*, S147–S153.

Manzoli, L., Villari, P., Pirone, G. M., & Boccia, A. (2007). Marital status and mortality in the elderly: A systematic review and meta-analysis. *Social Science & Medicine, 64*(1), 77–94.

McFarland, P. L., & Sanders, S. (2003). A pilot study about the needs of older gays and lesbians: What social workers need to know. *Journal of Gerontological Social Work, 40*, 67–80.

MetLife. (2011). *The MetLife report on American grandparents: New insights for a new generation of grandparents* (July 2011). Retrieved December 1, 2011, from http://www.metlife.com/mmi/research/american-grandparents-insights-new-grandparents.html#findings.

MetLife Mature Market Institute. (2006). *Out and aging: The MetLife study of lesbian and gay baby boomers*. Westport, CT: Metropolitan Life Insurance.

MetLife Mature Market Institute. (2010). *Still out, still aging*. Westport, CT: Metropolitan Life Insurance.

Moen, P., Erickson, M. A., & Dempster-McClain, D. (2000). Social role identities among older adults in a continuing care retirement community. *Research on Aging, 22*, 559–579.

Monserud, M. A. (2008). Intergenerational relationships and affectual solidarity between grandparents and young adults. *Journal of Marriage and Family, 70*(1), 182–195.

Moody, H. R. (2008). Environmentalism as an aging issue. *Public Policy & Aging Report, 18*(1), 3–7.

Moren-Cross, J., & Lin, N. (2006). Social networks and health. In R. Binstock & L. George (Eds.), *Handbook of aging and the social sciences* (6th ed.). New York: Academic Press.

Morrow-Howell, N., Sherraden, M., Hinterlong, J., & Rozario, P. A. (2001). *The productive engagement of older adults: Impact on later-life well-being*. St. Louis, MO: Longer Life Foundation.

Mueller, M., & Elder, G. (2003). Family contingencies across the generations: Grandparent–grandchild relationships in holistic perspective. *Journal of Marriage and Family, 65*, 404–417.

Muraco, A., & Fredriksen-Goldsen, K. (2011). "That's what friends do": Informal caregiving for chronically ill lesbian, gay, and bisexual elders. *Journal of Social and Personal Relationships, 28*, 1073–1092.

Neergaard, L. (2011, July 11). Aging boomers strain cities built for the young. *Seattle Times.* Retrieved from http://seattletimes.nwsource.com/html/health/2015572503_apusaginggamericaagefriendlycities.html.

Neugarten, B. (1964). *Personality in middle and late life: Empirical studies* New York: Atherton Press.

Neugarten, B., & Weinstein, K. (1964). The changing American grandparent. *Journal of Marriage and Family, 26*, 199–204.

Neville, S., & Henrickson, M. (2008). The constitution of "lavender families": A LGB perspective. *Journal of Clinical Nursing, 18*, 849–856.

Nunnelee, J. B. (2007). *Pets and the level of loneliness in community dwelling older adults*. (Doctoral dissertation.) University of North Texas. AAT 3254209.

Parker-Pope, T. (2005, June 20). The secrets of successful aging. What science tells us about growing older and staying healthy. *Wall Street Journal*. Retrieved January 14, 2012, from http://online.wsj.com/article/0,,SB111867751964458052,00.html.

Pew Research Center. (2010a). *The decline of marriage and rise of new families.* Retrieved July 15, 2011, from http://pewsocialtrends.org/2010/11/18/the-decline-of-marriage-and-rise-of-new-families/2/.

Pew Research Center. (2010b). *The return of the multigenerational family household*. Retrieved July 15, 2011, from http://pewresearch.org/pubs/1528/multigeneratioanl-family-household.pdf.

Pienta, A. M., Hayward, M. D., & Jenkins, K. R. (2000). Health consequences of marriage for the retirement years. *Journal of Family Issues, 21*(5), 559–586.

Pinquart, M. (2003). Loneliness in married, widowed, divorced and never-married older adults. *Journal of Social and Personal Relationships, 20*, 31–53.

Plotnick. R. (2009). Childlessness and the economic well-being of older Americans. *Journals of Gerontology: Social Sciences, 64B*, 767–776.

Porche, M. V., & Purvin, D. M. (2008). "Never in our lifetime": Legal marriage for same-sex couples in long-term relationships. *Family Relations, 57*, 144–159.

Prior, P. M., & Hayes, B. C. (2003). The relationship between marital status and health. *Journal of Family Issues, 24*, 124–148.

Project Visibility. (2011). *Project Visibility.* Retrieved November 15, 2011, from http://www.bouldercounty.org/help/adults/pages/projvis.aspx.

Reitzes, D. C., & Mutran, E. J. (2004a). Grandparent identity, intergenerational identity and well-being. *Journals of Gerontology, 59B*, S213–S220.

Reitzes, D. C., & Mutran, E. J. (2004b). Grand-parenthood: Factors influencing frequency of grandparent–grandchildren contact and grandparent role satisfaction. *Journal of Gerontology: Social Sciences, 59B*, S9–S16.

Rosenfeld, D. (2003). *The changing of the guard: Lesbian and gay elders, identity and social change.* Philadelphia, PA: Temple University Press.

Rothrauff, T., & Cooney, S. (2008). The role of generativity in psychological well-being: Does it differ for childless adults and parents? *Journal of Adult Development, 15*, 148–159.

Russell, D., & Taylor, J. (2009). Living alone and depressive symptoms: The influence of gender, physical disability, and social support among Hispanic and non-Hispanic older adults. *Journal of Gerontology: Social Sciences, 64*, 95–104.

Saito, T., Okada, M., Ueji, M., Kikuchi, K., & Kano, K. (2001). Relationship between keeping a companion animal and instrumental activity of daily living: A study of Japanese elderly living at home in Satomi village. *Nippon Koshu Eisei Zasshi, 48*, 47–55.

Salari, S. M. (2002). Intergenerational partnerships in adult day centers: Importance of age-appropriate environments and behaviors. *The Gerontologist, 42*, 321–333.

Sarason, I. G., & Sarason, B. R. (2009). Social support: Mapping the construct. *Journal of Social and Personal Relationships, 26*(1), 113–120.

Saxena, D., & Sanders, G. F. (2009). Quality of grandparent–grandchild relationship in Asian-Indian immigrant families. *International Journal of Aging and Human Development, 68*(4), 321–337.

Scafato, E., Galluzzo, L., Gandin, C., Ghirini, S., Baldereschi, M., Capurso, A., Maggi, S., Farchi, G., & for the IWG. (2008). Marital and cohabitation status as predictors of mortality: A 10-year follow-up of an Italian elderly cohort. *Social Science & Medicine, 67*, 1456–1464.

Schieman, S., & Meersman, S. (2004). Neighborhood problems and health among older adults: Received and donated social support and the sense of mastery as effect modifiers. *Journals of Gerontology, 59B*, S89–S97.

Shaw, B. A., Krause, N., Liang, J., & Bennett, J. (2007). Tracking changes in social relations throughout late life. *Journals of Gerontology: Psychological Sciences and Social Sciences, 62*(2), S90–S99.

Simon, R. W. (2002). Revisiting the relationship among gender, marital status, and mental health. *American Journal of Sociology, 107*, 1065–1096.

Social Security Administration. (2013). *Processing claims for same-sex couples*. Washington, DC: U.S. Social Security Administration. Retrieved September 23, 2013, from http://ssa-custhelp.ssa.gov/app/answers/detail/a_id/2492

Soliz, J., & Harwood, J. (2006). Shared family identity, age salience and intergroup contact: Investigation of the grandparent–grandchild relationships. *Communication Monographs, 73*, 87–107.

Stevens, N. L., Camille, M. S., Martina, M. A., & Westerhof, G. J. (2006). Meeting the need to belong: Predicting effects of a friendship enrichment program for older women. *The Gerontologist, 46*, 495–502.

Swift, M. (2009, January 24). All in the bigger family. *Seattle Times*, p. A4.

Theiele, D. M., & Whelan, T. A. (2008). The relationship between grandparent satisfaction, meaning, and generativity. *International Journal of Aging and Human Development, 66*(1), 21–48.

Thoits, P. A. (2011). Mechanisms linking social ties and support to physical and mental health. *Journal of Health and Social Behavior, 52*(2), 145–161.

Trenshaw, C. (2004). *A harvest of years: A Peer Spirit guide for proactive aging circles*. Langley, WA: Peer Spirit.

Turnbull, L. (2013, September 17). Summit will focus on LGBT aging issues. *Seattle Times*. Retrieved September 22, 2013 from http://o.seattletimes.nwsource.com/html/localnews/2021838918_lgbteldercarexml.html.

Uchino, B. N. (2004). *Social support and physical health: Understanding the health consequences of relationships*. New Haven, CT: Yale University Press.

Umberson, D., Pudrovska, T., & Reczek, C. (2010). Parenthood, childlessness, and well-being: A life course perspective. *Journal of Marriage and Family, 72*(3), 612–629.

Umberson, D., & Williams, K. (2005). Marital quality, health and aging: Gender equity? *Journals of Gerontology, 60B*, 109–113.

Umberson, D., Williams, K., Powers, D. A., Liu, H., & Needham, B. (2006). You make me sick: Marital quality and health over the life course. *Journal of Health and Social Behavior, 47*, 1–16.

U.S. Census (2010). *Current population survey Internet and computer use supplement public use file*. Retrieved November 30, 2011, from U.S. Census (2011).

U.S. Department of Health and Human Services. (2011). Better health and well-being: Making improvements for lesbian, gay, bisexual, and transgender Americans. *U.S. DHHS website*. Retrieved January 2013, from http://www.hhs.gov/secretary/about/lgbthealth_update_2011.html.

Vakalahi, H. F. O., Toafa, S. G., & Moala, K. O. (2008). Grandparenting in the Tongan community: A cultural model. *Journal of Intergenerational Relationships, 6*(3), 305–319.

Walker, R., & Luszcz, M. (2009). The health and relationship dynamics of late-life couples: A systematic review of the literature. *Ageing and Society, 29*, 455–480.

Watt, D., & Pachana, N. A. (2007). The role of pet ownership and attachment in older adults. *Australian Journal of Rehabilitation Counseling, 13*(1), 32–43.

Whitehouse, C., Fallcreek, S., & Whitehouse, P. (2005). Using a learning environment to promote intergenerational relationships and successful aging. In M. Wykle, P. Whitehouse, & D. Morris (Eds.). *Successful aging through the life span: Intergenerational issues in health*. New York: Springer.

Wienke, C., & Hill, G. J. (2009). Does the "marriage benefit" extend to partners in gay and lesbian relationships? Evidence from a random sample of sexually active adults. *Journal of Family Issue, 30*(2), 259–289.

Williams Institute. (2012). Newly released Census 2010 data show that same-sex couples are most likely to be interracial or interethnic. *Press release*. Retrieved January 2013, from http://williamsinstitute.law.ucla.edu/press/press-releases/newly-released-census-2010-data-show-that-same-sex-couples-are-most-likely-to-be-interracial-or-interethnic-2/.

Winefield, H. (2010). Grandparenting: Diversity in grandparent experiences and needs for healthcare and support. *International Journal of Evidence-Based Healthcare, 8*(4), 277–283.

Wu, Z., & Schimmele, C. M. (2007). Uncoupling in late life. *Generations, 31*, 41–46.

Yen, H. (2011). Share of children in U.S. hits record low. *Pittsburgh Post-Gazette*. Retrieved July 13, 2011, from http://www.post-gazette.com/pg/11194/1159987-115-0.stm?cmpid=healthscience.xml.

Youngkyeong, S. (2008). *The double ABCX model applied for Korean American grandparents: The effect of providing child care for their grandchildren on satisfaction with grandparenting and satisfaction with life* (Dissertation). University of South Carolina.

Zhang, Z. (2006). Routing in intermittently connected mobile ad hoc networks and delay tolerant networks: Overview and challenges. *IEEE Communications Surveys Tutorials, 8*(1), 24–37.

Zodikoff, B. D. (2006). Services for lesbian, gay, bisexual and transgender older adults. In B. Berkman (Ed.), *Handbook of social work in health and aging*. New York: Oxford University Press.

7 Informal and Family Caregiving

learning objectives

7.1 Identify the kinds of family/informal caregiving that exists in communities, including the benefits and costs of care giving.

7.2 Understand caregiver burden, its consequences, and approaches to relieve it.

7.3 Discuss services and supports available to caregivers as well as future service directions.

Listen to the Chapter Audio

When we think of someone who needs a caregiver, we often picture an older person, like a grandparent or great-grandparent. But the reality is that people of any age may need the help of a family or informal caregiver due to injury, disease, disability, or another condition that impairs their ability to function. Care recipients could include a wounded middle-aged soldier returning from combat duty, a teenager with an inherited muscular disorder that progressively worsens with age, or an older person with dementia living at home. Sometimes these people would also receive formal care—such as paid services from home health aides, physicians, nurses, and physical therapists—but the bulk of care is performed by relatives and friends and is largely uncompensated financially. This chapter includes:

- Benefits and costs of caregiving and objective and subjective burden
- The gendered nature of informal care
- Different types of caregivers
  - Partners and adult children
  - Caregivers in families of color
  - Caregivers of elders with dementia
  - Grandparents and great-grandparents as caregivers of grandchildren
- Policies, programs, and services to support family caregivers
- Caregiving when the care recipient relocates to a long-term care facility
- Elder mistreatment
- Direct care workers as underpaid caregivers

Although caregiving can be stressful, it also entails positive and often reciprocal benefits.

What Is Informal Caregiving?

Caregiving, whether informal or formal, denotes supportive, nonmedical, mostly low-tech services, such as help with bathing or eating, and some medical services, such as administering medications and attending to surgical wounds. Throughout this chapter, the terms family and **informal caregiving** are used interchangeably, although informal care can also be performed by friends and neighbors. We also use the term **care recipient** to refer to the person receiving paid or unpaid assistance.

Although a large number of care recipients are older people, you have learned that many elders are in relatively good health, have strong support networks, are capable of managing their daily tasks and remain engaged with others. In fact, older adults themselves are often caregivers to others, such as their partners or their grandchildren or even great-grandchildren. However, with increasing age, the likelihood that we will need assistance from an informal caregiver increases.

As people live longer with chronic illness, the issues of family caregiving will affect all of us in some way. You may be familiar with some aspects of caregiving because you or your family members are providing it to someone who needs assistance. Or you may be asked to help find a caregiver for a family or friend. At another point in your life, you may end up needing a caregiver. It is really in everyone's best interest that our society has an effective system of both formal and informal caregiver support so that we and our loved ones have access to quality care when we need it and, if we choose, are able to remain in our homes as long as possible.

What Kind of Informal Care Do Some Older Adults Need?

The kind of informal care that we might need as we age is wide-ranging and differs in intensity from person to person. Recall that in Chapter 3 you learned about the instrumental activities of daily living (IADLs) and activities of daily living (ADLs). Older adults with functional disabilities often have trouble performing ADLs and need a caregiver's help in getting dressed, eating, grooming, walking, toileting, or taking a bath. Sometimes the assistance needed is minimal, more in the form of verbal guidance and a little nudging. Or they require assistance with IADLs, such as grocery shopping and yard care. Other times, the assistance is more intensive, perhaps 24/7, because the care recipient is unable to perform basic tasks, even with coaching from others. These caregiving tasks may be temporary, until the older adult is able to recover from hospitalization or a short illness, or they may be permanent due to a progressive chronic condition such as multiple sclerosis or dementia.

If you think that all adults like Ruth, who have complex chronic care needs, reside in a long-term care

Ruth: When Care Needs Increase

Ruth was born in Arkansas in 1915. As a young woman, Ruth traveled with her husband as a migrant farm laborer. They eventually had two children, a daughter and a son, and settled down in a small town in Michigan. Although money was never abundant, they lived a comfortable life until the early 1960s, when their daughter developed a serious heart condition and died. Ruth was traumatized by this loss and never fully resolved her grief.

She worked as a nurse's aide at a skilled nursing facility prior to retirement. In addition, she was the primary caregiver for her husband who suffered from emphysema in his later years. His death seemed to renew her grief over their daughter. She became preoccupied with death and a major social outlet became going to funerals. She also attended church regularly and participated in activities at the local senior center.

Ruth lived alone in her own home but was unable to do much housework. Her house increasingly showed the signs of lack of attention to cleaning and maintenance. She also continued to drive her car to the store even though friends expressed concern about her safety due to her poor eyesight. She took medications for heart disease, hypertension, arthritis, and severe vertigo. Her son lived nearby and checked on her regularly by phone and in person, making sure she had her medications, driving her to medical appointments, taking care of yard work and other chores, and just visiting to have some enjoyable times together.

As she began to experience more limitations in her ability to carry out daily activities, her son tried to convince her to sell her house and move to an assisted living facility but she refused. She also resisted in-home services and home-delivered meals, stating that she preferred to "do for herself" as long as she could and did not want strangers in her home. Determined to be "independent," she fell while going to get her mail and fractured her hip. Following surgery and physical therapy, she reluctantly went to live with her son. Her memory has become very poor and she is frequently disoriented to time and place. She remains wheelchair bound and does not engage in any of the activities that she once enjoyed. Her son and his wife both have demanding jobs and feel that they have no time for themselves after work. Her son is contemplating placing her in a skilled nursing facility but feels guilty about it. What are some of Ruth's care needs? And what are some of the needs of her son and his wife as her caregivers? (Adapted from the National Center for Gerontological Social Work Education (Gero-Ed) Web site, www.Gero-Ed.org)

facility, you're not alone. That's a common misperception. Instead, approximately 66 percent of older people who receive long-term services and supports at home and need assistance with ADLs get all their care exclusively from family or other informal caregivers. Another 26 percent receive a combination of family care and paid help; only 9 percent receive paid help alone (see Figure 7.1). Because of informal assistance from their family, friends, and neighbors, the majority of older adults with chronic illness or disability are able to remain at home. Indeed, informal caregiving can prevent or delay the use of skilled nursing home care (Family Caregiver Alliance, 2012a; Feinberg, Reinhard, Houser, & Choula, 2011; Gibson, Kelly, & Kaplan, 2012; Mittelman, Haley, Clay, & Roth, 2006).

The primary forms of care provided by informal caregivers are as follows:

- Emotional support
- Help with instrumental activities (e.g., transportation, house work, meal preparation, grocery shopping)
- Personal care or direct assistance with ADLs (e.g., bathing, feeding, dressing)
- Financial help
- Contacting service providers and advocating for and coordinating services

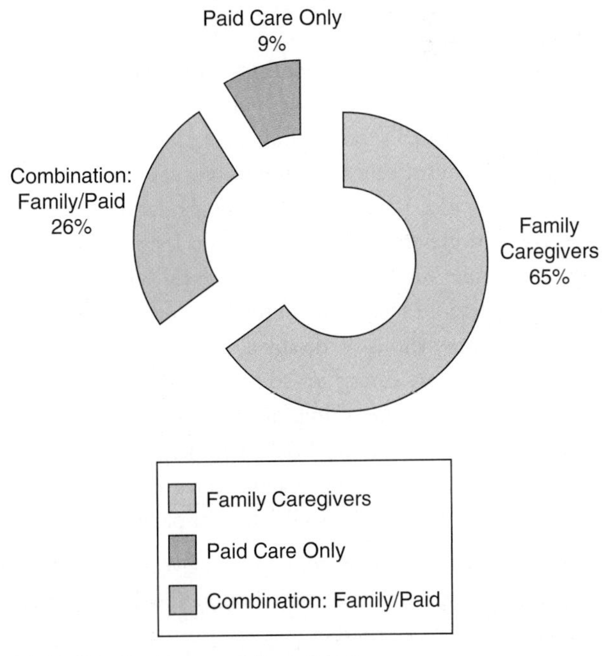

FIGURE 7.1 Forms of Caregiving

Source: Family Caregiver Alliance, 2012a

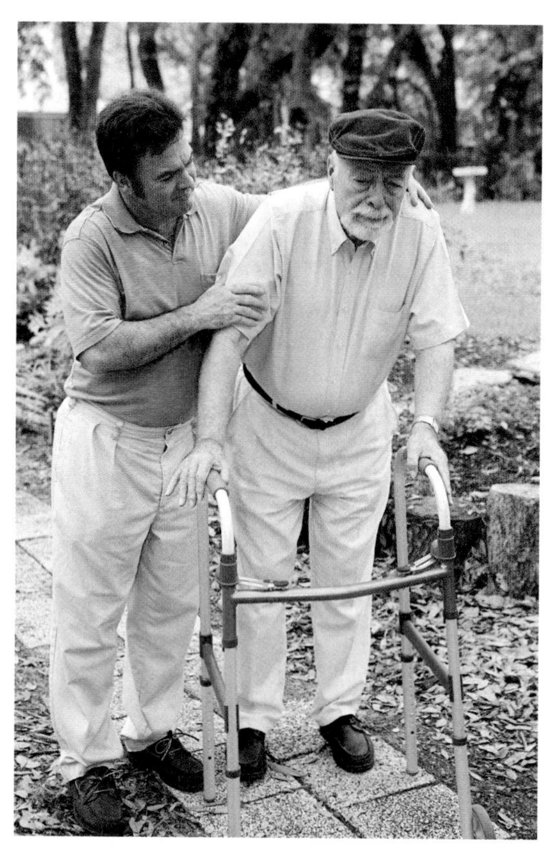

More sons today are caregivers to aging parents than in the past.

Who Are Informal Caregivers?

As already noted, family members, whether related by birth and marriage or friends, neighbors, or family of choice among LGBT populations, are the primary providers of long-term care not only in our country but also around the world. What do we know about these **family caregivers** in general? The bottom line is that there are a lot of people out there doing it! Nearly 66 million or almost 29 percent of all adults in the United States provide care to someone who is ill, disabled, or older. Of these, almost 44 million are caring for someone 50 years of age or older and 15 million are caring for someone with dementia (Family Caregiver Alliance, 2012a; Feinberg et al., 2011).

Here are some other facts about caregiving, which illustrate its centrality to the well-being of older adults:

- Approximately 66 percent of caregivers are female, with women providing more hours of assistance than their male counterparts.
- About 70 percent of caregivers are between the ages of 50 and 64 and likely to be among the 36 percent of those who are caring for parents, while caring for a partner is the most commonly reported care situation among those age 75 and older.
- Approximately 34 percent care for two or more people.
- Caregivers have performed their role for an average of 4.6 years, with about 30 percent giving care for 5 years or more.
- They devote about 20 hours per week, but those who live with the care recipient spend almost 40 hours per week. And the number of hours devoted to care increases with the caregiver's age.
- The average age of caregivers of adults is 48 years; this average age and that of their adult care recipients are edging upward, which is not surprising given increasing life expectancy. The number of hours of care and the length of care increase with the age of the care recipient and for persons with dementia, regardless of age. But the number of young caregivers age 8–18 helping parents or grandparents is also growing (Family Caregiver Alliance, 2012a; Feinberg et al., 2011; National Alliance for Family Caregiving & AARP, 2012).

These patterns are similar across cultures within the United States and in most developed societies. Families have always been the primary caregivers of elders, but until the mid-1980s, family care in the United States was perceived by policy makers as nonexistent and by researchers as largely invisible. It was just taken for granted that this was what families did out of love. After three decades of caregiver research and numerous testimonials, the central role played by families in the lives of elders and the stress they face are now widely documented, and the term family caregiver is used by policy-makers and the popular press. Just Google family caregivers and see the plethora of books, Web sites, and media on the topic. In many ways, it is the "new normal" to be a family caregiver. Nevertheless, the family's significant contributions to elder care are still at times unsupported, creating what is called a "shadow workforce" in geriatric health care (Bookman & Harrington, 2007; Gonyea, 2008; Reinhard, Feinberg, & Choula, 2012).

As you will see throughout this chapter, there is no single model of family caregiving as support varies with geographic proximity, gender, race, social class, sexual orientation, family structure, and the history and nature of the relationship between caregiver and care recipient. The caregiver and care recipient may not have shared a close emotional relationship in their younger years, which could affect the quality of caregiving later in life. In such instances, caregivers may be faced with caring for a parent who did not care for them. When caregivers may live too far away to provide regular direct care, they may spend most of their time worrying that they cannot do more and arranging for services from a distance. Regardless of the nature of the care arrangement, there are both losses and gains for the caregiver.

Losses and Gains of Informal Care

If families suddenly decided they would no longer provide care, how much do you think it would cost society to step in and cover the costs? You may be surprised by how much money informal caregiving saves the American health care system. The economic value contributed by family caregivers to society is estimated to be $450 billion, far more than the total expenditures for formal services and more than the annual revenue of some of America's largest companies (see Figure 7.2). In 2013, the Congressional Budget Office released a report estimating that the value of family caregiving specifically for people age 65 and older (not all adults, as the $450 billion figure above pertained to) was $234 billion in 2011, more than what is spent by Medicare, Medicaid, and private pay insurance for institutional care as well as home- and community-based services. Family caregivers of all adults and specifically of older adults thus constitute a large and often overlooked component of the American economy and systems of health care and long-term services and supports (Family Caregiver Alliance, 2012a; Feinberg et al., 2011; Redfoot, 2013).

This also means that without family caregivers, the formal "system" of long-term services and supports could collapse. This is especially true considering the trend of cutting government programs such as Medicaid home and community-based services. While families typically provide "high-touch" hands-on care, they also are increasingly expected to offer high-tech care because of policies to discharge patients quickly from hospitals to save money and to prevent rehospitalization. As a result, families, which typically are unprepared for caregiving and may receive little information or guidance from health care providers when their relative is discharged from a hospital, may find themselves providing medically oriented acute care (this means critical or urgent care) along with post-acute and rehabilitative care (such as intravenous drug therapy and ventilator assistance). Yet the majority of families may not know much about the particular illnesses or available resources, let alone have such technical skills. They frequently report feeling alone and overlooked by health care providers, especially when their relative is suddenly discharged from the hospital to home (Gibson et al., 2012; Given, Sherwood, & Given, 2008; Iecovich, 2008).

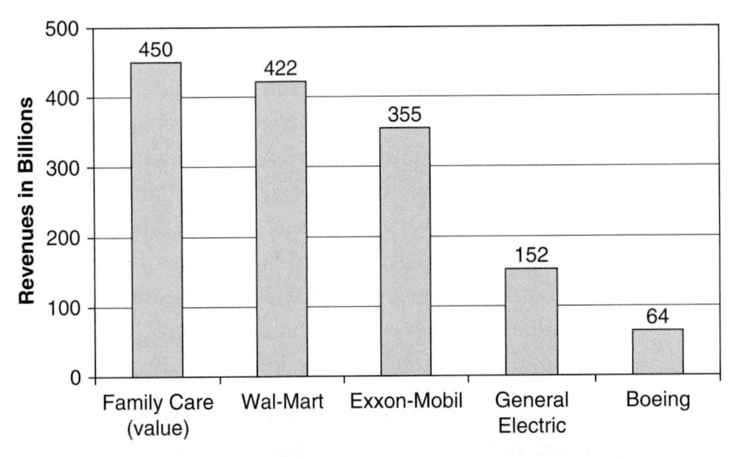

FIGURE 7.2 Comparative Economic Value of Family Caregivers

Source of Corporate Revenues (2011): CNN Money, "Fortune 500," http://money.cnn.com/magazines/fortune/fortune500/2011/full_list/. Corporate revenues rounded to the nearest billion.

Costs of Informal Caregiving Informal caregivers face at least two kinds of stressors—primary and secondary. **Primary stressors** are events that derive directly from the elder's illness, such as cognitive impairments and associated behavioral problems. **Secondary stressors** are not secondary in terms of their importance, but are so called because they do not arise directly from the older person's illness. Instead, they occur when primary stressors spill over into other aspects of the caregivers' life, such as their jobs or friendships. Common secondary stressors are role strains (e.g., difficulties adjusting to the caregiver role), financial losses, and deterioration of the caregivers' sense of mastery and self-esteem (National Alliance for Family Caregiving and AARP, 2012; Savundranayagam, Montgomery, & Kosloski, 2011).

These stressors create a sense of **caregiver burden**—the physical, emotional, and financial costs associated with care. **Objective burden** refers to daily physical tasks, such as managing the care recipient's symptomatic behaviors, driving them to doctor's appointments, and handling legal, employment, and financial problems. **Subjective burden** encompasses the family caregivers' emotions or feelings, such as grief, anger, guilt, worry, loneliness, and sadness. At times the caregiver's appraisal of what needs to be done is more salient—or more prominent in her mind—than the actual tasks that need to be performed. That appraisal contributes to subjective burden or the degree of stress experienced. It also explains why what is difficult for one caregiver may not be so for others. Programs that aim to reduce caregiver stress need to address how the caregiver assesses or appraises their situation in order to be effective (Sun, Hilgeman, Durkin, Allen, & Burgio, 2009; Zarit & Femia, 2008).

Caregiver Burden

Denise is a 45-year-old divorced mother of two teenage children. She is helping to care for her widowed mother, who is in the early stages of Alzheimer's disease and lives with Denise in her three-bedroom home. While her children take the bus to school, Denise drops her mother off at a community senior day health program in the morning and picks her up in the afternoon. On occasion, Denise must take off from her job to take her mother to a doctor's visit or other health-related appointment. She also does the grocery shopping, cooking, financial management, and simple home maintenance—trying her best to keep on top of everything despite holding down a demanding full-time job. She feels physically exhausted most of the time. She has little time for a social life and silently worries that her opportunities to find romance again are slipping away. Her stress levels are high and her emotions often overwhelm her, but she tries her best not to let them affect her work or family life. Torn by multiple and often competing demands, she feels tremendous guilt for not being a good enough mother to her children and not being a good enough caregiver to her mother. She wonders how long she can continue to care for her mother at home, and whether her children will resent her later for overlooking some of their needs and not spending enough quality time with them.

Can you identify the objective and subjective burdens that Denise is experiencing?

An estimated 30 percent of caregivers experience stress or burdens in three primary areas:

1. Poor physical and mental health outcomes, including increased risk of illnesses, such as hypertension, and depression and anxiety because of their compromised immune systems; lower physical stamina; sleep disorders; and inappropriate medication usage. Indeed, some studies have found increased mortality risks, particularly from strokes and heart disease, as a result of caregiving stress. Caregiving for a person with dementia, particularly a partner, tends to have the most negative effects on physical and mental health (Family Caregiver Alliance, 2012a; Feinberg et al., 2011; Haley, Roth, Howard, & Safford, 2010; Pinquart & Sorenson, 2007).
2. Financial: These encompass the direct costs for medical care, adaptive equipment, or hired help as well as indirect opportunity costs from lost income due to missed days from work, interruptions at work, forfeited promotions, needing to quit a job, and reduced retirement benefits. The employment of caregivers of persons with dementia is most negatively affected. Accordingly, low-income caregivers often experience more financial distress because they have fewer resources to meet care demands. Moreover, the recession has exacerbated these financial costs (Family Caregiver Alliance, 2012a; Feinberg et al., 2011).
3. Emotional: Subjective burdens tend to be the most deleterious, or draining on a caregiver's physical and emotional vitality. They encompass worry, anxiety, and feelings of being alone, isolated, and disconnected from others; feeling that one's identity is completely submerged in the care role; and feeling overwhelmed, out of control, inadequate, and fearful over the unpredictability of the future. Loss of time for oneself, family, and friends and giving up vacations, hobbies, and social activities intensify emotional stress. Of great concern is that 40–70 percent of caregivers have clinical symptoms of depression (Family Caregiver Alliance, 2012a; Family Caregiver Alliance and National Center on Caregiving, 2011; Rosalynn Carter Institute for Caregiving, 2010).

Caregiving burden is multidimensional—typically not due to any one single thing. Contrary to what you might assume, the care recipient's disability status or the amount or type of care provided are generally not the primary determinants of whether caregivers experience

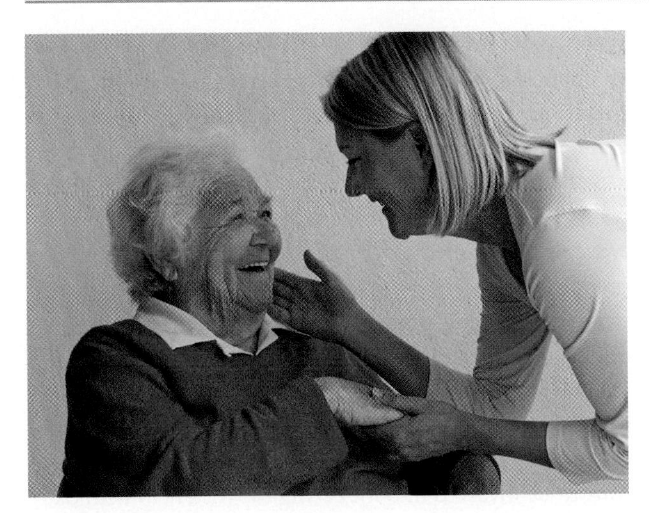

Growing numbers of younger women will assume both eldercare and employment responsibilities.

primarily costs or gains, except in when caring for a person with dementia. A wide range of other factors affect levels of caregiver stress:

- The nature of the relationship between the caregiver and recipient: A good relationship prior to caregiving can minimize stress, even in the face of heavy care demands.
- Whether living with the care recipient. This can reduce the stress of going back and forth between households, but being on call 24/7 can also increase the sense of burden.
- Limited financial resources generally increase the stress.
- The timing in a caregiver's life course, such as being faced with multiple demands from children, employment, and older parents at midlife.
- Gender, since women typically experience caregiving as more stressful and report higher levels of depression and anxiety and lower life satisfaction than men.
- Race and ethnicity: Caregivers of color generally use fewer formal services, but experience less stress and depression than Caucasian caregivers, perhaps because their religion and spirituality may help them cope with stress.
- Social support networks and degree of reciprocity between the caregiver and care recipient, which can buffer stress (Family Caregiver Alliance, 2012a,b; Norton et al., 2009; Savundranayagam et al., 2011; Schulz & Sherwood, 2008; Zarit & Femia, 2008).

Benefits of Informal Caregiving Because informal caregiving can be so stressful and costly, research has typically focused on its burdens or negative aspects. But caregiving encompasses positive experiences as well. Similar to other types of adversity throughout the life course, caregiving can be lonely, stressful, moving, and satisfying all at the same time. In other words, psychological well-being can coexist with distress under adverse life circumstances for both caregivers and care recipients. This means that caregivers may undergo losses of identity, privacy, and time for self, while simultaneously experiencing personal benefits, such as confidence, self-affirmation, pride, and greater closeness with the care recipient. These gains, which are more often experienced when care recipients express appreciation for their care, can buffer some of the stressors. And for parents and children who had a conflictual relationship, caregiving may offer an opportunity to work through these issues and become closer (Narayn, Lewis, Tornatore, Hepburn, & Corcoran-Perry, 2001; Richards, 2009).

Another gain for some caregivers is finding personal meaning to their role and a feeling of giving back to older generations. In fact, a greater sense of meaning in life can enhance caregiver well-being. These findings regarding caregiver gains reflect the concept of resiliency that you have learned about throughout this book as well as individual appraisal that we discussed earlier: what one caregiver experiences as stressful, another may find satisfying. In addition, benefits and costs vary over time in the care process, especially when beginning and leaving the role. These patterns also point to the need for practitioners to recognize how role gains and strains affect caregiver well-being and have implications for the design of interventions to support caregivers (Donovan & Corcoran, 2010; Narayn et al., 2001; Richards, 2009; Savundranayagam et al., 2011).

There is increasing recognition that strategies to reduce caregiver stress should aim to address both the caregiver and the care recipient. This is because caregivers are more likely to experience gains when there is reciprocity in the care relationship. To illustrate, an older person who can no longer manage daily chores can nevertheless read to a grandchild or listen with empathy. Interventions can foster reciprocity through strategies to improve communication and to share decision-making. Since many caregivers misperceive the care recipients' preferences for care, involving the older person in decision-making tends to benefit both members of the care dyad. But even caregivers of elders with dementia may experience mutual benefits, especially when there are deeply established attachments and rich memories (Whitlatch, 2008; Whitlatch, Piiparinen, & Feinberg, 2009).

points to ponder

What are some qualities that you possess that you think would make you a good caregiver to an older relative? What are some qualities about you that might interfere with your being an effective caregiver? As you think about your own strengths and challenges related to caregiving, what insights does that give you into caregiver stress?

We turn next to examining how the type of relationship—spouse/partner, adult children, or friend—affects the caregiving experience. You will also see how gender, race, and sexual orientation influence the level of burden experienced.

Adult Children as Caregivers

Parent care has become a predictable and nearly universal experience across the life course, yet many adults are typically thrust into the role with little advance warning and thus are not adequately prepared for it. Although often referred to as a "role reversal," an adult child never becomes a parent's parent. Instead, caring for parents involves letting go of outmoded patterns to meet current family needs, a process that can lead to feelings of loss and grief for the person who once cared for them and may persist for adult children even after a parent's death. Additionally, adult children often experience sibling conflict around caregiving decisions, or past conflicts may resurface.

The Gendered Nature of Caregiving Although gender roles are changing and the number of sons and husbands/male partners providing substantial care is growing, women are still the primary nurturers and kin-keepers. As you have learned, women—wives, daughters, daughters-in-law, nieces, granddaughters—form about 66 percent of all primary family caregivers; this means that they provide all or the majority of the care, 40 or more hours in a week, including the most difficult personal care tasks, such as bathing, toileting, and dressing. Indeed, female caregivers spend about 22 hours per week providing care compared to about 17 hours by male caregivers (Calasanti, 2009; Family Caregiver Alliance, 2012a; National Alliance for Caregiving & AARP, 2012).

These gender patterns are particularly evident in terms of caring for aging parents, where daughters are twice as likely as sons to be primary caregivers. Daughters predominate as the primary caregivers for older widowed women and older unmarried men, and they are the secondary caregivers in situations where an older partner is still alive and provides care. In contrast, when men are primary caregivers, they are usually husbands/partners, and secondarily sons. Moreover, daughters are more likely than sons to be involved in both **caring for** (i.e., help with daily personal care tasks that entail intimate contact), as well as **caring about** the care recipient (i.e., relational aspects of care that involve a sense of psychological responsibility or nearly constant worry) (Family Caregiver Alliance, 2012a).

Although such gender differences have been widely documented, some researchers contend that men as caregivers and their distinctive needs have been marginalized and overlooked in caregiving studies. Among spousal caregivers, both men and women are found to provide similar amounts of care. Men are most often the primary caregivers of people with HIV/AIDS, where they typically provide personal care, and gay men in general tend to provide more care compared to heterosexual men. With shifting gender expectations, there are growing numbers of sons who do become the primary caregiver of a parent (Family Caregiver Alliance, 2012a; Greenberg, Seltzer, & Brewer, 2006; Kramer & Thompson, 2002; Metlife, 2010).

Here are some patterns that characterize male caregivers. Although these generalizations are based on research, there are always exceptions to gender-based tendencies. You will undoubtedly think of some as you read through this list:

- As a whole, sons tend to focus on more circumscribed, instrumental, and sporadic tasks—house and yard maintenance, financial management, occasional shopping, and arranging care. Sons are more likely to adopt an attitude of "you do what you have to do" and use a "work" paradigm in approaching caregiving, looking for ways to do the job efficiently.
- Sons provide less personal care, especially to mothers, although they are more likely to perform personal care tasks such as bathing, meals, and dressing when they are their parent's primary caregiver.

- They tend to place less importance on emotional well-being and more on completing care goals. In other words, women more often approach caregiving with empathy, feel responsible for the care recipient's physical and psychological well-being, and perceive caregiving demands as more disruptive of their emotional and social lives than do men.
- In contrast, male caregivers are more likely to separate boundaries of employment and caregiving, to compartmentalize the losses associated with caregiving, and to engage in task-oriented self-care (such as exercise) than female carers (Calasanti, 2006, 2009; Family Caregiver Alliance, 2012a; Kramer & Thompson, 2002).

Women in the Middle If you have a mother who is still taking care of children, plus helping your grandparents, she is part of a growing category of caregivers. Middle-aged adult children, particularly daughters and daughters-in-law, are often referred to as the "sandwich generation" because of competing responsibilities of parental and child care. In many instances, **women in the middle** may be juggling extensive family responsibilities along with employment and their own age-related transitions (the term "men in the middle" is not yet used in the caregiving literature). This latter issue is particularly important because middle-age and young-old adults are most likely to be providing parent care. Women in the middle generation are also centrally involved in maintaining family communication and cohesion across generations, even if they are not directly involved in caregiving. Juggling multiple roles, however, may not always be a primary source of stress. In fact, some studies suggest that women who lack meaningful social roles may experience greater stress compared with women with multiple roles. Others' support for the woman's caregiving role may be more important for well-being than the multiplicity of roles per se (Brody, 2004; Family Caregiver Alliance, 2012a).

More recent data, however, suggest that daughters caring for older parents typically do not have dependent children (under age 18) for whom they are responsible. This means that they are more likely to face the competing demands of parental care and paid employment than the dual responsibilities of child and elder care. Nevertheless, middle-aged women may still feel psychologically and financially responsible for their young adult children, who frequently return home to "refill the empty nest" out of economic necessity or because of divorce or other disruptions in their lives. Even if the empty nest is not refilled, parents may be actively engaged in tangibly or emotionally assisting their adult children, especially as a result of the recession, during a prolonged period of "emerging adulthood," which has led to what is called "permaparenting" or "helicopter parenting" (Gonyea, 2008).

Reflecting the gender-natured of care, daughters generally experience more feelings of subjective burden than sons, even when they are both doing similar tasks across comparable time periods. Women caregivers have reported higher levels of depression, anxiety, psychiatric symptoms, and lower life satisfaction than men, although these mental health problems are probably due to more factors than caregiving strain alone. Women are also more likely to experience financial burdens, which have intensified as a result of the recession. Compared to adult sons, daughters are more likely to give up employment, which results in a loss of income (both current and in retirement) and a source of identity and self-esteem. Remember the concept of cumulative disadvantage from Chapter 5; overall, women experience greater economic costs from the undervalued work of caregiving for dependents across the life course than do men. In Chapter 10, we will discuss further how caregiving is a primary factor for women's higher rates of poverty than men's across the life course and into old age (Calasanti, 2006, 2009; Family Caregiver Alliance, 2012a,b; Gonyea, 2008).

Reflection Break

The research on caregiving has consistently shown that women provide more unpaid care than men in our society, and that this disparity can have long-term negative implications. Think about people you know who are family or informal caregivers. Are there more women in this role than men? What are some societal or cultural reasons that women have been traditionally overrepresented as unpaid caregivers? Now imagine being an unpaid caregiver and spending 5 years or more caring for a family member without financial compensation. How would this affect you in the long term? Would this influence your employment opportunities? Your social life? Your health? Your social status? Your retirement? Many caregivers willingly provide unpaid care and do so with much compassion and generosity, but they may still have a price to pay in various ways. This reflection break should encourage you to empathize with what caregivers—and especially female caregivers—sacrifice when they accept the often demanding and time-consuming responsibilities of caregiving.

Sandwich Generation Includes Daughters-in-Law

A woman in her mid-fifties with teenage children and a full-time job, Annette had cared for her parents-in-law, who lived with them, for over 5 years. Her mother-in-law was disabled with rheumatoid arthritis, and her father-in-law had suffered a major stroke and had difficulty talking. Annette's teenagers and her husband rarely helped with their care but instead resented the amount of time she devoted to his parents. Annette and her husband rarely even had a night out alone together. And they had not had a vacation in 5 years. As an employed caregiver, Annette frequently missed work and was distracted on the job whenever she had to consult doctors or take her parents-in-law for physical therapy during normal business hours. She felt alone, isolated, and overwhelmed by the stress. She was physically and mentally exhausted from trying to meet too many demands—unaware that some support services were available in her community—and feeling that as the daughter-in-law, she had to handle these responsibilities on her own.

Spouses/Partners as Caregivers

Whether a person is married or not can strongly affect his or her emotional and economic well-being because it influences living arrangements and the availability of informal caregivers. As you learned in Chapter 6, men age 65 and older are much more likely to be married than are women. Since women on average outlive men, they are more likely to have been caregivers for their husbands, often for long time periods, than men caring for their wives.

Most caregiving studies have focused on heterosexual couples, so the word "spouse" is often used here in our discussion. But same-sex couples also experience caregiving challenges and rewards. As you saw in Chapter 6, LGBT partners' caregiving experiences are sometimes made more difficult by legal and structural barriers. For example, they may be denied visitation rights in hospitals or skilled nursing facilities or overlooked by health care providers as the primary support (Zodikoff, 2006).

Of all family caregivers of older adults, it is usually the spouse or partner age 75 and older who performs up to 80 percent of care tasks, spending 40–60 hours per week on household chores and personal care. Older men receive more care on average, typically from only one person—their wife. In contrast, older women are helped by a larger number of caregivers, including children and grandchildren. Not surprisingly, wife caregivers were more likely to experience negative health effects (Family Caregiver Alliance, 2012a,b; Johnson & Wiener, 2006).

As you learned in our discussion of gender differences, when men are primary caregivers, it is typically as husbands; they comprise nearly 40 percent of spousal caregivers and are predicted to grow in the future because of gains in men's life expectancy. As is true of daughters and sons, men and women spouses/partners experience care responsibilities differently; this appears to result from the way they go about their caregiving work, with men, for example, focusing more on managing tasks like a "business" than expressing their feelings about the process. This means that they are less likely to experience subjective burden. Regardless of gender, caring for a partner or spouse brings added challenges. It is not easy to see someone you have lived with for so many years go through a decline, which may be coupled with the caregiver's own age-related physical and cognitive changes, illness, or reduced finances that can exacerbate the stress of caregiving and increase the risk of physical illness (Calasanti, 2006, 2009; Haley et al., 2010; Leland, 2008; Russell, 2004).

Family Caregivers of Color

As you learned in earlier chapters, multigenerational households are more common among populations of color than among Caucasians, and have been a source of strength historically. For example, African American, Latino, and Asian American families report higher levels of informal assistance to elders and generally positive parent–adult child relationships when compared to Caucasian counterparts. Taking care of older relatives, friends, and neighbors is often a strongly held cultural value. For both African Americans and Latinos, however, caregivers are more likely to be another family member—a sister, adult child, or niece—or a friend than a spouse/partner (Haley et al., 2004; National Alliance for Caregiving and AARP, 2012; Pinquart & Sorenson, 2006; Weiss, Gonzalez, Kabeto, & Langa, 2005).

Here are some other variations in family caregiving across different races and cultures:

- African American caregivers tend to be older than their counterparts, to provide higher levels of care, to live with the care recipient, to assist a wider range of extended family members, and to be more economically disadvantaged than their white counterparts. Yet they are less likely to use formal supports. Despite these greater objective burdens, African American caregivers typically report lower subjective burden: less stress, anxiety, feelings of "bother," and depression; higher levels of self-efficacy; and greater rewards compared to other groups. Their greater satisfaction and perceived gains (e.g., pride, belief that they will be rewarded by God) may be partially due to the mediating effects of religion, spirituality, prayer, and faith; strong cultural beliefs about filial support and families; and more positive, respectful views of elders than in Caucasian families. As you have learned, such beliefs and values can promote resilience.

- Grandparents and "fictive kin" of friends and neighbors among African American households have traditionally played a central caregiving role. Such extended family arrangements may have developed out of experiences with discrimination by service providers or out of economic necessity, especially since older African American women are less likely to be married and more likely to be poor than any other group among the older population. Such arrangements may carry financial and emotional costs and divert elders from accessing formal supports. These patterns may change as younger generations experience greater economic and geographic mobility, however, and turn to services to help assist them with parental care (Chadiha, Brown, & Aranda, 2006; Dilworth-Anderson, Williams, & Gibson, 2002; Foley, Tung, & Mutran, 2002; Roff et al., 2004).
- On the other hand, younger African American caregivers who are facing financial and other pressures (e.g., juggling more than one job to get by) may experience a contradiction between cultural expectations about what they should do for relatives and what they can actually do. In some instances, holding strong beliefs about the centrality of families may predispose some African American women caregivers to higher levels of psychological distress (Dilworth-Anderson et al., 2005; Family Caregiver Alliance, 2012a; Rozario & DeRienzis, 2008).
- Cultural values of familism and collectivism mean that Latinos typically feel obligated to provide care and may put the needs of family and community above their own well-being. In some studies, they are identified as experiencing greater burden and higher rates of physical health problems and depression and less positive appraisals and feelings of competence than whites or African Americans. This pattern may occur because of Latinos' high rates of poverty, poor health, and limited access to insurance and other services across the life course. Fear of deportation may also prevent some of them from accessing services that could reduce caregiving stress (Adams, Aranda, Kemp, & Takagi, 2002; Family Caregiver Alliance, 2012a; Magana, 2006).
- Seeking help within the family remains a strong Asian American value. Some studies have identified that Chinese American, Korean American, and Vietnamese American caregivers have relatively positive caregiving experiences, including role satisfaction and meaning and reduced stress and depression, in part because of strong beliefs of filial piety. Spirituality, religion, and prayers—and a belief that caring for aging parents is a higher calling—are widely used coping strategies, especially among Vietnamese Americans. Nevertheless, Asian American adult children who have adopted Western values may not feel as strong a sense of filial responsibility to care for their parents as prior generations. This sense of obligation may be threatened by daughters-in-law entering the paid workforce and sons' developing financial independence. Overall, however, cultural values of obligation for parents remain relatively strong, reducing the extent to which Asian American families rely on formal services for support (Funk, Chappell, & Liu, 2011; Lai, 2010; Liu, Hinton, Tran, & Hinton, 2008; Tang, 2011; Wong, Yoo, & Stewart, 2006).
- Among American Indians, providing care for elders is a core cultural value, but this may place a strain on the community as a whole, not only on individual caregivers, because of additional stressors faced by American Indian caregivers. These stressors include poverty, lack of access to support services, and caring for elders with high levels of functional disability. They may also be caring for grandchildren or great-grandchildren (Goins, Moss, Buchwald, & Guralnik, 2007; Jervis & Manson, 2002).

As you saw in Chapter 1, non-Hispanic whites will decrease as a percentage (from 80 to 59 percent) of the older adult population, while the percentage of African Americans, Asians, and especially Latinos will increase in the next four decades, pointing to a corresponding growth in family caregivers. Programs and service geared toward family caregivers will need to reflect their greater diversity and be culturally appropriate (Federal Interagency Forum, 2012).

Caregiving is an intergenerational responsibility in many cultures.

Friends as Caregivers

As noted earlier, when family members are unavailable or unwilling to provide care, many older adults turn to friends and neighbors. Indeed, even when families assist, friends and neighbors are still well suited to provide some supports. This is frequently the case for LGBT elders who have created families of choice composed of friends to provide assistance as they age. Unlike the general population, about the same proportion of gay men and lesbians serve as caregivers. In one study, both performed care management and care provider tasks, which suggests greater role flexibility and egalitarian relationships than in the heterosexual population. LGBT caregivers' time commitment is also found to be greater than in the population as a whole. The extent to which these greater time demands result from caring for persons with HIV/AIDS is not clear. Unfortunately, many government or private employer family leave policies typically do not recognize and therefore benefit extended family members or friends who are caregivers (Calasanti, 2009; Frediksen-Goldsen et al., 2011; Heaphy, 2007; MetLife, 2010).

Caregiving for Persons with Dementia

We focus here on the distinctive burdens faced by caregivers of elders with AD. They provide the most difficult kinds of personal care (bathing, feeding, and dealing with incontinence), spend more hours per week giving care ("constant care"), and do so for longer periods of time without any break compared to caregivers of non-AD relatives. They are more likely to be faced with the unpredictability of care tasks as well as disruptive behavioral problems—sharp personality changes, emotional and verbal abuse, and greater aggressive or violent behavior—that they may lack the skills to manage. The person with dementia may be physically present but psychologically absent. A particularly painful situation is when the person with AD no longer recognizes their caregiver. Not surprisingly, caregivers of persons with dementia are at higher risk of emotional stress, mental and physical health problems, and family conflicts. Because of this, many interventions or programs to reduce stress have been first targeted to caregivers of persons with Alzheimer's disease or other dementias (Belle et al., 2006; Gitlin, 2011; Mittleman et al., 2006; Parker, Mills, & Abbey, 2008).

Grandparents as Primary Caregivers

Increasingly, older people are the caregivers not only to their spouses or partners, but also to their grandchildren or even great-grandchildren. Although grandparents have traditionally assisted with child care, the number of grandparents who are primary or sole caregivers to their grandchildren has grown dramatically in the past three decades. This is because their adult children are unable or unwilling to care for their children, typically because of substance abuse, incarceration, child abuse, or military deployment. As you learned in Chapter 6, the absence of the parental generation is captured in the term **skipped-generation households** composed of grandparents and grandchildren, which are the fastest-growing type in the United States.

points to ponder

Let's say you know someone who is caring for a relative, friend, or community member. Perhaps you don't feel you can help too much with the demanding caregiving tasks right now, but you may be able to help the caregiver in ways that make her or his life a little easier. For example, you can invite that person out to do something enjoyable now and then, prepare a meal for the caregiver, run a short errand, or just send a card or an e-mail letting them know you are thinking of them and sharing any news the caregiver might find interesting. What else can you do to help the caregiver?

At the same time, the number of children living in a home with both a parent and grandparent present has declined (Generations United, 2012; Livingston & Parker, 2010).

Here are some startling figures about grandparent caregivers to consider:

- Over 6 million grandparents have grandchildren under age 18 living with them.
- About 2.7 million of these grandparents—62 percent are grandmothers, over 38 percent grandfathers—are responsible for most of the basic needs (i.e., food, shelter, and clothing) of the grandchildren living with them.
- Sixty-six percent are married.
- Thirty-six percent have provided care for more than 5 years.
- Sixty percent of grandparent caregivers are in the labor force.
- Yet 21 percent of grandparent caregivers live below the poverty line.
- Fifty-three percent are white, while 24 percent are African Americans, 18 percent are Latinos, and 3 percent are Asians. While disproportionately black and Latino, the greatest increase in the past decade has been among white grandparents.
- A total of 655,000 grandparents are caring for grandchildren with a disability (Generations United, 2012; Livingston & Parker, 2010; U.S. Census Bureau, 2010, 2012).

Still Taking Care

Mary long ago earned her stripes as a mom. She raised five children alone, in a tough Los Angeles neighborhood, and managed to put them through college or vocational training. She had looked forward to retirement and, being a loving grandmother, to spoiling her grandchildren on visits and then sending them home. But her life has not turned out as expected. Instead, she's raising her 10-year-old grandson, James, alone, since the incarceration of her daughter and the boy's father for selling drugs.

When Mary's daughter was charged for possession of drugs, Mary could not bear the thought of her grandson being raised by strangers in the foster care system. She petitioned the courts to become his guardian. Her daughter has only contacted her son twice in the past 4 years. This has made the adjustment difficult for Mary and James, who often lashes out at his grandmother. Mary tries to provide as much love and stability for him as possible, helping him with his homework, assisting with his Cub Scout troop, and attending all his school events. She derives some emotional rewards from these activities with James, but misses out on activities with her peers. Many of her friends have dropped away, as they have more freedom to "take off and do things." She also struggles with guilt about her daughter and her situation. She has turned her anger and grief into organizing local support groups for others like herself and pressuring legislators to recognize caregiving grandparents' needs.

As you can imagine, being the primary or sole caregiver has both rewards and challenges for both the grandparent and grandchild. Most grandparents assume the primary caregiving role willingly, often acting out of a deep sense of duty and obligation, and gain tremendous pride, love, and feelings of being valued. But there are numerous economic, emotional, and physical stressors that may come into play when grandparents are primarily responsible for their grandchildren, as illustrated by Mary in the box on this page.

Mary's story captures some of the costs for grandparent caregivers. This may not be how people their age planned to spend their lives after raising their own children, and they may regret not having a child-free time in their lives to do what they want. They may end up using up resources that were being saved for their retirement years or health care emergencies. Some may feel guilt, embarrassment, and shame from their adult children's inability or unwillingness to care for their own children. Moreover, they may grieve losses if their children's absence is due to death, incarceration, drug use, or sickness and feel that they failed as parents. What can be especially painful is when other family members and friends pull away and fail to help out. This can intensify the grandparent caregivers' sense of loss of family connections and their isolation and loneliness. It is not surprising that grandparent caregivers report more strain and conflict with other family members than their peers who are not providing daily care. Despite these stresses, most grandparent caregivers do not seek help for themselves but rather for their grandchildren (Byers, 2010; Kelch-Oliver, 2008; Letiecq, Bailey, & Kurtz, 2007; Lumpkin, 2007; Winefield, 2010).

Other feelings of loss may occur when grandchildren are embarrassed by having an older relative care for them and repeatedly long for their parents. In public, grandparents may try to appear to be the parents—perhaps coloring their hair or wearing more youthful clothing—to try to reduce their grandchild's embarrassment and increase the probability of younger parents' support. Public institutions, such as the schools, and service providers, are often not equipped to deal with grandparent caregivers, leaving the grandparent feeling unrecognized and even unappreciated for their hard work.

Some older adults may also have to cope without assistance with a grandchild's death, chronic illness, or developmental disabilities. Grandparents may also try to be "strong" to protect their adult child who is struggling with their own issues. When grandparents play an invisible, behind-the-scenes role of "taking care of everything," they are not taking care of their own pain, or it may be overlooked by others. As a result, they are at high risk for developing health or mental health problems (Misuk & Gardner, 2010; Woodbridge, Buys, & Miller, 2009; Youngblut, Brooten, Blais, Hannan, & Niyonsenga, 2010).

While social support is vital, the major need remains economic. Some low-income grandparents can turn to Temporary Assistance for Needy Families (TANF), but the child-only benefit has been reduced in recent years. Others can qualify for foster care payments, but this means transferring custody of the children to the state; they give up their own parental authority and must become formal "foster parents," a status that many grandparents do not want to assume. Ironically, if they do undergo foster care training and licensing, in many states they receive a lower foster care rate than do unrelated foster parents, and do not qualify for federal subsidies for adoption that are available to other low-income families. In an effort to encourage permanent family placements, the Kinship Caregiver Support Act of 2005 gives states the option to use federal funds for subsidized guardianship payments to relative caregivers of children in foster care. This makes it easier for grandparents to become legal guardians and reduces some barriers to services (Goodman, Potts, Pasztor, & Scorzo, 2004; Hayslip & Kaminski, 2005; Letiecz, Bailey, & Porterfield, 2008; Livingston & Parker, 2010).

Fortunately, child welfare policy-makers have worked to develop services to support grandparent caregivers outside the traditional foster care. Education and support groups, often offered through senior centers, as well as Internet resources are available to help grandparents, including Kinship Care Navigators and 1-800 information and assistance. Support groups tend to be most effective when they provide information on how to access resources, enhance parenting skills, build on strengths, use a constructive problem-solving focus, and are combined with respite or child care.

Sometimes individuals who have first-hand experience with the challenges and rewards of caregiving want to reach out to others who are experiencing similar life circumstances. This was the case with Sylvie de Toledo, a social worker who founded an organization in California called Grandparents as Parents in 1987. Sylvie's sister died, leaving an 8-year-old grandson to live with his grandparents (Sylvie's parents). Grandparents as Parents offers support groups, crisis counseling, workshops and educational programs, advocacy, respite care, emergency referrals for food, clothing, and shelter, and more. CNN profiled Sylvie as one of its "Heroes" for starting the nonprofit, but Sylvie said the real heroes are the grandparents and other relatives who serve as caregivers to young care recipients (Grandparents as Parents, 2013; Torgan, 2013).

points to ponder

Do you have a friend, neighbor, or relative who was raised by their grandparents or great-grandparents or other kin? If so, talk to them about their experience—both the positives and the challenges they faced. Try to learn about the nature of their relationship with their kinship caregiver and what the caregiver experienced.

Adult grandchildren raised by their grandparents might understandably feel closeness as well as an obligation to care for the grandparents or great-grandparents who took care of them when they were growing up. But even grandchildren who were not raised by their grandparents may enjoy a special bond with their grandparents and choose to be their caregivers. While the grandchild-caregiver's maturity level and life circumstances are likely to be factors in their ability to care for an older adult, grandchildren require access to similar resources and support that are available to other caregivers.

Legal Issues Related to Grandparent Caregiving

Grandparent (or great-grandparent) caregivers typically face legal challenges that add to their burden and stress. The legal system can be difficult to navigate, as well as expensive and emotionally draining, but legal action is often necessary to provide what is best for the child. Here are just a few examples of the legal complexities—or, in some cases, catch-22's—that grandparents may face. In order to enroll their grandchild in care, they must complete the legal paperwork to obtain educational consent. Additionally, they need to obtain medical consent to be able to attain health care for their grandchildren. Physical custody is the easiest and least expensive route for most grandparents, but then they have no formal rights or legal authority to make decisions regarding the child; these are retained by birth parents, which is a problem if the biological parents are not competent to make decisions. If grandparents become legal foster parents, they can qualify for state support, but legal custody of their grandchild resides with the state. Some grandparents adopt the grandchildren in order to have full legal custody, but this can exclude the birth parent if they are eventually able to care for the child. The best option for most grandparents is to obtain legal custody, whereby the grandparents assume legal authority to make decisions, but birth parents remain financially responsible for the children and have the right to visitation. Laws vary from state to state, making it even harder for grandparents to determine the options best for them and their grandchild. Fortunately, there are Web sites that provide an overview of these legal issues, and kinship care navigators can also help grandparents sort through these legal issues.

The Grandfamilies State Law and Policy Resource Center

Are you doing research on grandparents as caregivers or just interested in learning more? Here's a Web site that can help. The Grandfamilies State Law and Policy Resource Center Web site (http://www.grandfamilies.org/) is a collaboration between Casey Family Programs, the American Bar Association's Center on Children and the Law, and Generations United. This Web site is a national legal resource created to educate individuals about state laws, legislation, and policies in support of grand-families and to assist interested state legislators, advocates, caregivers, attorneys, and other policy-makers in exploring policy options to support relatives and the children in their care both within and outside the child welfare system.

Legislation and Policies to Support Family Caregivers

Although there are government policies to assist caregivers, they have limitations related to funding and who is covered. Two major federal policy initiatives to support families specifically include caregivers of older adults: the **Family and Medical Leave Act** of 1993 **(FMLA)** and the **National Family Caregiver Support Program** of 2000 **(NFCSP)**. Under the **FMLA**, businesses with 50 or more employees are required to grant up to 12 weeks of unpaid leave annually when a child is born or adopted, when a child, spouse, or parent (not in-laws) with a serious health condition needs care, or when the employee is unable to work because of a serious health condition. Employers must provide health coverage and reinstate employment after the leave. Because the FMLA does not apply to small employers, which employ almost 60 percent of American workers, less than 10 percent of private sector worksites are covered. Additionally not all workers of covered employers are eligible for FMLA benefits because of requirements related to duration and amount of work. The greatest limitation is that the leave is not paid, unlike family policies in many industrialized countries. Low-income workers simply may not be able to afford to take an unpaid leave. A few states have adopted paid leave, but most businesses oppose any such proposals at the state level because of the costs involved (Feinberg, 2013; Wisensale, 2009).

The NFCSP is funded by the Administration on Aging (AoA). This law requires that the Aging Network, which is funded by AoA, must serve not only older adults but also family caregivers age 18 and older who are caring for an adult age 60 and older and older-kin caregivers of grandchildren. Each state may use up to 10 percent of its total funds to help grandparent caregivers over age 55 who are caring for a child under age 18 or an adult age 18–59 with disabilities. The NFCSP represents a shift in public policy by formally recognizing the central role of informal elder care and that family caregivers are also "clients" who need supports. The NFCSP gives highest priority to services for low-income, older caregivers and for those caring for persons with developmental disabilities (AoA, 2012).

When the NFCSP was first implemented, some social service and health care providers had difficulty

Services Funded by the National Family Caregiver Support Program

- Information and referral assistance
- Individual counseling
- Peer support groups and caregiver training
- Respite care or temporary relief from care responsibilities
- Supplemental services to complement family care

thinking of informal caregivers as "clients" whose own needs should be assessed. They viewed their role as serving the older adult, not the family. But that shift in thinking is occurring, with a greater emphasis on **family-centered care**, and most states have designed caregiver assessment tools as a basis for developing a care plan for family caregivers. An early evaluation of the NCFSP found that it enabled 77 percent of caregivers to care for their loved one longer than otherwise would have been possible, and nearly 50 percent of caregivers of elders who were nursing home eligible would have been unable to keep them at home without the support services (Family Caregiver Alliance and the National Conference on State Legislatures, 2004; Feinberg, 2008; Montgomery & Kwak, 2008).

Some employers have developed flexible work hour policies for family caregivers, because they recognize the difference this can make in terms of work productivity. But this is the exception, not the norm. Both federal and state governments could better promote such policies by giving tax incentives to family-friendly corporations that offer generous leave policies, flexible work hours, and resource and referral to services to support elders and their family caregivers. Through funding demonstration projects, the federal government could stimulate states to implement such family-friendly initiatives. Even more important policy changes would be federal or state requirements for earned sick leave that could be used for caregiving and paid family and medical leave insurance. The development of such family-friendly workplace policies is unlikely to happen, however, in the face of pressures to cut the deficit and the lobbying power of businesses that do not want to make such changes because of the costs involved (Feinberg, 2013; Wisensale, 2009).

Services and Support for Caregivers

So far, you've read a lot about the challenges that caregivers face. However, there are things that can be done to support family caregivers, such as providing information or linking them to services. These are called **interventions**. An assessment of caregivers' needs is the first step toward identifying services that they will perceive as supportive and will reduce their burden. This means that families are evaluated for whether they have sufficient internal and external resources to provide the level of care necessary as well as for their own needs for supports. Internal resources could be healthy coping mechanisms (e.g., strength drawn from a belief system or regular meditation practice); external resources are from outside the person (e.g., adequate income or access to strong informal networks). For example, such assessment can identify family members at risk of negative health effects from caregiver stress and determine eligibility for additional supports. As noted in our discussion of the NFCSP, family caregivers benefit from having their own care plan that addresses their needs. When caregivers' needs and strengths are assessed, they are more likely to feel valued as part of the health care team and to experience less burden and depression. Such

What Is Family-Centered Care?

- Family caregivers' roles are viewed as essential to their older relatives' well-being, not secondary.
- Both older adults and family caregivers are "clients."
- Caregivers are not just a resource to their older relatives, but individuals who may need information, training, and other support.
- The caregiver's own health and well-being should be assessed as part of the care plan.
- The care plan should reflect the goals and preference of both the older adult and the caregivers.
- Family caregivers are part of the care team and should be involved in decision-making (Feinberg, 2012; Reinhard et al., 2012).

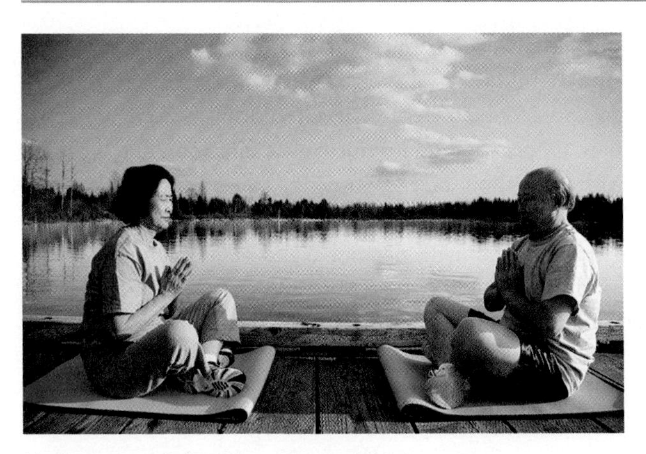

Meditation can help reduce caregiver stress.

assessments should reflect culturally competent practice, by taking into account aspects of the caregiver's culture that may enhance or make more difficult the caregiver experience. An example of a caregiver assessment tool, TCARE®, is described in the box on this page (Family Caregiver Alliance, 2012b; Montgomery, Kwak, Kosloski, & Valuch, 2011; Reinhard et al., 2012).

Why Don't Caregivers Use Services?

Perhaps surprising to you is that many family caregivers do not use most services. In some instances, they are unaware of services, cannot afford them, or resist accepting help, thinking they can "do it on their own." In other instances, families use them selectively to supplement informal care for limited time periods, but discontinue them after a short trial period—or they wait until services are absolutely necessary. When they do use services, they most often turn to transportation and financial assistance, and the least often to respite that would give them a break from caregiving. Whether reliance on informal networks results in or causes underutilization of formal services is unclear. Some families—especially families of color—do not identify themselves as caregivers needing support—or only do so when they have burned out or there has been a crisis in caregiving. In their minds, providing care is simply what people do for relatives they love. Moreover, services tend to be underutilized even by caregivers who perceive a need for greater formal support (Doty, 2010; Family Caregiver Alliance, 2012a; Feinberg et al., 2011; Montgomery & Kwak, 2008; Rosalynn Carter Institute for Caregiving, 2010; Zarit & Femia, 2008).

points to ponder

How would you explain the contradiction that families might not use existing services, even when they know about them? Have you ever known a caregiver who refused to use services, even if they were told the supports could make their job easier? What might be the reasons that they would insist on doing it on their own?

Effective Evidence-Based Interventions

The most effective interventions, tested by researchers, incorporate several strategies and types of services, such as problem-solving therapies, information about the disease and resources, access to services, building skills to respond to behavioral problems, peer support groups, and altering the physical environment to support in-home care. They are targeted to specific needs and risk factors, flexible, long-term (e.g., at least 8–12 weeks in duration and provide mechanisms for follow-up over time), and tailored to fit the care context. Effective treatments are also characterized by a psychosocial rather than a purely educational approach in order to address psychological barriers to service use; incorporate culturally based knowledge and beliefs and engage staff who are culturally competent and, where needed, bilingual. Such interventions have

TCARE®—Tailored Caregiver Assessment and Referral

- A personal family caregiver survey allows for comprehensive assessment of caregivers' experiences, such as how they feel about their care responsibilities and the types of care they provide.
- Care managers use a decision-making protocol and algorithm to integrate extensive information about the caregiver and care context and services available in local communities.
- The care plan focuses on strategies to help families achieve their goals and to provide them with critical information to empower them to make informed decisions (Kwak, Montgomery, Kosloski, & Lang, 2011).

been found to increase caregivers' competence and subjective well-being as well as reduce depression and, to a lesser extent, anxiety. The most significant effects are found when caregivers actively participate in the process. If you are interested in learning more about interventions that work to reduce caregiver stress, we suggest the Rosalynn Carter Institute for Caregiving's Caregiver Intervention Database of more than 65 effective interventions (http://www.rosalynncarter.org/caregiver_intervention_database/) and the Administration on Aging (www.aoa.gov). Despite the proliferation of proven interventions, many families continue to be underserved or receive services that are not evidence based (Belle et al., 2006; Brodaty, Green, & Koschera, 2003; Gitlin, Hauck, Dennis, & Winter, 2005; Kwak, Montgomery, Kosloski, & Lang, 2011; Mittelman, Roth, Haley, & Zarit, 2004; Schulz, Martire, & Klinger, 2005).

Psychoeducational Groups, Skills Training, and Treatments Caregivers' demand for information, especially related to keeping their loved one safe, has increased in the past 5 years. Psychoeducational groups, which usually combine education and social support, are found to be one of the most effective interventions to enhance caregiver well-being. In instances where caregivers often do not know how to access services, they benefit from understanding the nature of the illness and learning about relevant resources. In psychoeducational treatment, a counselor uses therapeutic techniques to encourage and overcome barriers to behavior change. In group treatment, the leader uses group processes to build cohesion and model new behavior. Individual therapeutic interventions, especially short-term cognitive-behavioral therapy, tend to be more effective than groups in addressing issues such as family conflict, emotional stress, and challenges resulting from a care recipient's cognitive disorders. Family-level interventions should address not only how much other members do to provide care but also the manner by which assistance is given. The REACH (Resources for Enhancing Alzheimer's Caregiver Health) program is one of the most successful psychoeducational programs using a combination of cognitive-behavioral and mood management skills (Family Caregiver Alliance, 2012b; Gallagher-Thompson & Coon, 2007; Parker et al., 2008).

Support Groups Caregiver support groups may be led by professionals or peers and are generally not highly structured. They typically build socio-emotional support among participants and create a space in which to discuss feelings and problems as well as exchange successful strategies. Although findings are mixed, peer support groups for caregivers are found to be effective in reducing caregiver burden if they are part of a multidimensional intervention (combined with education and counseling, for example); organized around particular illnesses or needs, such as specific to caregivers of elders with dementia; and more than eight weeks in duration. Most caregivers rate respite—finding time for themselves—and reducing their own stress lower than finding activities for their loved one (Chien et al., 2011; Family Caregiver Alliance, 2012a,b; Gallagher-Thompson & Coon, 2007).

Support group facilitators should take into account the different needs of spouses/partners and adult children caregivers and the fact that men typically prefer to talk to other men. They also need to provide respite care for elders—or in the instances of grandparent caregivers, child care—so that caregivers can attend meetings. Without such resources, support groups may be perceived as an additional burden by caregivers who have to travel and arrange respite care for their elder in order to attend. Or the group may add to stress if it focuses primarily on the negative aspects of caregiving.

Modifying the Home Environment Other interventions modify the home living space to be more supportive of the older person, especially those with dementia, and to reduce the environment demands and subsequent stress on the caregiver. In one model, the Home Environmental Skill Building Program (ESP), an occupational therapist visits the home for modifying the physical environment (e.g., remove hazardous objects, set up a memory board). Educational problem-solving, stress management techniques, and communication strategies enhance the social environment. These modifications were found to increase the caregiver's ability to provide care and to reduce their being upset with memory problems (Gitlin, 2011; Gitlin et al., 2005).

Respite Care **Respite care** is planned or emergency short-term relief for caregivers from the demands of ongoing care. Accessible and affordable respite care can provide caregivers with a break from their daily demands, thereby reducing both caregiver stress and nursing home placement. Respite encompasses a range of services and may be in- or out-of-home care—for example, through adult day health or overnight care in a long-term care facility.

Many caregivers state that they would like respite services, but often face barriers to their use, including their own reluctance to entrust their relative's care to someone else or guilt over taking a much-needed break. Some caregivers resist in-home respite because they do not want "strangers" coming into the home. The amount of respite provided appears to be a critical variable in whether its use makes a difference. When respite is used at least twice a week for three months, caregiver depression, role overload, and strain are reduced, and nursing home admission may be delayed (Gaugler et al., 2003; Kagan, 2006; Zarit & Femia, 2008).

The federal government has made funds available to selected states via the Lifespan Respite Care Act. States can use these funds to plan, establish, and expand or enhance Lifespan Respite Care systems in their areas. For example, programs developed with these funds could train and recruit respite workers and volunteers to help caregivers.

Electronic Supports Toll-free information and referral lines are vital, such as a national Eldercare Locator Service sponsored by the Administration on Aging. The Internet has emerged as a way for caregivers to acquire information, typically on behalf of their loved one, and share their experiences with others facing similar burdens. Many Web sites include advice and updated information from experts (such as the Alzheimer's Association's suggestions for managing behavioral issues and educational materials for caregivers), while others encourage caregivers to offer support to their caregiver peers. A growing number of Web sites through AARP, AoA, and Leading Age, an association comprised of a range of residential homes, allow caregivers to complete an interactive assessment online to determine the services they need most. Telehealth technology allows communication with heath care providers, especially in rural areas, to answer concerns as they arise.

Camps for Caring

The National Family Caregiver Alliance offers camps for caregivers of adults with cognitive impairments. This gives caregivers 48 hours of respite while their loved one enjoys a two-night stay with trained staff and volunteers in a noninstitutional, scenic bay area setting. Persons who are frail, incontinent, noncommunicative, or nonambulatory are welcome to participate.

"Smart" Devices Aid Caregivers

With a busy work life demanding a lot of her attention, Linda appreciates whatever assistance she can get when it comes to caring for her father, Roy, who has a long list of medications that he takes for multiple medical problems, including early-stage dementia, and who has recently become increasingly confused on his walks through the neighborhood. Sometimes that assistance has come in the form of Linda's smartphone, which has an app that allows her to easily keep track of her father's medications: what he takes, when he takes them, and at what dosages. Since this information is on her smartphone, she always has it with her and can conveniently update or share the information at a moment's notice.

Another electronic tool in her caregiver toolbox is a device that her father keeps on him so that Linda can remotely follow his movements using GPS tracking technology when they are not together. It helps Linda locate her father at all times—as long as he has the device with him—and reassures both of them that help is in reach should he ever get lost or begin to wander.

Teleconferencing is being used to create virtual support groups among caregivers and can be accessed through caregiver Web sites. The opportunity to log on to a chat room on the Internet avoids the need to find alternative care or respite for the care recipient at home while the caregiver attends support groups or trainings in person. Outcomes from accessing the Internet include caregivers' increased sense of control, confidence, and support as well as greater involvement of distant family members. Not surprisingly, caregivers under age 50 are more likely than older adults to use caregiving technology. As you will learn in Chapter 12, the use of technological supports will grow in the future, especially for baby boomers who tend to be Internet-savvy (Czaja & Schultz, 2006; Davis, Burgio, Buckwalter, & Weaver, 2004; Family Caregiver Alliance, 2012a,b; Smith, 2008).

Future Service Directions

Regardless of the specific service configuration, support services should be culturally competent and accessible, such as in primary care and neighborhood health clinics, the workplace, senior and community centers, faith-based institutions, and schools. Ideally, assistance is provided early in the caregiving cycle or even before it begins. This enables caregivers to plan before they are abruptly thrust into a burdensome role, often due to a medical crisis. General information sessions about services and supports for older adults and their caregivers are typically not well attended, often because few people like to think about these late-life challenges or face the prospect of their loved one's death. An effective early preventive strategy would engage the caregiver in planning shortly after experiencing the first acute incident or receiving the diagnosis of a chronic disease.

Self-care for caregivers is an essential component in reducing stress and preventing out-of-home placement. As noted earlier, most caregivers put a lower priority on time for themselves than on taking care of their loved one, however. Learning how to accept limits and asking others to help, attending to physical and spiritual needs through exercise, meditation, or time for reflection, and creating moments of joy with friends or family are critical to both self-care and to giving effective care over the long haul. Self-care activities are most realistic when they can be integrated with other daily routines. Organizations such as the Family Caregiver Alliance have developed Caregiver Bills of Rights as a way to encourage caregivers to take care of their own health in order to sustain quality care for their loved ones (Family Caregiver Alliance, 2012a; The National Alliance for Caregiving and AARP, 2012).

points to ponder

Imagine that you have a close friend or relative who is a caregiver and appears to be experiencing burnout? What can you recommend to them as strategies for self-care? What types of resources or services might you suggest that they consider? What would you do if they resist suggestions to take better care of themselves?

Self-Care

If you know someone who is a caregiver to an older adult or person with disabilities, encourage them to take good care of themselves. Their keeping healthy is vital to their ability to continue to provide care. Here are a few self-care suggestions for caregivers.

- Learn to accept help.
- Take time for relaxing and pleasurable activities by asking others for help or by utilizing respite/adult day care.
- Find ways to incorporate exercise into daily routines.
- Take time to eat healthy food.
- Set limits on the care recipient's demands.
- Attend to spiritual needs.
- Participate in caregiver support groups.

Some groups educate and empower caregivers to advocate for policy and programmatic changes. The need for a grass-roots caregiver movement to make caregiver voices heard by policy-makers and press for a national strategy to support family caregivers is increasingly recognized by caregiver advocates. The obvious barriers to such mobilization are the multiple demands on caregivers that reduce their time for such activities. In some instances, caregivers have turned to activism after the death of their loved one. For example, caregivers of persons with AD have become advocates for more federal money for research on dementia. In the economic downturn and passage of health care reform, caregiver activists may need to frame their messages in terms of effectiveness and cost reduction. An additional challenge is projected future declines in the availability of family members to shoulder these care demands (Redfoot, Feinberg, & Houser, 2013; Reinhard et al., 2012).

When Caregiving Becomes Too Much

By now it is clear that families provide the majority of in-home long-term care to older relatives, often on a daily basis for years and at cost to their own physical and mental well-being. Even when they are able to access formal services, they may reach a point where the intensity and stress of care is too much for them to continue to offer. Or the primary caregiver may become ill or even die. At that point, families may make the difficult decision to place their relative in a skilled nursing facility. In some instances, caregivers may become so stressed that they mistreat their older relative, although caregiver stress in itself is not the primary cause of elder mistreatment.

Placement in Long-Term Care Facilities

The move to a long-term care facility, such as intermediate or skilled nursing home care, is often the result of a breakdown in the balance between the older person's care needs, the primary caregiver's resources, and the larger support network. For instance, characteristics of the caregiving context—especially perceived burden, negative family relationships, and low confidence in care—are found to be stronger predictors of whether an Alzheimer's patient will enter a skilled nursing facility than is the nature of the care recipient's illness (Gaugler, Kane, Kane, Clay, & Newcomer, 2005; LoSasso & Johnson, 2002).

Most people hold negative attitudes toward skilled nursing facilities, even though many of them offer quality care. Given these attitudes, moving an older relative to a nursing home is typically a stressful family event; this is especially the case for wives who vowed to care for their husbands "in sickness and in health" and feel that they may have failed as caregivers, and for families of color with strong cultural values about caring for parents and parents-in-law. Accordingly, the placement decision often arouses feelings of grief, loss, guilt, and fear, and may renew past family conflicts. However, some families experience improved relationships with their relatives and continue to visit and assist with hands-on care in long-term care facilities. In other words, the role of caregiver does not completely cease after out-of-home placement, but the nature of tasks and stressors change (Gaugler, Kane, & Kane, 2002; Polivka, 2005; Seltzer & Li, 2000).

Families typically still feel psychologically responsible, even though they must relinquish control over daily care decisions to staff and learn how to be "visitors" rather than primary caregivers. These role changes can initially trigger the family's dissatisfaction with their elder's care. However, when staff–family partnerships develop, families generally experience less stress and are more satisfied with the care received by their elder (Schulz et al., 2003).

With the growth of the oldest-old population with multiple chronic illnesses, placement in a long-term care setting may come to be viewed as a natural transition in the life cycle. Geriatric care managers can assist with the timing of this transition and with negotiating a positive role for the caregiver's continued involvement in the facility. To ease the transition to the post-placement phase, many skilled nursing facilities have developed support and educational groups for families and special training for staff. Internet-based services can also assist families with knowing what qualities to look for and locating an appropriate long-term care facility.

Elder Mistreatment

In some cases, informal caregivers may mistreat older care recipients, although this is not typically due solely to caregiver stress. Instead, it is most often connected to the caregivers' own emotional or behavioral problems and to power inequities, such as financial dependence between the caregiver and care recipient. Abusers typically have more mental or physical health problems, alcohol or drug dependence, financial troubles, and resentment toward and social isolation from the older person compared to non-abusers (Lachs & Pillemer, 2004; Schofield & Mishra, 2003; Tomita, 2006).

Elder mistreatment encompasses any knowing, intentional, or negligent act by a caregiver or other person that harms or causes risk of harm to a vulnerable adult. Often invisible, elder mistreatment became a public issue only after the 1987 Amendments to the Older Americans Act provided guidelines for identifying it and as a result of the visible advocacy of the National Center for the Prevention of Elder Abuse (National Center on Elder Abuse, 2007).

Our focus here is on domestic abuse in the home, but elder abuse also occurs in long-term care settings such as skilled nursing facilities and adult family homes. Types of mistreatment range from physical, sexual, or emotional to financial or material exploitation and neglect/abandonment (either self-imposed or by another person) that result in unnecessary suffering. It is difficult to know precisely how many older adults are being mistreated, since abuse remains largely hidden. One study characterized the problem as prevalent, with the number as high as 5 million elder abuse victims. A 2011 Government Accountability Office (GAO) report stated that 14.1 percent of noninstitutionalized older adults experienced some type of abuse in the past year, suggesting that this figure was most likely an underestimate. A recent study points to 10 percent of older adults experiencing mistreatment. Regardless of the specific percentage, elder mistreatment appears to be increasing, but this may be partially a result of greater public awareness about it. Separate from incidence rates, what is of concern is that only a small percentage of abusive situations are referred for help (Acierno et al., 2010; General Accounting Office, 2011; National Center on Elder Abuse, 2007; Sewell, 2013; Taylor, Ghassan, Evans, & Jackson-Johnson, 2006; Tomita, 2006).

Sometimes elder abuse is not as clear-cut as hitting an older person or stealing their money. It could be more subtle, such as neglecting to take care of an older person or leaving them for long periods of time. **Neglect** accounts for most of the reported cases of elder mistreatment. Even more prevalent but less often reported is **self-neglect**, which falls under the legal definition of mistreatment. It occurs when the older adult engages in behavior that threatens his or her safety, even though he or she is mentally competent and understands the consequences of decisions. In some instances, the inability to perform essential self-care activities (e.g., providing for food, shelter, medical care, and general safety) may reflect a lifelong lifestyle choice and a way of preserving identity and remaining in one's home.

Hoarding, which is a persistent difficulty in discarding or parting with an excessive number of personal possessions, is an extreme case of self-neglect that may threaten elders' health, safety, and dignity, particularly because its private nature means it may remain unseen by others. Unfortunately, hoarding behavior, which is categorized as a mental disorder, is very difficult to change. Simply clearing out an older person's cluttered unsafe space is generally ineffective, as the individual will replace past possessions with new ones. Use of cognitive-behavior interventions such as in-home coaches, motivational techniques to support change, and skills training for decision-making and organization have had some success (Poythress et al., 2006; Steketee, 2012).

Although financial and emotional abuse and self-neglect are the most common types of mistreatment, neglect and physical abuse (e.g., slapping, hitting, bruising) are reported most frequently. Emotional mistreatment, neglect, sexual assault, and abandonment are harder to document and often unreported. Underreporting also occurs because some abusive behavior is enmeshed within complicated familial relationships (e.g., a family that has always yelled at one another) and because elders who are dependent on their abusers fear retaliation if they report mistreatment. Psychological and financial abuse is even further complicated by the victim's dependency on the abuser or the perpetrator's economic dependency on the victim. A 2011 General Accounting Office report found that physical and cognitive impairments, mental problems, and low social support all appear to place older adults at greater risk for abuse (GAO, 2011; Muehlbauer & Crane, 2006; Teaster & Roberto, 2004).

Undue influence is an abusive behavior that is especially difficult to detect. It occurs when a person uses his or her role and power to exploit the trust, dependency, and fear of another, often isolating and creating a world controlled by the abuser. If the abuser is a family member, older victims have trouble separating their feelings of care and love from the loss and trauma experienced at the hands of the abuser. The abusive situation becomes more complicated when the abuser is dependent on the older victim financially, emotionally, and for housing. A web of mutual dependency is created when both the abuser and the victim rely on each other for a portion of their livelihood. Abuser dependency occurs more often than the reverse; for example, the dependent caregiver relies on the elder's financial resources, but the older person accepts such exploitation over being placed in a skilled nursing facility (Setterlund, Tilse, Wilson, McCawley, & Rosenman, 2007; Wilber & Nielsen, 2002).

Research on **intimate partner violence** among older couples is relatively limited compared to that of younger populations. Yet partner violence may have more adverse effects on physical and mental health and may be more severe than among younger partners. Although men are also victims of abuse, women are most frequently the victims of spousal or partner violence. In general, older women underreport partner abuse compared to older men. Professionals in the domestic violence and aging networks should be trained to look for signs of intimate partner violence to ensure that older victims' needs are addressed (Desmarais & Reeves, 2007; Logan, Walker, Jordan, & Leukefeld, 2006).

Whether a behavior is labeled as abusive or neglectful depends on its frequency, duration, intensity, and severity,

points to **ponder**

As you are learning, elder mistreatment can come in several different forms, including emotional abuse. Words play a significant role in how we relate to other people. We use words to establish intimacy, to cause people to laugh, and to make people feel good about themselves. Words can also be used to hurt, to demean, and to coerce people to do things that they don't want to do and thus be a form of emotional or psychological abuse. In some cases, words can lead to violence.

When you see a family member interacting with an older person, pay attention to their words. Are they supportive or demeaning? Do they seem to be expressing negative emotions, even anger, toward the older person, for no apparent reason? What constructive actions, if any, could you take if you saw their negative emotions escalating toward an older adult? Do you know any strategies to de-escalate a verbal conflict?

and varies across states. Lacking a national policy on elder mistreatment, each state determines standards for what constitutes abuse, who should be protected, and how. Regardless of state statutory definitions, however, the older person's perception of the action and the sociocultural context of the mistreatment also affect its identification and consequences. Although ethnic and cultural groups vary in their opinions about what constitutes abuse, cultural differences should never be used as a justification for harming an older person. Nevertheless, culture, degree of acculturation, and filial values and beliefs can influence the definition of abuse and the elder's response to it (Lachs & Pillemer, 2004).

Not surprisingly, elders who are mistreated experience a high level of psychological distress and negative effects on their health and even their life expectancy. Although research is limited, clinical accounts suggest that elders who are abused or financially exploited by their children may experience grief over some of the following losses:

- The family member whom the elder loved, but who is now abusive.
- The person they had hoped their child would become and their pride in their own parenting.
- Their sense of mastery and control of their situation.
- Their anticipated security and safety in old age.
- Their capacity to trust others and even to trust themselves for allowing themselves to be mistreated (GAO, 2011; Gaugler, Kane, & Langlois, 2000; Wolf, 2000).

Older abuse victims generally do not ask friends or family for help. They may believe that living in a familiar but abusive situation is preferable to reporting the abuse and thus admitting that their child is mistreating them—or having to face the unknown of where they would live. Or they may fear being placed in a skilled nursing facility. If the abuser is arrested, restrained from the home, or abandons the elder, the older adult will suffer the loss of that relationship, no matter how bad it may have been. Moreover, few community-based living options and in-home supports exist specifically for elders removed from high-risk situations. In addition, professionals are often biased toward keeping an older person in the home and resist placing her in a long-term care facility, even when the latter would be safer.

What Is Happening to Mrs. Carlson?

Mrs. Carlson is fiercely proud of her ability to live in her own apartment that she had shared with her late husband after their children left home. However, since her husband's death, her level of worrying and isolating herself at home has increased dramatically. She shows no interest in any activities and sometimes stays in bed nearly all day, not eating or getting dressed. Her once immaculate apartment is now dusty, run-down, and crowded with old newspapers, shopping catalogs, and unopened mail, but she refuses to accept the help of chores services or to throw anything away. She thinks her son wants to move in to her apartment and take over power of attorney so he can get her money. What concepts previously discussed in this section may be applicable in discussing Mrs. Carlson's case? What further information would you like to find about her situation? What kinds of questions should you be asking to ascertain whether elder mistreatment may be occurring?

Financial Abuse and Exploitation **Financial abuse** is the improper use of an elder's funds, property, or assets. It is frequently the underlying motive for other forms of abuse as well (Jayawardena & Liao, 2006; Setterlund et al., 2007).

Three common types of financial exploitation are as follows:

- Door-to-door scams: Scammers contract for services they do not provide, double-bill for services, or collect money for false charities.
- Professional swindles by insurance or investment agents who promise wealth and security in exchange for a bogus financial investment.
- Caregiver, relative, or acquaintance abuse.

As noted above, this is the most prevalent and predatory type, and encompasses psychological abuse, including deceit, intimidation, threats, and insults to establish power and control over the elder. It is often the result of the abuser's distorted sense of entitlement in managing the elder's finances.

Reporting and Other Legal Requirements All 50 states have procedures for reporting domestic abuse (including 24-hour toll-free numbers for receiving confidential reports of abuse), and nearly all states have made such reporting mandatory for health care providers. This means that providers' failure to report elder abuse to public agencies is a criminal offense. In fact, some states require any person—not just professionals—to report

Beware of Predators Preying on Older Adults

Betsy was a 78-year-old widow living alone in her own home in the suburbs. For most of the 10 years since her husband died, Betsy had been able to maintain her home and yard. However, in the last couple of years, her property had been showing signs of neglect.

Although it was not evident to Betsy's grown children—who were living away from home and had busy lives of their own—Betsy was beginning to show early signs of dementia. Her short-term memory was poor, and she had problems managing her finances. She knew her property needed fixing up but was reluctant to "bother" her children with it.

One day a man knocked on her door and said that it appeared she needed some work done around the house. He spoke kindly to her and quickly won her confidence. She thought he was the answer to her prayers. He realized that Betsy had some cognitive problems and told her not to worry, that he would help her with things that needed to get done and would give her a special deal. Taking advantage of her confusion and trust, he had her sign a contract and began asking for money right away so that he could buy supplies and get started. He asked Betsy to write him a check made out to "cash," which she did.

Over the next week, this man politely asked Betsy for more checks. He always had a reason for needing more money, and Betsy believed him. To avoid raising suspicion, he did not ask for a large sum at one time. Instead, he had her write a series of checks on different days. Betsy became confused about what she was paying for, but it never crossed her mind that this nice man was swindling her until he stopped showing up to complete the work. By the time Betsy's daughter became involved, the man was nowhere to be found and had cashed all of her checks. A police investigator told Betsy and her daughter that he had seen an increase of cases in recent years in which vulnerable older adults are victims of fraud. Betsy's children finally realized that their mother needed more of their support, and they have worked out a system in which Betsy remains in her own home while allowing her children to help with specific tasks, like check-writing and decision-making.

suspicion of mistreatment. All states have established Adult Protective Services (APS) programs, described in the following box. Every state also has a long-term care ombudsman to investigate and resolve complaints about nursing home abuse, but not all states require APS investigation in institutional settings.

Despite a growing awareness of elder mistreatment, government funding to deal with it has not kept pace with the scope of the problem. When Congress passed the Elder Justice Act (EJA) in 2010, elder abuse advocates were hopeful since approximately $190 million was authorized for elder abuse prevention and programs. This was to provide more funding for APS, expansion of the Long-Term Care Ombudsman Program, training for nursing home surveyors, and support for a number of elder abuse forensic centers. But implementation has been slow. At a March 2011 Congressional hearing, Dr. Mark Lachs, a geriatrician at Cornell University, called for a more centralized system such as a national database for tracking elder abuse. Among other things, this database would help federal agencies network with each other on a national level to combat the various forms of elder abuse through legal means (Acierno et al., 2010; GAO, 2011; Pham, 2011; Quinn & Benson, 2012).

Preventing elder mistreatment requires a multipronged approach involving a wide range of individuals and organizations, including law enforcement, social service agencies, researchers, clinicians, case workers, policy-makers, advocacy groups, businesses, nonprofit organizations, concerned community members, and others. The National Committee for the Prevention of Elder Abuse (NCPEA)—a nonprofit

Getting to Know APS

When a child's well-being is thought to be in danger, Child Protective Services is the name of the government agency that is to be alerted and is supposed to investigate and take action, if necessary. The agency may also be known as Child and Family Services or something similar.

There is an agency that performs a similar service when older adults are in danger. **Adult Protective Services** is the state or county system that investigates reported cases, evaluates risk, assesses the elder's capacity to agree to services, develops and implements care plans, and monitors ongoing service delivery. APS may also refer cases to appropriate legal authorities such as district attorneys. Since mandatory reporting laws require that APS accept all reports, heavy caseloads typically are filled with complex and difficult cases that other agencies are unwilling or unable to accept. Where exactly APS is housed in state or local government varies from state to state, as does the specific ages of the population served. What is known is that almost nine out of 10 APS programs have seen increases in the reports of elder abuse and expanding caseloads in recent years (Quinn & Benson, 2012).

organization and association of individuals and entities committed to preventing elder abuse—has a Web site that is both informative and action oriented. NCPEA has collected best-practice models from across the United States showing ways that elder mistreatment is being tackled. For example, the Massachusetts Bank Reporting Project provides training to bank personnel about how to identify and report financial exploitation. Another example is the Los Angeles Fiduciary Abuse Specialist Team (FAST), which provides expert consultation to train to APS, case workers, ombudsmen, public guardians, and others about complex financial abuse cases.

It should be noted that elder abuse is not confined to the United States or developed countries. The World Health Organization (WHO) reports that elder abuse occurs throughout the world, and that in many places it evokes little recognition or response, considered largely a private matter. WHO maintains that even if prevalence rates are elusive, the moral and societal consequences are obvious, and has called for a global, multifaceted response to protect the rights of older persons (World Health Organization, 2013).

points to **ponder**

Think about how difficult it is for a prosecutor to deal with neglect cases in court. Such cases are generally difficult to prosecute because of the challenge of proving "failure to act." Investigating cases of elder neglect can also be complicated by the victim's underlying disease: Was the disease or neglect responsible for the person's death? A fire department aid crew found a woman's mother in her garbage-littered, foul-smelling suburban home. She was lying in the fetal position, her head and body covered with feces. She was taken to the hospital, where she died a week later of dehydration and hypothermia. The daughter said she had stopped by her mother's house to bring her shampoo, assumed she was bathing, and had not noticed any unusual smells about her mother. She eventually called 911 and reported that her mother had fallen. It was the first time the county medical examiner had declared a death to be homicide by elder neglect, and it sent an aggressive new message that crimes of neglect would no longer be ignored. The daughter was convicted of first-degree manslaughter through reckless neglect.

Underpaid Caregivers: Direct Care Workers

We turn now to the largest group of health care workers and the largest component of the paid long-term care workforce—**direct care workers**. They are second only to families as the primary providers of long-term care in both the community and skilled nursing facilities. As the "hands, voice, and face" of the long-term care system, direct care workers provide "high-touch" intimate, personal, and physically/emotionally challenging care. These hands-on providers are expected to be compassionate in their care, yet often do not feel prepared, respected, or valued—similar to the experiences of many family caregivers. In many ways, they share with families' similar joys and burdens from care and blur the distinction between paid formal and unpaid informal care (Harahan & Stone, 2009; Institute of Medicine, 2008; Seavey, 2010–2011, 2011).

The direct care workforce is comprised of three groups of over 3 million workers and is now statutorily defined by the 2010 Patient Protection and Affordable Care Act (health care reform) as follows:

1. nursing assistants, aides, orderlies, and attendants, typically in skilled nursing facilities, assisted living, or hospitals;
2. home health aides, typically in the elders' home or other community settings; and
3. personal care aides and attendants, including homemaker aides in both private and group homes.

Since 1998, there has been slightly over a 50 percent increase in the number of direct care workers, at more than seven times the rate of overall new job growth. And the demand for direct care workers will grow dramatically in the next few decades (Seavey, 2011).

If you have ever been in a hospital, you probably interacted most with nurse aides and attendants who may have brought you your food, helped you to the bathroom, or periodically checked your vital signs. However, the majority of direct care workers are now in home and community-based settings. A growing number also work directly for consumers and their families rather than be employed through an agency. In these home-based settings, direct care workers may require more autonomy, responsibility, and skill, since they do not have direct supervision (Seavey, 2010–2011, 2011).

Direct care workers are on the frontlines of long-term care.

The intersections of gender, race, and immigration status are reflected in the defining characteristics of direct care workers.

- Ninety percent are women (average age of 42), oftentimes single mothers responsible for dependent children. They have minimal education (55 percent have only a high school education or less), frequently hold more than one job but still live in poverty or near-poverty, and increasingly are dependent on food stamps and other public benefits to supplement their income. Many are women transitioning from welfare to work and facing significant barriers to moving out of poverty. These conflicting pressures may affect their work performance.
- Racial inequities in terms of education and employment opportunities across the life course partially explain the predominance (51 percent) of African American, Asian, and Latina women (many of whom are immigrants) among such hands-on care providers. African Americans form 30 percent of the workforce and Latina or other workers of color comprise over 16 percent.
- Foreign-born women, generally educated in another country, comprise 20–25 percent of the direct care workforce, with the highest rates among immigrants from Mexico, Haiti, Puerto Rico, Jamaica, and the Philippines. Immigrant women are especially vulnerable to financial exploitation because such work is often paid under the table, which means local labor laws may not be enforced. The wide variation by race, ethnicity, and culture among direct care staff are reflected in language and cultural differences in communication. This may result in miscommunication and conflict with other staff, older care recipients, and family members, which may interfere with meeting older persons' needs. Over 12 percent of nurses' aides, for example, report that they speak English poorly or not at all.
- As a result, low-income younger women of color are often caring for low-income Caucasian older women. Both groups of women are negatively impacted by the adverse work environments faced by their low-income female direct care workers (Browne & Braun, 2008; Harahan & Stone, 2009; Institute for Women's Policy Research, 2013; Leutz, 2007; Polson, 2013; Redfoot & Houser, 2005; Seavey, 2010–2011, 2011; Stone, 2011).

It is important to note however that these characteristics vary by region and state. For example, in California and New York, up to 50 percent of the workforce is foreign-born and nearly 70 percent are non-white. In contrast, in the Midwest, 75 percent of direct care workers are white, which reflects lower immigration rates to these states (Seavey, 2010–2011).

Our society as a whole does not value the socially and economically important work of caregiving; this lack of public recognition is, in turn, reflected in relatively negative working conditions. These include poverty-level wages and part-time employment with no or limited benefits (particularly health insurance); little training (for more than 20 years, federal law has required only 75 hours of training, but this is shifting under health care reform); inadequate supervision; and low status.

Economic and Health Disparities Faced by Direct Care Workers

Direct care workers struggle to support themselves and their families on an average income of $17,000 a year, well below the median wage for all U.S. workers. Indeed, they often earn less per hour than the typical veterinary assistant. Not surprisingly, they are twice as likely as other workers to be low-income. Additional problems faced by direct care workers include unpredictable hours, lack of full-time work, and limited or nonexistent health and other types of benefits. About half of direct care workers are so poorly paid that they qualify for public assistance (Direct Care Alliance, 2012; Miller, 2012; Seavey, 2010–2011, 2011).

Although many people are drawn to direct care work from a desire to help people, such work is physically and emotionally draining. Direct care staff face significant on-the-job risks to their own personal safety and health. The heavy workload is often a repetition of single tasks, and the risk of personal injury from physical work is among the highest of any occupation, by one estimate second only to truck drivers. The highly stressful nature of direct care work may explain higher than average rates of depression among personal care workers. Workers of color may be treated disrespectfully, called "girl" or "maid," even verbally and physically abused by some older care recipients, either because of racism or cognitive impairment. In addition, there are few incentives for direct care workers to obtain more training or education to enhance quality of care. Fortunately, some education and advocacy groups such as PHI (formerly Paraprofessional Health Institute) are proposing career ladders for advancement of direct care staff (Squillace, Bercovitz, Rosenoff, & Remsburg, 2008; Seavey, 2010–2011; Stone & Dawson, 2008; Tak, Sweeney, Alterman, Baron, & Calvert, 2010).

The low societal value placed on caregiving can create problems not only for the workers but also for older adults, families, and formal care providers. Quality of care is diminished when morale among direct care workers is low, turnover high, and labor shortages persistent. Staff turnover rates in home care range from 40 to 60 percent, and in nursing homes are as high as 66 percent in some job categories. This "workforce churning" not only disrupts continuity of care but also is expensive, entailing that employers pay more for recruitment, training, and lost productivity (Harahan & Stone, 2009; Miller, 2012; Seavey, 2010–2011; Stone, 2011; Wiener, Squillace, Anderson, & Khatursky, 2009).

An Honest Day's Work Deserves Full Pay

Della was a home health aide from West Africa, who came to the United States when her husband was in graduate school. This was the only job she could find. She worked in home care for 5 years. During that time, her basic rights as home care worker were not guaranteed by the federal Fair Labor Standards Act, so she did not get compensated for overtime and made only the minimum wage. Fast food workers, by contrast, were covered by the Fair Labor Standards Act. This inequity existed because home care workers, who often provide intensive skilled care, were considered by the Department of Labor to be only "companions."

Once a month, Della drove about 300 miles to take the man she cared for to his monthly medical treatment. She stayed with him for five days and was available to him 24/7 but was only paid for 12 hours of work a day. While she was out of town, she had to pay a friend to watch her children. Because she barely made enough money during those time periods to cover child care and other expenses, she took on other part-time jobs to get by. She loved working with older people, but the only way she could make more money was to quit and find another job where she would be guaranteed benefits and minimum wage. She became involved with several national advocacy groups to support a proposal from the Department of Labor that would extend basic labor protections to home care workers.

On September 17, 2013, their advocacy efforts paid off. On that day, Della learned that home care workers would also be covered by Fair Labor Standards Act protections! Future home care workers nationwide would have to be paid minimum wage and overtime. Congress finally recognized that an honest day's work deserves full pay (U.S. Department of Labor, 2013).

Future Demand

A majority of states face a shortage of direct care workers. Such labor shortages will be exacerbated as the aging population increases. By 2018, it is estimated that an additional 1.3 million direct care staff will be needed primarily for home and community-based care settings, and they will outnumber residential facility workers by nearly two to one. Home health aides and personal care aides are projected to be the third and fourth fastest-growing occupations in the country. Indeed, there are expected to be more direct care workers in the United States in 2018 than K–12 teachers, law enforcement and public safety workers, or registered nurses. At the same time, there will be a graying of the current direct care workforce with over 33 percent age 65 and older, compared to 20 percent now (Seavey, 2010–2011).

But in order to recruit and retain a direct care workforce, certain changes need to be made:

- Competitive wages that reward longevity and skill improvement
- Health care benefits

- Scheduling and staffing practices that support stable hours and income
- Improved orientation and training based on core competencies, including effective interpersonal communication skills
- Involvement in decision-making, since direct care staff often know the older residents better than the professional staff
- Creation of opportunities for advancement and job enrichment, such as a career ladder and the concept of an advanced care aide
- Supervisory practices that will promote retention, such as a coaching style of supervision (Harahan & Stone, 2009; Seavey, 2010–2011, 2011; Stone & Dawson, 2008; Wiener et al., 2009).

Fortunately, employers and policy-makers are beginning to recognize the centrality of direct care workers to quality care. Indeed, both the 2001 and 2008 Institute of Medicine reports on the geriatric workforce emphasized that the quality of long-term care depends on the performance of the caregiving workforce and recommended more attention to education, training, and supports for direct care workers. This represented a shift from past reports' emphasis on regulations and staffing levels. Indeed, the societal need to improve the elder care workforce and to create more jobs is interconnected. Moreover, the Affordable Care Act (health care reform) funds training and incentives for more people to join the long-term care workforce. And national advocacy groups such as PHI and the Direct Care Alliance are proposing changes to benefit direct care workers at both federal and state levels, including increased wages. Direct care jobs are plentiful, are among the fastest growing, and cannot be outsourced at a time when most states are faced with the need to move the unemployed into jobs with strong growth potential. Given this, some of you might want to consider pursuing direct care work as a way to make a positive difference in older adults' lives (Seavey, 2010–2011).

summary

Most of the caregiving in the United States is provided by informal caregivers as opposed to paid care. Informal caregivers include adult children, spouses/partners, other family members, friends, grandparents, and even great-grandparents. Family and friends provide about $450 billion of financially uncompensated care. They assist older adults with ADLs and IADLs above and beyond what the formal health care system would be able to manage and thus are considered to be essential and significant contributors to enhancing the quality of life for elders. Informal caregivers experience both benefits and costs. But objective and subjective burdens tend to be greatest when caring for a relative with dementia, and women are more likely to experience high levels of stress compared to their male counterparts. Caregivers of color often have strong extended networks to help share responsibilities, but have less awareness of and access to formal services. LGBT families of choice often rely on friends for care and support.

When grandparents and great-grandparents take on primary care responsibilities for their grandchildren, they experience a wide array of challenges. Financial and legal issues often complicate their ability to provide what is best for the child. Trying to navigate the legal system can be overwhelming, but there are organizations and resources to support grandparent caregivers.

Service providers are increasingly aware that caregivers are "clients" whose needs should be assessed, and more communities are funding caregiver support services to support family-centered care. Information and referral services are critical for caregivers in finding out about resources available to them in their area. Where resources are available, they come in many forms, from support groups, problem-solving counseling, respite services, and home modifications, to Internet advice. There is a growing body of research to determine what interventions, such as psychoeducational programs, are effective at reducing caregiver burden and promoting their well-being. In some instances, families may not utilize services, believing that caregiving is just what they should do out of love for their relative. Continued and increased national support for caregivers is essential as the older adult population grows in the decades ahead. At times, informal care is not the best option, either because of elder mistreatment or caregiver burnout, and placement in long-term care facilities may improve the quality of care for the older care recipient.

Closely related to the central role of unpaid family caregivers, underpaid direct care workers are major providers of home and community-based long-term care, and face critical needs for additional training, higher wages and benefits, and quality supervision. The needs of unpaid and underpaid caregivers are clearly a growing concern for social and health care providers and policy-makers at the national level.

key terms

Adult Protective Services, p. 216
caregiver burden, p. 197
caregiving, p. 194
care recipient, p. 194
caring about, p. 200
caring for, p. 200
direct care workers, p. 217
elder mistreatment, p. 213
Family and Medical Leave Act (FMLA), p. 207
family caregivers, p. 196
family-centered care, p. 208
financial abuse, p. 215
hoarding, p. 214
informal caregiving, p. 194
interventions, p. 208
intimate partner violence, p. 214
National Family Caregiver Support Program (NFCSP), p. 207
neglect, p. 214
objective burden, p. 198
primary stressors, p. 197
respite care, p. 210
secondary stressors, p. 197
self-neglect, p. 214
skipped-generation households, p. 204
subjective burden, p. 198
undue influence, p. 214
women in the middle, p. 201

review questions

1. Discuss some reasons that informal and family caregiving is so essential to the American health and long-term care systems.
2. List four of the physical, psychological, and economic costs of caregiving.
3. Discuss at least three ways in which informal caregiving differs for women and men.
4. What is the approximate monetary value of caregiving services provided by informal caregivers? What might be the reasons that our society does not fully value caregiving work?
5. What is meant by subjective burden (as opposed to objective burden) as experienced by informal caregivers? What is a primary reason that feelings of subjective burden can vary among caregivers who are doing the same tasks?
6. What are some positive aspects of being an informal caregiver?
7. What kinds of services are funded by the National Family Caregiver Support Program (NFCSP)?
8. Identify three types of interventions that have been found to reduce caregiver stress and enhance their well-being.
9. Define different types of elder mistreatment: psychological abuse, financial exploitation, undue influence, and self-neglect.
10. Describe the role that direct care workers play in our long-term care support environment.
11. List three of the primary types of challenges that direct care workers face in the workplace.

media resources

Watch

- Sandwich Generation
- Caring for Elderly Parents

View

- Number of Persons 65+, 1900–2030 (millions)

Read

- Zook, Lee J. Mutual Aid and Elders in Amish Society.

references

Acierno, R., Hernandez, M. A., Amstadter, A. B., Resnick, H. S., Steve, K., & Muzzy, W. (2010). Prevalence and correlates of emotional, physical, sexual, and financial abuse and potential neglect in the United States: The National Elder Mistreatment Study. *American Journal of Public Health, 100*, 292–297.

Adams, B., Aranda, M., Kemp, B., & Takagi, K. (2002). Ethnic and gender differences in distress among Anglo-American, African American, Japanese American and Mexican American spousal caregivers of persons with dementia. *Journal of Clinical Geropsychology, 8*, 279–301.

Administration on Aging. (2012). *National Family Caregiver Support Program (OAA: Title IIIE)*. Retrieved February 2012 from http://www.aoa/gov/AoAprogram/HCLTC/Caregiver/index/aspx.

Belle, S. H., Burgio, L., Burns, R., Coon, D., Czaja, S. J., Gallagher-Thompson, D., et al. (2006). Enhancing the quality of life of dementia caregivers from different ethnic or racial groups: A randomized controlled trial. *Annals of Internal Medicine, 145*, 727–738.

Bookman, A., & Harrington, M. (2007). Family caregivers: A shadow workforce in the geriatric health care system? *Journal of Health Politics, Policy and Law, 32*, 1005–1041.

Brodaty, H., Greene, A., & Koschera, A. (2003). Meta-analysis of psychosocial interventions for caregivers of people with dementia. *Journal of the American Geriatrics Society, 51*, 657–664.

Brody, E. (2004). *Women in the middle.* New York: Springer.

Browne, C. V., & Braun, K. L. (2008). Globalization, women's migration and the long-term care workforce. *The Gerontologist, 48*, 16–24.

Byers, L. (2010). Native American grandmothers: Cultural tradition and contemporary necessity. *Journal of Ethnic and Cultural Diversity in Social Work, 19*(4), 305–316.

Calasanti, T. (2006). Gender and old age: Lessons from spousal caregivers. In T. Calasanti & K. Slevin (Eds.), *Age matters: Re-aligning feminist thinking*. New York: Routledge.

Calasanti, T. (2009). Theorizing feminist gerontology, sexuality and beyond: An intersectional approach. In V. L. Bengtson, D. Gans, N. M. Putney, & M. Silverstein (Eds.), *Handbook of theories of aging*. New York: Springer.

Chadiha, L. A., Brown, E., & Aranda, M. P. (2006). Older African Americans and other black populations. In B. Berkman & S. D'Ambruoso (Eds.), *Handbook of social work in 367 health and aging* (pp. 247–256). New York: Oxford University Press.

Chien, L.-Y., Chu, H., Guo, J.-L., Liao, Y.-M., Chang, L.-I., Chen, C.-H., & Chou, K.-R. (2011). Caregiver support groups in patients with dementia: A meta-analysis. *International Journal of Geriatric Psychiatry, 10*, 1089–1098.

Czaja, S. J., & Schultz, R. (2006). Innovations in technology and aging: Introduction. *Generations, 30*(2), 6–8.

Davis, L., Burgio, L., Buckwater, K. & Weaver, M. (2004). A comparison of in-home and telephone-based skill training interventions with caregivers of persons with dementia. *Journal of Mental Health & Aging, 10*, 31–44.

Direct Care Alliance.(2012). *Fair pay for quality care.* New York: Direct Care Alliance. Retrieved January 2, 2013, from http://www.directcarealliance.org/index.cfm?pageId=538.

Desmarais, S. L., & Reeves, K. A. (2007). Gray, black, & blue: The state of research and intervention for intimate partner abuse among elders. *Behavioral Sciences & the Law, 25*, 377–391.

Dilworth-Anderson, P., Brummett, B. H., Goodwin, P., Williams, S. W., Williams, R. B., & Siegler, I. C. (2005). Effects of race on cultural justification for caregiving. *Journal of Gerontology: Social Sciences, 60B*, S257–S262.

Dilworth-Anderson, P., Williams, I. C., & Gibson, B. E. (2002). Issues of race, ethnicity, and culture in caregiving research: A 20-year review. *The Gerontologist, 42*, 237–272.

Donovan, M. L., & Corcoran, M. (2010). Description of dementia caregiver uplifts and implications for occupational therapy. *American Journal of Occupational Therapy, 64*, 590–595.

Doty, P. (2010). The evolving balance of formal and informal, institutional and non-institutional long-term care for older Americans: A thirty-year perspective. *Public Policy & Aging Report, 20*(1), 3–9.

Family Caregiver Alliance. (2012a). *Fact sheet: Selected caregiver statistics.* San Francisco, CA: Family Caregiver Alliance.

Family Caregiver Alliance. (2012b). *Selected caregiver assessment measures: A resource inventory for practitioners* (2nd ed.). San Francisco, CA: Family Caregiver Alliance.

Family Caregiver Alliance & National Center on Caregiving. (2011). *Family caregiving 2010: Year in Review.* San Francisco, CA: Family Caregiver Alliance.

Federal Interagency Forum on Aging-Related Statistics. (2012). *Older Americans: 2011.* Washington, DC: Government Printing Office.

Feinberg, L., Reinhard, S. C., Houser, A., & Choula, R. (2011). *Valuing the invaluable: 2011 update: The growing contributions and costs of family caregiving.* Washington, DC: AARP Public Policy Institute.

Feinberg, L. F. (2008). Caregiver assessment. *Journal of Social Work Education, 44*, 39–41.

Feinberg, L. F. (2012). *Moving toward person and family-centered care.* Washington, DC: AARP Public Policy Institute.

Feinberg, L. F. (2013). *Keeping up with the times: Supporting family caregivers with workplace leave policies.* Washington, DC: AARP Public Policy Institute.

Foley, K. L., Tung, H. J., & Mutran, E. J. (2002). Self-gain and self-loss among African American and white caregivers. *Journal of Gerontology: Social Sciences, 57*, S14–S22.

Fredriksen-Goldsen, K. I., Kim, H.-J., Emlet, C. A., Muraco, A., Erosheva, E. A., Hoy-Ellis, C. P., Goldsen, J., & Petry, H. (2011). *The aging and health report: Disparities and resilience among lesbian, gay, bisexual, and transgender older adults.* Seattle, WA: Institute for Multigenerational Health, University of Washington.

Funk, L. M., Chappell, N. L., & Liu, G. (2011). Associations between filial responsibility and caregiver well-being: Are there differences by cultural group? *Research on Aging,* 1–18.

Retrieved September 22, 2013, from http://roa.sagepub.com/content/early/2011/11/18/0164027511422450.full.pdf+html.

Gallagher-Thompson, D., & Coon, D. W. (2007). Evidence-based psychological treatments for distress in family caregivers of older adults. *Psychology of Aging, 22*, 37–51.

Gaugler, J. E., Jarrot, S., Zarit, S., Stephens, M., Townsend, A., & Greene, R. (2003). Adult day service use and reductions in caregiving hours: Effects on stress and psychological well-being for dementia caregivers. *International Journal of Geriatric Psychiatry, 18*, 55–62.

Gaugler, J. E., Kane, R. A., & Langlois, J. (2000). Assessment of family caregivers of older adults. In R. L. Kane & R. A. Kane (Eds.), *Assessing older persons: Measures, meaning and practical applications* (pp. 320–359). New York: Oxford University Press.

Gaugler, J. E., Kane, R. L., Kane, R. A., Clay, T., & Newcomer, R. (2005). The effects of duration of caregiving on institutionalization. *The Gerontologist, 45*, 78–89.

Generations United. (2012). *Grandfamilies statistics*. Retrieved January 1, 2013, from http://www.gu.org/OURWORK/Grandfamilies/GrandfamiliesStatistics.aspx.

Gibson, M. J., Kelly, K. A., & Kaplan, A. K. (2012). *Family caregiving and transitional care: A critical review.* San Francisco, CA: Family Caregiver Alliance.

Gitlin, L. N., Hauck, W. W., Dennis, M. P., & Winter, L. (2005). Maintenance effects of the home environmental skill-building program for family caregivers and individuals with Alzheimer's disease and related disorders. *The Gerontologist, 66A*, 368–374.

Gitlin, L. N. (2011). *Skills2Care (Environmental skill building program)*. Retrieved August 13, 2011, from http://rosalynncarter.org/caregiver_intervention_database/dementia.

Given, B., Sherwood, P., & Given, C. (2008). What knowledge and skills do caregivers need? *Journal of Social Work Education, 44*, 28–34.

Goins, R. T., Moss, M., Buchwald, D., & Guralnik, J. M. (2007). Disability among older American Indians and Alaska Natives: An analysis of the 2000 Census public use microdata sample. *The Gerontologist, 47*, 670–696.

Gonyea, J. (2008). Foreword: America's aging workforce: A critical business issue. *Journal of Workplace Behavioral Health, 23*(1/2), 1–14.

Goodman, C. C., Potts, M., Pasztor, E. M., & Scorzo, D. (2004). Grandmothers as kinship caregivers: Private arrangements compared to public child welfare oversight. *Children & Youth Services Review, 26*, 287–305.

Government Accounting Office. (2011, March). *Elder justice: Strong federal leadership could enhance national response to elder abuse.* Report to the Chairman, Special Committee on Aging, U.S. Senate.

Grandparents as Parents. (2013). *About us.* Canoga Park, CA: Grandparents as Parents. Retrieved September 24, 2013, from http://www.grandparentsasparents.org/aboutus/index_aboutus.php.

Greenberg, J., Selzter, M., & Brewer, V. (2006). Caregivers to older adults. In B. Berkman (Ed.), *Handbook of social work in health and aging.* New York: Oxford University Press.

Haley, W. E., Gitlin, L., Wisniewski, S., Mahoney, D., Coon, D., Winter, L., et al. (2004). Well-being, appraisal and coping in African American and Caucasian dementia caregivers: Findings from the REACH study. *Aging and Mental Health, 8*, 316–329.

Haley, W. E., Roth, D. L., Howard, G., & Safford, M. M. (2010). Caregiving strain and estimated risk for stroke and coronary heart disease among spousal caregivers. *Stroke, 41*, 331–336.

Harahan, M., & Stone, R. (2009). Who will care? Building the geriatric long-term care labor force. In R. B. Hudson (Ed.), *Boomer Bust. The boomers and their future (Vol. 2)*. Westport, CT: Praeger.

Hayslip, B., & Kaminski, P. (2005). Grandparents raising their grandchildren. In R. K. Caputo (Ed.), *Challenges of aging in U.S. families: Policy and practice implications.* Binghamton, NY: Haworth Press.

Heaphy, B. (2007). Sexualities, gender and ageing: Resources and social change. *Current Sociology, 55*, 193–210.

Iecovich, E. (2008). Caregiving burden, community services, and quality of life of primary caregivers of frail elderly persons. *Journal of Applied Gerontology, 27*(3), 309–330.

Institute for Women's Policy Research. (2013). *Increasing pathways to legal status for immigrant in-home care workers.* Washington, DC: Institute for Women's Policy Research.

Institute of Medicine. (2008). *Retooling for an aging America: Building the health care workforce.* Washington, DC: National Academies Press.

Jayawardena, K. M., & Liao, S. (2006). Elder abuse at end of life. *Journal of Palliative Medicine, 9*(1), 127–136.

Jervis, L. L., & Manson, S. S. (2002). American Indians/Alaska Natives and dementia. *Alzheimer Disease and Related Disorders, 16*, S89–S95.

Johnson, R. W., & Wiener, J. M. (2006). *A profile of frail older Americans and their caregivers.* Washington, DC: Urban Institute, The Retirement Project. Occasional Paper Number 8.

Kagan, J. (2006). *Lifespan Respite Act now goes to President's desk to be signed into law.* Annandale, VA: National Respite Coalition. Press Release from Hilary Rodham Clinton.

Kelch-Oliver, K. (2008). African American grandparent caregivers: Stresses and implications for counselors. *Family Journal, 16*(1), 43–50.

Kramer, B. J., & Thompson, E. H. (2002). *Men as caregivers: Theory, research and service implications.* New York: Springer.

Kwak, J., Montgomery, R. J., Kosloski, K., & Lang, J. (2011). The impact of TCARE® on service recommendation, use and caregiver well-being. *The Gerontologist, 51*, 704–713.

Lachs, M., & Pillemer, K. (2004). Elder abuse. *Lancet, 364*, 1263–1272.

Lai, D. W. L. (2010). Filial piety, caregiving appraisal, and caregiving burden. *Research on Aging, 32*(2), 200–223.

Letiecq, B. L., Bailey, S. J., & Kurtz, M. A. (2007). Depression among rural Native American and European American grandparents rearing their grandchildren. *Journal of Family Issues, 29*(3), 334–356.

Letiecz, B. L, Bailey, S., & Porterfield, F. (2008). "We have no rights, we get no help": The legal and policy dilemmas facing grandparent caregivers. *Journal of Family Issues, 29*(8), 995–1012.

Leutz, W. (2007). Immigration and the elder: Foreign-born workers in long-term care. *Immigration Policy in Focus, 5*, 1–11.

Liu, D., Hinton, L., Tran, C., Hinton, D., & Barker, J. C. (2008). Reexamining the relationships among dementia, stigma, and aging in immigrant Chinese and Vietnamese family caregivers. *Journal of Cross-Cultural Gerontology, 23*, 283–299.

Livingston, G., & Parker, K. (2010). *Since the start of the Great Recession, more children raised by grandparents.* Washington, DC: Pew Research Center. Retrieved from http://www.pewsocialtrends.org/2010/09/09/since-the-start-of-the-great-recession-more-children-raised-by-grandparents/.

Logan, T., Walker, R., Jordan, C., & Leukefeld, C. (2006). *Women and victimization: Contributing factors, interventions, and implications.* Washington, DC: American Psychological Association Press.

LoSasso, A. T., & Johnson, R. W. (2002). Does informal care from adult children reduce nursing home admissions for the elderly? *Inquiry, 39,* 279–297.

Lumpkin, J. R. (2007). Grandparents in a parental or near-parental role: Sources of stress and coping mechanisms. *Journal of Family Issues, 29*(3), 357–372.

Magana, S. (2006). Older Latino family caregivers. In B. Berkman (Ed.), *Handbook of social work in health and aging.* New York: Oxford University Press.

MetLife Mature Market Institute. (2010). *Still out, still aging. Study of lesbian, gay, bisexual and transgender baby boomers.* Westport, CT: MetLife Mature Market Institute.

Miller, E. A. (2012). The Affordable Care Act and long-term care: Comprehensive reform or just tinkering around the edges. *Journal of Aging & Social Policy, 24,* 101–117.

Misuk, L., & Gardner, J. E. (2010). Grandparents involvement and support in families in children with disabilities. *Educational Gerontology, 36,* 467–499.

Mittelman, M. S., Roth, D. L., Haley, W. E., & Zarit, S. H. (2004). Effects of a caregiver intervention on negative caregiver appraisals of behavior problems in patients with Alzheimer's disease. Results of a randomized clinical trial. *Journals of Gerontology: Psychological Sciences, 59B,* P27–P34.

Montgomery, R., & Kwak, J. (2008). TCARE®: Tailored caregiver assessment and referral. *Journal of Social Work Education, 44*(3), 59–64.

Montgomery, R. J., Kwak, J., Kosloski, K., & Valuch, C. (2011). Effects of the TCARE® intervention on caregiver burden and depressive symptoms: Preliminary findings from a randomized controlled study. *Journals of Gerontology: Psychological and Social Sciences, 66B,* 640–647.

Muehlbauer, M., & Crane, P. (2006). Elder abuse and neglect. *Journal of Psychosocial Nursing, 44,* 43–48.

Narayn, S., Lewis, M., Tornatore, J., Hepburn, K., & Corcoran-Perry, S. (2001). Subjective responses to caregiving for spouses with dementia. *Journal of Gerontological Nursing, 27,* 19–28.

National Alliance for Caregiving and American Association of Retired Persons (NAC/AARP). (2012). *Caregiving in the U.S.* Bethesda, MD and Washington, DC: National Alliance for Caregiving and AARP.

National Center on Elder Abuse. (2007). *Major types of elder abuse.* Retrieved May 2009, from http://www.ncea.aoa.gov/ncearoot/Main_Site/FAQ/Basics/Types_Of_Abuse.aspx.

Parker, D., Mills, S., & Abbey, J. (2008). Effectiveness of interventions that assist caregivers to support people with dementia living in the community: A systematic review. *Journal of Evidence-Based Health, 6,* 137–172.

Pham, S. (2011, March 3). Government report finds elder abuse on the rise. *New York Times.* Retrieved January 2013, from http://newoldage.blogs.nytimes.com/2011/03/03/government-report-finds-elder-abuse-on-the-rise/.

Pinquart, M., & Sorensen, S. (2006). Gender differences in caregiver stressors, social resources and health: An updated meta-analysis. *Journal of Gerontology: Psychological Sciences, 61B,* P33–P45.

Polivka, L. (2005). Always on call: When illness turns families into caregivers: caring for our elders. *The Gerontologist, 45,* 557–561.

Polson, D. (2013). *By our sides: The vital work of immigrant direct care workers.* Washington, DC: The Direct Care Alliance.

Poythress, E. L., Burnett, J., Pickens, S., & Dyer, C. B. (2006). Severe self-neglect: An epidemiological and historical perspective. *Journal of Elder Abuse and Neglect, 18,* 5–12.

Quinn, K. M., & Benson, W. F. (2012). The state's elder abuse victim services: A system still in search of support. *Generations, 36,* 66–72.

Redfoot, D. L., Feinberg, L., & Houser, A. N. (2013). *The aging of the baby boom and the growing care gap: A look at future declines in the availability of family caregivers.* Washington, DC: AARP Policy Institute.

Redfoot, D. L., & Houser, A. N. (2005, October). *We shall travel on: Quality of care, economic development, and the international migration of long-term care workers.* Washington, DC: AARP Policy Institute.

Redfoot, D. (2013). *Just how valuable is family caregiving?* Washington, DC: AARP Policy Institute. Retrieved September 22, 2013, from http://blog.aarp.org/2013/07/19/just-how-valuable-is-family-caregiving/.

Reinhard, S., Feinberg, L., & Choula, R. (2012). *A call to action: What experts say needs to be done to meet the challenges of family caregiving.* AARP Public Policy Institute.

Richards, M. (2009). *Care sharing.* Woodstock, VT: Skylight Paths.

Roff, L. L., Burgio, L., Gitlin, L. Nichols, L., Chaplin, W., & Hardin, J. M. (2004). Positive aspects of Alzheimer's caregiving: The role of race. *Journals of Gerontology: Psychological Sciences, 59B,* P185–P190.

Rosalynn Carter Institute for Caregiving. (2010). *Averting the caregiving crisis: Why we must act now.* Retrieved September 7, 2011, from http://www.rosalynncarter.org.

Rozario, P. A., & DeRienzis, D. (2008). Familism beliefs and psychological distress among African American women caregivers. *The Gerontologist, 48,* 772–780.

Russell, R. (2004). Social networks among elderly men caregivers. *Journal of Men's Studies, 13,* 121–143.

Savundranayagam, M. Y., Montgomery, R. J., & Kosloski, K. (2011). A dimensional analysis of caregiver burden among spouses and adult children. *The Gerontologist, 51,* 321–331.

Schofield, M., & Mishra, G. (2003). Validity of self-report screening for elder abuse: Women's Health Australia Study. *The Gerontologist, 43,* 110–120.

Schulz, R., Burgio, L., Burns, R., Eisdorfer, C., Gallagher-Thompson, D., Gitlin, L., et al. (2003). Resources for Enhancing Alzheimer's Caregiver Health (REACH): Overview, site-specific outcomes and future directions. *The Gerontologist, 43,* 514–520.

Schulz, R., Martire, L. M., & Klinger, J. N. (2005). Evidence-based caregiver interventions in geriatric psychiatry. *Psychiatric Clinics of North America, 28,* 1007–1038.

Schulz, R., & Sherwood, P. R. (2008). Physical and mental health effects of family caregiving. *Journal of Social Work Education, 44,* 105–113.

Seavey, D. (2010–2011). Caregivers on the front line: Building a better direct-care workforce. *Generations, 34*, 27–35.

Seavey, D. (2011). *Who are direct care workers?* New York: Paraprofessional Health Institute (PHI).

Seltzer, M., & Li, L. W. (2000). The dynamics of caregiving: Transitions during a three-year prospective study. *The Gerontologist, 40*, 165–178.

Setterlund, D., Tilse, C., Wilson, J., McCawley, A. L., & Rosenman, L. (2007). Understanding financial elder abuse in families: The potential of routine activities theory. *Ageing and Society, 27*, 599–614.

Sewell, D. (2013). *Aging America: Elder abuse, use of shelters rising.* Retrieved September 23, 2013, from http://news.msn.com/us/aging-america-elder-abuse-use-of-shelters-rising.

Smith, C. (2008). Technology and Web-based support. *Journal of Social Work Education, 44*, 75–82.

Smith, K., & Bauman, R. (2007). Caring for America's aging population: A profile of the direct care workforce. *Monthly Labor Review,* 20–26.

Squillace, M., Bercovitz, A., Rosenoff, E., & Remsburg, R. (2008). *An exploratory study of certified nursing assistants' intent to leave.* Washington, DC: U.S. Department of Health and Human Services. Retrieved August 2008, from http://aspe.hhs.gov/daltcp/reports/2008/intent.htm.

Steketee, G. (2012). *Hoarding and older adults.* Presented at the Annual Program Meeting of the Council on Social Work Education, November 9. Washington, DC: CSWE.

Stone, R. I. (2011). *Long-term care policy: Yesterday, today, and tomorrow.* Testimony prepared for "Aging in America: Future Challenges, Promise and Potential" Forum convened by the Senate Special Committee on Aging, December 14, 2011. Retrieved February 2012, from http://aging.senate.gov/events/hr241rs.pdf.

Stone, R. I., & Dawson, S. L. (2008). The origins of Better Jobs Better Care. *The Gerontologist, 48*, 5–13.

Sun, F., Hilgeman, M. M., Durkin, D. W., Allen, R. S., & Burgio, L. D. (2009). Perceived income adequacy as a predictor of psychological distress in Alzheimer's caregivers. *Psychology and Aging, 24*, 177–183.

Tak, S. W., Sweeney, M. H., Alterman, T., Baron, S., & Calvert, G. M. (2010). Workplace assaults on nursing assistants in U.S. nursing homes: A multilevel analysis. *American Journal of Public Health, 11*, 1938–1945.

Tang, M. (2011). Can cultural values help explain the positive aspects of caregiving among Chinese American caregivers? *Journal of Gerontological Social Work, 54*, 551–569.

Taylor, D., Ghassan, B., Evans, J., & Jackson-Johnson, V. (2006). Assessing barriers to the identification of elder abuse and neglect: A community survey of primary care physicians. *Journal of the National Medical Association, 98*, 403–404.

Teaster, P., & Roberto, K. (2004). Sexual abuse of older adults: APS cases and outcomes. *The Gerontologist, 44*, 788–796.

Tomita, S. (2006). Mistreated and neglected elders. In B. Berkman (Ed.), *Handbook of social work in health and aging.* New York: Oxford University Press.

Torgan, A. (2013). Grandparents step up, save families. *CNN.com.* Retrieved on September 24, 2013, from http://www.cnn.com/2013/07/25/living/cnnheroes-de-toledo-grandparents/index.html?hpt=hp_t3.

U.S. Census Bureau. (2010). *Facts for features: Grandparents day 2010.* Retrieved July 12, 2010, from http://www.census.gov/newsroom/releases/archives/facts_for_features_special_editions/cb10-ff16.html.

U.S. Census Bureau. (2012). *Households and families: 2010. 2010 Census Briefs.* Washington, DC: U.S. Department of Commerce.

U.S. Department of Labor. (2013). Minimum wage, overtime protections extend to direct care workers by U.S. Labor Department. *News release.* Retrieved September 24, 2013, from http://www.dol.gov/opa/media/press/whd/WHD20131922.htm.

Weiss, C., Gonzalez, H., Kabeto, M., & Langa, K. (2005). Differences in the amount of informal care received by non-Hispanic whites and Latinos in a nationally representative sample of older Americans. *Journal of the American Geriatrics Society, 53*, 146–151.

Wiener, J. M., Squillace, M. R., Anderson, W. L., & Khatursky, G. (2009). Why do they stay? Job tenure among certified nursing assistants in nursing homes. *The Gerontologist, 49*, 198–210.

Wisensale, S. K. (2009). Aging policy as family policy: Expanding family leave and improving flexible work policies. In R. B. Hudson, *Boomer Bust?* (pp. 253–270). New York: Praeger Perspectives.

Whitlatch, C. J. (2008). Informal caregivers: Communication and decision-making. *Journal of Social Work Education, 43*, 89–95.

Whitlatch, C. J., Piiparinen, R., & Feinberg, L. F. (2009). How well do family caregivers know their relatives' care values and preferences? *Dementia, 8*, 223–243.

Wilber, K. H., & Nielsen, E. K. (2002). Elder abuse: New approaches to an age-old problem. *Public Policy & Aging Report, 12*, 24–26.

Winefield, H. (2010). Grandparenting: Diversity in grandparent experiences and needs for healthcare and support. *International Journal of Evidence-Based Healthcare, 8*(4), 277–283.

Wisensale, S. (2009). Aging policy as family policy: Expanding family leave and improving flexible work policies. In R. Hudson (Ed.), *Boomer Bust: Perspectives on the boomers Vol. 1.* Westport, CT: Praeger.

Wolf, R. (2000). The nature and scope of elder abuse. *Generations, 24*, 6–12.

Wong, S., Yoo, G., & Stewart, A. (2006). The changing meaning of family support among older Chinese and Korean immigrants. *Journal of Gerontology, 61B*, S4–S9.

Woodbridge, S., Buys, L., & Miller, E. (2009). Grandparenting a child with a disability: An emotional roller coaster. *Australasian Journal on Ageing, 28*, 37–40.

World Health Organization. (2013). *Elder abuse.* Geneva: World Health Organization. Retrieved September 24, 2013, from http://www.who.int/ageing/projects/elder_abuse/en/.

Youngblut, J. M., Brooten, D., Blais, K., Hannan, J., & Niyonsenga, T. (2010). Grandparent health and functioning after a grandchild's death. *Journal of Pediatric Nursing, 25*, 352–359.

Zarit, S., & Femia, E. (2008). Behavioral and psychosocial interventions for family caregivers. *American Journal of Nursing, 108*, 47–53.

Zodikoff, B. D. (2006). Services for lesbian, gay, bisexual and transgender older adults. In B. Berkman (Ed.), *Handbook of social work in health and aging.* New York: Oxford University Press.

8 Productive Aging: Leisure, Spirituality, and Civic Engagement

learning objectives

8.1 Describe the concept of productive aging, and how leisure, spiritual, and civic engagement activities can contribute to a meaningful life in old age.

8.2 Discuss the types of activities older adults can participate in to foster their intellectual, emotional, and civic engagement.

8.3 Articulate how older adults might expand their collective engagement to influence the well-being of all generations.

Listen to the Chapter Audio

When you see older adults in your community or even in your own family, you may wonder how they ever "fill up" their days now that they are retired or employed for fewer hours than when they were younger. As you learned in Chapter 6, role and activity theories pointed to keeping active and busy as ways to experience life satisfaction in old age. Indeed, some older adults will say that they are even busier in retirement than when they were employed—or they wonder how they ever managed to fit a job into their lives now that their days are full of "nonwork" activities. Consider Max who moved to Sun City after retiring from a factory job in the Midwest. He joins biking and hiking clubs, swims daily, volunteers at his local temple, and helps his neighbors with yard work. Others may feel that they deserve a chance to "relax and rest," not wanting to commit to "obligatory" activities such as volunteering or babysitting grandchildren. In some instances, their adult children may worry that they are not engaged with others, pushing them to go to the local senior center or to help out in their community. For example, Adelaide is content to read, work in her garden, and putter around the house; she has no interest in going to the community center for exercise classes or helping out at the local school. Her daughter nags her to be more active and get out with other people. Just as there is heterogeneity in how younger adults spend their time outside of school or work, even greater differences exist among older adults' leisure time pursuits and, specifically, their religious involvement, volunteer initiatives, and civic participation.

In this chapter, we will start with a brief discussion of what gerontologists mean by productive aging, summarize the ways older adults spend their leisure time, and identify how nonwork activities benefit older adults' physical and mental health well-being. It includes:

- Productive aging: how it is defined and viewed
- Leisure: typical patterns of "nonwork" activity among older adults
- Religion, religiosity, and spirituality
- Three domains of civic engagement—voluntary association membership, volunteering, and political activity

Defining Productive Aging

An emphasis on activity is congruent with Western values of being productive. We typically think of productivity in economic terms—how much we earn or how many hours we work. But proponents of active aging use a much broader definition of **productive aging** to include not only paid but also unpaid activity that produces benefits for society—such as caregiving, volunteerism, and contributing informally to family, friends, neighbors, and the community. This strengths-based approach maximizes older people's capacity to contribute to meet their own and societal needs. It contrasts with problem-focused approaches that emphasize older adults' deficits, illness, or impairments. Some proponents of a broader definition of productive aging also include social or leisure activities that are religious, spiritual, artistic, or recreational. Regardless of the specific definition, what is most important is that productive activities provide older adults with choice of opportunities for meaningful engagement with others, contributions to society, continued growth, and are inclusive—available to all elders, not just those with adequate financial resources. Additionally, some gerontologists

What Is Productive Aging?

Yakov, a 67-year-old retired mathematics teacher and immigrant from Eastern Europe, volunteers in the Senior Companion Program, which pairs an older friendly visitor with an elder who is limited by age-associated physical changes or illness. He spends a day each week with Harry, a retired mail carrier who is legally blind. Yakov receives a stipend for helping with Harry's household tasks while Harry helps Yakov with his English. Theirs is a reciprocal relationship: each is convinced that he is the helper and the other is the recipient. They often go out to lunch at the local Burger King, their favorite restaurant. The waiter who takes their order looks to be about their age, but he is wearing an orange and blue polyester outfit and a Burger King beanie and working for minimum wage alongside giggling 15-year-olds acquiring their first job experience. Which of these three older adults fits your definition of productive aging and why? (Adapted from Freedman (2001, p. 246)).

prefer not to use the term "successful" aging because it implies a right or wrong way to age, with the right way resulting in success. They often prefer the broad definition of productive aging instead (Hao, 2008; Morrow-Howell, 2011; Morrow-Howell, Hong, & Tang, 2009).

Leisure

Leisure is defined as any nonwork activity characterized by the absence of obligation or what one "should" do; not having to do a leisure activity is what makes it inherently satisfying. People's leisure experiences are influenced, in part, by cultural and societal values attached to paid work. Because of American values on being productive through hard work—held especially by the World War II cohort of elders—many of the oldest-old have not experienced satisfying nonwork activities earlier in their lives. They may even have been socialized to mistrust time spent in "nonwork" activities that are viewed as frivolous and believe that they should be "busy" all the time. Societal values are changing, however, with more legitimacy given to leisure across the life course. One indicator of this shift is the growing number of businesses that market classes, group travel, and adventure programs for higher-income middle-age and young-old adults. On the other hand, leisure may be a meaningless concept for elders of color, women, or others with low incomes who work long hours in poorly paid jobs simply to survive and lack resources for satisfying recreational time (Holstein, 2007).

Disagreement regarding the value of leisure pursuits for older people is reflected historically in the gerontological literature. An early perspective, shown in theories of role loss, was that leisure roles could not substitute for employment. Since work was a dominant value in our society, it was argued that individuals cannot derive self-respect from leisure. A closely related view was that retirement was legitimated only when it is filled with "keeping busy"—which is consistent with the activity theory of aging. Engaging in productive work-like activities was viewed as essential to retirement satisfaction. Indeed, the prevalence of the "busy" ethic is reflected in a question commonly asked of retirees: "What do you do all day?" It assumes that if a person is not engaged in paid work, then what can they possibly be doing of value?

A counterargument is that leisure can replace employment roles and provide satisfaction and meaningful engagement. In fact, leisure activities that challenge people's cognitive and physical abilities, such as dancing, gardening, playing a musical instrument, using the computer, and exercising, can enhance their sense of control and mastery. Although these may not seem to others to be "productive" activities, they can nevertheless benefit individuals, their families, and communities.

Ironically, the millennial generation (those born between the mid-1970s and 2000) may be better prepared to pursue leisure in old age in the future, because many of them have faced periods of unemployment and devised satisfying nonwork activities. Moreover, these children of baby boomers typically strive for a better balance between work and leisure than their hardworking parents who were seeking to "have it all" (Cohen, 2005).

points to **ponder**

Imagine yourself retired. How do you envision spending your time? How do you think your values, class, culture, and even how your parents or grandparents spent their time may influence your leisure in retirement? Will you be engaged with others or doing things by yourself? Do you think you will be participating in activities that you currently enjoy or do you see yourself trying out new adventures? Do you see yourself engaging in activities primarily with other retirees or seeking out intergenerational leisure opportunities?

Although wide variations exist, some patterns of meaningful leisure activities in old age are identified in the literature:

- Most activity changes are gradual, reflecting a consistency and a narrowing of activities. Older adults become more selective about how—and with whom—they choose to spend their free time.
- Compared to younger people, older adults are more likely to engage in solitary and sedentary pursuits—reading, listening to music, or sitting in quiet reflection.
- The oldest-old typically spend more time on routine errands, household and yard tasks, hobbies, and "doing nothing in particular." While you may perceive this as "boring and nonproductive," the ability to perform such relatively mundane tasks can be critical to

maintaining feelings of competence, self-esteem, and life satisfaction—and even provides social interaction (Johnson & Schaner, 2005; Prisuta, 2004).

Unpaid or leisure activities also vary by gender and social class in the current cohort of older adults.

- Older men do more household repairs and yard maintenance, while women perform more housework and grandchild care, volunteer, and participate in voluntary associations and religious institutions. This gender-based pattern may change with future cohorts, however.
- Not surprisingly, higher-income older people engage in more active leisure pursuits than low-income elders.

Such differences by social class probably result from the costs of pursuing or having ready access to such activities, such as those who live in middle- to upper-income planned retirement communities. But there are age-based programs designed to reduce financial barriers to leisure activities. For instance, elders can purchase Golden Passports at national parks to give them reduced admission fees. Most cities or counties as well as AARP membership offer lower rates to parks, museums, and cultural activities, and discounted prices from businesses and transportation services.

Leisure activities can have multiple benefits such as

- building social support systems,
- creating new sources of personal meaning and being valued, and
- enhancing a positive identity, self-concept, and life satisfaction.

But leisure activity in itself may not create well-being, because older people who engage in numerous activities also tend to be healthier and have a higher income—both factors that are themselves associated with subjective well-being. Moreover, the quality of social interactions in nonwork activities seems to be more salient for well-being than the number of interactions (Menec, 2003).

Religious Participation, Religiosity, and Spirituality

Of the various options for such interactions, affiliation with a religious institution—mosque, temple, synagogue, or church—is the most common choice for older people and offers both tangible and emotional support for them.

The Changing Landscape of Research on Religion and Aging

Forty years ago, the number of significant studies on religion and aging could be counted on one's fingers. And spirituality was rarely discussed. Today, religion, spirituality, and aging are popular topics of discussion, and there are hundreds of research studies and practice articles across a range of disciplines. Moreover, health and social service providers pay attention to these aspects of older consumers' lives. These shifts reflect increasing recognition of the benefits of religion and spirituality on elders' well-being (Sapp, 2010).

This is not surprising since the United States is a religious nation, where almost 90 percent of Americans report affiliation with a religious organization, 93 percent believe in God or a higher power and 54 percent say religion is very important in their lives. Nearly 60 percent of persons over age 65 and 43 percent of those ages 50–64 attend a religious institution in an average week and many more do so less frequently (Gallup, 2010; Gillum, King, Obisesan, & Koenig, 2008).

Defining Religion, Religiosity, and Spirituality

Although the terms religion, religiosity, and spirituality are related to each other, there are important differences. **Religion** refers to an organized formal system of spiritual belief, values, rituals, and practices, such as Islam, Christianity, Hinduism, Buddhism, and Judaism. Within these religions, there are sects or denominations. These will differ in observable behaviors that characterize their community of believers—the way they worship, interpret the written word such as the Bible or Koran, and structure their organization. Religion encompasses communal ties and practices within formal religious institutions—churches, synagogues, temples, and mosques—rather than individual informal behavior.

Religiosity is a broader concept than religion. It assumes belief in a divine being, faith in a higher power, and it typically involves prayer; additionally, it embraces values of hope, gratitude, and forgiveness that generally are associated with religions worldwide. The concept of religiosity can apply to a person who rarely or even never participates in a formalized religious community. For example, someone who was raised a Buddhist but no longer goes to a temple may still find great comfort in Buddhist teachings and meditate privately in the hopes of achieving enlightenment.

Spirituality is the broadest of the three concepts, and may or may not encompass elements of both religion and religiosity. It is not uncommon today to hear people say, "I am spiritual but not religious." What they often mean is that they do not practice any one form of religion or belong to an organized religious community, but they believe in a spiritual domain, perhaps largely discovered through a personal journey of spiritual searching. The "higher power" in spirituality may be similar to one described in an organized religion, or it may be very different. For example, the "higher power" could be in the form of nature or a flow of energy.

What these three concepts—religion, religiosity, and spirituality—share is the necessity of faith. How people practice that faith—and how observable it is to others—can vary tremendously across the life course and even within individuals at different points in time (Kim, Nesselroad, & McCullough, 2009).

points to ponder

How would you characterize yourself in terms of a faith? Are you religious or spiritual without participating in a formal religious community? Or perhaps you are all three—or none of these. Has your sense of religiosity or spirituality varied across time—or even within yourself at certain points in your life?

As we discuss religion and spirituality, it is important to keep in mind our society's increasing cultural and spiritual diversity. Communities across the United States represent a wide variety of cultural and religious backgrounds—Christianity, Judaism, Islam, Buddhism, Hinduism, Sikhism, and others—as well as denominations or branches within each broad religious category. Spiritual practices may integrate some of these or take a unique approach that emphasizes discovering the divine in nature. If you work with older adults and their families, you will encounter a wide spectrum of belief systems. For example, religious and spiritual beliefs and practices surrounding dying, death, and the afterlife may vary widely among cultural groups and can affect how older adults and their families view end-of-life care. While it is beyond the scope of this book to explore these varied approaches, we encourage you to seek out other resources to learn about these diverse religions and spiritual practices that may affect how people experience the aging process and respond to health and social service providers.

Religious Affiliation: Age, Gender, and Race

Whether people become more religious with age is not clear-cut, since there are multiple ways that older adults express their religious behaviors. We do know that among the current cohort of older adults, the meaning and importance of religion tend to be stronger in old age than in the earlier phases of life. For many elders such as Mrs. Judkins in the box on p. 231, belonging to religiously affiliated groups and participating in religious activities offer a loving, supportive community. This also provides ways to contribute to others—qualities likely to enhance mental and physical well-being. Moreover, leadership positions in churches, temples, and synagogues are often concentrated among older members, offering them respect and status. You may recall the concept of resilience from the Introduction and Chapter 4. Religiosity and spirituality are examples of inner capacities that can protect or buffer adults from adversities that they encounter across the life course and promote resilience. Others posit that spirituality is a central component of successful aging (Crowther, Parker, Achenbaum, Larimore, & Koenig, 2002; Faigin & Pargament, 2011; Law & Sbarra, 2009; Lawlor-Row, 2009).

Although rates of participation in religious institutions tend to increase with age, they often decline among the oldest-old. But this decrease may result from disability, poor health, functional limitations, or transportation difficulties that occur more often among those age 85 and older rather than changes in religiousness and spirituality per se. The oldest-old may adapt by turning to individual internal religious practices in their own homes—reading the Bible, Koran, or other religious books, listening to or watching religious broadcasts, praying and meditating, or studying religion. For the oldest-old who are still able to participate in religious activities, such as Mrs. Judkins, quality of life in their last years of life is, however, found to be positively related to involvement in a religious community (Idler, McLaughlin, & Kasl, 2009).

Community Support and Religious Life

Mrs. Judkins, age 76, attends church every Sunday and leads her women's prayer group every Thursday evening, with about 20 women she has known for many years. Mrs. Judkins has increasing difficulty getting around because of her arthritis, diabetes, and heart problems, but she is determined to get to church for these two gatherings. Fortunately for her, church friends are happy to drive her to and from church. Last year when she had bypass surgery, these friends said prayers for her and sent her cards, flowers, and meals, and several took turns staying with her after her hospitalization. She attributes the success of her surgery and her complete recovery to the prayers of her church friends as well as her own during that difficult time.

Prayer can be a source of comfort and strength.

Both formal participation and informal religious activities such as prayer and personal devotions vary by gender and race. Older women have higher rates of involvement in formal religious organizations than men. They also tend to hold their beliefs more firmly, practice their faith more consistently, and work more vigorously for the religious community. In many instances, religious participation offers opportunities for women to build upon and deepen social relationships—to have a best friend in their congregation—which they tend to value more than men. Indeed, the social connectedness of religious affiliation is often central to older women's well-being (Gallup, 2010; MacKinlay, 2008; Taylor, Chatters, & Levin, 2004).

Organized religion appears to be especially vital to the well-being of older Latinos and African Americans, enhancing their sense of meaning, life satisfaction, self-worth, and community involvement. Mexican American elders may turn to faith communities and religious practices for emotional support and tangible assistance rather than use formal social services. Many are members of families who have been Catholic for generations. Mexican elders tend to identify strongly with Catholicism and its teachings and maintain a rich devotional practice, with elaborate home altars and religious symbolism that help them cope with the challenges of old age. In one study, older Mexican Americans who used their religious belief to find something positive in the face of suffering, compared to those who suffered in silence, tended to rate their health more favorably (Hill, 2008; Idler, 2006; Krause & Bastida, 2011).

African Americans more frequently attend church and turn to religion as a source of help than do whites. African American churches often serve multiple roles that promote well-being and are a basis for social and political activities in the community. One reason for these benefits is that African American elders are generally held in high esteem in the church. Historically, African Americans had more control, social support, and leadership opportunities in their religious lives than other aspects of their daily lives. The black church also traditionally provides social services such as in-home visitation, counseling, meals, household help, and transportation for older members, and may link them with formal agencies. This type of support reflects the African American church's historical responsibility for improving its parishioners' socioeconomic conditions. Within the heterogeneous black American community, immigrant churches play central roles in integrating people within the fabric of the community. For example, the church has been a vital resource for new black Caribbean immigrants and subsequent generations. Black Caribbean women typically place great emphasis on religion, sharing strong religious ties and a sense of loyalty, moral obligation, and respect for the church and its teachings. Spirituality separate from organized religious affiliation is also central to the well-being of many African Americans (Roff et al., 2006; Skarupski, Fitchette, Evans, & Mendes de Leon, 2010; Taylor, Chatters, & Jackson, 2007).

Religiosity

Religiosity, as contrasted with attendance at formal religious events, appears to be relatively stable from the late teens until age 60, and to increase thereafter. Older adults typically report higher levels of subjective religious experiences than other age groups, thinking of themselves as religious or spiritual persons. This means that some older people may appear to be disengaged from religious organizations (e.g., stop attending religious services), but fully engaged in nonorganizational ways; in other words, they still experience strong and meaningful subjective ties to religion (Idler, 2006; Law & Sbarra, 2009; Nelson-Becker, Nakashama, & Canda, 2006).

Some older adults may not participate in religious institutions because they do not feel welcome or accepted. But they may nevertheless be religious. This has been the case for many LGBT elders. Arnold's difficult choices about religious participation are shared by many LGBT elders. This is an example of religiosity because Arnold's belief system is based on his religious upbringing, but he no longer attends church.

Gay Elder Remains Religious without Church

Arnold is a 66-year-old gay man who attended a Christian church from the time he was a child until his young adult years. As he grew older and came to terms with his sexual orientation, he realized that his romantic feelings were in conflict with the moral teachings of his family's church. He stopped going to this church as he felt increasingly alienated from some of its doctrines and offended by homophobic sermons. While he no longer felt the need to go to church, he still identifies as a Christian and values many of the ideas learned from his years of attendance. He continues to pray, read the Bible, and nurture a relationship with God in his private life. Future cohorts of LGBT older adults may find greater acceptance from some churches that promote an inclusive membership approach, however.

Benefits of Religious Participation and Religiosity for Older Adults The well-documented benefits of religion and religiosity are receiving growing attention by gerontological researchers, educators, and practitioners—along with increased visibility in the popular press. As you have been learning in this chapter, religious participation generally has protective effects on physical and mental well-being and helps older adults cope more effectively. In fact, the strength of these relationships between religious involvement and well-being appears to increase over time (Idler, 2006; Lawlor-Row, 2009).

Perhaps the most compelling finding is that religious participation is associated with a lower prevalence of physical illness and may even reduce the risk of mortality. Because religion provides a world view that infuses the present with meaning and the future with hope, it may help people effectively cope with health problems. For example, among patients undergoing cardiac surgery, religious involvement and its importance have been shown to decrease distress and time of recovery (Ai, Park, Huang, Rodgers, & Tice, 2007).

In addition to lower risk of mortality—and higher probability of survival—here are other striking physical benefits of religiosity found for African Americans, Latinos, and white older adults:

- Longer life expectancy
- Later onset of disability
- For those with disability, increased likelihood of improving physical functioning and better health outcomes
- Better cognitive functioning
- Improved immunity to disease
- Lower blood pressure
- Enhanced quality of life, including at end of life (Atchley, 2008, 2009; Chida, Steptoe, & Powell, 2009; Hill, 2008; Idler, 2006; Lawlor-Row, 2009; Roff et al., 2006, 2007; Turesky & Schultz, 2010)

There are also benefits for older adults' mental well-being:

- Improved self-esteem, life satisfaction, and self-concept; feelings of internal control, usefulness, purpose, and being of value; and higher morale
- Decreased prevalence of depression, anxiety, substance use, and suicide
- Lower rates of loneliness
- Reduced fear of dying

- In instances of depression, a greater likelihood of recovery and a shorter recovery time (Idler, 2002, 2006; Koenig, 2002; Schieman, Bierman, & Ellison, 2010; Van Ness & Larson, 2002)

Similar to formal religious participation, religiosity in itself also has positive effects on mental and physical well-being, coping effectively with adversity, quality of life at end of life, and facing one's mortality (Daaleman & Dobbs, 2010; Idler, McLaughlin, & Kasl, 2009; Parker et al., 2003).

Other Factors to Consider regarding Religion and Health Be careful not to imply that religious involvement causes well-being. The association between religious involvement and physical and mental well-being must be interpreted cautiously, since religious characteristics are not the only factors responsible for good health. Indeed, religion has beneficial effects on health precisely because there are so many different pathways to well-being. These pathways include the following:

- Changes in health behaviors that reduce risk factors for poor health
- A sense of belonging and social support derived from religious participation
- A sense of control over unhealthy behaviors and belief systems for coping with adverse circumstances
- Regular opportunities for interaction and informal support from church members as well as more formal support from religious leaders
- The use of religiously based coping strategies (e.g., prayer) when confronted with stressful life situations
- Opportunities to care for and serve others in need, especially among women who volunteer within religious settings (Idler, 2006; Taylor, Chatters, & Levin, 2004)

So...Does This Mean That Religious Participation Is "Good for You"?

Some proponents of faith-based initiatives would claim that "going to church is good" for you. What evidence can you cite in support of that claim? What do you think is beneficial about attending religious services? What caveats, if any, would you suggest about the claim that religion is good for elders?

Religious institutions often encounter the paradox that as their congregation ages and faces increased need for support, fiscal resources diminish, in part because of fewer younger members. Fortunately, a growing number of religious institutions are now more actively reaching out to their aging members by offering transportation, minimizing physical barriers such as stairs, making large-print publications and hearing-assistance devices available, visiting those who are homebound or in hospitals, and organizing healthier members to accompany elders to worship services. Some churches are even offering exercise classes to recruit elders in a setting more comfortable to them than a gym. Religious institutions are also distinctive for having memberships that cut across the life course, creating opportunities for intergenerational interaction and reciprocity. As public social services continue to lose their funding, faith-based institutions are expected to play a greater role in providing basic services (Cnaan, Boddie, & Kang, 2005; Idler, 2006; Koenig & Brooks, 2002; Nelson-Becker, 2005a, 2005c; Roff et al., 2006).

Spiritual Well-Being

Spirituality emphasizes an individual's subjective experience, while religiosity refers to a person's experience within the context of a religion. Spirituality provides an interpretive framework for us to make sense of the world—who we are and how we should live. Most definitions of spirituality capture the notion of connectedness—with self, others, nature, the earth, or that which transcends all of these (Atchley, 2009; MacKinlay, 2008).

Some of these definitions listed below may fit with your own experience; others may not resonate with you. Or you may want to add your own perspective.

- a human quest for meaning, sense of purpose, and moral principles
- a relationship with what is considered sacred in life and that transcends the ordinary limits of the body, linear space, and time
- a sense of being supported by some power greater than ourselves
- a sense of the depth and wholeness of life and connectedness to the universe, nature, and a higher power
- wisdom in which we try to achieve balance in life, compassion, and gratitude

- wonder, awe, or unconditional joy about life or our concept of reality
- intuitive nonverbal understanding of how to cope with life's circumstances (Atchley, 2009; Hodge, 2003; Nelson-Becker et al., 2006)

points to ponder

When you hear the term spiritual, what immediately comes to your mind? Can you think of someone whom you consider spiritual but not religious? Do you consider yourself to be a spiritual person? If so, what does that mean to you? Next ask an older person—a relative, neighbor, or close friend—whether he or she perceives himself or herself as spiritual. What does spirituality mean to the individual? And how has that meaning developed over time?

We may express spiritual needs in both religious and nonreligious forms. Elders may experience a sense of spirituality through privately seeking meaning and purpose in their lives, perhaps through mentoring others, examining the significance of past events or contemplating the legacy they hope to leave behind. Indeed, aging itself can be characterized as a spiritual journey in which a person aims to integrate the biological, psychological, social, and spiritual aspects of their lives. An ageless self—that is, a person who is not preoccupied or discouraged by aging—has an identity that maintains continuity and is on a spiritual journey in time. For such an individual, being old is neither a central feature of the self nor the source of its meaning.

You learned in Chapter 4 about the importance of life review techniques. Similarly, **spiritual reminiscence** is a way of telling a life story by emphasizing what gives meaning to life and what has given joy or brought sadness. This process may bring to the surface issues of anger, guilt, or regret. It can also help people to reframe some of these events and come to a new understanding of the purpose of their lives, thereby promoting well-being (MacKinlay, 2006).

For other elders, spirituality is a state of being—of approaching others with kindness, openness, forgiveness, and grace without judging or evaluating them. Confronting negative images of aging, loss, and death is believed to be essential for psychological-spiritual growth and healthy aging. As captured by Lustbader (2011) in her interviews and practice with elders, "Our yearning for something overarching like the divine to explain what is going on is never greater" (p. 62). In fact, dealing with helplessness, loss, and suffering can be one of the greatest spiritual challenges for elders—as you will learn in Chapter 9 (Lustbader, 2011).

While the spiritual journey can be a profound experience, it does not always have to be serious and solemn. For those who have been on the path of spirituality for a long time, a sense of humor can actually be helpful as they struggle with the contradictions they discover along the way. Many spiritual journeyers also learn to be patient and not to force issues or events. Waiting, and not necessarily "waiting for," is often an important part of the spiritual process, along with commitment, self-discipline, and regular spiritual practice (Atchley, 2009).

As is true of religiosity, high levels of spirituality are associated with a range of benefits for mental well-being, including a sense of purpose in everyday life; increased self-esteem, life satisfaction, and perceived quality of life; and lower rates of depression. These benefits overlap with those of religiousness, because private forms of religiosity and spirituality are sometimes similar (Atchley, 2008; Harvey & Silverman, 2007; Keyes & Reitzes, 2007; Koenig, 2007; Yoon & Lee, 2007).

Baby boomers are less likely than the pre-World War II cohort to say they are "religious and spiritual" or "religious only," but they are more likely to say "spiritual only" and to reject prescribed and structured belief systems. Just as boomers redefined lifestyles earlier in life, some are creating distinctive approaches to spirituality, "mixing and matching" ideas and practices from a variety of religious and spiritual traditions. In this more

Meditation as an Expression of Spirituality

Carl, age 68, is an active volunteer and employed part-time. No matter how busy he is, however, he always manages to set aside a half-hour in the morning to sit in silence and meditate. Since he started meditating at age 62, his blood pressure has decreased; he has fewer health problems and maintains a calm, positive outlook on life. He describes his meditation to his friends as the center of his spiritual journey. And his family notices these changes as well.

"open-systems" approach, adherence to religious authority and fixed doctrines is less important than viewing spirituality as an evolving, flowing process. Some connect with small groups of spiritual seekers through prayer, meditation, appreciating nature, and practicing positive emotions such as gratitude and forgiveness. With increased spiritual and religious diversity in our society, associated with the immigration of growing numbers of Muslims, Hindus, and Buddhists, baby boomers and future cohorts of older adults are likely to relate to a wider set of both religious and spiritual possibilities than prior cohorts (Ano & Vasconcelles, 2005; Atchley, 2009; Ardelt & Koenig, 2006; Okon, 2005; Smith & Seokho, 2005).

points to **ponder**

Imagine that you are working in a skilled nursing facility where an older women tells you that she has a spiritual life that involves belief in a higher power, prayer, and meditation. She confides that she does not feel comfortable praying or meditating in her room because she is afraid of staff interrupting her or her roommate's family making fun of her. How would you, as a staff member, try to support her spiritual practices?

Implications for Health Care Providers The central role of religion, religiosity, and spirituality in older adults' lives has numerous implications for professionals working with them. Historically, the medical profession has focused largely on biological and medical aspects of elders' lives, overlooking psychological, emotional, and spiritual factors. Their past failure to address spirituality and people's search for meaning also ignored a source of patients' strength (Awara & Fasey, 2008; Harvey, 2009; Lee, 2011).

Now there is increasing acceptance that health care providers should introduce questions of religion or spirituality—and be respectful of cultural and religious differences—when they treat an older adult with chronic illness or who is dying. Providers have become more competent in gauging the elder's comfort level about these topics, displaying a genuine and caring attitude, and actively listening to patients' spiritual concerns when they surface.

Compared to a relatively short time ago, the curriculum for health care providers now generally includes competencies in addressing older adults' religious and spiritual lives across different cultures. For example, providers need to be competent in handling their own values and feelings in professional relationships with older adults of different beliefs and religions. When practitioners are open to talking about spirituality with elders, they can create common experiential ground that transcends specific faith traditions, opens opportunities for incorporating spirituality into all aspects of everyday life, and allows treatment interventions that take account of spiritual variations. For instance, patients, staff, and families can experience profound togetherness out of shared silence in hospice programs, where having a sense of purpose positively affects a dying person's subjective well-being. Practitioners also need to respect and accommodate spiritual practices in health and long-term care settings, such as creating a space for Muslim ablutions or private places for Buddhists to meditate (Cullinane, 2008; Klemmarck et al., 2007; Schwarz & Cottrell, 2007; Snodgrass, 2009).

A spiritual assessment of personal values, philosophy, and sense of purpose, conducted by health care providers in an open, inquiring manner, can include questions such as the following:

- What helps you experience a deep sense of meaning, purpose, and moral perspective? How might this affect your current experience with illness?
- Do you consider yourself religious, a person of faith, or spiritual?
- If so, what terms for referring to spirituality, religion, or faith do you prefer that we use?
- Would you like to incorporate spirituality or religion in our work together (Nelson-Becker, 2005b; Nelson-Becker, Nakashima, & Canda, 2007)?

Listening carefully to what gives a person meaning and promotes their quality of life, health care providers may encourage elders to seek religious support or reconnect with a spiritual community. They also will learn ways to ensure culturally appropriate spiritual interventions that take account of the diversity of religious beliefs (Harvey, 2009; Lee, 2011; Nelson-Becker et al., 2006; Parker et al., 2002; Tanyi, McKenzie, & Chape, 2009).

Stages of Spiritual Growth Many people as they age arrive at a metaphorical crossroads where they realize that there must be more to their existence than what they have. They may have material possessions and professional achievements, and yet feel as though something is missing,

The End of the Journey

Mrs. Tanaka ended up in the hospital after fracturing her hip. While there, her other chronic health problems worsened, and her kidneys were beginning to shut down. Several physicians concurred that aggressive treatment would prolong Mrs. Tanaka's suffering and that she was not likely to live beyond a few weeks. With Mrs. Tanaka's understanding and consent, supported by an advanced health directive, the family asked that all measures be taken to ensure Mrs. Tanaka's comfort but that no further medical treatments be administered. She was transferred to a residential hospice facility in her own community.

The Tanaka family members were not religious people. None of them went to church or observed religious practices, but at a time like this, they felt the need for spiritual comfort. The hospice staff put them in contact with a spiritual counselor who practiced what is called an open-systems approach. This counselor helped Mrs. Tanaka and her family talk about end-of-life issues in a way that was both comforting and comfortable. As it turned out, the Tanakas were a very spiritual family. They believed in the existence of the soul and felt that Mrs. Tanaka's soul was destined for a place of eternal peace and love after her physical body had died. In the final hours of Mrs. Tanaka's life, each of her family members felt genuinely connected to her, soul to soul, and conveyed their love, gratitude, and warm thoughts to her. After Mrs. Tanaka died, the spiritual counselor helped the Tanakas prepare a service that focused on the meaningfulness of her life and their loving memories. The family felt the service was an appropriate and spiritually nourishing way to say goodbye.

something much deeper and more meaningful. They may also sense that time is running out. Some mental health professionals may refer to this as a psychological phenomenon, but others describe this yearning as part of a process of spiritual growth in which our thoughts are focused away from the external world and toward the inner life of the soul That soul, which is connected to a higher power in the universe, is presumed to communicate with the conscious self and awaken it to "new and extraordinary faculties within us." The end result is thought to be a spiritual fulfilment that transcends worldly and material rewards (Moody & Carroll, 1997, p. 34). Mrs. Tanaka and her family in the box above illustrate such spiritual growth at the end of life.

In sum, for many older adults and their families, religiosity and spirituality are central components of active aging, and may involve giving back to others. We turn next to other ways that older adults give back to the community and find meaning and purpose in their lives through volunteering, membership in voluntary associations, and political activity.

Civic Engagement

Civic engagement is a process in which people actively participate in the life of their communities through individual and collective activities associated with civic life, such as voting, being a political activist, joining community groups, and volunteering, oftentimes with nonprofit organizations. Broadly defined, it encompasses a wide array of activities to benefit others, such as cleaning up a local park, assisting a homebound friend or neighbor, joining in neighborhood mutual aid activities, staying informed about current events, and even caregiving of young and old (Hinterlong & Williamson, 2006–2007; Kaskie, Imhof, Cavanaugh, & Culp, 2008; Morrow-Howell et al., 2009).

Proponents of civic engagement initiatives view older adults as our society's most underutilized social asset—not as a problem to be addressed. Baby boomers represent the first generation reaching retirement age in which a large proportion of men and women have amassed a lifetime of knowledge and skills that can be used to benefit communities and society as a whole. Recognizing this potential, the reauthorization of the Older Americans Act in 2006 called for strategies to utilize older adults to address critical local and national concerns. Additionally, major national professional associations in aging, such as the Gerontological Society of America and the American Society on Aging, have civic engagement initiatives that aim to benefit American communities as well as provide fulfillment and

points to ponder

What does civic engagement mean to you? Do you consider yourself to be civically engaged? What about your parents, grandparents, or other older adults you know? How would you characterize their extent and types of civic engagement?

purpose for older participants. And some foundations and corporations fund civic engagement initiatives (Kaskie et al., 2008; Morrow-Howell et al., 2009).

Civic Engagement: Toward What End?

Just as most social issues divide Americans by ideological differences, political conservatives and progressives advocate for civic engagement, especially volunteerism, for very different reasons. Conservatives frequently favor volunteerism as a way to address social problems rather than turning to governmental solutions. Older adults as volunteers, often through faith-based organizations, are viewed as a way to fill gaps created by cuts in services or to reduce the need for such programs. In contrast, progressives advocate for elders to be politically active and to promote social justice in order to ensure that public policies safeguard the rights of vulnerable elders. Progressives also contend that a narrow focus on individual volunteerism detracts from grassroots civic activism and minimizes the need for broader social change. This distinction is illustrated by the following statement: "volunteering in a soup kitchen will help hungry individuals in a town, but will do nothing to address broader problems of homelessness and poverty" (Theiss-Morse & Hibbing, 2004, pp. 237–238). This tension between individual and government responsibility for basic human needs continues to surface in current political debates, which we discuss more in Chapter 13 (Holstein, 2007; Hudson, 2006–2007, 2007; Martinson, 2006–2007).

Others argue that the concept of civic engagement itself may overlook less visible ways of attaining meaning and fulfillment in later life. They contend that civic engagement should be broadly defined as whatever ways are possible for and desired by older people in order to grow and live a good old age. They also point to the benefits of a wide range of activities that foster social connectedness; for instance, they posit that local exchanges—keeping an eye on each other's house or on neighborhood children—may be more salient for both individual and community well-being than formal volunteering. In fact, what people actually do may matter less than the fact that they are involved in their community and experience a feeling of belonging. Because most elders seek meaning and purpose—spiritual, religious, artistic, political—in their lives, our society needs to create purposeful roles, which may or may not be formal civic engagement activities, and which crosscut racial, ethnic, and class groupings (Emerman, 2006; Holstein, 2007; Martinson, 2006–2007).

points to **ponder**

Where do you fall on the debate about the meaning and role of civic engagement? Do you advocate the use of volunteers rather than social and health services to meet human needs? Or would you argue that older adults should be more active in social change and political activities rather than volunteering? Or perhaps you agree that it is more important for elders to find meaning through inner well-being rather than focusing on formal civic engagement. Where you come down on this spectrum probably reflects some of your own views of active aging.

Membership in Voluntary Associations

Given our societal emphasis on being active and productive, voluntary association membership is presumed to be a "good" leisure activity. Such involvement is believed to have countless physical and mental health benefits for older participants. Voluntary associations range from recreational, ethnic, and fraternal clubs, vocal or drama programs, community organizations, and faith-based initiatives, to senior centers. Opportunities for politically active participation are found in senior advocacy groups such as the Older Women's League (OWL) and state chapters of AARP, or in organizations such as advisory boards to Area Agencies on aging where older people must, by law, be in leadership roles.

Patterns of Membership Overall, older people tend to be more involved in voluntary organizations than younger adults. But membership is most closely tied to social class, not age, and varies among cultures. When socioeconomic status is taken into account, older adults show considerable stability in their general level of voluntary association participation from middle age until their sixties. Age, gender, race, ethnicity, prior activities and memberships, and health also influence voluntary association membership. Consistent with the continuity theory discussed in Chapter 5, adults who were members of such associations earlier in life "become more of what they already were" and remain active as they age. Much of what we know about voluntary association membership, however, is based on the World War II cohort that preceded the baby boom generation and may change dramatically with the aging boomers (Cutler & Hendricks, 2000).

Here are some typical patterns of organizational membership:

- Older women are more active in voluntary associations than men, and usually have been across the life course.
- Older African Americans have higher rates of organizational membership than do whites or other elders of color, typically in church-related groups and social and recreational clubs.
- Latino elders often participate in fraternal and service-oriented organizations, mutual aid societies, and "hometown" clubs.
- Older whites are more likely to be members of nationality organizations and senior citizen groups.
- Regardless of race, ethnicity, or gender, membership is highest among those with better health and higher income and education levels.

Benefits that older adults experience from involvement in voluntary associations include the following:

- Social relationships and connections with others
- An expanded sense of control
- Improved health, fewer doctor visits, and reduced prescription use
- Increased morale and decreased loneliness (Cohen, 2005; Cohen et al., 2006; Newson & Kemps, 2005)

However, some of these benefits from participation may be due to the participants' higher levels of health, income, and education—factors that may influence their decision to become involved in the first place. The most satisfied members of voluntary associations are those who join in order to have new experiences, achieve goals, be creative, attain leadership roles, and help others (Greenfield & Marks, 2007).

Reflection Break

Becoming engaged with your community to enhance the social welfare of your fellow community members is as much a habit of mind as it is a social behavior. As you think about the community that you live in, can you identify social problems or needs that would benefit from a group of concerned citizens acting in "common good"? Are people already getting involved with activities and projects that help make their community a better place? These activities could be as simple as occasionally joining others to pick up trash in a public area, or it could be more complex such as joining coalitions to address and try to resolve problems like homelessness. Developing a state of mind when you are young that emphasizes the importance of grassroots, community-based solutions may help you remain civically engaged throughout your life, including when you become an older adult. Can you think of one or two things you can get involved with now to help your community? If you are already involved, what has that experience been like for you? How can you get others to join you, or to become more civically engaged in other areas of community need?

Senior Centers: Are They Prepared for Changing Demographics? Senior centers are age-based voluntary associations that offer not only recreational events but also social and health services, such as nutrition programs, home-delivered meals, fitness and wellness programs, educational and arts classes, volunteer opportunities, support groups for caregivers and grandparents, and counseling. Despite the range of activities and benefits offered, only about 1 million older adults participate in senior centers. Furthermore, centers typically draw from a relatively narrow population, reaching primarily healthy, lower- to middle-class individuals with a lifetime of joining groups but who are now aging into the oldest-old population. Approximately 70 percent of participants are women, half of whom live alone. The majority are Caucasians. Nationwide, elders who are generally less advantaged, but not the least advantaged, are most likely to join in senior center activities. Already socially active, they view centers as arenas for enhanced social interaction (National Council on Aging, 2012; Pardasani, 2004a, 2004b).

Although there are numerous center participants like Rhonda as illustrated in the box on p. 239, some elders simply are not interested in the types of activities offered, or the programming does not meet the diverse needs of the heterogeneous older adult population, is not culturally appropriate, or is not accessible to those for whom English is a second language. Other elders may have health problems or a level of disability that makes it difficult for them to get to a center, especially if there is no van service. Because of the predominance of women and of Caucasians, men and elders of color may be reluctant to participate in an activity where they will be a numerical minority. And last, some older adults do not want to identify themselves as "seniors" or to be only with old people.

Senior Centers as Vital Sources of Support

Ever since her husband died eight years ago, Rhonda, age 83, has sought companionship at the senior center nearest her. She depends on the hot lunch three times a week for both the prepared food as well as the social interaction, since she hates eating alone at home. She goes on nearly every trip sponsored by the center, whether to see the fall tree colors, shopping at outlet malls, and even the local casino. Rhonda feels useful by helping to run the center's thrift shop and making gift baskets for the annual fund-raiser auction. More recently, she has enjoyed the center's initiatives to bring in younger community members. Four times a year, the center sponsors an intergenerational dance night that represents the diverse culture of her neighborhood, and the center's board is considering leasing part of their space to an after-school program, where she hopes to volunteer. Rhonda often comments to her children, who live at a considerable distance, that she does not know how she would get by without the center staff and friends, whom she considers to be like family.

They may themselves hold ageist stereotypes or they may simply prefer age-integrated activities (National Council on Aging, 2012).

For those, like Rhonda, who do participate in senior centers, they often experience benefits such as

- enhanced physical and mental well-being, and health benefits, including delaying the onset of chronic illness;
- improved functional and cognitive status; and
- a sense of belonging and expanded social interactions and friendships, higher morale, and increased health-promoting behaviors—all of which can be conducive to active aging (Fitzpatrick et al., 2008; Greenfield & Marks, 2004; 2007; NCOA, 2012).

Some senior center staff and boards worry whether baby boomers will participate in the future, particularly because of the stigma of being involved in a "senior" center. In fact, some centers are eliminating "senior" from their names and marketing or are developing more inclusive language, such as "community, friendship, or intergenerational centers." They may offer new fee-based programs, such as fitness, falls prevention, continuing education, and a non-institutional-looking environment to attract the young-old

Group dances among young and old at senior centers foster intergenerational contact.

while using more traditional programming to try to retain their current participants who are increasingly frail.

While many senior centers are targeting the young-old as a way to revitalize their membership, they also are testing new ways to reach out to the oldest-old, many of whom may be homebound. One such innovation is Senior Center without Walls, which offers friendly conversations, classes, and support groups to isolated homebound elders and others who find it difficult to travel to a senior center. Participants attest to the value of having something to look forward to and someone with whom they can share. As noted by one participant, Senior Center without Walls is about removing the walls and creating connections on the phone or by Skype with people who otherwise would not know one another (Senior Center without Walls, 2011).

The funding legislation, the Older Americans Act, requires that centers concentrate on offering services to

Neighborhood Gathering Spots, Not Senior Centers

When senior centers were started in the 1960s and 1970s, hot midday meals and companionship drew older adults to participate. But now they are no longer the draw they once were. Competition for the older American market underlies a search for new models to change negative perceptions of senior centers. In Chicago, senior centers feature neighborhood cafés with a lively ambiance and healthy menus that draw all ages. Adjacent to the café are yoga classes, Spanish lessons, computer access, and exercise classes with state-of-the-art equipment. Designers have created a "neighborhood place, not a senior place" (Gross, 2008).

those most in need, who tend to be low-income, rural, people of color, or frail elders. But elders of color are typically underrepresented in senior centers, even in culturally diverse communities. Some of the issues listed above—lack of transportation, inadequate facilities, language differences, staff with limited cultural competence, and programming perceived as irrelevant—are barriers to the participation of elders of color. However, increasing the representation of culturally diverse and bilingual staff and providing culturally specific and linguistically appropriate programming and meals can foster their participation (NCOA, 2012).

The challenge for senior centers is to reach out to the broadest cross section of the older population while expanding the participation of young-old and elders from diverse backgrounds. African American elders are slightly more likely than whites to attend when center programs take account of their specific needs and mutual aid networks. Similarly, Latino participation increases when staff speaks Spanish and centers serve ethnic-specific congregate meals on-site and offer socialization opportunities with members of their own communities. Asian American elders are more likely to participate when they are in relatively good health and senior centers are located in their own neighborhood and offer programs in their native language. The box on this page, "Culturally Appropriate Congregate Meals," highlights the importance of serving ethnic specific meals at centers (Lai, 2001; NCOA, 2012; Pardasani, 2004b).

Although many voluntary associations have paid staff, they may also rely on volunteers, especially when budgets are cut and membership costs rise. Volunteering is increasingly viewed as a central component of active aging, resilience, and healthy communities.

Becoming Inclusive of All Older Adults

The board of a senior center that prided itself on its racially and ethnically diverse programs and membership came face to face with the need to address all types of diversity in order to be inclusive of neighborhood residents. A transgender elder who lived nearby wanted to participate in the center, but was uneasy using restrooms designated only as male and female. She went to the board with her request for a gender-neutral restroom with a lock. At first the board resisted, saying the lock would cost too much. But as their executive director talked with them about different levels of discrimination and stigma, they gradually saw the importance of the inclusive statement made by a gender-neutral restroom. Other senior centers are now following their lead.

Culturally Appropriate Congregate Meals

Staff at senior centers that serve meals (this is known as congregate meal sites) could not understand why Asian Americans in the surrounding neighborhoods did not participate, especially since many of them were living on small fixed incomes and the meals were free. But this pattern changed dramatically when they started offering white rice with every meal. Now there is a waiting list of Vietnamese, Cambodian, and Chinese American elders waiting to access the meals.

Volunteering

Volunteering is distinguished from other forms of civic engagement by choosing to serve or help others, and can be formal (within an organization) or informal (such as time spent helping others in one's neighborhood or community). Volunteering has value both to the individual and their families and to society.

Within the past 40 years, a number of public and private initiatives have fostered greater volunteer service by older persons. Indeed, with the recession and cutbacks in social services, volunteering has become increasingly important as a way to serve others. Corporations often expect their employees to volunteer; for example, workplace volunteering allows companies to improve their local communities while enhancing their corporate public image.

Here are just a few examples of volunteer opportunities available specifically to the older population, which is just as heterogeneous in their volunteer interests as they are in other aspects of their lives.

- Environmental Alliance for Senior Involvement promotes environmental activities.
- Family Friends advocates for and mentors children.
- **Foster Grandparents** offers support to children with special needs.
- Programs funded by the government through the Older Americans Act rely heavily on volunteers to assist at meal sites and to offer transportation services, home repair, delivery of meals, counseling, and legal aid.

- Peace Corps places older volunteers to meet needs in other countries.
- **Retired and Senior Volunteer Program (RSVP)** funds volunteers in schools, hospitals, and other community settings.
- Service Corps of Retired Executives (SCORE) assists small businesses and first-time entrepreneurs.
- Volunteers-in-Parks are found in most national parks.
- The **Senior Companion Program** gives financial support to low-income adults age 60 and older to provide in-home services to frail elders in need.
- The **Senior Community Service Employment Program** places older adults in community service activities that are often a bridge to employment.
- Single Volunteers brings single adults together for service events and indirectly as a way to make new friends.

And there is increasing public recognition of the central roles performed by older volunteers. Here are a few examples. **Civic Ventures** is a think tank on baby boomers, work, and meaning that promotes postretirement **encore careers**, many of which include volunteerism. It offers the national Purpose Prize to recognize older individuals for exemplary service and the Breakthrough Award for innovative organizations. The National Council on the Aging's Respectability initiative provides technical assistance to nonprofits to more effectively utilize older volunteers (Freedman, 2001).

Volunteering across the Life Course

Mary, a homemaker and mother of four children, spent her early adult years involved with Scouts and PTA and teaching Sunday school. Her last child left home when Mary was 52, and she felt "lost" because there was no one who "needed" her in the same ways her children had. At 53, she began volunteering, answering the phone for a community center that served children and elders, and found a new role. When she was widowed at age 70, she increased the hours of volunteering to fill the lonely hours when she especially missed her husband. But the volunteering also gave her a sense of being useful and was a source of pride to her. Because she has never driven, she takes the bus to the community center. Now age 80, she was recently honored by the city at a special reception for her 8,000 hours of volunteer service through the years.

Who Volunteers?

- About 25 percent of all adults age 65 and older do so, a rate that is slightly lower than adults as a whole (nearly 29 percent).
- When volunteering is redefined to include informal contributions (e.g., helping neighbors), an additional 50 percent volunteer informally.
- Volunteerism rates (about 50 percent) are highest among adults at midlife (45–64 years), climb slightly among those 65–74 years, and then, not surprisingly, decline to only 9 percent among those age 75 and older.
- Women and professionals in the age range of 55–64 express the most interest in volunteering (Cheung, Michel, & Miller, 2010; Population Reference Bureau, 2011; Rozario, 2006–2007; Wilson & Hawlow-Rosentraub, 2008; Wilson & Simpson, 2006; Windsor, Anstey, & Rodgers, 2008).

Although volunteerism rates are slightly lower for adults age 65 and older than for adults in their forties and fifties, elders' level of involvement in terms of time spent volunteering (approximately 96 hours a year) is greater than the younger age group (about 50 hours a year). It is striking that the time older people devote to formal volunteer activities has been valued at about $45 billion. This is money that agencies otherwise would have to find to offer the same level of services (Butrica, Johnson, & Zedlewski, 2007; Population Reference Bureau, 2011).

Higher volunteerism rates earlier in life are often associated with employment and family roles, and thus with having more rather than fewer obligations and commitments. This pattern suggests that volunteering is not just a matter of having the time. Think about how younger and middle-aged parents volunteer in programs that benefit their children, such as being an officer in Parent–Teacher–Student Associations (PTSAs), coaching sports teams, or fund-raising for their children's schools. After their children have grown up, many parents, such as Mary (in the box above), continue to volunteer but for other types of organizations.

You learned in Chapter 6 that older adults tend to become more selective about how—and with whom—they spend their time. Consistent with this concept of **socio-emotional selectivity**, older volunteers place a higher value on meaningful relationships and deriving satisfaction from helping others. Most elders want roles that fully engage their capacities, and in ways that matter to their communities. However, many organizations also need volunteers who can do mundane tasks, like stuff envelopes and make phone calls—tasks that are essential but often not personally meaningful. Fortunately, many elders will pitch in and do whatever needs to be done. The primary sites where older adults volunteer are religious organizations, followed by social and community service nonprofits and hospitals. Whether volunteering is a continuation of earlier patterns, a substitute for prior roles, or a way to try out new roles, it illustrates the concept of generativity in old age, an important aspect of Erickson's stage theory of personality that you learned about in Chapter 4 (Cartensen, Mikels, & Mather, 2006; McNamara & Gonzales, 2011; Prisuta, 2004).

Volunteering as a Substitute for Past Roles

Ted was a teacher of sixth-grade science in an inner-city public school for 35 years. When he retired at age 57, he began a successful second career selling real estate. Now, at age 72, he continues to work on average two days per week. He enjoys the contact with people and finds his work very different from teaching. Because he believes it is important to give back to his community, he also volunteers as a tutor in an after-school program run by his church for neighborhood "latchkey" children. He enjoys performing an educational role again, but likes the tutoring outside a traditional classroom.

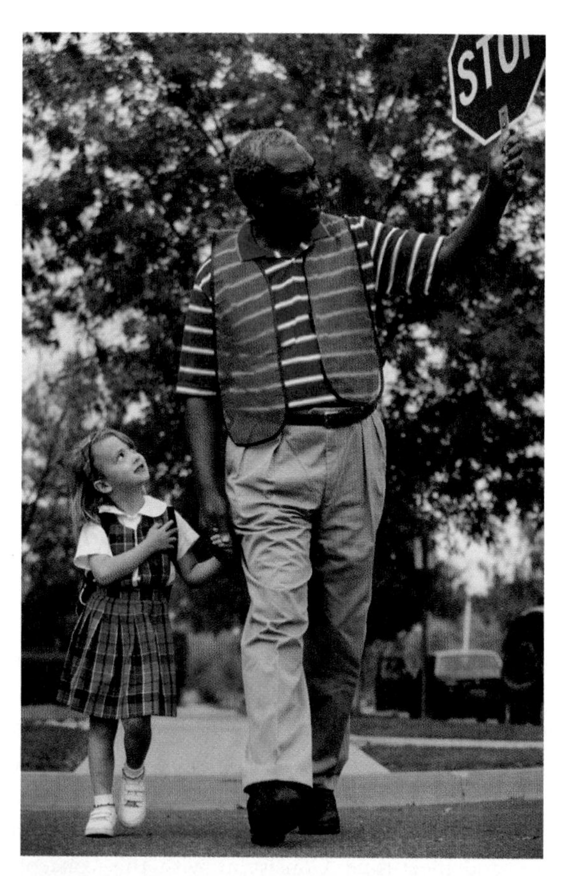

Volunteering with children can provide satisfaction and meaning.

Benefits of Volunteerism Regardless of the reasons or motivations for volunteering, the benefits are numerous and well documented. This is because socio-emotional benefits, particularly self-efficacy and self-esteem, appear to have positive physiological effects such as buffering stress reactions and protecting health.

Emotional and Mental Well-Being

- greater life satisfaction, sense of accomplishment, and feelings of usefulness, meaning, purpose, and personal growth. Older volunteers often talk about how important it is for them to make a difference in others' lives and to be able express values related to humanitarian concerns.
- positive self-efficacy—feelings of mastery, personal control, and self-determination
- lower rates of depression
- higher levels of cognitive functioning

Physical Well-Being

- higher self-rated health, levels of physical functioning, and muscular strength
- lower rates of functional disability and pain
- lower and delayed mortality rates

Social Well-Being

- expanded social networks, and social integration and social support
- reduced loneliness and greater structure to their lives (Donnelly & Hinterlong, 2010; Hinterlong & Williamson, 2006–2007; Li & Ferraro, 2006; Lum & Lightfoot, 2005; Morrow-Howell et al., 2009; Morrow-Howell, Hinterlong, Sheraden, Rozario, & Tang, 2003; Siegrist, Knesebeck, & Pollack, 2004; Tang, Choi, & Morrow-Howell, 2010; Wilson & Harlow-Rosentraub, 2008; Windsor, Anstey, & Rodgers, 2008)

The extent of organizational support—skills training, ongoing administrative and social support, and supervision—appears to enhance volunteers' commitment to the role as well as the benefits from volunteering. The chance to learn new skills, having some control over choice of activity and schedule, and access to flexible options also increase the benefits experienced (Morrow-Howell et al., 2009; Morrow-Howell, 2011; Tang et al., 2010).

points to **ponder**

Perhaps you have an older relative or friend who spends a lot of time alone at home whom you have tried to convince to volunteer. And you can't understand why they are not volunteering when there are so many community needs. If older adults do not volunteer, a major reason is that no organization or member of their social network has asked them to do so. If you are a volunteer or work in an organization that relies on volunteers, think about this factor when you hear statements about "why don't more older adults volunteer?" Maybe they just need to be asked!

Race, Social Class, and Volunteering Just as you learned about how race affects participation in formal religious institutions and voluntary associations, it also influences the rate and motivation for volunteerism. Elders of color are more likely to volunteer informally through churches and mutual aid associations than formal volunteering with nonprofit organizations. Immigrant groups often value helping others, but the concept of volunteering is uniquely American and may not readily translate into their familiar concept of informal helping in their communities.

- When informal volunteering is included in definitions, African American elders report slightly more hours of volunteering than whites.
- The Latino community has the lowest rates of formal volunteering, but informal volunteering, such as self-help, mutual aid, and neighborhood assistance, is rooted in Latino culture.
- Mutual aid (e.g., providing food and lodging to older persons) is frequent in American Indian communities.
- Volunteer activities among Asian and Pacific Islander elders reinforce the continuation of their value systems. Older Chinese Americans, for example, often work through family associations or benevolent societies. Some Japanese American elders participate in clubs that are an extension of the "family helping itself," which is a concept rooted in traditional Japanese culture.

Another reason for lower rates of formal volunteerism among elders of color is that the terms "volunteering" and "community service" can have negative connotations in some communities of color, evoking images of court-ordered community service. Organizations that seek to recruit more diverse volunteers need to consider all these factors and modify their strategies accordingly (Carlton-LaNey, 2006–2007; Rozario, 2006–2007; Zedlewski & Schaner, 2006).

Organizational support is especially important among low-income groups and elders of color and to people who experience barriers to volunteering, such as lack of transportation, costs, or poor health or who need some types of accommodations to remove physical barriers. A modest stipend that covers gas, bus fare, or other expenses incurred by time away from employment or caregiving can make a difference in the ability of low-income elders to volunteer. While some might argue that such paid public service is not volunteerism in the pure or traditional sense (i.e., nonpaid work), offsetting the costs of volunteering is the only way to ensure a racially and economically diverse pool of volunteers. The compelling rationale for designing accessible strategies and offering such supports is rooted in the documented benefits from volunteering. Fortunately, more programs are recognizing that they need to assist volunteers in underserved communities by addressing their economic needs so that volunteerism can be a realistic option for all elders (Morrow-Howell et al., 2009; Musick & Wilson, 2008; Tang, Morrow-Howell, & Hong, 2009; Tang et al., 2010).

A research finding that may surprise you, however, is that lower-income and less-educated older volunteers are found to perceive more benefits from their volunteer experience than higher-income elders. This may occur for a variety of reasons: Volunteer roles that are structured to promote self-esteem, meaningful engagement, and a sense of empowerment may offer them experiences that they lacked in poorly paid employment roles. They may simply have more to gain from the valued role of volunteer. Another finding that may be contrary to what you would expect is that the oldest-old and those with functional limitations benefit more from volunteering than healthier and younger volunteers. This may occur because elders who might otherwise have less social interaction in their

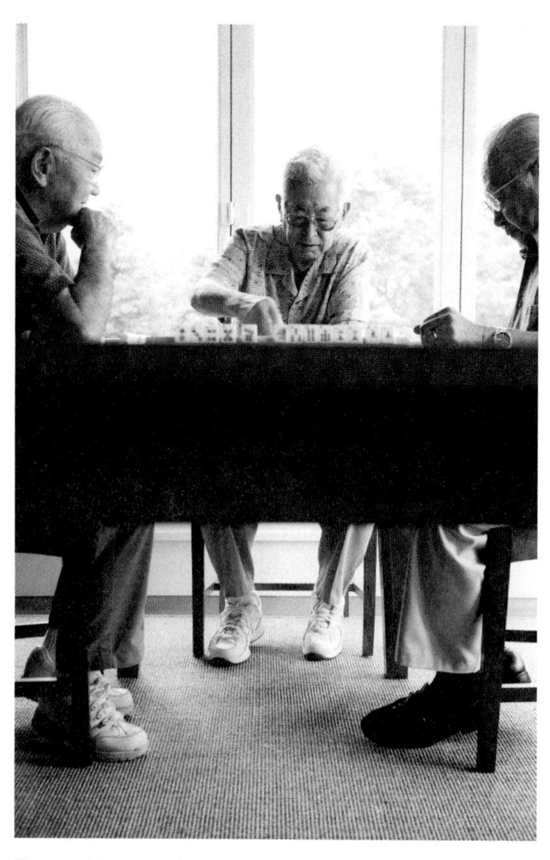

These older men playing cards are keeping their brains active as well as engaging in social interaction.

daily lives experience a protective effect from volunteering, particularly in terms of physical well-being (Martinez et al., 2006; McBride, 2007; Morrow-Howell et al., 2009; Tang, Chen, & Morrow-Howell, 2009; Tang, Morrow-Howell, & Hong, 2009).

The Senior Companion Program, Foster Grandparents, the Senior Community Service Employment Program, and **Experience Corps** all offer modest stipends to low-income older adults. Experience Corps is one example of a highly successful intergenerational project involving lower-income, less-educated elders of color, many of whom had mobility problems. You learned in Chapter 4 about some of the cognitive benefits experienced by Experience Corps volunteers (McNamara & Gonzales, 2011; Mozsw-Howell et al., 2009).

Given the diverse meanings of volunteering, some organizations are changing how they define and promote volunteering by emphasizing "neighboring" and "community involvement." A number of trends will influence the meaning and functions of volunteerism for older persons in the future. With increased national attention on self-help and mutual aid, some people may choose to become more active in cross-generational grassroots neighborhood and community activities. You will learn more about such neighboring approaches to volunteering in Chapter 11 when we discuss age-friendly communities.

Experience Corps

Experience Corps brings older adults into public elementary schools in well over 20 cities. They are there to perform an important job: to improve students' academic achievement through one-on-one tutoring, small-group academic help, and assisting teachers. Volunteers are required to commit about 15 hours per week during the school year. Students experience gains in their reading abilities and self-confidence. But their older tutors also benefit: they report improved self-esteem, an expanded circle of friends, even better cognitive and physical functioning, and fewer symptoms of depression (Barron et al., 2009; Carlson et al., 2009; Tan et al., 2009; Washington University, 2008).

Lifelong Learning Programs

Another important source of social and civic engagement for older adults is **lifelong learning**. In fact, you may know older adults in your classes, or family members who are taking regular or continuing education classes at a community college or university. In the past 40 years, creative learning initiatives for midlife and older adults have developed nationally and internationally. Most of these are entrepreneurial, or part of the "silver industry" geared to the young-old who have the resources to participate in them. You may have seen participants in Osher Lifelong Learning Institutes or Road Scholar eating in the dining hall at your college or university.

points to ponder

Hazel is a 78-year-old neighbor. Because she uses a walker and is fearful of falling, she rarely leaves her home. Her mind is sharp, however, and she tells you that she would like to contribute to the neighborhood in some way. Can you think of some civic engagement activities that she could realistically participate in?

Since 1975, the **Road Scholar** program (formerly Elderhostel) has involved over 150,000 adults age 50 and older in over 8,000 programs at over 1,500 different academic institutions. The oldest participant to date is 103! Programs take place in all 50 states and in 150 countries, such as studying architecture in London, seals in Antarctica, monkeys in Belize, antiquities in Greece, or archaeology in the Southwest United States. Many are physically challenging, involving biking, hiking, or kayaking. Their Web site characterizes its participants as adventuresome, curious, fun, and open to experiencing the world through travel. They also offer intergenerational learning programs for grandparents and grandchildren (Moody, 2004–2005; Road Scholar, 2012).

The **Osher Lifelong Learning Institutes (OLLIs)** are also associated with many colleges and universities. They are based on a financial model that requires participants to provide labor and leadership to pay for their own continuing education. Older learners make all the decisions about course offerings and many of them volunteer to teach courses. The Osher Lifelong Learning programs host a journal and national conferences to bring together members of diverse communities (Manheimer, 2008).

Some gerontology certificate programs prepare middle-aged and older people for roles as advocates and service providers. Community colleges, because of their accessibility, are ideal settings in which to design human service programs that offer older adults ways to be of service to others or to retool for new careers. Retirement communities associated with colleges and universities are likely to grow as well, along with the number of older adults taking advantage of tuition-free courses in a wide range of academic settings. A few states recognize the market for lifelong learning and are funding a range of programs, including liberal arts education, peer learning groups, health promotion, training, and intergenerational service learning. A growing number of organizations now offer leadership training for older persons in advocacy and nonprofit organizational management.

Lifelong learning programs for all elders represent an area ripe for further development and funding, especially as baby boomers seek new learning challenges. With the growth of distance learning and Web-based instruction, baby boomers also provide a market for online educational programs. As this cohort ages, they will increasingly learn by sitting at their computers, relying on online courses that they can take anywhere in the world and not have to attend classes on-site. But they may miss the social interaction of being with other students in a classroom.

Some older people who cannot get to a classroom can take courses online.

As suggested in Chapter 4, educational programs need to take account of older learners' particular needs, such as self-paced learning and accommodation of hearing and vision decrements. As lifelong learning options increasingly become a function of the marketplace, strategies are needed to make such programs accessible to low-income and historically disadvantaged populations who may have had limited educational experiences earlier in life. Certificate programs and vocational education will also be in demand as older adults move into second and third careers, whether out of economic necessity or choice, perhaps with an emphasis on technical training needs.

Political Participation

When you hear the term civic engagement, you may immediately think of political activity. And as we saw above, progressives view political action as a more effective form of civic engagement than volunteerism. Political acts range from voting to participation in a political party or a political action group, to grassroots campaign work, to running for or holding elective office.

Do Older Adults Become More Politically Conservative with Age? Age differences in political ideology are less a matter of people becoming more conservative or liberal than of their maintaining these values throughout life. Successive generations entering the electorate since World War II were comparatively more liberal, with older people more likely in the past to identify with the Democratic Party. This was partly because of that party's greater support for Social

Security and Medicare. More recently, older voters have been more conservative on policy issues and less supportive of the Democratic Party. On the other hand, older voters across all racial and ethnic groups were part of President Obama's winning coalition in 2008, although younger voters were decisive in Obama's win and white boomers age 45 to 64 favored his opponent John McCain. Moreover, older voters can be swayed by interest groups, such as the Tea Party, and away from their more liberal roots, especially when they feel their benefits through programs such as Social Security are threatened. This happened in the 2010 elections for senators, representatives, and governors, where more elders voted for Republican candidates (Fisher, 2008; Lynch, 2010).

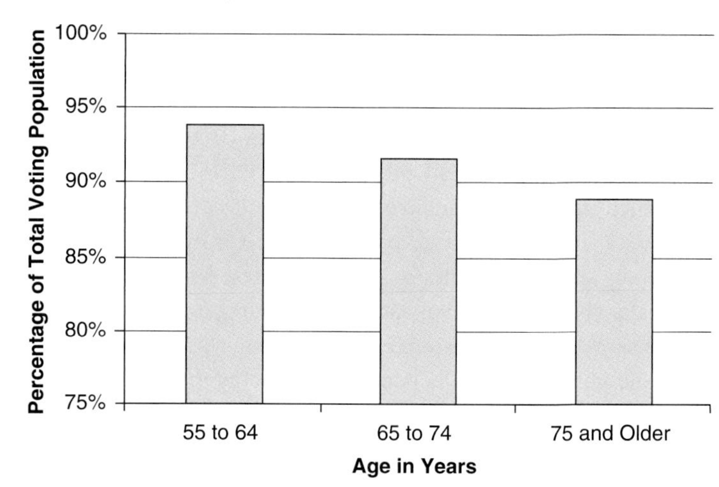

FIGURE 8.1 Percentage of Older Adults Voting in 2008 Presidential Election

Source: Lynch, 2010.

Not surprisingly, older voters are highly heterogeneous, with voting differences greater within than between age groups. For example, various cohorts of older adults during the past 60 years have distributed their votes among presidential candidates in roughly the same proportions as other age groups. However, this pattern is beginning to change, with increasing numbers of older adults shifting to support the Republican Party in the 2012 election, even though the Romney–Ryan ticket was likely to dramatically change Social Security and Medicare, compared to their past support of Democratic candidates in the 1990s. In other words, individuals of all ages are not ideologically consistent in their preferences on specific issues, such as Medicare, Social Security, or taxes. Furthermore, both young and old may hold beliefs on specific issues that contradict their views on more general principles. Given the older population's increasing heterogeneity, differences of opinion on any political issue are likely to equal or exceed variations between age groups. So when you hear someone say "he's conservative because he is old," remember that social class, race, ethnicity and party affiliation are generally more important than age in terms of political views (Binstock, 2006; Lynch, 2010).

Voting Behavior Regardless of how they vote, older Americans are more likely to go the polls than younger adults. The voting rates of older adults have remained steady or have increased over the past 35 years. Even more striking is that their voting rates are significantly higher than those of the population on average—nearly 63 percent as contrasted with approximately 36 percent of adults under the age of 55, although rates decline with age, as shown in Figure 8.1. Moreover, elders' participation rate in the last eight presidential elections has been higher than the rates for all other age groups; although in the historic 2008 presidential election, all age groups—particularly young voters—turned out in higher proportions than in previous decades. However, in 2012, youth voter turnout rates declined slightly, while the over 65 rate rose (Hudson, 2008; Lynch, 2010; Taylor & Lopez, 2013; U.S. Census Bureau, 2010).

In non-presidential elections where voter turnout among older adults is low, factors other than aging are probably the reason. These include gender, race, ethnicity, immigration status, education, and generational variables, as well as being able to physically get to the polls where mail-in ballots are not possible. Here are examples of how voting rates vary by race and ethnicity among older adults:

- nearly 72 percent of whites,
- 68 percent of African Americans,
- 56 percent of Latinos, and
- 45 percent of Asian Americans.

Let's look at some of the reasons for these differences. Limited political acculturation of some older Latinos appears to influence their relatively low rates of voting, even in the historic 2008 presidential election. Mexican American elders, if fearful of deportation, tend to be more cautious and conservative in their political involvement, but this pattern will shift dramatically with the increasing political clout of younger Latinas. On the other hand, older African Americans who are active in their communities, with a strong sense of social responsibility, a Democratic identity, and higher levels of education, are more likely to vote than other historically underserved groups. Similarly, Cuban American elders represent a strong voting bloc in Florida, where they have long influenced local, state, and national policies. It is important to recognize that lower rates of political participation rates among some elders of color do not reflect age or race per se, but rather cohort and immigration experiences, lower educational levels, feelings of powerlessness, and real or perceived barriers to voting and other political activities. With the increased racial and ethnic diversity of the baby boomers, some of these voting patterns among elders of color may shift (Lynch, 2010).

Older adults tend to have higher rates of other types of political participation as well.

- They demonstrate greater levels of "civic competence"; this means that they are more likely than younger age groups to pay attention to the current news—often still through newspapers and evening news shows—and to be more knowledgeable about politics and public affairs.
- They have the highest level of interest in political campaigns and public affairs generally.
- They identify with the major political parties more strongly than do younger persons. Strong partisanship increases the likelihood of voting regardless of age.
- They make campaign contributions at higher rates than younger people and are active in contacting their representatives regarding proposed legislation.
- They participate more in political organizations (Binstock, 2006, 2007; Lynch, 2010).

Given these patterns of political participation, there are divergent views about how powerful older voters are. To public officials and the media, the older electorate is viewed as exerting substantial political influence, especially on policies directly affecting them such as Medicare. But others think that the political power of older adults is overstated and, in fact, diminishing, as reflected in the following perspectives on "senior power."

Are Older Adults a Powerful Political Constituency? Those who agree with this position point to the following patterns:

- Older people come out in large numbers as voters and often are political leaders, so legislators and appointed officials pay attention to them.
- Over 1,000 separately organized groups for older adults exist at the local, state, and national levels, with approximately 100 major national organizations involved in political action on behalf of older persons.
- Age-based organizations are effective at building memberships, conducting policy analyses, marshaling grassroots support, and utilizing direct mail and political action. AARP, for example, has significant political influence and can mobilize their members in large numbers to contact policy-makers and register displeasure.
- Because of common cohort values and experiences, older people often develop a shared political consciousness; this is predicted to increase with the aging of the baby boomers, who will be more likely to take collective action based on their age, in part because they have been a strong organizational presence throughout their lives. Think of the political activity of boomers during the Vietnam War and Civil Rights era.
- Even if older people cannot affect the passage of legislation, they are seen as effective at blocking changes in existing policies. Policy-makers and politicians do not want to alienate the "senior vote." Indeed, they often invite representatives of age-based groups to special political events so that they appear to be "in touch with" older adults.
- Similarly older adults have relatively easy informal access to public and administrative officials, legislators and their staff, and the media. Some of this is due to what is called "the electoral bluff." Indeed, the perception of being powerful is, in itself, a source of political influence, even though, as you have learned, older adults do not always vote as a block (Binstock, 2007; Hudson, 2006, 2008; Lynch, 2009).

Others argue that older people are *not* a significant age-based political force. They point to the following patterns:

- Age is only one of many personal characteristics that affect political behavior. It cannot predict age-group consciousness or activity.
- Since the older population is more heterogeneous than any other age group, they do not have shared interests around which to coalesce as a voting bloc. Instead, differences by social class, race, education, religion, and immigration status increasingly influence older people's political interests.
- The increasing diversity of organizations representing older adults—the National Caucus for the Black Aged, National Hispanic Council on Aging,

points to ponder

Political power is often concentrated among older adults. In the 111th Congress, the average age of members of both houses was 57.0 years; of Representatives, 55.9 years; and of Senators, 61.7 years. You may recall Senator Robert Byrd, who served for 50 years before stepping down at age 90 from the chair of the powerful Senate Appropriations Committee and died at age 93. Senator Daniel Inouye was the second-longest-serving U.S. Senator, in Congress for 50 years before his death at age 88. Or Ronald Reagan, the oldest President to be elected at age 69. Do you consider age when you vote for political candidates? Do you see age as a virtue or disadvantage in how well someone performs in political office? Do you think that there should be an age limit when it comes to holding political office at the federal level?

National Asian-Pacific Center on Aging, National Indian Council on Aging, and Senior Action in a Gay Environment (SAGE)—also reduces their ability to act together in a unified manner on the basis of age.

- Both older and younger people are more likely to form alliances along social class, racial, ethnic, sexual orientation, gender, and ideological lines than to unite on the basis of age.
- Many older people, especially the young-old, do not identify themselves as "old" or define problems as stemming from their age. Not perceiving benefits from voting as a block, older adults distribute their votes among candidates in roughly the same proportion as the electorate as a whole.
- Cross-age collaborations will be increasingly important around issues such as climate change, preserving the environment, and affordable health care. Older adults will also join with other movements such as disability rights. For example, **Generations United**—a cross-generational national organization—unites groups as diverse as the Child Welfare League and AARP around a wide range of issues affecting multiple generations (Binstock, 2007; Hudson, 2006, 2007; Lynch, 2010).

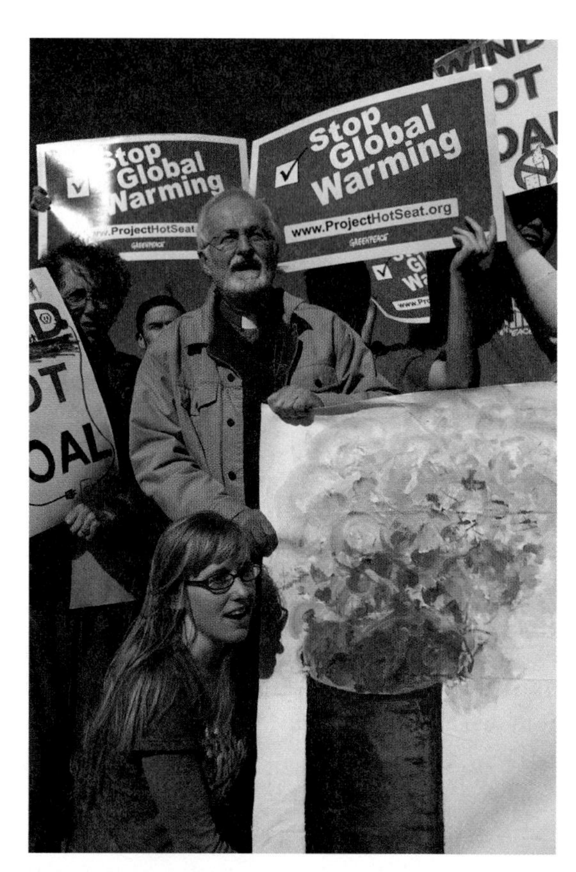

Older and younger generations unite around environmental actions that will benefit future generations.

AARP—The Largest Membership Organization in the Country One reason that older adults are perceived as politically powerful is the dramatic influence of **AARP**. By actively soliciting anyone over age 50 to join as an aging American, AARP seeks to promote age-based consciousness and is the primary mass membership organization that advocates on behalf of older adults. Imagine an organization that has a membership of over 40 million, ranging in age from 50 years to over 100! Over 50 percent of the nation's population age 50 and older and more than 13 percent of the U.S. population comprised its membership in 2012. For just $16 a year, adults age 50 and older can benefit from its many services. This low membership fee gives its members access to lower-cost health insurance, public policy alerts, credit cards, travel, rental car discounts, discount prescriptions by mail, and a myriad of other services.

Initially founded in 1958 to provide health insurance for school teachers, AARP has changed dramatically and sought to recreate its image as the older population

A Sample of Services Offered by AARP

- tax preparation services
- peer grief and loss counseling
- legal counsel for older adults
- driver safety courses
- classes on personal safety
- a money management program
- home, auto, long-term care, and life insurance at reduced rates
- mobile home insurance
- Grandparent Information Center
- AARP Health Care Options (supplemental health insurance)
- fraud prevention courses

has shifted. It has a wide array of diversity initiatives to historically underrepresented groups and seeks to attract both the young-old and the oldest-old. It even changed its name from the American Association of Retired Persons to just AARP, not wanting to be seen as an organization only for those who are retired. More recently, it has focused on addressing the needs of elders adversely affected by the recession, including homelessness and hunger.

Over 100 other national associations seek to influencing education, practice, policy, and research to improve the lives of older adults, their families, and their paid caregivers. We cite a few that have the greatest national presence.

- The **Gerontological Society of America (GSA)** (which now also encompasses the **Association for Gerontology in Higher Education**) and the **American Society on Aging (ASA)** are composed primarily of gerontological researchers, educators, and practitioners from many disciplines and professions.
- Numerous largely discipline-specific national organizations, such as the American Geriatrics Society, the Association for Gerontological Education in Social Work, the American Geriatric Dental Society, and the American Association of Geriatric Nursing represent professional providers and often become involved in influencing workforce policies.
- The **National Council on Aging (NCOA)** encompasses over 3,500 affiliates—senior centers, senior housing, faith-based groups, and area agencies on aging, consumers, and leaders in academia, business, and the human services.
- The **Older Women's League (OWL)** brings together people concerned about issues affecting older women, especially health care and insurance, Social Security, pensions, and caregiving.
- The **Gray Panthers**, founded by the late Maggie Kuhn, aims to form grassroots intergenerational alliances around social justice issues affecting all ages. Since Maggie Kuhn's death, the Gray Panthers' visibility has declined, but they are still involved in social change and grassroots democracy that benefits multiple generations.

Is AARP for *All* Older Adults?

Yes...

- It seeks to represent the age diversity of the population age 50 and older, particularly the young-old and baby boomers who may not perceive themselves as retirees or old.
- It continues to publish three slightly different versions of *The Magazine* to appeal to cohorts in their fifties, sixties, and beyond, although age is never made explicit on the magazine cover.
- It also publishes in Spanish to reach out to the rapidly growing young-old Latino population.
- It recognizes the huge market for its products with the baby boomers, and spends millions to advertise in popular magazines with images of healthy, robust, and often physically attractive older adults. AARP sponsors 10K runs, marathons, a wide range of fitness activities, and adventure travel.
- The political arm of AARP speaks out for or against bills that affect the health and social well-being of older adults, most recently in support of the 2010 Patient Protection and Affordable Care Act.
- The AARP Foundation has made eliminating poverty hunger, homelessness, and social isolation its top priorities.

But...

- Its membership is primarily middle- and upper-working-class Caucasians.
- Critics contend that AARP has become "big business," concerned primarily with marketing its products and services and influenced by drug companies and insurance interests.

In spite of the growth of age-based organizations, the senior-power model appears to have little validity with respect to older adults' voting behavior and political attitudes. Old age per se is currently not a primary basis for political mobilization, despite images of homogeneous senior groups put forth by politicians, the media, and age-based organizations. With regard to the future, we can predict that baby boomers will cast a higher total vote in national and local elections than voting rates today, but the heterogeneity of the baby boom cohort suggests that age will not form the primary basis for political behavior.

Looking toward the Future of Productive Aging

Considering future patterns of productive activity, it is likely that baby boomers will find numerous opportunities to engage in mutually beneficial relationships, to contribute to society, or to pursue solitary creative or educational activities. As you have seen throughout this book, as boomers have moved through life, they have continued to reshape many of the social conventions around marriage and family, sexuality, parenting, and workplace behavior and seek opportunities that provide them with a sense of meaning and purpose. Accordingly, they will undoubtedly shape patterns of leisure, spirituality, religion, and civic engagement in old age. They epitomize the concept of the **Third Age**, which denotes the stage in life that occurs after middle age but before the final stage, and is conceptualized as a time of continued involvement and growth in areas of life beyond employment and family. It is argued that our society must find ways to build upon the vitality of the older population to utilize their skills and wisdom for the benefit of society and of older adults themselves. Advocates of a productive aging society argue for placing a real value on unpaid volunteer and caregiving activities. Volunteer efforts, including political activity and grassroots activism, may be perceived as contributing more to the common good than paid work and therefore as deserving greater rewards than currently exist. Indeed, volunteerism is often defined as a second or third career. However, flexible options for productive activity and for Third Age opportunities by older adults are unevenly distributed across all sectors of society. Therefore, initiatives to encourage unpaid productive contributions must occur within a broader framework that seeks to eliminate economic inequities across the life course and in old age.

summary

Older adults often experience meaningful involvement and develop new opportunities and skills through a range of productive activities: leisure pursuits, formal and informal religious involvement, and civic engagement through voluntary association membership, volunteering, education, and political involvement.

Past research on religious and civic participation has pointed inaccurately to declines in old age. Although formal religious participation such as church, mosque, or synagogue attendance appears to diminish slightly among the oldest-old, other private informal activities such as reading religious texts, listening to religious broadcasts, and praying increase. Religiosity appears to be an effective way of coping, particularly among elders of color. Spirituality is differentiated from religion in that it does not imply affiliation with a specific religious group or activity. Often conceptualized as a journey, spirituality can have a positive broad impact on older people's physical and mental well-being, and can enhance active aging. Health care providers now recognize the importance of conducting a spiritual assessment to ensure that treatment and services are congruent with elders' spiritual and religious values.

Civic engagement has become akin to a social change movement, with proponents advocating for elders to help solve societal problems such as climate change, while critics worry that civic engagement, particularly volunteerism, can perpetuate reductions in publicly funded services and expect older volunteers to pick up the slack. The meaning and functions of participation in these areas are obviously highly individualized. Participation may be a means to strengthen and build informal social networks, influence wider social policies, serve other persons, substitute new roles, and acquire new sources of meaning and purpose. The extent of involvement is influenced not by age alone, but also by a variety of other salient factors including gender, race, ethnicity, health, religious affiliation, marital status, social class, and educational level.

Because of the number of interacting variables, age-related patterns in participation are not clearly defined. There are some general age-associated differences in types of leisure pursuits. With increasing age, the current cohort age 65 and older tends to engage in somewhat sedentary, inner-directed, and routine pursuits. But this pattern may shift with the baby boomers, who are more likely to travel extensively and seek out new learning experiences and productive roles than previous cohorts. Changes in organizational participation, such as senior centers and volunteering, are less clearly age related. Participation in voluntary associations stabilizes or diminishes only slightly with old age; declines that do occur are associated with poor health, inadequate income, and transportation problems. Volunteering, which is increasing among today's older population, tends to represent a lifelong pattern of community service that peaks in middle age and then remains relatively stable until after age 70.

Voting by older people has increased since the 1980s. Declines in voting and political participation in the past may have been a function of low educational status or physical limitations, not age per se. In fact, older persons' skills and experiences may be more valued in the political arena than in other spheres. The extent to which older people form a unified political bloc that can influence politicians and public policy is debatable. Some argue that older adults are cohesive, with a strong collective consciousness; others point to their increasing diversity and differences on public policy. As a whole, it appears that older adults are not a homogeneous voting bloc and often react to policies rather than initiate them, but many politicians still court them as if they all had common objectives.

Most forms of organizational involvement appear to represent stability across the life course. The knowledge and skills necessary for a varied set of activities in old age are generally developed in early or middle adulthood and maintained into later life. On the other hand, preretirement patterns of productivity are not fixed. Individuals can garner new interests and activities in later life, often with the assistance of senior centers, lifelong learning programs, and community organizations.

key terms

AARP, p. 248
American Society on Aging (ASA), p. 249
Association for Gerontology in Higher Education (AGHE), p. 249
civic engagement, p. 236
Civic Ventures, p. 241
encore careers, p. 241
Experience Corps, p. 244
Foster Grandparents, p. 240
Generations United, p. 248
Gerontological Society of America (GSA), p. 249
Gray Panthers, p. 249
leisure, p. 228
lifelong learning, p. 244
National Council on Aging (NCOA), p. 249
Older Women's League (OWL), p. 249
Osher Lifelong Learning Institutes (OLLIs), p. 245
productive aging, p. 227
religion, p. 229
religiosity, p. 229
Retired and Senior Volunteer Program (RSVP), p. 241
Road Scholar, p. 245
Senior Community Service Employment Program, p. 241
Senior Companion Program, p. 241
socio-emotional selectivity, p. 241
spirituality, p. 230
spiritual reminiscence, p. 234
Third Age, p. 250

review questions

1. How is productive aging defined? What types of activities typically characterize productive aging?
2. What does it mean when a baby boomer says that they are spiritual, but not religious?
3. List three benefits of religious participation/religiosity for older adults.
4. What types of activities are included under the broad concept of civic engagement?
5. Identify some of the benefits of volunteerism for older volunteers and for the organizations they serve.
6. How would you respond to someone who says that older people become more politically conservative as they age?
7. Imagine that you were the director of an agency that depends largely upon older adults as volunteers. What factors should you consider in recruiting and retaining older volunteers?

8. What are some of the major challenges facing senior centers today? If you were the director of a senior center, what kinds of programmatic changes might you want to make?
9. What evidence would you cite to argue that older adults today are no longer as powerful a political constituency as they were in the past? What are some limitations of age-based organizations versus intergenerational alliances to influence policies and programs?
10. How do patterns of civic engagement often differ by race and gender?
11. Religion, religiosity, and spirituality, volunteering and senior center engagement all have benefits for physical and mental well-being. What reasons might explain why these different types of activities have similar benefits for elders?

media resources

Watch

- A 92-Year-Old Volunteer
- Discovering Optimism and Resilience: Renee Firestone
- Successful Aging, Independent Lifestyle: Thelma, 81 Years Old

Listen

- NPR: Older Love

references

Ai, A., Park, C., Huang, B., Rodgers, W., & Tice, T. N. (2007). Psychosocial mediation of religious coping styles: A study of short-term psychological distress following cardiac surgery. *Personality and Social Psychology Bulletin, 33*, 867–882.

Ano, F. F., & Vasconcelles, E. B. (2005). Religious coping and psychological adjustment to stress: A meta-analysis. *Journal of Clinical Psychology, 61*, 461–480.

Ardelt, M., & Koenig, C. S. (2006). The role of religion for hospice patients and relatively healthy older adults. *Research on Aging, 28*, 184–215.

Atchley, R. C. (2008). Spirituality, meaning, and the experience of aging. *Generations, 32*, 12–16.

Atchley, R. C. (2009). *Spirituality and aging.* Baltimore. MD: Johns Hopkins University Press.

Awara, M., & Fasey, C. (2008). Is spirituality worth exploring in psychiatric out-patient clinics? *Journal of Mental Health, 17*, 183–191.

Barron, J. S., Tan, E. J., Yu, Q., Song, M., McGill, S., Fried, L. P. et al. (2009). Potential for intensive volunteering to promote the health of older adults in fair health. *Journal of Urban Health, 86*(4), 641–653.

Binstock, R. H. (2006). Older voters and the 2004 election. *The Gerontologist, 46*, 382–384.

Binstock, R. H. (2007). Older people and political engagement: From avid voters to "cooled-out marks." *Generations, 30*, 24–30.

Butrica, B. A., Johnson, R. W., & Zedlewski, S. R., (2009). Volunteer dynamics of older Americans. *Journals of Gerontology Series B: Psychological Sciences and Social Sciences, 64*, 644.

Carlson, M. C., Erickson, K. I., Kramer, A. F., Voss, M. W., Bolea, N., Mielke, M., (2009). Evidence for neurocognitive plasticity in at-risk older adults: The Experience Corps program. *Journals of Gerontology Series A: A Biological Sciences and Medical Sciences, 64*(12), 1275–1282.

Carlton-LaNey, I. (2006–2007). "Doing the Lord's work": African American elders' civic engagement. *Generations, 30*, 47–50.

Cartensen, L. L., Mikels, J. A., & Mather, M. (2006). Aging and the intersection of cognition, motivation and emotion. In J. Birren & K. W. Schaie (Eds.), *Handbook of the psychology of aging* (6th ed.). San Diego, CA: Academic Press.

Cheung, S., Michel, M., & Miller, D. (2010). *Volunteerism: Give a little, gain a lot.* Georgian College Research Analyst Program. Retrieved September 2011, from http://planeterra.org.

Cnaan, R. A., Boddie, S. C., & Kang, J. J. (2005) Religious congregations as social service providers for older adults. *Journal of Gerontological Social Work, 45*(1/2), 105–130.

Cohen, G. D. (2005). *The mature mind: The positive power of the aging brain.* New York: Avon Books.

Cohen, G. D., Perlstein, S., Chapline, J. Kelly, J., Firth, K., & Simmens S. (2006). The impact of professionally conducted cultural programs on the physical health, mental health and social functioning of older adults. *The Gerontologist, 46*, 726–734.

Crowther, M. R., Parker, M. W., Achenbaum, W. A., Larimore, W. L., & Koenig, H. G. (2002). Rowe and Kahn's model of successful aging revisited: Positive spirituality—The forgotten factor. *The Gerontologist, 42*, 613–620.

Cullinane, B. D. (2008). Guest at the door: Spirit waiting to be invited. *Generations, 32*, 17–19.

Cutler, S. J., & Hendricks, J. (2000). Age differences in voluntary association memberships: Fact or artifact. *Journals of Gerontology, 55B*, S98–S107.

Daaleman, T. P., & Dobbs, D. (2010). Religiosity, spirituality, and death: Attitudes in chronically ill older adults. *Research on Aging, 31*(2), 224–243.

Donnelly, E. A., & Hinterlong, J. E. (2010). Changes in social participation and volunteer activity among recently widowed older adults. *The Gerontologist, 50*(2), 158–169.

Emerman, J. (2006). On life's new stage—And its challenge to the field of aging. *Aging Today*, 3–4.

Faigin, C. A., & Pargament, K. I. (2011). Strengthened by the spirit: Religion, spirituality, and resilience through adulthood and aging. In B. Resnick, L. P. Gwyther, & K. A. Roberto (Eds.), *Resilience in aging: Concepts, research, and outcomes* (pp. 163–180). New York: Springer.

Fisher, P. (2008). Is there an emerging age gap in U.S. politics? *Society, 45*, 504–511.

Fitzpatrick, S., Reddy, S., Lommel, T., Fischer, J., Speer, E., & Stephens, H. (2008). Physical activity and physical function improved following a community-based intervention in older adults in Georgia senior centers. *Journal of Nutrition for the Elderly, 27*, 135–154.

Freedman, M. (2001). Structural lead: Building new institutions for an aging America. In N. Morrow-Howell, J. Hinterlong, & M. Sherraden (Eds.), *Productive aging: Concepts and challenges.* Baltimore, MD: Johns Hopkins University Press.

Gallup Poll. (2010). *Near-record high see religion losing influence in America.* Retrieved September 20, 2013, from http://www.gallup.com/poll/145409/near-record-high-religion-losing-influence-america.aspx.

Gillum, R. F., King, D. E., Obisesan, T. O., & Koenig, G. (2008). Frequency of attendance at religious services and mortality in a U.S. national cohort. *Annals of Epidemiology, 18*, 124–129.

Greenfield, E., & Marks, N. (2004). Formal volunteering as a protective factor for older adults' psychological well-being. *Journal of Gerontology: Social Sciences, 59B*, S258–S264.

Greenfield, E., & Marks, N. (2007). Continuous participation in voluntary groups as a protective factor for the psychological well-being of adults who develop functional limitations: Evidence from the National Survey of Families and Households. *Journal of Gerontology: Social Sciences, 62B*, S60–S68.

Gross, J. (2008). Its appeal slipping, the senior center steps livelier. *New York Times.* Retrieved September 20, 2013, from http://www.nytimes.com/2008/03/25/us/25cafe.html?pagewanted=print&_r=0.

Hao, Y. (2008). Productive activities and psychological well-being among older adults. *Journal of Gerontology: Social Sciences, 63B*, S64–S72.

Harvey, I. S. (2009). Spiritual self-management: A look at older adults with chronic illness. *Journal of Religion, Spirituality & Aging, 21*(3), 200–218.

Harvey, I. S., & Silverman, M. (2007). The role of spirituality in the self-management of chronic illness among older African Americans and whites. *Journal of Cross-Cultural Gerontology, 22*, 205–220.

Hill, T. D. (2008). Religious involvement and healthy cognitive aging: Patterns, explanations, and future directions. *Journals of Gerontology, 63*, 478–479.

Hinterlong, J. E., & Williamson, A. (2006–2007). The effects of civic engagement on current and future cohorts of older adults. *Generations, 30*, 10–17.

Hodge, D. R. (2003). The intrinsic spirituality scale: A new six-item instrument for assessing the salience of spirituality as a motivational construct. *Journal of Social Service Research, 31*, 41–61.

Holstein, M. (2007). A critical reflection on civic engagement. *Public Policy & Aging Report, 16*, 21–26.

Hudson, R. B. (2006). The 2005 White House Conference on Aging: No time for seniors. *Public Policy & Aging Report, 16*, 1–3.

Hudson, R. B. (2006–2007). Aging in a public space: The roles and functions of civic engagement. *Generations, 30*, 51–58.

Hudson, R. B. (2007). Terms of engagement: The Right and Left look at elder civic activism. *Public Policy & Aging Report, 16*, 17–18.

Hudson, R. B. (2008). Public policy and the boomers: An expanding scope of conflict. In R. B. Hudson (Ed.), *Boomer bust? Economic and political issues of the graying society* (Vol. 1). Westport, CT: Praeger.

Idler, E. L. (2002). The many causal pathways linking religion to health. *Public Policy & Aging Report, 12*, 7–12.

Idler, E. L. (2006). Religion and aging. In R. Binstock & L. K. George (Eds.), *Handbook of aging and the social sciences* (6th ed.). New York: Academic Press.

Idler, E., McLaughlin, J., & Kasl, S. (2009). Religion and the quality of life in the last year of life. *Journal of Gerontology: Social Sciences, 64B*(4), 528–537.

Johnson, R., & Schaner, S. (2005). Value of unpaid activities by older Americans tops $160 billion per year. *Perspectives on productive aging.* Brief no. 4. Washington, DC: The Urban Institute.

Kaskie, B., Imhof, S., Cavanaugh, J., & Culp, K., (2008). Civic engagement as a retirement role for aging Americans. *The Gerontologist, 48*, 368–377.

Keyes, C. L. M., & Reitzes, D. C. (2007). The role of religious identity in the mental health of older working and retired adults. *Aging and Mental Health, 11*, 434–443.

Kim, J., Nesselroade, J. R., & McCullough, M. E. (2009). Dynamic factor analysis of worldviews/religious beliefs and well-being among older adults. *Journal of Adult Development, 16*, 87–100.

Koenig, H. G. (2002). An 83-year-old woman with chronic illness and strong religious beliefs. *Journal of the American Medical Association, 288*, 487–493.

Koenig, H. G. (2007). *Spirituality in patient care* (2nd ed.). Philadelphia, PA: Templeton Foundation Press.

Koenig, H. G., & Brooks, R. G. (2002). Religion, health, and-aging: Implications for practice and public policy. *Public Policy & Aging Report, 12*, 13–19.

Krause, N., & Bastida, E. (2011). Religion, suffering, and self-rated health among older Mexican Americans. *Journals of Gerontology, 66B*(2), 207–216.

Klemmarck, D. L., Roff, L. L., Parker, M. W., Koenig, H. G., Sawyer, P., & Allman, R. M. (2007). A cluster analysis typology of religiousness/spirituality among older adults. *Research on Aging, 29*, 163–183.

Lai, D. (2001). Use of senior center services by elderly Chinese immigrants. *Journal of Gerontological Social Work, 35*, 59–79.

Law, R. W., & Sbarra, D. A. (2009). The effects of church attendance and marital status on the longitudinal trajectories of depressed mood among older adults. *Journal of Aging and Health, 6*, 1202–1823.

Lawlor-Row, K. A. (2009). The role of religious activity and spirituality in the health and well-being of older adults. *Journal of Health Psychology, 14*(1), 43–52.

Lee, K. H. (2011). The role of spiritual experience, forgiveness, and religious support on the general well-being of older adults. *Journal of Religion, Spirituality & Aging, 23*(3), 206–223.

Li, Y., & Ferraro, K. F. (2006). Volunteering in middle and later life: Is health a benefit, barrier or both? *Social Forces, 85*, 498–519.

Lum, T., & Lightfoot, E. (2005). The effects of volunteering on the physical and mental health of older people. *Research on Aging, 27*, 31–55.

Lustbader, W. (2011). *Life gets better: The unexpected pleasures of growing older*. New York: Penguin.

Lynch, F. R. (2010). Political power and the baby boomers. In R. Hudson (Ed.), *The new politics of old age policy*. Baltimore, MD: Johns Hopkins University Press.

MacKinlay, E. (2008). *Ageing, disability and spirituality: Addressing the challenge of disability in later life*. Philadelphia, PA: Jessica Kingsley.

MacKinlay, E. (2006). *Spiritual growth and care in the 4th age of life*. London: Jessica Kingsley.

Manheimer, R. J. (2008). Gearing up for the big show: Lifelong learning programs are coming of age. In R. B. Hudson (Ed.), *Boomer Bust? Economic and political issues of the graying society* (Vol. 2). Westport, CT: Praeger.

Martinez, I., Frick, K., Glass, T., Carlson, M., Tanner, E., Ricks, M., et al. (2006). Engaging older adults in high impact volunteering that enhances health: Recruitment and retention in the Experience Corps Baltimore. *Journal of Urban Health: Bulletin of the New York Academy of Medicine, 83*(5), 941–953.

Martinson, M. (2006–2007). Opportunities or obligations? Civic engagement and older adults. *Generations, 30*, 59–65.

McBride, A. (2007). Civic engagement, older adults, and inclusion. *Generations, 30*, 66–71.

McNamara, T. K., & Gonzales, E. (2011). Volunteer transitions among older adults: The role of human, social & cultural capital in later life. *Journal of Gerontology: Social Sciences, 66B*, 490–501.

Menec, V. (2003). The relation between everyday activities and successful aging: A 6-year longitudinal study. *Journal of Gerontology: Social Sciences, 58B*, S74–S82.

Moody, H. R. (2004–2005). Silver industries and the new aging enterprise. *Generations, 28*, 75–78.

Moody, H. R., & Carroll D. (1997). *The five stages of the soul: Charting the spiritual passages that shape our lives*. New York: Anchor Books.

Morrow-Howell, N. (2011). *The potential of an aging society*. Presented at the Active Aging Symposium, Case Western Reserve University, October 2011.

Morrow-Howell, N., Hinterlong, J., Sheraden, M., Rozario, P., & Tang, F. (2003) Effects of volunteering on well-being. *Journals of Gerontology: Social Sciences, 58B*, S137–S145.

Morrow-Howell, N., Hong, S. I., & Tang, F. (2009). Who benefits from volunteering? Variations in perceived benefits. *The Gerontologist, 49*(1), 91–102.

Musick, A. M., & Wilson, J. (2008). *Volunteers: A social profile*. Bloomington, IN: Indiana University Press.

National Council on Aging. (2012). *Senior centers: Fact sheet*. Retrieved December 27, 2012, from http://www.ncoa.org/press-room/fact-sheets/senior-centers.

Nelson-Becker, H. (2005a). Religion and coping in older adults: A social work perspective. *Journal of Gerontological Social Work, 45*, 51–68.

Nelson-Becker, H. (2005b). Development of a spiritual support scale for use with older adults. *Journal of Human Behavior in the Social Environment, 11*, 195–212.

Nelson-Becker, H. (2005c). Religion and coping in older adults: A social work perspective. *Journal of Gerontological Social Work, 45*, 54–67.

Nelson-Becker, H., Nakashima, M., & Canda, E. R. (2006). Spirituality in professional helping interventions with older adults. In B. Berkman (Ed.), *Handbook of social work in health and aging*. New York: Oxford Press.

Nelson-Becker, H., Nakashima, M., & Canda, E. R. (2007). Spiritual assessment in aging: A framework for clinicians. *Journal of Gerontological Social Work, 48*, 331–347.

Newson, R., & Kemps, E. (2005). General lifestyle activities as a predictor of current cognition and cognitive change in older adults: A cross-sectional and longitudinal examination. *Journal of Gerontology: Psychology, 60B*, P113–P120.

Okon, T. R. (2005). Palliative care review: Spiritual, religious, and existential aspects of palliative care. *Journal of Palliative Medicine, 8*, 362–414.

Pardasani, M. (2004a). Senior centers: Focal points of community-based services for the elderly. *Activities, Adaptation and Aging, 28*, 27–44.

Pardasani, M. (2004b). Senior centers: Increasing minority participation through diversification. *Journal of Gerontological Social Work, 43*, 41–56.

Parker, M. W., Bellis, J. M., Bishop, P., Harper, M., Allman, R. M., Moore, C., & Thompson, P. (2002). A multidisciplinary model of health promotion incorporating spirituality into a successful aging intervention with African American and white elderly groups. *The Gerontologist, 42*, 406–415.

Parker, M., Roff, L. L., Klemmack, D. L., Koenig, H. G., Baker, P., & Allman, R. M. (2003). Religiosity and mental health in Southern, community-dwelling older adults. *Aging & Mental Health, 7*, 390–397.

Population Reference Bureau. (2011). Volunteering and health for aging populations. *Today's research on aging, 21*, 1–7.

Prisuta, R. (2004). Enhancing volunteerism among aging boomers. Harvard School of Public Health and MetLife. *Reinventing aging: Baby boomers and civic engagement.* Boston, MA: Harvard School of Public Health, Center for Health Communication.

Road Scholar. (2012). *Road Scholar: Adventures in lifelong learning.* Retrieved December 27, 2012, from http://www.roadscholar.org/.

Roff, L. L., Klemmack, D. L., Simon, C., Cho, G. W., Parker, M. W., Koenig, H. G., Sawyer-Baker, P., & Allman, R. M. (2006). Functional limitations and religious service attendance among African American and white older adults. *Health and Social Work, 31*(4), 246–55.

Rozario, P. A. (2006–2007). Volunteering among current cohorts of older adults and baby boomers. *Generations, 30*, 31–36.

Sapp, S. (2010). What have religion and spirituality to do with aging? Three approaches. Book reviews. *The Gerontologist, 50*, 271–275.

Schieman, S., Bierman, A., & Ellison, C. G. (2010). Religious involvement, beliefs about God, and the sense of mattering among older adults. *Journal for the Scientific Study of Religion, 49*(3), 517–535.

Schwarz, L., & Cottrell, R. F. (2007). The value of spirituality as perceived by elders in long-term care. *Physical & Occupational Therapy in Geriatrics, 26*, 43–62.

Senior Center without Walls. (2011). *Senior Center without Walls: Who we are.* Retrieved September 29, 2011, from http://www.seniorcenterwithoutwalls.org.

Siegrist, J., Knesebeck, O., & Pollack, C. (2004). Social productivity and well-being of older people: A sociological exploration. *Social Theory and Health, 2*, 1–17.

Skarupski, K. A., Fitchett, G., Evans, D. A., & Mendes de Leon, C. F. (2010). Daily spiritual experiences in a biracial, community-based population of older adults. *Aging & Mental Health, 14*(7), 779–789.

Smith, T. W., & Seokho, K. (2005). The vanishing Protestant minority. *Journal for the Scientific Study of Religion, 44*, 211–223.

Snodgrass, J. (2009). Toward holistic care: Integrating spirituality and cognitive behavior therapy for older adults. *Journal of Religion, Spirituality and Aging, 21*, 219–236.

Tan, E., Rebok, G., Yu, Q., Frangakis, C., Carlson, M., Wang, T., et al. (2009). The long-term relationship between high-intensity volunteering and physical activity in older African American women. *Journal of Gerontology Series B: Psychological Sciences and Social Sciences, 64*, 304–311.

Tang, F., Choi, E., & Morrow-Howell, N. (2010). Organizational support and volunteering benefits for older adults. *The Gerontologist, 50*(5), 603–612.

Tang, F., Morrow-Howell, N., & Hong, S. (2009). Institutional facilitation in sustained volunteering among older volunteers. *Social Work Research, 33*, 172–182.

Tanyi, R. A., McKenzie, M., & Chapek, C. (2009). How family practice physicians, nurse practitioners, and physician assistants incorporate spiritual care in practice. *Journal of the American Academy of Nurse Practitioners, 21*, 690–697.

Taylor, R., Chatters, L., & Levin, J. (2004). *Religion in the lives of African Americans.* Thousand Oaks, CA: Sage.

Taylor, R. J., Chatters, L. M., & Jackson, J. S. (2007). *Journals of Gerontology Series B: Psychological Sciences and Social Sciences, 62*(4), S251–S256.

Taylor & Lopez (2013). *Six take-aways from the Census Bureau's voting report.* The Pew Research Center. Retrieved February 2014, http://www.research.org/fact-tank/2013.

Theiss-Morse, E., & Hibbing, J. (2004). Citizenship and civic engagement. *Annual Review of Political Science, 8*, 227–249.

Turesky, D. G., & Schultz, J. M. (2010). Spirituality among older adults: An exploration of the developmental context, impact on mental and physical health, and integration into counseling. *Journal of Religion, Spirituality & Aging, 22*(3), 162–179.

U.S. Census Bureau. (2010). *Voting and registration in the election of November 2008.* Retrieved September 21, 2013, from http://www.census.gov/hhes/www/socdemo/voting/publications/p20/2008/tables.html.

Van Ness, P., & Larson, D. (2002). Religion, senescence and mental health. The end of life is the not the end of hope. *American Journal of Geriatric Psychiatry, 10*, 386–397.

Washington University. (2008). *Experience Corps: Benefits of volunteering. George Warren Brown School of Social Work,* Center for Social Development. Retrieved September 29, 2011, from http://www.gwbweb.wustle.edu/csd.

Wilson, L., & Simpson, S. (Eds.) (2006). *Civic engagement and the baby boomer generation. Research, policy and practice perspectives:* Binghamton, NY: Haworth Press.

Wilson, L. B., & Harlow-Rosentraub, K. (2008). Providing new opportunities for volunteerism and civic engagement for boomers: Chaos theory redefined. In R. B. Hudson (Ed.), *Boomer Bust: Economic and political issues of the graying society* (Vol. 2). Westport, CT: Praeger.

Windsor, T. D., Anstey, K. J., & Rodgers, B. (2008). Volunteering and psychological well-being among young-old adults: How much is too much? *The Gerontologist, 48*(1), 59–70.

Yoon, D. P., & Lee, E. K. O. (2007). The impact of religiousness, spirituality, and social support on psychological well-being among older adults in rural areas. *Journal of Gerontological Religion, Spirituality and Aging, 48*, 281–298.

Zedlewski, S., & Schaner, S. (2006). Older adults engaged as volunteers. *Perspectives on productive aging.* Washington, DC: Urban Institute, The Retirement Project.

9 Loss and Grief in Old Age

learning objectives

- **9.1** Differentiate the kinds of loss that older adults may experience, including non-death-related losses.
- **9.2** Describe phases of the grief process along with responses to grief.
- **9.3** Identify end-of-life care options—palliative care, hospice and Right to Die legislation—and meaning of a "good death."

Listen to the **Chapter Audio**

All of us experience losses in our lives. Loss is typically produced by an event that we perceive to be negative and that results in unwanted changes—whether in our social relationships, living situations, or roles and social status. Loss always involves some kind of deprivation—we no longer have someone or something that we used to have. Losses are often experienced during transitions from one role or setting to others. Even positive transitions typically involve giving up something. For example, if you moved away from home to go to college, you were undoubtedly excited about being on your own. But such a move brought the loss of what was familiar—your family, your room, your pets.

Older adults are more likely than younger persons to have experienced multiple negative losses—and grief—in their lives simply because they have lived longer. Not all losses are due to deaths of loved ones. Some may result from physical changes (e.g., declines in vision, hearing, or mobility) and illnesses, and others from changes in one's community or social networks. For example, social relationships are often lost when an older person moves to a new living situation or retires especially if the person did not choose these changes.

In this chapter, we first discuss the nature of loss and grief within the context of aging, and then address losses, other than death, that are commonly experienced in old age and often cause grief reactions. This chapter includes:

- Typical non-death losses faced by older adults
- Death of loved ones: partners, siblings, and friends
- Approaching one's own death and the dying process

We use the word order of loss and grief, since loss precedes grief. Grief is a natural reaction to loss, and loss is an inevitable part of being human. But not every loss gives rise to grief. Some losses may be experienced as positive, such as giving up the parent or grandparent caregiving role when it means no longer being responsible 24/7 for small children. Or leaving one's job through a long-planned-for retirement—and no longer bound by a suit, tie, and structured schedule. Other losses may bring a sense of relief: the death of a distant relative who has always been hostile or of a family caregiver who mistreated an elder. In such instances, however, relief may be tinged with feelings of grief such as guilt, ambivalence, or anxiety. We turn next to examine how most losses in old age are experienced as negative; however, some elders are depleted or embittered by them, while others are resilient and have a capacity to grow from and find meaning in their losses.

Loss and Grief within the Context of Aging

Old age—the phase of life when one is most apt to die—has often been characterized as a time of primarily loss and detachment. Recall our discussion of disengagement theory in Chapter 5. Additionally, the losses associated with normal age-related changes are often intensified by ageism, or Western societies' tendency to stereotype and minimize older adults' value. Ageist assumptions may mean that family members and health care providers presume that loss in old age is "not a big deal," and devalue older adults' grief. When others minimize their grief, older adults are at increased risk for secondary losses, such as depression and social isolation.

Remember the concept of life course that you learned about in the Introduction. Many older people have to deal with the cumulative effect of losses created by lifelong inequities as a result of their age, race, social class, sexual orientation, gender, or ability. They bring a lifetime of coping with loss to old age. Additionally, losses in old age, even when expected as "normative," tend to have a greater negative impact on an elder's physical and psychosocial well-being than when we are younger. This is generally because of the cumulative impact of multiple losses over a lifetime that may deplete an elder's psychological, physiological, and social reserves. Even losses much earlier in life, such as a child's death, may continue to cause emotional pain in old age. Grief from profound earlier losses that may have been

Cumulative Impact of Loss

One older woman described grief as kind of like eating grapes: you have one or two, then pause before having some more. She recounted how she could still think of times in her life when a new loss brought up past losses and how the grief of losing her father as a teen would come into the present.

Multiple Losses

Mrs. Luna, an 88-year old widow, still lives in her isolated rural home in Montana. She uses a kerosene heater to heat her small cinder-block home, because she cannot afford to pay for utilities. Her vision is poor, and she uses a walker because of her arthritis. She cooks her one meal of the day on a two-burner hot plate. This is a far cry from her life when her husband was alive. Although he did not earn much as a carpenter, he was able to keep up their rural home and provide her with a comfortable life as she raised their three children. When a neighbor went to check on her, Mrs. Luna reported a lengthy story about her children stealing her land from her and wanting to put her in a nursing home to die there. She repeatedly said that she needs a lawyer but cannot afford one. But she also said that her children don't really want her to go to a nursing home, because it would use up all her money and property. She was tearful and worried about her future, wondering how she will take care of herself. She reported that she often goes for as much as a week or two without getting out of the house or having a visitor. When she becomes too cold or lonely, she just goes to bed. What types of losses has Mrs. Luna experienced? Did reading about Mrs. Luna change what you consider to be losses in life? What sources of strength or resilience do you think Mrs. Luna has?

buried for years may resurface in later life. Some elders who have experienced multiple deaths of loved ones may feel overwhelmed by their accumulated negative effects and are at higher risk of depression (Hooyman & Kramer, 2006).

Several theories attempt to explain why grief from earlier losses may intensify as we age. Erikson's psychosocial theory of development, which you learned about in Chapter 4, proposed that individuals in later life try to integrate earlier life's experience and achieve ego integrity or a sense of wholeness. Failure to do so can result in despair or profound dissatisfaction with one's life. Additionally, some of today's oldest-old may find it difficult to engage in such a self-reflective process. When they were children and young adults, they may have been socialized to "be strong" and not to express painful feelings in order to cope with life's hard blows. For example, many World War II veterans felt they needed to keep their horrific experiences to themselves and never talked about them. In such instances, it is not surprising if older adults resist encouragement from family members or helping professionals to share earlier memories. Instead, they may take painful experiences or unresolved grief with them to the grave (Erikson, 1982; Erikson & Erikson, 1981; Erikson, Erikson, & Kivnick, 1986; Kastenbaum, 1969).

But other elders with multiple successive losses during their lives may display considerable resilience, especially if their community, family, and cultural and religious/spiritual supports are strong, as you learned in Chapter 4. Many elders possess an inner strength and wisdom that helps them adapt to grief and reframe their losses. For example, they may reappraise negative events to find something positive in them, and lower their expectations of what life has in store for them. As you are learning throughout this book, even when age-related losses limit a person's options, aging adults can still grow and find purpose and satisfaction in their lives. When any of us confronts loss, we are challenged to create meaning where none seems to exist. This intensely personal process can mean weaving an entirely new picture and story about ourselves, our world, and what it means to live with loss. And sometimes the story we weave is one we like even better (Hooyman & Kramer, 2006; Moss, Moss, & Hansson, 2001; Ramsey & Blieszner, 2000).

Elders' experiences with loss are also influenced by their proximity to death, spirituality and/or religiosity, and culture. If an adult has achieved peace with the thought of his or her own death, other losses, including the death of friends and family, may not be as devastating as they are for younger people for whom death is still far away.

points to **ponder**

Think about an older adult you know who has experienced multiple losses but still radiates peacefulness and joy in living. What do you think has occurred in their life that has made this possible? Perhaps they have successfully engaged in what is called **life review**—a process you learned about in Chapter 4 of introspection, self-reflection, and reminiscence that commonly includes reflecting on themes of loss. As earlier memories resurface, some older adults review, evaluate, and perhaps reinterpret past experiences in order to achieve a new sense of meaning, both as an accounting to oneself of one's past life and as a preparation for death (Butler, 1963).

The oldest-old, especially among elders of color, are often characterized as "hardy survivors," who have managed to find ways to compensate for age-associated losses and have come to terms with their mortality.

The Nature of Grief

Although we may fear it, grief is the normal psychological, social, and physical reaction to loss. It is experienced through our feelings, thoughts, and attitudes, behavior with others, and even our health and physiological changes. Intensely personal, our grief is based on how we perceive the loss and its meaning to us. Accordingly, no two people grieve in the same way. Well-meaning friends and professionals may try to encourage an elder "to get over" their loss or falsely assure them that their grief will end in six months, a year, five years. But a fixed timetable or sequence of stages does not exist. Instead, grief is more like a roller coaster as its intensity and form ebb and flow over time. To grieve requires a great deal of time, energy, and attention (Hagman, 2001; Rando, 1988).

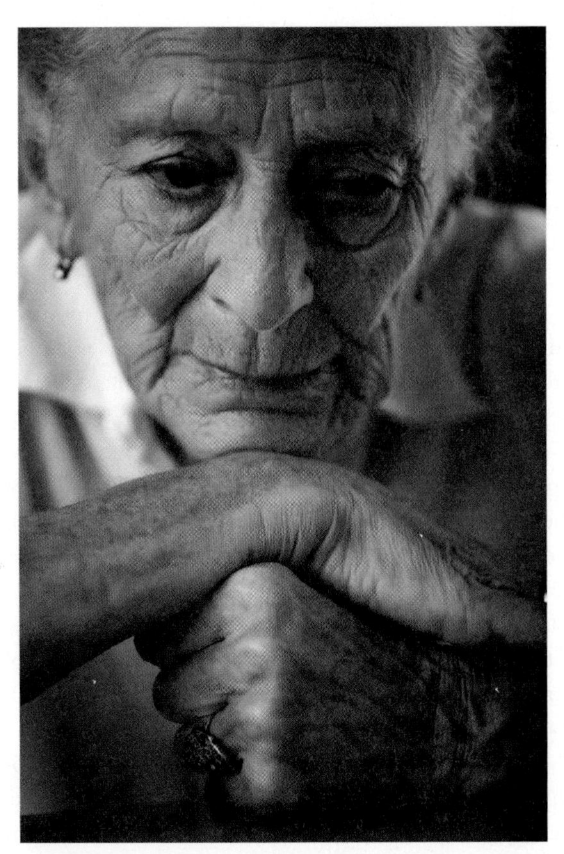

Self-reflection and reminiscing can be helpful later in life as elders review their life's journey.

Although grieving has no fixed stages, a constellation of feelings generally accompanies a significant loss. These typical feelings encompass:

- Fear, including the fear of expressing one's feelings: "If I start to cry, will I ever be able to stop?"
- Numbness, shock, disbelief, and denial: "This is a bad dream that I just need to wake up from."
- Guilt, anger, rage, and questioning of faith: "Why do bad things happen to good people?"
- Being overwhelmed, powerless, and anxious about one's ability to carry on with life: "How can I ever manage my life or be happy again?"
- Intense sadness, loneliness, fatigue, loss of appetite, and sleeplessness, which may be symptoms of depression: "I just can't get out of bed in the morning or I have lost 25 pounds in the two weeks after a major loss."

Within a matter of hours, a person who is grieving may experience anger, guilt, helplessness, loneliness, and uncontrolled crying along with strength, pride in their coping, and even laughter.

Most losses also entail the symbolic loss of dreams. When a dream has been abandoned, something inside a person is lost. This is also true of the non-death losses associated with life's transitions that we next discuss. If you are working with older adults, it is important to recognize the multiple symbolic losses they may face that entail abandonment of dreams of their future (Klass, 1996, 1999b; Walter, 2003).

Typical Losses Faced by Older Adults

You may still be wondering why we are including topics such as relocation, retirement, and caregiving in a chapter on loss and grief. Admittedly, physical loss—the death of a loved one—is generally presumed to be the greatest

points to ponder

As you are learning, loss does not always involve death. Take a moment to consider some of the transitions in your life that have been accompanied by losses. Can you think of a non-death loss in your life that resulted in a grieving process? What type of loss was it? What were some of the feelings you experienced?

loss—and what geriatric practitioners most often deal with. But losses other than death can also be as devastating in their impact on elders' well-being. As you have just learned, many of these are symbolic losses, such as loss of status after unemployment or retirement, or a decline in one's network after widowhood or divorce, which affect a person's identity and social interactions. Losing our health, our job, or our memory can be like losing a part of ourselves—which is also what happens when someone we love dies.

As we noted above, non-death losses are often associated with life transitions that can include both positive and negative changes. For example, relocation to a new living situation may entail gains in feelings of safety and comfortable surroundings but also giving up one's sense of place or home, cherished possessions, or way of life. As another example, caring for a relative with a chronic illness or living with a disability allows caregiversto express their love and gain a greater appreciation for the preciousness of life. Yet in the process, they may also lose their self-esteem, identity, income, or mobility.

Relocation Place defines our sense of space and how we feel in that space and adds predictability to life. Consider the emotional connotation of being able to "go home," no matter what phase of life we are in. Many older adults are attached to their living spaces, belongings, yards, animals, and neighborhoods. And the importance of the home can be even more significant in later life than at earlier phases.

points to ponder

As a student, you may occasionally long for home or count the days until a break when you can come home. What does going home mean to you? What is it about home that you have missed? Do you think any of your feelings might be shared by older adults?

Losing the space that is "home" can throw older adults psychologically off base, making it even more difficult for them to handle secondary losses often associated with residential moves.

One example of an unanticipated secondary loss is role changes that shift power within family systems. For example, a move to a retirement facility that is closer to children and grandchildren can result in increased dependency on adult children, which may be exactly what older parents have been trying to avoid. Or recall that you learned in Chapter 2 about the stress and loneliness faced by older immigrants who have left behind all that is familiar to them to join their adult children in the United States, often in suburban areas where they are socially isolated. Their children who are busy earning an income may not have time to spend with their older parents, who lack the informal social supports that they enjoyed in their home country (Longino, 2004; Oswald & Rowles, 2006; Robinson, Reid, & Cooke, 2010; Sergeant & Ekerdt, 2008).

Even active older adults who voluntarily move to a retirement community may grieve. They may not understand why they initially feel disoriented or distressed by what they had anticipated to be a positive transition. The changes of physical location, possessions, daily routines, and social support can cause them to experience insecurity and diminished control over their lives, feel cut off from their memories, and, in some cases, lose their sense of belonging and identity. However, the majority of older people who relocate gradually adjust to their new surroundings, and the benefits of the move begin to outweigh the losses (Capezuti, Boltz, Renz, Hoffman, & Norman, 2006; Dupuis-Blanchard, 2007; Walker, Curry, & Hogstel, 2007).

Unwanted moves, such as losing one's home to foreclosure or entering a skilled nursing facility, tend to cause the most emotional stress from relocation. Forced moves often occur on top of other losses associated with chronic illness, reduced income, or outliving immediate family, and

Moving Closer But Apart

Mrs. Thomas moved across country to be closer to her son, daughter-in-law, and three grandchildren. At the time of the move, she was relatively independent and looking forward to being able to share birthdays, holidays, and other special events with her family. But once she settled into her condo, she found herself more isolated and lonely than when she lived 2,000 miles away from her family. Her son and daughter-in-law had busy jobs and her grandchildren were all in school during the day. She had few friends, was unable to drive safely in the city, and couldn't keep up with her grandchildren's busy weekend schedules of sports and lessons. She became more and more dependent on her son to drive her places and her family to provide her with a social life. This strained what had been a good relationship when they saw each other only a few times a year and sent e-mails or enjoyed Skype between visits.

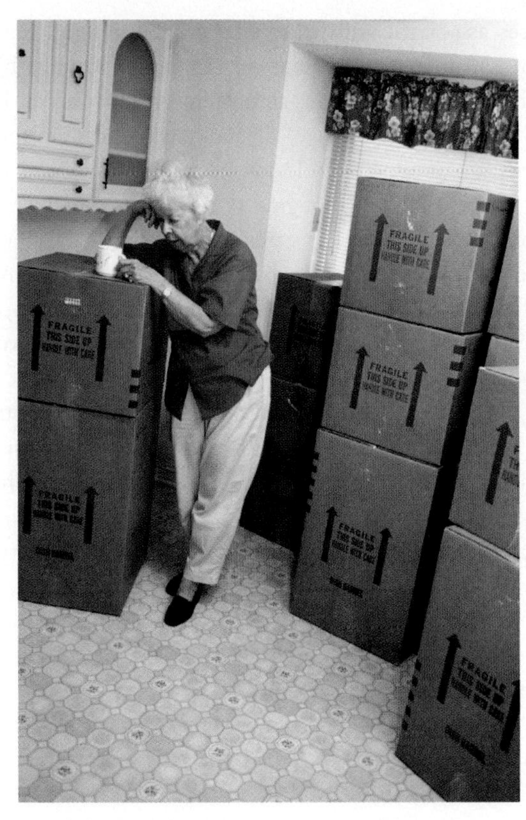

Relocation generally entails a loss of familiar surroundings and possessions.

can result in fear, devaluing of self, and feeling a burden to others. Some elders may view placement in a skilled nursing facility as a punishment or a death sentence and experience much higher rates of depression and further declines in their health, and even die sooner than elders in community-based settings. Such feelings are exacerbated when older adults have no input into relocation decisions. For instance, older individuals who feel they had no control about moving to a skilled nursing facility may beg to come home or berate family members for abandoning them (Chen, Zimmerman, Sloane, & Barrick, 2007; Nelson, 2001; Oswald & Rowles, 2006).

Because of the multiple losses entailed by a move to a long-term care facility, families and staff should seek to involve elders as much as possible in planning for the transition and take account of what the experience means to them. Staff can help in this process by learning about the elder's personal history and their sources of identity in the past. Additionally, they can encourage personalization of space through favorite furniture pieces and pictures and respect privacy as much as possible, such as always knocking on closed doors.

points to ponder

If you had a major injury, such as a spinal cord injury, and had to move to a skilled nursing facility, what would be most important to you to be able to still do or have? What objects would you want to have in your room? What would be one part of your current daily routine that you would want to preserve?

In instances when families decide on nursing home placement contrary to their elder's wishes, they may also experience losses—feeling guilty, perceiving themselves as failures as caregivers, and needing to adjust to dramatic changes in their relationship with their relative. Staff can assist grieving caregivers by acknowledging their feelings of guilt, asking if they have questions and answering them as best as possible and involving them in decisions that range from the minutiae of everyday life to end-of-life preferences.

Retirement For most adults, retirement is an exciting transition, planned for and eagerly anticipated. For others, who may feel "forced" to retire because of caregiving demands, poor health, or layoffs, retirement may precipitate a deep sense of loss. In our society with its value on work deriving in part from America's Christian heritage, a job provides not only income but also social legitimacy and a

Creating a New Nest

A study of older women who moved to an assisted living facility found that this experience initially threatened their identities. They became increasingly aware of their diminished self-reliance, often due to widowhood, declining health, loneliness, and sense of isolation. They described a process of reestablishing themselves both physically—getting accustomed to the smaller space—and psychosocially—reaching out to other residents. By building a "new nest," they created a new sense of well-being. For them, this "building" involved three phases: parting with a meaningful past, shaping a desired future, and settling into an altered present. In effect, they created a "home beyond the house" as a way to foster a sense of community and belonging (Dupuis-Blanchard, 2008; Robinson et al., 2010).

Guilt over Nursing Home Placement

One family caregiver who continued to carry a burden of guilt after many years recounted: "And the girls [staff] actually tell me this. They say 'You shouldn't feel guilty. One person cannot do what two of us are doing all the time as our job. One person can't do it 24 hours a day. You can't do it. You are going to break ... Your doctor knows it, everybody knows it; we all know it. So trust us and lay aside your guilt and enjoy your visits when you come'" (Dupuis-Blanchard, 2008).

principal source of personal identity. Work can provide a structure for the day, week, and year, a purpose for getting up in the morning and going somewhere.

In contrast, retirement means that an individual can no longer define themselves or be defined by others by their work. Even the loss of the physical space of an "office" can be devastating. Older adults who consider themselves not retired but unemployed may feel a particularly profound loss of dignity, status, purpose—along with income. Most retirement planning seminars tend to focus on financial planning and rarely address feelings of grief that may accompany this transition. But it is essential to help people proactively cope with such feelings before they make the decision to retire.

Caring for a Relative with Chronic Illness or Disability Some retirees may also find themselves caring for a partner or an adult child with a chronic illness or disabilities; as caregivers, they may experience numerous losses, although, as you learned in Chapter 7, there are also often gains in the relationship with their loved one. In many ways, loss and grief are the price that people pay for love and commitment to one another (Kramer, 1997; McLeod, 2001).

Let's review some of the losses that caregivers experience:

- Family members as they once knew them;
- Financial security
- Dreams or what they hoped and expected their lives to be in retirement or what is considered a "normal" life
- Self-esteem and self-worth
- Time, privacy, leisure, and social life
- A sense of justice and fairness in life

Losses associated with caregiving can be physical (e.g., a partner to help run the house or to communicate with) or symbolic (one's identity as competent breadwinner or how one had imagined old age). If family caregivers are forced to give up productive roles as worker or volunteer, they may lose a sense of belonging to a larger community and become isolated. Grief in caregivers is often misdiagnosed as depression but these are distinct processes. For example, the focus in grief is on the loss experience; in depression, it is an overall negative interpretation of oneself and one's world (Sanders, Ott, Kelber, & Noonan, 2008).

Spouses and partners tend to experience more stress and loneliness from caregiving than adult children; this is partially due to losses in marital and family relationships, shared social activities and identity, and physical or emotional intimacy as a couple. Spousal or partner grief is typically characterized by a yearning for the past, isolation, and restricted freedom, and such losses may escalate over the course of a disease (Meuser & Marwit 2001; Sanders et al., 2008; Seltzer & Li, 2000).

Losses tend to be most intense for caregivers of persons with Alzheimer's disease (AD), especially when the person

Days without Structure

As a vice president in a major national bank for over 20 years, Jake arrived at his office each day, even on weekends, by 6 a.m. His evenings were filled with dinners and special events associated with his responsibilities for corporate-community relations. This arrangement worked well for his wife, who was busy with her own career. But when the bank failed during the recession, Jake, who had just turned 67, was given one day's notice to clean out his desk. His pension with the bank—along with the structure to his days—abruptly disappeared. The only assistance provided by the bank to long-term employees like Jake was a seminar on job hunting and how to collect unemployment. Wanting to work, Jake put a lot of energy into the job hunt, applying for any job for which he qualified. On other days, however, he could barely manage to get out of bed by noon and get dressed. After two years of unemployment and only three job interviews, he has resigned himself to the fact that he will never be employed again. He spends his days reviewing his retirement investments, and preparing meals and cleaning house so his wife can concentrate on her career and income. But he misses the intellectual stimulation and social engagement of work. And he is increasingly irritable with his wife and adult children.

A daughter comforts her mother with her words, gentle touch, and compassionate presence.

is psychologically absent and no longer able to recognize the caregiver. Caregivers of adults with other types of neurological disorders, a brain injury, or a personality disorder caused by a stroke may experience similar types of losses. The grief reaction of family caregivers for people with AD has some distinctive characteristics, however. As the dementia progresses, family members must continually redefine their relationships. The concept of "learning to bend without breaking" refers to the family's need to accommodate the ongoing unpredictability inherent in living with a relative with AD. Feelings of loss can be particularly profound and the grief process prolonged for years when the personalities of persons with dementia change so much that new disruptive behaviors, such as verbal abuse or violent actions, emerge (Dupuis, 2002; Sanders & Corley, 2003; Schulz, Boerner, Shear, Zhang, & Gitlin, 2006).

Living in a state of "quasi-widowhood," caregivers of relatives with dementia refer to their loved one's dying twice: first the psychological death of the person they knew and loved and then the physical death. The psychological death can last years, since the person with AD dies slowly as a result of the dementia's progression before actual death occurs. This process is referred to as **chronic sorrow**: caregivers' grief is unending and unpredictable because it is associated with the living, not with the deceased. Moreover, grief is intensified when the person with dementia is unable to say good-bye or achieve closure with family members (Albinsson & Strang, 2003, p. 231; Dupuis, 2002; Gwyther 1998, Sanders, Butcher, Swails, & Power, 2009).

When caregivers' **anticipatory grief** for a loved one prior to his/her death is not acknowledged by professionals or friends, caregivers may experience what is called **disenfranchised grief**—a loss that is not openly acknowledged by others, publicly mourned, or socially supported. Their friends and family, feeling uncomfortable with the caregivers' grief and not knowing what to say or do, may visit less frequently, thus further reducing their social support when they most need it (Narayn, Lewis, Tornatore, Hepburn, & Corcoran-Perry, 2001; Sanders et al., 2008; Sanders et al., 2009).

When a relative with AD dies, caregivers may experience both relief and sadness. For some, their own well-being may improve. But those who were socially isolated while providing care may suffer long-term negative consequences, such as depression and poor health. Professionals may misdiagnose their grief as depression, recommending medications rather than helping them to express their grief and integrate the loss into their lives. A good question to begin with is to ask a caregiver, "In what ways has your life changed since you began to provide care?" A professional or caring friend can then help them find ways to regain what they have lost during the caring process (Ahmed, 2003; Carr, 2003; Doka, 2004; Schulz et al., 2003, 2008).

Caring for Adult Children with Chronic Illness or Disabilities Improved health care has resulted in a better quality of life and greater longevity for persons born with physical and intellectual disabilities. But for their parental caregivers, their child's increased life expectancy means that their grief (or chronic sorrow that is associated with grieving the living) continues much longer; they constantly face adjustments throughout their child's life and grieve for years at what might have been a milestone (e.g., birthdays, school graduations, first jobs, and nowadays even retirement) when they reflect on "what might have been." Older parents caring for adult children with disabilities are out of sync with their peers, since they have not "launched" their children. They may also face financial losses through the actual costs and lost employment opportunities of caring for their child for 40–50 years. As parents age and "wear out" from years of caring for a child with a disability, some may become "depleted caregivers," disillusioned, isolated, and vulnerable (Heller, 2011; Roos, 2002, p. 124).

Most aging adults with developmental disabilities continue to live in their parents' homes, in part because of few community-based residential care options. Their parents may become increasingly anxious about the future as they worry about who will care for their adult child when they become ill or die. But despite such worries, many parents do not plan for their adult child's future care. Talking about dying and transferring care responsibilities to other family members may only remind them of their ongoing sorrow. Family discussions about future plans may also provoke siblings' and other relatives' past resentment and grief over the child's disabilities or disrupted family life. An older caregiver may then try to avoid such conflicts by simply not preparing for the future (Heller & Caldwell, 2006; Roos, 2002).

As is true in caring for a relative of any age, there are gains in caring for an adult child with disabilities. In fact, many older caregivers care deeply about their child and cannot imagine life without them. Ricky and Ed's mutual dependence and benefits show that older parents may also experience support and caring from their adult children with disabilities.

Aging parents caring for an adult child with a chronic mental illness also experience grief. Because the average age at onset for depression, bipolar disorder, and schizophrenia is the early to mid-twenties, middle-aged and young-old parents, who anticipated launching their young adult child through college or employment, may suddenly be faced with caring for a child with chronic mental illness—something they never imagined having to do, particularly in old age. They grieve the loss of their child's potential, personality, family role, and hoped-for future. In fact, they may also mourn the physical loss of their child if he or she joins the chronically mentally ill homeless on the streets, is institutionalized, or is incarcerated. Their own plans for enjoying an empty nest and retirement without child-rearing responsibilities are thwarted.

Because the losses with mental illness are largely psychological and social rather than physical, the community often does not recognize the parents' loss or provide additional social support, which may result in disenfranchised grief. Older parents of an adult with mental illness may also experience chronic sorrow, because of hopelessness about their adult child's progress. Their energies are often absorbed in a frightening care situation of never-ending responsibilities, including medication management, and responding to their child's unreasonable actions and demands. They may also struggle with negotiating with health and mental health care providers and systems.

Their grief response may initially parallel those of parents whose adult child has died: avoidance and denial, anger, guilt, blaming of self and others, and, over time, the reorganization of their lives, belief systems, and self-perception to incorporate the loss. But unlike the parents of a child who died, they are dealing with a child who is alive but very different from earlier in life. Guilt may be especially intense as parents struggle with what they might have done to prevent the onset of a disease whose cause is not well understood. Additionally, feelings of grief are often worsened by the stigma of mental illness and by anxiety over whether their adult child may harm others.

Under these conditions, the final phase typical of grief—the reinvestment of energy in other relationships—may not be possible. In fact, some researchers have found

No Longer Able to Care

Now 41, Ricky was diagnosed with autism as a child. He's needed constant monitoring his entire life, which his dad, Ed, has committed to give, even after his wife of 50 years died. But there is a constant strain, etched in the wrinkles on Ed's face, the resignation in his voice, and his empty social calendar. And it's likely that Ricky will outlive his dad. Ed's health is declining, which has forced him to face the burden of who will take care of Ricky when he is gone. Ed is tired of the constant care, of feeling hopeless, of thinking no end is in sight. He yearns to play golf, or to go to the senior center or the movies. He constantly struggles with questions such as "Do I take care of him forever or take care of myself by finding a place for him to live? But what if the group home abuses him?" And he has had to admit that as much as Ricky relied on his dad, Ed depended on his son. Ricky got loving care; Ed got company, a routine, and a purpose in his life.

He couldn't turn to his two other sons, who are successful businessmen outside the area and still carry childhood resentment from being embarrassed by Ricky's behavior. In fact, his other sons are constantly urging him to find a group home for people with disabilities for Ricky. As happens in many caregiving situations, the caregiver's poor health precipitated a change. Ed had a heart attack and required open heart surgery. His other sons used this crisis as a time to force a change—and find a group home for Ricky. When Ed was released from the hospital, he rationalized that he would be removing a burden for his two other sons and that he was doing a service by making a decision now.

He tries to be positive about the move, but when he goes to visit, he worries about the care Ricky is receiving, compared to what Ed was able to provide at home. He often leaves the group home in tears. Back home, his four-bedroom house feels empty. He has all the free time in the world, but he does not feel like going to a movie or out to dinner. He feels lonely, worried, and confused. With tears in his eyes, he muses, "I don't know how Ricky's going to do in this group home" and then "I don't know how I am going to do without him" (O'Hagan, 2008).

that older parents with schizophrenic adult children had more chronic grief than did parents of an adult child who died. Those who are able to come to terms with their responsibilities and integrate their grief into their lives are generally ablc to construct some positive meaning out of the illness experience. For instance, they may become involved in education and advocacy organizations, such as the National Alliance on Mental Illness (Ha, Hong, Seltzer, & Greenberg, 2008).

points to ponder

Do you have any friends or acquaintances who have been diagnosed with a mental disorder in their twenties or thirties? If so, how has this affected the family dynamics between parents and other siblings? What supports are available to this young adult? To their family, especially as their parents age? How do you think that coping with an adult child with mental illness may differ from dealing with physical illness?

Living with Chronic Illness or Disability Losses associated with one's own physical disability may have even greater adverse long-term consequences on a person's well-being than the loss of a loved one. One reason for this is that elders with disabilities continue to experience their effects on a daily basis. Additionally, they may lose not only their physical health but also their self-esteem and sometimes their support networks. Their self-confidence and sense of self as an active person who is interdependent with others is usually replaced by a new self-image as a "dependent" patient. Moreover, their informal family and community supports may decline if they lose their employment, social life, and relationships. Symbolic losses encompass no longer feeling attractive and desirable to others, and abandoning dreams of what their old age would be (Harvey, 1998; Hooyman & Kramer, 2006).

It is not surprising that elders with chronic disabilities are prone to depression, negative thinking, and a sense of being misunderstood, especially if others discount their grief. Feelings of depression can worsen other conditions, leading to greater cognitive and physical impairment. Their family caregivers, faced with physical, financial, and emotional burdens, may also become depressed, which then harms their relationships (Adamek, 2003; Katz and Yelin, 2001).

Facing a nearly continuous sense of loss, elders living daily with pain and illness must mourn their old self and then reconstruct their identity. In doing so, they may be able to discover new strengths, capacities, and positive meaning from how their life has changed. For example, stroke victims typically lose taken-for-granted freedoms, abilities, and ways of relating to others. But over time, they are often able to develop a new perspective on life, finding enjoyment and beauty in ordinary things and using phrases such as "fortunate to be alive" (Kelley, 1998; Pilkington, 1999).

Death of Loved Ones

When we think of the losses of old age, we inevitably think of death—and the process of dying. Consider how you respond to news of the death of a child compared to that of an older person. A child's death is more likely to be seen as an unimaginable tragedy, while an elder's death as to be expected, perhaps even a blessing. But death in old age can be devastating for the survivors, since death is the only loss that can never be recovered; it lasts forever.

Death of a Partner

A spouse or partner's death, no matter when or how it occurs, can adversely affect well-being. This is because it involves multiple losses of

- a many-layered relationship—best friend, lover, companion, and confidant;
- rituals, traditions, and interdependencies;
- a central part of the surviving partner's identity, forcing them to shift from "we" to "I";
- a shared past and a future of growing older together, such as traveling during retirement or reminiscing about a shared life; and
- social supports, particularly friends once shared as couple (Carr, 2003, 2008).

The closer the attachments and bonds between partners, the greater the distress, since the grieving partner must reconstruct a new concept of self as alone. One widow in a support group captured this difficulty by her comment: "My husband is just the person I need to help me get through his death." Both men and women, especially if the marriage was harmonious, cite lack of physical and emotional intimacy, loneliness, and being alone as their greatest problems, much greater than managing practical challenges of daily life. The terms widow and alone are almost synonymous, at least during the early phases of widowhood. Moreover, such loneliness may be intensified if the widowed person is isolated at home (Carr et al., 2000; Cicirelli, 2002; Richardson, 2005a; Utz, Carr, Nesse, & Wortman, 2002; Worden, 2002).

The death of a partner often triggers "cascading effects," bringing back sadness associated with earlier losses. Additionally, grief may interact with other age-associated physiological changes or chronic illness. Older widowed persons are more likely than younger widowed adults to become sick or die, often within the first six months of a partner's death. This occurs in part because their immune systems are weakened due to hormonal responses to the stress of loss. They tend to experience more symptoms of depression and anxiety, including thoughts of suicide. Dramatic changes in their moods, obsessive thoughts of the deceased, disorientation, memory problems, and difficulties concentrating are nearly nine times as high among the newly bereaved as among married individuals. Older widows and widowers more often visit physicians and use other forms of health care and are more likely to be hospitalized or spend time in a skilled nursing facility. The rates of such physical and mental problems and of death are higher for widowers than widows. However, over the long term (i.e., more than two years), the negative effects of a partner's death on physical and mental health generally decline (Carr, 2003, 2008; Hall & Irwin, 2001; Laditka & Laditka, 2003; Sonnega, 2002).

Despite the stresses, many widowed persons are highly resilient. Over time, they are able to balance the positive (e.g., involvement with neighbors, meeting new people, dating) and negative aspects (e.g., loneliness, "feeling down") of their lives. For example, some widows feel pride, self-confidence, and usefulness in mastering new roles related to finances or home maintenance. They may build stronger relationships with adult children, friends, and other relatives. And for women who have been in an abusive, neglectful, or tightly controlled relationship, their partner's death may give them newfound freedom to pursue new goals (Walter, 2003).

If you have ever visited a senior center or any type of long-term care facility, you probably noticed the predominance of single women. Here are some facts that underlie what you observed.

- Eighty-five percent of wives outlive their husbands, because women generally marry men older than themselves and live longer than men.
- More than three times as many women age 65 and older are widowed as are older men (40 and 13 percent, respectively).
- Among the oldest-old, these rates increase to 73 percent of women and 36 percent of men.
- Among elders of color, the proportion of widows is twice that of whites. Also, women of color are widowed earlier, which reflects the shorter life expectancy of men of color.
- Women also spend more years as a widow and less often remarry compared to men (AoA, 2012; Redfoot, Feinberg, & Houser, 2013).

Although overall rates of widowhood have declined since 1990, these statistics nevertheless convey that for women, widowhood can be an anticipated or normative life course transition. This means that many older women assume they will outlive husbands, which may serve to better prepare them for widowhood. When death was anticipated as a result of long illness, the partners may have been able to share good memories for the wife to draw upon after her husband dies and to talk about her future. Another strength for older women to draw upon is extensive networks of friends formed across the life course—and now largely composed of other widows. Such networks

The Experience of Widowhood

Darlene became a widow at age 58. Although she was too young to qualify for her husband's Social Security, her teenage children received a monthly benefit of approximately $1,000 per child. A successful career woman, Darlene sought refuge in her work, her friends, and her children. She learned new skills, such as home and car repairs, and appeared to be self-sufficient and "moving on" to her friends and children. During the day, she functioned well. It was only at the end of the day that she would be overcome by feelings of intense loneliness, hopelessness, and regret. At times, she felt overwhelmed at the thought of all the years ahead when she would bear both responsibilities and pleasure alone, lacking a partner with whom to share joys and sorrows. For more than two years, she cried every night before she fell asleep.

These older women regularly gather to play mah-jongg, laugh, and socialize.

appear to vary with social class, race, and culture. For example, Asian American widows are more likely to live with others and thus to have more active support systems than Caucasian widows, and African American women tend to have extended kinship networks throughout their lives, although they often live alone. Regardless of racial and cultural differences, women's greater likelihood of being socially connected can buffer some of the adverse effects of widowhood, including the increased risk of health problems and hospitalization that we described earlier. In general, personal feelings of control in their lives, an attitude of learning from experience, and involvement with others all seem to decrease negative effects of loss for widows (AARP, 2006; Cheng, 2006; Laditka & Laditka, 2003; Miller, Smerglia, & Bouche, 2004; Redfoot, Feinberg, & Houser, 2013; Rossi, Bisconti, & Bergeman, 2007).

Developing New Roles in Widowhood

Martha had always seen her role as wife and mother and left the "business" aspects of family life to her husband. Her "job" was to keep the home a comfortable place for him and their daughter. Widowed at age 65, she felt ill prepared to take on paying the bills and budgeting. She sought the advice of her banker on the best way to set up a bookkeeping system. After paying the bills and taking care of the Medicare paperwork for the past few years, she now sees herself as being in the role of "manager" for herself (even arranging home repairs) and is pleased with what she has learned.

Despite such social supports, older widows are generally worse off than widowers in terms of finances, years of education, legal problems, and prospects for remarriage. Women over age 65 who were economically dependent on their husbands throughout the marriage typically find their incomes drastically reduced—sometimes to the point of poverty. They may have depleted their savings by caring for a partner during a long illness or last years in a nursing home. But regardless of gender, income makes the most difference in how widowed men and women cope. Not surprisingly, higher income is associated with better bereavement outcomes (Schulz et al., 2006).

Men tend to have a tougher time emotionally adjusting to widowerhood than women do and are more likely to

- suffer from physical health problems and depression and to die within six months after their wife's death;
- complain of loneliness, make slower emotional recoveries, and be less satisfied with their lives;
- think about their wives nearly constantly—but typically not share their feelings with others;
- struggle with issues of self-identity (who are they if not husband and breadwinner?) and find it difficult to build new informal networks that substitute for the sociability they typically enjoyed in marriage; and
- remarry—in some instances, rather quickly.

You can probably think of some reasons that men have a tougher time. As we discussed earlier, men in the current cohort of oldest-old adults—the World War II or Korean War generation—were not socialized to express feelings. They focused largely on their jobs and depended on their wives to arrange their social lives. Accordingly, they may express their grief through action—keeping busy and solving problems. Because men's grieving pattern generally involves fewer words and emotions, it may not be evident and perceived as grief by others. Moreover, their need to grieve may even be met with discomfort by family, friends, or professionals who expect the man to "be strong and take charge" (Ajrouch, Blandon, & Antonucci, 2005; Berg, Hoffman, Hassing, McClearn, & Johansson, 2009; Martin & Doka, 2000).

Whether grief from death of a spouse is greater for the young than for the old is unclear. Because of the unanticipated nature of death, younger widows/widowers typically show more intense grief initially, but older partners generally experience emotional and physical distress longer. This may be the case because the end of

The Wife as the Social Organizer

At age 88, Harry had had three wives die; his first died in child birth when he was only in his thirties; the other two when he was age 77 and 82. He admitted that he needed a wife to help him have a social life. Now, he was dating a woman in her early eighties who lived in the same assisted living facility, although he had just been diagnosed with terminal cancer. Even as he faced death, he needed a woman in his life.

a lifelong relationship results in greater disorganization of roles, commitments, and daily routines, compared to younger bereaved partners. Older widows and widowers tend to have fewer social and community supports, especially if they have outlived friends, colleagues, and even adult children or if their family is at a geographic distance. Moreover, older people are more likely to experience other losses simultaneously (this is called **bereavement overload**), which may prolong their grief. Overall, the duration and intensity of grieving probably depend less on age per se and more on the quality and length of the partner relationship, the extent of social support after the death, and whether earlier inequities, such as being low-income, interfered with the development of resilience to adapt to loss in later life (Kastenbaum, 2004, 2008; Moss, Moss, & Hansen, 2001).

Another factor that may intensify loss among older widowed persons is that well-meaning friends and professionals may minimize a partner's death, commenting, "He lived a long life" or "She is free from her suffering." Such answers that look for the "silver lining" are not helpful to elders trying to redefine their lives in the context of multiple losses. In some instances of widowhood, there are disenfranchised grievers— LGBT partners, secret lovers, former partners, and others rejected by the immediate family who have to mourn their loss with little family or community support. Older adults' same-sex relationships may become public only with their partner's death, so they must deal with both their grief and their family's reaction to their sexual orientation. They may have to struggle alone with their mourning and feelings of ambivalence, guilt, and isolation. In other relationships that are not socially sanctioned, such as that of lover or former partner, the disenfranchised bereaved person may not be permitted even to participate in funeral or memorial arrangements or to reach out to the extended family for support.

Death of Siblings

As you learned in Chapter 6, sibling relationships represent the one family bond that can last a lifetime. As one older person acknowledged, "It is the one relationship that you are stuck with all of your life." Most adults will not lose a sibling to death until they are past 70 years of age. The sibling relationship in old age is characterized by a shared history, relatively equal relationships, and increasing closeness. As a result, siblings usually have very close bonds, whether positive or negative. When a sibling dies, there is not only the physical loss but also losses of shared family memories and stories, and the surviving sibling is painfully reminded of their own mortality. A sibling's death often realigns family roles and responsibilities. For example, if the middle sister who was always the peacemaker or nurturer of other family members dies, a surviving sibling may feel they need to assume that role (Connidis, 2001; Uhlenberg, 1996).

There is relatively little research on the impact of a sibling's death on the surviving sibs. Some studies suggest that bereaved siblings experience more health problems than a bereaved husband or wife does. In addition, social supports for bereaved siblings are often limited. This is because our society tends to minimize a sibling's loss, assuming that a partner's death is more difficult. Grieving siblings may feel pushed to the sidelines when others' attention during mourning goes to their sibling's partner or children. When siblings are overlooked as grievers, they may also experience disenfranchised grief (Hays, Gold, & Pieper, 1997; Moss et al., 2001; Walter, 1996).

Sibling relationships may change throughout the life course but often are especially important later in life.

How Professionals and Families Can Support the Grieving Process

Here are some suggestions of how professionals and families can be supportive of a person who is grieving. You may be able to draw upon this list when you know someone who has experienced the death of a loved one.

- Listen, without judging or giving advice, to the bereaved individual's expression of feelings—guilt, anger, and anxiety—rather than suggesting what he or she should feel or do.
- Realize that grieving is a natural response to loss that can be a lengthy and emotional roller coaster, not a fixed progression.
- Avoid endless chatter or simplistic statements ("I know just how you feel." "She is happier now." "God loved him more than you did." "You should feel better in six months." "You can marry again/you'll meet someone else").
- Encourage sharing of memories and stories, and resist telling your own stories.
- Provide time and space for the bereaved to cry, rather than telling them not to be sad.
- Listen carefully to the silences, to what is not said as well as what is said.
- Simply "to be there" for the bereaved—to be present—is sometimes the most helpful response.
- Identify concrete tasks by which to help—such as organizing meals, pet care, yard work, and house cleaning—so the bereaved has time and space to grieve.
- Respect gender and cultural/racial/religious differences in grieving.
- Encourage meditation, deep breathing, self-care, and exercise.

Time itself does not heal. Healing occurs through dealing with grief, which can be painful and exhausting. But it is important to recognize that some mourners never engage in "grief work," and that this cannot be forced.

Death of Friends

As we grow older, the number of friends' dying inevitably increases. In some instances, such as a childhood friendship with a history of memories intertwined over many years, a friend may have been a closer confidant than a partner. With a friend's death, older adults lose a past that can never be recaptured with anyone else. Because women especially value close friendships, it is not surprising that they express more grief over a friend's death than do their male counterparts, who tend to have fewer intimate friendships.

Friends are typically accorded fewer rights as mourners than are distant members of the deceased's family, making this another form of disenfranchised grief. Indeed, the friend "who was always there for us" may not be recognized in obituaries or eulogies nor be included in family grief rituals. This may be particularly poignant when the extended friendship networks of LGBT individuals are excluded from the formal mourning process. We know relatively little about the cumulative effects of numerous friends' deaths in old age on physical or mental well-being (Archer, 1999).

Approaching One's Own Death and the Dying Process

Although we know that aging does not cause death and younger people also die, it is not surprising that dying is associated with old age in Western society. This is because older adults constitute the majority of the total deaths each year, as a result of medical advances and increased life expectancy. In preindustrial societies, death rates were high in childhood and youth, and parents could expect as many as half of their children to die before the age of 10. As we saw in Chapter 3, most deaths now occur from chronic disease. Accordingly, death in old age has come to be viewed as a predictable event, the completion of the life cycle.

Western societies tend to view death as an unnatural event that is to be fought off as long as medically possible. Prior to the twentieth century, the period of time spent dying was relatively short, due to infectious diseases

The Importance of Cross-Generational Friendship Networks

Recognizing that one's age peers will die as we age, Maggie Kuhn, the founder of the intergenerational advocacy group Gray Panthers, urged adults to make sure they had some younger friends, who could be there to support them in old age. As she aged, she always lived in intergenerational households, whose members then cared for her as she was dying.

points to ponder

What thoughts, feelings, or images do you experience when you hear that a baby has died? What about the death of a young adult just graduating from college? A 50-year-old mother whose last child has left home? A 7-year-old who is hit by a car while crossing the street? An 85-year-old who has advanced dementia? A 93-year-old who dies in their sleep? What variables or factors might explain differences in your reactions? What does your reaction tell you about how you deal with death and dying?

and catastrophic events, which typically brought death on suddenly. With improved diagnostic techniques, early detection, and life-prolonging technology, individuals with terminal and chronic illnesses are often kept alive long beyond the point at which they might have died naturally and peacefully in the past. Since medicine focuses on "curing" diseases, physicians and families may see death as a defeat, not as an inevitable and natural culmination of life.

The surroundings in which death occurs have also changed as medical interventions to keep people alive have expanded. In preindustrial societies, most people died at home, with the entire community often involved in rituals surrounding the death. Today, about 90 percent of adults indicate that they want to die at home, without pain, surrounded by friends and family. Yet most adults experience the exact opposite: around 60 percent of all deaths—regardless of age—occur in hospitals where aggressive and costly life-prolonging treatment is common. African American and less-educated older adults are even more likely than other groups to die in a hospital. Some recent data, however, indicate that more of the oldest-old are dying at home rather than in a hospital, although this may reflect efforts to cut hospital costs through discharging patients earlier than in the past rather than quality end-of-life care (Gruneir et al., 2007; Span, 2012; Weitzen, Teno, Fennell, & Mor, 2003).

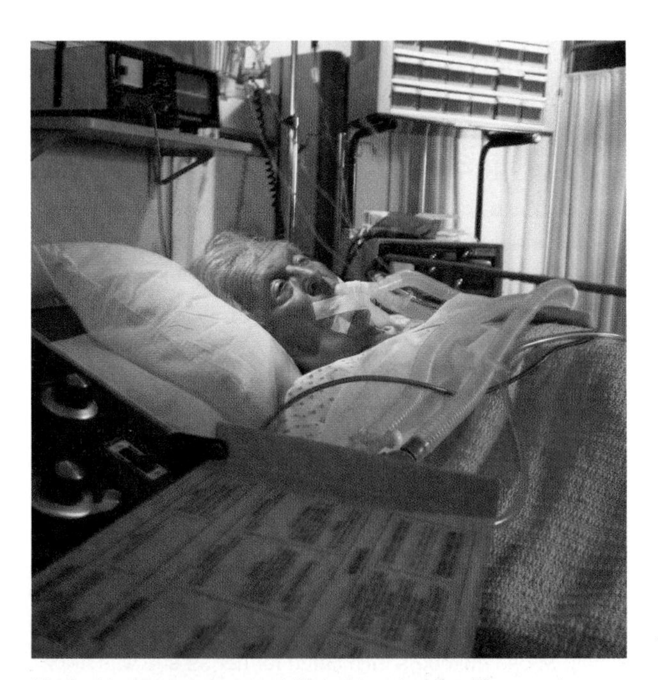

Medical technology has contributed to extending life expectancy, but not always quality of life.

A reason why many elders do not experience death in settings of their choice is that most people, if they discuss death at all, do so on a rational, intellectual level. They rarely talk openly and prepare for their own deaths or those of loved ones. Dying is one of the few events in life certain to occur, but for which we rarely plan. Both acceptance and denial reflect the basic paradox surrounding death: we recognize its universality but cannot comprehend or imagine our own dying. However, the oldest-old generally think and talk in a matter-of-fact way about death—even joke about it—and appear to be less afraid of their own death compared to midlife and young-old adults, who have "unfinished business" and goals they still want to accomplish (Cicirelli, 2006).

points to ponder

We may spend more time planning for a two-week vacation than we will for our last two weeks of life. What factors might explain this? What does this suggest about your own ability—or that of your loved ones—to talk about death and dying?

A number of factors may explain the apparent paradox of elders' lessened fear of death as it approaches. If they have internalized the ageism in our society, older persons may see their lives as having ever-decreasing social value and lower any positive expectations of the future. If they have lived past the age they expected to, they may view themselves as living on "borrowed time." In general, older adults accept the inevitability of their own death, even though they tend to be concerned about its impact on loved ones. Regardless of age, however, a near-universal fear is the suffering and pain of dying—not death itself (Cicirelli, 2002, 2006; Lamberg, 2002; Thorson & Powell, 2000; Tomer & Eliason, 2000).

The Dying Process

Extensive research and clinical practice have addressed how to minimize the pain and suffering of dying. For many years, the "stages of dying" was the primary framework for understanding this process. Advanced by Kübler-Ross (1969, 1981), this model identifies five stages that represent a form of coping with the **dying process**.

1. Shock and denial over the prognosis of death
2. Anger ("why me?"), resentment, and guilt about what is happening
3. Bargaining, such as trying to make a deal with God; if I become a better person, will you let me live longer?
4. Depression and withdrawal from others, including close family members
5. Adjustment and acceptance of one's death

Although Kübler-Ross cautioned that these stages were not fixed or universal, she nevertheless encouraged health care providers to help their patients advance through them to achieve the final stage.

This widely debated perspective has been empirically rejected. Family members and health care providers are now encouraged to be cautious about implying that the dying person must or "should" move through each stage. Dying is more "messy" than may be suggested by these sequential linear stages. Some people remain stuck at an early stage, while others move readily into accommodating the reality of their death. For others, there is no sequencing; the dying person moves back and forth across a wide range of sometimes contradictory feelings: guilt, protest, anger, fearfulness, and despair intermeshed with humor, hope, acceptance, and gratitude (Hooyman & Kramer, 2006; Walter, 2003; Weiss, 2001).

points to **ponder**

If you have experienced the dying process of someone close to you or for whom you provided care, what phases—if any—did you observe? Did you view the dying process as flowing, alternating between different stages, or moving in a sequential manner?

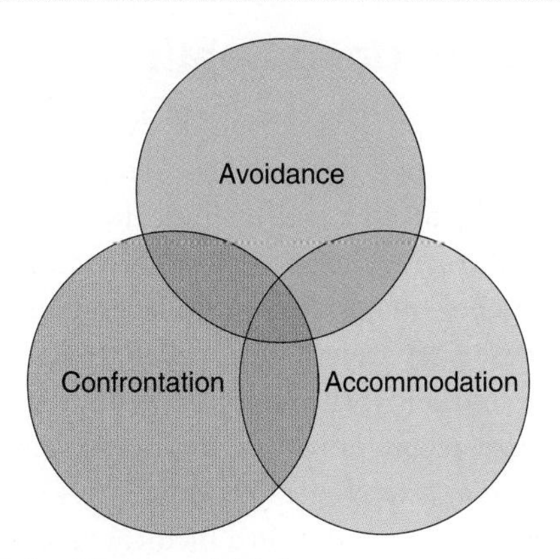

FIGURE 9.1 Clusters of Grief

Similar to the grief process associated with other losses, there are clusters of feelings typically experienced by a dying person. These can be broadly conceptualized as avoidance, confrontation, and accommodation. Remember, however, that there are exceptions and variations to these clusters.

1. **Avoidance** encompasses a wide range of feelings, which often occur when a person first learns they are dying:
   - Shock, numbness, disbelief (how can this be happening to me?), denial, and inability to comprehend the situation
   - Fear, anxiety, and dread
   - Attempt to gain a sense of control by gathering facts about the disease through the Internet or getting a second medical opinion
2. **Confrontation,** or trying to change the "death sentence one has been given," includes the following:
   - Guilt and blaming oneself or others
   - Helplessness, panic, confusion, powerlessness, and an intense sadness
   - Unfocused anger, rage, and despair
   - Loss of faith, a sense of injustice, or becoming disillusioned with religious beliefs
3. **Accommodation**:
   - Accepting the reality of death and integrating it into one's identity
   - Saying good-bye
   - Organizing a will, other legal documents, and possessions
   - Gradually letting go of the physical world
   - Drawing upon one's religious or spiritual beliefs

Desire for a Good Death

Just as most people fear a painful dying process, they also wish for a good death. This preference highlights the importance of how end-of-life care is provided. As you learned earlier, older people typically die where they least want to be—in hospitals or skilled nursing facilities, often because they experienced an unexpected medical crisis. Despite their wishes, they may find themselves in intensive care, where providers use life-sustaining treatments that may exacerbate the elder's suffering. There are often few opportunities in a medical crisis to discuss with health care providers their end-of-life preferences for a good death and quality of life. When there is time to do so, here is what most people want: respectful affirmations of their identity and the meaning and value of their life; participation in the decision-making process; and appropriate and adequate care.

According to the Institute of Medicine, which often recommends national guidelines for medical practice, a "good death" is characterized by the dying person's

- ability to maintain dignity and reasonable control over what happens,
- understanding of what to expect physically and emotionally,
- adequate control of pain and other symptoms,
- choice about where death occurs,
- access to information and expertise of whatever kind is needed,
- supports to minimize spiritual and emotional suffering,
- access to hospice or palliative (or comfort) care in any location, and
- sufficient time to say good-bye (Dula & Williams, 2005; Richardson & Barusch, 2006).

If these principles and guidelines were fully followed, health care at end-of-life would be radically changed in our society. Fortunately, palliative care and hospice have emerged as ways to ensure a "good death" for older adults who are aware of and choose these options, and there is growing agreement that the dying person's self-determination and right to be free from physical pain are essential to humane care. In fact, the U.S. Supreme Court ruled in 1997 that Americans have a constitutional right to palliative care.

Guidelines for Health Care Providers to Ensure a Good Death

- Focus on the person who has the disease, not on the disease.
- Promote self-determination, particularly regarding pain management.
- Support autonomy: the answer to "who should decide" is "the patient decides."
- Honor personal beliefs.
- Inform patients of institutional or personnel policies that affect their end-of-life care preferences.
- Allow informed consent—a written or oral document that states reasons for treatment, its benefits, risks, and alternatives—and provide the patient with adequate information to make decisions.
- Empower the patient to make decisions based on their assessment of quality versus quantity of life (Lee, 2009).

End-of-Life Care: Palliative Care and Hospice

Palliative care is for patients of all ages with life-limiting illnesses; it focuses on relief of pain and other symptoms by addressing the patient's emotional, social, and spiritual needs, not on lifesaving measures. Interdisciplinary teams use both medications, especially pain management, and counseling to help patients cope with symptoms. It can be delivered in hospitals, skilled nursing facilities, home care, and hospice. Palliative care is often considered to be the same as hospice care, but there are some important distinctions between the two: palliative care is about making the most of life with a serious illness and can be delivered while the person is receiving treatment and can still recover; hospice care is typically delivered to a person with less than six months to live and is oriented to a good death, although there are some exceptions to the six-month eligibility criteria. Even though the two services differ somewhat, hospice is a primary system for the delivery of palliative care (Center to Advance Palliative Care, 2011; National Consensus Project for Quality Palliative Care, 2009; Rafinski, 2011).

Hospice aims to help individuals who are beyond medicine's curative power to maintain personal dignity and some control over their dying process, often by remaining in familiar surroundings. In addition to pain management, hospice offers integrated physical, medical, emotional, and spiritual care to dying persons, their family, and other informal supports. Hospice is not always a "place," but a philosophy of care; it is offered primarily in the dying person's home, but also in hospital and long-term care settings, such as skilled nursing or assisted living facilities. In fact, the availability of hospice care along with state funding for home care and caregiver support often determines whether an older person is able to die at home (Muramatsu, Hoyem, Yin, & Campbell, 2008).

Hospice professionals and volunteers, working as an interdisciplinary team, try to design supportive environments in which people can tell their life stories, resolve relationships with family and friends, and find meaning in their deaths. Listening to and touching the dying person, enjoying music and art, and celebrations of special events such as birthdays and weddings are all encouraged. For those who value spirituality, the staff supports them in their quest for meaning and dignity in the last stage of life.

Distinguishing Characteristics of Hospice

- Focus on quality of life and a good death
- Service availability 24 hours per day, 7 days per week, as needed
- Respite care and support for the family
- Management of pain and other physical symptoms
- Full information and psychological, social, and spiritual counseling for patients and their families
- Physician direction of services delivered by a multidisciplinary team
- Coordination among providers of skilled services (home healthcare, hospitals, skilled nursing facilities) and homemaker/personal care services
- Use of volunteers as team members
- Inpatient care when needed
- Bereavement counseling for family and friends

Culturally Appropriate End-of-Life Care

Some racial disparities persist even into end-of-life care and death. Low-income individuals and persons of color—particularly African Americans and Latinos—are often underserved by both palliative care programs and hospice and more likely to die in hospitals. This is of concern since groups such as African Americans have a higher overall incidence of death from cancer, inadequate pain treatment, and greater financial strain. African Americans and Latinos are less likely than other groups to complete legal arrangements or spend time talking with physicians about their end-of-life care preferences. In some instances, they prefer to die in a hospital with the best possible medical care rather than receiving hospice care at home; in others, they may not have adequate information about end-of-life choices (Cohen, 2008; Gert & Burr, 2008; Kwak, Haley, & Chiraboga, 2008).

There are historical, economic, cultural, and religious reasons that many of the current cohort of elders of color prefer aggressive life-saving treatments in a hospital setting. They may mistrust health care providers based on past discriminatory experiences with inadequate care earlier in life. They may have heard of examples of unethical research conducted on persons of color in the past. Or they may think that palliative care and hospice mean that providers do not value their lives or are "giving up" on them. Aggressive medical treatment ("fighting while going down" as an expected part of life's ongoing struggle) is often viewed as a sign of respect among older African Americans, even if it means feeding tubes, pain, and loss of life savings (Payne, Lackan, Eschbach, et al., 2009; Welch, Teno, & Mor, 2005).

Another factor is they may view hospice as not respecting their cultural and personal values. For example, African American elders are more likely than whites to believe that God is the ultimate decision-maker regarding

Facing Death on One's Own Terms

Ruth, age 85, was diagnosed with incurable cancer. She told her family and doctor that she wanted to live long enough (five months) to see her first granddaughter married. Her doctor arranged for low-dose chemotherapy that did not cause much discomfort, and she experienced a remission. After her granddaughter's wedding, the doctors found that the cancer had returned and spread. Her response was that she was now ready to die. She received excellent palliative care, lived three months without pain with the help of morphine, and was alert almost to the end, sharing memories and saying good-bye to her family.

The Comfort Provided By Hospice Care

Three months of chemotherapy followed by six weeks of radiation was not working for Mr. Frank. His last hope was a stem cell transplant, but those prospects were dimming each day as he became weaker. Mr. Frank decided that he did not want to spend his final days in a losing battle with his rapidly advancing and painful lymphoma. He preferred to be as comfortable as possible by leaving the hospital and returning home.

Mr. Frank and his wife, Jean, contacted a local hospice that helped them set up a range of services at home that would assist both of them through the final months of his life. A nurse and physician were assigned to his care. The hospice staff trained Jean, friends, and family in ways to make him more comfortable, such as using tiny ice chips to help him deal with his extremely dry throat and mouth. They also taught Jean how to tell when Mr. Frank's pain was increasing, so that he could be given a high dose of morphine before it became unbearable.

The hospice team social worker talked with Mr. Frank about resolving some issues with his daughter, who held considerable anger toward her father. When the hospice team estimated that Mr. Frank would probably die in three days, they encouraged Jean to contact family and friends who lived at a distance so that they would have time to visit and say their good-byes. In those last three days, Mr. Frank was lucid and able to talk, laugh, and cry with those who loved him, including his daughter.

His family and friends all commented later that they felt Mr. Frank had a "good death." They appreciated being able to be part of his peaceful death in the comfort and familiar surroundings of his home. Mr. Frank's daughter was especially grateful for the opportunity to reconcile with her father before he died. The hospice social worker kept in touch with Jean for a year after her husband's death, encouraging her to express her grief and learn new coping skills.

the time, manner, and place of death. They tend to have more religious prohibitions against speeding up the timing of death by limiting life-sustaining treatment. Health care providers must take account of such historical, institutional, cultural, and religious and spiritual differences in order to ensure a good death for all their patients while not conveying that they are giving up hope. Fortunately, more programs are using culturally appropriate methods for communication and education about end-of-life care options, particularly with Latinos and African Americans. The Balm of Gilead Project and Harlem Palliative Care Network, end-of-life care programs that originated in African American communities, are examples of culturally competent approaches to hospice care that are more likely to be trusted (Condon, Miller, Quasem, & Looney, 2008; Dula & Williams, 2005; Hampton, 2008; Johnson, Elbert-Avila, & Tulsky, 2005; Washington, 2007).

The influence of culture on the meaning and experience of death and dying can affect pain management, advance care planning, and grief counseling. Cultures and religions vary greatly in their communication or "truth-telling" of a patient's diagnosis and prognosis, end-of-life preferences, and use of life-sustaining technologies. Local traditions, customs, core spiritual values, and family

Culturally Competent Palliative Care Programs

The Balm of Gilead Project in Alabama was created to meet the palliative care needs of low-income African Americans. It aims to be responsive to the community's economic and social realities, where dying patients often lack appropriate caregivers to remain at home and where distrust of the medical system is pervasive. The Balm of Gilead offers an array of services to address the holistic needs associated with terminal illness in each of its stages and treatment settings. These include:

- Hospital-based services—with an inpatient palliative care unit, palliative care consultation, and educational efforts with hospital staff focused on pain management
- Home care services
- Long-term residential care through palliative care at a local skilled nursing home
- Community outreach and education involving care teams, civic groups, faith communities, and education

The Harlem Palliative Care Network assumes that an effective palliative care program must come from, and be part of, the community. Organizers first established a base of expertise in palliative medicine at a community hospital and networked with community organizations—churches, social groups, and nursing homes. These networks helped to identify patients and families with advanced illnesses who could benefit from palliative interventions, including pain management early in the course of an illness. The network also provides nonmedical services to support patients and families emotionally and spiritually.

dynamics all influence communication about illness and dying. In some non-Western cultures, such as East Indian and Chinese, relatives may ask the doctor to provide them with relevant information about a terminal disease but not to disclose such information to the patient. Health care providers may view this withholding of the truth from the dying person as a problem, but for the relatives, it is an act of caring and love. In these cultures, promoting the patient's welfare and avoiding harm to them are central values, which cause them to want to preserve the patient's hope. This contrasts with Western cultural values on individual decision-making and self-determination in end-of-life care. Traditional gender roles in some cultures, where men are the primary decision-makers or view themselves as protecting their wives, may also affect communication about dying. Understanding cultural, spiritual, and gender differences is essential for health care providers seeking to communicate effectively and in a culturally appropriate way with family members and dying individuals. These communication challenges are even greater when family members do not speak English. Interpreters are essential at end-of-life care, but may not convey the nuanced meaning of a family or group's approach to death and dying (Chaturvedi, Loisell, & Chandra, 2010; Sharma & Dy, 2011; Thornton, Pham, Engelberg, Jackson, & Curtis, 2009).

Guidelines for Communicating about End-of-Life Care in Diverse Population

- Create opportunities for the patient to be involved: Ask the patient "How would you prefer to get information?" Some patients want to know everything about their condition; others prefer that their doctors talk primarily to their families. Use trained medical interpreters and take time to meet with them before and after meetings with the patient and the family in order to be clear about accurate translation.
- Attend to spirituality and religion: "What is important for us to know about your faith and spiritual needs? How can we support your needs and cultural practices?"
- Assess the patient's preferences for family involvement: "How should decisions be made about your care? What role should your family play in decision-making?"
- Emphasize that you, the patient, and their family will all try to work together to achieve the best possible care.
- Reiterate that palliative care does not mean "giving up on the patient."
- Respect the desire for more aggressive care when it is medically possible (Sharma & Dy, 2011).

The Right to Die

You have learned that health care providers now give increased attention to the ways in which people choose to die, including pain management and whether aggressive treatment should be withheld. We turn now to the **right to die**, which refers to helping someone die as they wish. Whether others have a right to help people die a "good death," and under what conditions, has been discussed throughout history. The **Dying Person's Bill of Rights**, developed nearly 40 years ago, states that individuals have the right to personal dignity and privacy; informed participation (having their end-of-life choices respected by health care professionals); and considerate, respectful service and competent care during their dying process. Moreover, the right to die with dignity and without pain is currently supported by laws, public policies, and clinical practice more than it was at the time the Dying Person's Bill of Rights was passed.

But debates about the ethical, social, and legal issues raised by the right-to-die movement have intensified with increased medical advances to prolong life and the legal recognition of patients' decision-making autonomy. Proponents of the right to die maintain that prolonging excruciating pain simply to keep a person alive in a hopeless situation threatens a person's dignity and does not serve public interests. Notably, the American Geriatrics Society has clearly stated that dying persons should be provided with opportunities to make the circumstances of their dying consistent with their preferences and values. But decisions about how people die become even more complex when an elder is mentally incompetent, such as suffering from advanced dementia, or is comatose. As noted above, cross-cultural differences also affect how life-sustaining treatment and palliative care are interpreted and the value and respect accorded to elders' wishes (American Geriatric Society, 2007).

Hastened Death and Physician Aid-in-Dying **Euthanasia** refers to a painless or peaceful death. However, advocates of the right to die generally use the term **hastened death**—what they view as speeding up the inevitable—rather than euthanasia. Hastened death can be passive (allowing death) or active (causing death). In **passive euthanasia**, treatment is withdrawn, and nothing is done to prolong the patient's life artificially, such as using a feeding tube or ventilator. Stopping medical interventions (this is also known as physician aid-in-dying) allows the natural dying process to occur, but no active steps are taken to bring about death. Medications to relieve pain are sometimes given that may hasten death, but the object is to relieve suffering, not to bring about death. Withholding or withdrawing useless or unwanted medical treatments, or providing adequate pain relief, even if it hastens death, have been determined to be legal and ethical and are generally accepted by the vast majority of Americans.

Active euthanasia refers to deliberate steps taken to bring about someone else's death by administering a lethal injection or some other means. It can be voluntary (at the dying person's request) or involuntary (without consent). Sometimes called mercy killing, the legality of active euthanasia has been tested by several highly controversial court cases, voter initiatives, and state legislation. You may have heard about instances of active euthanasia in the media in which a partner seeks to relieve their loved one's pain.

The Controversial Dr. Kevorkian and Assisted Suicide

You may have heard of Dr. Jack Kevorkian, whose assistance to over 100 people in ending their lives was widely publicized. In the first case, involving a woman with Alzheimer's disease, the court dismissed the murder charges on the grounds that no law in Michigan prohibited assisting in a death. Subsequently, the legislature passed a bill to stop Dr. Kevorkian's activities. While prior cases were dismissed on the grounds that the law against physician-assisted suicide (PAS) is unconstitutional, Kevorkian was charged with second-degree murder in 1999. He was sentenced to 10–25 years in prison because he directly administered a lethal injection to an adult in the final stages of amyotrophic lateral sclerosis (ALS) rather than the dying individual taking the final action. Although controversial, Kevorkian's crusade to legalize active euthanasia pushed the debate on PAS to the forefront of public awareness. He was paroled in 2007 with the stipulation that he must abstain from assisting terminally ill patients and that he could not provide care for anyone age 62 or older, or anyone with a disability. Dr. Kevorkian lectured widely since his parole, seeking to persuade states to change their assisted suicide laws. He died in a hospital in 2011.

Family Members Supporting the Right to Die

In some instances, family members may assist their loved one to end their life. Consider the situation described by John West, in his book *The Last Goodnights*, whose 74-year-old father asked him to help him commit suicide. He recognized that his father, a renowned psychiatrist, would know what he wanted. So when the cancer had spread everywhere, his father said "It's time." Then John helped his father take a cocktail of pills, and by morning, he was dead. Months later, his mother, who had Alzheimer's disease, osteoporosis, and emphysema, asked for the same kind of help. For more than a decade, he kept the secret to himself (West, 2010)

A subject of intense controversy is **physician-assisted suicide (PAS) or physician-assistance-in-dying**, which removes the connotation of suicide. PAS occurs when someone else provides the means by which a terminally ill individual who chooses to can end his or her life. For example, a physician may prescribe medication, typically barbiturates, knowing that an individual intends to use it to end his or her life. But it is the dying person who decides when and whether to take the medication.

Conflicting state rulings and pressure from right-to-die advocacy organizations brought the issue of PAS to the U.S. Supreme Court. In June 1997, the Court ruled that there is no constitutional or fundamental "right to die." However, states can decide on their own to pass laws allowing PAS. This was the case in Oregon, the first state to legalize PAS as a choice for patients who are diagnosed by two doctors as having less than six months to live. As of this writing, four states have legalized PAS, although one requires a court order. Debates among medical care providers, lawmakers, and patient rights advocates continue, but public opinion overall remains in support of physician assistance-in-dying for terminally ill patients in severe pain, even if it is not legalized. Most Americans believe that forcing people to endure prolonged suffering is inhumane and cruel, although this pattern shifts among people with conservative religious affiliations (Lee, 2009).

The increased visibility of right-to-die legislation, court rulings, and individual cases means that more people know about their legal rights and have thought about what they might choose for themselves or other family members when faced with a terminal illness. It has also raised the issue of training health care providers in end-of-life and palliative care.

Is This Assisted Suicide?

An 89-year-old man was in tremendous pain from the end stages of pancreatic cancer. He had been diagnosed only six weeks earlier, and nothing could be done to halt the spread of this deadly cancer. His daughter flew him cross-country to her home in order to provide daily care and to have his beloved grandsons nearby. The day before his 90th birthday, he cried out for relief from the pain. His daughter called the hospice doctor, who delivered a bottle of morphine to her home. He advised the daughter to start a heavy dosage right after dinner. While leaving, he gently said to her, "and if he does not wake up, that may be a blessing." The next morning, her father did awaken, but he was disoriented, appeared to have suffered a mild stroke during the night, and was crying from the pain. Anxious to relieve the pain, his loving daughter gave him another dose of morphine. Within a few hours, he was dead. Did the morphine hasten his death? What was the doctor's role? The daughter's? What is your reaction in reading this?

As you learned earlier, health care providers must also be sensitive to cultural differences related to end-of-life choices and decision-making (Chaturvedi, Loisell, & Chandra, 2010).

Patients' Legal Options regarding Their End-of-Life Care An array of legal arrangements now allow people to make known their preferences about how they want to die. Here are the most frequently used ones.

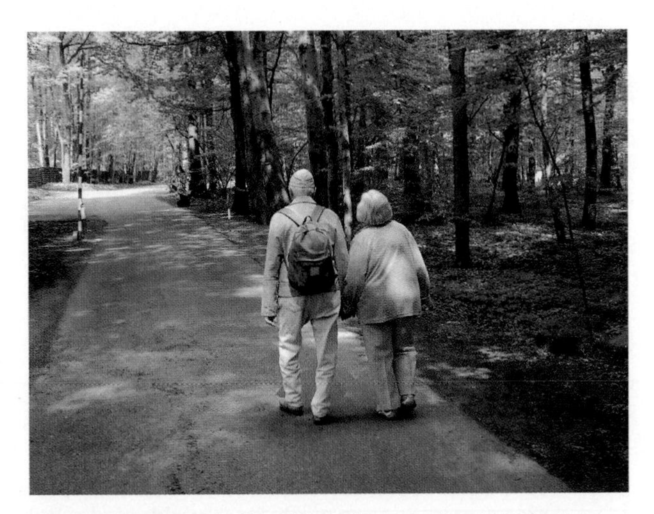

Elders can make their end-of-life preferences known to family members and health care providers.

- **Advance directives**, legal in all 50 states, refer to patients' oral and written instructions about end-of-life care and someone to speak on their behalf if they become incompetent.
- The **Patient Self-Determination Act**, a federal law, requires health care facilities that receive Medicaid and Medicare funds to inform patients in writing of their rights to create advance directives regarding how they want to live or die. But this law does not require a patient to actually take action to make an advanced directive.
- A **living will** is the most common type of advance directive. An individual's wishes about medical treatment are put into writing in the case of irreversible terminal illness or the prognosis of a permanent vegetative (unconscious) state.
- **"Five Wishes"** is another example of a living will. Unlike other advance directives, Five Wishes is written in everyday language and is designed to encourage conversation about broader questions related to health care decisions than those covered in most advance directive documents. It is available in 26 languages and Braille, and meets the legal requirements for an advance directive in 42 states.
- **Health care power of attorney** designates a surrogate decision-maker when there is no living will and the patient is not mentally competent. This person has a duty to act according to the patient's known wishes. If those are not known, the surrogate must act according to what they consider to be in the patient's best interest.

Dying persons and their families can access their state's particular law and forms for living wills through the Web sites of national organizations such as Compassion

points to ponder

Have you and the people you love ever discussed how to die, your preferences, and fears? Perhaps with your parents or if you have a partner or adult children? If not, how could you initiate such a discussion? Do you ever talk about death—your own or that of others—with someone else? If so, with whom do you discuss it? What kinds of concerns, fears, hopes, or questions do you express? How comfortable are you with such conversations about death? What might increase your feelings of comfort?

Compassion and Choices

Compassion and Choices is now the largest and most comprehensive end-of-life organization in the country, with over 60 chapters and over 30,000 members. It seeks to support, educate, and advocate for choice and care at the end of life, while pursuing legal reform to promote pain control, advance directives, and legalized physician assistance-in-dying. Its Web site (http://www.compassionandchoices.org/) is a comprehensive resource for information about the right-to-die movement, and a user-friendly place to download advance directive packages geared to the laws and regulations of a particular state.

and Choices, local hospitals, state attorneys general's offices, their physicians, or the Internet.

This discussion about the complex issues surrounding end-of-life care highlight that advancements in medical technology are not matched by refinements in the law and the ethics of using technology to keep people alive. This is the case even though **bioethics**, or medical ethics—which focuses on procedural approaches to questions about death, dying, and medical decision-making—has grown in the past 50 years. Assisted suicide raises not only complex ethical and legal dilemmas, but also resource allocation issues. Both policy-makers and service providers face the challenge of how to balance an individual client's needs for personal autonomy with the community's demand to conserve health care resources and funding.

Regardless of the laws, however, some elders and their families will continue to make decisions on their own to hasten death. Internet resources on dying, including information on how to hasten death, foster the debates taking place at the grassroots level and empower families and their older relatives. Such Internet resources, which once were unimaginable, will increase in number and detail in the future. These legal and ethical debates—whether in courtrooms, ethics committees, or cyberspace—translate into daily practice and hard choices for those who are caring for chronically ill and dying elders. Questions of who should control decisions about life and death will continue to be argued philosophically and legally, but it is doctors, nurses, social workers, and families who will be faced with the tough clinical decisions for timely practical solutions.

Will Boomers Redefine End-of-Life Care?

Baby boomers, who are better educated and more accustomed to having control over their lives than previous cohorts of elders, are more likely to complete advance directives and to be outspoken about their end-of-life preferences. As boomers seek to make decisions about remaining at home to die, our society will be faced with the question of how to allocate community services such as hospice and home care in the face of shrinking public resources for such programs.

summary

This chapter emphasizes that losses in old age encompass more than death. Losses may result even from positive changes, but most often when a person feels little control over decisions about changes—from relocation and retirement to caring for someone with chronic illness or coping with one's own disabilities. In some instances, such as caring for a person with dementia or an adult child with disabilities, older adults experience chronic sorrow that is continuing. Or some elders experience disenfranchised grief, such as when a gay or lesbian partner dies and others do not recognize the legitimacy of the loss.

Most older adults are remarkably resilient and able to reconstruct their altered lives to create meaning, purpose, and self-esteem, despite their loss. They often find new ways to be involved in their communities and culture, through voluntarism, civic engagement, or care for family members. In doing so, they strengthen their inner capacity to derive life's lessons and meaning from their losses. But even what may appear to be relatively minor losses, such as the move of a supportive neighbor or the closure of a local senior center, can negatively impact elders' physical and mental well-being.

While loss through death is typically the hardest, its magnitude varies markedly depending upon the nature of the relationship. Although the death of a partner/spouse is often the most devastating, the death of siblings and friends, which may be minimized by others, can also have negative impacts on well-being. There are numerous challenges associated with facing one's own death—cycling through the waves of grief, coping with end-of-life pain through palliative care or hospice, and making one's wishes for end-of-life care known through legal documents, such as advance directives. Fortunately, health care providers along with the general public are more attentive to ensuring a "good death," although far too many elders still die in pain and in hospitals rather than in their homes and are unable to maintain decision-making control about their end-of-life care. We hope that this discussion has been useful to you not only if you work with older adults in the future, but also to you as you face issues of loss with your own families and friends.

key terms

active euthanasia, p. 276
advance directives, p. 277
anticipatory grief, p. 263
bereavement overload, p. 268
bioethics, p. 278
chronic sorrow, p. 263
Compassion and Choices, p. 278
disenfranchised grief, p. 263
Dying Person's Bill of Rights, p. 275
dying process, p. 271
euthanasia, p. 275
"Five Wishes", p. 277
hastened death, p. 275
health care power of attorney, p. 277
Hospice, p. 272
life review, p. 258
living will, p. 277
palliative care, p. 272
passive euthanasia, p. 276
Patient Self-Determination Act, p. 277
physician-assisted suicide (PAS) or physician-assistance-in-dying, p. 276
right to die, p. 275

review questions

1. Identify three types of loss other than death that many older adults are likely to face.
2. Define the concept of "right to die."
3. What are three distinguishing characteristics of hospice?
4. What are the primary ways that hospice differs from other types of palliative care programs?
5. Define the terms chronic sorrow and disenfranchised grief. Cite one way that each of these differs from other types of grieving.
6. Discuss three ways that women's experience with widowhood often differs from men's.
7. If you have a friend or relative who is grieving the death of someone they love, what are three things you could do that they are likely to experience as helpful?
8. List three clusters of grief typically experienced by a person who is dying.
9. Identify three characteristics of what is considered to be a "good death" by the Institute of Medicine.
10. Define hastened death, physician aid-in-dying, and physician-assisted suicide.
11. List three legal options that adults have regarding their end-of-life care.

media resources

View

- Death of a Spouse
- Grieving a Spouse, Parts I and II
- Planning for the End of Life

Read

- Place of Death of Patients under Hospice Care
- The Elderly Who Are Widowed
- Gordon, Suzanne and Timothy McCall. Healing in a Hurry: Hospitals in the Managed-Care Age.

references

AARP. (2006). Looking at act II of women's lives: Thriving and striving from 45 on. *The AARP Foundation Women's Leadership Circle Study.* Retrieved September 21, 2013, from http://assets.aarp.org/rgcenter/general/wlcresearch.pdf.

Adamek, M. (2003). Late life depression in nursing home residents: Social work opportunities to prevent, educate and alleviate. In B. Berkman & L. Harootyan (Eds.), *Social work and health care in an aging society.* New York: Springer.

Administration on Aging (AoA). (2012). *A profile of older Americans: 2011.* Retrieved September 21, 2013, from http://www.aoa.gov/AoARoot/Aging_Statistics/Profile/2012/docs/2012profile.pdf.

Ahmed, I. (2003). *Coping with the burden of caregiving.* Paper presented at the Conference on Aging and Diversity, University of Hawaii, Honolulu, June.

Ajrouch, K., Blandon, A., & Antonucci, T. (2005). Social networks among men and women: The effects of age and socioeconomic status. *Journals of Gerontology, 60B,* S311–S317.

Albinsson, L., & Strang, P. (2003). Existential concerns of families of late-stage dementia patients: Questions of freedom, choices, isolation, death, and meaning. *Journal of Palliative Medicine, 6,* 225–235.

American Geriatrics Society. (2007). *The care of dying patients.* Washington, DC: Author.

Archer, J. (1999). *The nature of grief: The evolution and psychology of reactions to loss.* New York: Routledge.

Berg, A. I., Hoffman, L., Hassing, L. B., McClearn, G. E., & Johansson, B. (2009). What matters, and what matters most, for change in life satisfaction in the oldest-old? A study over 6 years among individuals 80+. *Aging and Mental Health, 13*(2), 191–201.

Butler, R. N. (1963). The life review: An interpretation of reminiscence in the aged. *Psychiatry, 26,* 65–76.

Capezuti, E., Boltz, M., Renz, S., Hoffman, D., & Norman, R. G. (2006). Nursing home involuntary relocation: Clinical outcomes and perceptions of residents and families. *Journal of the American Medical Directors Association, 7,* 486.

Carr, D., House, J. S., Kessler, R. C., Nesse, R. M., Sonnega, J., & Wortman, C. (2000). Marital quality and psychological adjustment to widowhood among older adults: A longitudinal analysis. *Journal of Gerontology: Social Sciences, 55B,* S197–S205.

Carr, D. (2003). A good death for whom? Quality of spouse's death and psychological distress among older widowed persons. *Journal of Health and Human Behavior, 44,* 215–232.

Carr, D. (2004). Gender, preloss martial dependence and older adults' adjustment to widowhood. *Journal of Marriage and the Family, 66,* 220–235.

Chaturvedi, S. K., Loiselle, C. G., & Chandra, P. S. (2009). Communication with relatives and collusion in palliative care: A cross cultural perspective. *Indian Journal of Palliative Care, 15,* 2–9.

Chen, C. K., Zimmerman, S., Sloane, P. D., & Barrick, A. L. (2007). Assisted living policies promoting autonomy and their relationship to resident depressive symptoms. *American Journal of Geriatric Psychiatry, 15,* 122–129.

Cheng, C. (2006). Living alone: The choice and health of older women. *Journal of Gerontological Nursing, 32,* 24–25.

Cicirelli, V. G. (2002). *Older adults' views on death.* New York: Springer.

Cicirelli, V. G. (2006). Fear of death in mid-old age. *Journals of Gerontology: Psychological Sciences, 61B,* P75–P81.

Cohen, L. L. (2008). Racial/ethnic disparities in hospice care: A systematic review. *Journal of Palliative Medicine, 11,* 763–768.

Condon, J. V., Miller, K. M., Le, A. H., Quasem, M., & Looney, S. W. (2008). Acute myocardial infarction and race, sex, and insurance types: Unequal processes of care. *Health Care Manager, 27,* 212–222.

Connidis, I. A. (2001). *Family ties and aging.* Thousand Oaks, CA: Sage.

Doka, K., (2004). Grief and dementia. In K. Doka (Ed.), *Living with grief: Alzheimer's disease* (pp. 139–153). Washington, DC: Hospice Foundation of America.

Dula, A., & Williams, S. (2005). When race matters. *Clinical Geriatric Medicine, 21,* 239–253.

Dupuis, S. L. (2002). Understanding ambiguous loss in the context of dementia care. *Journal of Clinical Epidemiology, 45,* 861–870.

Dupuis-Blanchard, S. M. (2007). Building a new nest: The experience of women relocating to a seniors-designated apartment building, *Canadian Journal of Nursing Research, 39*(4), 136–153.

Erikson, E. H. (1982). *The life cycle completed: A review.* New York: Norton.

Erikson, E. H., & Erikson, J. M. (1981). On generativity and identity: From a conversation with Erik and Joan Erikson. *Harvard Educational Review, 51,* 249–69.

Erikson, E. H., Erikson, J. M., & Kivnick, H. Q. (1986). *Vital involvement in old age.* New York: Norton.

Gert, K., & Burr, J. A. (2008). Planning for end-of-life care: Black–white differences in the completion of advance directives. *Research on Aging, 30,* 428–449.

Gruneir, A., Vincent, M., Weitzen, S., Truchil, R., Teno, J., & Roy, J. (2007). Where people die: A multilevel approach to understanding influence on site of death in America. *Medical Care Research & Review, 64,* 351–378.

Gwyther, L. (1998). Social issues of the Alzheimer's patient and family. *American Journal of Medicine, 104*(4A), S17–S21.

Ha, J.-H., Hong, J., Seltzer, M. M., & Greenberg, J. S. (2008). Age and gender differences in the well-being of midlife and aging parents with children with mental health or developmental problems. Report of a national study. *Health and Social Behavior, 49,* 301–316.

Hagman, G. H. (2001). Beyond decathexis: Toward a new psychoanalytic understanding and treatment of mourning. In R. A. Neimeyer (Ed.), *Meaning reconstruction and the experience of loss* (pp. 13–32). Washington, DC: American Psychological Association.

Hall, M., & Irwin, M. (2001). Physiological indices of functioning in bereavement. In M. S. Stroebe, R. O. Hansson, W. Stroebe, & H. Schut (Eds.), *Handbook of bereavement: Consequences, coping and care.* Washington, DC: American Psychological Association.

Hampton, T. (2008). Studies address racial and geographic disparities in breast cancer treatment. *Journal of the American Medical Association, 300,* 1641.

Harvey, J. H. (1998). *Perspectives on loss: A sourcebook.* Philadelphia, PA: Brunner/Mazel.

Hays, J. C., Gold, D. T., & Pieper, C. F. (1997). Sibling bereavement in late life. *Omega, 35,* 25–42.

Heller, T, & Caldwell, J. (2006). Supporting aging caregivers and adults with developmental disabilities in future planning. *Mental Retardation, 44,* 189–202.

Hooyman, N., & Kramer, B. (2006). *Living through loss: Interventions across the lifespan.* New York: Columbia University Press.

Johnson, K., Elbert-Avila, K., & Tulsky, J. (2005). The influence of spiritual beliefs and practices on the treatment preferences of African Americans: A review of the literature. *Journal of the American Geriatrics Society, 53,* 711–719.

Kastenbaum, R. J. (1969). Death and bereavement in later life. In A. H. Kutscher (Ed.), *Death and bereavement* (pp. 27–54). Springfield, IL: Charles C. Thomas.

Kastenbaum, R. (2004). *On our way: The final passage through life and death.* Berkeley, CA: University of California Press.

Kastenbaum, R. (2008). Grieving in contempory society. In M. S. Straube, R. O. Hansson, H. Schut, & H. Stroebe (Eds.), *Handbook of bereavement research and practice* (pp. 67–87). Washington, DC: American Psychological Association.

Katz, P. P., & Yelin, E. H. (2001). Activity loss and the onset of depressive symptoms. *Arthritis and Rheumatism, 44,* 1194–1202.

Kelley, P. (1998). Loss experienced in chronic pain and illness. In J. Harvey (Ed.), *Perspectives on Loss: A Sourcebook* (pp. 201–212). Philadelphia, PA: Brunner/Mazel.

Klass, D. (1996). The deceased child in the psychic and social worlds of bereaved parents during the resolution of grief. In D. Klass, P. R. Silverman, & S. L. Nickman (Eds.), *Continuing bonds: New understandings of grief* (pp. 199–216). Washington, DC: Taylor & Francis.

Klass, D. (1999a). Developing a cross-cultural model of grief: The state of the field. *Omega, 293,* 153–178.

Klass, D. (1999b). *The spiritual life of bereaved parents.* Philadelphia, PA: Brunner/Mazel.

Kramer, B. J. (1997). Gain in the caregiver experience: Where are we? What next? *The Gerontologist, 37,* 218–32.

Kübler-Ross, E. (1969). *On death and dying.* New York: Macmillan.

Kübler-Ross, E. (1981). *Living with dying.* New York: Macmillan.

Kwak, J., Haley, W. E., & Chiraboga, D. A. (2008). Racial differences in hospice use and in-hospital death among Medicare and Medicaid dual-eligible nursing home residents. *The Gerontologist, 48,* 32–41.

Laditka, J., & Laditka, S. (2003). Increased hospitalization risk for recently widowed older women and protective effects of social contacts. *Journal of Women and Aging, 15,* 7–28.

Lamberg, L. (2002). "Palliative care" means "active care": It aims to improve quality of life. *Journal of the American Medical Association, 288,* 943–944.

Lee, B. C. (2009). *Should euthanasia or physician-assisted suicide be legal? Compassion and Choices.* Retrieved November 12, 2011, from https://www.compassionandchoices.org/sslpage.aspx.

Martin, T. L., & Doka, K. J. (2000). *Men don't cry, women do.* Philadelphia, PA: Brunner/Mazel.

McLeod, B. W. (2001). Self-care: The path to wholeness. In K. J. Doka (Ed.), *Caregiving and loss: Family needs, professional responses* (pp. 195–207). Washington, DC: Hospice Foundation of America.

Meuser, T. M., & Marwit, S. J. (2001). A comprehensive stage sensitive model of grief in dementia caregiving. *The Gerontologist, 41,* 658–670.

Miller, N., Smerglia, V., & Bouche, N. (2004). Women's adjustment to widowhood: Does social support matter? *Journal of Women and Aging, 16,* 149–167.

Moss, M., Moss, S., & Hansson, R. (2001). Bereavement in old age. In M. Stroebe, R. Hansson, W. Stroebe, & H. Schut (Eds.), *Handbook of bereavement research.* Washington, DC: American Psychological Association.

Muramatsu, N., Hoyem, R. L., Yin, H., & Campbell, R. T. (2008). Place of death among older Americans: Does state spending on home and community-based services promote home death? *Medical Care, 46,* 829–838.

Narayn, S., Lewis, M., Tornatore, J., Hepburn, K., & Corcoran-Perry, S. (2001). Subjective responses to caregiving for spouses with dementia. *Journal of Gerontological Nursing, 27,* 19–28.

National Consensus Project for Quality Palliative Care. (2009). *Clinical practice guidelines for quality palliative care.* Retrieved May 2009, from http://www.nationalconsensusproject.org.

Nelson, J. C. (2001). Diagnosing and treating depression in the elderly. *Journal of Clinical Psychiatry, 62*(24), 18–22.

O'Hagan, M. (2008). Aging father agonizes over fate of his son. *Seattle Times.* Retrieved September 10, 200, from http://www.seattetimes.com.

Oswald, F., & Rowles, G. D. (2006). Beyond the relocation trauma in old age: New trends in today's elders' residential decisions. In H.-W. Wahl, C. Tesch-Römer, & A. Hoff (Eds.), *New dynamics in old age: Environmental and societal perspectives* (pp. 127–152). Amityville, New York: Baywood Publishing.

Pilkington, F. B. (1999). Publishing a qualitative study of life after stroke. *Journal of Neuroscience Nursing, 31,* 336–347.

Rafinski, K. (2011). Easing pain: Palliative care is not what you think. *AARP Bulletin, 52,* 14–15.

Ramsey, J. L., & Blieszner, R. (2000). Transcending a lifetime of losses: The importance of spirituality in old age. In J. H. Harvey & E. D. Miller (Eds.), *Loss and trauma: General and close relationship perspectives* (pp. 225–236). Washington, DC: Taylor & Francis.

Rando, T. A. (1988). *Grieving: How to go on living when someone you love dies.* Lexington, MA: Lexington Books.

Redfoot, D., Feinberg, L., & Houser, A. (2013). *The aging of the baby boom and the growing care gap: A look at future declines in the availability of family caregivers.* Washington, DC: AARP Public Policy Institute.

Richardson, V. E., & Barusch, A. S. (2006). Bereavement in later life. In V. E. Richardson & A. S. Barusch (Eds.), *Social work practice with older adults.* New York: Columbia University Press.

Robinson, C. A., Reid, R. C., & Cooke, H. A. (2010). A home away from home: The meaning of home according to families of residents with dementia. *Dementia: International Journal of Social Research and Practice, 9*(4), 490–508.

Roos, S. (2002). *Chronic sorrow: A living loss.* New York: Brunner-Routledge.

Rossi, N. E., Bisconti, T. L., & Bergeman, C. S. (2007). The role of dispositional resilience in regaining life satisfaction after the loss of a spouse. *Death Studies, 31,* 863–883.

Schulz, R., Mendelsohn, A. B., Haley, W. E., Mahoney, D., Allen, R. S., et al. (2003). End of life care and the effects of bereavement on family caregivers of persons with dementia. *New England Journal of Medicine, 349,* 1936–1952.

Schulz, R., Boerner, K., Shear, K., Zhang, S., & Gitlin, L. N. (2006). Predictors of complicated grief among dementia caregivers: A prospective study of bereavement. *American Journal of Geriatric Psychiatry, 14,* 650.

Seltzer, M. M., & Li, L. Q. (2000). The dynamics of caregiving: Transitions during a three-year prospective study. *The Gerontologist, 40,* 165–78.

Sergeant, J. F., & Ekerdt, D. J., (2008). Motives for residential mobility in later life: Post-move perspectives of elders and family members. *International Journal of Aging and Human Development, 66*(2), 131–154.

Sanders, S., Butcher, H. K., Swails, P., & Power, J. (2009). Portraits of caregivers of end-stage dementia patients receiving hospice care. *Death Studies, 33,* 521–556.

Sanders, S., & Corley, C. S. (2003). Are they grieving? A qualitative analysis examining grief in caregivers of individuals with Alzheimer's disease. *Health and Social Work, 37,* 37–53.

Sanders, S., Ott, C. H., Kelber, S. T., & Noonan, P. (2008). The experience of high levels of grief in caregivers of persons with Alzheimer's disease and related dementia. *Death Studies, 32,* 495–2008.

Sharma, R. L., & Dy, S. M. (2011). Cross-cultural communication and use of the family meeting in palliative care. *American Journal of Hospice and Palliative Medicine, 17,* 212–215, 1–8.

Sonnega, J. (2002). *Survey evidence of clinical wisdom: Special occasions and grief in the elderly widowed.* Lecture. Ann Arbor, MI: University of Michigan.

Span, P. (2012, April 18). Where the oldest-old die now. *New York Times.* Retrieved December 31, 2012, from http://newoldage.blogs.nytimes.com/2012/04/18/where-the-oldest-die-now/.

Tomer, A., & Ellison, G. (2000). Attitudes about life and death. Toward a comprehensive model of death anxiety. In A. Tomer (Ed.), *Death attitudes and the older adult: Theories, concepts and applications.* Philadelphia, PA: Taylor & Francis.

Thornton, J. D., Pham, K., Engelberg, R. A., Jackson, J. C., & Curtis, J. R. (2009). Families with limited English proficiency receive less information and support in interpreted intensive care unit family conferences. *Critical Care Medicine, 37,* 89–95.

Thorson, J., & Powell, F. C. (2000). Death anxiety in younger and older adults. In A. Tomer (Ed.), *Death attitudes and the older adult: Theories, concepts and applications.* Philadelphia, PA: Taylor & Francis.

Uhlenberg, P. (1996). The burden of aging: A theoretical framework for understanding the shifting balance of caregiving and care receiving vs. cohort ages. *The Gerontologist, 36,* 761–67.

Utz, R., Carr, D., Nesse, R., & Wortman, C. (2002). The effect of widowhood on older adults' social participation: An evaluation of activity, disengagement, and continuity theories. *The Gerontologist, 42,* 522–533.

Walker, C., Hogstel, M. O., & Curry, L. C. (2007). Hospital discharge of older adults: How nurses can ease the transition. *American Journal of Nursing, 107,* 60–70.

Walter, T. (1996). A new model of grief: Bereavement and biography. *Mortality, 11,* 7–27.

Walter, T. (2003). *The loss of a life partner: Narratives of the bereaved.* New York: Columbia University Press.

Washington, H. (2007). *Medical apartheid: The dark history of medical experimentation on Black Americans from colonial times to the present.* New York: Doubleday.

Weiss, R. S. (2001). Grief, bonds and relationships. In M. Stroebe, R. Hansson, W. Stroebe, & H. Schut (Eds.), *Handbook of bereavement research: Consequences, coping and care.* Washington, DC: American Psychological Association.

Weitzen, S., Teno, J., Fennell, M., & Mor, V. (2003). Factors associated with site of death: A national study of where people die. *Medical Care, 41,* 323–335.

Welch, L. C., Teno, J. M., & Mor, V. (2005). End-of-life care in black and white: Race matters for medical care of dying patients, and their families. *Journal of the American Geriatrics Society, 53,* 1145–1153.

West, J. (2010). *The last goodnight: Assisting my parents with suicides: A memoir.* Berkeley, CA: Counterpoint.

Worden, J. W. (2002). *Grief counseling and grief therapy: A handbook for the mental health practitioner.* New York: Springer.

10 Economic Well-Being: Retirement, Employment, and Poverty

learning objectives

10.1 Describe how baby boomers are changing the expectations, timing and economic status of retirement.

10.2 Discuss challenges that older adults face when searching for employment and building their retirement income.

10.3 Demonstrate knowledge of the various sources of income available to older adults as well as concerns about their economic well-being.

Listen to the Chapter Audio

All of us are concerned about how we are doing financially—although we may have very different criteria by which we measure our economic well-being. Some of you may be employed while in school, while others benefit from federal loans and scholarships. Our economic status—specifically our income and job—often influence how we feel about ourselves. And you are probably determined to complete college as a way to improve your economic status and ensure your future economic well-being.

Similarly, well-being in old age is profoundly influenced by economic status or social class, whether a person is poor or wealthy, is retired from a professional or service position or still employed out of financial necessity, or receives a private pension or only the minimum amount of Social Security. Even though having financial resources does not guarantee quality of life and satisfaction, it does affect physical and mental health in multiple ways. Because of this, economic status is an important consideration for both research and practice with older adults and their families.

This chapter focuses on three primary economic conditions that are central to older adults' financial well-being:

- Retirement as a status and a social process that affects not only income but also identity, roles, and activities
- Employment status and barriers to finding jobs when unemployed
- Socioeconomic status or social class, the extent of poverty and near-poverty among older adults, and how these are influenced by the primary sources of income in old age, particularly Social Security

As you learned in Chapter 8, many older adults are productive without being paid for their contributions. This chapter emphasizes both the opportunities and constraints that older adults face related to the concept of productivity as defined specifically by their paid work, their retirement or unemployment, and their sources of income. We close by briefly reviewing some of the innovations in new careers—paid or volunteer—for midlife and older adults.

Retirement

The concept of **retirement** is a relatively recent phenomenon in Western society. Prior to the industrial revolution, most people worked—often as farmers—until they died, typically in their forties or fifties. Retirement developed along with industrialization, surplus labor, and a rising standard of living. Social Security, passed in 1935, established the right to financial protection in old age on the basis of past economic contributions to society. It was also a way to support people of all ages unable to work because of illness or disability. At the same time, Social Security created jobs for younger people by "removing" adults age 65 and older from the workforce.

Some societal and individual consequences of retirement are negative, however. Earlier retirement, combined with longer life expectancies, prolonged elders' relying on Social Security and other retirement benefits and meant a loss of older workers' skills and knowledge. Because retirement is associated in the public mind with the chronological age of 65 for over 40 years, the age of eligibility for full Social Security and Medicare benefits, it may also carry the connotation of being "old" and no longer physically or cognitively capable of employment or even other activities. This perception may inadvertently limit job and retraining options for older adults as well as negatively affect their sense of well-being.

As individuals live longer, a smaller proportion of their lifetime is typically devoted to paid employment, even though the number of years worked is longer. Someone who retires at age 62 may live 30 more years—but 40 percent of people do not do extensive planning for this long phase of retirement. Adults generally hold age-related expectations about the rhythm of their careers—when they should start working, when they should be at their career peak, and when to retire. They typically assess whether or not they are "on time" according to these socially defined schedules. Upon retirement, their thinking often shifts from how much time has passed to how much time is left. Increasingly, however, retirement is not a single irreversible event; instead, more adults are moving in and out of the workforce either by

points to ponder

How does your view of work and retirement differ from that of your parents and/or grandparents? What does retirement mean to you and how can you assure a successful retirement, including enough income? Will you even want to retire? How many careers do you anticipate having? It's never too early to be thinking about these issues.

choice or financial necessity than occurred 30 years ago (Carstensen, 2009; Charness & Czaja, 2011).

The value placed on paid productivity in our society shapes how individuals approach employment and retirement. Most adults derive much of their identity from their jobs. Think about how often the first question asked of someone at a social gathering is what they do for a living. Those over age 75 today—the World War II generation—were socialized to a traditional view of hard work, job loyalty, and occupational stability. Many of them were in the same job for 40 or more years, retiring with a pension that rewarded their company loyalty. As a whole, they have been less affected by the recession than other age groups, because most of them had already retired and simplified their lifestyles. Even so, 33 percent of adults age 65 and older in a 2011 national survey had cut back on their spending and reported that the recession has caused stress in their family. And many among the cohort age 65 and older, such as the O'Brians below, have been hard hit by declining retirement investments (AARP, 2011; Charness & Czaja, 2011; Pew Research Center, 2009).

Baby Boomers and Changing Expectations of Retirement

In contrast to earlier generations, most boomers had assumed that they would enter old age with adequate economic resources—and that if they continued to work in their "retirement," it would be for a sense of productivity and satisfaction, not because they had to. Many baby boomers were able to earn six-figure salaries, a pattern resulting from economic and demographic shifts such as deferred marriage, reduced and later childbearing, higher levels of educational attainment, longer work hours, and women's increased labor force participation. They also acquired more real estate and invested in the stock market more than prior cohorts.

Additionally, baby boomers that are just now in their early sixties tend to have a different view of retirement than the current cohort of older adults. They are more likely to have pursued multiple careers, switched jobs voluntarily or involuntarily, often reinventing themselves in middle age. As you have seen throughout this book, boomers reshaped many of the social conventions around marriage and family, sexuality, and workplace behavior and sought out opportunities that provided them with meaning and purpose. It was anticipated that the generation of workers currently in their fifties and sixties would redefine the notion of retirement, moving by choice into new "retirement jobs" or encore or second or third careers to enjoy a sense of productivity, social contacts, and life satisfaction. They anticipated options such as flex time positions and partial or phased retirement, giving them discretion to choose how much and where they worked (Brown, Aumann, Pitt-Catsouphes, Galinsky, & Bond, 2010; Charness & Czaja, 2011; Metlife Mature Market Institute, 2008; Rix, 2011a, 2011b).

However, with the global economic downturn and the U.S. recession, baby boomers now face a very different future and are more likely to remain employed for financial reasons, not psychological and social ones. In a 2011 national survey, 25 percent of the respondents said they will need to work until at least age 80 because they will not have enough money to retire comfortably. A record high number of adults age 45–75—nearly 75 percent—were already employed or looking for work. This shift of continued employment for financial reasons is because baby boomers have been more negatively impacted by the recession than prior cohorts. The reasons for this disproportionate negative impact on the boomers are numerous (Charness & Czaja, 2011; Pitt, 2011; Rix, 2011a, 2011b).

They typically borrowed more and saved less than their parents; as a result, they hold fewer assets than prior generations and have seen their private investments, particularly their individual retirement accounts or IRAs, decimated by the economic downturn. In one survey, over 60 percent of boomers reported significant losses in their retirement funds after 2008—through no fault of their own. In many instances, boomers simply stopped contributing to their dwindling retirement savings because they

Retirees' Increasing Economic Worries

Mary O'Brian, 76, and husband Robert, 77, retired without pensions and with modest Social Security benefits, counting on income from their stocks. But the bulk of their investments were relatively high-risk stocks in a major bank, which declined dramatically. Their "safe investments" of certificates of deposit also now have a lower interest rate, producing a minimal income stream. They no longer follow their stocks closely because it only makes them feel discouraged and worried. Having worked hard all their lives, they are bitter that their economic security was taken away by the bursting of the stock market bubble in 2008.

no longer trusted the stock market or had prematurely withdrawn some of it. A shocking figure is that 16 percent of middle age and young-old adults in a 2010 survey stated they have no savings at all while 27 percent said they have less than $1,000 in savings. In a 2011 study, the median savings was $25,000 among middle-class older adults, just 7 percent of what is considered to be an adequate retirement financial goal to maintain a comfortable standard of living. Additionally, many boomers who acquired real estate watched property values decline to levels below their current mortgage and the real estate market glutted with homes and condominiums (Helman & VanDerhei, 2010; Pitt, 2011).

The recession not only adversely impacted baby boomers' retirement plans and employment options but also their daily choices. In one national survey, about 33 percent of adults age 45 and older were postponing medical or dental care and about 20 percent were having difficulties paying for essentials such as food and utilities. Quite simply, more older adults have been looking for work out of a sense of urgency as retirement portfolios and home values have gone down, reducing their long-term financial security while other immediate expenses, such as health insurance, property taxes, utility bills, and family caregiving responsibilities, have gone up (AARP, 2010; Pew Research Center, 2009; VanHorn, Corre, & Heidkamp, 2011).

If baby boomers do retire or lose their jobs because of company closures and downsizing, they face numerous barriers to finding work during a time period of high unemployment. Accustomed to being successful at changing jobs in the past, baby boomers are now encountering obstacles to reentry to the workforce. For some, this may be one of the first times they are not successful at achieving their career goals. After hearing stories about how difficult it is to find work at their age, many older workers are reluctant to give up the security they have. Workers who had planned on retiring at their age of eligibility are often rethinking their futures and deciding to keep working, especially if they already have a job (Pitt, 2011; Rix, 2011a).

Reflection Break

Some people say it's never too early to plan for retirement—that we should start doing so from the time of our first jobs. Retirement probably seems a long way off for many of you, especially if you are struggling to pay for college and cover basic living expenses of you and perhaps your family members. But the advantage of thinking about retirement while you are younger is that you have many more years to plan for it financially. Those who put off planning for retirement are often surprised by how quickly it creeps up on them—and how many years they may have ahead of them. At what age do you see yourself retiring, and what will you do after you retire? While financial security is often people's primary concern, it is also important to plan for how you will spend your nonwork time—hobbies, volunteering, travel, taking classes, or keeping fit. Would you want to work for pay or do volunteer work after age 65, 66, or 67?

What sources of income do you expect to have in retirement? Are you starting to put money aside now for retirement, and if so, in what ways? If not, when do you plan to start? What do you know about Individual Retirement Accounts (IRAs), Social Security, Medicare, and investing your money? Make a detailed list of all the expenses you think you'll have when you retire. Don't forget to include entertainment and recreational activities. Do you think you'll have enough money to pay for all these expenses? If you want to see just how much you should be saving to be financially secure, you can get an estimate by Googling Retirement Calculator and plugging in your age and current income. Based on what you find, could you imagine yourself living on that amount?

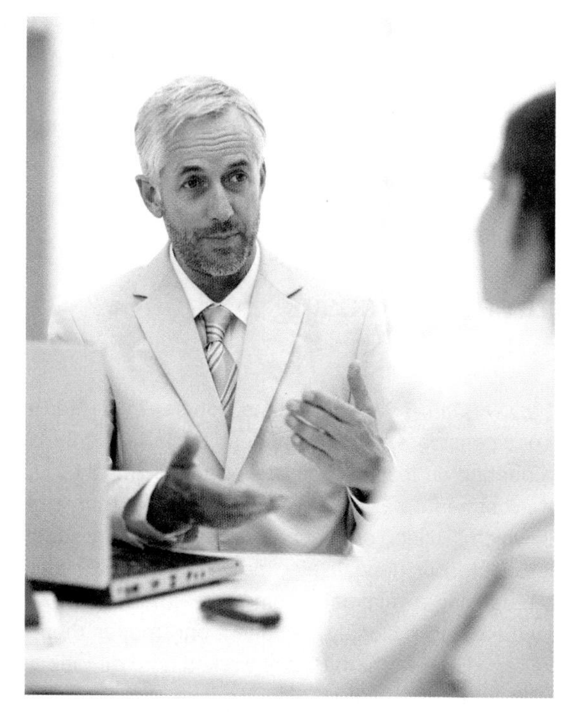

Baby boomers often face obstacles when trying to reenter the workforce after being laid off or deciding to return to work after retirement.

Time-Tested Thriftiness Returns

In a national survey in England, 70 percent of people over age 50 have resorted to wartime thriftiness to endure the current economic downturn. The methods used to stretch their financial resources are varied, from buying food at discount prices to growing their own vegetables and preparing food from scratch. They sew and mend clothing for themselves and family members and save leftovers.

One retiree said she refuses to waste anything, including water, and keeps her washing to a minimum, always putting in a full load. She makes homemade compost for her garden using vegetable peelings, shredded newspaper, and coffee grinds. She knits and sews new zippers into old clothes, and cuts her own hair rather than go to the hairdresser. Most of those surveyed said younger generations could learn from their thriftiness, which was honed in harsher times when resources had to be stretched. How do some of these thrifty behaviors correspond with what you may know about the importance of recycling and composting garbage waste? In many ways, thriftiness can be the "new green" lifestyle (*Telegraph*, 2009).

The Timing of Retirement

Prior to 1986, retirement at age 65 was mandatory for most jobs, although the majority of people retired sooner between the ages of 60 and 64. Even after mandatory retirement ended, very few adults continued to work past age 70 and most retired in their early sixties (the average age of retirement in 2013 was 61, up from 57 two decades ago). In other words, factors other than chronological age—such as health, social relationships, economic status, extent of financial preparation, and geographic location—determined when most workers left the labor force (Adams & Rau, 2011; Gallup, 2013).

For generations retiring in the 1980s and 1990s, early retirement was in part due to employer incentives to move older workers out of the labor force. One incentive was receipt of Social Security. Each year, 75 percent of all new Social Security beneficiaries retired shortly after they became eligible for partial benefits at age 62. Another incentive was generous retirement and pension plans and employer-sponsored health insurance, particularly for white-collar workers, offered by companies since the 1900s and until the beginning of the twenty-first century that encouraged early retirement. The result in the 1980s was a group of well-off retirees with generous pensions. Even employees who were not planning to retire were often offered benefits too attractive to turn down. Workers in the past accumulated a significant proportion of their retirement funds in the decade preceding retirement, presumably when their earnings were the highest. But this pattern is no longer the case, and now the average American plans to retire at age 66 or 67, compared to age 60 in 1995 (Gallup, 2013; Rix, 2008).

points to ponder

If you still have a grandfather—or father over age 70—alive, ask about his experience with pensions and other retirement incentives. Then talk to someone in their early sixties about their sources of income in retirement. What differences do you see in their experiences?

Over time, the shift to a later retirement age may have societal benefits, because more workers will be paying into Social Security for a longer time period and spending fewer years in retirement drawing down Social Security. This could help to reduce the future projected shortfall in Social Security. Nevertheless, most workers age 50 and older do not favor a later retirement age to qualify for benefits. This response is not surprising since raising the full retirement age just 2 years would mean at least a 13 percent cut in Social Security benefits, no matter what age an eligible worker retires. Workers may expect and even want to work well past age 65, but they want to choose the timing of it themselves. You will learn more about the controversies surrounding proposed changes to Social Security, including

Why We Consider Age 65 as the Normal Retirement Age

Ironically, the emergence of age 65 as the benchmark for "normal" retirement age was an artifact of a decision made by Social Security planners based on what seemed appropriate and affordable; 60 seemed too low, 70 too high, given that average life expectancy in 1935 was about 60 years. This is a striking example how a relatively arbitrary decision can become institutionalized as "old age" (Kingson & Altman, 2011; Social Security Administration, 2011a).

raising the retirement age in Chapter 13 (Butrica, 2011; Herd, 2011; Kingson & Altman, 2011).

You read in Chapter 2 about the street protests and political controversies in recent years in many European countries, such as France, that attempted to raise the age of eligibility for retirement benefits. Workers protested against legislation to increase the minimum age for reduced retirement benefits from 60 to 62 and for full benefits from 65 to 67. Workers viewed early retirement as something to which they were entitled—and rational arguments about longer life expectancy and mounting debt meant nothing to them (Norris, 2010).

Factors other than age of eligibility for retirement benefits also affect the timing of retirement. Poor health, when combined with an adequate retirement income and health insurance, usually results in early retirement. In contrast, poor health, an inadequate income, and lack of health insurance generally delay retirement, as is often the case with low-income workers, who are disproportionately employees of color and who must keep working out of financial necessity despite health problems. If these workers lose their jobs because of business closures, their poor health often acts as a barrier to their being able to reenter the labor force (Angel & Mudrazija, 2011).

In some cases, retirement due to poor health and adverse work conditions results in older adults perceiving their early retirement as forced—that is, they had to leave the workforce earlier than they had planned or wanted to. About 20 percent of retirements are involuntary or not by choice. And in the current economy, more low-income workers with limited education or technical skills feel forced to retire—or to take part-time positions, because of job displacement, layoffs, or downsizing. Conversely, good health, at least a college education, and the skills to work in occupations that are not physically strenuous increase the chances of finding paid work in retirement (Charness & Cazja, 2011; Rix, 2011b).

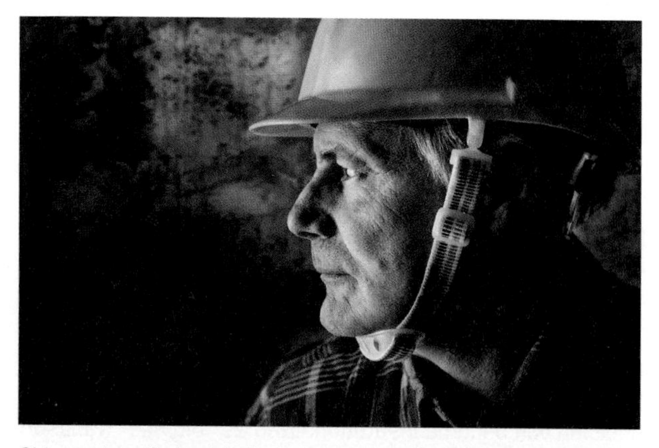

Older workers facing job displacement, layoffs, and forced retirements may seek part-time jobs in occupations that are lower pay and more physically demanding than their prior positions.

It is not the phasing of retirement (e.g., a gradual reduction of work hours vs. a sharp break), but rather the degree of control that people feel they have over the process that typically affects their postretirement well-being. Involuntary retirement tends to have negative consequences for both physical and mental health. In such cases, retirees are unlikely to be positive about their new lifestyle of "imposed" leisure. As jobs disappear and income declines in the current economy, more older adults are lacking choice about their retirement age (Charness & Czaja, 2011; VanHorn et al., 2011).

points to ponder

What are your concerns, if any, when it comes to retirement? These do not necessarily have to be economic concerns—any concerns. If you can't think that far in advance, what do you think a person nearing the age of retirement is thinking about as he or she gets closer to that time?

As is true with many opportunities across the life course, gender and race also appear to affect the timing of retirement. Although both men and women have chosen early retirement in the past, older women are less likely to be fully retired than their male counterparts. Women who may have entered the labor force after years of child rearing may reach the peak of their careers later than their male peers. For other women who moved into the workforce in middle age or later because of divorce or widowhood, they may have to remain in low-wage jobs just to get by financially. Compared to Caucasian women, African American women are more likely to have been employed steadily most of their adult lives, but they are also more likely to retire later, primarily for economic reasons. Single African American women, when poorly paid, tend to remain underemployed and get caught in a situation in which they lack adequate resources to retire. Regardless of race, unmarried women face the most negative economic prospects for retirement now and for at least the next 20 years (Angel & Mudrazja, 2011; Holden, 2009; Harootyan & Sarmiento, 2011; James & Wink, 2008).

Lifetime employment patterns experienced by many low-income adults of color often create an unclear line between paid work and nonwork, where elders of color movc in and out of the labor force across the life course; this is sometimes referred to as "unretirement–retirement." For example, job reductions during the recession may have "pushed" adults of color into retirement. Additionally, lengthy periods of unemployment or underemployment at an earlier age limit their access to retirement benefits in old age. Since African Americans and Latinos tend to have a greater likelihood of chronic illness and disability than other groups, they are more likely to retire for health reasons than are whites. Indeed, 36 percent of African Americans and 32 percent of Latinos age 60–61 report a health condition that limits their ability to continue to work (Government Accountability Office, 2010).

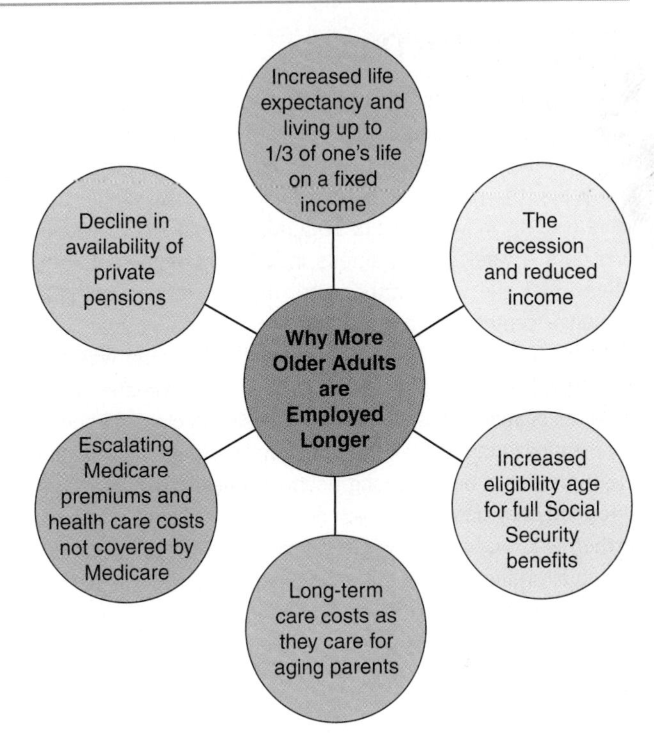

FIGURE 10.1 Why More Older Adults Are Employed Longer

Source: Cawthorne, 2010; Uraban Institute, 2009

Employment

Given the growing numbers of middle age and older adults who cannot afford to retire, we turn next to employment—and conversely unemployment of older workers. As noted above, the vast majority of older adults in the past chose to retire early, and therefore the employment rate of workers age 55 and older had been declining since the 1950s up until about 1993. This low rate was also due to past Social Security eligibility rules that discouraged labor force participation.

However, since about the late 1990s, the number of adults age 55 and older who are employed has increased steadily to about 20 percent in 2013. Here are some striking statistics of this change. Employment of workers age 65 and older increased 101 percent since 1977. That's almost double the 59 percent increase for total employment of workers age 16 and older during the same time period. Moreover, the increase in the number of women 65 and older who were employed since 2000 was nearly twice as much as for men. This shift also reflects that women in the baby boom cohort are more likely to have been in the labor force throughout adulthood than prior generations. Not surprisingly, labor force participation is greatest among those ages 65–69 and those who have highest levels of education—the group that might have chosen early retirement in the past. While the number of employed people age 75 and over is relatively small, this group nevertheless had the most dramatic gain in employment, increasing by more than 172 percent in the past 30 years (Federal Interagency Forum, 2012; Fleck, 2012; Gallup, 2013).

The proportion of part-time and full-time employment has also shifted, with older adults now more likely to be employed full-time than was true in the past—even though the majority of older individuals would prefer part-time flexible work. These trends toward growing rates of full-time employment among older workers began well before the worldwide economic downturn, but whether this pattern will continue beyond the recession is unclear. And as you will see below, more older workers stay on the job because they enjoy their work (AoA, 2013; Employee Benefits Research Institute, 2011; Federal Interagency Forum, 2012; Harootyan & Sarmiento, 2011; Sok, 2010).

Unemployment

As is true of all age groups, the unemployment rate for adults age 55 and older is at record high levels—over 7 percent, the highest it has been since 1948—and higher

Retirees Who Don't

Some older adults are continuing to work into advanced old age not so much for financial reasons, but because being employed is part of how they define active aging. Over the years, the percent of older people in the workforce has increased as shown in Figure 10.2. Marge, age 79, still works two days a week as a waitress in a family restaurant. She states that she would rather work than go to a social club or senior center. Marge brings a strong work ethic and commitment to the job. Waldo began working when he was 13, guiding a lead team of horses pulling a wheat thresher. After a series of varied jobs, he started a business cleaning seeds for planting in the 1950s and ran it until he was 91 years old. He then took a decades-long hobby of beekeeping and went into the honey business, which he is still running at age 104. Arthur, who worked 72 years repairing Los Angeles buses, eventually retired at age 100. And Elinor Otto, who was part of the famous "Rosie the Riveter" brigade that put women into the workforce producing planes to help the World War II effort, is still working today at age 93, helping produce Boeing C-17 cargo planes.

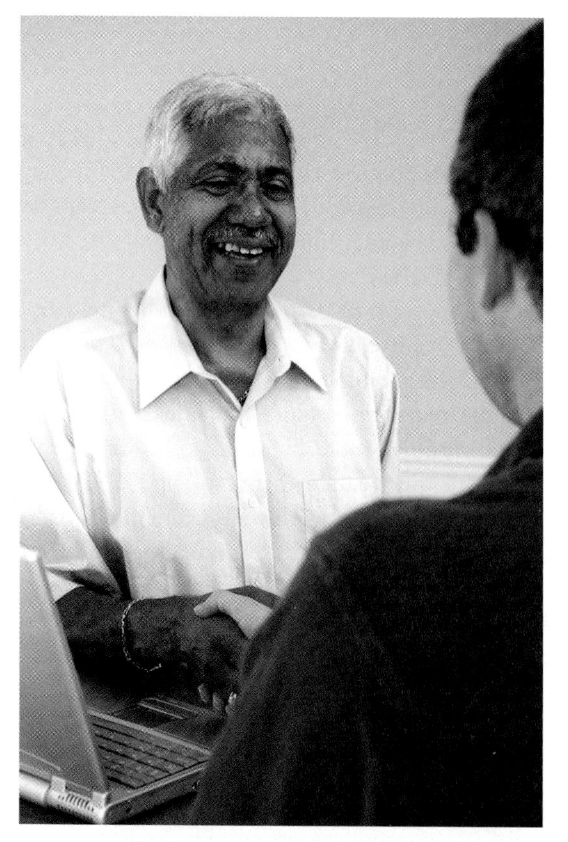

As retirement income shrinks, older employees may remain longer in the workforce.

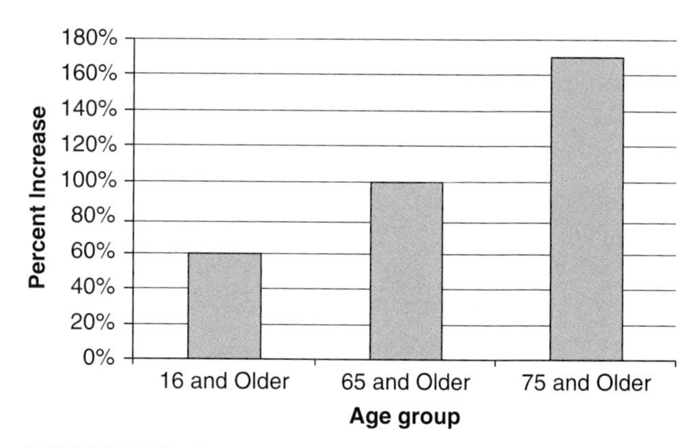

FIGURE 10.2 **Percent Increases of Older People in the Workforce, 1977–2007**

Source: Fleck, 2012

for men than for women. Indeed, the unemployment rate among older adults has doubled since 2007. These rates are even higher for those with low levels of education and for African Americans and Latinos. Additionally, this increased proportion of unemployed older adults does not include the many young-old who call themselves retired simply because they have given up on finding a job or who are underemployed and working fewer hours than they would like. Due to ageism, older workers often find it especially difficult to get hired during an economic downturn, especially when pursuing the same jobs as much younger applicants who are willing to work for less and may be perceived by employers as having more relevant skills or as more easily trainable. Being unemployed generally makes it harder for them to compete successfully compared to those who hold a job but are seeking to change. Faced with numerous barriers, older workers are more likely to get discouraged and drop out of the labor force. For many young-old adults, like Carol in the box on p. 291, the job competition is so intense that they fear they may simply age out of the labor force before the economy improves and they can find a job (AARP, 2011; Harootyan & Sarmiento, 2011; Rix, 2011b; Sok, 2010; VanHorn et al., 2011).

When older adults are unemployed, even by choice, they are more likely to remain unemployed for longer time periods than younger workers. This is even more the case for low-income workers. In a 2011 study, unemployed workers age 55 and older had been searching for work for an estimated 52.7 weeks on average—a whole year—compared to 36.5 weeks for younger unemployed. Because of earlier life disadvantages in terms of education and employment, men of color—particularly Latino

Too Young to Retire, Too Old to Get Hired

Joan is a 55-year-old woman who majored in marketing during college and had a successful career in the software industry for many years. She was earning more than $60,000 a year when she was laid off as part of her former company's reorganization strategy. Because of her excellent work history, she was not too worried about finding a new job. She assumed she would make use of her unemployment benefits but would find new employment fairly quickly. As a marketing professional, she knew how to present herself in the best possible light. Joan applied for jobs, made phone calls, and tapped into her network of professional colleagues, but to her disappointment, she was not getting any offers. She had difficulty even getting the occasional interview. As her unemployment benefits began to run out, she started using funds from her savings account and began cashing in some retirement savings, which she never thought she would have to do. Now she is willing to take a job that pays far less than what she was making before she was laid off just so she can make ends meet and not dip further into her retirement savings. She is too young to retire but thinks she is being rejected for jobs because others think she is too old. Her story is not unique.

males—face the highest unemployment rates and longest job searches (GAO, 2011; Rix, 2011b; Sok, 2010; VanHorn et al., 2011).

points to ponder

Next time you are talking socially to an employer, ask whether the firm has older workers and how they define an "older worker." Is it people in their fifties, sixties, or older? How are older workers' skills utilized? Are they given opportunities for training and promotions? Or are they employed part-time in lower-paying positions? What have the firm's experiences with older workers in terms of absenteeism, productivity, and morale? Did you learn anything about older workers from this conversation that surprised you?

Barriers to Employment

Why do unemployed older workers have a particularly difficult time with their job search? Here are a few of the primary reasons:

- They may have been in one occupation for many years and therefore lack job-hunting and technological skills expected in today's information- and services-dominated economy. As a result, they may not feel confident. One older job-seeker noted that "going back to work is not just about skills. It's also in our heads. It's about lacking confidence." Fortunately, some local governments offer skills training, interview preparation, and assistance in the job search as well as career coaching. And many older adults handle the job search better than others, saying that "We're not as fearful as some of the other generations. It may be our age. We've seen the hard times and we've already suffered some losses. We've been around the block. We're determined and nothing is going to stop us" (Luck, 2010).
- With rising unemployment levels across all ages, businesses are less likely to modify work environments, such as allowing part-time work, and to provide job retraining for older workers. In the current tight economy, their focus is on efficiency and reducing costs, not accommodating older workers' needs. Fortunately, some companies see the value of older workers as captured in the box below.
- Even though mandatory retirement policies are illegal for most jobs, age-based employment discrimination persists, often going "underground." The **Age Discrimination in Employment Act (ADEA)** of 1967 reduced blatant forms of age discrimination (e.g., advertisements that explicitly restrict jobs to younger

Best Places to Work

Some companies recognize that older workers make up a very important part of the workforce. They want to hire older workers because they will bring leadership, experiences, and skills to the job. Recognized by AARP as best places to work for employees age 40 and older, they range from Home Depot, Toys R Us, and La Quinta Inns to MetLife, New York Life Insurance Company, the IRS, and the Peace Corp. Or consider the Vita Needle factory in Needham, MA, where the average age of the employees is 74, with the oldest worker 100 years old. Vita Needle thinks that hiring older employees part-time with flexible hours has boosted their profits. They praise their older workers for their loyalty and reliability. And most of the employees value the chance to be productive and not feel useless (AARP, 2011; PBS, 2013).

people) and, in 1986, eliminated mandatory retirement for most occupations. But it has been less effective at promoting the hiring and retraining of older workers who have lost their jobs. In fact, age discrimination alleged as the basis for loss of employment is now the fastest-growing form of unfair dismissal complaints submitted to the Equal Employment Opportunity Commission. Some studies have found that older workers are less likely to get called for an interview compared to younger applicants with identical resumes. Ageism in the workplace may also emerge when older adults are passed up for promotions or raises. And subtle forms of ageism endure, such as expectations of attractiveness in dress, makeup, and hairstyle, or making jobs undesirable to older workers by downgrading the title or salary (Herd, 2011; Johnson & Mommaerts, 2011; McCann & Ventrell-Monsees, 2010; Schulz & Binstock, 2006).

- Negative stereotypes about aging and productivity persist. Despite decades of evidence to the contrary, some employers still assume that older workers will not perform as well as younger ones because of poor health, declining energy, lack of computer and other technical skills, diminished intellectual ability, or different work styles. Additionally, they may presume that hiring older workers will result in higher training and health care costs (Borie-Holtz, VanHorn, & Zukin, 2010).

Is this Age Discrimination?

A bank announces that it is opening a new branch and advertises for tellers. Jane Feld, age 53 with 22 years of banking experience, applies. The employment application includes an optional category for age. Rather than pausing to think about whether to indicate her age, she answers the question voluntarily and truthfully. The next week, Ms. Feld receives a polite letter from the bank complimenting her on her qualities but turning her down, because she is overqualified. She later finds out that a 32-year-old woman with only 4 years' experience has been hired.

Sarah Nelson, age 55, is a manager with a large advertising company. For the past 5 years, she has received outstanding performance reviews. Two months after a strong review and pay increase, she was abruptly fired for "poor performance." Her replacement, age 35, started a week after she was fired.

A 65-year-old man, who had held a high-level managerial position in a bank before it closed, interviewed for a project manager position in a nonprofit for which he was overqualified. All the interviewers were in their late twenties. They told him that "people here work really hard and have a lot of energy," implying that they doubted his energy for work because of his age. When he told them that he was accustomed to working 10-hour days, six days a week, they just looked past him. He was not invited back for a second interview.

Organizations such as AARP and government employment assistance programs have been offering retraining classes to help older job-seekers enhance their skills, such as computer technology, but federal programs for workforce development have generally not responded well to older workers' needs. Only a few programs, such as the federal **Senior Community Service Employment Program (SCSEP)**, specifically target low-income older adults through retraining, job placement, a stipend, and part-time subsidized employment. A typical SCSEP job might be as a van driver for persons with disabilities or a nurse's aide. However, this program enrolls only a small proportion of elders annually, uses strict eligibility requirements, and has experienced budget cuts in recent years (Gonyea & Hudson, 2011; Harootyan & Sarmiento, 2011).

points to ponder

Due to the poor economy, some older adults are remaining in the workforce longer and others are coming out of retirement to look for work. What qualities can older workers—say in their sixties and older—bring to the workplace? What stereotypes are they up against in the hiring process?

Economic Status

Patterns of retirement, employment, and unemployment along with the larger economic and political context, such as the recession, are the primary determinants of the major sources of income in old age—and in turn of economic status or social class. We briefly review these income sources before turning to a discussion of social class, poverty, and hunger in old age.

What Are the Major Sources of Income for Older Adults?

If you are tuned into contemporary media discussions about cutting federal expenditures, you probably hear or read a lot about the major source of income for older adults: **Social Security**.

Social Security benefits account for about 36 percent of the aggregate income of the older population. The remainder is

- earnings—32 percent,
- assets—11 percent,
- other pensions—18 percent, and
- other—3 percent (Social Security Administration, 2013a).

Social Security provides a foundation of retirement protection for nearly every American, and its benefits are not means tested (e.g., eligibility is not determined by your income, but rather by what you have paid into the Social Security system through your payroll taxes as an employee). But as you have learned, the average benefits are modest—about $14,144 a year—and the maximum benefit was just over $30,000 in 2013 (Social Security Administration, 2013a).

Not surprisingly, the distribution of income sources varies widely: women, elders of color, and the oldest-old, who fall at the bottom of the income range, are most likely to rely on Social Security—and to depend on it as their only source of income—because they often lack pensions and other assets. Since benefits are tied to a worker's wage and employment history, women and people of color who worked intermittently or part-time, often because of discrimination or caregiving responsibilities, also tend to receive less than the average monthly Social Security benefit.

But Social Security was never intended to provide an adequate retirement income; it was to be only a minimum floor of protection or the first tier of support to prevent poverty. When you listen to media reports about Social Security, you may hear the concept of a three-legged stool. This refers to the assumption that other pensions and individual savings would help support people in their later years. This assumption has not been borne out; instead, retirees now receive proportionately lower income from savings and private pensions compared to Social Security than they did 10 years ago (AoA, 2012).

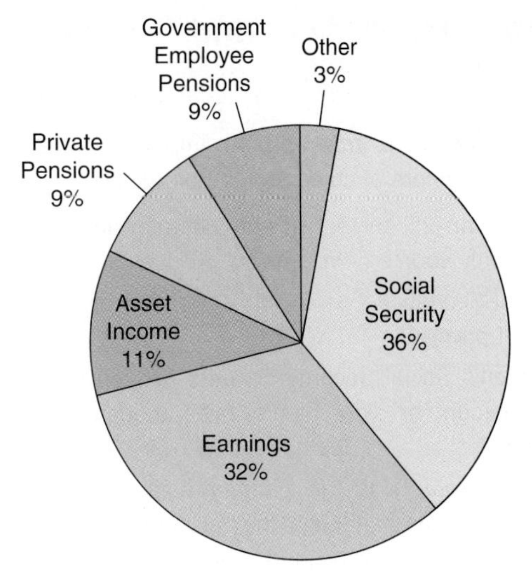

FIGURE 10.3 Sources of Older Adults' Aggregate Income

Source: Social Security Administration, 2013a.

Social Security Consider these statistics to get a sense of how important Social Security is to getting by financially in old age.

- Social Security is the major source of income for about 66 percent of older beneficiaries.
- For approximately 24 percent of beneficiaries, they depend on Social Security for 90 percent or more of their income.
- About 35 percent of older adults would be poor without the safety net of Social Security.
- Almost 30 percent of those kept out of poverty by Social Security are under age 65 and include over 3 million children who receive benefits as dependents of workers who are retired, disabled, or deceased.
- Reliance on Social Security as the primary source of income increases with age (Caldera, 2012a; Center on Budget and Policy Priorities, 2012; Shelton, 2013b; Social Security Administration, 2013a; Van de Water & Sherman, 2010).

Social Security is so critical to low-income retirees because it is what is called a guaranteed progressive benefit that keeps up with increases in the cost of living. This means that lower-income workers benefit proportionately more from Social Security when they retire—they receive benefits equal to 55 percent of their working wages, while high-income workers collect only 27 percent of their prior salary. On the other hand, higher-income workers receive

Gender, Race, Age, and Social Security

Social Security is an even more important safety net for women, elders of color, and the oldest-old.

- More than 25 percent of older women depend on it as their only source of income.
- Social Security keeps about 40 percent of older women out of poverty.
- Women's Social Security benefits are, on average, just 75 percent of older men's, even though they rely on it more.
- Social Security is the primary source of income for elders of color, although they are less likely to receive benefits than Caucasians.
- Older Latinas and African Americans are more likely than whites to rely on it for 90 percent or more of their income.
- Latina and Asian older women are least likely to receive Social Security, in part because many of them are immigrants who may not be eligible (Caldera, 2012a, 2012b; Center on Budget and Policy Priorities, 2012; Shelton, 2013a, 2013b; Social Security Administration, 2011b; Waid & Koenig, 2012).

more Social Security income in absolute dollars. But it is also a regressive benefit (i.e., both the rich and the poor pay the same payroll rate of 12.4 percent). This means that low-income workers, often women and people of color, pay a larger proportion of their monthly salary for the Social Security tax compared to higher-income workers. So the system is both fair and unfair for low-income retirees. On average, Social Security replaces about 40 percent of what a person earned before retirement, far below the 70 percent of preretirement income that is typically required to get by financially in retirement (Caldera, 2012b; Center on Budget and Policy Priorities, 2012; Shelton, 2013b).

If you are a younger person and listening to media stories about retirement, you might assume that you will never receive Social Security. The answer is not clear-cut—and depends upon the economy, Congressional policy decisions, and political will. You are very likely to receive Social Security benefits when you retire, although it probably will be at a lower rate and a later age. You will learn about both the myths and facts about the future solvency of Social Security in Chapter 13.

Until recently, certain categories of people were excluded from Social Security benefits. LGBT partners, for example, could not qualify for benefits based on their partner's earnings, since Social Security was based on a traditional model of marriage between a man and a woman. However, things are changing as a result of the 2013 Supreme Court ruling striking down the Defense of Marriage Act. The Social Security Administration is now processing some retirement spouse claims for legally married same-sex couples and will pay benefits when due. With guidance from the Department of Justice, the agency has been hammering out policies and procedures to deal with claims from same-sex couples in states where same-sex marriages or civil unions are prohibited or not recognized. Despite the current ambiguities, individuals in such relationships may submit an application for benefits (Social Security Administration, 2013b).

Another inequity is that 60 percent of older women currently receive benefits as wives and widows, rather than as paid workers, because the benefits they would receive as employees would be smaller. This is projected to be the case for the next several cohorts of women as they reach old age, despite more women having longer work histories and moving into higher-paid positions than in prior cohorts. The primary reason that women will continue to depend on their husband's Social Security is because women as a whole still earn only about 80 cents for every dollar earned by men; their lower wages reduce their own lifetime earnings as a basis for calculating their Social Security benefits (Caldera, 2012a; Johnson and Wilson, 2010; Meyer, 2010).

Calculating What Your Social Security Benefits Might Be

You can calculate your own Social Security benefits for your anticipated age of retirement. Go to the Social Security Administration (http://www.ssa.gov/) Web site. What was your reaction to the projected Social Security that you might receive? Do you think you could live on just your Social Security? If not, what changes do you think you might need to make in your life to be financially secure when you are old? You may now understand why financial planners generally agree that young adults should start saving now for their retirement (Bernard, 2010).

Assets **Assets**, third most important income source for elders, include

- interest-bearing savings and checking accounts that typically generate low earnings,
- investments,
- home equity, and
- personal property.

About 54 percent of older adults receive asset income. To put it more starkly, this means that 46 percent of older households that have earned low wages throughout their lives—typically the oldest-old; women, particularly unmarried women; and persons of color—report no asset income. Moreover, 60 percent of workers report that they and their partners have saved less than $25,000 for retirement (excluding their homes and pension plans), suggesting that retirement is going to be a tight squeeze. All age groups have seen their assets decline during the recession. But older workers and retirees who were relying on investments for retirement income have less time to recover from the recent major stock market losses, simply because they will not live long enough to do so (AoA, 2012; Helman, Greenwald, Copeland, & VanDerhei, 2012; Social Security Administration, 2013a).

Home equity represents the most important component of older people's assets, and has typically been about 50 percent of their net worth. In terms of quality of life, home equity is not liquid wealth or cash and cannot be relied on to cover daily expenses, however. Approximately 80 percent of older people own their homes compared to about 60 percent in the overall population. But this percentage of homeownership is lower among elders of color, and has declined since 2008 among all groups of older adults as a result of the recession. Only 40 percent of these older homeowners own their homes free and clear—they no longer have to pay a mortgage. About 16 percent of older adults owe more on their house than it is worth, a pattern found especially among those who moved to Sunbelt states, such as Arizona or Florida. If they are unable to sell their home, it is no longer a financial safety net as was true in the past, but instead is a financial burden. Additionally, equity-rich and cash-poor elders are attractive targets for unscrupulous mortgage lenders who capitalize on their need for cash by offering high-rate and high-fee loan products (Cawthorne, 2010; Harrell, 2011; Johnson and Wilson, 2010; NCOA, 2012).

As we look toward the future, boomers are less likely than the current cohort of elders to have paid off their mortgages and more likely to have refinanced multiple times as a way to reduce monthly expenses and increase their cash flow. This puts them at higher risk of foreclosure—losing their home to the bank, which would greatly threaten their economic security. Overall, many older adults who viewed a home as their retirement nest egg are finding that they cannot sell it—or can do so only at a loss. They have become what is commonly known as "house rich but cash poor" (AoA, 2012; Harrell, 2011; Pynoos, Cicero, & Nishita, 2010).

Pensions Other Than Social Security Although nearly all jobholders are covered by Social Security as a general public pension, only about 28 percent of employees receive other pensions, which are tied to a specific job and administered by an employer, union, or private insurance company. Pension benefits are generally based on earnings or a combination of earnings and years of service; traditionally intended to supplement Social Security, they rarely provide the replacement rate of income necessary for retirement. Up until the 1990s, those who did receive pensions knew that they could count on it as long as they worked for the same company for 30 years. They typically were covered by **defined benefit pension plans**—a specified amount is guaranteed by the company as a lifetime annuity. For example, autoworkers could count on a generous pension and retire relatively young. Now pensions are typically **defined**

Facing Foreclosure

Stories about older adults facing foreclosure on their homes abound. Consider Mercedes Robinson-Duvallon, 82, who did not have the money to fix a leaky roof, so she agreed to refinance her home a second time when a telephone salesman called with an offer. It turns out she agreed to an "interest-only" loan, and she saw her loan payments balloon from $700 to $2,800 per month. Such payments far exceed her monthly fixed income. Then the company that refinanced her home went under and was bought by another bank, which initiated the foreclosure. Her attorneys said she owed a total of $50,000 on her home because she refinanced it in the past. After the story was publicized by a Miami TV station, several community members came to her support, including a lawyer who helped postpone her eviction while a solution was hammered out. The television station set up a fund on her behalf. Robinson-Duvallon, who uses a cane and walks slowly, tearfully told the TV reporter: "I love my home" (WSVN.com, 2011).

Inequities by Pension Coverage

- Among older workers in the top earnings brackets, slightly over 60 percent have private pensions.
- Among the lowest-income workers, less than 20 percent do.
- Almost twice as many men as women receive pensions, and their pensions tend to be nearly twice the size of women's.
- Women, workers of color, and lower-income workers in small nonunion plants and low-wage industries have the lowest rates of pension coverage (Meyer and Estes, 2009; Myles, 2010).

With limited assets and rising health care costs, many older adults are literally counting their pennies.

contribution plans such as a 401(k), in which the amount of the benefit depends on an individual's investment returns; this creates a greater financial risk for employees who may not be skilled at managing investments. In the past three decades, the share of employees in large and medium private sector jobs who are covered by defined benefit pensions—the ones assuring the greatest economic security—declined from 84 to less than 30 percent (Angel & Mudrazija, 2011; Employee Benefit Research Institute, 2010; Harootyan & Sarmiento, 2011; Myles, 2010).

As shown in the box above on pension inequities, the recession and escalating health care costs have also reduced pension assets. The marked decline of employee pension coverage is a problem for older adults' future well-being. Just as we have seen with other sources of income, pension coverage varies by social class, race, gender, and age.

Being able to keep employer-provided health insurance may be a primary consideration for the young-old who are contemplating retirement but do not yet qualify for Medicare. Among employed adults ages 55–64, only about 20 percent have health coverage by their own employer. This low rate is not surprising since very few firms offer health care insurance to their retirees. Fortunately, the Patient Protection and Affordable Care Act will offer this age group health benefits at lower rates that they can use until they qualify for Medicare. Health insurance benefits have also been jeopardized by company bankruptcies. Think about airline pilots and flight attendants who have lost pensions and other benefits when their company declared bankruptcy (Brandon, 2009; Jacobson, Schwartz, & Neuman, 2009).

Earnings Current job earnings form approximately 32 percent of the total income of older households; they are reported by about 18 percent of men and 13 percent of women. The median income of married adults age 65 and older who are employed is around $45,500, although this declines dramatically among unmarried elders to slightly less than $20,000. The proportion of income from earnings may grow slightly in the future, because of increased employment among older people, along with a drop in interest and dividend income. On the other hand, low wages may keep job earnings a relatively small percent of a person's total income (AoA, 2012; Koenig & Walker, 2011; Pension Rights Center, 2014; Social Security Administration, 2013a).

points to ponder

Imagine that your annual income is the median income for a single older adult—around $20,0000. Consider what you now pay for rent, food, utilities, health care, gas, insurance, and any leisure activities. Total the amount that you spend each year on your basic living expenses. Are you able to live on that amount? If not, what would you have to give up in order to do so?

Although earnings are an important income source to the young-old and to those with the highest income from assets and pensions, they diminish with age. Additionally, with the increasing numbers of older Americans who are finding themselves unemployed, they are likely to have filed for Social Security benefits earlier than they had initially planned. In such instances, earnings have declined as a proportion of their income while Social Security has grown in importance as an essential safety net (AoA, 2012; Aversa & Rugaber, 2009; Hicks and Kingson, 2009; Johnson and Wilson, 2010).

Public Assistance Only about 5 percent of older adults, primarily single women, women who are divorced, and persons of color, receive public assistance in the form of **Supplemental Security Income (SSI).** The average monthly benefit for older recipients in 2013 was only $417, but most older recipients also have Social Security (Congressional Budget Office, 2012; Social Security Administration, 2013a).

SSI was established in 1974 to provide a minimum guaranteed income for elders living on the margin of poverty (or as you will learn in our discussion of poverty below, were "economically insecure"), and for older adults and persons of all ages who are visually impaired or disabled. Unlike younger recipients, older adults do not need to be disabled to qualify for SSI but instead must meet the income eligibility requirements. In contrast to Social Security, SSI does not require a history of covered employment contributions. Instead, eligibility is determined by a strict means test based on monthly income and assets. For those who qualify, the federal SSI benefits fall substantially below the poverty line. Indeed, SSI supplies only about 14 percent of the income of poor older people. Those who receive SSI may also qualify for Medicaid and food stamps, but only about 30 percent of eligible elders receive food stamps, in part because they are embarrassed to do so. This participation rate, lower than other age groups, is of concern as growing numbers of older adults are dealing with hunger because of the recession and ongoing cuts to the food stamp program (AARP, 2010; AoA, 2012; Food Research and Action Center, 2010; Fuller-Thomson & Redmond, 2008; Wu, 2009).

Many eligible older poor do not participate in SSI. One reason is that proving financial eligibility for SSI is a difficult, time-consuming, and often demeaning process, requiring extensive documentation and dealing with conflicting criteria for benefits from SSI, Medicaid, and food stamps. Additionally, legal immigrants are denied access to these programs. Of great concern is the number of states that have reduced SSI, food stamps, and Medicaid benefits during the economic downturn and budget cuts. This has occurred while the numbers of "poor" or "near-poor" older adults who are eligible for public assistance and lack the income to meet their basic needs have grown.

Social Class and Poverty in Old Age

Social class as one indicator of economic status in old age—whether we are upper-income, middle class, or low-income—is influenced by the larger economy, past and current employment patterns, and resultant retirement income and benefits. Social class, in turn, largely shapes what is possible in old age, including the option to decide how to spend one's time in work or retirement. Moreover, social class is related to every measure of health, illness, and disability, not just in old age but across the life course. It also affects access to medical and dental care, out-of-pocket health care costs, living situations and social networks, transportation, and opportunities to experience productive activities, such as volunteering and contributing to others. In other words, the income we have across the life course profoundly affects our choices in old age (Johnson & Wilson, 2010).

The widely held public perception is that older adults are financially better off than other age groups—and to some extent, this is true. Older adults have benefited from policies designed to give them a minimum standard of income and health care—particularly Social Security and Medicare, which we discuss fully in Chapter 13. As you have just learned, they are more likely to own their homes

points to ponder

How would you define the social class of your family—both your immediate and extended family? How has your family been affected by the recession? If you have older relatives, how are they doing economically? What kind of changes have they made in their lives as a result of the recession? Have they cut back on certain purchases, been unable to retire, tried unsuccessfully to sell their home? What do you think might be some of the long-term effects of the recession on their economic well-being? And how has the recession affected the middle class in America?

and to have other assets such as savings and retirement benefits than younger adults—even though home values, saving, and investments dramatically declined during the worldwide economic downturn. As a result, their net worth (all sources of income) tends to be greater than for those under age 35. But those assets do not necessarily translate to disposable income—or money that they can spend.

A common myth is that older adults are benefiting financially at the expense of younger generations. In some scenarios, older adults who receive Social Security and Medicare are even blamed for the increasing poverty among children under age 6. However, the decline in the income status of children is caused by economic, political, and demographic forces—especially cuts in Medicaid, child welfare, and income maintenance programs—and not by the income growth of the older population. As is true of the general population, the gap between rich and poor within the aging population has rapidly increased in recent years; a relatively small percent of older adults are wealthy, while many elders struggle to get by financially (AoA, 2012).

points to ponder

Imagine yourself as a 70-year-old woman with a fixed income from Social Security of $1,200 a month. Your monthly expenses for rent, utilities, and food come to almost $1,100. What would you give up if you had a health emergency one month and had to spend $900 for medical expenses not covered by Medicare?

Moreover, among older adults, women, elders of color, those over age 85, those who live alone, and elders in rural areas and in the South are most likely to be low-income. As a result, social class inequities are actually greater among the older population than among other age groups. And a growing proportion of older adults are caught between high- and low-income older people—not well enough off to be financially secure but not poor enough to qualify for the means-tested safety net of SSI and Medicaid, which would qualify them for some health and social services (AARP, 2010).

One reason many older adults struggle financially, even when they have Social Security or a private pension that raises them above the poverty level, is that they need about 80 percent of their preretirement income to maintain their living standard in retirement. But retirement can reduce individual incomes by one-third to one-half. This means that retirees who do not fall into upper-income brackets must markedly adjust their standard of living downward—while their out-of-pocket spending for items such as health care and medications typically goes up with age. Indeed, a 65-year-old couple retiring in 2012 with only Medicare needed about $240,000 to cover future medical costs, assuming a life expectancy of early to mid-eighties (Brady, 2010; Fidelity.com, 2012).

Are Older Adults Poorer Than Other Age Groups? Slightly less than 10 percent of adults who are 65 and older currently live at or below the federal poverty level; this level for one person was $11,490 for two, $15,510 in 2013. Another 5.8 percent are what is considered "near-poor" (income between the poverty level and 125 percent of this level). Admittedly, the overall proportion of older adults who are poor is much lower than among children under age 18 and adults age 18–64 (15 percent of those younger than age 65 are poor). But the percent of older people who are poor actually rose slightly in 2010, the first time since the 1950s, another sign of the negative impacts of the recession. These rates may rise in the near future if Social Security cost of living increases are not given, if cuts are made to Medicare benefits, or simply because of rising health care costs. Not surprisingly, older adults who are poor also have the poorest health (AoA, 2012; Levinson, Damico, Cubanski, & Neuman, 2013; National Council on Aging, 2012; U.S. Department of Health and Human Services, 2012).

Poverty statistics do not tell us the whole picture. This is because the official poverty threshold does not capture the 36 percent of older adults who are considered **economically insecure**—this means that they are living at

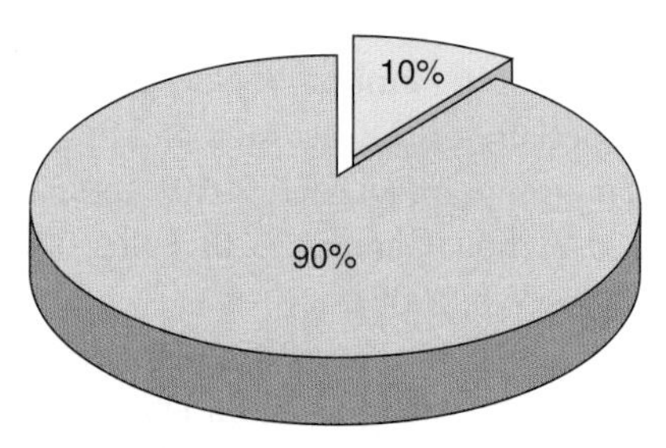

FIGURE 10.4 Percent of Older Adults in Poverty According to Official Poverty Statistics

Source: AoA, 2012

or below 200 percent of the poverty level, which makes them at high risk of becoming poor. A crisis, such as the death of a partner, a major illness not fully covered by Medicare, or a rise in monthly expenses, such as a spike in gasoline or home heating fuel prices, can quickly push them into poverty. In addition, the hidden poor—those living with relatives or in long-term care facilities—are not counted in official census statistics. When all these factors are taken into account, more elders are at marginal levels of income and at greater risk of poverty than the population 18–64 years. And as you will see next, there are some problems with what are considered the official poverty statistics (Institute on Assets and Social Policy, 2011a).

Limitations of Official Poverty Statistics Poverty statistics are static or fixed at one point in time. But people's lives are constantly changing, which cannot be fully captured by statistics. Older people are more likely than younger age groups to move in and out of poverty over time, often because of health and long-term care costs. And once an older person moves into poverty, she or he is less likely to return to financial adequacy than are younger cohorts. Their risk of economic vulnerability is increased because they are unlikely to have reserve funds to cover emergencies such as catastrophic medical expenses or caregiving for a partner. As a result, low-income elders often face impossible trade-offs, such as giving up medications or food in order to pay for heat. Additionally, older people facing major health care needs or living alone in inadequate, poorly maintained housing may have greater difficulty coping with economic hardship than younger adults, which can then affect their sense of self and well-being. In fact, AARP has estimated that the poverty rate is as high as 16.8 percent when health care costs are taken into account; the oldest and poorest Medicare beneficiaries spend about 25 percent of their income on health care, which can then tip them below the poverty line. Indeed, out-of-pocket medical spending rises dramatically with age, and nearly doubles for low-income adults age 75 and older (Koenig & Walker, 2011).

Yet another way that poverty statistics of older adults can be misleading is that the federal poverty standard for a single adult age 65 and older is 8–10 percent lower than for younger adults. In setting this lower threshold for elders to qualify for benefits as "poor," the Census Bureau assumes that the costs of food and other necessities are less for older people. But this is often not the case, especially since elders spend proportionately more on housing, utilities, transportation, and health care than do younger groups. And of course this pattern is intensified when the cost to live in a particular city or state is higher than the national average. For instance, an older adult in New York City or San Francisco will have a much harder time covering the cost of housing and food than someone living in a small Midwestern town. If the same poverty standard were applied to the older population as to the other age groups, the poverty rate among older people is estimated to double to nearly 20 percent (AARP, 2010; Munnell, Wu, & Hurwitz, 2009).

In 2011, the Census Bureau announced a new supplemental measure of poverty that takes into account current economic conditions such as health care costs better than the official poverty measures. When this supplemental measure accounts for such costs, the poverty rate among elders is estimated to be 16 percent—higher than for other age groups. However, some economists counter that this new supplemental measure overestimates poverty among elders because it does not consider their income from savings, the stock market, and other accumulated wealth. What is clear

How the High Cost of Living Can Lead to Poverty

Californian elders need at least twice the income calculated by the federal government to make ends meet, because of the high cost of housing. In 2007, nearly 50 percent of older Californians did not make enough money to cover basic needs, even though just 8 percent fell below the official federal poverty level. The recession has meant that even more elders must rely on SSI and food stamps and other services to get by. An 80-year-old widow from the Philippines works part-time at a nursery school, earning $215 a month. With $845 a month in SSI, she takes home less than $13,000 a year, but according to federal standards, she is not poor. Yet her daily life is that of a poor person. She goes from food pantry to food pantry with a suitcase in search of enough to eat, and rents out the tiny rooms in her rundown home to two widows and a couple to help cover her $1,800-a-month rent. Each person's space overflows with pieces collected over a lifetime—part of an old army uniform, sheets of scripture, family photographs. None of the renters makes enough money to live independently, and is resigned to their crowded living conditions. The widow concludes that "America is a nice place for the young, but for the old, it is no good" (Zavis, 2010).

Poverty: A Frequent Outcome from Caregiving

Consider an older woman who has never been poor until her partner's death. Not only is she struggling to get by financially, but she is also coping with her altered sense of someone who had been middle class and economically secure all her life. But all that changed rapidly because of high medical expenses and because she had to quit her job to take care of him. Next time you pass an older woman with bulging garbage bags on the streets, stop to think that she may not always have been poor and homeless. She may have been doing what is expected of many women—to care for others—and now is paying the economic price.

is that regardless of how poverty is measured, there are more older people in distress nowadays than in the recent past. Another limitation of the "official" poverty rate is it does not adequately capture the high rates of poverty among older adults who have been historically disadvantaged: women and elders of color (Tavernise & Gebeloff, 2011).

Poverty Variations by Race, Gender, and Sexual Orientation As you have seen in earlier discussions of the life course, inequities throughout life often lead to what is called **cumulative disadvantage**—inequities experienced in old age are piled onto disparities faced as early as childhood, intensifying the gap between rich and poor. You learned about this concept in Chapter 5 where we discussed the life course. And it is a concept you will see played out in the higher rates of poverty among older women and elders of color compared to their white counterparts in old age. If one starts out poor and with limited opportunities, reversing this pattern is difficult—and the inequities typically become worse as we age (Cawthorne, 2010; Johnson and Wilson, 2010; Werner, 2011).

Across all racial and ethnic groups, older women are more likely to be poor and near-poor than men. The poverty rate among older women—often the result of widowhood—is almost twice that among older men, while men's economic status tends to improve when they are widowed. And almost 38 percent of women are more likely to fall into the category of being economically insecure than men (about 23 percent) and to rely on SSI. This is due in part to their fewer sources of retirement income, less net worth, and lower Social Security benefits that result from lower earnings and time away from employment to care for family members. Some women become poor after depleting their assets while caring for a dying partner. You learned in Chapter 7 how caregiving has numerous economic costs, which is captured in the box on this page (AoA, 2012; Caldera, 2012a; Congressional Budget Office, 2012; Johnson and Wilson, 2010).

Many African American elders experience poverty resulting from a lifetime of lower wages, less private pension coverage, and fewer assets than white older adults. Even before the recession, nine out of 10 African American and Latino older adults did not have sufficient resources to sustain themselves throughout their projected lifetime. Indeed, many African Americans across all ages have experienced an economic depression (not just a recession), with an unemployment rate of 16.5 percent, compared with 9.7 percent for the nation as a whole. This has meant that middle-age and young-old blacks have had to raid their "nest eggs" (for those who had them) to get by during what should be peak earning years. More than twice as many African Americans ages 45 and older compared to all older adults responding to a large national survey reported having to cut back on necessities such as medications and to borrow money to pay monthly living expenses. This pattern then increases the likelihood of their being poor when they are among the old-old and oldest-old (AARP, 2011; VanHorn et al., 2011).

Facing both gender and racial disparities, women of color are the most economically vulnerable. Contrary to the public perception that children are the poorest group in our society, it is actually Latina and African American

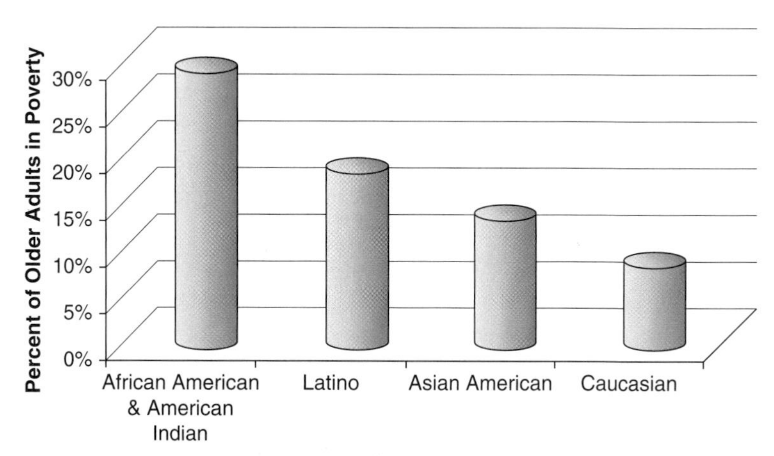

FIGURE 10.5 Poverty by Racial/Ethnic Groups

Source: AARP, 2011.

Economic Disparities among Elders of Color

- The poor: approximately 7 percent of older whites, 18 percent of older African Americans, 19 percent of older Latinos, and 12–14 percent of Asian Americans in 2011
- The economically insecure (living at or below 200 percent of poverty): around 30 percent of whites, 52 percent of older African Americans, and 56 percent of older Latinos
- Those living alone: 16 percent, versus 5 percent living with families
- Those in cities: 11 percent, versus 10 percent in rural areas
- Those ages 85 and older: 15 percent (AoA, 2012; Dumez & Derbew, 2011; Institute on Assets and Social Policy, 2011b; Johnson and Wilson, 2010; Waid & Koenig, 2012)

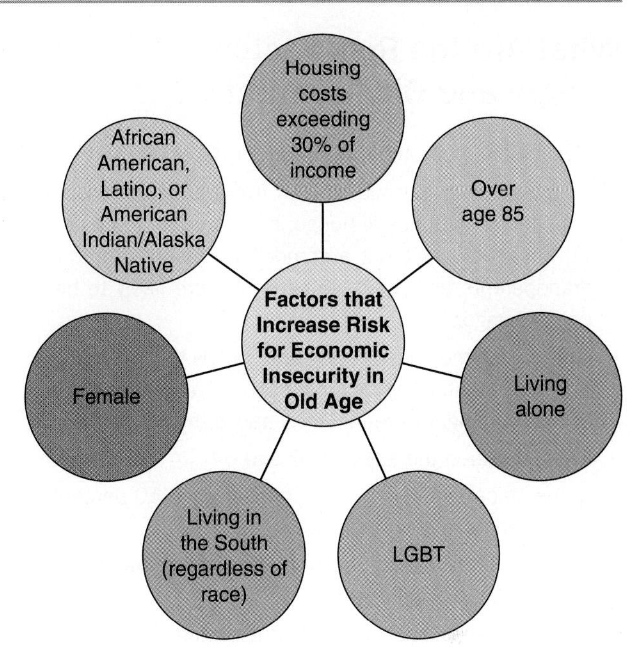

FIGURE 10.6 Factors That Increase the Risk of Economic Insecurity in Old Age

women age 65 and older and living alone (approximately 41 and 31 percent, respectively) who are the poorest. The level of economic insecurity, hovering just above poverty, also increases dramatically among older women of color (AoA, 2012; Johnson & Wilson, 2010).

One reason that income declines with age and gender is because there are more unmarried women among the oldest-old; additionally, women on average live longer but earn less income than men. Moreover, single women who have never married are likely to have earned less than single men, and cannot draw upon a husband's retirement benefits. Reflecting the process of cumulative disadvantage, unmarried women have a lower median income than unmarried men or married couples in every successively older age group. It may surprise you to learn that this pattern is unlikely to improve dramatically in the future (AoA, 2012).

Homelessness among older adults has increased in recent years with declines in affordable housing.

The poverty rate among lesbian, gay, bisexual, and transgender (LGBT) older adults increased during the recession and is higher than the rate for heterosexual elders; this may result in part from social stigma, unequal legal treatment, and greater dependence on informal networks than their heterosexual counterparts. Overall, economic hardships faced by older LGBT cohorts are often compounded by a lifetime of discrimination, by historical patterns such as working at jobs with no pensions, and by recent events such as loss of a partner or declining health (Badgett, Durso, & Schneebaum, 2013).

In summary, despite the overall improved financial situation of the older population since 1955, large pockets of poverty and near-poverty persist and economic inequities are widening.

Hunger Is Increasing among Older Americans

Look at these startling facts about hunger among older adults—so contrary to the image many of us hold that elders are financially secure.

What Are the Risk Factors for Being Hungry and Old in America?

- Living alone—divorced, widowed, or never married
- Living with a grandchild: One in five grandparent-headed households is at risk of hunger compared to about one in 20 households without a grandchild present, and these grandparents are about 50 percent more likely to be at risk of hunger.
- Limited income and/or living at or below the poverty line. But this is a startling fact: over 50% of all elders who are at risk of hunger have incomes above the poverty line.
- Being between the ages of 60 and 64
- Being African American or Latino, although 50 percent of elders who are hungry are white
- Being a renter makes one twice as likely to be at risk of hunger than homeowners.
- Being a high school dropout. But having a high school diploma protects against hunger on a scale comparable to being married (Jaret, 2010).

- Over 5 million older adults—11.4 percent of all elders—experience some form of **food insecurity**—which is the government's official name for hunger and refers to households that are uncertain of having enough food for all household members.
- Of these, about 2.5 million are at risk of hunger.
- One in six older adults in New York City received food from soup kitchens and food pantries, and more than one in three had trouble affording food in 2009, a 65 percent increase since 2003 (AARP, 2013; Jaret, 2010).

Concerned about the rising rates of hunger, AARP teamed with highly visible and seemingly unlikely spokespersons, such NASCAR's Jeff Gordon, to publicize the plight of hungry elders. In addition to speaking out about the issue, Gordon's race car has a logo promoting AARP's cause "Drive to End Hunger." Viewers have lots of time to see the logo in a 500-mile race! Part of the campaign's goal is to reduce the stigma for elders' accepting government assistance, like food stamps.

Going hungry at any age has negative consequences for one's health and overall well-being. Squeezed by rising health care costs and living expenses, more people are forced to choose between paying for medications and putting food on the table. People struggling to eat are almost 3 times more likely to skip pills, delay refilling prescriptions, or stop taking a medication entirely. Similarly, older Americans faced with hunger are more likely to report poor health and to experience vitamin deficiencies than those with enough to eat. They are also more likely to be hospitalized, to have longer hospital stays, and to have limitations in their ability to carry out activities of daily living. Most striking is the fact that being marginally food insecure is roughly equivalent to being 14 years older chronologically (AARP, 2013; Jaret, 2010; Lee, Fischer, & Johnson, 2010; Ziliak & Gundersen, 2011).

Hunger cuts across the income spectrum, and is not always due to low income. In some instances, an older adult may have the money to purchase food, but is unable to readily get to the grocery store, lacks the sociability of eating with others, is unable to cook for themselves, or may be experiencing some of types of mental disorder or cognitive impairment that affects their appetite.

Changing Conceptions of Work and Retirement

This chapter has focused on economic challenges facing older adults. But not all older adults continue to work out of financial necessity, and many choose to experience active aging through new productive opportunities in their retirement, which you learned about in Chapter 8. We close this chapter with some examples of positive directions for retirement.

Many older adults genuinely enjoy their jobs and get satisfaction from working, regardless of whether

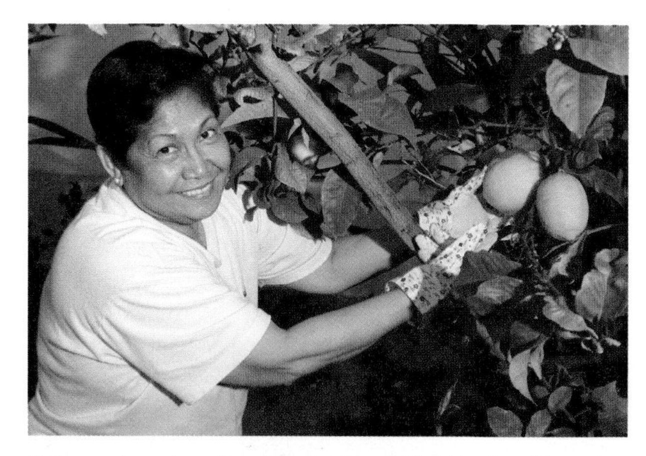

Retirement can be a time to enjoy favorite hobbies for elders who feel financially secure.

they need the money. Others are making valuable contributions to their organizations and to society at large. They keep on working to feel productive and a sense of meaning and purpose. This is often the case for those in academic and research settings, or engaged in creative pursuits, where they can exercise some control over their work conditions. Some adults may have changed careers multiple times throughout their lives, making them more flexible as job markets change. Others have shifted into new "retirement jobs," or what have been called encore careers, with an emphasis on working by choice and for enjoyment. An illustration is that of a businessman who retires from the corporate world and moves into teaching—something he wanted to do all his life, but felt he could not do so because of the need to earn more money while raising his family. Because they have shifted into a new job, they may earn less than those who have never retired. But they have traded income for work they find challenging and meaningful, experiencing new learning opportunities, and feeling respected. Many such workers in their encore careers hope to work until advanced old age (Carstensen, 2007, 2009).

points to **ponder**

There is a saying: "Don't retire. Rewire!" What are the ways that older adults can "rewire"—that is, discover something to do with their lives, which is different from what they were doing as working adults? Do you have any examples of retired adults who have "rewired"?

The Encore Careers Movement has spawned growing numbers of nonprofit groups and programs that aim to help older workers find public service jobs that benefit society. Civic Ventures is the leading national think tank promoting encore careers for adults ages 55–80; it is based on the value that age is an asset—to both the private and public sectors. As noted by its founder, Marc Freedman, on the Civic Ventures Web site, "people are hitting the reset button. There is a tremendous feeling of returning to earlier ideals." Rather than a problem to be solved, Civic Ventures sees the longevity revolution as the springboard for an America made better by experience (Brown et al., 2010; Civic Ventures, 2011).

Encore Career Changers

Gary rose to become president of a major food brokerage company, earning a six-figure salary but always frustrated that he was not able to "give back" to society. At age 56, he joined the VISTA program as a $7,000-a-year food bank employee. Six years later, he founded the Farm to Family program, which delivers millions of pounds of fresh produce to California food banks. Jack, a retired physician, was not satisfied spending his days golfing. He started Volunteers in Medicine, a network of free clinics staffed by medical professionals over age 55. Hazel received her college degree in art history at age 94. She plans to work as a docent in a local museum. Raising six children and working full-time, she never had the time in the past to get her degree. Through her experience, she hopes to inspire others to realize it's never too late to get a college education (Chea, 2010; Civic Ventures, 2011).

From a societal perspective, a sequential process of education, work, and retirement for a population with a longer life expectancy—and the possibility of over 30 years in retirement—requires modifying expectations about lifelong education and training. Changing values about the "appropriate age" for education, employment, retirement, and leisure demand a reexamination of employment policies and norms. As Freedman argues, we need a major shift in thinking, culture, social institutions, and public policies from what worked in the past to what can carry us into the future. The traditional linear life cycle of education for the young, employment for the middle-aged, and retirement for the old is already undergoing major changes. This is occurring as more middle-aged and older persons enter or reenter college, take online courses, move into new careers, or begin their studies for graduate or professional degrees. Freedman and other proponents of "rewiring" rather than "retiring" argue that these changes in the workplace can benefit all ages (Freedman, 2011).

Many countries are well ahead of the United States in fostering new models of work and retirement. A "gliding-out" plan of phased retirement in Japan and some European countries permits a gradual shift into a part-time schedule and for older workers to train younger ones. Some Scandinavian countries give workers year-long sabbaticals every 10 years as a time to reevaluate their careers or to take a break instead of working straight through

The Benefits of an Age-Integrated Workforce

Older and younger adults working together can provide reciprocal benefits to each other and to the organization, with the older worker bringing experience and institutional knowledge to the relationship, and the younger worker enriching the organization with innovation and a fresh perspective. That is one scenario. Another could be that the older worker is the newer employee in the organization with a much younger supervisor. In this and other scenarios, there are opportunities for people from every age category to learn from each other and enjoy each other's company.

to retirement. Jobs can also be restructured, gradually allowing longer vacations, shorter workdays, and more opportunities for community involvement during the preretirement working years. Barriers to such changes in our society, however, include the fact that Americans have fewer vacation days than any other Western industrialized society, and some do not even use their earned vacation days. In addition, the current climate of unemployment, cuts to public sector jobs, and business failures makes it unlikely that employers will create alternative employment models for older workers.

New jobs in the future are likely to be in the service sector (e.g., health and social services, food, and recreation) and information technology. For example, older workers could fill a growing labor gap in the long-term care sector, often in direct care positions, especially in home care. But these types of jobs may not provide older workers with adequate financial security. Whether technological advances will produce new jobs or result in net job losses is also unknown. What is certain is that there will be greater labor market diversity among the older population and greater variations in the reasons for retirement, employment, and economic well-being.

summary

This chapter addressed three primary economic conditions that profoundly shape older adults' well-being, roles, and activities: retirement, employment/unemployment, and social class, particularly poverty and near-poverty. A long-term pattern of early retirement is now shifting, with more adults working into their seventies and even eighties as a result of economic necessity or their desire for a sense of purpose and identity through their work. In many ways, working longer makes sense, given increased life expectancy. Health status, degree of education, the nature of one's occupation, and gender and race all affect the timing of retirement and the degree of satisfaction experienced, but income and whether one has a sense of control over the retirement decisions are the most important factors.

When the majority of older adults in the past chose to retire early, the employment rate declined. However, since about the late 1990s, the number of employed adults age 55 and older has increased steadily, reaching the highest rate since 1962. The proportion of part-time and full-time employment has also shifted, with older adults now more likely to be employed full-time than was true in the past.

As result of the economic downturn since 2008, an increasing number of older adults feel that their retirement has been forced, and are unemployed. Older adults tend to face more barriers, including age discrimination, in seeking employment, and are unemployed longer than younger adults. Many simply give up looking, or settle for low-paying jobs just to get by financially.

Economic status or social class in old age is determined by public and private pensions, assets, earnings, and public assistance. For the majority of older people, especially women and elders of color, Social Security is their primary—and in some instances, their sole—source of income. The oldest-old tended to have been employed in jobs with private pensions, but future cohorts will depend on their own personal investments and Social Security rather than employer-provided pensions. Compared to younger people, older adults are more likely to have assets—especially a home, although the value of their home has probably declined since 2008. Additionally, a home is not a "liquid" asset that provides immediate income and may entail extensive maintenance costs.

Although a smaller percent of older people have incomes below the poverty line than was true prior to the passage of Social Security and its automatic annual cost of living increase (COLA), the poverty rate among the older population increased slightly in 2010, the first time since the 1950s. In addition to the approximately 10 percent of older adults who are counted as living below the poverty line, many others hover just above this level or are "hidden poor," who live in long-term settings or with their families and not counted as poor in the official statistics. A new supplemental poverty figure suggests that the poverty rate may be as high as 16 percent among older adults, primary due to health care costs. The poverty rate increases among women, the oldest-old, elders of color, and those living alone, with African American and Latina women the poorest groups in our society. One of the most striking indicators of older adults' marginal economic status is the growing hunger rate. Public assistance programs such as Supplemental Security Income and food stamps have not removed the very serious financial problems of the older poor, in part because they are underutilized and are becoming more restrictive with state budget cuts.

The numbers of economically vulnerable elders will not diminish dramatically in the future. Instead, a permanent underclass of boomers is projected, with a disproportionate representation of persons of color, those with a sporadic employment history, single women, and those with limited education. In fact, the baby boom cohort is characterized by more income inequality, with a disappearing middle class, than any prior cohort. Women continue to face more financial challenges in old age than men, despite the growing number who have entered the paid labor force and worked longer than in the past. These inequities among the boomers are unlikely to change without interventions earlier in the life course to prevent poverty and chronic illness and to ensure educational and employment opportunities in young adulthood and middle age. On a more positive note, however, middle-age and young-old adults who have the financial resources often are pursuing new encore careers, returning to school, and redefining traditional work patterns as they age.

key terms

Age Discrimination in Employment Act (ADEA), p. 291
assets, p. 295
cumulative disadvantage, p. 300
defined benefit pension plans, p. 295
defined contribution plans, p. 295
economically insecure, p. 298
food insecurity, p. 302
retirement, p. 284
Senior Community Service Employment Program (SCSEP), p. 292
Social Security, p. 293
Supplemental Security Income (SSI), p. 297

review questions

1. How have patterns of work and retirement changed in the past 10 years? What are some of the primary reasons that older adults are working longer than in the past?
2. List three factors that affect the timing of retirement. Then list three factors that affect whether retirement is a positive experience or not.
3. Describe some of the primary barriers to employment of older individuals. What are some of the myths or misconceptions about older workers? What are some reasons that older adults are unemployed longer on average than younger age groups?
4. Imagine that you were the Director of Human Resources for a business that wanted to hire and retain older workers. What kinds of workplace changes would you recommend to make that possible?
5. List the primary sources of income for older adults. How do these vary for women and elders of color?
6. How does Supplemental Security Income (SSI) differ from Social Security?
7. Based on your reading of this text, do you think that all older adults are financially better off, especially compared to younger adults? Why?
8. What are some of the limitations of the official measures of poverty when they are applied to the increasingly heterogeneous population of older adults?
9. List three risk factors for food insecurity or being hungry.
10. What are some of the ways that patterns of work and retirement may be changing for the baby boom generation, especially for those who have adequate financial resources?
11. Give an example of what would characterize an encore career.

media resources

View

- Seniors Say No
- Transitioning to Retirement: Mary and George

Read

- Total Retirement Income Claims on the Economy
- The Economist. A Gradual Goodbye: If People Are Living Longer, They Will Have to Work Longer, Too.

references

AARP. (2010). *AARP closer look survey of June 2010.* Retrieved from http://assets.aarp.org/rgcenter/general/closer-look-econ-0610.pdf.

AARP. (2011). *African Americans hit harder by the recession than whites.* Retrieved February 19, 2011, from http://www.aarp.org/money/budgeting-saving/info-02-2010/economyaa.html.

AARP. (2013). *Why we created the drive to end hunger.* Retrieved September 26, 2013, from http://www.aarp.org/aarp-foundation/our-work/hunger/about-drive-to-end-hunger/.

Administration on Aging (AoA). (2012). *Profile of older Americans: 2011.* Washington, DC: Administration on Aging.

Adams, G. A., & Rau, B. L. (2011). Putting off tomorrow to do what you want today: Planning for retirement. *American Psychologist, 66,* 180–192.

Angel, J., & Mudrazija, S. (2011). Raising the retirement age: Is it fair for low-income workers and minorities? *Public Policy & Aging Report, 21,* 12–19.

Aversa, J., & Rugaber, C. S. (2009, October 3). Recovery: Job market bleakest since 1983. *Post Standard.*

Badgett, M. V., Durso, L. E., & Schneebaum, A. (2013). *New patterns of poverty in the lesbian, gay and bisexual community.* Boston, MA: The Williams Institute. Retrieved September 26, 2013, from http://williamsinstitute.law.ucla.edu/wp-content/uploads/LGB-Poverty-Update-Jun-2013.pdf.

Bernard, T. S. (2010). *Social Security jitters? Better prepare now.* Retrieved November 5, 2010, from http://www.nytimes.com/2010/07/31/your money/31money.html.

Bortie-Holtz, D., VanHorn, C., & Zukin, C. (2010). *No end in sight: The agony of prolonged unemployment.* New Brunswick, NJ: John J. Heldrich Center for Workforce Development, Rutgers University.

Brady, P. J. (2010). Measuring retirement resource adequacy. *Journal of Pensions, Economics and Finance, 9,* 235–262.

Brandon, E. (2009, March 12). Baby boomers are changing their retirement plans. *U.S. News & World Report.* Retrieved from http://tinyurl.com/av4pcw.

Brown, M., Aumann, K., Pitt-Catsouphes, M., Galinsky, E., & Bond, J. T. (2010). *Working in retirement: A 21st century phenomenon.* Retrieved November 5, 2010, from http://www.bc.edu/research/agingand work/all_feeds/2010-20-06.html.

Butrica, B. (2011). Making a case for working longer at older ages. *Public Policy & Aging Report, 21,* 20–24.

Caldera, S. (2012a). *Social Security: A key retirement resource for women.* Washington, DC: AARP Public Policy Institute.

Caldera, S. (2012b). *Social Security: Who's counting on it?* Washington, DC: AARP Public Policy Institute.

Carstensen, L. L. (2007). Growing older or living long: Take your pick. *Issues in Science and Technology, 23*(2), 41–50.

Carstensen, L. L. (2009). *A long bright future: An action plan for a lifetime of happiness, health and financial security.* New York: Random House.

Cawthorne, A. (2010). *The not-so golden years: Confronting elderly poverty and improving seniors' economic security.* Washington, DC: Center for American Progress. Retrieved November 5, 2010, from http://www.americanprogress/org/issues/2010/09/not_so_golden_years.

Center on Budget and Policy Priorities. (2012). *Policy basics: Top ten facts about Social Security.* Retrieved December 4, 2012, from www.cbpp.org/cms/?fa=view&id=3261.

Charness, N., & Czaja, S. J. (2011). Raising the minimal retirement age: Psychological issues. *Public Policy & Aging Report, 21,* 29–32.

Chea, T. (2010, May 16). College dream fulfilled at 94. *Seattle Times,* p. A2.

Civic Ventures. (2011). *The next chapter: Helping society achieve the greatest return on investment.* Retrieved October 3, 2011, from http://civicventures/org.

Congressional Budget Office. (2012). *Supplemental Security Income: An overview.* Washington, DC: U.S. Congressional Budget Office.

Dumez, J., & Derbew, H. (2011). *The economic crisis facing seniors of color: Background and policy recommendations.* Berkeley, CA: The Greenlining Institute.

Employee Benefit Research Institute. (2010). *EBRI databook on employee benefits (Chapter 10).* Retrieved June 13, 2011, from http://www.ebri.org/pdf/publications/books/databook/DB.Chapter%2010.pdf.

Employee Benefit Research Institute. (2011). *New research from EBRI: Higher percentage of older workers in the work force in 2010.* Retrieved from http://www.ebri.org/pdf/PR913%2017Feb11%20LbrFrcPar1.pdf.

Federal Interagency Forum on Aging-Related Statistics. (2012). *Older Americans 2011: Key indicators of well-being.* Washington, DC: U.S. Government Printing Office.

Fidelity.com. (2013). *Fidelity® estimates couples retiring in 2012 will need $240,000 to pay for medical expenses throughout retirement.* Retrieved January 13, 2013, from www.fidelity.com/inside-fidelityindividual-investing/retiree-health-care -costs-2012.

Fleck, C (2012). *Reasons for optimism among older workers.* Washington, DC: AARP. Retrieved September 21, 2013, from http://blog.aarp.org/2012/12/03/reasons-for-optimism-among-older-workers/.

Food Research and Action Center. (2010). *Seniors and SNAP food programs.* Retrieved September 26, 2013, from http://frac.org/initiatives/addressing-senior-hunger/seniors-and-snapfood-stamps/.

Freedman, M. (2011). *The big shift: Navigating the new stage beyond midlife.* New York: Public Affairs.

Fuller-Thomson, E., & Redmond, M. (2008). Falling through the social safety net: Food stamp use and nonuse among older impoverished Americans. *The Gerontologist, 48,* 235–244.

Gallup Economy and Personal Finance Survey. (2013). *In U.S., average retirement age up to 61.* Retrieved September 26, 2013, from http://www.gallup.com/poll/162560/average-retirement-age.aspx.

Gonyea, J., & Hudson R. (2011). Promoting employment and community service among low-income seniors: The successes and challenges of the Senior Community Service Employment Program. *Aging & Public Policy Report, 21,* 40–47.

Government Accountability Office. (2010). *Raising the retirement age would have implications for older workers and SSA disability rolls.* Washington, DC: U.S. Government Printing Office.

Harootyan, B., & Sarmiento, T. (2011). The future for older workers: Good news or bad? *Public Policy & Aging Report,* 21, 3–9.

Harrell, R. (2011). *Housing for older adults: The impacts of the recession.* Washington, DC: AARP Public Policy Institute.

Helman, R., Greenwald, M., Copeland, C., & VanDerhei, J. (2012). The 2012 Retirement Conference Survey: Job insecurity, debt weigh on retirement confidence, savings. *ERBI Issue Brief,* 369. Retrieved January 13, 2013, from http://www.ebri.org/pdf/briefspdf/EBRI_IB_03-2012_No369_RCS2.pdf.

Helman, R., & VanDerhei, J. (2010). The 2010 Retirement Confidence Survey: Confidence stabilizing, but preparations continue to erode. *EBRI Issue Brief,* 340. Retrieved January 13, 2013, from http://www.ncbi.nlm.nih.gov/pubmed/20369455.

Herd, P. (2011). Does Betty White have it right? The implications of raising the retirement age for women. *Public Policy & Aging Report, 21,* 25–28.

Hicks, J., & Kingson, E. (2009). The economic crisis: How fare older Americans. *Generations, 33*(3), 6–11.

Holden, K. C. (2000). The boomers and their economic prospects. In R. B. Hudson (Ed.), *Boomer bust? Economic and political issues of the graying society* (Vol. 1). Westport, CT: Praeger.

Institute on Assets and Social Policy. (2011a). *From bad to worse: Senior economic insecurity on the rise.* Retrieved December 19, 2012, from http://iasp.brandeis.edu/pdfs/FromBadtoWorse.pdf.

Institute on Assets and Social Policy. (2011b). *The crisis of economic insecurity for African-American and Latino seniors.* Retrieved September 21, 2013, from http://www.demos.org/sites/default/files/publications/IASP%20Demos%20Senior%20of%20Color%20Brief%20September%202011.pdf.

Jacobson, G., Schwartz, K., & Neuman, T. (2009). *Health insurance coverage for older adults: Implications of a Medicare buy-in.* Kaiser Foundation, Focus on Health Care Reform.

James, J. B., & Wink, P. U. (2008). *The crown of life: Dynamics of the early post-retirement period.* New York: Springer.

Jaret, P. (2010). *The challenge of having enough to eat intensifies in these hard economic times.* Retrieved February 12, 2011, from http://www.aarp.org/giving-back/charitable-giving/info-11-2010/hungry_in_america_2010.2.html.

Johnson, R., & Mommaerts, C. (2011). *Age differences in job loss, job search and reemployment.* Washington, DC: The Urban Institute, The Program on Retirement Policy.

Johnson, K., & Wilson, K. (2010). *Current economic status of older adults in the United States: A demographic analysis.* Washington, DC: National Council on Aging (NCOA). Retrieved from http://www.ncoa.org/assets/files/pdf/Economic-Security-Trends-for-Older-Adults-65-and-Older_March-2010.pdf.

Kingson, E., & Altman, N. (2011). The Social Security retirement age(s) debate: Perspectives and consequences. *Public Policy & Aging Report,* 21, 1–7.

Koenig, G., & Walker, L. (2011). *How many older Americans live: Ten facts to consider.* Washington, DC: AARP Public Policy Institute.

Lee, J. S., Fischer, J. G., & Johnson, M. A. (2010). Food insecurity, food and nutrition programs and aging. *Journal of Nutrition for the Elderly, 29,* 116–149.

Levinson, Z., Damico, A., Cubanski, J., & Neuman, P. (2013). *A state by state snapshot of poverty among seniors: Findings from analysis of the Supplemental Poverty Measure.* Retrieved September 26, 2013, from http://kff.org/medicare/issue-brief/a-state-by-state-snapshot-of-poverty-among-seniors/.

Luck, K. (2010). *Back to work after retiring? Help is available.* Retrieved November 5, 2010, from http://www.journal-newspapers/com/artcies/2919/11/92.

McCann, R. A., & Ventrell-Monsees, C. (2010). Age discrimination and employment. In R. Hudson (Ed.), *The new politics of old age policy* (2nd ed., pp. 356–372). Baltimore, MD: Johns Hopkins University Press.

Metlife Mature Market Institute. (2008). *Boomers: The next 20 years.* Palo Alto, CA: Institute for the Future.

Meyer, M. H. (2010). Shifting risk and responsibility: The state and inequality in old age. In R. Hudson (Ed.), *The new politics of old age policy* (2nd ed., pp. 21–42). Baltimore, MD: Johns Hopkins University Press.

Meyer, M. H., & Estes, C. L. (2009). A new Social Security agenda. *Public Policy & Aging Report, 19*(2), 7–11.

Myles, J. (2010). What justice requires: Normative foundations for U.S. pension reform. In R. Hudson (Ed.), *The new politics of old age policy* (2nd ed., pp. 64–86). Baltimore, MD: Johns Hopkins University Press.

National Council on Aging. (2012). *Economic security for seniors: Fact Sheet.* Washington, DC: National Council on Aging.

Norris, F. (2010). *Rethinking early retirement in Europe.* Retrieved November 5, 2010, from http://www.nytimes.com/2010/10/30/business/30charts.html.

PBS. (2013). *Manufacturer Vita Needle finds investment in older workers turns a big profit.* Retrieved January 13, 2013, from www.pbs.org/newshour/bb/business/jan-june13.making-sesne_01-02.html?print.

Pension Rights Center. (2014). *Income of today's older adults.* Retrieved from http://www.pensionrights.org.

Pew Research Center. (2009). *The oldest are most sheltered. Different age groups, different recessions,* May 14. Retrieved from http://pewsocialtrends.org/assets/pdf/recession-and-older-americans.pdf.

Pitt, D. (2011). *More Americans expect to retire in their 80s.* Associated Press. Retrieved December 5, 2011, from http://today.msnbc.msn.com/id/45329778/ns/today-money/#.TsUzFnFXs00.

Pynoos, J., Cicero, C., & Nishita, C. M. (2010). New challenges and growing trends in senior housing. In R. Hudson (Ed.), *The new politics of old age policy,* 324–337. Baltimore, MD: Johns Hopkins University Press.

Rich, M. (2010). *For the unemployed over 50, fears of never working again.* Retrieved November 6, 2010, from http://www.nytimes/com/2010/09/20/business/economy/20older.html.

Rix, S. E. (2008). Will the boomers revolutionize work and retirement? In R. Hudson (Ed.), *Boomer bust? Economic and political issues of the graying society* (Vol. 1). Westport, CT: Praeger.

Rix, S. E. (2011a). Boomers sail into retirement—Or do they? *Public Policy & Aging Report, 21,* 34–39.

Rix, S. E. (2011b). *The employment situation, July 2011: Little improvement for older workers.* Washington, DC: AARP Public Policy Institute.

Schulz, J. H., & Binstock, R. H. (2006). *Aging nation: The economics and politics of growing older in America.* Westport, CT: Praeger.

Shelton, A. (2013a). *Social Security: A key retirement resource for women.* Washington, DC: AARP Public Policy Institute.

Shelton, A. (2013b). *Social Security: Who's counting on it?* Washington, DC: AARP Public Policy Institute.

Social Security Administration. (2011a). *Increasing the social security retirement age. Social Security on-line.* Retrieved June 21, 2011, from http://ssa-custhelp.ssa.gov/app/answers/detail/a_id/233.

Social Security Administration. (2011b). *Social Security fact sheet: Social Security is important to women.* Baltimore, MD: Department of Health and Human Services, Social Security Administration.

Social Security Administration. (2013a). *Fast facts & figures about Social Security, 2013.* Washington, DC: Office of Retirement and Disability Policy, Social Security Administration.

Social Security Administration. (2013b). *Benefit eligibility for couples in states that prohibit or do not recognize same-sex marriages or other legal same-sex relationships.* Retrieved September 26, 2013, from http://ssa-custhelp.ssa.gov/app/answers/detail/a_id/2503.

Sok, E. (2010). Record unemployment among older workers does not keep them out of the job market. *Issues in labor statistics.* Retrieved from http://www.bls.gov/opub/ils/summary_10_04/older_workers.htm.

Tavernise, S., & Gebeloff, R. (2011). New way to tally poor recasts view of poverty. *New York Times,* November 7. Retrieved December 4, 2011, from http://www.ongo.com/v/2265917/-1/239FBE015C8DE494/new-way-to-tally-poor-recasts-view-of-poverty.

Telegraph. (2009). *Elderly turn to wartime thriftiness during recession, says Age Concern. May 11.* Retrieved February 20, 2011, from http://www.telegraph.co.uk/finance/recession/5303320/Elderly-turn-to-wartime-thriftiness-during-recession-says-Age-Concern.html.

U.S. Department of Health & Human Services. (2012). *2012 HHS poverty guidelines.* Washington, DC: Office of the Assistant Secretary for Planning and Evaluation, U.S. Department of Health and Human Services. Retrieved September 21, 2013, from http://aspe.hhs.gov/poverty/12poverty.shtml.

Van de Water, P., & Sherman, A. (2010). *Social Security keeps 20 million Americans out of poverty: A state by state analysis.* Washington, DC: Center on Budget and Policy Priorities.

VanHorn, C. E., Corre, N., & Heidkamp, N. (2011). Older workers, the Great Recession, and the impact of long-term unemployment. *Public Policy & Aging Report, 21,* 29–33.

Waid, M., & Koenig,G. (2012). *Social Security: A key retirement income source for older minorities.* Washington, DC: AARP Public Policy Institute.

Werner, C. (2011). *The older population 2010: 2010 Census briefs.* Washington, DC: U.S. Census Bureau.

Williamson, J. B., & Wattersroy, D. M. (2009). Aging boomers, generational equity and the framing of the debate over Social Security. In R. Hudson (Ed.), *Boomer Bust?* (pp. 153–172). New York: Praeger Perspectives.

WSVN.com (2011). *Community helps elderly woman in foreclosure.* Retrieved February 19, 2011, from http://www.wsvn.com/news/articles/local/21003576742857/.

Wu, A. (2009). *Older women's economic well-being: Income, consumption and leisure before and after retirement.* University of Chicago, Harris School of Public Policy, unpublished paper.

Zavis, A. (2010). *For the elderly, poverty doesn't cut it.* Retrieved November 7, 2010, from www.chicagotribue.com/news/local/la-me-elderly-poverty-20101017.story.

Ziliak, J. P., & Gundersen, C. (2011). *Food insecurity among older adults—Policy brief.* Washington, DC: AARP Public Policy Institute.

11 Community Well-Being: Living Arrangements and Social Interactions

learning objectives

11.1 Articulate how elders' living situation affects their well-being.

11.2 Discuss the various types of housing and long-term care living arrangements for older adults, including aging in place, age-friendly communities, and culture change.

11.3 Demonstrate knowledge of housing policy for older adults and how this affects patterns of homelessness.

Listen to the Chapter Audio

You may have particular images about where older adults prefer to live; similar to other aspects of their lives, there is no one pattern, but rather tremendous heterogeneity. Elders' decisions about where they live are influenced by many factors—their health status, functional ability, geographic location, activity interests, finances, and families. The vast majority wants to remain in their own homes, but others are eager to move to a smaller apartment or condo in a retirement community, or to know that someone will be watching out for them in an assisted living facility. Few choose to live in a skilled nursing facility, but for some, this allows them to receive the care they need and is a good option.

Regardless of where elders live, we know that the physical (or built) and social environments can make a profound difference in their sense of well-being. No environment is inherently good or bad. What matters is the extent that the environment fits with their physical, cognitive, and emotional needs and allows them to maintain a degree of control over their surroundings. Increasingly, architects, computer specialists, and urban designers are taking account of how to modify environments to foster older adults' maximum choice, autonomy, and life satisfaction for as long as possible. Such environmental changes take place not only in community settings, but also in long-term care facilities that recognize the value of creating a home-like culture, including for cognitively impaired elders. Even the prison system, which is faced with a growing number of older inmates with health care needs, has to make changes in its physical and social environments to accommodate the graying of its population.

This chapter will cover the following topics:

- Options in housing and community-based long-term care to help elders remain in the community
- The importance of designing age-friendly livable communities, including those that promote aging in place
- Organizational cultural change in skilled nursing facilities
- Federal government housing policy affecting low-income older adults
- Homelessness among older adults and
- aging prisoners

The concept of **life-space** is central to our discussion of living arrangements and age-friendly neighborhoods and communities. It is defined as the distance a person travels to perform activities over a specified time (e.g., one week, one month). An individual's life-space can range from the immediate surroundings of one's bedroom to the home, neighborhood, or citywide. For active elders, the usual pattern of mobility extends beyond the town where they live. Researchers who have created a tool to assess life-space note that the larger an older person's life-space, the better their physical and psychological well-being. Similarly, older adults whose life-space constricts over time experience declines in their functional abilities. You may be able to recall a time when your life-space was largely restricted to a dorm room or your parents' home. How did such limited space affect how you felt and functioned (Allman, Sawyer, & Roseman, 2006; Brown et al., 2009; Crowe et al., 2008)?

The Aging Experience in Rural, Urban, and Suburban Areas

As you have learned, over 80 percent of older Americans live in metropolitan areas (i.e., urban and suburban communities), compared with only 5 percent in rural communities with fewer than 2,500 residents. Elders of color are more likely to live in central cities (AoA, 2012).

How and Where Elders Live Affects Their Well-Being

The living arrangements of older adults are linked to their income, health status, availability of caregivers, and urban/rural/suburban location. Older persons who live in rural areas or small towns generally have lower incomes and poorer health than those in metropolitan areas. Limitations in mobility and activity are greatest among elders in rural communities and least among those in suburbs. The greater availability of services, such as hospitals, clinics, senior centers, private physicians, and transportation, in urban and suburban communities compared to rural settings may partially explain this pattern. Transportation is a critical issue for older rural residents, whether to take them to medical and social services or for providers to travel to their homes.

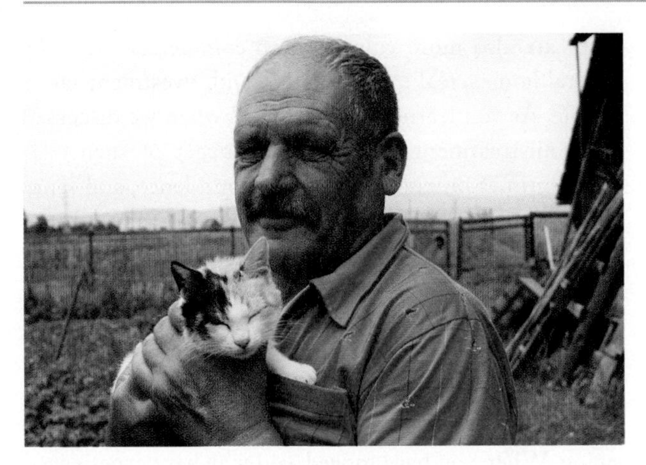

An older farmer with his cat after a hard day's work on his rural farm.

Despite their lower income and poorer health, older persons in small communities tend to interact more with neighbors and friends than do those in urban settings. Indeed, friendship ties among elders appear to be stronger and more numerous in rural than in urban settings. Greater social interaction may result from increased proximity to neighbors, stability of local residents, and shared values and lifestyles. Proportionately few rural elders live near their children or receive financial and social support from them. Even though older persons in rural areas and small towns experience more limitations of income, health, and service accessibility than those in metropolitan areas, they often benefit from robust informal support systems as well as a strong sense of community. The population of older adults as distributed among metropolitan and smaller communities is depicted in Figure 11.1.

There is also a phenomenon known as the "**graying of the suburbs**"; this means that a greater proportion of people who moved into suburban developments in the 1960s and 1970s have raised their children and remained in these communities after retirement combined with fewer younger families moving into these areas. Compared to their urban counterparts, elders in suburban communities tend to have higher incomes, are less likely to live alone, and report themselves to be in better functional health. Some choose to move to retirement homes built in the suburbs.

Even though suburban living may seem attractive, many suburban communities are not good places to grow old; they were designed around the automobile, with giant malls and big box stores often at a geographic distance, roads that are not pedestrian friendly, and limited sidewalks. The lower density of housing, greater distance to services, and fewer mass transit options can make it difficult for older adults to remain there if they become frail or unable to drive. Over two-thirds of older suburban residents say that public transportation is not available in their communities; this means that they have to be able to drive and afford the expenses of car ownership or find volunteer or paid drivers. Indeed, transportation costs have been described as a hidden cost of home ownership. About 50 percent of suburban communities are responding to their changing resident needs by developing community transit programs (e.g., vans or special buses) to take older adults and persons with disabilities to social and health services, senior centers, shopping, restaurants, and places of worship, as illustrated in the box on p. 312 (Gray, Harrell, & Sykes, 2010; Scharlach, 2012).

Urban elders are more likely to have public transportation, sidewalks conducive to walking, and access to social and health services. Many of them live in apartment buildings or condominiums or in neighborhoods that have basic services—all physical environments conducive to aging in place. But urban areas may also place elders at risk of crime victimization. Fear of victimization may partially explain why those in urban areas are twice as dissatisfied with the safety of their neighborhoods as their counterparts in suburbs and rural areas. Their fear may be greater than the reality, however, since national surveys by the U.S. Department of Justice consistently show that people age 65 and older have the lowest rates of all types of victimization among all age groups over age 12, whether as victims of an assault, robbery, or purse snatching (Bureau of Justice Statistics, 2012).

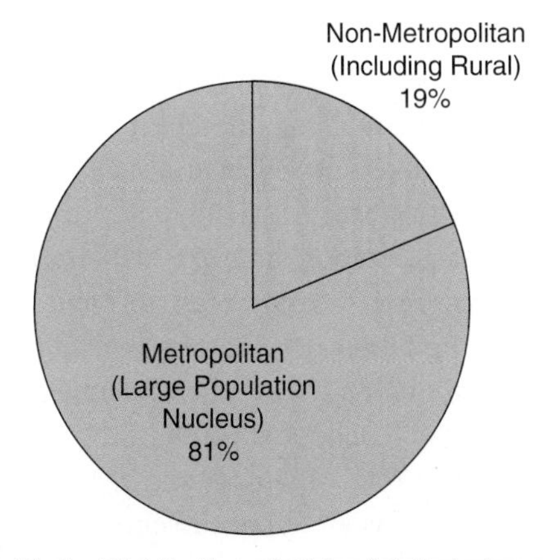

FIGURE 11.1 Distribution of Older Adults between Large and Small Communities

Source: AoA, 2012.

An Innovative Transportation Program

Public transit is not always available or convenient, particularly outside of large cities, and carries its own challenges for older adults. Bus stops, for example, can be blocks away and require standing outside in bad weather. Bus schedules and routes do not provide the independence and mobility most people experience with their own private cars. Because they think they have no alternative, many people continue to drive longer than they should. ITNAmerica, a nonprofit offering more than 500,000 door-to-door rides for elders in eight states, was designed to meet these challenges. Riders purchase an annual membership along with ride credits to be placed in a Personal Transportation Account™, based on an estimate of how much travel is needed. ITNAmerica charges about 50 percent of the cost of a taxi for each ride. Since riders do not pay cash and only private automobiles are used, using ITN vehicles is more like riding with a friend than taking a taxi. Unlike publicly funded transportation for older adults, which provides trips only to doctors, churches, and grocery stores within restricted hours, ITNAmerica is available 24/7, 365 days a year, with "door-to-door" service to wherever its riders want to go. Older people can trade use of their own cars to pay for rides and volunteer drivers can store credits for their own future transportation needs. Local businesses get involved through the Ride & Shop™ promotion, helping to pay for rides for shoppers who buy from them. And doctors' offices and clinics help out the program and their patients through the Healthy Miles™ donation program (http://www.itnamerica.org/).

Nevertheless, some segments of the older population are at slightly greater risk for being crime victims as shown in Figure 11.2.

Overall, the significance of their fear of crime is not whether it is warranted, but the effect it has on elders' psychological and social well-being, such as restricting their activities. On the other hand, older persons report feeling safe going outdoors in urban neighborhoods that have police nearby, with easy access to public transportation, coexisting businesses and housing, and "green features" such as trees and clean streets (Beard et al., 2009; Lachs et al., 2006).

In contrast to rates of violent crime, older people in urban areas are more susceptible to economically devastating crimes by con artists and high-pressure salesmen. Medical quackery and insurance fraud are also common. They are also more vulnerable to commercial fraud by funeral homes, real estate brokers, and investment salespeople. As you learned in Chapter 7 when we discussed elder mistreatment, the negative impact of such economic crimes on elders' trust, self-confidence, and sense of community safety can be as devastating as the financial consequences.

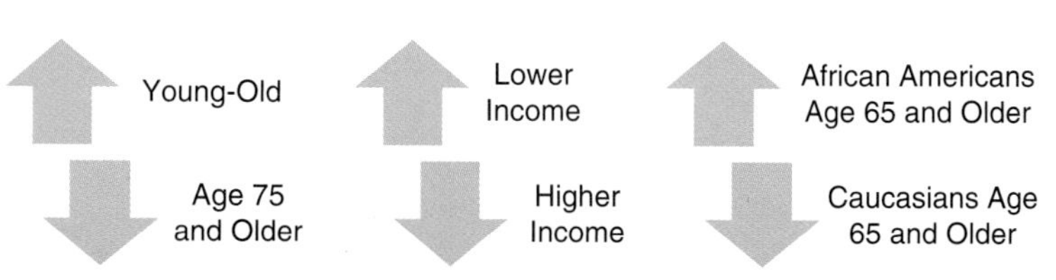

FIGURE 11.2 Crime Victim Comparative Risk Among Older Adults

Source: Bureau of Justice Statistics, 2012.

Relocation

Moving from one city or house to another can be difficult, even when the move is chosen—and even if you are young. When you have moved, you may have experienced times when you felt disoriented or out of place or lonely. An older person who has lived in the same home or community for many years will typically require more time to adapt than a young person, even if the move is perceived as an improvement to a better, safer, or more comfortable home. Moreover, a relocation that entails extensive lifestyle changes, such as to an assisted living facility, generally requires even more time to adapt. Regardless of the nature of the move, many elders experience feelings of loss associated with giving up a familiar setting, as you saw in Chapter 9.

Contrary to images of older adults moving to warm climates or to be near children or grandchildren, they are actually less likely to change residence than other age groups. Moreover, relocation rates decline with increasing age. Consider the bar graph in Figure 11.3 on p. 313.

In general, older people are less likely to move to a new area than are younger families. But they are more likely to move to a different type of housing within the same neighborhood or community—such as to a retirement community near their family home. Older people generally relocate in response to major changes in their lives, such as retirement, poor health, or loss of a partner, which has meant that their existing home environment no longer fits their needs. This also means the type of housing they

Neighborhood Crime Prevention Programs

In response to concerns about crime in urban areas, Neighborhood Watch and other programs encourage neighbors to become acquainted and to look out for signs of crimes. Such crime prevention programs increase older people's access to their neighbors. They break down perceptions of neighbors as strangers and apprehension of being isolated in a community, both of which foster fear of crime. Some large communities have established special police units to investigate and prevent crimes against older people. These units often train police to understand processes of aging and to communicate better with elders to help them overcome the trauma of a theft or physical assault. Improvements in community design can also create a sense of security. For example, brighter and more uniform street lighting, especially above sidewalks and in alleys, can deter many would-be criminals.

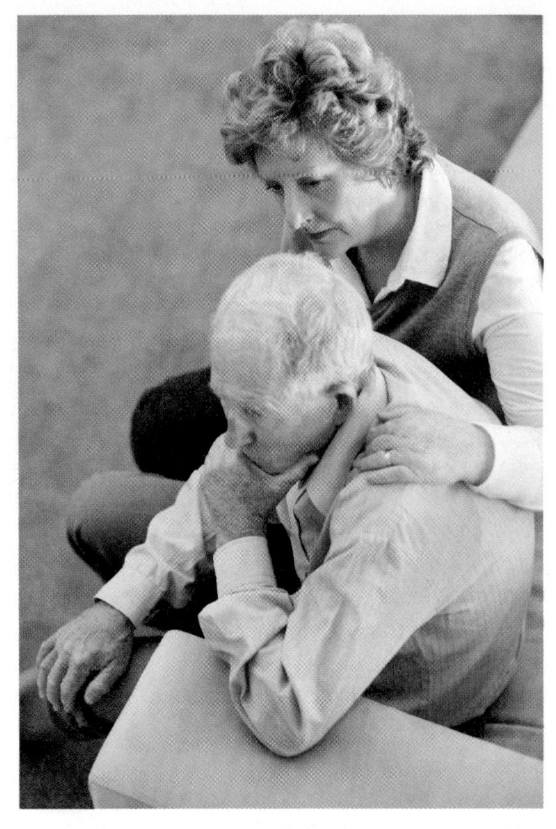

Many older adults experience feelings of loss and grief when they must move from their longtime home or live in an area where they do not feel safe.

choose varies according to the reasons for the move (AoA, 2012; Longino & Bradley, 2006; Longino, Bradley, Stoller, & Haas, 2008).

Not surprisingly, relocation is more difficult for elders with multiple or severe physical or cognitive disabilities. But even though their home may be too large, difficult to negotiate, or need extensive repairs, many frail elders resist a move to a safer environment. To family members or service providers, their resistance may seem irrational in the face of in such seemingly obvious needs to relocate. However, families need to take account of the meaning of home to the older person as a symbol of identity and control. Additionally, the stress of adapting to a new setting can be reduced if the older adult is involved in the decision-making process and able to express some preferences, such as selecting the facility and what possessions to keep.

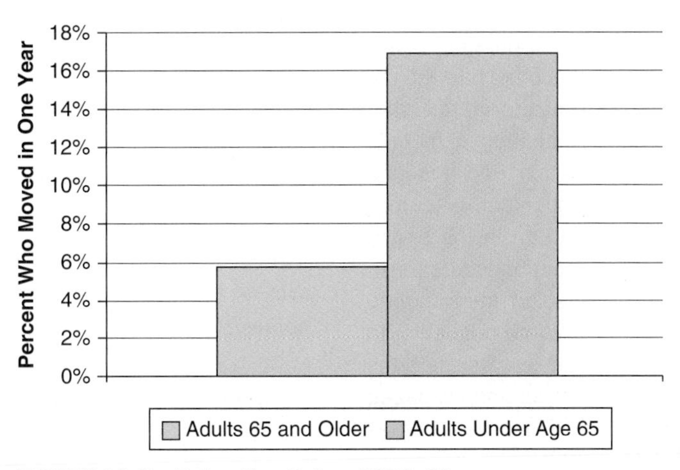

FIGURE 11.3 Relocation Rates, 2009–10

Source: AoA, 2012.

A Three-Stage Model of Migration among Older Adults

This model is useful for recognizing that adults often make multiple moves as their health, income, and social relationships alter with age.

- Stage 1, known as amenity or lifestyle-driven moves, occurs largely among the young-old and recent retirees, often to retirement communities in areas such as the Sunbelt. This may include "snowbirds" (or "sun birds") that spend their winters in warmer climates and the remaining months in their home states. Such moves have meant a significant increase in the population age 65 and older in Sunbelt states—Florida, California, Arizona, or Texas—in the past 40 years. However, this pattern is shifting as more older homeowners are unable to sell existing homes to move to warmer areas and Sunbelt communities seek to attract younger families as a way to survive financially. Increasingly, elders who seek a retirement setting for "active seniors" are moving to smaller facilities closer to their home community.
- Stage 2 assistance moves are often precipitated by chronic illness that limits elders' abilities to perform their daily activities. They may move to nearby retirement communities that have some supportive services or assisted living facilities that offer some amenities (e.g., meals, housekeeping), but still seek to remain as self-reliant as possible. Others move closer to family members when they need help with daily tasks.
- Stage 3 assistance move occurs when severe or sudden disability (e.g., stroke), chronic illness, or loss of partner makes it impossible to live even semi-independently. For example, a frail older person relocates from a Sunbelt community to a skilled nursing facility near family members (e.g., they become part of the "counter-stream migration"). One indicator of this shift is that Florida has the highest population of people age 65 and older. But this proportion declines dramatically among those age 85 and older, who may move back to home communities, often in the snowy Midwest or Northeast, when they need skilled care or to be near family. For some elders, an intermediate stop may be an adult child's home before relocating to a long-term care facility. In other cases, older persons receive some home care and other community-based services that allow them to remain in their homes (Longino, 2004; Longino et al., 2008).

We turn next to reviewing the various types of living arrangements available to older adults. These range from remaining in their own homes (or being able to age in place) to securing some degree of assistance with daily activities through assisted living facilities to daily assistance through skilled nursing facilities. Throughout you will learn about some innovative approaches to creating home environments for older adults.

Housing Patterns of Older People

The most common residential arrangements of older persons are independent housing, planned housing, and residential long-term care. Within these options, there are new approaches to support elders' remaining in their own homes and communities or to make long-term care facilities as homelike as possible.

Independent Housing

By far the most common type of housing for older adults is traditional independent housing; over 90 percent of those 65 and older live in such housing. Even among the oldest-old, 75 percent still live in independent units. The desire to remain in one's own home is nearly universal. About 80 percent of adults age 45 and older in a 2010 survey wanted to be able to stay in their own home as they age. It is not surprising that fewer than 10 percent thought that long-term care facilities were the best living arrangement (AoA, 2013; MetLife Mature Market Institute, 2010).

Of the over 23 million older households, 80 percent are homeowners and 20 percent renters. Elders may own condominiums or mobile homes, or buy into cohousing or cooperatives, but single-family homes are by far the most common. The median value of their homes, however, tends to be less than that of younger homeowners, perhaps because they are more likely to have lived in their current homes, which are often older houses in need of repair, for at least 30 years (AoA, 2012; Harrell, 2011).

Rates of home ownership are highest among

- married households compared to single elders (over 90 and 69 percent, respectively),
- Caucasians compared to elders of color,

- higher-income elders, and
- those living in rural areas (Federal Interagency Forum, 2012).

Older homeowners are more likely than any other age group to own their homes free and clear of a mortgage (e.g., they have paid it off), but this percent has declined as a result of the recession. Even more alarming is the number of older adults who have lost their homes to foreclosures in recent years, even if they have paid off the mortgage. This is because they are more likely to be living alone and in older homes, often poorly built before 1960 and now in need of maintenance and plagued by high energy costs. Additionally, older homes are often multiple stories, with steep entrance steps, narrow hallways, and no bedroom or bathrooms on the first floor. As noted by one researcher of housing options, "many older adults live in 'Peter Pan' housing apparently designed for someone who will never grow old" (Scharlach, 2009, p. 6).

High maintenance and utilities costs, mortgage payments, taxes, and insurance may partially explain why more older householders (almost 40 percent) spend more of their income (at least 30 percent) on housing costs than younger adults. This is of concern since economists maintain that spending this much of one's income on housing costs is an indicator of economic vulnerability, meaning that this could push older homeowners into poverty. Even if older homeowners want to be free of these household costs, the recessionary collapse of the housing market has meant that they cannot sell their homes—or do so at a significant loss. As you learned in Chapter 10, for growing numbers of older homeowners, their homes are no longer a safety net as they had once assumed (Federal Interagency Forum, 2012; Harrell, 2011; Scharlach, 2009).

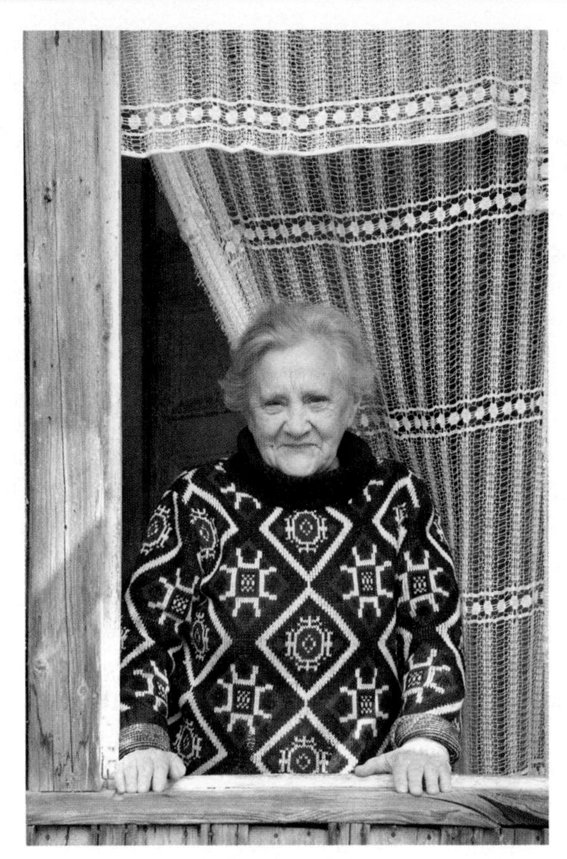

Because older homes often need repairs and upkeep, some older adults end up spending a substantial portion of their retirement income for home maintenance.

What to do with a Lifetime of Possessions?

Older adults who move to a smaller home—whether a condo, apartment, assisted living, or nursing home—are typically faced with the task of disposing of a lifetime of objects. The memories and sentimental value associated with favorite possessions can result in wrenching decisions, intensifying elders' feelings of loss associated with a move. This task can be even more daunting for older adults from the Depression-era cohort, who have saved material items throughout their lives. For other elders who are classified as hoarders, their living spaces are so cluttered that they are not usable and can pose a fire risk. Another complicating factor in disposing of lifelong possessions is when family members disagree over who should inherit which cherished items. To assist with this process, new services have recently emerged, including senior move managers, professional organizers, consultants to help arrange home furnishings, and even support groups for hoarders.

An older home often lacks adequate weatherproofing and other energy-saving features, frequently for large spaces that are costly to maintain. And it is not unusual to hear news stories during winter months of fires in older homes that result from faulty wiring, overloaded circuits, and the use of space heaters because of inadequate furnaces. Some communities attempt to prevent these problems by offering free or low-cost home assistance to older persons to make their homes more energy efficient (e.g., no-interest loans for weatherproofing and installing storm windows). Cities that have experienced sudden increases in their electricity and natural gas rates have also developed energy assistance programs to aid low-income people of all ages, but this type of service is strained as energy costs rise dramatically and publicly funded services are cut.

Aging in Place

A major reason for so many elders preferring to remain in their own home, regardless of its condition, is the almost universal desire for **aging in place** in one's community as long as possible. Older adults want to be where the environment is familiar, neighbors can be relied on for assistance and socializing, and they have some sense of control. In many ways, this reflects the well-known phrase that "home is where the heart is." And aging in place has documented benefits; it is found to be associated with better health, life satisfaction, and self-esteem. As more adults live to their eighties or even their nineties, however, a growing number of services are likely to be required to allow aging in place. To the extent that supportive services are accessible in the neighborhood or local community, people are more likely to remain there and to avoid or delay relocation to a long-term care facility. On the other hand, many communities do not have the services needed to foster aging in place and some elders may become socially isolated as they age in place in their single-family homes (MetLife Mature Market Institute, 2010; Salomon, 2010).

We turn now to a number of neighborhood and housing innovations aimed to support older adults' preferences to age in place.

Age-Friendly/Livable Communities

A community-level strategy to support aging in place is that of **age- (or elder-) friendly communities**. These are also often referred to as **livable or lifelong communities**, where residents of all ages can comfortably live their whole lives. This approach recognizes the importance of the built environment, particularly housing and transportation, along with social and recreational activities to promote social engagement and healthy choices. To illustrate, such communities promote healthy activities by building walking or biking trails or curb cuts at every corner, which are enjoyed by young parents with babies in strollers, active elders riding a bike, as well as persons with disabilities who use wheelchairs or walkers. Communities with pedestrian-friendly streets, safe, bikeable and walkable neighborhoods, and benches in parks can promote the health of residents of all ages. But age-friendly communities are not just about physical features. They also aim to foster interdependence and cross-generational exchanges among community members, regardless of age or functional ability. For instance, older adults volunteer as school cross guards, "Citizens on Patrol" with the police department, and the "Neighbor Helping Neighbor" program with transportation, yard work, and home repairs. Indeed, some research suggests that social relationships, connectedness, and contributing to others are more important aspects of age-friendly communities than physical design. This may not surprise you after learning about the importance of informal social supports in Chapter 6 (Atlanta Regional Commission, 2013; Emlet & Moceri, 2011; Gray et al., 2010).

Older adults should be able to live out their entire lives in elder-friendly communities, supported by multigenerational residents who are civically engaged.

Here is a summary of the major characteristics of age-friendly communities. Does the neighborhood or community where you live have any of these features?

- Zoning that allows a range of housing options that are affordable, accessible, and environmentally sound, and take account of residents' changing needs
- User-friendly mobility options: public transportation and ride match programs, but also walkable neighborhoods to promote health and reduce dependence on cars and greenhouse gas emissions
- Convenient and walkable access to social and health services; preventive and health promotion activities; and key amenities such as grocery stores with healthy produce, local farmers markets, and pharmacies
- Social interaction and civic engagement initiatives for older adults to contribute to others through employment, volunteering, and cross-generational activities
- An environment that not only promotes physical activity but also supports efforts to improve air quality and reduce pollution

Age-Friendly Traffic Lights

Traffic lights that change from green to red too quickly at crosswalks can signal unsafe conditions for those who are not able to walk fast enough. These quickly changing signals might also lead to jaywalking if pedestrians take too long to cross and find themselves still in the crosswalk when the walk light turns red. Elders—many of whom no longer drive and must walk more to get around in their communities—sometimes find themselves in situations when they feel rushed to cross the street or risk being hit by a moving vehicle or ticketed for jaywalking. Fortunately, some cities are designing roads to be more pedestrian friendly. They are implementing countdown clocks, lengthened time to cross streets, and "refuge islands" so those crossing the streets do not have to do it all at once. Elders are not the only ones benefiting from such changes. Who else might benefit from pedestrian-safe crosswalks and age-friendly traffic lights?

- Preservation of open space, farmland, natural beauty, critical environmental areas, even intergenerational community gardens on donated land, ensuring that livable communities are also environmentally sustainable ones
- Community input and collaboration in making decisions about development (Atlanta Regional Commission, 2011; Gray et al., 2010; Salomon, 2010)

Flexible Housing and Universal Design Designing housing that is adaptable to elders' changing needs is another central component of many age-friendly communities that promote aging in place. **Universal design**, first proposed by activists for the rights of persons with disabilities, is the design of products and places that allow choice and flexibility by people of all ability levels. In other words, universal design means that homes are useful over time as changes occur with aging or with disability at any age. What began as an attempt to design street "curb cuts" and hallways and bathrooms in homes accessible to people in wheelchairs has grown to a movement that makes all environments—parks, wilderness areas, automobiles, and computer workstations—promote the autonomy and dignity of people who are able-bodied as well as those with limited mobility, vision, and hearing (MetLife, 2010). In Chapter 12, you will learn about how technology promotes universal design. But other "low- or non-tech" design features can also be built into housing to support aging in place, including the following:

- bathrooms with roll-in showers
- hands-free sensors on faucets
- nonskid flooring
- low-pile carpeting
- uniform lighting throughout the house
- elevator shafts that are built into the home and used as closets until they are needed as elevators
- computerized controls (portable keypads) for heat, artificial lighting, and window shades

The most common modification is to install grab bars in bathrooms. Other changes are far less frequent, in part because of their cost. Ironically, spending money on such modifications to keep older adults in their own homes is likely to be far less expensive than moving to a residential facility with services. It is anticipated that baby boomers will increasingly demand—and be able to afford—such universal design features.

New home buyers are also increasingly interested in **flexible housing**—homes that can be built and remodeled for use throughout a lifetime. For example, movable walls can expand or shrink a room as needs change, or plumbing can be added to convert a small room on the main floor of a house into a bathroom. The number and size of bedrooms can be modified by using a cluster design so that multiple generations and even unrelated renters can live under the same roof while retaining their privacy. Main-floor hallways and doorways in private homes can be built to be wide enough for wheelchair access. All of these give families the flexibility to adapt their homes in the future as they assume caregiving roles or require in-home care. Even though the Americans with Disabilities Act (ADA) does not require accessibility in private homes, these shifts are occurring because builders recognize the growing market for such housing features.

points to **ponder**

Think of the physical arrangement of where you currently live. If you were to become disabled because of an accident and had to use a wheelchair, what kinds of modifications would you need to make to your current living situation? Would you have the financial resources to utilize high-tech modifications?

Planning for Aging in Place

When Mr. and Mrs. Pond bought their last home, they were in their late sixties. They chose a house on one level and installed grab bars in the bathroom and nonslip surfaces, had additional lighting and switching, and had kitchen counters and cabinets that could be easily reached, even by someone in a wheel chair or electric scooter. When Mr. Pond was 78, he had a stroke that restricted his mobility. Because their home was on one level, building a ramp to the front door was relatively easy. Mrs. Pond's vision became more impaired but she was able to move about safely because of the nonslip surfaces. With help from a weekly chore worker, daily meals delivered to their home, and twice-weekly visits to an adult day care facility, they were able to remain in their home until they died, he at age 82, she at 85.

Additional Innovations for Aging in Place Some organizations working with older adults engage in a community development approach called **asset mapping**. This means that they involve residents in a process to identify their community's strengths and capacities. Most importantly, older people are viewed as valuable resources rather than a problem to be solved. By doing such mapping, communities identify, appreciate, and manage these resources to promote their older residents' quality of life. For example, they may shift from a traditional focus on delivering services to accommodate deficits to an asset development approach through health and wellness programs, community development, and civic engagement. With such an approach, neighbors organize to help each other through offering transportation, yard work, home maintenance, pet walking, or just checking in on each other on a regular basis. Take the time to look around your neighborhood and try to identify its strengths and assets, which we often overlook on a daily basis.

Many elders live in apartment buildings that were not planned for an aging population. But because people have lived in the structures for many years, they have become **naturally occurring retirement communities (NORCs)**. NORCs are defined as a community where over 50 percent of the residents are age 65 and older. Many of these settings were originally built for young families in the 1950s and 1960s. Over the years, they attracted adults who aged in place. Some of these buildings are now deteriorating in terms of maintenance and may pose access challenges for residents with chronic care needs, such as numerous steps or hallways too narrow to accommodate a wheelchair or walker (Cohen-Mansfield, Dakheel-Ali, & Frank, 2010).

Some state and local governments are offering expanded supportive services for NORC residents who are ill or disabled. For example, in Queens, New York, city funds and philanthropic grants pay for an on-site team of social workers and nurses to care for elders in an apartment complex where more than 60 percent of residents are age 60 and older. The paid staff includes older residents who work on community-building and identifying problems in the NORC's physical environment, such as inadequate bus routes to health clinics and home repair needs. The social support in NORCs is found to be the key to sustaining residents' quality of life, keeping them physically active and socially connected to the larger world outside their homes, and preventing depression or other threats to well-being (Cohen-Mansfield et al., 2010; Kirk, 2009; United Hospital Fund, 2009).

The virtual **village** concept is an innovative, intentional model for supporting aging in one's community and building

An Asset-Based Model of Service Exchange

Partners in Care (PIC) in Maryland provides a network of support for older adults to promote self-sufficiency and volunteerism in the community. Involving over 2,600 individuals, PIC uses the tool of time banking or service exchange. People volunteer their time and talents to help each other accomplish the many tasks involved in everyday living. Assets that are already in the community are used to "accomplish more with less." Older adults are empowered as they not only earn the help they need, but also give back. In exchange for sharing their time and skills, they receive rides to medical appointments, pharmacies, and grocery stores, and help with home repairs.

To illustrate, a 70-year-old woman drives another person to the doctor periodically. She earns hours in her "bank" and can receive partial fuel reimbursement. When her arthritis prohibits her from installing her storm windows, two volunteer members go out to put up the windows. One volunteer who performs the task donates his hours to an older neighbor so that she will have "time in the bank" to call in if she needs groceries. His partner donates his hours to the general pool. Elders living in their own homes are grateful to have someone donating on their behalf but may also give back by making telephone calls or giving financial contributions. Having credits in the bank makes it easier to ask for help when it is needed (http://www.partnersincare.org).

What Defines a Village?

Three primary characteristics of village communities are as follows:

1. People of all ages interact and support one another.
2. Social engagement through helping your neighbor is a way of life.
3. There is a commitment to safety and ease in getting around and living in one's own home.

on existing social networks. It is not a provider model or a specific physical location, which is why it is often referred to as virtual. Community members come together with the common desire to stay in their neighborhood as they age. They generally incorporate as a nonprofit, with members paying an annual fee. These fees typically support a staff person to help coordinate volunteers, link to professional services, and seek discounted rates from local businesses, such as plumbers, home health agencies, and financial advisors. However it is the volunteers, providing whatever an elder needs to remain safely in their own home, who are central to the success of a village. In some cases, volunteers can "bank" their hours to "spend" when they need help themselves. In other instances, younger volunteers provide opportunities for intergenerational connections. Some villages, such as the Beacon Hill Village model in Boston, charge higher fees and provide a "concierge" level of services, such as group transportation to special events, pet-sitting services, and help with paying bills or doing taxes. Over 100 such villages exist nationwide, but a major need is to replicate the model in low-income communities (Accius, 2010; Anderson, 2009; Ginzler, 2009; Krishman, 2010; Scharlach, 2012; Wick & Zanni, 2009).

Cohousing is another type of collaborative community where people can age in place. Those who have started cohousing projects refer to a seemingly contradictory approach of "living together on one's own." First adapted from Denmark in the late 1980s, cohousing communities are clusters of 10–30 individually owned housing units (attached or single-family homes) where families of all ages, or older adults only, live interdependently. But they share a "common house" for social and recreational activities, community meetings, and occasional group meals. Residents typically share cooking, cleaning the common house, yard care, and physical maintenance. The value that unites "cohousers" is what they can give back to the community rather than what is in this for themselves. A key element for successful cohousing is that both owners and future residents are involved in the community's planning and construction (Co-Housing Association of the U.S., 2012; Durrett, 2009; McManus & Durrett, 2011).

Most existing cohousing communities are primarily younger residents, although there are a growing number of intergenerational communities in the United States. Cohousing for elders is sometimes built nearby younger communities, but with fewer units and more physical features and social services that take account of age-associated changes. Elders who participate in cohousing are motivated by remaining active and preventing loneliness through building a community of neighbors and friends. They may be engaged in teaching classes, volunteering, and sharing travels—but also help care for other residents who are coping with chronic diseases and cognitive decline. But cohousing may present challenges distinctive to older adults. Physical barriers such as multistory dwellings may become difficult for older residents with mobility limitations. Additionally, the principles of participatory decision-making and resident management that characterize cohousing may be challenging for those experiencing cognitive decline. To meet frail residents' care needs, guest rooms in the common house may be designated as a residence for paid caregivers, who may assist several occupants and become part of the community.

Intentional (or niche) communities are another recent housing model that encourages aging in place. These are communal housing projects, both intergenerational and targeted only at older adults, where people with common interests (e.g., religious, artistic, political, professional, or sexual orientation) collaborate in the construction of a community of apartments, townhouses, or detached single-family homes. Residents of intentional communities generally share more activities than those in cohousing. These housing models are typically geared to healthy adults but often have an assisted living units and, in some instances, memory care units for those with dementia. The fastest-growing niche community sector is university-based retirement communities, sited

points to **ponder**

At this point in your life, if you were looking for a new place to live and had an opportunity to move into a multigenerational cohousing community, would you do so? What would appeal to you about cohousing? What might you find to be disadvantages?

Is Cohousing Viable as We Age?

Yvonne moved into cohousing when she was in her late sixties, when she helped establish the community garden and served on numerous planning and work communities. Now in her eighties, newer and younger members have no memory of the services she has provided or a long-term connection with her. Instead, they complain that she is not holding up her end on workdays. She had anticipated years of support from others, but instead feels isolated and relatively invisible. When she has brought up issues of aging, others ignore her and want to focus on more pressing issues of simply running the community. She wants to stay in the community, so she has made arrangements for care and support from friends outside the cohousing. But Yvonne's experience is not universal since many elders enjoy the cross-generational benefits of cohousing (deLaGrange, 2011; Durrett, 2009).

near college campuses. Residents can readily take classes and attend athletic or cultural events, and students can volunteer at these communities (Abrahms, 2011; Yeoman, 2006).

Elder cottages—also known as auxiliary dwelling units or mother-in-law units—are another growing option, particularly in urban areas. An elder cottage is typically a factory-built, self-contained, energy efficient, and aesthetically appealing dwelling of around 800 square feet that is specifically designed for older adults and people of all ages with disabilities. They are built with a modular design that makes them easy to move and are a low-density approach to use land efficiently to expand housing stock. Such cottages are generally placed on the property of a family member's home, allowing proximity to assistance but also privacy. A granny pod or MedCottage is a high-tech cottage that uses the latest in biometric and communications technology and universal design, almost a portable hospital room. Look around your own community—do you see units that could be elder cottages? You may walk or drive by them daily but have not noticed them because most communities want these units to "blend into" the environment (Dobkin, 2011; Kunkle, 2012).

Last, **home sharing** is a common sense approach to helping people stay in their homes, save money, and help others find affordable housing. A homeowner opens up their home to others, typically for rent, but also with the understanding that they will share household responsibilities. Since the recession, interest in this affordable housing model has grown. There are many benefits beyond rental income for people who share their home with others: feeling safer, happier, and less lonely, and enjoying one's home more. The key to successful home sharing is the "match," which must meet the needs of both parties. Not surprisingly, a poor match is the major reason for home sharing not working. Although home sharing initially focused on helping elders remain in their homes, it has also been adapted to helping single-parent households, the homeless, and individuals with special needs (Dunn, 2010).

We have covered a lot of different housing innovations here. What we hope you will take away from this review is that just as older adults are more heterogeneous than other age groups, there is a vast array of housing options to meet different life styles, levels of functional ability, and social relationships in age-friendly environments. And older adults, particularly baby boomers, are increasingly involved in planning creatively for how they will age in place. We turn now to some of the types of retirement homes or long-term care facilities.

Planned "Retirement" Housing

Planned housing specifically for older persons encompasses government-subsidized housing for low-income elders and age-segregated housing such as assisted living, often geared to middle- and upper-income older persons.

An Innovative Model of Rural Affordable Housing

Vermont's Support and Services at Home (SASH) Program offers housing plus services to support residents, many of whom have lived 20–30 years in their apartments, to age in place. In many facilities, services coordinators, provided by the local Area Agency on Aging, work with low- to moderate-income residents to ensure they are getting needed services—from helping residents understand a cable bill to making sure supports are in place after a hospital stay. Most housing complexes have a SASH team—on-site clinics operated by a local hospital, with a primary care physician, a wellness nurse, a geriatric psychiatrist, and physical, occupational, and speech therapy available on certain days of the week. Others contract with home care agencies. Informal supports are fostered as well. Residents monitor each other's safety through the "I'm Okay" check. They put an "I'm Okay" sticker outside their apartment door in the morning if all is well. If no sticker appears, security personnel can check that nothing is amiss. This housing plus services model has had dramatic results: reductions in hospital admissions and readmissions, falls, and number of residents who are physically inactive or at moderate nutritional risk (Molvig, 2011).

While most of us think we would prefer to remain in our own homes, we need to be careful not to assume that this is always the best option or preference for elders. Those who are frail and coping with chronic diseases and functional limitations may require more assistance than is possible in a home care setting, particularly if they do not have the resources to purchase such services Additionally, some elders become socially isolated and lonely in their own homes, especially if they live in neighborhoods difficult for them to maneuver physically. In such instances, a planned residential setting, which offers services to prevent or manage disabilities and promotes social activities and relationships, may be most conducive to quality of life.

For older adults with chronic illness and disabilities or for those who simply prefer a more structured, safe environment, the number and variety of residential options have grown dramatically in the past decade. At the simplest level, such retirement communities free residents from home and yard maintenance, offer companionship and some social services and health promotion activities, and may provide limited health care. And in many instances, relocation to such planned housing can improve older adults' quality of life and well-being. Unlike the Vermont model, many low- to moderate-income independent living retirement complexes—often called affordable or subsidized rent housing—are not able to offer extensive health or social services to support their residents' aging in place (MetLife, 2010; Oswald, Jopp, Rott, & Wahl, 2011).

Two major categories of older adult residential facilities are available to those with financial resources:

1. **"Active adult" or lifestyle** communities. These relatively exclusive and expensive retirement communities offer a wide range of activities—computer access, health spas and fitness centers, club houses, golf courses, hiking trails, and meal options. But they do not offer health care or other types of assistance with daily tasks. Instead, such developments may provide vans for their older residents to obtain medical and social services. Although the potential buyers of such complexes tend to be the young-old, many of them have lost retirement savings due to the recession or cannot sell their homes and thus cannot afford such a move. As a result, for the first time in years, many lifestyle communities now have vacant units and some developers are instead exploring how to offer services that will enable elders to age in place and even selling units to younger adults (Jackson, 2010; Maag, 2012).
2. **Service-enriched housing**—assisted living, continuing care retirement communities, and skilled nursing facilities—packages housing and care, and offers different levels of care on-site or with easy access to services. For the most part, moves to service-enriched housing are precipitated by a health crisis or recognition of the need for more assistance with daily activities. These facilities offer a defined set of services that theoretically matches residents' needs, but sometimes there is a disconnect between the two, since needs change and may necessitate other move(s) to higher levels of care. Slightly less than 3 percent of older adults live in some type of senior housing with at least one supportive service available (Federal Interagency Forum, 2012).

Retirement communities offer opportunities for social interaction and physical activity.

points to ponder

Flip through newspapers or magazines, check out TV ads, and surf the Internet, and you will see numerous ads for "active retirement communities." Many are inviting people to meals, events, and tours. Who do these ads seem to target?

Continuing Care Retirement Communities

Continuing care retirement communities (CCRCs)—also known as life care communities and continuum of care facilities—are the broadest type of service-enriched housing that recognizes that residents may need increasing levels of care over time. You have probably seen such attractive complexes in your community. These multilevel facilities offer a range of housing, social, and health services on the

Philosophy of Care of ALFs

- appear residential in character and small in scale
- provide residents with privacy
- recognize each resident's uniqueness
- encourage independence and interdependence
- emphasize health maintenance, prevention, mental stimulation, and physical activity
- support involvement by residents' families
- maintain contact with the immediate community

same campus, from independent apartments to assisted living arrangements, and intermediate to skilled nursing care. This means that older residents can first live in their own separate apartment. But when their needs for assistance increase, they can remain in the same CCRC but move to assisted living or other types of intermediate care, and later to a skilled nursing facility on-site or nearby. When several levels of care are available at one site, older partners can feel assured that they can remain near each other, even if one needs to be placed in intermediate or skilled care. The extent to which LGBT partners feel that such options are available to them and their partners varies widely, however (Voisine et al., 2009).

Reasons that older adults typically choose a CCRC include

- a desire to plan ahead if care is needed in the future,
- not wanting to be a burden on family members,
- guaranteed health care, and
- availability of supportive services and social, educational, and exercise programs (Zarem, 2010).

CCRCs are expensive, especially where there is a life care contract requiring a substantial nonrefundable entry fee based on projections of life expectancy, extent of care needed, and size of the living unit. In order to recruit more residents, CCRCs are now offering different and less costly ways to pay. Some are waiving or reducing the buy-in fee, but then restricting the long-term services and supports available. Others charge fees for services as needed, which may become quite costly if care is required for long periods (AAHSA, 2011).

Regardless of the type of payment, access to CCRCs is typically limited to the small percentage of older people who have considerable cash assets. Assisted living is a growing option in community residential care that is less expensive than CCRCs, although still not readily available to low-income older adults. Less than 3 percent of older adults live in CCRCs or assisted living (Federal Interagency Forum, 2012; National Center for Assisted Living, 2011; Zarem, 2010).

Assisted Living

Assisted living facilities (ALFs) are a model of group housing with additional services, such as at least one meal a day, basic health care, 24-hour security, and some personal assistance. They target older adults who need help with personal care and some ADLs, but who are not so severely impaired that they require 24-hour skilled medical care. ALFs are not necessarily a specific building type but a philosophy of care.

To implement this care philosophy, ALFs usually provide private apartments, and offer meals in a common dining room, as well as housekeeping, and help with some ADLs, such as medication use. ALFs often develop individual service plans, based on each resident's functional

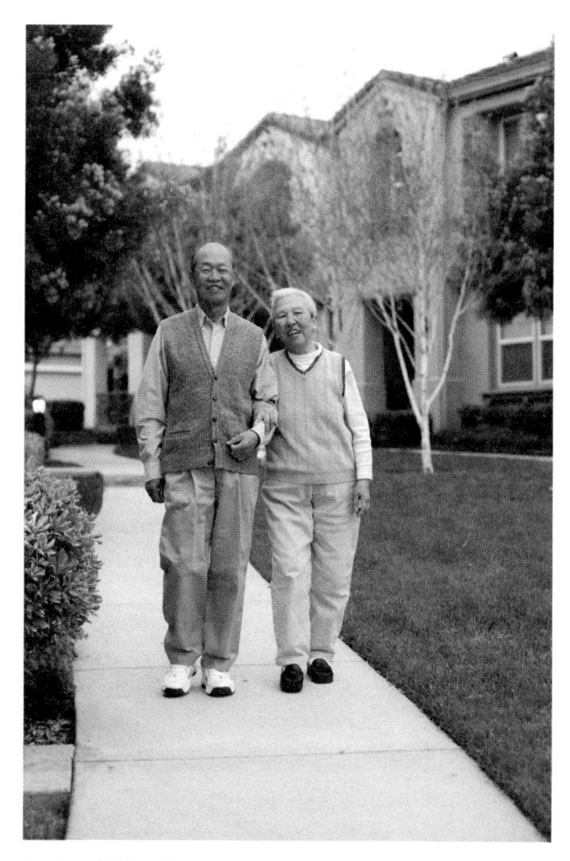

Assisted living facilities provide private residences in a community setting with additional support such as congregate dining, cleaning services, transportation, safety monitoring, and other services as needed.

abilities and their participation in care decisions. Staff generally includes at least one nurse and someone to provide case management services. Access to health care is typically offered by the facility contracting the services of physicians, physical therapists, and mental health specialists to meet specific needs. As a result, staffing costs are considerably lower than in skilled nursing facilities and CCRCs. Not surprisingly, the costs increase for those requiring higher levels of care. Indeed, elders in ALFs today, with an average age of 87 years, are frailer and often requiring more help with tasks such as bathing and dressing than was intended when this type of housing was first built. As a result, some "high-end" facilities with extensive amenities and health services can end up costing as much as a skilled nursing facility (SNF) (Mollica, 2009; Mollica & Houser, 2011; Wilson, 2007).

ALFs are not regulated in ways that SNFs are. As a consequence, there can be unevenness in the quality of care. Additionally, elders and their families assume greater "risk" in ALFs in exchange for having greater choice and decision-making than is possible in SNFs. Some ALFs can accommodate older people with multiple disabilities, who might traditionally be placed in SNFs. On the other hand, ALFs may not be good settings for aging in place if they are unable to provide adequate services when residents need more help with ADLs (MetLife, 2010; Zimmerman, Munn, & Koenig, 2006).

Although the use of ALFs is growing dramatically, their costs are typically prohibitive for many low- and middle-income elders. Moreover, only some facilities accept elders who depend on Medicaid, the primary public funding for long-term care, because Medicaid's reimbursement rates are lower than fees charged to private pay residents. In some cases, elders must move out if they have run out of funds and must turn to nursing homes that accept Medicaid. A few states offer Medicaid waivers for assisted living as an alternative to SNFs, where elders dependent on Medicaid are able to remain in ALFs (Mollica, 2009; Mollica & Houser, 2011; NSCLC, 2010).

ALF Low-Income Residents Organize

Eleven long-time residents of an ALF were told that they had two months to move since the facility owners decided that they would no longer accept Medicaid reimbursement for patients who have exhausted their savings and are poor. Meanwhile, management was carpeting and painting vacant rooms in order to attract higher-income residents. ALF residents organized to protest the corporation's decision but without success. For most, their only option was a skilled nursing home facility, which will disrupt valued friendships—and cost the state more.

points to ponder

Based upon what you have learned so far, what living arrangements would you recommend for your parents or grandparents who are living in a home that is too large for them and costing them more in maintenance, utilities, and taxes than they can afford. How would you respond when they insist they want to stay in their own homes as long as possible, even though they are becoming socially isolated?

Private Homes That Offer Long-Term Supports

Adult family homes (AFHs) are another option for older persons who do not need the 24-hour medical care available in skilled nursing facilities. In some states, they are known as adult foster homes, board and care homes, or group homes. Care is provided in a private home by owners who may have some health care training but are not required to be professionals in the field. The owner and, in some cases, auxiliary staff provide housekeeping, help with some ADLs, personal care, and some delegated nursing functions. Like ALF residents, older residents in AFHs can generally decide for themselves whether to take their medications or to exercise, unlike the more structured skilled nursing home schedule. These homes are licensed to house up to five or six residents. Some specialize in caring for adults with physical disabilities or mental disorders; others refuse to care for people with advanced dementia, while still others offer services to dementia patients only. Families and elders both tend to like the small family-like atmosphere of AFHs, even though quality among AFHs varies widely.

With the rapid growth of AFHs as a less regulated and less expensive option than SNFs, concerns about quality of care have intensified. Medicaid reimbursement rates for AFHs are one-third to one-half the rates paid to nursing homes. AFHs work well for residents who do not require heavy care (e.g., those who are not bedridden or with severe behavioral problems due to dementia). However, for those who have become more impaired while living in an AFH, the reimbursement rates do not reflect the time and effort required of the facilities' caregivers, which can negatively

Reflection Break

Your older neighbor Esther is in her eighties and lives alone. Esther has always prided herself on being a good planner. Right now she's able to manage living by herself, but she anticipates a time when she may need more assistance, perhaps in a setting other than her current home. She knows there are different kinds of living arrangements for older adults, but she's not familiar with the specifics. She asks for your advice. Can you explain to Esther what are age-friendly communities, cohousing, intentional communities, continuing care retirement communities, assisted living facilities, adult family homes, and skilled nursing facilities? Maybe Esther has not considered in-home care or home modification. What can you tell her about those?

affect the overall quality of care. With more elders and families seeking alternatives to SNFs, increasing numbers of AFH residents have multiple diagnoses, take large numbers of medications, and need qualified staff to monitor their care. Not surprisingly, instances of abuse and neglect have been found in AFHs. Aging in place in less restrictive and expensive long-term care settings can have benefits but also risks for older residents. Families need to monitor care and advocate in order to ensure that their loved one is receiving quality care.

Regardless of the type of residential facility, certain characteristics promote quality of life. These can serve as a checklist for families and older adults visiting facilities to make a decision about the next move. Does the facility promote:

- a sense of safety, security, and order
- physical comfort and freedom from pain
- enjoyment of daily life
- meaningful activities and interpersonal relationships
- functional ability
- a sense of individuality, dignity, and choice
- spiritual well-being
- a sense of privacy, and
- opportunities for intimacy and expressing one's sexuality?

Even in high-quality residential settings that further these qualities, functional decline may require relocation to an SNF.

Skilled Nursing Facilities (SNFs) **Skilled nursing facilities (SNFs)** offer skilled nursing care, rehabilitation, subacute care, and long-term care. People who are unfamiliar with the residential patterns of older adults mistakenly assume that the majority live in SNFs. In 1985, 5.4 percent of older adults lived in SNFs, but this proportion has decreased to only about 4 percent of the population 65 and older. The lifetime risk of admission to a SNFs increases with age, however. Not surprisingly, the oldest-old are most likely to live in SNFs, where the average age of residents is mid-eighties. Indeed, almost 50 percent of residents are age 95 and older. The lower rates of nursing home admissions will probably continue, despite the significant growth of the oldest-old. This is because of the trends you have been learning about—the increasing number of community-based options for long-term service and supports and a preference for aging in place as long as possible (AoA, 2012; Federal Interagency Forum, 2012).

Because of negative stereotypes and media stories about poor-quality facilities, few older people initially choose to live in a skilled nursing home. Most enter after receiving informal care from family members and formal home care services and, in some cases, following a stay in ALFs or AFHs. Nevertheless, skilled nursing facilities are often the best choice for the oldest, frailest, and most vulnerable segments of the population.

SNFs are also often the best option when the demands of care become too great for families to manage. It is not surprising that elders with severe dementia, incontinence, hallucinations, impaired communication, and several ADL and IADL limitations are more likely to move to an SNF, even if they have a family caregiver. Fortunately, there has been an increase in the number of homes offering special

points to ponder

What is your perception of nursing homes? You may be surprised to learn that they can offer some advantages over other types of care:

- social interaction
- accessible social activities
- intensive rehabilitation services
- access to skilled health care
- relief from the stress of caregiving on family

You may find it useful to visit a skilled nursing facility in your community to see some of these benefits first-hand. Be sure to look beyond your initial impressions of just the physical features to see the "life" within.

care units (SCUs) or **memory care units** for residents with dementia; such units offer a high level of care for residents who are likely to have disruptive behavioral problems, such as wandering.

Not surprisingly, women predominate among SNF residents due to their longer life expectancy, greater risk of multiple chronic and disabling illnesses, and higher likelihood of being unmarried. The last factor is a critical one, since the absence of a partner or another caregiver is a major predictor of nursing home placement.

Some older adults use SNFs only briefly at some point in their lives, often for a short stay after hospitalization. For example, an older adult who has broken a hip and requires surgery is rarely able to be discharged to their home, instead requiring rehabilitation and monitored care. Each year more than 1 million older persons leave long-term care facilities—almost evenly divided among discharges to the community, transfers to other health facilities, and death. Keep in mind the statistic of 4 percent is a static picture of the population in nursing homes that does not take account of movement into and out of such settings.

It is striking that the decline in overall nursing home use has occurred predominantly among white elders. What has shifted from the past historical patterns is an increase among Latinos, Asians, and African Americans in SNFs, as depicted in Figure 11.4. In the past, it was assumed that elders of color did not choose nursing homes for cultural or familial reasons, cost, or discrimination. But this recent shift is not necessarily a desired change, since most older adults prefer to age in the least restrictive setting. Instead, it appears that elders of color have less access to the home and community-based supports that you are learning about in this chapter. For example, assisted living facilities are more likely to be built in high-income areas and serve well-educated residents, making them less available to elders of color, who as a whole have fewer financial resources than whites. For some elders of color, their "last resort option" may be a bed in a poor-quality nursing home that accepts low-income patients on Medicaid (Feng, Fennell, Tyler, Clark, & Mor, 2011).

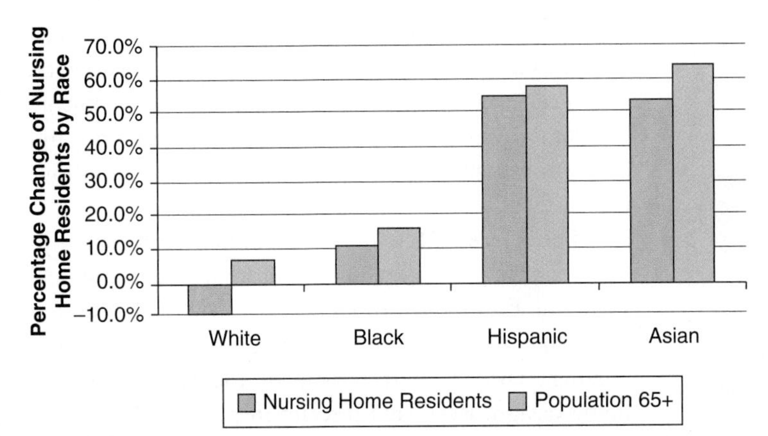

FIGURE 11.4 Percent Change of Whites and Elders of Color in Nursing Homes, 1999–2008

Source: Tyler, Clark, & Mor, (2011).

On the other hand, in some communities with highly diverse populations, ethnic-specific nursing homes that offer quality culturally appropriate care are now built under the auspices of nonprofit organizations or faith-based groups. For example, in cities such as San Francisco and Seattle, Japanese and Chinese American elders can enter nursing homes operated and staffed by people who speak their language and serve culturally specific foods. In most of the Chinese facilities, for example, employees communicate with residents in many dialects of Chinese.

Although the media often report instances of abuse and violation of regulations in nursing homes, you are learning that there are many excellent SNFs. Increased efforts to improve quality of care and the development of innovative options signal an important change in skilled nursing facilities. Increasingly, residents and their families have more influence over their lives through resident councils, patients' bills of rights, nursing home ombudsman, complaint resolution units, and the advocacy of groups such as the National Citizens' Coalition for Nursing Home Reform (NCCNHR). In its resident surveys, the NCCNHR found that a major concern of cognitively intact older people is to be involved in decisions about their daily lives in the facility. Through such efforts, along with increased gerontological training, nursing home staff are also implementing ways to involve family, friends, and the larger community in their policies, procedures, and activities and thus to promote elder residents' self-determination.

Culture Change in Long-Term Care New models for the care of elders in long-term care settings, particularly in SNFs, are growing. Since the 1990s, there has been a major **culture change** and an emphasis on person-centered care. Culture change focuses

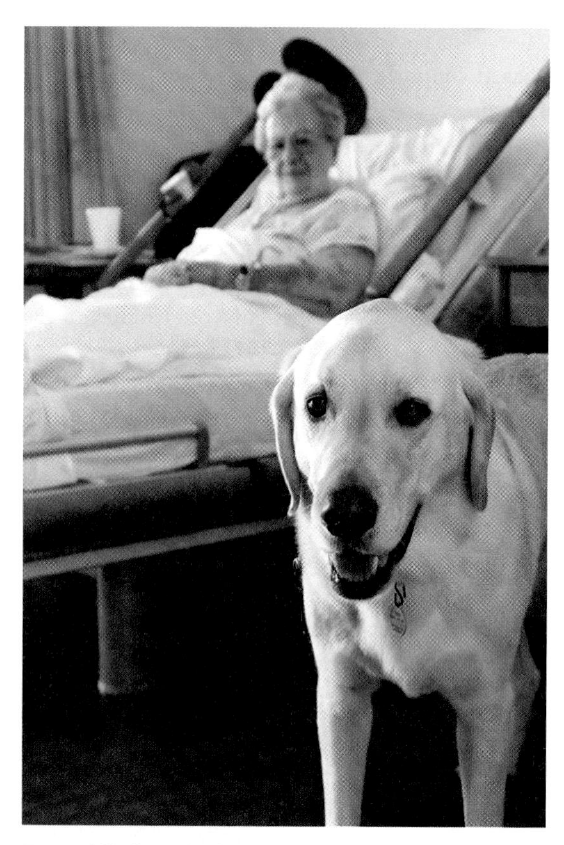

Some skilled nursing facilities provide care in a more homelike environment, sometimes even including pet visitors for patients who would like them.

not just on the physical environment, but also on decision-making that moves away from a hierarchical bureaucratic structure and encourages more input by residents, family members, and staff. Such initiatives emphasize the "home" aspect of SNFs as a place where residents can continue to grow, rather than institutions where they come to die. **Person-centered care** means individualizing services to each resident's needs and preferences, offering choices in waking, eating, and bathing times, and in some cases even selecting which staff members serve them. You will learn about person-centered care in community settings in Chapter 13.

points to ponder

Of all the living arrangements that you have learned about, which one(s) would you seek out later in life, assuming you have adequate financial resources and you were healthy and active? What might you consider if you were no longer able to live alone due to illness or disability? What are the reasons you might choose these options?

The **Eden Alternative** is one of the first national efforts aimed at changing nursing home culture. It is characterized by involving elders in decision-making and engaging them in meaningful activities, including caring for plants and pets in the home or volunteering in a child care center if there is one on-site. Facilities that have adopted the Eden Alternative deemphasize strictly scheduled activities and focus on humanizing staff–elder interactions. It has been found to benefit both the residents and the staff (Bergman-Evans, 2004; Schmidt & Beatty, 2005).

points to ponder

Imagine that your health and functional ability have declined to the point that you need to enter a skilled nursing facility. What would be your greatest fears? If you could choose one aspect of nursing home life over which you could have full control, what would that be?

Similar models of organizational culture change are promoted by the **Pioneer Network**, a growing national coalition of long-term care administrators, practitioners, and advocates working to improve the quality of care in long-term care facilities. The Pioneer Network also emphasizes person-centered care rather than rigid adherence to institutional regulations. It modifies the physical environment to be more homelike, creates "neighborhoods," and offers residents more privacy. Culture change, as promoted by the Pioneer Network, can occur even without extensive physical restructuring by promoting residents' decision-making autonomy and by improved supervision, training, and work conditions for staff.

The **Green House** has a similar philosophy of decentralization and choice but a different physical structure. Eight to 10 residents share a small home that looks like a single-family dwelling and does not have nursing stations characteristic of the typical nursing home design. Residents interact in a shared living and dining area, but have private rooms and bathrooms. These smaller houses are linked together organizationally and share backyards or outdoor access. All staff

A Model of Culture Change

One of the first nursing homes in the country to effectively implement these types of physical and organizational changes was Mt. St. Vincent Home in Seattle. Each floor is divided into "neighborhoods" or households, each encompassing a cluster of residents' rooms and a large kitchen/dining/activities area for 6–25 residents. These neighborhoods are characterized by resident-directed care and the integration of cognitively alert elders and those with dementia. Staff is permanently assigned to a neighborhood and is trained to share roles and responsibilities rather than follow a traditional medical model. A child care center offers numerous opportunities for intergenerational contact. Not surprisingly, there is often a long waiting list to live and work there (Anderson, 2009; Angelelli, 2006; Boyd, 2003; Grant, 2006; Nelson, 2010).

is taught to provide direct or hands-on care, including meal preparation, personal care, and housekeeping, rather than specializing in one task (Lustbader & Williams, 2006; NCBCapital Impact, 2013; Rabig, Thomas, Kane, Cutler, & McAlilly, 2006).

Even without physical modifications, empowering direct-line workers (specifically certified nurse aides or CNAs) can enhance resident care and staff cooperation and job satisfaction. Modifying workloads and improving supervision and training can also reduce staff turnover, as you learned in our discussion of direct care workers in Chapter 7. Under the overall framework of the Pioneer Network, these significant shifts in organizational philosophy and structure, physical design, and staff caregiving practices are improving the quality of care for frail elders in skilled nursing homes (Angelelli, 2006; Yeatts & Cready, 2007).

Social and Health Services to Promote Aging in Place

Long-term services and support have evolved in the past 20 years from an emphasis on institutional care to a broad range of **home and community-based services (HCBS)** to help older adults age in place in the least restrictive environment possible. Under this broader definition, homemaker services, nutrition programs, adult day care, and home health care are all long-term care services and supports. Some of these services (e.g., home care) are brought to the older person's residence, whereas others (e.g., adult day health) require the individual to leave home to receive services.

Here's a list of community-based services, which are not health care services, that can promote aging in place:

- personal assistance, such as chore services to maintain the home
- personal care to help the person perform ADLs
- home-delivered meals
- home repair and modification
- respite care, either in the home or in a facility, which gives family caregivers a break
- automatic safety response systems that alert a caregiver if an older adult needs help

But even when these services are available and affordable, aging in place may be difficult because services are not organized into an easily managed system and may not work in coordination with each other. Even families with resources and knowledge of benefits for their older relative may find it nearly impossible to navigate a system with lots of different funding streams, eligibility criteria, and qualifications (MetLife Mature Market Institute, 2010).

Technology Promoting Resident-Centered Care

Oatfield Estates, or Elite Care, near Portland, Oregon, uses technology to promote a resident-centered model of long-term care. The campus is comprised of multiple houses with 12 private suites. Family members are encouraged to visit and volunteer, and they can monitor their elder's daily activities 24 hours a day (with the resident's permission). Residents wear an unobtrusive electronic monitoring device that can track their activities. Such monitoring also allows elders to wander throughout Oatfield Estates' gardens and houses without concerns about getting lost. This combination of technology and **resident-centered care** has allowed the facility to care for even the frailest elders with dementia who would ordinarily be placed in a more restrictive setting.

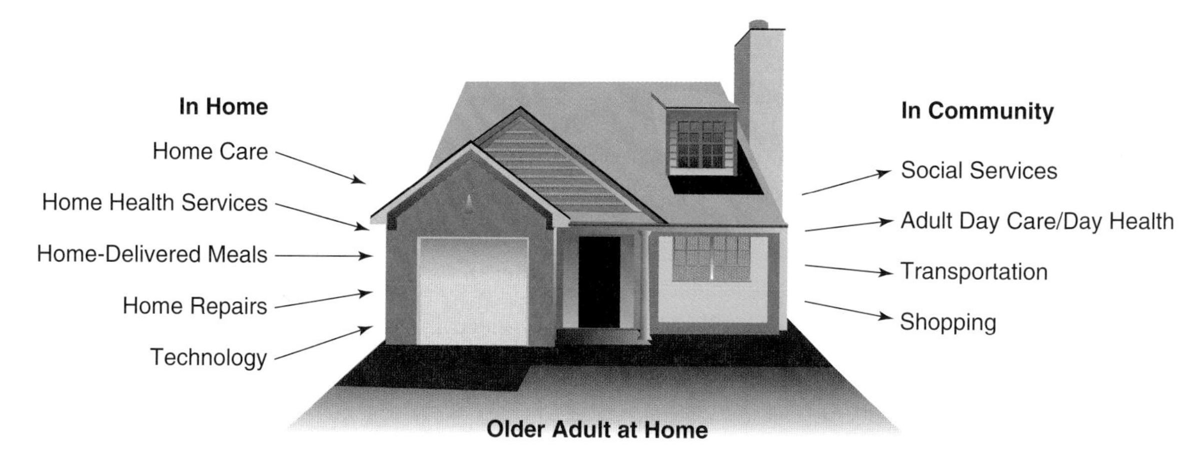

FIGURE 11.5 Services to Support Aging in Place

Figure 11.5 captures the array and complexity of services needed to support aging in place as well as service-enriched housing.

We briefly describe home care and adult day care/adult health care in this chapter; other HCBS services are addressed in Chapter 13.

Home Care

While some home care alternatives are motivated by elders' desire to age in place, cost concerns drive other changes. As Medicare seeks to reduce escalating hospital and nursing home costs, home care services have grown dramatically. Medicare reimburses some **home health care** services, defined as skilled nursing or rehabilitation benefits that are provided in the patient's own home and prescribed by a physician. Most non-health care services, such as chore workers, are covered by older adults' and family members' paying out of pocket, or if they are low-income, these may be reimbursed through Medicaid. You will learn more about home care, especially under health care reform, in Chapter 13.

Chore workers and other home and community-based services can help older people remain in their homes.

Adult Day Care and Adult Day Health Care

Adult day care (ADC) allows the older person to remain at home but receive some health and social services outside the home. In this case, elders attend a local ADC center one or more times per week, for several hours each day. ADC goes beyond senior centers by providing structured health and social services for older people with cognitive and functional impairments, including those with dementia, as well as for younger people with disabilities. These facilities are smaller than most senior centers, with an average daily attendance of fewer than 25 elders.

Adult day health care, or ADHCs, are similar to ADCs, but are based on a health rehabilitative model of long-term care with individualized care. Although both ADCs and ADHCs provide recreation, meals, transportation to and from the facility, and memory-retraining programs, ADHCs are more likely to offer nursing care, physical and speech therapy, health monitoring, and scheduled medication distribution. The greatest advantage of both ADCs and ADHCs over home health care is bringing older people together for social interaction.

Use of ADCs and ADHCs may delay moving an elder into a nursing home, but this also depends on the characteristics and stress level of the elder's family caregivers. Such services are not suitable for the most impaired older person,

points to ponder

We talked earlier about what you might recommend to parents or grandparents who are "aging in place" in a home too large and expensive for them. If they insist in staying in their own home, even as their health declines, what services might you recommend them to support their "aging in place"?

but they are an invaluable resource for elders with moderate levels of dementia or with serious physical impairments and chronic illnesses who can access transportation to the center. These services also benefit families, by providing them with respite for rest and relaxation or allowing them to keep their jobs (Cho, Zarit, & Chiriboga, 2009).

Housing Policy and Growing Housing Needs

Housing policy for older people is less well developed than in the areas of income security and health care. This is due, in part, to the influence of well-organized interest groups such as builders and real estate developers, which have typically opposed public funding for housing.

The major housing programs that benefit older adults involve subsidies to suppliers of housing to enable them to sell or rent housing for less than the prevailing market price. Since 1959, two special housing programs administered by the federal Housing and Urban Development (HUD) for low-income older people and those with disabilities have given long-term loans for the construction of housing and to offset the rent. **Section 202**, the only program specifically for older adults, provides housing for people age 62 and older whose incomes are less than 50 percent of the median income in their areas. Loans to private nonprofit organizations or consumer cooperatives for the financing, construction, or rehabilitation of housing for older people do not need to be repaid as long as the housing is available to very low-income elders for at least 40 years. These subsidized housing projects must provide some support services such as meals and transportation.

Section 8 housing programs represent an additional form of housing subsidy for very-low-income families and individuals, regardless of age. Qualifying elders or families of persons with disabilities receive vouchers to subsidize their rent in the private housing market. Unfortunately, federal budget cuts mean that relatively few older households currently benefit from Section 8 vouchers, and federal funding for new housing has been almost nonexistent since 1997. With markedly reduced funding for low-income housing, some landlords have converted their buildings into higher-rent apartments or condominiums, hotels, or office spaces or have sold the property outright to local developers. These changes in federal funding and local priorities have significantly reduced the supply of housing for low-income elders (National Coalition for the Homeless, 2009).

As a result, less than 5 percent of older people benefit from federally funded housing assistance programs. The demand for subsidized housing for elders far outpaces the planned development, resulting in long waiting lists. This has become a crisis for the many older persons who cannot afford market rate housing, and, as a result, some become homeless in their later years (Pynoos, Cicero, & Nishita, 2010).

Homelessness: Aging in Place on the Streets

A growing segment of the older population is homeless, often unable to afford or access funds for basic housing and unaware of services to which they are entitled. Today's

The Increasing Population of Homeless Elders

The global economic crisis that emerged in late 2008 resulted in job losses and home foreclosures for many middle-class families. Older adults were not immune from this crisis. With their shrinking pensions and dependence on Social Security, some older persons can no longer afford their homes or pay for apartments and have been relegated to living in their cars and pickups. The long waiting lists for public housing and homeless shelters that are filled to capacity cannot provide them with better housing options. Many churches and businesses have opened their parking lots to these homeless elders living in their cars. According to the executive director of the National Coalition for the Homeless, "The homeless population is graying along with the general population, and we're seeing more elderly people living out their final years on the streets" (Michael Stoops, *Seattle Times*, April 8, 2009, p. 1).

homeless elders (defined as age 55 and older because they are often 10–20 years older physiologically than their chronological age) comprise 8–10 percent of the homeless population, although this is likely to be an underrepresentation. The percentage is significantly higher in major cities such as New York and San Francisco. While these percentages may seem low to you, any level of homelessness among older adults is of concern, given their greater vulnerability. Additionally, rates of homelessness among elders are projected to increase markedly, an ongoing effect of the recession (Sermons & Henry, 2010).

Homeless elders are composed of two markedly different groups:

1. The chronic homeless, who have lived on the streets for many years, lost contact with their families, and often suffer from persistent psychiatric disorders, alcoholism, drug abuse, or cognitive impairment. Older homeless men have generally lived this way longer than their female counterparts. As a result, this vulnerable segment of the homeless population has a life expectancy of 42–52 years, far lower than the national average.
2. Lower- and middle-income Americans—many of whom are women who never expected to be homeless—who are living on the streets or in their vehicles because of the recession, the loss of affordable housing, reductions in HUD's housing assistance programs for elders, and the record foreclosure rate (National Coalition for the Homeless, 2009; Sermons and Henry, 2010).

Homeless people also generally lack food, clothing, medical care, and social supports. Such a disorganized lifestyle can magnify the usual age-related declines in biological and psychological processes described in earlier chapters. Due to their unstable lifestyles and frequent disruptions to mental well-being, homeless elders with chronic health problems often do not have the capacity to seek regular medical care for these conditions, or even to follow the necessary medication schedules and dietary restrictions. The prevalence of chronic diseases in this group is higher than for other segments of the older population, yet their access to health services is inadequate and sporadic. They generally obtain health care through public hospital emergency rooms; clinical appointments and follow-up visits are rarely kept. Because they are more likely to be sick and frail, they are also more likely to be victims of crime. As a result, they often die because of diseases that are neglected, accidents or victimization on the streets (Sermons & Henry, 2010).

Homeless shelters are typically ill prepared to deal with the distinctive needs of frail elders who are homeless, although some shelters specifically for this population are being developed. The McKinney–Vento Homeless Assistance Act provides limited funds. But these funds are inadequate for most communities to respond to the growing homeless population. Homelessness is projected to increase by 33 percent from 2010 to 2020, and more than double between 2010 and 2050, in part because of the growth in younger persons with risk factors of lifelong poverty, substance abuse, incarceration, and family disruption, who will then age into place on the streets. An additional concern is that many cities have responded to the growth of homelessness among older adults by making it increasingly difficult, if not illegal, to live on the street, enforcing no-sleeping and no-camping ordinances (Sermons & Henry, 2010).

A Novel Temporary Solution to Elder Homelessness

In the ultra-affluent city of Santa Barbara, California, a dozen parking lots throughout the city are transformed into relatively safe outdoor lodging for homeless to sleep in their vehicles (for the homeless who still have a vehicle). Two social workers check the lots each night as part of the safe parking project. One "resident" is a 55-year-old woman who earns $8 an hour at a local coffee shop and had owned two homes worth nearly $2 million, purchased when she was earning a substantial income as a realtor. Unable to sell her homes or manage the $10,000-a-month mortgage, she declared bankruptcy and lost both properties to foreclosure. Another resident is a 66-year-old mother of three, who became homeless after she lost her job and couldn't afford $2,150-a-month rent, even with Social Security and a part-time job. Because she had lived in Santa Barbara all her life, she was reluctant to leave what was familiar. But after living in her car for three months, she reluctantly moved to a less expensive community. Both women said that they never dreamed this would happen to them (Fleck, 2008).

points to ponder

Next time you see a homeless person who "looks" older, consider what life experiences may have brought them to this point. Contrary to what the media often suggest, they are not necessarily alcoholics or drug users.

Because of rising housing costs, even the oldest-old may find themselves homeless for the first time in their lives.

Aging in Place among Older Prisoners

You may not think of geriatric needs within the prison population. But prisoners are literally "aging in place," albeit involuntarily. The number of older adult inmates has quadrupled in the past 25 years; this is because of the large numbers who have aged in prison with life terms or longer sentences than in the past and mandatory minimum sentences with no parole. In some cases, prison is a "haven" for those who intentionally commit new crimes to avoid life on the streets and to have regular meals and health care. As with younger populations of prisoners, African Americans are disproportionately represented among older inmates (Center on Sentencing & Corrections, 2010; Phillips et al., 2011).

Prisoners 50 and older are classified as "old." This is because inmates generally age faster as a result of more chronic diseases and a history of substance abuse. Due to a lifetime of poor health practices, older inmates have higher rates of common chronic diseases—hypertension, arthritis, and chronic obstructive pulmonary disease. Although these are typical in the older population generally, rates are 25 percent higher among prisoners and occur at younger ages. Many inmates have been exposed to trauma and other stressful events earlier in their lives—as well as to a culture of violence in prison—which negatively affects their mental health as they age. Mental health problems, especially depression, are often lifelong and go untreated in up to 50 percent of prisoners. Because of these needs, prisons spend 2–3 times more on health care for older than younger inmates under age 50. But even with these high costs, many inmates with serious chronic health conditions fail to receive adequate care, especially as the budgets of correctional services are being cut (Center on Sentencing and Corrections, 2010; Haugebrook, Zgoba, Maschi, Morgan, & Brown, 2010; Maschi, Gibson, Zgoba, & Morgen, 2011; Pew Center on the States, 2008; Wilper et al., 2009).

Several recommendations have been offered to improve older prisoners' health status and reduce health care costs. These include reallocating budgets to provide more preventive health services to older inmates; designing separate geriatric health facilities and hospice services; making physical accommodations in older inmates' cells and in bathrooms (e.g., installing handrails, removing top bunks); and training younger inmates to be caregivers to older inmates with functional impairments (this would also provide job training for future parolees).

A more controversial issue is early release, known as **geriatric or compassionate release**, for nonviolent older inmates who have major medical needs or at end of life. Although not widely used, proponents believe that geriatric release is ethically and legally justifiable for a subset of prisoners with life-limiting illnesses, and when the financial costs from continuing incarceration outweigh the benefits. Critics contend that the risk is too great, especially since medical prognoses can be flawed. What is your opinion about compassionate relief (Center on Sentencing and Corrections, 2010; Williams, Sudore, Greifinger, & Morrison, 2011)?

summary

This chapter emphasized how the built or physical environment affects older people's well-being. Some environments are more conducive for achieving active aging among some people, while other older adults need an entirely different set of features. Most older adults live in urban and suburban areas, with those in rural and suburban areas often facing the most difficulty remaining in their homes because of lack of public transportation and accessible services. In urban areas, the neighborhood takes on greater significance as a source of social interactions, health and social services, and access to small businesses. But elders in urban areas may become isolated in their homes if they are fearful of crime; however, their fear tends to be much greater than the actual incidence of crime. Contrary to what we may assume about elders' moving to sunny climates, older people are less likely to move to a totally new area than are younger families. But they are more likely to move to a different type of housing geographically close by within the same community. When they do relocate, they often experience feelings of grief over losing a longtime home and their sense of place. Regardless of the type of living situation, being able to have some control over relocation decisions is paramount.

The vast majority of older adults lives in independent housing—and wants to continue to do so. But they often face high maintenance costs and, when they do have to move, difficulties selling their homes for something more manageable because of the current poor housing market.

Fortunately, there are growing numbers of choices in living environments, particularly related to the concepts of elder- or age-friendly communities and aging in place for those who want to stay in their own homes or apartments. More cohousing and intentional communities, as well as virtual communities such as villages that do not require relocating but provide services to a network of elders for a small annual fee, are emerging for groups of older adults who choose to live near people who share their interests and lifestyle, but where they can age in place in their own homes. Aging in place becomes an even more viable option as more homes are built according to the principles of universal design. Homes with elder-friendly home design—including bedroom, bath, and kitchen facilities on the entry floor, easy-to-operate mechanical and electronic devices, and temperature controls for each area of the home—can create a supportive environment for aging, but will be limited to those who can afford them. Middle-aged adults who are building new homes or remodeling existing homes to accommodate their aging parents often find that the home can benefit them as they age in place as well. Initiatives to create age-friendly intergenerational and "green" communities that benefit all age groups are also growing nationwide.

For older adults who can no longer remain in independent housing, there are a growing number of residential living situations. Continuing care retirement communities (CCRCs) provide choices in housing and long-term services and supports, including skilled nursing care, as aging residents' needs for assistance change, but serve only a small proportion of financially secure seniors. Assisted living and adult family homes are rapidly becoming cost-effective options to nursing homes for older people who need help with ADLs but not necessarily 24-hour care. These less institutional options provide greater autonomy and privacy, and less direct supervision than nursing homes.

Home care is now the fastest-growing component of personal health care expenditures. It allows older people to age in place while bringing services such as skilled nursing care, rehabilitation, and personal and household care to the person's home. Adult day care or adult day health care, as both a social and rehabilitative model, provides social and health care opportunities for frail older people who are living at home alone or with a family caregiver. Unfortunately, as states have faced the need to curtail Medicaid spending, home health and adult day health have increasingly been a victim of budget cuts.

Only about 4 percent of older adults—typically the oldest-old—live in skilled nursing facilities, but for some elders and their families, this is the best living option. And skilled nursing facilities increasingly seek to initiate organizational culture change to create more homelike environments by changing both the decision-making structure and the living arrangements to promote resident-centered care. Funding for low-income housing for older adults has always been limited, but even more so in the current economic context. And such housing typically does not offer enough services for residents to age in place. In recent years, the number of homeless adults age 55 and older has been growing. They often face chronic medical, psychiatric, and cognitive disorders that go unattended because of inadequate access to health services. As a result, homeless elders grow physiologically old more rapidly and have a shorter life expectancy than do more affluent elders.

Another concern is increased numbers of elders in prisons, mostly because many have aged in place. By age 55, many of these prisoners have chronic diseases and disabilities found in chronologically older adults in the community. The escalating costs of care for this population, as well as the incongruence between prison environments and the needs of frail older persons, have stimulated discussions about the need for geriatric facilities in prisons, physical accommodations, and even early release.

Health and social service providers need to be informed of the growing options in housing and long-term care and how to effectively utilize them to support older adults' aging in place and control over their environment. These professionals must be sensitive to the impact of the home and neighborhood on elders' well-being, social engagement, and ultimately their quality of life and know how to make modifications to support aging in place. Accordingly, the need for community-based long-term services and supports that allow elders to age in place will grow. Although future cohorts of elders will have more options, these will depend on their financial resources. Adults now in their thirties or early forties who cannot afford to purchase a home and anticipate renting most of their lives may have fewer housing options in their old age.

key terms

"active adult" or lifestyle, p. 321
adult day care (ADC), p. 328
adult day health care, or ADHCs, p. 328
adult family homes (AFHs), p. 323
age- (or elder-) friendly communities, p. 316
aging in place, p. 316
asset mapping, p. 318
assisted living facilities (ALFs), p. 322
cohousing, p. 319
continuing care retirement communities (CCRCs), p. 321
culture change, p. 325
Eden Alternative, p. 326
elder cottages, p. 320
flexible housing, p. 317
geriatric or compassionate release, p. 331
graying of the suburbs, p. 311
Green House, p. 326
home and community-based services (HCBS), p. 327
home health care, p. 328
home sharing, p. 320
intentional (or niche) communities, p. 319
life-space, p. 310
livable or lifelong communities, p. 316
memory care units, p. 325
naturally occurring retirement communities (NORCs), p. 318
person-centered care, p. 326
Pioneer Network, p. 326
resident-centered care, p. 327
Section 8, p. 329
Section 202, p. 329
service-enriched housing, p. 321
skilled nursing facilities (SNFs), p. 324
universal design, p. 317
village, p. 318

review questions

1. What is meant by the term "graying of the suburbs"? List some disadvantages of suburban living for older adults.
2. Describe the prevalence of crime against older adults. What factors might account for the difference between the actual crime rate and older adults' perception of crime? What type of crime is most common against older adults?
3. How would you describe the village concept of aging in place? What are some of its advantages?
4. How does cohousing differ from the village concept?
5. List four characteristics of an age-friendly community. How can age-friendly communities also benefit younger adults?
6. Define the terms continuing care retirement communities, assisted living facility, and skilled nursing facility. What are the distinctions between them?
7. What does the term culture change mean when applied to a long-term care facility? List three characteristics of such culture change.
8. Although most older adults prefer not to live in a skilled nursing facility, identify three advantages of such facilities for some older adults.
9. Discuss some home and community-based service options available to an older person who does not wish to move to retirement housing but prefers to stay in her long-term home.
10. What are the reasons why a prisoner or person who is homeless is considered to be "old" when they are 50? What are three of the primary causes of homelessness among older adults?

media resources

Watch

- Active Seniors
- Late Adulthood: Happiness, Molly

Read

- Successful Aging, Extended Family: Maria, 68 Years Old
- Blumer, Herbert. The Nature of Symbolic Interactionism.

references

Abrahms, S. (2011). *Finding your niche housing in retirement—Or before. The rise of affinity communities. AARP fact sheet.* Washington, DC: AARP Public Policy Institute.

Accius, J. C. (2010). *The village: A growing option for aging in place. AARP Fact Sheet 177.* Washington, DC: AARP Public Policy Institute.

Administration on Aging (AoA). (2012). *A profile of older Americans: 2012.* Retrieved February 2014, from http://www.aoa.gov/stats/profile.

Allman, R. M., Sawyer, P., & Roseman, J. M. (2006). The UAB study of aging: Background and prospects for insights into life-space mobility among older African Americans and whites in rural and urban settings. *Aging and Health, 2,* 417–428.

American Association of Homes and Services for the Aging (AAHSA). (2011). *Continuing care retirement communities.* Retrieved October 2011, from http://www.aahsa.org/consumer_info/homes_ svcs_directory.

Anderson, D. (2009). The village movement comes home to Seattle. *Seniors Digest, Seattle-King County Division on Aging.* Retrieved May 23, 2010, from http://www.poststat.net/pwp008/pub.49/issue.1044/article.4309.

Angelelli, J. (2006). Promising models for transforming long term care. *The Gerontologist, 46,* 428–430.

Atlanta Regional Commission Area Aging on Aging. (2013). *Lifelong communities handbook: Creating opportunities for lifelong living.* Retrieved September 22, 2013, from www.atlantaregional.com/File%20Library/Aging/ag_llc_designhandbook.pdf.

Beard, J. R., Blaney, S., Cerda, M., Freye, V., Lovasi, G. S., Ompad, D., et al. (2009). Neighborhood characteristics and disability in older adults. *Journal of Gerontology: Social Sciences, 64B,* 252–257.

Bergman-Evans, B. (2004). Beyond the basics: Effects of the Eden Alternative model on quality of life issues. *Journal of Gerontological Nursing, 30,* 27–34.

Boyd, C. (2003). The Providence Mt. St. Vincent experience. *Journal of Social Work in Long Term Care, 2,* 245–268.

Brown, C. J., Roth, D. L., Allman, R. M., Sawyer, P., Ritchie, C. S., & Roseman, J. M. (2009). Trajectories of life-space mobility after hospitalization. *Annals of Internal Medicine, 150,* 372–378.

Bureau of Justice Statistics. (2012). *Criminal victimization in the United States 2010: Statistical tables.* Washington, DC: U.S. Department of Justice.

Center on Sentencing and Corrections. (2010). *It's about time: Aging prisoners, increasing costs, and geriatric release.* Retrieved January 11, 2012, from http://www.vera.org/centers/center-sentencing-corrections.

Cho, S. Zarit, S.H., & Chiriboga, D. A. (2009). Wives and daughters: The differential role of day care use in the nursing home placement of cognitively impaired family members. *The Gerontologist, 49,* 57–67.

Cohen-Mansfield, J., Dakheel-Ali, M., & Frank, J. K. (2010). The impact of a naturally occurring retirement communities service program in MD, USA. *Health Promotion International, 25,* 210–220.

Co-Housing Association of the U.S. (2012). *What is co-housing?* Retrieved December 3, 2012, from http://www.cohousing.org/.

Crowe, M., Andel, R., Okonkwo, O., Wadley, V., Sawyer, P., & Allman, R. M. (2008). Life-space and cognitive decline in a community-based sample of African American and Caucasian older adults. *Journal of Gerontology: Medical Sciences, 63,* 1241–1245.

deLaGrange, K. (2011). *Elder cohousing: How viable is cohousing for an aging population?* Retrieved October 10, 2011, from http://www.eldercohousing.org.

Dobkin, L. (2011). *Elder cottages.* Retrieved March 30, 2011, from http://www.ncoa.org/strengthening-community-organizations.

Dunn, K. (2010). *Future of home sharing.* Home Sharing Vermont. Retrieved September 21, 2013, from http://www.bos.frb.org/commdev/.

Durrett, C. (2009). *The senior cohousing handbook* (2nd ed.). Gabriola Island, BC: New Society Publishers.

Emlet, C. A., & Moceri, J. T., (2011). The importance of social connectedness in building age-friendly communities. *Journal of Aging Research,* 10, 303–320.

Federal Interagency Forum on Aging-Related Statistics. (2012). *Older Americans 2011: Key indicators of well-being.* Washington, DC: U.S. Government Printing Office.

Feng, Z., Fennell, M. L., Tyler, D. A., Clark, M., & Mor, V. (2011). Growth of racial and ethnic minorities in US nursing homes driven by demographics and possible disparities in options. *Health Affairs, 30*(7), 1358–1365.

Fleck, C. (2008). A growing number of lower and middle-income Americans are finding themselves homeless. *AARP Bulletin.* Retrieved March 30, 2011, from http://www.aarp.org/home-garden/housing/info.

Ginzler, E. (2009). *It takes a village: An innovative model for aging in your community.* Retrieved September 2011, from http://www.aarp.org.home/gardening/info.

Gray, R., Harrell, R., & Sykes, K. (2010).The built environment: Planning healthy communities for all ages: Community design, neighborhood change and impact on older adults. *Public Policy & Aging Report, 20,* 22–26.

Grant, L. (2006). *Culture change in for-profit nursing homes.* The Commonwealth Fund. Retrieved November 2006, from http://www.cmwf.org/spotlights/spotlights_show.htm?doc.

Harrell, R. (2011). *Housing for older adults: The impacts of the recession.* Washington, DC: AARP Public Policy Institute.

Haugebrook, S., Zgoba, K. M., Maschi, T., Morgan, K., & Brown, D. (2010). Trauma, stress, health and mental health issues among ethnically diverse older adult prisoners. *Journal of Correctional Health Care, 16,* 220–229.

Jackson, M. (2010). Recession slows elders' moves into retirement communities. *Denver Post.* Retrieved September 22, 2013, from http://www.denverpost.com/business/ci_14394851.

Kirk, P. A. (2009). Naturally occurring retirement communities, thriving through creative retrofitting. In P. S. Abbott, N. Carman, J. Carman, & B. Scarfo (Eds.), *Re-creating neighborhoods for successful aging* (pp. 115–143). Baltimore, MD: Health Professions Press.

Kunkle, F. (2012). Pioneering the granny pad: Fairfax County family adapts to high-tech dwelling that could change elder care. *Washington Post.* Retrieved December 3, 2012, from http://www/washingtonpost/com/local/dc-politics.

Lachs, M., Bachman, R., Williams, C. S., Kossack, A., Bove, C., & O'Leary, J. R. (2006). Violent crime victimization increases risk of nursing home placement in older adults. *The Gerontologist, 46,* 583–589.

Longino, C. F. (2004). Socio-physical environments at the macro level: The impact of population migration. In H. W. Wahl, R. J. Scheidt, & P. G. Windley (Eds.), *Annual Review of Gerontology and Geriatrics, 23,* 110–129.

Longino, C. F., & Bradley, D. E. (2006). Internal and international migration. In R. H. Binstock & L. K. George (Eds.), *Handbook of aging and the social sciences* (6th ed.). San Diego, CA: Academic Press.

Longino, C. F. Bradley, D. E., Stoller, E. P. & Haas, W. H. (2008). Predictors of non-local moves among older adults: A prospective study. *Journal of Gerontology: Social Sciences, 63B,* S7–S14.

Lustbader, W., & Williams, C. C. (2006). Culture change in long-term care. In B. Berkman & S. D'Ambruoso (Eds.), *Handbook of social work in health and aging.* New York: Oxford Press.

Maag, S. (2012). *CCRCs today: The real deal about retirement communities.* Retrieved September 22, 2013, from http://www.leadingage.org.

Maschi, T., Gibson, S., Zgoba, K. M., & Morgen, K. (2011). Trauma and life event stressors among young and older adult prisoners. *Journal of Correctional Health Care, 17,* 160–172.

McManus, K., & Durrett, C. (2011). *Creating cohousing: Building sustainable communities.* Gabriola Island, BC: New Society Publishers.

MetLife Mature Market Institute. (2010). *Aging in Place 2.0: Rethinking solutions to the home care challenge.* Westport, CT: MetLife Mature Market Institute.

Mollica, R. (2009). *State Medicaid reimbursement policies and practices in assisted living.* Washington, DC: American Health Care Association.

Mollica, R., & Houser, A. (2011). *Assisted living and residential care in the states in 2010.* Washington, DC: AARP Public Policy Institute.

Molvig, D. (2011). Housing + services models preserve independence. *Leading Age Magazine,* 1. Retrieved January 19, 2013, from www.leadingage.org/magazine/Fetaure.aspx?/id=2108.

National Center for Assisted Living. (2011). *Resident profile.* Retrieved October 11, 2011, from http://www.ahcancal.org/ncal/resources/Pages/ResidentProfile.aspx.

National Coalition for the Homeless (NCH). (2009). *Homelessness among elderly persons.* Retrieved October 11, 2011, from http://www.nationalhomeless.org.

National Senior Citizens Law Center. (2010). *Medicaid payment for assisted living: Preventing discrimination against Medicaid-eligible residents.* Retrieved from http://www.nsclc.org/wp-content/uploads/2011/06/Medicaid-Payment-for-AL-White-Paper-11.17.10.pdf.

NCBCapital Impact. (2013). *The Green House project: What is the Green House project?* Retrieved September 27, 2013, from http://www.ncbcapitalimpact.org/home/expert-technical-assistance/green-house/.

Nelson, G. G. (2010). *Household models for nursing home environments. Presented at Creating Home in the Nursing Home,* a national symposium on culture change and the environmental requirements. Minneapolis, MN: Nelson-Tremain Partnership.

Oswald, F., Jopp, D., Rott, C., & Wahl, H.-W. (2011). Is aging in place a resource for or risk to life satisfaction? *The Gerontologist, 51,* 238–250.

Pew Center on the States. (2008). *One in 100: Behind bars in America, 2008.* Pew Center on the States' Public Safety Performance Project. Retrieved January 12, 2012, from http://www.pewcenteronthestates.org/news_room_detail.aspx?

Phillips, L. L., Allen, R. S., Harris, G. M., Presnell, A. H., DeCoster, J., & Cavanaugh, R. (2011). Aging prisoners' treatment selection. *The Gerontologist, 51,* 663–674.

Pynoos, J., Cicero, C., & Nishita, C. M. (2010). New challenges and growing trends in senior housing. In R. Hudson (Ed.), *The new politics of old age policy* (pp. 324–336). Baltimore, MD: Johns Hopkins University Press.

Rabig, J., Thomas, W., Kane, R. A., Cutler, L. J., & McAlilly, S. (2006). Radical redesign of nursing homes: Applying the Green House concept in Tupelo, Mississippi. *The Gerontologist, 46,* 533–539.

Salomon, E. (2010). *Fact sheet: Housing policies to suppport aging in place.* Washington, DC: AARP Public Policy Institute.

Scharlach, A. (2009). Creating aging-friendly communties. *Generations, 33*(2), 5–11.

Scharlach, A. (2012). Creating aging-friendly communities in the United States. *Ageing International, 37,* 25–38.

Sermons, M. W., & Henry, M. (2010). *Demographics of homelessness series: The rising elderly population.* Washington, DC: National Alliance to End Homelessness.

Schmidt, K., & Beatty, S. (2005). Quality improvement: The pursuit of excellence. *Quality Management in Health Care, 14,* 196–198.

Seattle Times. (2009). Backyard houses in Seattle, pp. B1, B9.

Susman, T. (2011, June 11). Cross-walks are increasingly deadly for the elderly. *Los Angeles Times,* Retrieved December 3, 2012, from http://www:articles.latimes.com/print.

United Hospital Fund. (2009). *What is a NORC?* Retrieved July 2009, from http://www.norcblueprint.org.

Voisine, J. M., Walker, L. M., & Jeffrey, S. M. (2009). Home is where the heart is: Living arrangements for older adults. *Consultant Pharmacist, 24,* 134–145.

Wick, J. Y., & Zanni, G. R. (2009). Aging in place: Multiple options, multiple choices. *Consultant Pharmacist, 24,* 804–806, 808–809, 811–812.

Williams, B. A., Sudore, R. L., Greifinger, R., & Morrison, R. S. (2011). Balancing punishment and compassion for seriously ill prisoners. *Annals of Internal Medicine, 155,* 122–126.

Wilper, A. P., Woolhandler, S., Boyd, J. W., Lasser, K. E., McCormick, D., Bor, D. H., & Himmelstein, D. U. (2009). The health and health care of U.S. prisoners: Results of a nationwide survey. *American Journal of Public Health, 99,* 666–672.

Wilson, K. B. (2007). Historical evolution of assisted living in the U.S.: 1979 to the present. *The Gerontologist, 47* (Special Issue), 8–22.

Yeatts, D. E., & Cready, C. M. (2007). Consequences of empowered CNA teams in nursing home settings. *The Gerontologist, 47,* 323–339.

Yeoman, B. (2006). Rethinking the commune. *AARP Magazine.* Retrieved December 2006, from http://www.aarpmagazine.org/lifestyle/rethinking_the_commune.html.

Zarem, J. E. (Ed.). (2010). *Today's continuing care retirement community.* Washington, DC: American Seniors Housing Association.

Zimmerman, S., Munn, S., & Koenig, T. (2006). Assisted living settings. In B. Berkman & S. D'Ambruoso (Eds.), *Handbook of social work in health and aging.* New York: Oxford University Press.

12 Enhancing Older Adults' Well-Being through Technology

learning objectives

12.1 Describe how elders' physical and mental well-being can be enhanced through the use of technologies, including home monitoring systems and computer games.

12.2 Discuss how technologies can promote intergenerational communication, lifelong learning, and civic engagement.

12.3 Articulate the limits and challenges of using technologies to benefit elders' lives.

Listen to the Chapter Audio

Most of us use some form of technology every day. In fact, some of you probably use technology throughout the day—texting your friends, checking your e-mail and social networking sites, watching YouTube, and taking online classes. You also use technology when you withdraw or deposit money at an ATM, make travel reservations via the Internet, heat up food in a microwave, play video games, and engage in numerous other activities that are part of our daily routines.

A growing number of technologies help older adults maintain their autonomy and promote their physical and mental well-being. **Telemonitoring**, for example, allows caregivers or health professionals to keep an eye on care recipients from a distance by using electronic communication devices; it can enable older adults to remain at home safely and provide families with peace of mind or alert them to potential problems before they become crises. Relatedly, remote patient monitoring devices collect health information (e.g., weight, glucose levels, blood pressure readings, etc.) for evaluation by health professionals who are geographically distant but can summon assistance if needed. Other technologies provide audible or visual reminders to elders to take medications, or to order medications at the appropriate time. If widely adopted, these kinds of technologies can improve home- and community-based care for elders. With the advent of sophisticated mobile technologies such as smartphones, an emerging field called **mobile health**, or **mHealth**, is aims to improve self-management of care and facilitate communication among patients, caregivers, and clinicians (Center for Technology and Aging, 2009, 2011).

In this chapter you will learn about technologies that can benefit older adults. These include:

- Information and communication technologies
- Online health management
- Technology in the workplace
- Technologies to promote aging in place
- Computer games

Some of these technologies are essential to an older person's health and safety, and enable that person to age in place rather than move to a long-term care facility. Other technologies are just for fun or for maintaining relationships, important activities at any age. Like you, many older adults enjoy e-mailing their friends and family members, or associating with others who share similar interests on social networking sites. Maybe you have been "friended" by an older relative or keep in e-mail contact with a grandparent. Many of you are familiar with technologies that are used for information-seeking, communication, and entertainment in our everyday lives. These same technologies can be commandeered by elders for such things as getting more exercise (e.g., video game console), telecommunications (e.g., Web camera), reading and keeping up with current events (e-readers), entertainment (e.g., video-on-demand services or online movie rentals), and more (Grobart, 2011).

Information and Communication Technologies

Information and communication technologies or ICTs is a broad category encompassing telecommunication devices or software that either provide electronic access to information or enable communication, or both. Many technologies fall under this category—the Internet; e-mail; social media such as Facebook, Twitter, and YouTube; cell phones; smartphones; iPads; Skype; and much more. Although younger people are most likely to use social networking sites like Facebook and Instagram, Internet users age 74 and older have shown the biggest growth in use in the past decade (Lloyd, 2010; Madden, 2010).

One 2012 survey found that slightly more than half of American adults age 65 and older were using the Internet or e-mail. This finding represented a critical turning point, because older adults were often assumed to be behind the curve when it came to Internet use. While their rate of adoption might have been slower than younger age groups, they are making dramatic gains (Zickuhr & Madden, 2012).

Figure 12.1, on p. 338, illustrates how Internet and e-mail use has been steadily increasing by all adult groups over the past decade or so, and depicts a trend that suggests continued growth in coming years.

Internet usage among older adults will probably increase even more because many baby boomers have used the Internet, e-mail, and other ICTs in the workplace. It is understandable, however, that a generation that did not

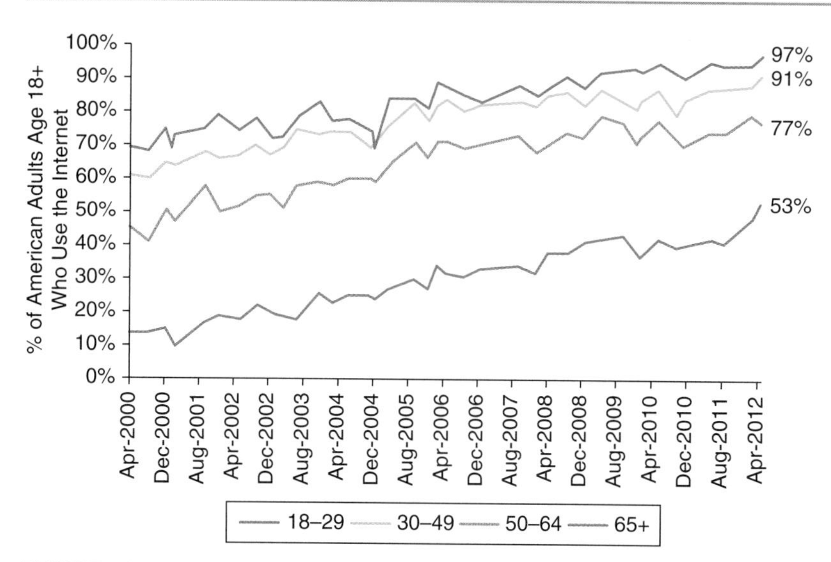

FIGURE 12.1 Internet Use by Age Group, 2000–2012

Source: Pew Internet & American Life Project Surveys, 2000–2012

grow up surrounded by personal computers, smartphones, and other devices may take longer to adopt or become comfortable using those technologies. That is why after age 75 (the old-old), Internet usage drops off considerably (Zickuhr & Madden, 2012).

Although we may think that young adults are the primary users of smartphones, which enable Internet access among other things, a 2013 study showed that older adults are also adopting this technology. Of those 65 years and older who were surveyed, 18 percent owned smartphones, and of those between the ages of 55 and 64, 39 percent did so. From these data, we can surmise that as the younger age group ages, the number of smartphone owners 65 and older will increase. However, there are some differences in smartphone ownership when younger adults are compared to older adults. For adults 65 years and older, the survey data suggest that those who earn $75,000 or more are more likely to own smartphones. For younger adults, their income is less of a factor when it comes to smartphone ownership (Pew Internet and American Life Project, 2013).

These findings suggest that one reason older adults may be more hesitant to adopt new technologies is cost. Often on fixed incomes, they may not have the resources to buy ICTs or subscribe to ICT services; however, the good news is that Internet access, computer hardware and software, and ICT training are increasingly available through community settings such as public libraries and senior centers, as will be discussed later in this chapter.

Despite the costs, more than 50 percent of older adults in the United States live in a house where there is Internet access. What do they use the Internet for when they go online? According to Madden (2010) of the Pew Internet & American Life Project, over 50 percent of them are using e-mail. Other activities include visiting news sites, online banking, and social networking (see Figure 12.2).

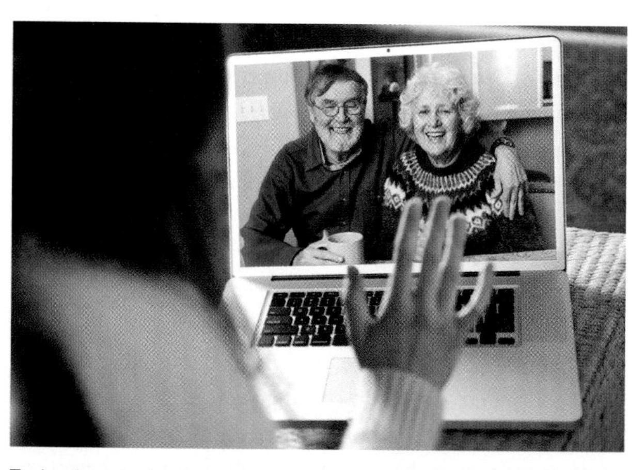

Technology makes it possible for faraway family members to stay connected with friends and relatives, as these grandparents are doing in a videoconference with their granddaughter.

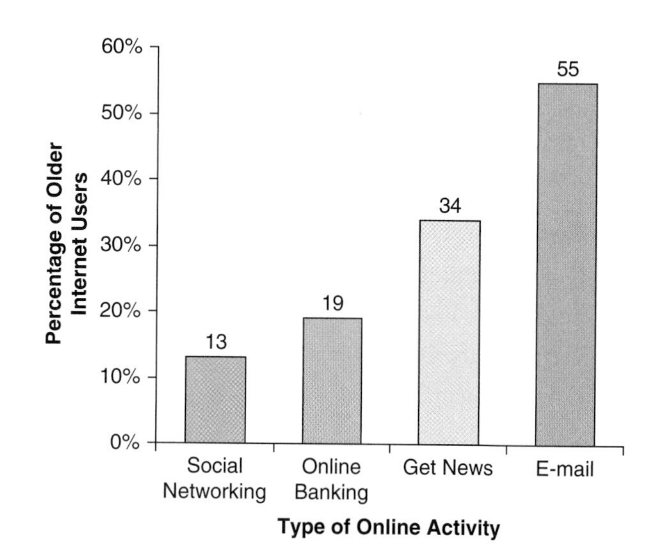

FIGURE 12.2 What Older Adults do Online on a Typical Day

Source: Pew Research Center's Internet & American Life Project, April 29–May 30, 2010 Tracking Survey

Profile of One State's Social Networking Activities

AARP Washington State conducted a survey in 2011 to find out how the state's Internet-using residents age 45 years and older were using social networking. Here's some of what they found:

- Seventy-three percent of Internet-using Washington adults age 45 and older access the Internet at least one time a day for personal use.
- Sixty-five percent say social networking Web sites are a great way for people to stay in touch.
- Forty percent say they are a waste of time.
- Seventy percent have at least one social networking account.
- Sixty-nine percent have heard of video chat; of those, 7 percent have used it at least once.
- Nonusers of video chat say they would be likely to use it to talk to their children, grandchildren, and health care or service providers (Nelson, 2011).

Older adults interested in getting "wired" have a variety of options. Libraries, community centers, senior centers, and assisted living residences offer classes to get older people started online. Local AARP offices often sponsor or cosponsor such classes with community partners. Many of these programs are well attended as elders discover the advantages and enjoyment of becoming more computer and Internet-savvy. Sometimes the best teachers are peers, elders who have become experts themselves about computers, the Internet, or other devices and thus can now teach others. In New York State, the Older Adults Technology Services (OATS) is a nonprofit organization that aims to help older adults live healthier, more connected, and socially engaged lives by empowering them to use technology in beneficial ways. One of OATS's projects is Senior Planet, an online community that connects older adults age 60 and older. Senior Planet's tagline is "Aging with Attitude." There are also intergenerational programs in many communities where younger people tutor older adults in the use of computers and the Internet. Additionally, these programs offer opportunities for cross-generational friendships and shared learning.

Although Washington State with its high-tech industries and large number of technologically literate residents may not be representative of the United States as a whole, this study provides a snapshot of middle-age and older adults' use of social networking in a geographically defined area. A majority of residents in this age group who are online are not only familiar with but also engaging in social networking.

Intergenerational Communication

More grandparents are communicating with their grandchildren online. In a *Wall Street Journal* article, for example, a writer observed that her three children were playing with their electronic gadgets one evening. As she was about to call them together for family time, she realized that they were already engaging in family time. Her 9-year-old son was playing Scrabble with his grandmother two time zones away. Her 11-year-old was video-chatting with his grandfather in another state. And her 14-year-old was on Facebook. Among his "friends" was his great-grandfather halfway across the country.

Staying in Touch through Facebook

Didi and Harry are a married couple in their sixties who use the Internet but never had any interest in Facebook. Then, their first grandchild Michael was born, halfway across the country. Didi and Harry's daughter and son-in-law began posting photos of Michael on Facebook with short messages about what it is like to be the parents of a newborn baby. Didi and Harry realized they would be missing out on a lot of these moments, even though they often talked by phone with Michael's parents. They signed up for a Facebook account and followed Michael's early life online. They were delighted by all the photos they could see of their grandson and the daily comments left by his tired but proud parents. Didi and Harry also wrote regularly on Michael's Facebook page, signing it "Grandma and Grandpa."

In addition to Facebook, Didi and Harry also use Skype. They can see and talk to Michael in real time, and they look forward to the day when he's old enough to respond to them and listen to stories that his Grandma and Grandpa read to him through Skype. Their daughter and son-in-law also use Pinterest and Instagram. Emboldened by their success with Facebook and Skype, Didi and Harry are interested to learn more about those social media tools, too. While they still look forward to phone calls and face-to-face visits, they are happy they can stay in touch daily and keep up with Michael's day-to-day activities and growth without having to be there physically.

Grandparents and grandchildren often have the time to use the Internet and are interested in staying in touch. Although the messages that get sent back and forth on the Internet may strike some people as being trivial at times, these types of communication can lead to closer relationships, especially for grandparents and grandchildren who live far from each other (Baker, 2011).

Lifelong Learning

The Internet and World Wide Web, which is a subset of the Internet, are online environments that can help elders remain intellectually engaged and connected to peers with similar interests. Some studies suggest a relationship between computer use and mental performance across adulthood, with computer users having a higher level of cognitive functioning than nonusers. One study based on a large national sample showed that frequent computer use was associated with better overall cognitive performance. There was also a positive relationship between computer use and executive function (as you learned in Chapter 4, this is the ability to plan and anticipate, make good judgments, and carry out multiple tasks simultaneously) and task switching (the ability to move from one task to another). The direction of causation is unclear, however. It could be that those with higher cognitive ability were more likely to use computers in the first place. More studies are needed to determine the specific relationship between computer use and mental functioning, but regular computer usage does seem to have some cognitive benefits (Tun & Lachman, 2010).

The Internet and Web are suited to lifelong learning activities for older adults who have access to a networked computer. People can study at their own pace in their own home and can be connected to others all over the world who share their interests. Organizations such as **SeniorNet**, whose mission as stated on its Web site is to "provide older adults education for and access to computer technologies to enhance their lives and enable them to share their knowledge and wisdom," have online courses that help elders learn more about their computer, get connected, and explore the world. Older adults learn how to use technologies such as e-mail, Facebook, and Skype through SeniorNet programs online or at community learning centers. These are important for ensuring Internet access to elders who do not have the financial means to own a computer. Check out the SeniorNet Web site at www.seniornet.org to learn more about this organization and what it offers.

points to ponder

Do you communicate via e-mail, Facebook, or another technology with any older family members? If so, when did you first start doing this and how have you benefited from the experience? And what do your older relatives view as benefits from this type of communication?

Is there an older family member or friend who you think wants to learn about the Internet and e-mail but has not yet taken that first step? Can you find out if there is a program in your area that offers computer classes for older adults?

Perhaps you know an older adult who does not use the Web. But she would like to look up information on the web once in a while. How can you help her?

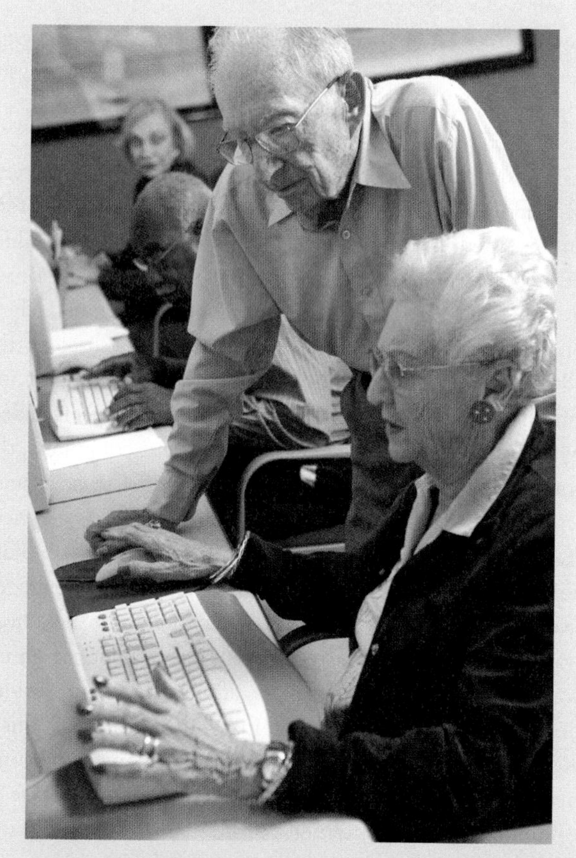

Computer-savvy elders can help other elders understand and use technology.

The act of regularly searching for information and exploring the Web is a new form of lifelong learning since the Web contains a bounty of content for self-directed study. An unfamiliar word can be quickly deciphered using an online dictionary. Topics can be further explored, in many cases rather extensively, by entering a relevant search term in Google, Bing, or other search engines. Music and videos dating back decades can be discovered (or rediscovered) on YouTube and evoke nostalgic memories of a bygone era. And Wikipedia, while not necessarily an authoritative or always accurate source, can be a helpful starting point for expanding one's knowledge and understanding of a myriad of topics. As will be discussed later, a large number of Internet users also look up online health information for themselves or their loved ones.

As most of you know, the Web is a massive information source. As far back as 2008, Google identified a trillion unique Web addresses or URLs. That's a lot of information at people's fingertips. People could literally spend hours pursuing their interests online, whether those interests relate to a hobby, an intellectual pursuit, or a desire to communicate with others. As more older adults embrace the Web, the medium can serve as a continuing education tool of sorts, although it is always important to keep in mind that not everything on the Web is trustworthy and accurate.

News and Information

Older adults in general are heavy consumers of news. Those who study the demographics of newspaper readership know that people age 55 years and older represent the largest percentage of daily print newspaper readers. In fact, it may be people in this age category who are keeping the newspaper industry alive! However, print newspaper readership has been in decline for years among all age groups. Online newspaper readership, on the other hand, has been increasing. Baby boomers are an important part of this growing online readership demographic (Newspaper Association of America, 2010; Pew Research Center, 2010, 2011).

Online newspapers represent a vast resource of news and information that older adults can tap into on a regular basis. Adults age 65 and older represent a relatively small percentage of online news readers, but that is because they are also less likely to use the Internet in general when compared to their younger counterparts.

Goodwill's Internet Café: Providing Access to Low-Income Older Adults

When you think of Goodwill, the organization that collects clothing, household items, and other goods for resale to help people with disabilities or disadvantages, you might not think of online learning. But the Goodwill Lifelong Learning Internet Café serving southeastern Wisconsin offers free computer classes to people 60 and older. The goal of the class is to teach basic computer skills, and no experience is necessary. Older students learn how to send e-mail to family and friends, safely navigate the Internet, and download photos. Students also have access to computers during open lab times. Are there similar programs in your community for older adults (http://www.goodwillsew.com)?

Let's look at who uses the Internet for their main source of news.

- Sixty-five percent of adults younger than age 30
- Almost 50 percent of those 30–49, and about 30 percent of those 50–64
- About 14 percent of those 65 and older

As the number of baby boomers with computer skills and others who learn these skills through training programs increases, the number of older adults who gravitate to the Internet for their news and information will likely grow. However, most of the old-old, the current cohort age 70 and older, will continue to rely on print versions of news and information rather than the Internet (Pew Research Center, 2011). Also, it should be noted that more online newspapers are charging for "premium" news content, employing an online subscription revenue model. How this will impact consumer use in the future is uncertain.

There is concern that the use of new media technologies may decrease the level of civic engagement as people withdraw into their private worlds and disengage from public life. On the other hand, the consumption of news and information actually may lead to more civic participation and interpersonal trust as people take an interest in their social and political environments and communicate with others about key social issues. As noted in Chapter 8, older adults vote at higher rates than people in younger age groups. As older adults use online news and information to form opinions and increase their knowledge of current events, they have the potential to play an important role in politics through their voting behavior and civic activism.

One thought-provoking proposition is that if people save time by doing more of their business online (e.g., banking), that will free up time for more social interaction and civic engagement. It is not clear at present what the social consequences will be for older adults—positive or negative—as more and more use the Internet, but these are questions for us to think about in the midst of our rapidly evolving media environment (Vergeer & Pelzer, 2009).

Even if the increased use of ICTs and other technologies does not result in dramatically higher levels of civic engagement, it might lead people to discover things in common that they can discuss both on- and offline. News Web sites provide plenty of material for discussions about politics, sports, world affairs, health, technology, entertainment, business, the weather, and lifestyle. Keeping up with current events by reviewing selected online news sites each day, for example, can help older adults engage others in conversation, regardless of where they live or how mobile they are. A good conversationalist is a well-informed individual, and electronic news sources can help with that objective for people of any age—as well as provide them with a means to connect with informal supports vital to their well-being, as you learned in Chapter 6.

Books of the Future?

As you are undoubtedly aware, Amazon, Samsung, and Barnes & Noble have their own versions of the electronic book, or e-book. A benefit of e-books for older adults is that the text size on the lighted screen can be enlarged for those with visual impairments. Personal electronic libraries can be stored in these devices for reading on the porch, in bed at night, on airplanes, in a waiting room, on the bus, or even at the beach. Some of the e-book content is free but most of it must be purchased. The devices are lightweight, so they make reading a large novel easier (and less demanding of arthritic fingers). The e-book market for people of all ages is predicted to grow dramatically. As newer cohorts of elders emerge, e-books will become more popular and acceptable. Current cohorts of older persons, however, may be less likely to accept this different way of reading a novel, which lacks paper pages and perhaps is more difficult to "thumb through" the book. And of course, some people just prefer the look and feel of a "real" book, copies of which can be stored on bookshelves and loaned out to family and friends, or given as gifts. Nevertheless, e-books provide a growing alternative to the traditional book in print.

Managing Health Online

As you have learned throughout this book, few things in life are more personally significant than our physical and mental well-being. Health-conscious people seek ways to remain active and live life fully, and those with health problems want to know what can be done to resolve or effectively manage those challenges. At one time, access to reliable health information may have involved consulting an expert (like a physician, nurse, or other health specialist) or visiting a medical library or the health section of a public library, assuming these libraries were accessible to someone with health problems. Now, extensive health information is available online, and research shows that health-related Web sites are popular.

Technology can enhance elder health in numerous ways. The Center for Technology and Aging released a draft position paper in 2011 entitled *mHealth Technologies: Applications to Benefit Older Adults*. The concept of "mHealth" relates to mobile technologies used in the service of health care. The vast majority of Americans carry and use mobile communication devices like smart phones or digital tablets. In the future, these technologies may be increasingly used for elder health care applications relating to chronic disease management, medication adherence, safety monitoring, access to health information, and wellness (Center for Technology and Aging, 2011).

Health Information on the Internet

For almost a decade, about 80 percent of Internet users have reported searching for health information online—and are continuing to do so. Indeed, searching for health care information is the most popular reported online activity after e-mail and using a search engine, although using a search engine may also involve searching for health care information (Fox, 2011; Pew Research Center, 2010).

What kinds of health information do Americans in general, not just older adults, look up online? Here is what the Pew Center/California HealthCare Foundation study found listed in order of frequency.

- A specific disease or medical problem: 66 percent.
- A certain medical treatment or procedure: 56 percent.
- Physicians or other health professionals: 44 percent.
- Hospitals or other medical facilities: 36 percent.
- Health insurance: 33 percent.
- Food safety or recalls: 29 percent.
- Drug safety or recalls: 24 percent.
- Environmental health hazards: 22 percent.
- Pregnancy and childbirth: 19 percent.
- Memory loss, dementia, or Alzheimer's: 17 percent.
- Medical test results: 16 percent.
- How to manage chronic pain: 14 percent.
- Long-term care options: 12 percent.
- End-of-life decisions: 7 percent (Fox, 2011).

Not surprisingly, family caregivers were found to be one of the largest categories of Internet users who search for health information online. Other research has shown that just because many Internet users seek health information online does not mean they consult their health care providers less frequently. Online health information generally supplements information provided by a person's health care provider. People also find peer support online, including support groups for specific diseases or health conditions, which can be especially helpful if they lack adequate social support in their daily lives. Legitimate health care providers are also venturing online to provide consultations and other services via Internet-based teleconferencing (Fox, 2007; Pew Internet & American Life Report, 2011; Tu & Cohen, 2008).

One of the drawbacks to seeking health information online is the lack of quality control. One relatively reliable source can be mainstream news Web sites that have a separate section that contains news articles related to health. For example, if you go onto the CNN Web site (www.cnn.com), you will find a link to articles only about health topics. CNN also features the Chart Blog, with postings by medical experts. Internet users need to be cautious about medical advice given by nonexperts on Web sites that are unaffiliated with trusted sources of news and information. The old Latin phrase "*caveat emptor*" means "let the buyer beware." It should be modified for Internet users to read: "Let the health information seeker beware of online information."

Improving Web Pages for Older Users

You may be in a position to use Web sites as a way of communicating with consumers about health and wellness information. If so, remember that readers are diverse. As you have learned, some older users may have visual or cognitive impairments that may make it difficult to read or comprehend Web site content. There is good information available on how to design Web sites so they are maximally beneficial to older users. Here are some of their suggestions:

- Avoid a patterned background behind text material.
- Use dark type or graphics against a light background.
- Avoid excess graphics and animation.
- Use a consistent layout in different sections of the Web site.
- Avoid pop-up menus that can confuse the main text.
- Limit how much information is presented on each page.
- Distinctly identify all links with a specific convention, such as underlining or a unique graphic.
- Clearly identify the content that is included under each heading.
- If animation or video is used, select short segments to reduce download time.
- Provide a telephone number and e-mail address for users who want direct contact for assistance in using the Web site.

(Adapted from Mead, Lamson, & Rogers (2002) and National Library of Medicine (2002).)

If you find yourself looking for health information online or being asked for assistance by an older adult family member or friend, keep in mind that not all such information online can be trusted in terms of quality, accuracy, or usefulness. In particular, watch out for sites that are clearly advertising a product or service by a Web developer who has no expertise in that area, and ask for personal information from the viewer in order to "send them special gifts or products." So-called "anti-aging" ads are particularly suspect. Remember that claims of "reversing" or "stopping" aging are probably false or greatly exaggerated. When first searching for health information, go with reputable sources. **Health literacy**—the capacity to obtain, process, and understand basic health information and services needed to make appropriate health decisions—is essential in the online environment. When people do not understand basic health information and services, their health outcomes are jeopardized (U.S. Department of Health & Human Resources, 2013).

The Medical Library Association (2010), a nonprofit educational organization founded over 100 years ago, is comprised of more than 1,100 member institutions. What follows is a list of its top health Web site recommendations relevant to adults of all ages. You may want to search through some of these sites for further study and understanding of health information online and evaluate how "elder-friendly" these sites are:

- **Cancer.gov** (http://www.cancer.gov/) is the official Web site for the National Cancer Institute (NCI), a component of the National Institutes of Health (NIH). The NIH is one of eight agencies that compose the Public Health Service (PHS) in the Department of Health and Human Services (DHHS). The NCI, established under the National Cancer Act of 1937, is the federal government's principal agency for cancer research and training.
- **Centers for Disease Control and Prevention** (http://www.cdc.gov/), an agency of the Department of Health and Human Services, is dedicated to promoting "health and quality of life by preventing and controlling disease, injury, and disability." Its Web site includes an up-to-date section on evidence-based health promotion programs as well as other healthy aging initiatives.
- **Familydoctor.org** (http://familydoctor.org/) is operated by the American Academy of Family Physicians (AAFP), a national medical organization representing nearly 94,000 family physicians, family practice residents, and medical students. All of the information on this site has been written and reviewed by physicians and patient education professionals at the AAFP.
- **Healthfinder®** (http://www.healthfinder.gov/) is a gateway consumer health information Web site whose goal is "to improve consumer access to selected health information from government agencies, their many partner organizations, and other reliable sources that serve the public interest." Menu lists on its home page provide links to online journals, medical dictionaries, minority health, and prevention and self-care.
- **HIV InSite** (http://hivinsite.ucsf.edu/) is a project of the University of California San Francisco (UCSF) AIDS Research Institute. Designed as a gateway to in-depth information about particular aspects of HIV/AIDS, it provides numerous links to many authoritative sources.
- **Mayo Clinic** (http://www.mayoclinic.com/) is an extension of the Mayo Clinic's commitment to provide health education to patients and the general public. Editors of the site include more than 2,000 physicians, scientists, writers, and educators at the Mayo Clinic, with more than 100 years of history in patient care, medical research, and education.
- **MedlinePlus®** (http://medlineplus.gov/) is a consumer-oriented Web site established by the National Library of Medicine, the world's largest biomedical library and creator of the MEDLINE database. An alphabetical list of "Health Topics" consists of more than 300 specific diseases, conditions, and wellness issues. This is also an excellent resource to find out about new scientific publications in health topics of interest to users.
- **Geriatric Mental Health Foundation** (http://www.gmhfonline.org/gmhf/) was established by the American Association for Geriatric Psychiatry to raise awareness of psychiatric and mental health disorders affecting older adults, eliminate the stigma of mental illness and treatment, promote healthy aging strategies, and increase access to quality mental health care for older adults.

The Medical Library Association (MLA) also recommends specialized Web sites for cancer, diabetes, and heart disease. If you have an older relative or friend who is seeking information about an illness or effective treatments, this list of Web sites is the best place to begin. Search mlanet.org Web site and click on the Resources for Health Consumers link (Medical Library Association, 2010). Last, one particularly useful site for older adults is NIH **SeniorHealth**; an example of how someone might use this Web site is presented in the box on p. 345.

Health Plans Online

A number of health insurance companies have their own Web sites with extensive health care information as well as customized interactive features that can help members feel like partners in their own health and wellness program. Members log in and can read about common health problems, such as high blood pressure, asthma, different kinds of cancer, depression, diabetes, and the flu. They can get advice about screening, treatment, prevention, finding a participating physician or specialist, and so forth—all in

NIH SeniorHealth Web Site

Loretta is afraid. Her husband has been diagnosed with diabetes, and although his physician tried to talk to her about the disease, she was too distressed to take in all the details. Her husband has dementia, and Loretta is his caregiver. He does not fully understand what is going on. Now back at home, Loretta is at the computer wondering where to find some reliable online information about diabetes. A nurse at the clinic gave her a Web site address for the NIH SeniorHealth Web site (nihseniorhealth.gov) as a place to start learning more about diabetes. The Web site, designed specifically for older adults, contains information from the National Institutes of Health, which is a reliable and unbiased source of health information. There are settings on the Web site to make the text bigger, change text color, and even hear the text read aloud. Loretta knows that she needs to work with her husband's physician and care team to help manage her husband's diabetes. She and her husband have an appointment later to talk with a diabetes specialist at her husband's clinic. Until then, however, Loretta is trying to learn more about diabetes on her own, using information from sources she trusts on the Web, and feeling less anxious about his care.

simple, nontechnical language. Members can even review plan benefits and claims for payment from health care providers and other account information.

Here's how one online health promotion service worked. The service was free to members of a particular health insurance plan. Participants filled out an extensive health risk assessment questionnaire either online or on paper and then met with a health care professional (e.g., a registered nurse) to review results. Participants were also measured for height, weight, body mass index (BMI), waist circumference, body fat, blood pressure, pulse, cholesterol, and HbA1c (which tests for average glucose levels in the blood). Participants had access to a Web site that contained information about healthy lifestyles for men, women, children and teens, and seniors. On the program's Web site, participants found information about a variety of health topics as well as links to programs and services such as disease management, immunizations, prenatal care, smoking cessation, and health reminders. Appointments and follow-ups with a participant's primary care provider were encouraged when appropriate. This hybrid online/in-person program encouraged participants to take ownership of their own health care and self-monitor with the assistance of health professionals.

Telehealth

As you learned in Chapter 11, **assistive technology** refers to products, devices, or equipment that people with physical or mental limitations use to perform functions that might otherwise be difficult or impossible. While we often think of this technology as mobility devices such as walkers and wheelchairs, it also includes information technology, such as home monitoring for individuals with particular chronic illnesses, such as diabetes and hypertension. In this case, the person's relevant health variables (e.g., weight, blood pressure, blood glucose, and cholesterol) are transmitted to a centralized health care database. Indeed, the field of **telehealth**, where health information is transmitted electronically from the patient's home to his or her physician's office or from an ambulatory care setting such as a health clinic to a specialist's office, has grown 40 percent annually since 1997. These biometric, video phone, and telemonitoring systems can increase patients' compliance with medication regimens and reduce their hospitalization and nursing home placement rates. Telehealth is cost-effective not only because it reduces hospitalizations and ER visits, but it also improves patients' perceived control or self-efficacy over their health. Information about the elder's health status can also be transmitted online to specific family members who live or work at a distance from the elder. This allows long-distance surveillance by caregivers, but also enables the elder to decide who can and cannot receive their health information (Department of Veterans Affairs, 2009; Lehmann, 2003; Utterback, 2005).

The VA health system, for example, is at the forefront in using telehealth, enrolling more than 35,000 veterans in its home telehealth program. Patients with chronic diseases monitor and transmit their vital signs via a regular phone line to a secure central site; clinicians at VA hospitals can then review these data without having the patient drive hundreds of miles for a 30–60 minute visit, thereby saving time for both the patient and health professional. Only in the case of significant changes in the patient's vital signs and symptoms would the person need a face-to-face appointment.

The use of telehealth and other strategies for elders to take a greater role in managing their health assumes a level of health literacy. As noted earlier, this refers to the degree to which individuals have the capacity to obtain, process, and understand health information to make informed and appropriate decisions, reduce health risks, and increase quality of life. Researchers have found that

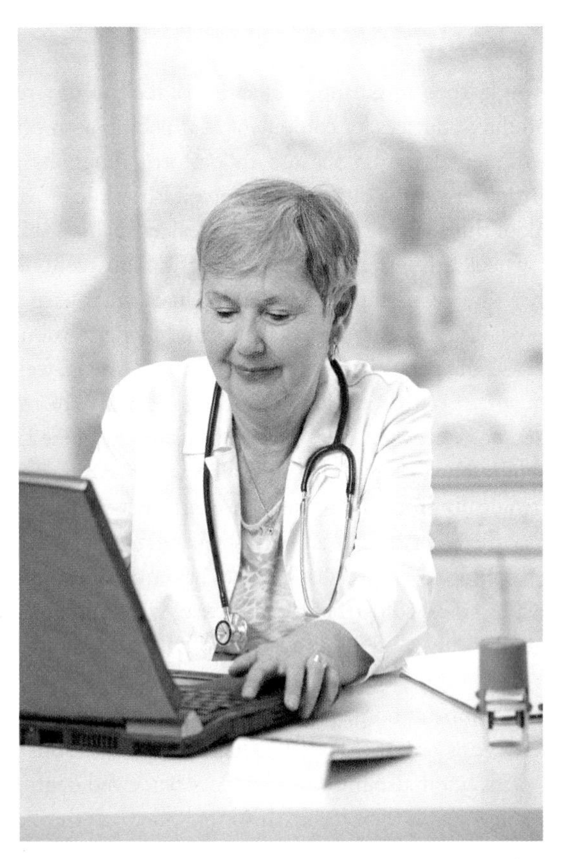

Health providers can communicate with their patients via telehealth technologies.

older adults generally have lower levels of health literacy than younger persons, in part because they have typically been less proactive in learning about their health and have relied on their health care providers to make decisions for them. However, baby boomers have higher levels of health literacy because they generally take a more active role in deciding about their treatment regimens than older cohorts. Indeed, they were the generation questioning authority in young adulthood, so they are likely to want to obtain as much information as possible and not just rely on an expert's advice (Nielsen-Bohlman, Panzer, & Kindig, 2004; Zarcadoolas, Pleasant, & Greer, 2006).

Health Consultation Online

Increasingly, physicians and nurses are communicating with their patients online. The convenience of asking simple questions through e-mail, following up on an office visit, or connecting with a doctor using Internet video makes it appealing to a number of patients, especially those in rural areas. Health information is going digital in other ways as well, including the conversion of patient records to electronic files that allows easy transfer and storage. The use of electronic health records that allow people to access their records from all their providers is a piece of the 2010 Affordable Care Act and aims to improve the coordination of care.

In some cases, online health consultation is used when a person is not available to provide health expertise. A rural hospital, for example, may lack a pharmacist or medical specialist 24 hours a day, 7 days a week. In these cases, information and communication technologies can be used to consult with health professionals over great distances.

Public and private organizations are using or experimenting with disease management and wellness apps for smartphones, online health coaching and pharmaceutical information, wireless breathing monitors, and health text messaging services on mobile phones. Health IT is a rapidly growing area that integrates both health and business interests and will likely continue to change dramatically conventional approaches to health care for years into the future.

Technology in the Workplace

A common ageist stereotype of older workers is that they are technophobic and unwilling to adapt to innovations in the workplace. A reporter for CBS Business News (BNET) reminds us that the baby boom generation put a man on the moon and a computer on every desk. Older workers, he writes, are not afraid of technology, but they may not have the same relationship to tools and gadgets that younger generations do. Of course, there are exceptions. Some older adults are actually ahead of the pack where technology is concerned. For older workers who are not "tech-savvy," particularly in the generation preceding the baby boom cohort, it is important to help them understand how new technologies relate to the jobs they need to get done, and then give them the chance to learn it. Unfortunately, older job-seekers often encounter employers who believe that older people are resistant to change and cannot become technologically savvy. It may be that some elders are indeed opposed to some changes, but there may be good reasons for this. Most elders believe

Computer Training for Work-Ready Elders

Elders eager for paid work but who need to enhance their computer skills can often find programs available at community centers and through government programs. For example, the Mayor's Office for Senior Citizens in Seattle offers a program called Seniors Training Seniors. The classes are taught by computer-savvy older adults and designed for students 50 and older. They learn in small classes (one-on-one tutoring is also available) and develop skills in word processing and using the Internet, including e-mail and sending attachments. These kinds of classes are essential for job-seeking older persons in order to broaden their skill sets and enhance their chances in the job market.

that change needs to make sense if it is to be adopted, and that change simply for the sake of change may be useless. As you learned in Chapter 4, rigidity is not an effect of age, but of personality. Even when older workers are not as comfortable with computer technology as younger cohorts, they still have much to contribute to an organization as it takes on newer technologies. For these reasons, organizations should take time to explain upcoming technological changes to their employees and invest in the necessary job training and retooling opportunities. Training programs for older adults need to take into consideration any constraints on their learning (as we discussed in Chapter 4) and preferred platforms for learning (Lee, Czaja, & Sharit, 2009; Turmel, 2010).

In short, to remain competitive in today's workplace that is characterized by the rapid pace of technological change in a knowledge-based economy, older workers would benefit from effective training and retraining. Furthermore, they should not be overlooked for new learning opportunities because of their age or assumptions that they cannot become technologically competent. Older workers may also be good candidates for telecommuting as it allows for a certain degree of work flexibility. True, sometimes workplace technology can present barriers for some older adults—for example, small mobile device display monitors with their tiny keyboards may be difficult for those with visual and dexterity problems—but with deliberate planning for a diverse workforce, these obstacles can be overcome (Githens, 2007).

Technologies to Help Aging in Place

As you learned in Chapter 11, designing housing that fits elders' changing needs is a central component in helping them to age in place, remaining in their homes and having necessary services brought to them as appropriate. The areas of flexible housing, **universal design**, assistive technology, and **gerontechnology**, which is a recent field of research and practice aimed at using technology to improve older adults' autonomy, are all exciting and rapidly changing developments to promote aging in place. In fact, whatever we can do to assist aging in place can enhance quality of life, since the majority of middle-aged and young-old people want to live in their own homes and communities as long as possible (AARP, 2011).

Universal Design and Smart Homes

As you learned in Chapter 11, the number and range of technologies, particularly assistive technology devices, for the home are growing rapidly. Homes are increasingly being designed and built or modified with the idea that they can be used throughout a lifetime.

Assistive technology is one aspect of universal design—designing the environment to allow the widest range of users possible (i.e., **inclusive design**) and to facilitate active aging. This concept is attracting the attention of architects, landscape architects, and interior

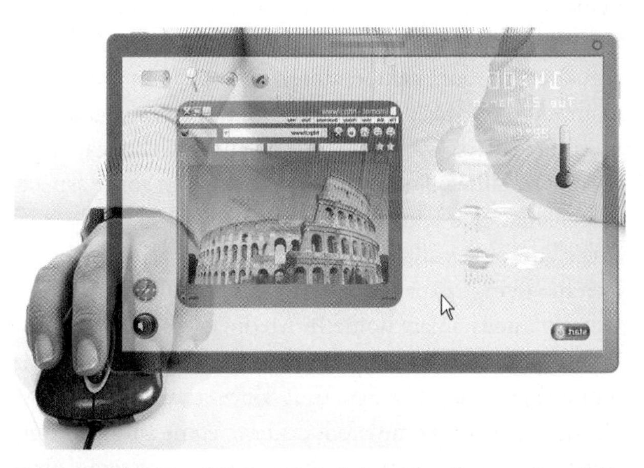

Computers enable quick access to information that can be used in the workplace, health care, design of one's living space or leisure and travel.

and furniture designers. What began as an attempt to make street curbs and home hallways and bathrooms accessible to people in wheelchairs has grown to a movement that allows all environments—parks, wilderness areas, automobiles, and computer workstations—to accommodate people who are able-bodied as well as those with limited mobility, vision, and hearing. As you learned in Chapter 11, universal design can benefit all age groups, not only older adults.

Architects are working on cost-effective means of applying new technology to the design of both homes and long-term care settings. For example, systems that make a room light up through sensors in the floor can help prevent falls when an older person gets up at night. Bed sensors that detect movement and sudden weight change can monitor how often an older adult gets out of bed during the night. These days, many homes already have motion sensors on the outside that turn lights on when movement is detected. This is primarily for security enhancement, but the same technology can be employed inside the home for safety so that occupants are not walking around in the dark. Portable keypads or remote controls for operating thermostats, windows, and their coverings can help an older adult change the room temperature as needed, as well as open and close windows and shades to manage the ambient temperature and to prevent glare from early morning sunshine.

Related to universal design is the concept of **smart homes**. These are residences equipped with technology that connects all the devices and appliances in a home to communicate with the residents. The residents can use their voice, a remote control, or a computer to command their home network to open doors, light a path for nighttime bathroom trips, turn on exterior lights, regulate the room temperature, play music in any room, or monitor people's movements. Smart homes can help monitor elders with care needs and reduce caregiver burden by allowing technology to help with some aspects of personal care and support. For healthy relatively self-sufficient older adults, smart homes can improve the overall living experience. Microsoft co-founder Bill Gates' famous smart home in Medina, Washington, was highly publicized when outsiders got a glimpse inside more than a decade ago. But since then many more affordable smart home products have come into the consumer marketplace, such as basic lighting systems, electronic security kits, and remotely controlled devices that can be purchased at home improvement stores.

Robotics will likely be part of the aging-in-place future. Researchers and engineers at the Massachusetts Institute of Technology, Sony, Honda, and other companies are testing robots that can be used by frail elders to perform routine housework and personal services, and can even socialize with their owners. The Intel Corporation is designing a digital photo frame that is activated when someone calls. If the caller's information is stored on the digital frame, it can identify the caller with a photo and a description of when they last called and what they discussed. Such memory reminders can be useful to people of all ages, but particularly to elders who are experiencing cognitive impairments.

Smart home and universal design principles are being studied in real-life settings by a number of researchers. The University of Florida, for example, has the Gator Tech Smart House, which studies how technology and design can assist older adults in maintaining quality of life in a home setting. Real people live in the house as part of the research to see how the technology and design affect people's lives in a more natural setting than a conventional laboratory. For more information about this project, go to http://www.icta.ufl.edu/gt.htm.

Another university-based project is Georgia Tech's Aware Home Research Initiative, an interdisciplinary research endeavor that looks at technological, design, and social aspects of home living. The laboratory for research is an actual three-story, 5,040-square-feet house. One of the areas being studied is the health and well-being of older adults in such a home and how a well-designed home can support caregiving, chronic disease management, and resource sharing. For more information on the project, including the possibility of touring the Aware Home, go to http://www.awarehome.gatech.edu/.

Robots for Frail Elders

Researchers at Waseda University in Tokyo have developed a bedside robot that can lift frail elders out of bed, carry them, and even serve them breakfast. Its delicate grip can hold a straw and bring it to an elder's lips. The software is being refined to respond to voice commands to bring medications and food. However, this type of robot costs far more than individuals or even a long-term care facility can afford; developers project its price to be around $200,000 when the robot becomes available within a decade (Binns, 2009).

The LeadingAge Center

Check this out: The LeadingAge Center for Aging Services Technologies (CAST) is "leading the charge to expedite the development, evaluation and adoption of emerging technologies that can improve the aging experience," according to its Web site at www.leadingage.org. The organization is a network of 5,500 nonprofit organizations dedicated to "expanding the world of possibilities in aging." Click on the Technology link on its Web site for resources on aging services and technologies.

Would older adults want robots in their homes to help with tasks? A Georgia Tech researcher found that adults age 65–93 who were shown a video of a robot's capabilities were willing to consider robotic assistance for routine household chores such as cleaning the kitchen, taking out the trash, and doing laundry, but they preferred humans for social activities and personal care such as bathing, eating, and getting dressed. These preferences may shift with future cohorts that have used technology throughout their lives (Georgia Tech, 2012).

Another concept related to smart homes and universal design is gerontechnology, which is not a mutually exclusive term but rather a complementary one, and thus some examples may overlap or be similar in purpose. This section elaborates on these related concepts.

Some of the products that fall under the rubric of gerontechnology have already been around for a while now and are designed to help people remember their medication schedules.

- One product uses verbal and tone reminders, as well as flashing lights and a single red button, to dispense medications on a predetermined schedule.
- Others utilize an automated system to call the person after the scheduled medication time and ask if the pill has been taken; if the elder does not respond or does not recall taking the medication, phone alerts are sent to family members or other contact persons. Families or health providers can set up a prescription routine on a specific schedule for up to 11 different drugs for 30 days.
- Other devices can be attached to each prescription container; a prerecorded voice announces the schedule and dose needed for that particular medication. This technique is especially useful for older people with dementia who would benefit from hearing a family member's voice reminding them what medications to take.
- For older adults who are cognitively alert and use personal data assistants (PDAs), software is available to call and remind them when it is time to take their meds.

These technologies for medication management are not necessarily better than hands-on care by caregivers, but they may allow the elder to remain self-sufficient longer, reduce caregiver burden, and are more cost-effective than paid caregivers. However, some of these medication management tools are costly and thus not yet accessible to all older adults, which can further inequities that you learned about in Chapter 10 (Agree & Freedman, 2003; Rialle, Duchene, Noury, Bajolle, & Demongeot, 2002).

Computer programs have also been designed to describe potential side effects of various medications and interactions among them. Currently, these software programs are aimed at physicians, pharmacists, and other health professionals. However, programs will soon be available, written in layman's language, where elders can type in the names and doses of medications they are taking and then obtain a printout of potential side effects and special precautions. This would be particularly useful to the many older adults who are using multiple prescriptions and over-the-counter medications.

Another growing technology is remote monitoring between a patient's home and a local health care facility for such information as blood pressure and heart-rate measurement. Sometimes referred to as **remote patient monitoring**, the system involves a person wearing a wristband or arm cuff attached to a computer or a cell phone that transmits health data to a centralized database in a hospital or health provider's office. This is consistent with the idea of telehealth described earlier, and expands the concept beyond hospitals to other health care settings.

After paying for the necessary hardware and software, however, the costs of regular monitoring by a health care provider may be prohibitive for many older adults. On the other hand, this approach to health care may still cost less and be less disruptive for elders than remaining in their own home. In the future, more accurate monitoring devices may be implanted as tiny sensors inside the body. Health insurances plans may cover the costs in the future if they see that these technologies will reduce health care expenditures by preventing hospitalizations and emergency room visits.

National Public Radio Series: Growing Old, at Home

National Public Radio (NPR) featured a series of radio reports in anticipation of the growing number of baby boomers who will want to grow old in their own homes. NPR explored this "quiet revolution" in a 2010 four-part series, which included the following programs featuring technology: "High-Tech Aging: Tracking Seniors' Every Move," "Wired Homes Keep Tabs on Aging Parents," and "Building Homes to Age In."

In the session on wired homes, a "telecaregiver" is featured. She checks in with an older couple during dinner time via a computer, visiting with them like a virtual guest. Except that she is in Indiana and they are in Georgia! Here's a description from the program: "The scene may not seem so strange in the era of Skype, when many people use the computer to keep in touch with far-flung relatives. But Cady [the telecaregiver] can see almost every move the Fitzgeralds [the older adult couple] make. Their house is wired with video cameras, like something out of a sci-fi movie, though, at first, you don't notice it." These long-distance caregivers can alert nearby relatives or friends if something appears out of the ordinary (e.g., the elder remains in the bathroom too long or seems to be engaging in unusual behavior). In one case, the telecaregiver even noticed that the older person had not cooked his meal thoroughly and warned him to cook the food longer before eating it!

Go to www.npr.org and search for "Ludden" and "aging" to find stories about creative technology to help elders age in place while at the same time maintaining their autonomy and privacy in their own home.

Monitoring systems allow elders with early-stage dementia to remain at home while their family caregivers are employed or involved in other activities outside the home. Known as **aware home technology**, these systems support aging in place for persons with dementia by monitoring daily activities such as medication use, mapping trends in ADLs, and assisting elders' communication. Caregivers can choose to obtain real-time data on their work computers or only emergency information. Alarms can alert family members if the frail elder has fallen, left the stove on beyond a predesignated time, or walked beyond the home's boundaries (e.g., "safe" doors may lead to a protected garden while "alarm" doors lead to the street). Sensors can be placed under mattresses to determine if the older person is sleeping, restless, or out of bed during the night. Because they work by detecting weight on the bed, these sensors can also track the elder's weight and notify caregivers if significant weight loss occurs. Despite its potential benefits, some caregivers reject home monitoring systems because they require the elder to learn about technology. Additionally, they may have concerns about their reliability or violating the older person's privacy, self-determination and dignity (Kinney & Kart, 2006; Rogers & Fisk, 2005).

Less invasive technologies that can enhance safety in the home are **medical alert systems**, which can help elders who have fallen or are injured. They wear a necklace or bracelet that serves as a communication device, alerting a monitor, emergency personnel, or a designated individual when help is needed. A number of different companies provide this service but services and costs vary. The obvious advantage to having a good medical alert system is that help can be summoned right away if everything is working properly. This often provides customers and their loved ones with peace of mind. In the future, with technological advances and public–private partnerships, more

Reflection Break

Let's say that you are interested in working in the field of gerontology, but you prefer not to have direct contact with older adults (i.e., "direct practice"). You believe that your strengths would be in the area that is called as gerontechnology, where you would work more closely with hardware and software than with patients or clients. Based on the information presented in this chapter, what are some of the jobs you might pursue where your primary responsibilities would be utilizing technology to be of service to older adults and their families? Think about this question before proceeding to the next paragraph.

Here are some suggestions: Assistive technologies to support older adults remaining in their own homes need to be invented, designed, tested, installed, and maintained. All of these stages require individuals who are capable of performing the relevant tasks. Similarly, Web sites geared toward older adults need designers who are knowledgeable about how older adults use the Internet and what their needs and desires are, and who can create "aging-friendly" sites. Additionally, remote monitoring equipment needs to be set up and maintained—skills that require specialized training. What else can you think of where you could help develop or monitor technology?

points to **ponder**

Picture this scenario. You are an older person living alone. It is in the middle of the day and you don't feel well. You say something out loud but notice that you are slurring your words. You try to get up but you have difficulty walking, are feeling dizzy, and feel a severe headache coming on. Your vision is blurring and you feel numbness on one side of your body. You want to get to the phone but don't think you can make it. You have enough awareness to remember that you are wearing a medical alarm bracelet and press the button that calls for emergency help—and not a moment too soon. Seconds later, you begin to lose consciousness. Now imagine what would happen if you did not have that medical alarm bracelet.

Internet connectivity between the home and community health systems will be possible and medical alert systems will become even more common.

Manufacturers and businesses are paying more attention to developing technologies suitable for elders. This could involve enabling text in larger font size or creating technologies that are not overly complex, such as a basic cell phone that is easy to use, has a long-lasting battery, and connects to 24-hour customer service in case of problems of questions. The Jitterbug Plus is one such phone and offers elder-friendly features such as the following:

- 5Star Urgent Response transforms your Jitterbug into your own personal safety device. In any situation, you can speak immediately with a 5Star Agent, who will quickly identify your location, evaluate your situation, and get you the help you need.
- Urgent Care app lets you have access to unlimited health care advice and a registered nurse who can escalate to a board-certified doctor, and even get a prescription for common medications right from your smartphone, 24/7.
- Medication Reminders is an award-winning service that calls you daily to remind you to take your medications at the correct time of day and when to refill your prescriptions.
- Brain Games gives you access on your Jitterbug Plus to fun, innovative games clinically proven to improve your memory and focus.
- MyWorld keeps you up to date with your personal interests and pastimes while you're on the go—from weather forecasts and sports scores to daily horoscopes and stocks right on your Jitterbug Plus (http://www.greatcall.com/jitterbug/).

As mentioned in Chapter 7, specialized apps for smartphones, laptops, and tablets can be a big help in the caregiving process. Caregivers often have to keep track of large amounts of information—from their care recipients' medications to personal health history to numerous appointments. Specialized apps can help to organize and keep updated all of this information to facilitate doctors' visits, hospital admissions, or ordering medications from a pharmacy.

Monitoring a loved one can be made easier through GPS technology. For example, an employed woman whose husband has mild dementia and sometimes stays at home alone can use a program called Comfort Zone, which sends out a signal from his GPS tracking device every 5 minutes. This information allows his wife to remotely "see" her husband's movements after she logs into a computer program from work. If the pattern of his movement suggests her husband is wandering or lost, she can take steps to assist as appropriate. Another program called Care Family can help match up paid caregivers and clients, monitor paid caregiver work attendance, send reminders about medications and appointments, and provide various ways to exchange information. Not all of these apps and computer programs are appropriate or financially feasible for all caregivers and care recipients, but they are examples of options increasingly available to help in the care process (Fitzgerald, 2013).

Relatedly, the development of high-speed Internet capability, also known as **broadband** technology, may help older adults age in place, possibly making the difference in some cases between whether an elder is able to remain at home or needs to move to a more structured residential environment. A 2013 AARP Public Policy Institute suggests that broadband can contribute to technologies that increase the potential for elders to live independently, safely, and comfortably in their own homes (Baker & Seegert, 2013).

As the fields of gerontechnology and telehealth grow, elders and their families must be alert to the ethical issues of privacy and confidentiality. They also must recognize that technology cannot substitute for personal attention and caring by a loved one. However, these new developments can lengthen the time a frail elder lives relatively independently and reduce caregiver burden. Although technology may seem too expensive for many elders, it costs far less than fees for skilled nursing facilities or even assisted living (Agree & Freedman, 2003; Pew & Van Hemel, 2004; Rogers & Fisk, 2005).

Can Computer Games Promote Elders' Well-Being?

Although older adults do play computer games, they do so in far smaller numbers than younger people. This may change as growing numbers of older persons continue to use computers after their retirement and more research emerges that links computer game-playing with cognitive health. Some research already looks promising. Consider this example of how a computer video game, "Rise of Nations," enhanced executive function in a research study. The game rewards users for building cities, feeding and employing people, maintaining an adequate military, and expanding their territories. It requires effective resource management and planning skills to perform well. The study participants who were trained in "Rise of Nations" showed improvements in switching between tasks compared to the control group that received no training. Their working memory, reasoning ability, and—to a lesser extent—short-term memory of visual cues also improved. However, the video game training had no effect on other functions, such as recalling a list of words in order. The researchers conclude that playing the video game may be one way of maintaining mental and cognitive fitness, but it should not be the only mental exercise performed by an elder (Basak, Boot, Voss, & Kramer, 2008).

Computer technology can enhance elders' quality of life in different ways, from encouraging intergenerational interaction to helping stimulate the mind through online puzzles and games.

Another game called "NeuroRacer" requires that players do different tasks simultaneously such as using a joystick to navigate a car along a road with challenging terrain and distractions. The player must steer the car, control the car's speed, and push certain buttons—but not others—that appear on the video screen. Players are scored by how quickly they accomplish these tasks. The game gets more difficult to keep it challenging as time goes by to keep it challenging. A small study conducted with regular players of NeuroRacer suggests that games like this might boost mental abilities, helping older people react better to signs while driving (Ritter, 2013).

As we discussed briefly in Chapter 4, the computer game market has been expanding to include so-called brain fitness products or **brain games** that promote cognitive stimulation and may improve memory, language, and thinking. Even homebound elders can have fun with games that will challenge them cognitively. Some of these games are designed for people who are already suffering from early stages of dementia, although more research needs to be done about whether brain games are of benefit specifically to adults with dementia. The scientific research linking specific computer games to improved cognitive function in people with dementia is currently not strong. Nevertheless, many elders enjoy playing computer games, whether or not there are demonstrated cognitive benefits (Haines, 2010; Pouter, 2009).

Today you can find dozens of computer brain games for sale or free on the Internet that claim to improve brain fitness. You can use a search engine to find examples of these games without cost, but be careful that the site is not trying to scam you. Sometimes Internet sites purport to offer something for free but are really trying to collect personal data for future marketing purposes.

Do you know of any relatives or friends who are alone for much of the time and might enjoy playing a board game, cards, or even a computer game that you set up for them on a laptop computer? The experience can be even

Bringing a Critical Eye to Brain Games

A critical review of computer games and their effectiveness in improving older adults' cognitive skills cautions us about expecting too much from brain fitness exercises. Even if people seem to improve cognitive function in a laboratory, critics warn this does not mean these improved skills will carry over into everyday life. On balance, however, there seems to be general agreement about the benefits of keeping older persons' brains engaged and challenged, whether with computer games or traditional board games like Scrabble, crossword puzzles, and sudoku (Van Pelt, 2011).

more enjoyable to you and the older person if you can share it. If an elder you know needs help finding mind-stimulating games on the Internet, you may be able to help. Search for crossword puzzles, Scrabble, sudoku, brain teasers, logic puzzles, IQ tests, and other brain games. AARP has a Web site specifically on brain games that is a good place to start. Visit the "Games" section of the AARP Web site at games.aarp.org, and look for *Brain Games*.

Here are a few of these fun-sounding options:

- Entangled Figures: Keep your brain in shape by identifying elements of a jumbled object.
- Split Words: Hone your language skills with this puzzle.
- Shapes and Colors: Boost your concentration by memorizing and then finding shapes.
- Private Eye: Sharpen your analytic skills by figuring out which letter or symbol does not belong.
- Writing in the Stars: Work your problem-solving abilities with this new twist on the crossword puzzle.

You can find dozens of other games on the AARP Web site, such as Multiple Player Checkers, Multiple Player Chess, Beach Sudoku, Crossword, Cryptogram, Decoder, and Mahjongg Toy Chest. But remember: Brains can be stimulated offline as well! Help elder family members and friends discover the brain exercises that are right for them. Or just engage them in conversation, which is both mentally and socially stimulating for many elders, and will allow you to exercise both your brain and "heart." And as noted in Chapter 3, even moderate amounts of exercise have benefits for cognitive ability. Simply walking 30 minutes a day is a less expensive way to gain some cognitive benefits than buying lots of brain games.

The takeaway point here is that people should attempt to keep their minds—and themselves—active and engaged throughout their lives. How we choose to do that will be based on our abilities, interests, financial resources, and knowledge of the options available.

Computer Games and Physical Exercise

If you go to a video arcade, you will likely see young people there—especially teenagers—playing games that require a lot of physical movement. For example, there is a game in which players take cues from lighted arrows on a platform to do dance steps in rhythm with recorded music. A pressure sensor on the ground records a player's steps

Getting Physical with Computer Video Games

Exercise-based computer video games, also known as **exergames**, can help elders literally kick-start their physical activity regimen while potentially boosting self-confidence and social interaction. A number of these console systems are made by the same manufacturers—for example, Nintendo, Sony, and Microsoft—that sell games to younger people but are designed with an older user in mind. They may be useful not only for routine physical exercise but also to help elders rehabilitate after a stroke or other debilitating illness by targeting certain areas for improvement such as upper body strength or balance.

You are probably familiar with how Wii, PlayStation, and Kinect work. Now imagine that an older person is connected to the console to enjoy an ability-appropriate game of virtual tennis, bowling, or another fun activity. Or imagine an elder doing exergames in a rehabilitation facility under the supervision of a physical therapist or another health care professional.

If played with others at a community center or group residential setting, these computer video games could help strengthen friendships while keeping both the body and mind engaged. The hope among advocates of exergames is that elders will continue doing physical exercise if they enjoy the way they are doing it. Of course, safety considerations must be taken into account with any exercise program, including asking a health care provider whether such exercise is appropriate. Research is currently being done to study the effectiveness of these technologies in health maintenance and rehabilitation.

and determines whether a player has passed the challenge. If so, a more complicated and longer series of dance steps is indicated by the lighted arrows. The goal is to keep mastering more challenging dance steps. Inaccurate steps, as judged by the game's computer system, will eventually lead to the end of the game.

Sensor-type games are being used for older adults as well. The games are not just for entertainment and recreation, however, but could also help collect data about a person's physical decline over time. The games may motivate older adults to exercise more, enhance rehabilitation, and possibly avoid falls. A multidisciplinary team from the University of Missouri is studying the effects of Microsoft's Kinect for Xbox 360 at an independent senior housing environment. Kinect can help researchers and the housing staff collect information about residents' movement and motion. At another location, Kinect is being used to aid with physical therapy and rehabilitation. The adaptation of games like Kinect to enhance older adults' well-being is still in its early stages of research, but initial feedback is promising (Microsoft, 2011).

summary

Maintaining as much autonomy as possible through aging in place is becoming a viable option, thanks to technological advances in information and communication technologies, health information and telehealth, workplace technology, smart homes, and computer games. Technology is enabling older adults to stay informed with news and information Web sites and to keep in touch with friends and relatives through social media. Technology also allows older people to communicate with family members and health and social service providers via the Internet and telehealth. These innovative technologies offer control and choice for the older user, which will be even more critical for the boomer generation than for current cohorts of elders because many boomers have been introduced to technologies in their workplace. New developments in home monitoring technology can provide electronic reminders to take medications, exercise, and eat healthy meals, as well as record and transmit vital signs to health care providers. Families may find that caregiving burdens are reduced if they can safely leave the elder at home and monitor them from a distance. As home monitoring technology becomes more affordable and easier to use, the likelihood of consumer adoption is greater. More research needs to be done on how to most effectively integrate technology into the day-to-day lives of older adults for a wide range of purposes. These may include entertainment and recreation, but also helping with exercise, rehabilitation, and the continuing assessment of an elder's health status through sensoring devices. Affordability and the ethical use of technology remain enduring concerns.

key terms

assistive technology, p. 345
aware home technology, p. 350
brain games, p. 352
broadband, p. 351
exergames, p. 353
gerontechnology, p. 347
health literacy, p. 343
inclusive design, p. 347
information and communication technologies or ICTs, p. 337
mobile health or mHealth, p. 337
medical alert systems, p. 350
remote patient monitoring, p. 349
SeniorHealth, p. 344
SeniorNet, p. 340
sensor-type games, p. 354
smart homes, p. 348
telehealth, p. 345
telemonitoring, p. 337
universal design, p. 347

review questions

1. What is mHealth?
2. Name two or three tools, technologies, or assistive devices that someone you know uses that enhance that person's quality of life.
3. What would be the purpose of using remote patient monitoring?
4. Research at Georgia Tech showed that older adults would not mind having robots help with routine tasks,

but they don't want robots taking the place of certain activities. What are those types of activities?

5. List three ways you can make a Web site more elder-friendly in its design?
6. Discuss ways that technology can help an elder remain safely in the home.
7. If an older adult who is not comfortable around computers wants to learn to use the Internet, what recommendations would you make to him or her?
8. If you're afraid of leaving an elder home alone due to problems with balance, what technologies might help ease your concerns?
9. What are some of the possible benefits of computer games for older adults?
10. Name a Web site that is devoted mainly to health-related information and briefly describe what is on that Web site.

media resources

Watch

- Social Interaction and Technology

View

- High Technology in Global Perspective

references

AARP. (2011). AARP and you. *AARP the Magazine,* 22.

Agree, E. M., & Freedman, V. A. (2003). A comparison of assistive technology and personal care in alleviating disability and unmet need. *The Gerontologist, 43,* 335–344.

Baker C., & Seegert, L. (2013). *A platform for aging in place: The increasing potential for high-speed Internet connectivity.* AARP Public Policy Institute. Retrieved September 29, 2013, from http://www.aarp.org/content/dam/aarp/research/public_policy_institute/cons_prot/2013/potential-of-high-speed-internet-connectivity-AARP-ppi-cons-prot.pdf.

Baker, M. (2011). OMG! My grandparents r my BFF! *Wall Street Journal,* Retrieved September 2011, from http://online.wsj.com.

Basak, C., Boot, W. R., Voss, M. W., & Kramer, A. R. (2008). Can training in a real-time strategy video game attenuate cognitive decline in older adults? *Psychology and Aging, 23*(4), 765–777.

Binns, C. (2009). Machines that heal. *Popular Science, 275,* 62–63.

Center for Technology and Aging. (2009). *Technologies to help older adults maintain independence: Advancing technology adoption.* Oakland, CA: Center for Technology and Aging, July 2009 Briefing Paper.

Center for Technology and Aging. (2011). *mHealth technologies: Applications to benefit older adults.* Oakland, CA: Center for Technology and Aging, March 2011 Draft Position Paper.

Department of Veterans Affairs. (2009). *Care coordination services: Telehealth.* Retrieved May 2009, from http://www.carecoordination.va.gov/telehealth/.

Fitzgerald, J. (2013). *Beleaguered caregivers getting help from apps.* Retrieved September 27, 2013, from http://news.yahoo.com/beleaguered-caregivers-getting-help-apps-182717113.html.

Fox, S. (2007). *E-patients with a disability or chronic disease.* Washington, DC: Pew Internet & American Life Project.

Fox, S. (2011). *Health topics.* Pew Research Center Internet & American Life Project and California HealthCare Foundation (CHCF). Retrieved April 2012, from http://www.pewinternet.org/Reports/2011/HealthTopics.aspx.

Georgia Tech. (2012). *Robots in the home: Will older adults roll out the welcome mat?* Press release, October 25, 2012. Retrieved January 2013, from http://www.gatech.edu/newsroom/release.html?nid=165041.

Githens, R. P. (2007). Older adults and e-learning: Opportunities and barriers. *Quarterly Review of Distance Education, 8*(4), 329–338.

Grobart, S. (2011). Staying in touch with technology. *New York Times,* March 2.

Haines, C. (2010). Non-medical therapies for Alzheimer's disease gets scientific backing. *AARP Bulletin,* March.

Kinney, J. M., & Kart, C. S. (2006). Somewhere between panacea and impossibility: Assessing the place of technology in facilitating caregiving to a relative with dementia. *Generations, 30,* 64–66.

Lee, C., Czaja, S. J., & Sharit, J. (2009). Training older workers for technology-based employment. *Educational Gerontology, 35*(1), 15–31.

Lehmann, C. A. (2003). *Economic benefits of telehealth in managing diabetes patients in ambulatory settings.* Paper presented at SPRY Foundation Conference on Technology and Aging, Bethesda, MD.

Lloyd, J. (2010). Seniors surge on social networks. *USA Today.* Retrieved April 2011 from http://www.usatoday.com/yourlife/parenting-family/2010-12-15-graytech15_ST_N.htm.

Madden, M. (2010). *Older adults and social media.* Pew Internet & American Life Project. Retrieved April 2011, from http://www.pewinternet.org/Reports/2010/Older-Adults-and-Social-Media.aspx.

Mead, S. E., Lamson, N., & Rogers, W. A. (2002). Human factors guidelines for Web site usability: Health-oriented Web sites for older adults. In R.W. Morrell (Ed.), *Older adults, health information, and the World Wide Web* (pp. 89–107). Mahwah, NJ: Lawrence Erlbaum.

Medical Library Association. (2010). *A user's guide to finding and evaluating health information on the Web.* Retrieved April 2011 from http://www.mlanet.org/resources/userguide.html.

Microsoft. (2011). *Kinect effect reaches into hospitals, senior centers.* Microsoft News Center, November. Retrieved December 2011, from http://www.microsoft.com/presspass/features/2011/dec11/12-19KinectEffect.mspx.

National Library of Medicine. (2002). *Making your Website senior friendly.* Retrieved from www.nlm.nih.gov/pubs/staffpubs/od/ocpl/agingchecklist.html.

Nelson, B. (2011) *The new social clicks: 2011 online survey of Washingtonians 45+ about social networking.* AARP report, October 2011.

Newspaper Association of America. (2010). *Newspaper readership and audience 2010.* Retrieved April 2011, from http://www.naa.org/TrendsandNumbers/Readership.aspx.

Nielsen-Bohlman, L., Panzer, A. M., & Kindig, D. A. (2004). *Health literacy: A prescription to end confusion,* Institute of Medicine report. Retrieved January 2009, from http://search.nap.edu/nap-cgi/skimchap.cgi?recid=10883&chap=1–18.

Pew Internet & American Life Report. (2011). *Profiles of health information seekers: Caregivers.* Retrieved March 18, 2012, from http://pewinternet.org/Reports/2011/HealthTopics/Part-2/Caregivers.aspx.

Pew Internet & American Life Report. (2013). *Smartphone ownership 2013.* Retrieved September 29, 2013, from http://pewinternet.org/Reports/2013/Smartphone-Ownership-2013/Findings.aspx.

Pew, R. W., & Van Hemel, S. B. (Eds.). (2004). *Technology for adaptive aging.* Washington, DC: The National Academies Press.

Pew Research Center. (2011). Pew Media Center's project for excellence in journalism. *The state of the news media 2011.* Retrieved April 2011, from http://stateofthemedia.org/2011/newspapers-essay/.

Pew Research Center for People & the Press. (2010). *Americans spend more time following the news.* Retrieved April 2011, from http://pewresearch.org/pubs/1725/where-people-get-news-print-online-readership-cable-news-viewers.

Pouter, S. (2009). Brain training like Nintendo DS "don't stave off dementia or Alzheimer's." *Mail Online.* Retrieved October 2011, from http://dailymail.co.uk/news/article-1156103/Brain-training-games-like-Nintendo-DS-don't-stave-dementia-alzheimers.html.

Rialle, V., Duchene, F., Noury, N., Bajolle, L., & Demongeot, J. (2002). Health "smart" homes: Information technology for patients at home. *Telemedicine Journal and e-Health, 8,* 395–409.

Ritter, M. (2013). *Video game boosts mental abilities in older folks.* Retrieved September 27, 2013, from http://news.yahoo.com/video-game-boosts-mental-abilities-older-folks-170707050.html.

Rogers, W. A., & Fisk, A. D. (2005). Aware home technology: Potential benefits for older adults. *Public Policy & Aging Report, 15,* 28–30.

Tu, H. T. & Cohen, G. R. (2008). *Striking jump in consumers seeking health care information.* Tracking report no. 20. Center for Studying Health System Change. Retrieved March 18, 2012, from http://www.hschange.com/CONTENT/1006/.

Tun, P. A., & Lachman, M. E. (2010). The association between computer use and cognition across adulthood: Use it so you won't lose it? *Psychology and Aging, 25*(3), 560–508.

Turmel, W. (2010). Get older workers to use technology whether they like it or not. *BNET* (*The CBS Business News Network*). Retrieved April 2011, from http://www.bnet.com/blog/virtual-manager/get-older-workers-to-use-technology-whether-they-like-it-or-not/453.

U.S. Department of Health and Human Services. (2013). *Health literacy.* Retrieved September 27, 2013, from http://www.health.gov/communication/literacy/.

Utterback, K. (2005). Supporting a new model of care with telehealth technology. *Telehealth Practice Report, 9*(6), 3–11.

Van Pelt, J. (2011). Brain fitness games for older adults—Strengthening minds or building false hopes...or both? *Social Work Today* (Web exclusive). Retrieved April 2011, from http://www.socialworktoday.com/archive/exc_020811.shtml.

Vergeer, M., & Pelzer, B. (2009). Consequences of media and Internet use for offline and online network capital and well-being: A causal model approach. *Journal of Computer-Mediated Communication, 15*(1), 189–210.

Zarcadoolas, C., Pleasant, A., & Greer, D. S. (2006). *Advancing health literacy: A framework for understanding and action.* San Francisco, CA: Jossey-Bass/Wiley.

Zickuhr, K., & Madden, M. (2012). *Older adults and Internet use.* Pew Internet & American Life Project. Retrieved January 2013, from http://www.pewinternet.org/Reports/2012/Older-adults-and-internet-use/Main-Report/Internet-adoption.aspx.

13 Policies to Promote Older Adults' Well-Being

learning objectives

13.1 Describe the most common policies, programs, and regulations relating to older adults.

13.2 Discuss the historical, economic, and political context of these policies, including the intergenerational inequity debate.

13.3 Identify limitations of current policies and future directions for long-term services and supports.

 **Listen to the Chapter Audio**

Social policy—typically a government policy designed to address a social problem or issue—may seem like an abstract complex concept—distant from your everyday lives. In fact, you may be wondering why you even need to learn about policies. But policies influence almost all aspects of our lives. You undoubtedly benefit every day from public policies: perhaps from student loan policies that help you attend college. Most policies seek to address certain problems. For example, unemployment insurance policies give unemployed adults a basic level of income while they hunt for jobs. And when we understand policies, we are better-informed citizens who can influence the policy-making process by our votes and advocacy. We hope by the end of this chapter that you will see how central policies are not only to older Americans' well-being but also to your own lives.

Understanding how policies affect the lives of older adults and their caregivers is important for practitioners, family members, and researchers. Since the 1930s, a wide range of public social and health policies and programs have evolved to improve older people's social, physical, and economic well-being. This chapter includes:

- The primary factors that affect the development of public policies (both federal and state) for older adults, particularly societal values and the larger historical, economic, and political context
- Social Security, the major source of income for older adults
- The Older Americans Act, which funds community-based direct services to elders and their family caregivers
- Medicare, which funds acute health care primarily in hospitals and some skilled home health care services
- Medicaid, which funds long-term services and supports in homes and in skilled nursing facilities
- Policies to promote innovative health and long-term services and supports, including the Patient Protection and Affordable Care Act (ACA)

Understanding Policies, Programs, and Regulations

One reason that policies directly impact our lives is that they exist at all levels of government (federal, state, county, city, or town) as well as within organizations or agencies. Policies typically result from legislation, which is then translated into regulations, programs, and services that determine how funds are allocated among different groups—who should receive what benefits, from which sources, and on what basis. Policies thus reflect society's decisions about what choices to make in meeting elders' needs and who should be responsible doing so—the government, non-profit service agencies, the private sector, or families. For example, federal legislation in 1965 established the Older Americans Act (OAA), the primary funder for social services for adults age 60 and older. Congress periodically authorizes funds for OAA programs, such as senior centers, adult day health, and Meals on Wheels. These programs at the local level have to follow federal and state regulations that determine what kinds of activities and even food they can offer and whether they can charge for any services.

Policies Affect Real People

In the months and years ahead, you will hear your elected officials at the national, state, and local levels talk about balancing their respective budgets, as well as about the challenges of providing programs and services for an aging population. These are not hypothetical or theoretical arguments conducted by people far removed from you. Instead, these are discussions that will lead to decisions that affect real people's everyday lives. They will influence your community members, neighbors, loved ones—and yourselves. They will affect how financially secure your parents and grandparents will be after retirement. They will shape when and if you will be eligible for those same protections when you retire. They will impact how we take care of those around us who do not have the financial means to care for themselves in terms of health care, food, transportation, housing, and so forth. If you haven't already done so, learn about what your elected officials and government policy-makers are thinking in terms of older adult programs and services—and how they are planning to spend the public's tax dollars. There are many ways to participate in this process, such as being an informed voter, joining an advocacy or educational organization, writing an op-ed piece for your local paper or blogging, attending lobby days at your state legislature or providing testimony at city council hearings, participating in campaigns, or even running for elected office yourself.

Separating Fact from Fiction about Age-Based Policies

We hear a lot in the media about entitlement programs that are based on age because they are viewed as responsible for much of the growth of the federal budget. Some policy-makers and citizens think that the older population benefits at the expense of other age groups and is "busting the budget." Not surprisingly, such age-based policies are often at the center of various proposals to reduce government spending.

It is true that federal expenditures for older adults are growing as life expectancy—and the older population—increases. Expanded spending for Social Security, Medicare, and Medicaid is estimated to outpace overall economic growth by two to three times by 2030. Because of this, policy-makers are debating different options for managing spending on these programs as part of a larger process of reducing the federal budget deficit (Center on Budget and Policy Priorities, 2012).

As you listen to such debates, it is important to recognize that while Social Security and Medicare are a big part of the federal budget, they are not the only drivers of the growing deficit. This is because they are financed by a dedicated payroll tax paid by employers and employees. In fact, the current reserves in the Social Security Trust Fund help pay for other federal expenditures because the government borrows from these to cover other expenses.

Is the Entitlement Society Rhetoric True?

In the 2012 election, fiscally conservative politicians predicted that we were becoming an "cntitlement" society and the work ethic was being destroyed. Although spending on entitlement programs has grown, 90 percent of the dollars go to older adults, persons with disabilities, and working households, not those who are "too lazy" to work. This funds medical care, unemployment insurance, and Social Security benefits or what is often called the safety net (Sherman, Greenstein, & Ruffing, 2012).

Instead, the fiscal challenges of federal programs are largely the result of tax cuts, escalating defense spending and health care costs, and the global economic crisis. For instance, since 2001, funding for defense has grown much faster than the average growth rate for Social Security, Medicare, and Medicaid combined. So the next time you hear someone blaming older adults for the deficit, remember that factors other than the growth of the older population are also at play. Figure 13.1 shows where our tax dollars go (Center on Budget and Policy Priorities, 2012).

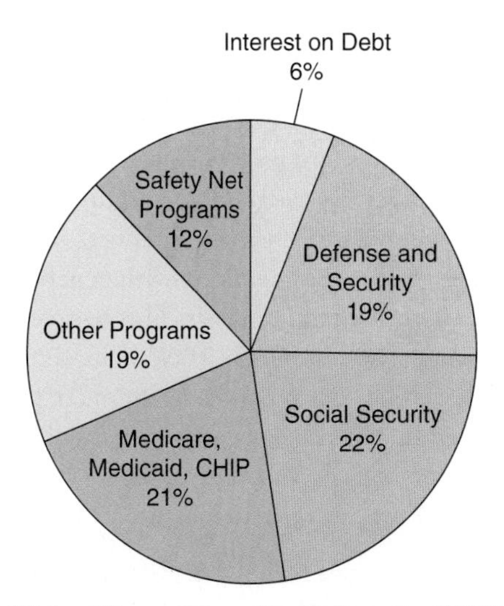

FIGURE 13.1 Where did our Tax Dollars Go, 2013?

Source: Center on Budget and Policy Priorities, 2013.

Note: Percentages may not total 100 due to rounding.

Criteria by Which Policies Vary

When you hear or read about policies, it is useful to know how they vary in terms of eligibility criteria and how they are funded. Figure 13.2 on p. 360 shows some of the primary criteria, which are often a focus of current policy debates.

Eligibility criteria (e.g., who can benefit) are typically age based or need-based.

Social Security and Medicare are **age-based entitlement programs**—meaning that all adults are automatically entitled to receive benefits based on their age, not on their financial or health needs. But older people receive these benefits based on their lifetime contributions as workers into these public insurance systems. Contrary to what the media may imply, these age-based programs are not "welfare" or a "free ride."

Age-based programs are also known as **universal and categorical benefits**; this means that they are available as a social right to all persons belonging to a designated category, for example, those over a certain age. Because government has to fund such programs for anyone who meets

Program Dimensions	Examples
Eligibility	
On basis of age	Medicare
On basis of financial need	Supplemental Security Income Medicaid
Form of benefits: Direct or indirect	
Cash	
Direct cash transfers	Social Security
Indirect cash transfers	Income tax exemption
Cash substitute	
Direct cash substitutes	Vouchers
Indirect cash substitutes	Medicare payments to service providers
Method of financing	
Contributory (earned rights)	Social Security
Noncontributory	Supplemental Security Income
Universal or selective benefits	
Universal - for all persons who belong to a particular category	Older Americans Act
Selective - determined on an individual basis	Food stamps
Who pays	
Mandatory contributions by paid workers	Social Security, Medicare
Discretionary funds from Congress	Temporary Assistance for Needy Families

FIGURE 13.2 How Policies vary by Eligibility, Funding, and Payment Structures

the age criterion and is thus entitled to benefits, spending on them will continue to grow as more Americans live longer, unless changes are made in eligibility criteria or the size of benefits.

In contrast, **need-based** (or means-tested) programs decide eligibility by financial need. Also known as **selective benefits**, these are determined on a case-by-case basis. Programs for children and for younger persons with disabilities are typically means based. But low-income elders also qualify for means-based programs, such as Medicaid, Supplemental Security Income, food stamps, and public housing. People have to apply for and extensively document their low-income status to receive need-based benefits. Many public debates have focused on whether aging services should continue to be universal by age—or whether they should be targeted only to low-income elders and subsidized by higher-income older adults. You will see this debate, still very timely today, throughout this chapter.

Another way that policies vary is how they are financed.

- Social Security and Medicare are **contributory** plans; an older adult is entitled to these benefits based on their mandatory contributions into the system as a paid worker throughout their lives.
- Or funding may be **discretionary**. Temporary Assistance for Needy Families (TANF) for low-income children and parents is a program with discretionary funding; Congress has to approve its funding annually and the amount typically varies from year to year.

Factors That Influence the Development of Public Policies

If you have followed the passage of any legislation at the federal level or in your state, you know the policy development process is not rational. For example, the 2010 **Patient Protection and Affordable Care Act (ACA)**—health care reform to improve quality of care and reduce costs—reflects countless compromises and last-minute changes to meet budget targets, not sound policy analysis. These were needed in order to ensure its passage—and resulted in a plan quite different than President Obama's original proposal. The public policy process is characterized by its shortsightedness—its general inability, because of annual budgetary cycles, the frequency of national partisan elections, and increasing bipartisan and ideological divisions, to deal adequately with long-term economic, demographic, and social trends, or to anticipate future consequences of current policies. We have seen many of these factors at play in all the efforts to repeal the ACA or Obamacare, despite the 2010 Congressional vote and the 2012 Supreme Court decision upholding the constitutionality of mandatory insurance.

This reflects how the funding and eligibility criteria for programs are often determined by prevailing social values, ideologies, and the political party in control of the presidency and Congress, not by a clear direction of what is good policy. As the number and diversity of older adults have grown, such shortsightedness has resulted in a fragmented array of services, with separate entitlements and eligibility requirements. This has created what is often referred to as separate silos of funding. In fact, this complexity can be so confusing to older people and their families that it has spawned the growth of private case or care managers, Web sites, and toll-free navigator phone and Internet services to locate, access, and coordinate services.

Values Affecting Social Policy We turn now to how values, beliefs, or ideology shape policy. Two contrasting core values regarding responsibility have been played out in U.S. policies—and are reflected in many current debates:

1. Individual welfare is essentially a *person's responsibility* within a free-market economy unfettered by government control. This belief in individualism, self-determination, personal choice, and privacy is deeply rooted in American history and culture.
2. Individual welfare is the responsibility *of both the individual and the larger community*. Government intervention, such as Medicaid and the ACA, is required to protect its citizens and compensate for the free market's failure to distribute resources equitably.

Indeed, the ongoing Republican and Tea Party opposition to Obamacare is really about the fundamental question of the role of government versus individual responsibility in promoting health.

Our society's emphasis on individual responsibility has resulted in government playing a residual or "backup" role to informal support systems, such as the family. This contrasts with the approach of many Western European countries, where health and welfare polices represent a national collective responsibility that all citizens are entitled to have basic needs met by the government. For example, in Scandinavian countries, public policies benefit citizens from "cradle to grave," including free health care. In contrast, even when our federal government intervenes, policies are often incremental and justified only because the market economy, the family, or the individual failed to provide for themselves or their relatives.

Since the New Deal of the 1930s, policy has oscillated between these two core values as the public mood, national administrations, and the larger political and economic context have shifted. From the 1930s to the 1980s, public perceptions of older people as more "deserving" than other age groups converged to create the universal categorical programs of Social Security, the Older Americans Act, and Medicare available to persons who meet age criteria.

In contrast, policies that use income (e.g., means-testing) to determine if a person is "deserving" of services reflect our society's bias toward productivity and economic self-sufficiency. Since the Reagan anti-tax era in the 1980s, some policy-makers have asserted that problems faced by elders cannot be solved with government programs alone. They argue that solutions must come from state and local governments, the private sector, and individuals responsible for their own well-being. These solutions encompass self-help, family caregiving, private retirement investments, faith-based organizations, and volunteerism. Over the span of five decades, the programs for older adults have shifted from government's ensuring adequacy and protection to cutting budgets, reducing government size, and increasing revenues (Hudson, 2010; Walker, 2009).

As you learned in our discussion of eligibility criteria, another ongoing debate that reflects societal values is whether services for older adults should be delivered on the basis of age or need.

Here is the argument for entitlement programs based on age:

- They are an efficient way to set a minimum floor of protection and transfer resources to the older population.
- They are less stigmatizing, since older people are viewed as deserving of public support solely because of their age.

And this is what critics of age-based programs argue:

- This approach is no longer economically feasible, because so many people now qualify for age-related benefits, because of increased life expectancy.
- Some Administration on Aging (AoA) network programs, such as senior centers, increasingly benefit the young-old who are relatively healthy and have enough income to pay for services.
- Age-based services reinforce the perception of "the old" as a problem.
- Because the older population is socioeconomically diverse, eligibility should be selectively determined on the basis of income and functional ability in order to provide a safety net for the most vulnerable elders.

Intergenerational Inequity versus Interdependence

The **intergenerational inequity perspective** also fuels debates about age- versus need-based policies. It first emerged in the 1980s, when fiscally conservative groups, such as Americans for Generational Equity (AGE), claimed that older citizens were "greedy geezers," thriving at the expense of younger age groups and selfishly concerned only with their retirement benefits. They viewed programs for older people as a cause of youth unemployment, inadequate schools, and increased child poverty. This view is heard again today when some groups, such as the Tea Party, contend that the growth of Social Security is jeopardizing future generations and making people less responsible for their own retirement. This argument is fueled primarily by advocates of reduced government size and spending and increased self-sufficiency and private sector responsibility (Williamson & Watts-Ray, 2008).

Proponents of this perspective, however, overlook the increasing income inequality among older adults—far greater than among any other age group. As you learned in Chapter 10, not all older adults have adequate finances. Moreover, there is little evidence of significant intergenerational conflict. In contrast, the **interdependence of generations framework** recognizes that younger and older generations support each other across the life course. As you learned in our discussion of social exchange theory in Chapter 5, assistance from young to old and old to young benefits all ages and supports families across the life course. This framework also recognizes that so-called age-based policies, such as Social Security, often benefit younger generations. Moreover, younger generations generally express support for programs that benefit older adults, while older generations recognize the necessity of government support for children and families. As noted in Chapter 8, national organizations such as Generations United build on this cross-generational interdependence in their advocacy (MacArthur Foundation, 2009).

We next discuss how the larger societal context intersects with values in influencing the types of policies developed for older adults across major time periods.

points to ponder

Imagine yourself as a policy-maker who has to take a position or participate in a debate about age-based versus need-based policies. What would your argument be? Would you support all older adults receiving benefits based on age regardless of need, or do you think that elders and their families should pay for services, based on their income? Would you propose changing Social Security and Medicare from age-based programs to ones based on income?

Historical, Economic, and Political Context

Policies are responsive to changing conditions in the larger environment, as well as public beliefs. Here are a few examples of this dynamic. The 2011 federal policy that continued unemployment insurance benefits and federal tax cuts for the wealthy reflects changing political and fiscal conditions caused by the recession and the election of Tea Party candidates. In contrast, the repeal of the military's "Don't Ask, Don't Tell" policy in 2011 or President Obama's support of gay marriage reflect more progressive values of the Democratic administration. You probably can think of other contemporary policies that reflect the rapidly changing social, political, and economic environment. Our focus here is how this larger context has shifted since the 1930s in shaping the types of policies specifically for older adults.

The First Policies to Benefit Older Americans, 1930s–1950s

Age-based approaches evolved in a very different historical time period, when life expectancy was shorter, chronic disease relatively rare, poverty of elders higher than other age groups, and federal deficits of less concern. The United States lagged behind most European countries in developing age-based policies. For example, Social Security was not passed until 1935, while Western European countries instituted such systems in the nineteenth century. You may wonder why the United States would be so slow to respond to older Americans' economic distress caused by the Great Depression. Factors such as the low percentage of older adults in the United States compared to Europe, a strong belief in individual responsibility, and the free-market economy are partial explanations. In the 1920s and 1930s, families, communities, charity organizations, and local governments (e.g., county work farms or poor farms) were expected to be responsible for elders.

But economic factors became the primary cause for increased government responsibility for older citizens. The Great Depression dislodged the middle class from financial security and from widely held beliefs that low-income older adults did not deserve public assistance.

Prior to Social Security, many elders lived in almshouses established to provide sanctuary for the poor.

Images of poor elders gradually aroused public sympathy and a favorable political response of protection simply by virtue of age. The Depression also fueled growing mistrust of the private sector. Additionally, Social Security as a public pension was assumed to cost less than reliance on local poorhouses. By encouraging retirement, it was seen as a strategy to reduce unemployment and create job opportunities for the young. Because older adults were only 5 percent of the population, and no one predicted medical advances that would result in dramatic increases in life expectancy, it was assumed that there would always be enough workers paying into Social Security to guarantee the reserves to finance it. Thus, contextual variables came together to create the necessary public and legislative support of partial government responsibility for its older citizens through a system of social insurance. These factors—values, demography, and the historical, political, and economic context—continue to influence our policies today.

Expansion of Age-Based Programs in the 1960s and 1970s: "Compassionate Stereotypes" about Older Adults

In contrast to the economic distress that gave way to Social Security in the 1930s, periods of economic growth can also be conducive to new policies. For example, Medicare and the Older Americans Act were passed in the 1960s and early 1970s, which was a time of economic progress and increased social consciousness about the needs of vulnerable populations. Federal spending for programs for older adults rapidly expanded, resulting in what has been called the **"graying" of the federal budget**—the creation of a wide array of major federal programs and interest groups directed toward older persons. Just a few of these are reflected in the box on p. 364.

Within this context of increased age-related programs, it is not surprising that some older Americans grew to expect that they were automatically entitled to receive benefits based on age (Binstock, 2008; Hudson, 2008; Meyer, 2010).

Cost Efficiency and Program Reductions in the 1980s and 1990s

While economic growth and compassionate stereotypes underlay this expansion of age-based entitlement programs, markedly different factors influenced policies in the 1980s and 1990s: a growing federal deficit and pressures to reduce government costs, an anti-tax mentality, and increasing concern about younger groups' economic well-being. Public support for universal age-based benefits began to erode, dismantling the priority on the common good established by the Social Security Act (Meyer, 2010; Schulz & Binstock, 2006).

Another change during the 1980s was the growing diversity of the aging population. Poverty among older citizens had declined as a result of Social Security, and the numbers of elders—typically white males—with generous private pensions and personal savings had grown. It then became more apparent that chronological age is not an accurate marker of financial status or functional ability. Accordingly, policies began to take account of older adults' differential capabilities to help finance publicly funded services. Services through the OAA were first targeted to

points to ponder

When you hear or read about contemporary policy debates, bring a critical eye to the arguments: What factors—values, the growth of older adults, the recession, increasing bipartisanship—are salient to these debates? Are facts or beliefs/ideology being debated? What do these debates mean for the well-being of all generations?

The "Graying" of the Budget

- The first White House Conference on Aging, 1961
- The establishment of the Senate Special Committee on Aging, 1961
- Passage of Medicare, Medicaid, and the Older Americans Act (OAA), 1965
- Efforts to strengthen the OAA, the second White House Conference on Aging, 1971
- Expansion of Social Security benefits and inclusion of cost-of-living adjustments (COLAs), 1973

low-income elders, and some federal funding was cut or transferred to state and local units.

With old age alone no longer considered sufficient grounds for public benefits, a major societal shift in attitudes toward the older population continued into the 1990s. National groups, which cut across the political spectrum, maintained that Social Security, Medicare, and Medicaid needed to be drastically curtailed to balance the federal budget and that older adults should finance their own retirement (Hudson, 2010; Kail, Quadagno, & Keene, 2009; Walker, 2009).

Since 2000: Market and Personal Responsibility and Reduced Government Spending

Age-based entitlements of Social Security and Medicare were further challenged during the Bush administration (2000–2008) and under the Republican majority in Congress in 2010–2012. Cost and intergenerational inequity issues that surfaced in the 1980s are still salient, but are secondary to beliefs about the appropriate role and size of government and individual responsibility for elders' well-being.

With a Democratic President and Congress elected in 2008, their value stance was to increase policy and programmatic supports for vulnerable populations of all ages, as reflected in the ACA and the extension of unemployment benefits. However, the recession, record high unemployment and deficit, and the Republican victories in 2010 made it difficult for Congressional Democrats and the Obama administration to act on their values to protect vulnerable citizens. As you learned in Chapter 8's discussion of political participation, older adults are now less likely to be perceived as a "politically sympathetic" group compared to children and young families. And proposals for private sector initiatives and personal responsibility for retirement income and health care have garnered more support. At the same time, the economic downturn has intensified disparities, with subgroups of poor, elders of color, women, and persons with disabilities more likely to join political alliances around class, race, gender, or ability, which may put them in conflict with groups of more affluent elders (Hudson, 2008, 2010; Kail et al., 2009; MacArthur Foundation, 2009; Meyer, 2010).

These different historical, economic, and political time periods illustrate how policy approaches to older adults vary widely across time—and will continue to do so in the future. We next review the four federal programs that have accounted for most of the age-based expenditures in the past 75 years—and that you probably hear about in the news:

1. Social Security: Old-Age, Survivors, and Disability Insurance (OASDI)
2. The Aging Network of the Older Americans Act (OAA)
3. Medicare
4. Medicaid

points to **ponder**

You may be affected by these programs if you are low-income or have disabilities, take care of an older relative with chronic illness, or one of your parents has died. Or perhaps you have a friend or relative who is receiving benefits from one of these programs. Stop and think if you—or someone you know—is benefiting from any of these four programs. How has this made a difference in their lives?

Social Security: An Income Security Program

As you learned in Chapter 10, the primary purpose of the 1935 Social Security Act was to establish a system of income maintenance for all older persons to protect against financial disaster. A secondary purpose was to ensure a basic level of protection for the neediest older adults, initially through state plans for OASDI and since 1974 through the federally funded Supplemental Security Income (SSI) program. A more recent objective is to provide compensatory income to persons of all ages who experience a sudden loss of income—such as widows, surviving children, and persons with disabilities, as reflected in Figure 13.3.

The Goals of Social Security

Social Security is characterized by dual goals of social adequacy and individual equity.

- **Social adequacy** refers to a shared societal obligation to provide a basic standard of living (a "safety net") for all who are eligible, regardless of the size of their payroll contributions. No one is excluded based on "risk," and benefits can be counted on regardless of inflation and market fluctuations. This universal protection is a fundamental difference from private insurance or discretionary income maintenance programs for children and families (Caldera, 2012b; Williamson & Watts-Ray, 2008).

  The goal of social adequacy is reflected in the statistics that we noted in Chapter 10, particularly the following:
  - Social Security covers over 90 percent of American workers.
  - Social Security benefits, albeit modest, are the largest source of income for the vast majority of older adults (Caldera, 2012b; Shelton, 2013a).

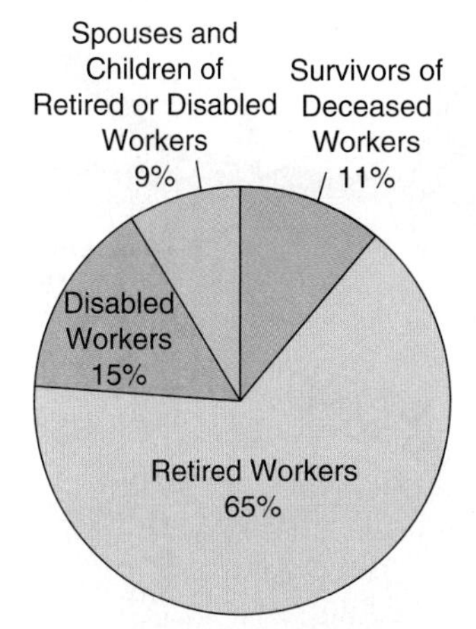

FIGURE 13.3 Who Benefits from Social Security?

Source: Social Security Administration, 2013.

Social Security—A Partial Success Story

In its 75-year history, Social Security has never missed a payment; without it, almost 50 percent of older Americans would be poor or near-poor. And it protects younger families as well through Survivors and Disability benefits. Social Security has been and continues to be an important source of economic stability for the broad middle class of Americans. But in some ways, it is only a partial success, since the poverty rate of approximately 10 percent among older adults in the United States is higher than in any other Western country (Caldera, 2012b; Gregory, Bethell, Reno, & Veghte, 2010; Shelton, 2013b).

- **Individual equity**. As you just learned earlier in this chapter, Social Security is based on the concept of earned rights as a result of a lifetime of paid work. It is financed with revenues raised equally from the mandatory payroll tax contributions of employees and employers, and by income based on current tax revenues. If you are employed, you are probably paying into the Social Security system and will be eligible when you are in your late sixties to receive benefits based on your employment record and what you paid as payroll taxes.

The Cross-Generational Nature of Social Security

One reason for strong public support is Social Security's cross-generational benefits. Although the media and many policy-makers portray Social Security as only an old-age program, it actually helps individuals across the life course. It is a myth that Social Security is a pension system in which retirees are merely paid back, with interest on the contributions of workers and their employers. Instead it is like a pipeline: payroll taxes from today's workers flow in, are invested in the Social Security Trust Fund, and simultaneously flow out to current retirees or workers with disabilities. Moreover, every worker contributing to Social Security, regardless of age, has disability and life insurance if they should need it.

Social Security is an example of cross-generational social compact to ensure well-being of multiple generations, since it is central to many younger families' economic well-being.

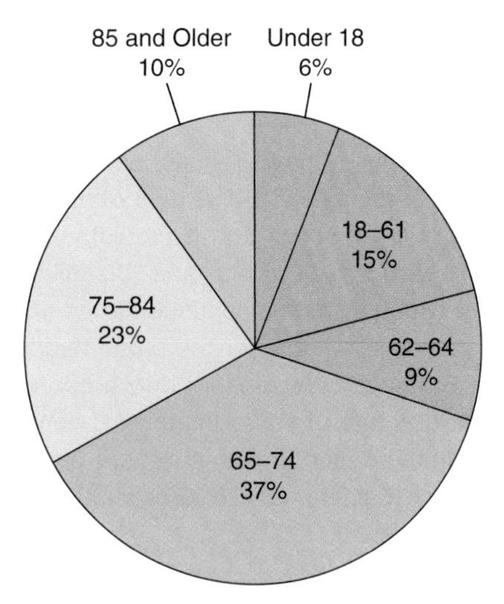

FIGURE 13.4 Social Security Beneficiaries by Age

Source: Social Security Administration, 2013.

- It frees the middle generation from financial support to older relatives.
- It ensures compensatory income, regardless of age, to those who experience sudden income loss (e.g., widows, surviving children under age 18 of beneficiaries, younger persons with disabilities). For example, Social Security lifts over a million children above the poverty threshold, and it is the largest source of cash benefits for grandparents who are raising their grandchildren and often living on very low incomes.
- It ensures basic protection for the neediest members of society, regardless of age, through the SSI program that you learned about in Chapter 10. Figure 13.4 shows how both young and old benefit from Social Security (SSA, 2013).

The Future of Social Security

As you have been learning, dire predictions about Social Security are not new. Since the 1980s, policy-makers have argued that "apocalyptic demography" will make it difficult to sustain such age-related benefits and that the "graying of the welfare state" is having catastrophic consequences for the living standards of working-age Americans. Others portray a picture of the government taking money from employees and not investing it wisely so that the system will collapse. When you hear statements like this, it is important to take a critical view: there are great risks of error in making long-range forecasts of nearly 75 years, and those dire projections are only speculations, not fact. Indeed, there are widely different interpretations of the same data about the financial stability of Social Security. Consider these facts.

- Yes, Social Security does face funding challenges; according to the Social Security Trustees, action needs to be taken sooner rather than later to allow younger generations to adequately prepare. But Social Security is not bankrupt, is not causing the federal deficit, and does not need "radical" reform.
- Yes, it is true that the Trust Fund will continue to grow only until about 2022, at which point the benefits payable will exceed the amount raised through employment taxes. This means that the Trust Fund will begin to be drawn down in order to pay full benefits. But Social Security currently has a surplus, which has actually helped to reduce the federal deficit.
- And a true funding shortfall—where the benefit payouts exceed taxes and interest so that Trust Fund reserves are drawn down—will not occur until at about 2033. Even if the Trust Fund is exhausted, this would not mean that benefits would stop altogether. The federal government would still be able to pay around 77 cents for every dollar of benefits promised to future retirees until about 2087. This is an important statistic for you to remember as it will affect you. It means today's younger workers will still benefit from Social Security but it will take them longer to recoup their contributions after they retire (Shelton, 2013b).

Despite these long-range funding challenges, about 80 percent of Americans—across party lines—agree that it is critical to preserve Social Security for future generations,

The vast majority of Americans are in favor of maintaining Social Security benefits for future generations.

even if it means raising the payroll tax. They value it for themselves, their families, and for the stability it provides others. Politicians advocating changes in Social Security must take account of this widespread support for protecting the program's fundamental principles (AARP, 2010b; National Academy of Social Insurance, 2012b; Smith, 2010; SSA, 2012).

The box below summarizes the demographic, economic, and political context that now frames ongoing debates about Social Security's future. You may find it useful to compare this context to our earlier discussion of factors that influenced the passage of Social Security in the 1930s.

Current Context of Social Security Debates

- Increased life expectancy: when Social Security was enacted, life expectancy was 61 years compared with over 78 years today.
- The changing age-dependency ratio from 50 workers to "support" 1 retiree in 1935 to between 4 and 5 currently, to only 3 to 1 by 2030, and approximately 2 workers to 1 retiree by 2034. Because of high rates of unemployment, even fewer workers than this ratio are projected as paying into the Social Security Trust Fund.
- A shift from a focus on adequacy of benefits to a preoccupation with financing Social Security.
- Increasing numbers of older adults who are healthier, better educated, and working longer, but oftentimes continuing to work largely out of economic necessity.
- Economic pressures on young adults, many of whom are underemployed or unemployed.
- Economic strains on elders who rely primarily on Social Security, but did not receive cost-of-living increases in 2010 and 2011 (Caldera, 2012b; SSA, 2013).

Proposed Changes to Social Security Despite strong public support, some fiscally conservative policymakers argue for **privatization** of Social Security by requiring employees to contribute to individual savings accounts such as IRAs. Other proposals would divert part of the payroll taxes paid into Social Security into private accounts managed by the government. Both approaches presume that private retirement accounts and stock market investments would result in higher rates of return. They also assume a strong economy and stock market, as well as individual knowledge and skills to make informed investment decisions. Yet think about how similar assumptions were undermined by the stock market's poor performance in 2000 and 2008–2011; additionally, most Americans are uneducated about investments and do not adequately plan financially for retirement. Moreover, a wide range of negative outcomes of privatization have been identified by the Social Security Administration presidential commissions, economists, and policy scholars. Here are a few of these:

- Privatization is a fundamental shift from universal government protection to individual responsibility, while not resolving Social Security's long-term financial problems. For example, the uncertainty of the stock market compared to the guaranteed security of U.S. treasury bonds would mean that investment income would be unlikely to be sufficient to last until a person dies.
- Privatization would not ensure coverage for younger groups of children whose parents died and for adults of any age who become disabled.
- Privatization would disproportionately negatively impact low-income workers, especially women and persons of color, who depend on Social Security more than other groups and who have limited resources to invest privately.
- The primary beneficiaries of a privatized system would be higher-income unmarried workers (Campbell & King, 2010; Gregory et al., 2010; Shelton, 2013b).

While points of view vary widely about proposed solutions to the Social Security "crisis," it is clear that there are ways other than privatization to ensure its future. In contrast to warnings of doom, a more optimistic view is that projected shortfalls can be addressed with relatively minor adjustments, since Social Security spending is relatively predictable as a share of the national economy. Here are the most commonly proposed strategies to extend full solvency of the Trust Fund beyond 2033 and what they would mean for different groups of older people:

1. *Raise the retirement age of eligibility for benefits.* The downside of this approach is that it could disadvantage persons of color, who have lower life expectancies and may be forced to retire from physically demanding jobs in their mid-sixties for health reasons.
2. *Increase payroll taxes.* These taxes have not changed since the mid-1980s. Raising the employer and employee's share each by less than 2 percentiles (from 12.4 to 14.4 percent) would keep the system fully solvent for

75 years. But this would hurt low-income workers, such as women and persons of color, since the increased tax would represent a greater share of their income.

3. *Reduce benefits across the board by 1 percent.* This also negatively affects the lowest-income workers, who depend on Social Security for a greater share of their retirement income than do higher-income retirees.
4. *Raise the cap on the amount of wages and salaries subject to payroll taxes.* Currently income above $110,000 is not subject to the Social Security payroll tax. This means that a worker who makes twice the Social Security wage cap of $229,000 per year still pays Social Security tax on only half of their earnings. Raising the cap—or eliminating it altogether—would mean that higher-income workers would help to close the Social Security funding gap while the relative value of benefits for lower-income workers would be increased. Indeed, there is a national campaign to "Scrap the Cap"—complete with YouTube videos—as a way to solve Social Security's financing challenges.
5. *Expand the number of workers paying Social Security taxes*, such as those government workers who currently do not participate.
6. *Reduce the annual cost-of-living adjustments* (an increase to take account of inflation); even reductions as small as 0.7 percent would, over time, result in enormous cost savings (Board of Trustees, 2012; Center for Economic and Policy Research, 2012; Center on Budget and Policy Priorities, 2012; National Academy of Social Insurance, 2012a; Shelton, 2013b).

You may have read or heard about other possible incremental ways to change Social Security. Although none of these is a perfect solution, we encourage you to bring a critical eye to think about the pros and cons of different proposals for groups of vulnerable citizens. It is important to recognize that any of these proposed changes would be political compromises between those who favor privatization and those who view Social Security as a "sacred entitlement." Accordingly, future benefits to older people will not rely solely on the proportion of workers to retirees. It will also depend on whether the economy generates sufficient additional resources to cover Social Security and whether the political will exists to transfer them to older adults, their survivors, and persons with disabilities (Myles, 2010).

points to ponder

With all the debates about entitlement programs like Social Security, what are your thoughts about the future of Social Security? Do you think our political leaders can find a viable solution to keep Social Security fully solvent for future generations? What do you think should be done?

AARP and Social Security

With the Republican majority in Congress and growing antigovernment sentiment in 2011–2012, there have been numerous proposals to cut Social Security. In response, the 50 million members of AARP launched a national television ad that reminded Congress that older adults are more than just numbers in a budget. Instead, Congress needs to understand that seniors have worked hard and paid into the system their whole lives to have secure health coverage and retirement income they can count on. Here are excerpts from the ad:

> "I'm not a number. I'm not a line item on a budget. And I'm definitely not a pushover. But I am a voter."
>
> So Washington, before you even think about cutting my Medicare and Social Security benefits, here's a number you should remember—50 million. We are 50 million seniors who have earned our benefits. And you will be hearing from us. Today and on Election Day. Tell Congress: cut waste and loopholes, not our benefits. (AARP, 2011a; Davidson, 2011)

Proposals to Reduce Gender Inequities in Social Security As you learned in Chapter 10, women—particularly women of color—tend to fare less well under Social Security than men. But relatively modest modifications could eliminate some gender inequities inherent in Social Security. Here are just a few proposals that could help reduce the high poverty rate among older women and, in some instances, benefit elders of color as well. Think about how some of these changes might benefit your mother, your grandmother, or other older women you know.

1. *Raise the minimum Social Security benefit to 125 percent of the poverty level.* This would benefit women and persons of color, because both groups are overrepresented in low-wage, part-time jobs with few or no benefits and in physically demanding jobs that often lead to an earlier departure from the paid labor force.

It would also help poor working women who never married or were married less than 10 years and thus receive a benefit based solely on their own employment histories, typically in lower-paid jobs (Caldera, 2012a; Shelton, 2013a).

2. *Increase benefits for the oldest-old*, who are likely to be economically vulnerable women, who are unable to continue working to supplement their Social Security.
3. *Raise widows' survivors benefits*. This would address the reality that many older women are not poor until their husband dies. This often happens because widows must choose benefits based on either their husband's earnings or their own, but not the combined earnings. A widow who works long enough to be eligible for benefits of her own essentially gets no credit for her own earnings if she selects benefits based on her husband's income, which among current cohorts of elders is generally higher than the wife's. She ends up with only one source of income. One option might be to pay a widowed spouse 75 percent of the combined worker benefits received by the two spouses. This proposal is a good example of how relatively small incremental change can have multiple benefits; it would cost a very small percent of taxable income, yet greatly improve the widow's economic status in old age (Caldera, 2012a; Entmacher, 2010; Estes, O'Neill, & Hartmann, 2012).
4. *Provide credit for caregiving years that women spend out of the paid labor force*. You have learned in earlier chapters how women are often financially disadvantaged in old age because of years devoted to family caregiving. This proposal would recognize women's disproportionate responsibilities for raising children, or what has been called the "motherhood penalty." Women would receive benefits based on their contributions to the economy through both their labor force participation and their unpaid work of caregiving (Rix, 2010).
5. *Allow earnings sharing*. Each partner in a marriage would be entitled to a separate Social Security account, regardless of which one is employed. Covered earnings would be divided between the two spouses, with one-half credited to each spouse's account.
6. *Place an economic value on taking care of dependents*. Dependent care credits, common in other Western countries, would represent a set amount of earnings to substitute for a certain number of years of low earnings. To illustrate, if there were a $15,000 care credit and a woman had two years across her lifetime where she earned only $8,000, she would be credited with an additional $7,000 (for a total of $15,000) for those years (Estes et al., 2012).

None of these changes would benefit all women, but more women would fare better under any of these proposals than they do now under the single-breadwinner model. Unfortunately, recommendations to reduce gender inequities are unlikely to be considered in the near future, given current pressures to reduce government spending and to privatize parts of Social Security (Estes et al., 2012; Shelton, 2013a).

points to ponder

Imagine living in a society in which there is no public pension like Social Security to provide a "safety net" for older adults. How do you think older adults would get by financially in such a society? What might their lives be like? What is their "safety net"?

We shift now from an age-based contributory program of earned rights to an entitlement program based solely on age—the Older Americans Act. Remember the concept of universality based on age rather than need that you learned about under our discussion of eligibility criteria.

Social Services through the Older Americans Act

Given all the media focus on age-based programs, you may be surprised to learn that only about 1 percent of the federal budget allocated to programs for older adults is spent on social services, primarily through the 1965 **Older Americans Act (OAA)**. At the federal level, the act charges the **Administration on Aging (AoA)** to oversee, support, and advocate for the services through the **Aging Network**. This is the system that plans, coordinates, and delivers direct services to older adults and increasingly to persons with disabilities.

Each state has a State Unit on Aging responsible for overall planning of age-based services. Then there are 629 local **Area Agencies on Aging (AAAs)**, 244 tribal organizations and two Native Hawaiian units that develop and administer service plans within regional and local areas. The advisory boards for each AAA must include older adults in decision-making roles. If you are trying to find services for an older adult, your local Area Agency on Aging information and assistance service is typically the best place to start. Approximately 30,000 direct service providers and 500,000 volunteers in local communities provide services that you often see—transportation, meals on wheels, or senior centers, to name just a few. Check out online or by phone the **Eldercare Locator**, which has for over 20 years connected more than 2.4 million older adults, caregivers, and professionals to local aging resources throughout the country and is administered by the National Association of Area Agencies on Aging (n4a) (AoA, 2013).

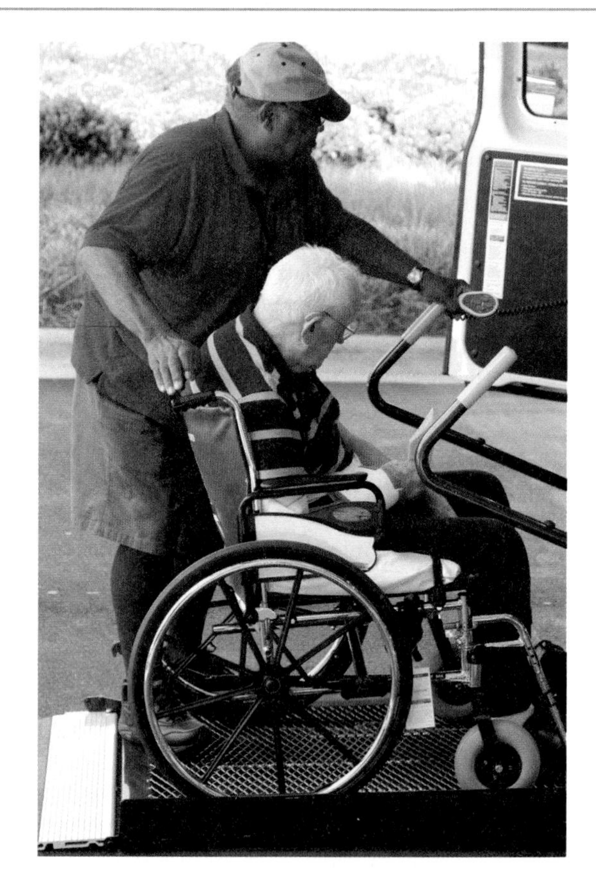

Many agencies funded by AoA provide free or low-cost transportation services.

In 2012, a major change took place with the creation of a new organization, the **Administration for Community Living (ACL)**, with the goal of increasing access to community supports and full participation across the life course, while focusing attention and resources on the unique needs of people with disabilities as well as older Americans. ACL includes the Administration on Aging, the Administration on Intellectual and Developmental Disabilities and the Center for Disability and Aging Policy in a single agency. It is intended to enhance policy and program support for crosscutting initiatives focused on the unique needs of individual groups such as children with developmental disabilities, adults with physical disabilities, or elders, including seniors with Alzheimer's. Not surprisingly, this was a controversial change, and some aging advocates fear that this will dilute funding for older adults, while others contend that it is important to be inclusive of issues of aging with disability (Putnam, 2012).

The growing numbers of older adults combined with reduced budgets means that the Aging Network faces challenges on how to fund and deliver adequate services to meet growing demand. Here are just a few of these challenges.

- Years of flat funding, rising operating costs, and, more recently, significant budget reductions have resulted in waiting lists, particularly for transportation, respite care, home-delivered meals, homemaker services, and homecare.

Services Provided Under the Older Americans Act

- Access services: information and assistance, care management and coordination, and transportation.
- In-home supportive services: homemaker assistance, emergency response systems, friendly visiting, minor home repairs, telephone reassurance, and nonmedical home health care and homemaker services.
- Senior center programs: social, physical, educational, recreational, and cultural programs, with a growing emphasis on health promotion and wellness.
- Nutrition programs: meals at senior centers or nutrition sites; in-home meals (Meals on Wheels).
- Caregiver supports: assessment, respite care, and counseling and support groups.
- Legal assistance advocacy: for individuals and on behalf of programs and legislation.

Meals on Wheels: More than Food

The Meals on Wheels program has delivered food to older adults and persons with disabilities since 1954. Sometimes the social contact can be as or more vital than the actual food. When volunteers deliver meals to 90-year-old Ann, they also remove rotting food from her refrigerator, check that the gas stove burners are turned off, and make sure that Ann's daughter has dropped by to visit. Harriet, who is age 85 and blind, says that she cannot pay the voluntary stipend that the agency now requests because she also has an $800 pharmacy bill that has yet to be paid. When a volunteer looks into this, she discovers that the pharmacist forgot to submit the paperwork for Medicare reimbursement. At a battered gray-shingle house, the volunteers leave meals on the front porch because 72-year-old Henry hates anything to do with the government and goes berserk if they enter his home. However, they call on their cell phone and watch from their car when he picks up the meals to make sure he is still functioning. Older adults such as Ann, Harriet, or Henry would lose both the food and the social contact without Meals on Wheels.

In part because of the recession, there are long waiting lists for Meals on Wheels in some parts of the country. Difficulties recruiting and retaining volunteers are one factor contributing to this in some locales. There is a shortage of drivers, partially due to rising fuel costs and the growing numbers of elders who need to work for pay instead of volunteering. Meals on Wheels programs typically give volunteers a modest payment and pay their mileage to deliver meals, but with reduced funding, such stipends are being cut. If you were director of a Meals on Wheels program and had a limited budget, how would you handle these budgetary challenges that reflect societal values about who should benefit?

- As a result, many AAAs supplement their federal funding by asking middle- and higher-income recipients to share the cost of services through sliding fee schedules and fees for services, such as making a donation for home-delivered meals. Others are developing business partnerships.
- Although its original goal was universal service based on age, AAAs also need to target outreach and services to low-income elders, elders of color, LGBT older persons, those in rural settings, and frail older adults at risk of nursing home placement.
- Coordination across disparate services is essential along with research to prove that such care management is cost-effective, especially during care transitions from one setting to another.
- There are no strong Congressional advocates for the Aging Network. And the most recent reauthorization of the OAA took 10 years! Legislation for reauthorization in 2011 and 2012 got lost in the short-term measures taken to prevent a government shutdown and avoid the fiscal cliff.

One way to ensure that services such as Meals on Wheels can meet growing demand is to charge for them, such as asking for a voluntary weekly contribution from those who can afford it. But this challenges the OAA's basic premise of universal entitlement based on age. It may hurt low-income elders who are embarrassed if they cannot contribute and may stop accessing the service. On the other hand, providing meals or home care to everyone who requests them raises questions of fairness when higher-income elders can afford to purchase such supports. Advocates of aging services are concerned that the OAA will become a two-tiered system, one for the poor and another for the well-to-do (Putnam, 2008).

A reason that the question of payment for services is difficult to answer is that the AoA is increasingly a primary provider of many long-term services and supports targeted to frail, homebound elders. As you learned in Chapter 11, these services aim to keep older adults out of nursing homes. But the Aging Network is doing so without the benefit of a comprehensive national long-term care policy or adequate funding.

Another change is the development of **Aging and Disability Resource Centers (ADRCs)**, which are jointly funded by the AoA and **Centers for Medicare and Medicaid Services (CMS)**, the federal agency that administers the Medicare and Medicaid programs. ADRCs aim to streamline community-based services into a single coordinated system to provide easier access to information and services through one entry point—"no

points to ponder

What do you think about charging a fee for Aging Network services? And would you charge by different types of activities, such as a fee for exercise classes but not for congregate meals? If so, what is your rationale? Can you see any downsides to differential fees?

wrong door"—for both older adults and adults of any age with disabilities. Compared to traditional information and assistance, they give more decision-making power to these populations through guided support for participant-directed care by options counselors. Services and support can be provided by phone or a home visit. Under the new ACL, the goal is that ADRCs will be in every region of every state so that every family caregiver and older adult knows where to turn for resources (Kunkel and Lackmeyer 2010; Putnam, 2008).

Some services available through the Aging Network are shifting to meet baby boomers' needs. There is a greater emphasis on evidence-based health promotion, age-friendly communities, and lifelong learning opportunities. Service providers are also seeking to reach middle-age caregivers willing to pay for assistance with caring for older family members. Already, the OAA includes several provisions with an intergenerational impact, such as health promotion and wellness services and programs to promote interaction between school-aged children and older individuals. As you learned in Chapter 7, the National Family Caregiver Support Act, through the AoA, funds services to caregivers across the life course, including grandparents as caregivers of grandchildren. The number of cross-generational programs with the potential for other private sector sources of funding may grow in the future, given the ACL's focus on inclusive cross-age group policies and programs.

points to ponder

How would you describe the Aging Network to a visitor from another country? What are the gaps or limitations that you might identify? How would you explain the recent shift to the Administration for Community Living?

Medicare and Medicaid

We turn next to the two major insurance systems for older adults' health: Medicare, a universal health insurance policy based on age that funds primarily acute care, and Medicaid, based on economic need, which has become the primary funder of long-term services and supports. You probably are hearing or reading a lot about both of these programs in the media but may not always understand the difference in the eligibility criteria of the two programs.

Medicare

To underscore the importance of Medicare to older adults' well-being, we first note the rising costs of health care. Indeed, the media, policy-makers, and the public are all concerned about a "crisis" in health care and often view Medicare as part of the cause of escalating health care expenditures. Contrary to what you may hear in the media, older adults are not the primary cause of these costs. Instead, the increasing use of technology and sophisticated, complex, and expensive medical treatments are major factors. These tend to be used in addition to rather than replacements for old technologies or procedures. For example, a patient now may receive X-rays, CAT scans, and MRIs to diagnose a problem, whereas only X-rays might have been used in the past. And Americans pay for more expensive procedures and tests than people in other countries (Rosenthal, 2013).

Societal values of individual and private sector responsibility also underlie these costs. These values guide a free market approach to health care that has been determined largely by the method of payment by private insurance companies and by a focus on treating illness rather than preventing it. People have been largely free to choose health care providers. In turn, physicians have been able to charge whatever they choose, as long as insurance companies approved, compared to many other countries that deliver health care on a fee-for-service basis or single payer. These and other factors have created the most costly health care system in the world—and one in which a Long Island resident might be billed about $6,000 for a colonoscopy while someone in North Carolina might be charged over $19,000. Whether we pay directly or through insurance, Americans pay more for almost every interaction with the medical system than any other country (Kaiser Family Foundation, 2012a; Rosenthal, 2013).

Medicare, or Title XVIII of the Social Security Act of 1965, is, like Social Security, a social insurance system based on age available to all adults age 65 and older. Similarly, beneficiaries earn access by virtue of paying payroll taxes throughout their years of employment.

Medicare is intended to provide financial protection against the costs of acute or short-term care by hospitals and physicians. Prior to its passage, only about 50 percent of older adults had health insurance. Now, almost all elders are covered by Medicare. In 1972, the program was expanded to include younger persons with permanent disabilities. Medicare in 2012 paid for about 22 percent of all health care expenditures for over 44 million people, 16 percent of whom were younger than age 65 and disabled. Indeed, Medicare currently provides coverage to about one out of every seven people! When the last of the boomers reaches age 65 in 20 years, more than 80 million people will be covered by Medicare. These costs are of concern since Medicare accounts for about 14 percent of the federal budget and over 20 percent of total national spending. Indeed, Medicare was one of the top issues in the 2012 presidential election (Kaiser Family Foundation, 2012a; Medicare Board of Trustees, 2012; Meyer, 2010; Multack, 2012).

Older adults and their families are often surprised to learn what Medicare covers or—more importantly—does not include. The box on this page shows its four primary components.

You may know someone on Medicare who is shocked to receive bills from their physician or hospital, having assumed Medicare would cover all costs. They are discovering that Medicare pays only 80 percent of the allowable charges, not the actual amount charged by health providers. A patient must pay the difference between "allowable" and "actual" charges, unless the physician accepts "assignment" and agrees to charge only what Medicare pays, as illustrated by the vignette about Mr. Connor on p. 374.

To address some of these gaps in Medicare funding, about 24 percent of beneficiaries purchase private supplemental Medigap insurance. These typically cover catastrophic costs of intensive care, numerous tests, extended hospitalization, and dental care, eye exams, and hearing aids. But they still do not cover what older adults often most want—home care, skilled nursing home care, and physician charges exceeding the amount approved by Medicare. As a result, paying a high monthly amount for supplemental insurance does not mean that the average out-of-pocket spending on health care has substantially declined (Kaiser Family Foundation, 2012a; Multack, 2012).

Despite Medicare's goal of financial protection, it covers only about 47 percent of older adults' health care expenses. The cumulative effect of gaps in coverage, increasing monthly premiums, annual deductibles, and levels of co-payments (the percent of costs beneficiaries must bear when they visit the doctor or pick up a prescription)

Summary of Medicare Parts

Hospital Insurance (Part A)

- Covers 99 percent of the older population
- Financed through a payroll tax of 1.45 percent
- Pays up to 90 days of hospital care and a restricted amount of skilled nursing care following at least a three-day inpatient hospital stay, rehabilitation, home health services (if skilled care is needed), and hospice care
- Inpatient psychiatric care for up to 190 days during a beneficiary's lifetime

Supplemental Medical Insurance (Part B)

- Covers 97 percent of the older population
- Financed through a combination of monthly premiums paid for by the older beneficiary and general tax revenues
- Has an annual deductible
- Covers physician services, one-time physical exam for new beneficiaries, and yearly wellness visit
- Outpatient hospital services and medical equipment
- Outpatient mental health services
- Outpatient occupational, physical, and speech therapy
- Preventive services such as mammogram and diabetes screening, flu shots
- Home health care is limited to certain types of health conditions and specific time periods

Part C (Medicare Advantage)

- Includes Parts A and B and requires an additional monthly payment to enroll in a private health plan, such as a health maintenance organization
- Provides more generous benefits than Medicare's traditional fee-for-service plans: preventive checkups, vaccines, eyeglasses, hearing aids, and prescription drug coverage
- Generally recruits healthier and wealthier older adults and does not accept those with multiple chronic illnesses or disabilities

Part D, private insurance for medications, under the Medicare Modernization, Improvement and Prescription Drug Act

- In 2012, Medicare enrollees paid a monthly premium and were responsible for the first $320 of drug costs each year.
- After that, Part D covered 75 percent of drug costs up to the first approximately $2,930 in purchases. Coverage then stopped (this is referred to as the **donut hole**) until the beneficiary had spent $4,700 out of pocket. After a person had spent that amount, then 95 percent of their drug costs were covered until the benefits started again the following year (Multack, 2012).

Medicare Pays Only Partial Health Care Costs

Mr. Connor went to his physician for a colonoscopy, a procedure to examine the large colon for polyps or cancer. Let's say that his physician charges $1,300 for his part of this procedure. Medicare determined that the typical fee for a colonoscopy in Mr. Connor's community is $1,000, which means that Medicare pays the physician 80 percent of that amount, or $800. If Mr. Connor's physician accepts the assignment, then Mr. Connor owes his doctor the difference between $1,000 and $800, or $200. Fortunately, Mr. Connor has private Medigap insurance that covers this difference. If Mr. Connor's physician had not accepted the assignment, then Mr. Connor would have been responsible for paying $1,300 less the amount paid by Medicare, or a total of $500. Of course you earlier learned how this routine one-hour procedure can cost up to $19,000 in some states!

means that the health expenses account for about 16 percent of household budgets of Medicare beneficiaries. Figure 13.5 shows how these extra health care costs are typically covered by older adults and their families (Kaiser Family Foundation, 2012a; Medicare Payment Advisory Commission, 2012; Multack, 2012).

As with all age groups, wide disparities in health care insurance coverage exist among older adults. For example:

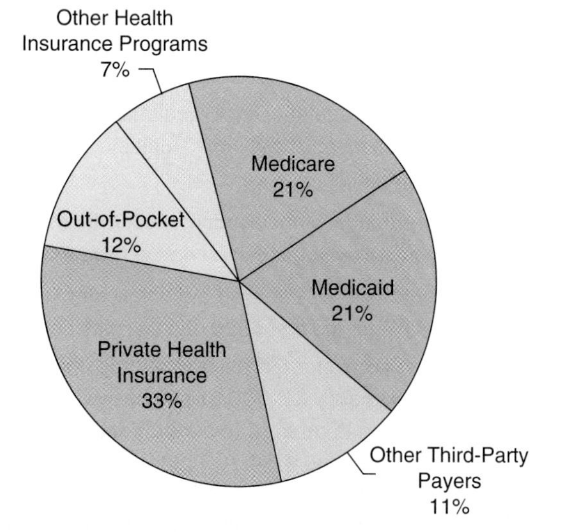

FIGURE 13.5 Sources of Spending on Personal Health Care in 2010

Source: Kaiser Family Foundation, 2012a.

- Approximately 12 percent of Medicare's recipients who are near-poor do not have assistance from Medicaid or supplemental coverage to help pay for Medicare's co-pays, deductibles, and non-covered services.
- Low-income women and persons of color and/or those who are in very poor health are least likely to have access to supplemental insurance through their jobs and most likely to have high out-of-pocket expenditures.
- The proportion of income spent on health care increases as income decreases.
- Older adults in rural areas often have difficulties finding physicians willing to take more Medicare patients.
- Some elders on tight budgets may try to save money by not going to the doctor and delaying preventive care, but this can result in higher health costs when they finally seek care (Kaiser Family Foundation, 2012a; Meyer, 2010; Morgan, 2010).

Another fundamental limitation is that Medicare covers acute or short-term care, typically within a hospital setting, but does not reimburse for long-term services and supports for older persons with chronic illness—which is what most people prefer for care. When Medicare was passed in 1965, medicine had limited ability to keep persons with chronic illnesses and disabilities alive, and medications to do so rarely existed. Medicare's focus on acute care was appropriate for that historical and demographic context. But advances in medicine in the past 50 years mean that the management of chronic diseases—diabetes, dementia, and heart disease—is older adults' primary health care need, and drugs a primary form of treatment, as you learned in Chapter 3. For example, older adults who suffer cardiac arrest will have their hospital costs covered by Medicare, but those living with chronic heart disease face barriers to accessing publicly funded in-home care and only under restricted

points to **ponder**

Talk to some of the older adults you know about their experiences with Medicare. Had they assumed that Medicare would cover all their health care when they turned 65? What surprises if any did they encounter when they got their first bill from their physician after moving onto Medicare? How have they managed to pay for the balance that Medicare did not cover?

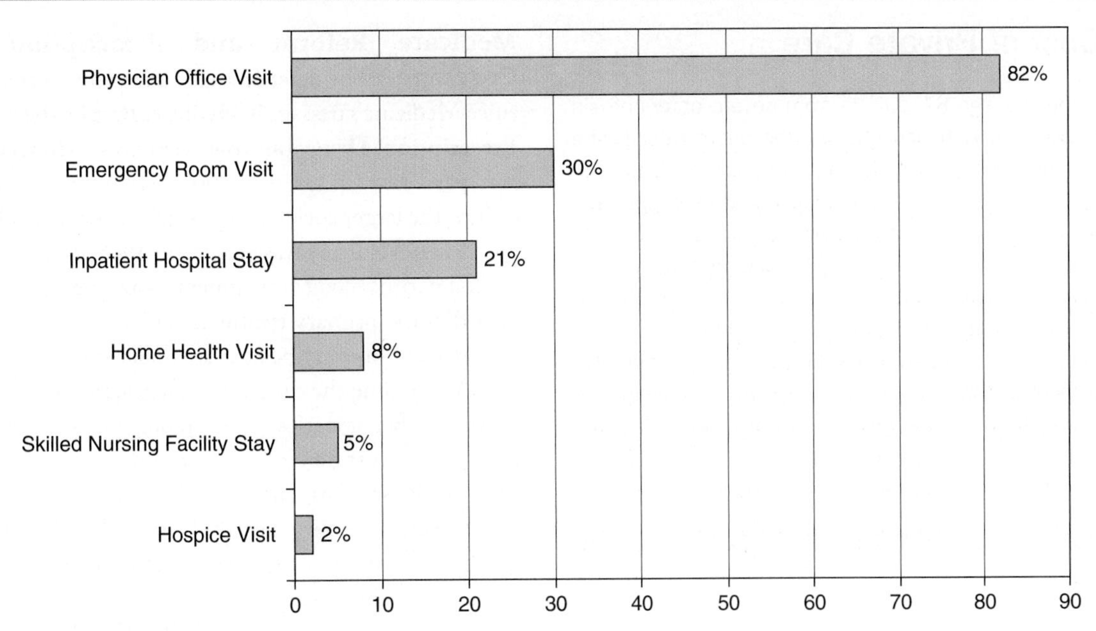

FIGURE 13.6 Medicare Beneficiaries' Utilization of Selected Medical and Long-Term Care Services

Source: Kaiser Family Foundation, 2013.

conditions—even though this is what they probably most need. In addition, Medicare funding for prevention, including annual physicals, has been relatively limited, although that is changing under the ACA that now covers annual wellness exams. Figure 13.6 shows how heavily slanted Medicare is to acute care in a physician's office, hospital, or emergency room.

Many older adults and their families also mistakenly believe that Medicare covers nursing home costs. But Medicare's coverage is limited to only 100 days of skilled care or rehabilitation services, typically for an acute illness or injury after hospitalization. This automatically excludes ongoing care for chronic conditions or disabilities. Indeed, Medicare covers the expenses of only about 6 percent of elders in skilled nursing homes. Unfortunately, some older adults become aware of the limited protection offered by Medicare only after they are discharged from a hospital to home or admitted to a skilled nursing facility (Jacobson, Neuman, & Damico, 2010).

Medicare-Funded Home Health Care Another limitation is that only about 4 percent of health care expenditures covered by Medicare are for home health care. This is a huge gap, since the majority of older adults prefer to remain in a home care setting, which is generally a lower-cost alternative to skilled nursing home placement. Additionally, older people typically require home care after hospitalization, or after a temporary placement in a rehabilitation unit or skilled nursing facility, and they recover faster at home when there is continuity of care. Over time, Medicare has partially responded to this need and can now fund home health care for a limited number of visits and fixed length of time by accredited provider agencies. But they will do so only under specific restricted conditions, as described in the following box (Kaiser Family Foundation, 2012a).

Eligibility for Medicare-Reimbursed Home Care and Home Care Aides

- Person must be homebound.
- Person must be capable of improvement/recovery within a reasonable and generally predictable time period.
- Person must require short-term intermittent nursing care, physical, occupational, or speech therapy, not long-term care.
- All services and medical equipment must be prescribed by a physician, who certifies that skilled services are medically necessary (Centers for Medicare & Medicaid Services, 2012).

The Cost of Private Care

Mrs. Roberts, age 87, suffers from severe osteoporosis and arthritis. Although she worries about falling, she wants to stay in her home as long as possible. Since she is not eligible for any publicly funded home care program, she must pay out of pocket for daily assistance with bathing, walking, and cooking. Her daughter is employed and has young children to care for, but tries to stay with her mother on weekends and assist her with household chores. Because the cost of personal assistance at home is so much greater than her income, Mrs. Roberts' savings are dwindling. She and her daughter worry that she will have to rely on Medicaid and have very little choice of nursing homes that will accept Medicaid patients after her savings have been depleted.

The criterion that many older adults are unable to meet is "being capable of improvement." As a result, Medicare home care is often not available to those who live with chronic illness for years, but with little likelihood of documented "recovery." Additionally, personal assistance funded by Medicare must be directly related to the medical treatment of an illness or injury. This means that Medicare home care does not fully address personal assistance with activities of daily living, which is typically needed by persons with chronic illness and disability. You will learn later in this chapter how Medicaid covers more home health care, but only for low-income elders.

Given elders' preference to obtain health care at home, it is not surprising that the number of people using home care and the average number of visits per user are increasing. As a result, home care is now the most rapidly growing Medicare benefit. In general, home health care is less expensive than hospital and skilled nursing care and comparable in cost to care provided by adult family homes. However, costs may equal skilled nursing home care if a person needs 24-hour care from a private agency.

For older adults who can pay privately, the number of for-profit home health companies that provide 24-hour daily care for an indefinite period, specialty services, and homemaker/home health aide care has grown. Even so, costs may become prohibitive when private agencies require families to pay for a minimum number of hours of care each day, even though the older person may not need all those hours. It is important to assess each elder's specific care needs to make sure that home care services as an alternative to skilled nursing care are affordable.

Medicare Reform and Prescription Drug Coverage The most dramatic and controversial change since Medicare's passage is **Medicare Part D, the Medicare Prescription Drug Improvement and Modernization Act**, passed by Congress in 2003. Here is another example of how the larger societal context affects what a policy covers. When Medicare was enacted in 1965, drugs were not a central part of medical treatment. Now, prescription drugs are often the primary treatment and account for a significant percent of every health care dollar spent.

At the time the drug reform legislation was proposed, Medicare beneficiaries spent more, on average, out of pocket each year on costly prescriptions than on physician care, vision services, and medical supplies combined. Of even greater concern, nearly 40 percent of beneficiaries had no prescription drug coverage at some point each year. As a result, they skipped filling prescriptions, split drug amounts (e.g., broke pills in half), eliminated doses, or relied on physician samples. These cost-cutting behaviors can result in adverse medication reactions for elders and, over time, increase health care costs.

Such costs and lack of coverage fueled the Congressional debate regarding the best way to solve the

Weaving Your Safety Net Now

There is a saying, "Hope for the best; prepare for the worst." No one knows for sure what the financial condition of the country will be 10, 20, or 30 years down the road, just as many people were taken by surprise when the U.S. economy began to decline in 2008. Public policies attempt to help us avoid problems in the future. For example, Social Security and Medicare provide a safety net for older adults so that they can avoid poverty and lack of health care. However, it seems increasingly clear that public policies alone will not be adequate to ensure quality of life and dignity for older Americans of the future. What can you do to start weaving a safety net now so that you can enjoy a comfortable (however you define that) lifestyle for yourself in your sixties, seventies, and beyond—assuming government support alone will be inadequate? Specifically, how can you integrate personal responsibility and public support for an optimum aging experience? (Think about things such as making lifestyle choices that provide the best potential outcomes for good health; planning for retirement early in your adult life; and making social connections that will serve you long into the future.)

problem, especially whether drug benefits should be age based (i.e., universal) or need-based (i.e., means tested). Another central issue was whether a vast array of private health care plans could deliver better care at lower cost than the traditional Medicare program. Our societal values of individual responsibility and competition to lower costs prevailed. The resulting drug benefit is provided entirely by private plans, making this the first time that beneficiaries must sign up with a private insurer to receive a portion of their Medicare benefits. This means that the nature of the benefit varies, depending on the private insurance chosen. And not surprisingly, some of the plans with the best benefits are too costly for low- and middle-income older adults.

Another major change is that for the first time in Medicare's history, higher-income beneficiaries (with annual incomes of more than $85,000) must now pay higher premiums for both Part D and Part B, which covers doctors' care. Applying means-testing to higher-income elders reflects a shift from Medicare's universal or age-based nature, although one could argue that it is a fair approach.

Overall, Part D has helped reduce out-of-pocket spending drugs of most Medicare enrollees. And the ACA includes some changes that improve drug coverage for low-income elders as well as greater access to important classes of drugs for all older adults (Kaiser Family Foundation, 2012b; Medicare Payment Advisory Commission, 2012).

The Future of Medicare Even with Medicare, older individuals and their families continue to pay more out of pocket for health care than do younger Americans. Indeed, they spend more in actual dollars, adjusted for inflation, now than they did before Medicare was established in 1965. Moreover, low-income elders spend even more of their income for health care compared to the total older adult population, and these percentages continue to rise each year (Meyer, 2010; Morgan, 2010).

At the same time that older adults are paying more, Medicare spending as the percent of the gross domestic product (GDP) is projected to double by 2030, just to provide the same level of services for a growing Medicare population. Even though policy-makers appear to be more concerned about Social Security, the threats to the Medicare Trust Fund are more immediate. By 2026, the system will only be taking in enough funds from payroll taxes to pay about 87 percent of hospital insurance costs (Rosenthal, 2013).

One reason for this more immediate fiscal challenge is that people over age 65 receive about three times more in Medicare benefits to cover their medical costs than what they paid in taxes as workers. Similar to Social Security, the number of workers paying taxes relative to the number of beneficiaries is declining. But to reiterate, the primary cause of Medicare's fiscal problems are the rising costs of health care and inefficiencies in health systems. The ACA includes several regulations to increase efficiencies, which we will discuss below. As of this writing, the ACA is actually slowing down health care spending and extending the solvency of Medicare—a fact that is overlooked by opponents of Obamacare (Alonso-Zaldivar & Fram, 2013; Moon, 2012).

Not surprisingly, political parties differ on the nature and size of cuts to Medicare. Fiscal conservatives advocate increased competition and privatization, such as individual health care accounts as a way to lower costs. But there is little evidence that expanded competition would reduce Medicare costs, as long as the overall cost of health care keeps rising.

As is true with Social Security, the majority of Americans agree that the federal government has a basic responsibility to guarantee adequate health care for older people and oppose significant cost cutting. Relatively modest strategies could reduce Medicare costs and ensure its long-term solvency: increase the age of eligibility; raise monthly premiums, coinsurance, and deductibles for high-income beneficiaries; or boost the combined payroll tax for Medicare and Social Security.

As you listen to debates about altering Medicare, remember that it has been effective in achieving its original goal of improving access to acute medical care for older adults. Like Social Security, Medicare is a success

Reflection Break

Let's say you just read an article about Medicare and Social Security on an online news site. At the end of the article, you decide to browse through the readers' comments in response to the article. One person wrote: "Why should old people get all their health care paid for by the government?" Another person wrote: "Social Security and Medicare are responsible for our skyrocketing federal budget deficit!" And still another person wrote: "Old people are rich. They are not entitled to these handouts." You know these comments are misguided and decide you should respond with a well-reasoned, thoughtful comment that corrects these misconceptions. What would you write?

story—but only partially since it covers less than half of beneficiaries' total annual health care costs, compared to most industrialized countries with universal health care. It is also noteworthy that Medicare is administratively far more efficient at controlling overall costs than private sector insurance plans (Morgan, 2010).

We last turn to Medicaid, which is the primary funder of long-term services and supports for low-income older adults. You learned that Medicare's acute care focus means that it does not address the needs of older adults with chronic illness or disability who require long-term supports either in their homes or as residential care. In the acute care setting, costs are determined by the number and intensity of services and the desired outcome is cure, while in long-term care settings, cost is determined by the length of care and the desired outcome is quality of life, despite living with chronic illness or disability.

Medicaid

The gap between acute care and the need for long-term support is partially addressed by **Medicaid**—a federal and state means-tested program of medical assistance for the poor, regardless of age.

When you hear the word long-term care, most people think of nursing homes. But **long-term services and supports (LTSS)** are much more than that. They encompass a range of types of personal assistance to individuals of all ages who are living with chronic illness or disability. They address not only medical needs but also social, financial, and cognitive well-being. LTSS, whether skilled nursing care or home health care, chore services or personal assistance in the home, typically aim to minimize, rehabilitate, or compensate for the loss of functional ability, so that a person can live as independently as possible and with the highest possible quality of life (Alkema, 2013).

Our focus here is on LTSS for older adults; approximately 70 percent of Americans who reach age 65 will need LTSS (both community-based and in nursing homes) for an average of three years. But adults and children with developmental and physical disabilities, traumatic brain injury, mental illness, and HIV/AIDS also require such long-term assistance with activities of daily living. Indeed, about 40 percent of people utilizing community-based LTSS are younger than age 65. Regardless of age, most Americans are not prepared financially or emotionally for the high likelihood of needing LTSS at some point in their lives (Alkema, 2013).

LTSS Challenges

- Financing, given Americans' limited financial preparation and ability to pay for the high costs of services, which can wipe out life savings
- Inadequate care coordination, which negatively affects both quality and costs of care
- Primary emphasis on institutional care, creating a lack of balance between community-based and residential options
- Recruitment and retention of direct care staff
- Uneven quality of care in some long-term care facilities

As you learned in Chapter 7, the majority of LTSS (over 60 percent) is provided by informal caregivers, particularly families. But family caregivers cannot do it all. For those who qualify, Medicaid has become the primary funder of formal LTSS. But Medicaid is only for the poor or those who become poor by using up their savings and other assets, often to pay for long-term or medical care for themselves or a partner. It is tragic that our policies mean that many people are forced into poverty in order to get LTSS. And those with income just slightly above the income eligibility level but without the resources to pay for private care are often out of luck in accessing LTSS (Redfoot & Fox-Grage, 2013).

Recall our earlier discussion of eligibility criteria and how they may reflect societal values. Medicaid is a means-tested program; eligibility is determined by strict income and asset requirements, regardless of age, in order to demonstrate the functional need for services.

Reflecting societal views of the poor as "underserving," there is a lot of complex paperwork to prove citizenship and that one's income and assets have been depleted in order to qualify for Medicaid coverage. In part because this application process is complicated and often experienced as demeaning and stigmatizing, many low-income older adults, who might be eligible, do not receive Medicaid.

For those who apply and meet the strict income requirements, Medicaid does offer LTSS benefits not possible through Medicare. Figure 13.7 on p. 379 illustrates how Medicaid is the primary funder of LTSS.

- It pays for in-home personal care, rehabilitation, and both intermediate and skilled levels of nursing home care.
- It is the primary public source of funding for both skilled nursing facilities and long-term home and community-based services.

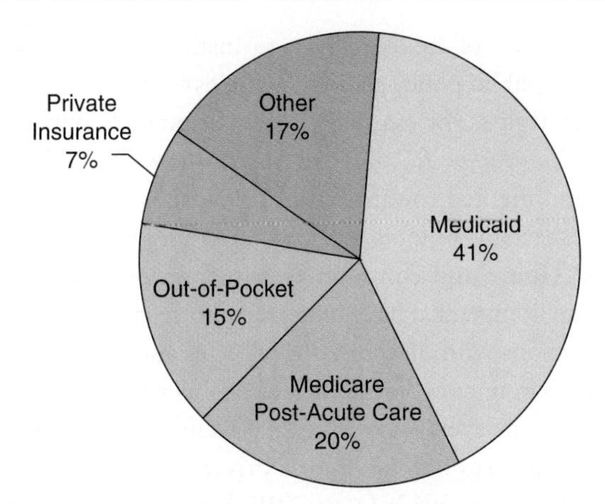

FIGURE 13.7 Medicaid as the Primary Funder of Long-Term Care

Source: Kaiser Family Foundation, 2013.

- It makes Medicare affordable for low-income beneficiaries by paying premiums, co-payments, and deductibles. This group is referred to as the **dual eligibles**, because they qualify for both Medicare and Medicaid. They are the poorest and sickest elders, have significant functional and cognitive limitations, and are the fastest-growing and highest users of health care services, particularly emergency room care, and nursing home care among beneficiaries. Because of their poor health status, their Medicare costs are 1.5 times higher than those of other beneficiaries. Additionally, although about 15 percent of Medicaid enrollees, they represent almost 40 percent of Medicaid funding. Women, African Americans, and Latinas—along with persons with disabilities under the age of 65—form the majority of the dual-eligible population. The ACA aims to more effectively integrate acute and long-term care and Medicare/Medicaid funding streams for dual eligible, which is a new resource for states struggling to finance LTSS (Grabowski, 2012; Jacobson et al., 2011; Kaiser Family Foundation, 2011a, 2013; Jacobson et al., 2011; Walls, Fox-Grage, Scully & Hall, 2013).

Medicaid has significant limitations, however. Reimbursement rates are far below prevailing fees—even lower than Medicare rates. As a result, some physicians refuse to take Medicaid patients, especially those with multiple complex conditions, or limit them to a small proportion of their patients. Federal funds are administered by each state, which results in considerable variation in the quality and types of services provided, particularly "optional" services such as dental services, eyeglasses, and physical therapy, and in reimbursement rates. Indeed, some states are even opting out of expanded federal funding for Medicaid under the ACA. As with Medicare, growth in Medicaid expenditures is due largely to price increases by health providers. For most states, Medicaid is the second largest budget item. Accordingly, in the current economy, Medicaid is often the first program to be cut by states. Indeed, without any substantive policy changes that will finance more LTSS for growing numbers of low income elders and persons with disabilities, Medicaid has the potential to "collapse" even before Medicare becomes insolvent (Alkema, 2013; Engquist & Johnson, 2010).

Another major limitation is its bias toward institutional care, even though care at home is typically less expensive. Ironically, Medicaid was never intended to be a major payer of nursing home care. When passed in 1965, it was viewed primarily as medical insurance for the younger poor. Yet Medicaid accounts for about 60 percent of the nation's long-term care expenditures, with more than 50 percent of this spending for institutional care (Alkema, 2013; CMS, 2011; Miller, 2012).

Medicaid-Funded Skilled Nursing Home Care Older adults who depend on Medicaid for skilled nursing home care often encounter a number of inequities. In order to control costs, most states have lower reimbursement rates for Medicaid residents. As a result, Medicaid recipients, especially those requiring high levels of care and who are typically older women and elders of color, often have more difficulty finding a nursing home bed—and wait longer to do so—than

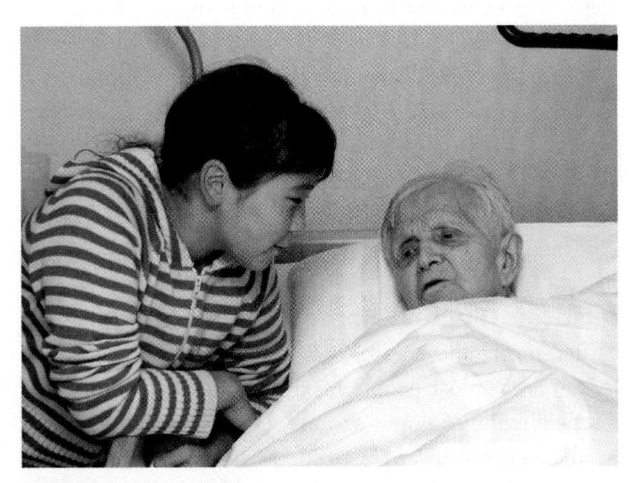

Medicaid pays for skilled nursing home care for those who qualify based on income, but at lower levels of reimbursement.

points to ponder

Older adults qualify for Medicaid-funded nursing home care if they spend down or deplete their income and assets. Among those who pay out of pocket at the time of admission to a skilled nursing home, well over 60 percent spend down their savings and have Medicaid as their only source of payment within a relatively short time period, because of the high cost of nursing home care (Redfoot & Fox-Grage, 2013).

What is your position on Medicaid "**spend down**"? Do you think that it unjustly impoverishes older people and their families? Do you think that those with assets should be able to hire lawyers to find ways to protect them and still be able to qualify for Medicaid to cover the cost of nursing home care? Reflect on family members or others you know who have had to spend down all their assets to access nursing home care. What were some of their experiences and how did they feel about becoming Medicaid-eligible in this way?

higher-paying private-pay clients. Or they may have access only to lower-quality facilities. Moreover, some nursing homes do not even accept Medicaid patients and discharge those whose private funding runs out. In fact, a relationship exists between low socioeconomic status and poorer quality of nursing home care. Paradoxically, although many skilled nursing facilities need Medicaid residents to survive financially, they often reduce services, especially staffing, and hours of direct care to maintain a profit. With the growth of the oldest-old, who are most likely to use skilled nursing homes but lack the resources to pay for it, Medicaid is faced with how to provide coverage for low-income and vulnerable populations at a time of intense pressure to limit public spending (Engquist & Johnson, 2010; Grogan & Andrews, 2010; Redfoot & Fox-Grage, 2013).

Medicaid-Funded Home Health Care As noted earlier, most older adults with chronic illness or disability—indeed, most people regardless of age—would prefer to remain at home as long as possible. Fortunately, Medicaid's bias toward institutional care is shifting toward home- and community-based services, including personal care, and away from skilled nursing homes, even though the majority of funds still go to institutional care. This shift in public policy toward home care is driven largely by civil rights. For example, a 1999 Supreme Court decision, *Olmstead vs. LC*, and the Americans with Disabilities Act are oriented toward returning persons with disabilities, especially younger persons, to community care settings. **Home and community-based services (HCBSs)** that are nonmedical have increased choices for both elders and persons with disabilities of all ages and are often less costly than nursing home care; as of this writing, personal care at home averages over $21,000 annually compared to an annual cost of $84,000 for a private room in a nursing home (Alkema, 2013; Doty, 2010; Harrington, Ng, Kaye, & Newcomer, 2009; Marek, Adams, Stetzer, Popejoy, & Rantz, 2010; Miller, 2012).

The **Medicaid Waiver Program** is intended to prevent or delay nursing home placement and keep low-income elders at home. It is a primary reason for the growth in Medicaid funding for HCBS, as shown in Figure 13.8 on p. 381. It allows Medicaid statutory requirements to be waived so that states can offer nonmedical HCBSs by targeting benefits to specific groups and number of beneficiaries in limited geographic areas. Care management, homemaker, personal care by a home health aide, and adult day care are examples of such services. However, states have stringent income eligibility criteria for receiving Medicaid-funded home care services. As noted earlier, those who are pre-Medicaid, just above the income eligibility level, must often become poor to get such services. Moreover, a person must be so ill that they would otherwise be in a skilled nursing facility and must require more care than homemaker services. Another constraint is that home care must not cost more than skilled nursing home care. As a result, only about 33 percent of Medicaid spending for LTSS currently goes toward HCBS, and younger persons with developmental disabilities are the primary recipients. The ACA offers incentives to states to fund more HCBSs, but this amount is still limited compared to mandated funding for institutional care (Harrington, Ng, LaPlante, & Kaye, 2012; Miller, 2012).

Because of these strict eligibility requirements for the Medicaid Waiver Program, states have had to limit services and number of recipients, which has resulted in long waiting lists for HCBS. And older adults who have too many assets to qualify for Medicaid but cannot afford private home care services typically lack access to these home care alternatives. Moreover, federal and state cuts in Medicaid

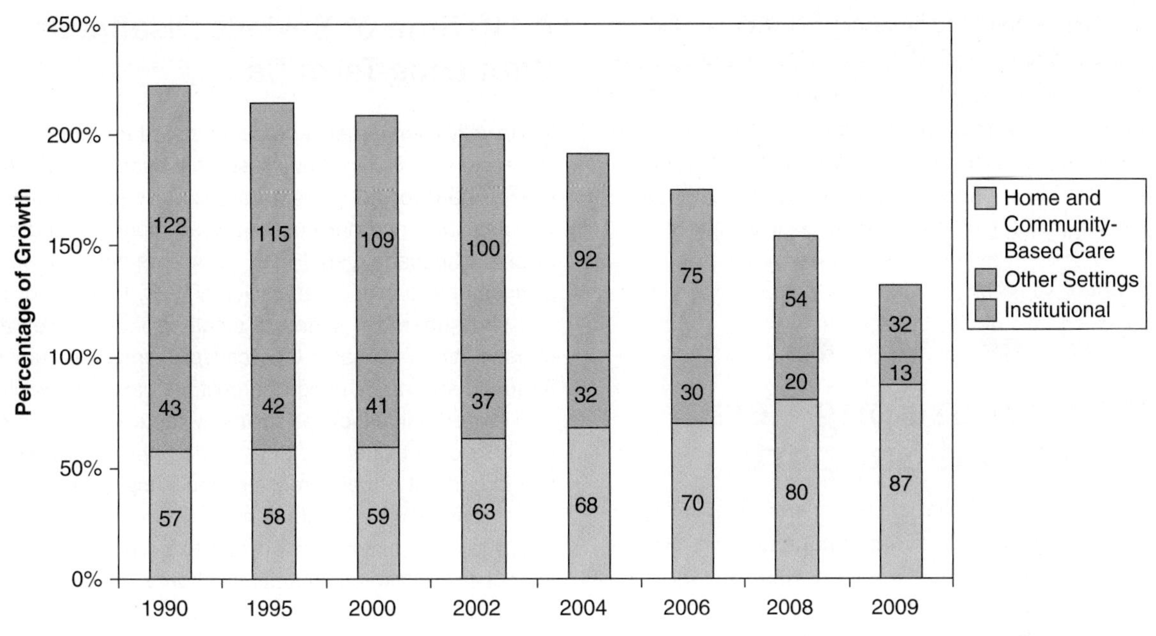

FIGURE 13.8 Growth in Medicaid Funding for Home and Community-Based Care

Source: Kaiser Commission on Medicaid and the Uninsured, 2011.

threaten the progress made by the use of Medicaid HCBS (Ng & Harrington, 2011).

Consumer-directed care is another Medicaid waiver program that supports decision-making choice for frail elders and adults of any age with disabilities. This approach reflects values of person-centered and participant-directed care rather than a traditional model in which the decision-making and managing authority rests with a professional. **Person-centered care** means that the individual is at the center of the planning process and the plan reflects what is most important to the person and their capacities, strengths and supports they require. **Participant-directed care** posits that consumers are experts about their service needs and have the right and ability to determine how to meet them, including "managing their own risk" and taking actions that professionals might disagree with. Consumers take on all worker management tasks, sometimes with assistance from family or a representative, including choosing their personal care attendant, with two exceptions: They do not receive a cash allowance to pay the worker directly and they cannot pay their spouse or partner. As another example reflecting our societal values about family care, it is assumed that a spouse or partner should provide care out of love and not receive any compensation (Doty, Mahoney, & Sciegaj, 2010; Simon-Rusinowitz, Loughlin, Ruben, Garcia & Mahoney, 2010).

Cash and counseling programs, a specific type of consumer- or participant-directed care with fewer restrictions, give consumers a monthly cash allowance, which they can use to hire, supervise, and fire their own caregivers. This can include paying family members. Because consumers control their own budget, they can decide whether to make their home wheelchair accessible, buy a pair of dentures, or hire a grandson to mow their lawn. Counselors are available to assist them with decision-making and states provide bookkeeping help, but the consumer retains control of the final decision. Being able to purchase services that fit their needs and to hire their

A home care visit by a nurse can allow elders to live at home and receive nursing care.

own caregivers is found to be associated with satisfaction and quality of life for both the care recipient and caregivers. This and other models of consumer-directed care are becoming more common in ACL programs, the Veterans Administration, and the ADRCs (Robert Wood Johnson Foundation, 2013; Simon-Rusinowitz, et al., 2010; Simon-Rusinowitz, Loughlin, Ruben, & Mahoney, 2010).

Directions in Long-Term Services and Supports

You have now learned that there are no adequate public funding mechanisms for a comprehensive system of long-term services and supports that provide different levels of care as adults' needs shift with age. Instead, adults of all ages with disabilities must rely on a patchwork of services increasingly subject to budget cuts. While public spending on LTSS is expected to increase by more than 2.5 times from 2000 to 2040, long-term care costs as part of older adults' overall personal health expenditures are growing from less than 4 percent in 1960 to over 12 percent today. This is not surprising, since only about 30 percent of older adults have enough assets to pay for 1 year of skilled nursing home care care. Indeed, most people have only about $50,000 saved for long-term care needs, yet about 22 percent of such costs are paid for out of pocket. And even people with the financial resources to pay for LTSS out of pocket still encounter problems with the lack of integration of acute and chronic care services. In short, the financial burdens of health and long-term care are expanding faster than the older population's capability to pay or government's willingness to fund. Continuing to develop innovative ways to deliver LTSS in the community will help but not solve the larger problem of how to finance long-term care. In 2013, an appointed Federal Commission on Long-Term Care had less than 100 days to recommend how best to deliver and finance LTSS. They came up with two very different approaches: private options for financial protection or a Social Insurance. Neither option is likely in the near future, given bipartisan divisions in Congress around public/private responsibility for health and long-term care (Alkema, 2013; Center for Medicare and Medicaid Services, 2012; Commission on Long-Term Care, 2013; Kaiser Family Foundation, 2012a).

A Lifetime of Savings Disappears With Long-Term Care

Virtually every American is unprepared for long-term care expenses. Helen thought she did everything right. She worked hard for 40 years as a secretary for churches and libraries. She and her husband lived modestly and saved. After her husband died, Helen felt secure because she had savings of well over a half-million dollars. In her early eighties, she suffered a series of small strokes as well as an unusual brain disease that caused temporary amnesia. Although she rarely needed a doctor's care and would live with her chronic illnesses for many more years, she could not take care of herself. She needed assistance with getting in and out of bed, dressing, and fixing her meals. After paying privately for personal care, it is not surprising that Helen ran out of money and had to go on Medicaid. She spent her last months in a nursing home, impoverished and sharing a small room with a stranger.

Long-Term Care Insurance

Private **long-term care (LTC) insurance** plans aim to address such gaps in home and skilled nursing care funding, but do not cover all LTSS costs. For example, they typically pay for only a fixed amount for each qualified day in a skilled nursing home and reimburse home health and adult day care services at lower percentages than the actual costs. Even though the majority of adults will need LTSS at some point in their lives, less than 10 percent have purchased LTC insurance. There are numerous reasons for this discrepancy (Ujvari, 2012).

Foremost, such insurance is very expensive. Even when people can afford it, they may be excluded because of preexisting conditions, including depression, or face higher rates due to their age or existing health or memory problems. Others may be overwhelmed by the complexity of options or the length of the process to be approved for insurance. Additionally, there is natural human tendency not to plan ahead for end-of-life issues or for illness. Not surprisingly, those who have purchased long-term care insurance tend to be among the young-old, with higher education and income, and in relatively good health. Given all these factors, private LTC insurance is likely to remain a relatively small market for the near future, and baby boomers who had once anticipated buying it may be less likely to do so because of losing funds during the

points to ponder

Talk to an older relative or friend about long-term care insurance. Do they have it? Have they thought about getting it or do they think they will never need it? If they don't have it, what are their reasons? If a person chooses not to buy long-term care insurance, what other ways can she or he prepare, financially and otherwise, for the possibility of very high health care–related costs later in life?

recession and not being able to afford the high premiums (Alkema, 2013; Curry, Robison, Shugrue, Keenan, & Kapp, 2009; Ujvari, 2012).

Policies to Promote Innovative Health and Long-Term Care Services

Remember how we began this chapter discussing how policies become implemented as regulations and programs that directly impact our lives. Having focused on so many limitations of health and LTSS policies and programs, we want to close with some promising innovations for care funded by Medicare and Medicaid, as well as how older adults are benefiting from the ACA.

You have learned that a major limitation of Medicare- and Medicaid-funded services is that acute and chronic care are not coordinated. But some models have worked for years to integrate these sectors together into a single system of social care. **On Lok**, begun in the 1970s, is the first such model. Meaning "peaceful happy abode" in Cantonese, it was initially implemented in San Francisco's Chinatown. By combining acute and chronic care into one agency, On Lok aims to prevent nursing home placement of frail elders certified as needing skilled care. A comprehensive day health program is coordinated with home care, meals, transportation, personal care, and respite care. A major strength of On Lok is its effectiveness at serving low-income older adults and elders of color, including immigrants, in their communities. It is replicated to varying degrees nationwide, often through the **Program of All-Inclusive Care for the Elderly (PACE)**.

Similar to On Lok, PACE focuses on reducing costs by coordinating primary and LTC within an adult day health model for frail adults eligible for nursing home placement. In addition to "one-door access" to a comprehensive care package of preventive, acute, and LTSS, adults may keep their own doctor. PACE must provide basic Medicare and Medicaid services but programs have flexibility to use less typical supports, including activities such as fishing trips and drama groups as preventive services. It also tries to address root causes of health care problems. For example, a Medicare beneficiary may show up frequently at an emergency room to be treated for skin infections due to flea bites. Rather than just treat the bites, the PACE team may fumigate her home and provide a flea dip for her dog. Interdisciplinary teams of physicians, nurses, social workers, aides, therapists, and even van drivers are central to coordinating care management at predetermined reimbursement rates. Both On Lok and PACE have decreased inpatient hospital admissions and hospital and nursing home days (and thus costs), and enhanced quality of life, satisfaction with care, functional status, and ability to live longer in the community. Unfortunately, these models are costly to implement and limited in number (Hansen, 2008; Hirth, Baskins, & Dever-Bumba, 2009).

Transitional care innovations funded by Medicare aim to address the lack of funded services when an older patient, often with multiple chronic illnesses, moves between different levels of care and across care settings and providers—from hospital discharge to skilled nursing to rehab and then home. Such transitions are typically unplanned; they often result from unanticipated medical problems, occur on nights or weekends, involve health care providers who may not know the older patient, and happen so quickly that support systems cannot adequately respond. Elders and their families may experience fragmented services, conflicting medical advice, care delays, medication errors, and inadequate follow-up, often ending up back in a hospital emergency room. Lack of continuity of care can be intensified by cultural differences, health literacy issues, and the lack of a single point person to ensure continuity of care. When transitions are not managed well, high rehospitalization rates and increasing costs often result. Transitional care models all point to the centrality of clear communication among patients, caregivers, and an interdisciplinary team of health care providers (Care Transitions Program, 2013; Coleman & Berenson, 2004; Golden & Shier, 2012–2013; Naylor & Keating, 2008; Schoen et al., 2011).

Effective Models of Transitional Care

In Care Transitions Intervention, a "transition coach" (a nurse, social worker, or trained volunteer) follows patients across settings for the first 30 days after leaving the hospital. The coach assists them with managing their medications, keeping a personal health record, follow-up care, and designing a plan for seeking further care if particular symptoms ("red flag" indicators) arise. The follow-up care includes pain management and rehabilitation services, visiting nurse services, home visits, and being available seven days a week by phone. Outcomes include improved functioning and high satisfaction among older adults, reduced hospitalizations, and lower health care costs (Coleman & Berenson, 2004).

Under the **Community-Based Care Transitions Program** in the ACA, hospitals with high rates of readmission may apply for funds for transitional care coordination with community-based organizations to make transitions smoother and safer. Anticipated outcomes are reduced risk for rehospitalization, improved quality of care, and decreased Medicare costs (Center for Medicare and Medicaid Innovations (CMMI) 2012; Golden, 2011; Lind, 2010).

Benefits of Health Care Reform for Older Adults

Debates in Congress about the 2010 ACA, which have continued every year since its passage, also illustrate conflicting societal values: whether our market approach to health care is the problem, or the core of what we should preserve. Compared to younger Americans, older adults are fortunate to have health insurance through Medicare. Accordingly, the ACA places priority on health care coverage for younger populations that lack health insurance and/or have preexisting health problems and are now able to access insurance either through their employers or health care exchanges. But the ACA also includes benefits for older adults. Some older adults mobilized against health care reform, because of some politicians' misrepresentations about health care rationing (advanced care planning and end-of-life counseling) and reductions to Medicare. But the act does not require such counseling, and the only cuts to Medicare are to eliminate the federal subsidy per enrollee in Medicare Advantage; it will also require these insurance companies to spend more on patient care rather than profits or overhead. These changes will slow the growth of Medicare spending and strengthen the Trust Fund's solvency, ultimately benefiting all people who live long enough to use Medicare (Miller, 2012; Moon, 2012).

Most of the act's benefits for older adults are oriented to using incentives to reduce hospital admissions (and readmissions), emergency room visits, and admission to skilled nursing facilities. The ACA creates a framework for doing so through innovative programs that shift health care from an emphasis on acute disease-focused episodes to person-centered coordinated care and to reduce the fragmentation that currently characterizes our health care system. Coordination of care over time and across multiple settings is a defining feature of the ACA, with several innovative programs to do so. **Accountable Care Organizations (ACOs)** are organizations of health care providers that are accountable for the quality, cost and overall care of Medicare beneficiaries. Providers are encouraged to develop creative approaches to cost-effective quality care. As an incentive, ACOs that meet specified quality performance standards will be eligible to receive a percentage of savings if the per beneficiary expenses are sufficiently low.

The Center for Medicare and Medicaid Innovation allows the testing of new ways to reduce costs while improving the quality of health care. A new Medicare **Independence at Home** demonstration pays physicians and nurse practitioners to deliver primary care services in the home to older adults with high-cost multiple chronic illnesses. States may also choose to offer **patient-centered medical homes (PCMHs)** for persons with complex health care needs, where each enrollee has a personal physician, who, with an interdisciplinary care team, coordinates care beyond the physical boundaries of the doctor's office. This includes comprehensive needs assessment, individualized care planning, improved coordination of care, transitional care between different health systems, and referral to community and social support services. **Health homes** offer similar services but with expanded coverage for mental health and substance use services, health promotion, and patient and family support services. Skilled nursing facilities are required to provide more information to consumers and regulators, and a national demonstration project on culture change in nursing homes and use of technology is funded (AARP, 2011; Miller, 2012; Moon, 2012).

For the first time, Medicare covers in full an annual wellness visit to a primary care physician, as well as other preventive services such as immunizations and screenings for diseases such as cancer, along with a personalized prevention plan. The ACA also improves Part D prescription drug coverage by eliminating the coverage gap (the donut hole) by 2020. In the meantime, older adults who fall in the donut hole receive a 50 percent discount on their brand name drugs, helping to reduce their costs. It expands prescription drug coverage for low-income elders and access to generic drugs for all beneficiaries. The ACA also enacts the Elder Justice Act to help prevent elder abuse, neglect, and exploitation and will fund a pilot test project in dementia management and abuse prevention (AARP, 2011; Moon, 2012).

A number of promising options and financial incentives are available to states to provide HCBS so people can receive quality LTSS in their homes or communities. We cite only a few of them here. Community First Choice funds states that elect to provide person-centered home and community-based attendant services so individuals with disabilities can remain the community. And the State Balancing Incentive Payment Program offers incentives to states that undertake structural reforms to increase access to non-institutional LTSS. Money Follows the Person provides individuals with LTSS that enable them to move out of institutions and into their own homes or other community-based settings. Recognizing the direct care workers' central roles in health care and LTSS, the ACA expands their health insurance benefits, training and career path opportunities, and reimbursement. Thus, contrary to the public perception that health care reform is largely for younger Americans, there are significant provisions related to LTSS that can benefit older persons and individuals with disabilities (Katz & Frank, 2012; Medicaid.gov, 2013; Miller, 2012).

One significant component of the act—the Community Living Assistance Services and Supports (CLASS) Act—will not be implemented. We mention this here because it was our society's first groundbreaking attempt to address the lack of insurance protection for LTSS. Its underlying value was that the government has a responsibility to provide LTC financing that is affordable and includes choice. Bringing together both the aging and disability communities, it shifted long-term care funding from welfare based (Medicaid) to insurance based. Unfortunately, because it was voluntary, only those already needing expensive care were likely to sign up. Without sufficient personal financing or government funding, the program was determined to be fiscally unsound. As noted in a 2011 Congress Blog, in the absence of CLASS Act, Medicaid will continue to be our de facto long-term care public policy. State Medicaid programs that require near, if not actual, impoverishment are like having an insurance policy with a deductible that is all your wealth! As an improvement over the status quo, some states are exploring a mandatory state payroll tax to fund long-term care insurance, recognizing that any type of social insurance of long-term care is unlikely to come out of the federal government in the near future (Goldberg, 2011; Kadlec, 2011; Miller, 2012; Tumlinson, Hammelman, Stair & Weiner, 2013).

Seek Solutions to Healthy Aging, Despite Challenges!

October 1, 2013, was a day many people will never forget. It was marked by two historic events, each related to the other, and both highly relevant to health and long-term care: the opening of health insurance enrollment under the ACA, and the first federal government shutdown in almost 20 years.

Health benefits exchanges opened, albeit with many Web site problems, around the country, offering insurance enrollment options to millions of Americans who lack health insurance. The vast majority of eligible people will receive these new benefits free or with subsidies. But not everyone views this as good news. In large part because of Republican efforts to dismantle health care reform, the Federal government partially shut down, following Congress's failure to come to agreement on a spending bill. The government shutdown had real consequences for real people, on a large scale, including 800,000 government employees thrown out of work, over a million more working without pay, offices that provide important services closed, and programs on which poor people depend cut off. Moreover, this shutdown furthered public disenchantment with government and the policy-making process. As we close this chapter on social and health policy, we encourage you—no matter where you are working or will work in the future—to foster public faith in collective solutions that assure the conditions for all people to age in a healthy manner across the life course.

summary

This chapter began with a framework of factors that affect the development of policies and programs, particularly values about individual versus societal responsibility and how the demographic, economic, and political context shapes the types of policies passed and the nature of eligibility criteria. Since Social Security's passage in 1935 as the first age entitlement program, the question of age-based versus needs-based benefits has been widely debated. Public beliefs that older people are deserving underlay the enactment of the two other age entitlement programs of Medicare and the OAA in 1965, a time period in which programs for older adults expanded. Medicaid was also passed in 1965, but it is a needs-based program.

Since the 1970s, the debate over age-based versus needs-based programs has intensified, with some arguing that older people are benefiting at the expense of younger age groups. This is known as the intergenerational inequity perspective. Accordingly, the pattern of support for programs for older adults shifted dramatically in the 1980s and 1990s, when federal allocations for age-based programs diminished. Proposals for reducing age-based entitlement programs, privatizing Social Security and Medicare, and means testing of the Older Americans Act programs grew during this time period.

Within this framework of how support for age-based programs changes as the larger social, political, and historical context alters, we reviewed the major federal programs that assist primarily older persons—Social Security, Medicare, the Older Americans Act, and Medicaid. Social Security is an example of an "earned right" based on workers' contributions through a payroll tax paid across the lives. But it also has benefits for younger generations, such as children of deceased workers and younger adults with disabilities. Because of the declining number of younger workers per retiree, the future solvency of the Social Security Trust Fund is jeopardized. But solvency could be restored through relatively modest changes to the payroll tax or age of eligibility. Moreover, Social Security is not a cause of the escalating federal deficit. Significant inequities by race and gender within Social Security are unlikely to be addressed, however, given current pressures to reduce government spending.

The Administration on Aging (now the Administration for Community Living) is the prime funder of community-based social services for adults age 60 and older, such as senior centers, respite care and meals programs, and, increasingly, LTSS for people of all ages with disabilities. As budgets have been cut, the question of whether to charge a sliding scale fee for such Aging Network services has intensified.

Medicare is the primary funder of acute care for older adults by hospitals and physicians but does not cover the full cost of care. Older adults with adequate resources purchase supplemental insurance to cover some gaps. Its major limitation is its failure to provide adequate protection against the costs of home and community-based care for chronic disease and disability, which is what most elders prefer. Medicare-funded home care is a rapidly growing area, but it is restricted in the types and amount of care provided. The 2003 Medicare Modernization Act or prescription drug bill addresses the problem of rising prescription drug costs, but also represents a marked shift by privatizing part of a once universal government program. Escalating hospital and physician costs are primarily responsible for rising Medicare expenditures. As is true with Social Security, the funding challenges of Medicare could be addressed with incremental modifications.

Although Medicare is almost absent from nursing home financing, the reverse applies to Medicaid. The largest portion of the Medicaid dollar goes to LTSS needed by older persons but not covered by Medicare—skilled nursing facilities, home health, and personal care. It is means-tested, which means that adults of any age qualify based on low income. Medicaid has traditionally been biased toward nursing home care for adults who have depleted their assets and other sources of income. Medicaid waivers have allowed state funding of some innovative home and community-based services for elders who are nursing home eligible. However, Medicaid has been increasingly subject to cost-cutting measures at the state level. Given the gaps in public funding for LTSS, private insurers are offering long-term care insurance, but these plans are beyond most elders' financial reach and are often misunderstood.

Some effective innovations are available to Medicaid and, in some cases, Medicare beneficiaries, such as On Lok, PACE, and consumer-directed care (also often referred to as person-centered and participant-directed care), but these have reached a relatively small number of elders. The ACA includes several benefits for older adults, oriented largely to preventing hospitalization and to improved coordination of acute care but with some provisions for home and community-based services. Although public spending for older adults has increased in terms of total dollars, it has declined when measured as a percentage of the gross national product. More importantly, older adults and their families now spend more on health and long-term care than they did before the passage of Medicare and Medicaid.

Our society is faced with complex and difficult policy choices related to income security, the services of the Aging and Disability Network, and health and LTSS. Debates about the role of government versus the private sector and the extent of societal responsibility toward vulnerable low-income elders are complex, heated, and often divided along party lines. Complicating the policy-making process is the fact that the older population is not one political constituency but several, in which race, gender, class, functional ability, sexual orientation, and rural/urban residence may be greater unifiers than age. A political agenda must be drafted that can unite different older constituencies as well as diverse populations with common needs that are not based on age. The probability of a comprehensive policy approach that can bring together diverse actors of all ages in the near future is extremely low, however.

Nevertheless, gerontologists must advocate for income maintenance, social services, and health and LTSS that benefit individuals across the life course and into old age. Translating gerontological research findings for policymakers and the general public is inherent within effective advocacy. This means that gerontologists need to be visible at the local, state, and federal levels in presenting evidence-based testimony and offering comprehensive, creative, and cost-effective solutions.

key terms

Accountable Care Organizations (ACOs), p. 384
Administration for Community Living (ACL), p. 370
Administration on Aging (AoA), p. 369
age-based entitlement programs, p. 359
Aging and Disability Resource Centers (ADRCs), p. 371
Aging Network, p. 369
Area Agencies on Aging (AAAs), p. 370
cash and counseling programs, p. 381
Centers for Medicare and Medicaid Services (CMS), p. 371
Community-Based Care Transitions Program, p. 384
consumer-directed care, p. 381
contributory, p. 360
discretionary, p. 360
donut hole, p. 372
dual eligibles, p. 379
eligibility criteria, p. 359
graying of the federal budget, p. 363
health homes, p. 384
home and community-based services (HCBSs), p. 380
Independence at Home, p. 384
individual equity, p. 365
interdependence of generations framework, p. 362
intergenerational inequity perspective, p. 361
long-term care (LTC) insurance, p. 382
long-term services and supports (LTSS), p. 378
Medicaid, p. 378
Medicaid Waiver Program, p. 380
Medicare, p. 373
Medicare Advantage, p. 372
Medicare Part D, the Medicare Prescription Drug Improvement and Modernization Act, p. 376
need-based, p. 360
Older Americans Act (OAA), p. 369
On Lok, p. 383
participant-directed care, p. 381
patient-centered medical homes (PCMHs), p. 384
Patient Protection and Affordable Care Act (ACA), p. 360
person-centered care, p. 381
privatization, p. 367
Program of All-Inclusive Care for the Elderly (PACE), p. 383
selective benefits, p. 360
social adequacy, p. 365
social policy, p. 358
spend down, p. 380
transitional care, p. 383
universal and categorical benefits, p. 359

review questions

1. What are the primary values that have influenced the development of policies and programs to serve older adults over the past 75 years?
2. How would you define entitlement programs?
3. Describe the difference between age-based and needs-based policies and programs.
4. During what time period did government programs for older adults grow most rapidly in our country?

5. What is the primary argument made by those who state there is increasing intergenerational inequity? How do those who support the perspective of intergenerational interdependence respond?
6. Based on your reading in this chapter, what is the likelihood, in your opinion, of the future solvency of Social Security?
7. Describe why women and persons of color benefit proportionately more from Social Security than other groups. Despite these benefits of Social Security, what are some of the inequities within Social Security, particularly for women?
8. List three types of services provided through the Aging Network.
9. Most Americans are concerned about the "crisis in health care." Are older adults responsible for the rising costs of health care? Why or why not?
10. What are the primary differences between the services covered and the populations served by Medicare and Medicaid? Which is the primary funder of long-term services and supports?
11. What does the Medicaid Waiver Program fund?
12. What is the major limitation of Medicare in terms of meeting the needs of older adults with chronic illness or disability?
13. Describe what is meant by models of transitional care. What are the benefits of this approach to care for older adults and their families?
14. In addition to cost, what are the other reasons that so few older adults purchase long-term care insurance?
15. What is a primary shared characteristic of consumer-directed care and cash and counseling programs?
16. List three ways that older adults are benefiting from the Affordable Care Act.

media resources

- U.S. Baby Boomer
- Social Security Payments to Beneficiaries

references

AARP. (2010a). $4 trillion package of spending cuts and new taxes proposed. *AARP Bulletin*. Retrieved December 14, 2010, from http://www.aarp.org/politics-society/government-elections/info-12-2010/deficit_commission_spending_cuts_and_new_taxes.html.

AARP. (2010b). *Social Security 75th anniversary survey report: Public opinion trends*. Washington, DC: AARP.

AARP. (2011a). *AARP to members of Congress: Don't cut Medicare, Social Security benefits*. Retrieved October 30, 2011, from http://www.aarp.org.

AARP. (2011b). *Health care reform: What's in effect, what's still to come*? Retrieved November 6, 2011, from http://aarp.org/health_law_benefits_2011.print.html.

Administration on Aging (AoA). (2013). *Older Americans Act and the Aging Network*. Retrieved September 30, 2013, from http://www.aoa.gov/AoARoot/AoA_Programs/OAA/Aging_Network/Index.aspx.

Alkema, G. (2013). *Current issues and potential solutions for addressing America's long-term care financing crisis*. Long Beach, CA: The SCAN Foundation.

Alonso-Zaldivar, R., & Fram, A., (2013). *A respite for Medicare; Social Security now worse*. Associated Press, Retrieved September 28, 2013, from http://news.yahoo.com/respite-medicare-social-security-no-worse-202356321.html.

Board of Trustees. (2012). *The 2012 annual report of the Board of Trustees of the federal Old-Age and Survivors Insurance and federal Disability Insurance Trust Funds*. Washington, DC: U.S. Government Printing Office.

Caldera, S. (2012a). *Social Security: A key retirement resource for women*. Washington, DC: AARP Public Policy Institute.

Caldera, S. (2012b). *Social Security: Who's counting on it*? Washington, DC: AARP Public Policy Institute.

Campbell, A. L., & King, R. (2010). Social Security: Political resilience in the face of conservative strides. In R. B. Hudson (Ed.), *The new politics of old age policy* (pp. 233–253). Baltimore, MD: John Hopkins University Press.

Care Transitions Program. *The Care Transitions Program: Health care services for improving quality and safety during care handoffs*. Retrieved September 29, 2013, from http://www.caretransitions.org/.

Center for Economic and Policy Research. (2012). *Who's above the Social Security payroll tax cap*? Retrieved December 28, 2012, from www.cepr.net/indexphp/publications/reports.

Center on Budget and Policy Priorities. (2013). *Policy basics: Where do your federal tax dollars go*? Washington, DC: Center on Budget and Policy Priorities. Retrieved October 1, 2013, from http://www.chpp.org.

Centers for Medicare & Medicaid Innovation (CMMI). (2012). *Community-Based Care Transitions Program*. Retrieved from http://www.innovations.cms.gov/initiatives/Partnership-for-Patients/CCTP/index.html?itemID=CMS1239313.

Centers for Medicare & Medicaid Services. (2012). *Medicare and home health care.* Washington, DC: U.S. Department of Health and Human Services.

Coleman, E. A., & Berenson, R. (2004). Lost in transition: Challenges and opportunities for improving the quality of transitional care. *Annals of Internal Medicine, 141*, 533–536.

Commission on Long-term Care. (2013, September 12). *Summary of Recommendations.* Retrieved October 1, 2013, from http://www.ltccommission.senate.gov/.

Curry, L. A., Robison, J. Shugrue, N., Keenan, P., & Kapp, M. B. (2009). Individual decision-making in the non-purchase of long-term care insurance. *The Gerontologist, 49*, 560–569.

Davidson, J. (2011). *Potential Social Security Administration budget cut paints bleak picture for aging population.* Retrieved October 30, 2011, from http://www.washingtonpost.com/politics/potential-social-security-administration-budget-cuts-paint-bleak-picture-for-aging-population/2011/10/03/gIQAZtbGJL_story.html.

Doty, P. (2010). The evolving balance of formal and informal, institutional and non-institutional long-term care for older Americans: A thirty-year perspective. *Public Policy & Aging Report, 20*(1), 3–9.

Doty, P., Mahoney, K. J., & Sciegaj, M. (2010). New state strategies to meet long-term care needs. *Health Affairs, 29*(1), 49–56.

Engquist, G. & Johnson, C., (2010). *Medicaid-funded long-term care: Toward more home and community-based options.* Hamilton, NJ: Center for Health Care Strategies.

Entmacher, J. (2010). Strengthening Social Security: A better benefit for widows. *Public Policy & Aging Research Brief.* National Academy on an Aging Society, 4–8.

Estes, C., O'Neill, T., & Hartmann, H. (2012). *Breaking the Social Security glass ceiling: A proposal to modernize women's benefits.* Washington, DC: National Committee to Preserve Social Security and Medicare Foundation.

Goldberg, L. (2011). It's time to start over on long-term care. *The Hill's Congress Blog*, October 21. Retrieved from http://thehill.com/blogs/congress-blog/healthcare/189145-its-time-to-start-over-on-long-term-care.

Golden, R. (2011). Coordination, integration and collaboration. A clear path for social work in health care reform. *Social Work, 36*, 227–228.

Golden, R., & Shier, G. (2012–2013). What does "care transitions" really mean? *Generations, 36*, 6–12.

Grabowski, D. (2012). Care coordination for dually eligible Medicare–Medicaid beneficiaries under the Affordable Care Act. *Journal of Aging & Social Policy, 24*, 221–232.

Gregory, J. M., Bethell, T. N., Reno, V. P., & Veghte, B. W. (2010). Strengthening Social Security for the long-run: *Social Security Brief, 35*, 1–16. National Academy of Social Insurance.

Grogan, C. M., & Andrews, C. H. (2010). The politics of aging within Medicaid. In R. H. Hudson (Ed.), *The new politics of old age policy*, pp. 275–307. Baltimore, MD: Johns Hopkins University Press.

Hansen, J. C. (2008). Community and in-home models. *Journal of Social Work Education, 44*, 83–88.

Harrington, C., Ng, T., LaPlante, M., & Kaye, S. (2012). Medicaid home and community-based services: Impact of the Affordable Care Act. *Journal of Aging & Social Policy, 24*, 169–187.

Harrington, C., Ng, T., Kaye, H. S., & Newcomer, R. J. (2009). Medicaid home and community-based services: Proposed policies to improve access, costs and quality. *Public Policy & Aging Report, 19*, 13–18.

Hirth, V., Baskins, J., & Dever-Bumba, M (2009). Program of All-Inclusive Care (PACE). Past, present and future. *Journal of the American Medical Directors Association, 10*, 155–160.

Hudson, R. H. (2008). Public policy and the boomers: An expanding scope of conflict. In R. Hudson (Ed.), *Boomer Bust?* vol. I (pp. 113–135). New York: Praeger Perspectives.

Hudson, R. H. (2010). Contemporary challenges to aging policy. *The new politics of old age policy* (2nd ed., pp. 3–20). Baltimore, MD: Johns Hopkins University Press.

Jacobson, G., Neuman, T., & Damico, A. (2010). *Medicare spending and the use of medical services for beneficiaries in nursing homes and other long-term care facilities: A potential for achieving Medicare savings and improving quality of care.* Washington, DC: The Kaiser Family Foundation.

Jacobson, G., Neuman, T., Domico, A., & Lyons, B. (2011). *The role of Medicare for the people dually eligible for Medicare and Medicaid.* Washington, DC: The Kaiser Family Foundation.

Kadlec, D. (2011). *The tragic bungling of a "Class" act.* Retrieved December 2011, from http:/moneyland.time.com/2011/.

Kail, B. L., Quadagno, B., & Keene, J. R. (2009). The political economy perspective of aging. In V. L. Bengtson, D. Gans, N. M. Putney, & M. Silverstein (Eds.), *Handbook of Theories of Aging* (pp. 555–572). New York: Springer.

Kaiser Family Foundation. (2011a). *Dual eligibles: Medicaid's role for low income Medicare beneficiaries.* Washington, DC: Henry J. Kaiser Family Foundation. Retrieved from http://www.kff.org/medicaid/upload/4091-08.pdf.

Kaiser Family Foundation. (2012a). *Medicare at a glance.* Retrieved December 28, 2012, from http://www.kff.org/medicare/upload/1066-15.pdf.

Kaiser Family Foundation. (2012b). *The Medicare prescription drug benefit.* Retrieved December 28, 2012, from http://www.kff.org/medicare/upload/7044-13.pdf.

Kaiser Family Foundation. (2013). *Medicaid's role in meeting the long-term care needs of America's seniors.* Washington, DC: Henry J. Kaiser Family Foundation. Retrieved September 28, 2013, from http://kff.org/medicaid/issue-brief/medicaids-role-in-meeting-the-long-term-care-needs-of-americas-seniors/.

Katz, R., & Frank, R. (2010–2011). A vision for the future: New care delivery models can play a vital role in building tomorrow's eldercare workforce. *Generations, 34*, 82–89.

Kunkel, S. R., & Lackmeyer, A. E. (2010). The role of the Aging Services Network in balancing and transforming the long-term care system. *Public Policy & Aging Report, 20*(1), 16–21.

Lind, K. D. (2010). *Health reform initiatives to improve care coordination and transitional care for chronic conditions.* Washington, DC: AARP Public Policy Institute.

MacArthur Foundation Research Network on an Aging Society. (2009). *Facts and fictions about an aging America.* Retrieved September 30, 2013, from http://www.macfound.org/media/files/aging-contexts-factfiction.pdf.

Marek, K. D., Adams, S. J., Stetzer, F., Popejoy, L., & Rantz, M. (2010). The relationship of community-based nurse care coordination to costs in the Medicare and Medicaid programs. *Research in Nursing and Health, 33,* 235–242.

Medicaid.gov. (2013). *Community-based long-term services and supports.* Retrieved September 29, 2013, from http://www.cms.gov.

Medicare Payment Advisory Commission. (2012). *A data book: Health care spending and the Medicare program.* Washington, DC: Medicare Payment Advisory Commission.

Meyer, M. H. (2010). Shifting risk and responsibility: The state and inequality in old age. In R. B. Hudson (Ed.), *The new politics of old age policy,* pp. 21–41 (2nd ed.). Baltimore, MD: Johns Hopkins University Press.

Miller, E. (2012). The Affordable Care Act and long-term care: Comprehensive reform or just tinkering around the edges? *Journal of Aging & Social Policy, 24,* 101–117.

Moon, M. (2012). Medicare and the Affordable Care Act. *Journal of Aging & Social Policy, 24,* 233–247.

Morgan, K. J. (2010). Medicare: Deservingness encounters cost containment. In R. B. Hudson (Ed.), *The new politics of old age policy,* pp. 254–274 (2nd ed.). Baltimore, MD: Johns Hopkins University Press.

Multack, M. (2012). *The Medicare Program: A brief overview.* Washington, DC: AARP Public Policy Institute.

Myles, J. (2010). What justice requires: Normative foundations for U.S. pension reform. In R. B. Hudson (Ed). *The new politics of old age policy,* pp. 64–86. Baltimore, MD: Johns Hopkins University Press.

National Academy of Social Insurance. (2012a). *Options to balance Social Security's finances.* Retrieved December 28, 2012, from http://www.nasi.org/learn/socialsecurity/balance-options.

National Academy of Social Insurance. (2012b). *Public opinions on Social Security.* Retrieved December 28, 2012, from http://www.nasi.org/learn/social-security/public-opinions-social-security pp. 64-86.

Naylor, M., & Keating, S. A. (2008). Transitional care. *Journal of Social Work Education, 44*(Supplement), 65–74.

Ng, T., & Harrington, C. (2011). *Medicaid home- and community-based service programs: Data update.* Washington, DC: Kaiser Family Foundation. Retrieved from www.kff.org/medicaid/upload/7720-04.pdf.

Putnam, M. (2008). Long-term care policy as an investment in baby boomers and future generations. In R. Hudson, *Boomer Bust?* (pp. 227–240). New York: Praeger Perspectives.

Putnam, M. (2012). Can aging with disability find a home in gerontological social work? *Journal of Gerontological Social Work, 55,* 91–94.

Redfoot, D., & Fox-Grade, W. (2013). *Medicaid: A program of last resort for people who need long-term services and supports.* Washington, DC: AARP Public Policy Institute.

Rix, S. (2010). Strengthening Social Security: What about the caregivers? *Public Policy & Aging Research Brief, 8.*

Robert Wood Johnson Foundation. (2013). *Cash & counseling. Program report, Grant ID# CAS.* Retrieved from www.rwjf.org/content/dam/farm/reports/program_results_reports/2013/rwjf406468.

Rosenthal, E. (2013, June 1). The $2.7 trillion medical bill. *The New York Times.* Retrieved September 28, 2013, from http://www.nytimes.com/2013/06/02/health/colonoscopies-explain-why-us-leads-the-world-in-health-expenditures.html?pagewanted=all&_r=0.

Schoen, C., Osborn, R., Squires, D., Doty, M. M., Pierson, R., & Applebaum, S. (2011). New 2011 survey of patients with complex care needs in eleven countries finds that care is often poorly coordinated. *Health Affairs, 30*(12), 2437–2448.

Schulz, J. H., & Binstock, R. H. (2006). *Aging nation: The economics and politics of growing older in America.* New York: Praeger.

Shelton, A. (2013a). *Social Security: A key retirement resource for women.* Washington, DC: AARP Public Policy Institute.

Shelton, A. (2013b). *Social Security: Who's counting on it?* Washington, DC: AARP Public Policy Institute.

Sherman, A., Greenstein, R., & Ruffing, K. (2012). *Contrary to "entitlement society" rhetoric, over nine tenths of entitlement benefits go to elderly, disabled, or working households.* Washington, DC: Center on Budget and Policy Priorities. Retrieved December 28, 2012, from www.cbpp/org/cms.

Simon-Rusinowitz, L., Loughlin, D. M., Ruben, K., Garcia, G. M., & Mahoney, K. (2010). The benefits of consumer-directed services for elders and their caregivers in the cash and counseling demonstration and evaluation. *Public Policy & Aging and Report, 20*(1), 27–31.

Simon-Rusinowitz, L., Loughlin, D., Ruben, K., & Mahoney, K. (2010). What does research tell us about a policy option to hire relatives as caregivers? *Public Policy & Aging Report, 20*(1), 32–37.

Smith, A. E. (2010). *U.S. attitudes toward Social Security.* Washington, DC: National Committee to Preserve Social Security and Medicare Foundation.

Social Security Administration. (2013). *Fast facts 2013.* Washington, DC: Office of Retirement and Disability Policy, Social Security Administration.

Tumlinson, A., Hammelman, E., Stair, E., & Wiener, J. (2013). *Insuring Americans for long-term care: Challenges and limitations of voluntary insurance.* Long Beach, CA: The SCAN Foundation.

Ujvari, K. (2012). *Long-term care insurance. 2012 update.* Washington, DC: AARP Policy Institute.

Walker, A. (2009). Aging and social policy: Theorizing the social. In V. L. Bengtson, D. Gans, N. M. Putney, & M. Silverstein (Eds.), *Handbook of theories of aging* (2nd ed.). New York: Springer.

Walls, J., Fox-Grage, W., Scully, D., & Hall, J. M. (2013). *Two-thirds of states integrating Medicare and Medicaid services for dual eligibles.* Washington, DC: AARP Public Policy Institute.

Williamson, J. B., & Watts-Ray, D. M. (2008). Aging boomers, generational equity and the framing of the debate over Social Security. In R. B. Hudson (Ed.), *Boomer Bust* (Vol. I). Westport, CT: Praeger.

14 Careers in Aging

learning objectives

14.1 Articulate the wide-ranging and growing careers in aging.

14.2 Discuss ways to explore, research, and prepare for a career in aging.

14.3 Articulate how knowledge of aging can affect all interactions with older adults, including as customers and colleagues.

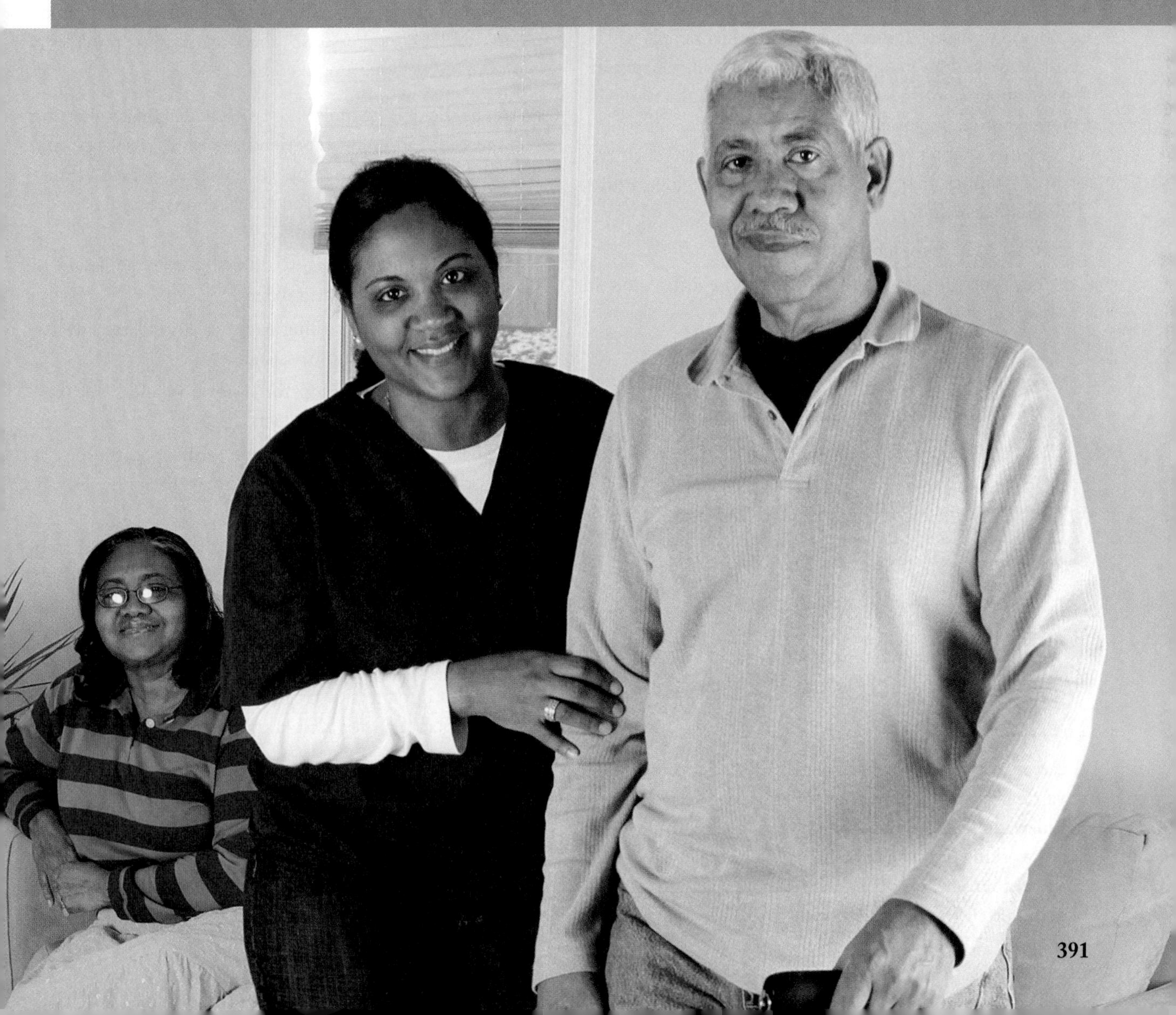

Listen to the **Chapter Audio**

By this point in the book, we hope you have learned why aging matters and are considering working with older adults in some capacity. Almost certainly, you will be working *alongside* older adults in just about any career that you choose. They will be among your colleagues, your supervisors, and possibly even your employees if you are in a management position. As you learned in previous chapters, many people are working beyond what was once considered to be conventional retirement age, because either they need the income and benefits, or they want to continue the work they enjoy or to pursue new career directions. With the growing number of older adults in our society, you will also encounter them as customers, clients, consultants, volunteers, neighbors, and associates. We hope this book has helped you better understand the issues, potential, and dimensions of older adulthood so that your interactions with older people will be constructive and meaningful. We also hope you are better informed about aging in a healthy manner throughout the life course—both for yourself and for those you love.

In this chapter, we consider the many different types of opportunities that involve working with older adults. This chapter includes:

- Reasons to consider a career in aging
- The kinds of jobs available for those interested in working with older adults
- Preparing for a career in aging
- Academic programs related to aging
- Internships and other training opportunities
- The value of a multidisciplinary perspective in your work
- Looking toward the future

Why Consider a Career in Aging?

A career in aging can be both personally and professionally rewarding for those who want to enhance the well-being of older adults and their families. One of the great aspects about working in the field of aging when you are a younger adult is that the positive changes you enact today will benefit you in the years ahead when you become an older adult. In other words, if you help create a better society for older people now, the dividends will pay off far down the road for you and your peers. Good citizens contribute to society in different ways, and working to build communities, services, and programs that support active aging as well as aging in place is a significant contribution that you can make at any stage of your life. You may also find that along the way you will acquire important life lessons from observing, working with, and listening to older adults, continuously learning why aging matters.

The **Association for Gerontology in Higher Education (AGHE)**, on its Web site, describes the field of aging as highly diverse, "offering many different employment opportunities." AGHE is a membership organization consisting of more than 280 colleges and universities that offer education, training, and research programs in the field of aging. In answer to the question "Why Study Aging and Older Persons?" the organization provides a series of answers, summarized here:

- The field is stimulating and challenging, reflecting people's different experiences, needs, resources, and abilities based on factors such as gender, race, ethnicity, immigrant status, functional ability, sexual orientation, and economic status.
- There is satisfaction in addressing the challenges of those who are growing older.
- Jobs can involve working with healthy elders as well as those who need more assistance.
- Opportunities abound for innovative ideas and creative programs and products.
- The field is multidisciplinary, with opportunities to work with professionals from other disciplines as well as family caregivers.
- People who work in the field of aging can positively influence agencies and organizations serving older persons, as well as the legislation and policies that affect elders' lives.
- Studying gerontology also provides a perspective and insight into one's own aging process and that of family members (AGHE, 2014a).

You already know that there are current and anticipated shortages of workers to fill many jobs related to aging, especially in rural areas. It is estimated that the United States will need an additional 3.5 million health care workers by 2030 just to maintain the current ratio of workers to the older population. The 2008 report *Retooling for an Aging*

Visit a Web Site, Join a Mailing List

If you go to the Association for Gerontology in Higher Education Web site (www.aghe.org) and click on the "Careers in Aging" link, you will be taken to a Web page that provides career development advice for those interested in working in aging, as well as free access to a database of job postings. Even if you are not ready to apply for a job in gerontology, it may be beneficial just to review the kinds of positions being posted across the country. You can also get information about the next "Careers in Aging Week" event and have the option of being added to a "Careers in Aging" mailing list. Your local gerontological organizations may have similar online services.

America: Building the Health Care Workforce, by the Institute of Medicine, was groundbreaking by documenting the need and pointing to educational and policy solutions to prepare the eldercare workforce. And the particular need for geriatric specialists is even greater than among health care providers generally. For example, because of the aging baby boom population, it is predicted that 36,000 new geriatricians (doctors with specialized training in geriatrics) will be needed by 2030, a number that cannot be met if current trends in medical student career choices are any indication. However, the American Geriatrics Society in its 2011 report *The Future of Geriatrics* acknowledges that producing such large numbers of new geriatricians is unrealistic. A more practical solution, however, may be to infuse geriatric competencies into the medical school curriculum to prepare primary care providers for working with older adults. In other words, rather than trying to recruit more medical students to specialize in geriatrics, the goal should be to get more medical schools to require geriatric education for all students who are training to become primary care physicians, because they treat the majority of older adults. Geriatricians could then focus on caring for frail older adults with complex needs as well as collaborate with primary care physicians who need consults for some of their older patients with chronic illnesses. Shortages among other health and social service providers—nurses, social workers, pharmacists, physical therapists, and psychologists—are also well documented, and these shortages are even greater when we look at how few providers are prepared to deliver geriatric mental health services. Recognizing the need for a qualified eldercare workforce, many health care professions are now developing geriatric competencies or knowledge, skills, and values for working effectively with older adults and their family caregivers. And increasing numbers of professional programs are working to infuse or embed aging in required curriculum so that all students graduate with a foundation of basic geriatric competencies (Bragg & Hansen, 2010–2011; Harahan, 2010–2011; Hooyman & Unutzer, 2010–2011; Institute of Medicine, 2008; Peterson, Bazemore, Bragg, Xierali, & Warshaw, 2011; Stone & Barbarotta, 2010–2011).

The anticipated shortage of geriatric or gerontological experts cuts across nearly all health specialties. Geriatric nurses, social workers, and pharmacists will be essential to quality care in community health clinics, home and community-based services, rehabilitation services, hospices, hospitals, and long-term care facilities. These systems and services also depend heavily on direct care workers such as nurse's aides and certified nursing assistants. Compensation and working conditions need to improve to attract and retain qualified people to work in these frontline eldercare positions.

The aging population is not the only reason that more jobs in the health care field are needed. The 2010 Patient Protection and Affordable Care Act (ACA as you learned in Chapter 13) aims to ensure that all Americans have

The need for health care providers with geriatric expertise is urgent and growing.

Compensating Geriatric Physicians

Although it is difficult to generalize across disciplines about compensation and work conditions for those working with older adults, various studies have identified financial compensation as one of the obstacles to recruiting people to gerontology. In the medical profession, for example, geriatric physicians typically earn less in annual pay than other medical specialists. One reason for this is because Medicare does not necessarily reimburse physicians for the length and intensity of care provided to older adults with multiple chronic illnesses compared to providers focused on acute care. Accordingly, geriatric physicians typically see fewer patients each day—and thus generate less revenue—than providers working with younger populations. Moreover, geriatric physicians require extra training beyond medical school. Given the additional time and financial investment, it is not surprising that geriatric medical fellowships are typically not full (American Geriatrics Society, 2011; Bragg & Hansen, 2010–2011).

access to affordable health insurance. As more people utilize health care services as a result of this law, there will be an increased need for primary care providers. Moreover, the health care context is rapidly changing to focus on preventing hospitalization and rehospitalization, managing chronic care (including self-management), and strengthening the coordination of care, particularly as older adults transition across acute and long-term care settings. All health care providers—nurses, social workers, pharmacists, and doctors, to name a few—will be expected to show that their interventions with older adults work—and save taxpayers' money. This is often referred to as cost effectiveness, accountable care, or evidence-based practice (e.g., providing the evidence that something works). The ACA also statutorily defined the direct care workforce as central to cost-effective care (Seavey, 2010–2011; Stone & Barbarotta, 2010–2011).

The bottom line is that an aging population combined with major changes in health care delivery will dramatically increase the need for people who are prepared with the knowledge and skills to work with elders. Fortunately, there are national organizations, such as the **Eldercare Workforce Alliance (EWA)**, that are actively working to influence federal legislation to expand the geriatric workforce. For example, this alliance of nearly 30 different professions has been advocating Congress for loan forgiveness for health care providers who work with older adults. This means that the amount owed on a student loan could be waived for graduates making a commitment to work with elders for a certain number of years. Although not yet successful, EWA continues to make loan forgiveness and other strategies to recruit and retain a strong eldercare workforce visible to federal and state policy-makers.

The examples we have just discussed involve working with older adults and their families in health care and long-term services and supports. But as you have seen in our discussion of active aging throughout this book, the majority of older adults are reasonably healthy and engaged in their communities. As our society prepares for the aging of the baby boomers, the number of jobs in community- and neighborhood-based settings, such as senior and community centers, to promote elders' health and civic engagement, will grow. In addition to clinical skills, the active aging workforce will require competencies in health promotion, community organizing and development, and policy advocacy to create age-friendly policies, services, programs, and communities.

Even if you are not sure exactly what you might want to do in the field of aging, just knowing that you want to work in some capacity with older adults is a good start. Remember that there are jobs in both the public and private sectors. Public sector jobs include working for a government agency or department, which could be at the national, state, or local level, such as the services delivered by the Area Agencies on Aging through the Aging and Disabilities Network. Private sector jobs encompass working for a business, large or small. Persons with gerontological training are also needed in academic research or teaching positions as well as nonprofit organizations and nongovernmental organizations. Or perhaps you are interested in policy-making. Many politicians at all levels of government come out of the helping professions or community organizing, including longtime U.S. Senator Barbara Mikulski, a social worker, and a handful of members in the U.S. House of Representatives.

Gerontologists also serve in staff positions in government in everything from program administration to legislative research to constituent relations. Champions of services for older adults are especially needed nowadays in Congress and state legislatures that are faced with tight budgets for health and human services. These advocates can help prepare and introduce key legislation to benefit older adults, such as the Positive Aging Act of 2013. The intent of the bill is to bolster mental health services to older adults through an amendment to the Public Health Service Act. Although proposed legislation such as this one must go through a number of stages and may never

Powerful U.S. Senator and Advocate for Aging

U.S. Senator Barbara Mikulski began her early career as a social worker in Baltimore, Maryland. She helped at-risk children and older adults, and she engaged in community activism to impact the social welfare of her community's citizens. Her life as an elected official began in 1971 when she ran for office as a city council member. Eventually she ran for national office and served as a member of the House of Representatives and the U.S. Senate. On March 17, 2012, she became the longest-serving woman in the history of the United States Congress. In Congress, she has been a strong supporter of the Older Americans Act, programs for family caregivers, and related legislation.

Senator Mikulski became chair of the powerful Senate Appropriations Committee soon after the death of 88-year-old U.S. Senator Daniel K. Inouye of Hawaii. The Appropriations Committee oversees spending of discretionary money by the U.S. government and, as such, is considered to be one of the most powerful committees in Congress. Barbara Mikulski, who was 76 years old at the time of her appointment, is the first female Senator in U.S. history to chair this committee and an example of women's growing influence in the U.S. Congress as well as of active aging. Both Senators Mikulski and Inouye have had public service careers spanning decades from middle age to older adulthood (Pershing, 2012; http://www.mikulski.senate.gov/about/biography.cfm).

be passed into law, it is important to have legislators and policy makers at all levels of government—federal, state, and city—who are knowledgeable about challenges facing older adults and drafting solution-focused legislation and policies to meet such needs (GovTrack.us, 2013).

Many roles must be filled in the eldercare workforce, each requiring different skill sets and levels of preparation. If you are thinking of going to medical school or getting a master's degree in social work or advanced training in physical therapy, pharmacy, or nursing, that's great. But you do not need to have an advanced degree to work with older adults. You can also enhance elders' quality of life with a bachelor's degree, an associate's degree, or even a high school education. Many direct care workers—people who have the most hands-on contact with care recipients and are critical to the quality of their lives—have a high school or community college degree. They generally have been trained as home care aides, personal care attendants, nursing assistants, and personal assistants to provide appropriate care in a safe environment to elders, although in some states, the amount of required training is inadequate. As noted on p. 393, the 2008 Institute of Medicine report on the eldercare workforce drew particular attention to the growing need for the preparation of more direct care workers. National organizations such as the Direct Care Alliance and PHI are striving to improve the training for direct care workers and other conditions in the work environment and have made advances toward that goal. They also advocate for career ladders, such as an advanced aide who would have greater care coordination and clinical responsibilities, for workers such as Maria who bring diverse skills to long-term care settings. Maria will use knowledge and skills garnered as a direct care worker to move into another job in health care but still work with older adults (PHI, 2012; Seavey, 2010–2011).

Career-Building Opportunities in the Direct Care Workplace

The Domingo family in Tucson, Arizona, filed a petition with the U.S. government to sponsor Maria, a family member living in another country, to permanently immigrate to the United States. The process was lengthy and involved a lot of paperwork and fees, but the Domingos were happy when Maria's visa was finally approved. Soon after Maria arrived in Tucson, she was interested in finding a job so that she could be self-supporting and save for her future. She was bilingual and liked working with people. She enrolled in a Certified Nursing Assistant training program and earned a certificate, which made her eligible to take the CNA exam overseen by the Arizona Board of Nursing. She was thrilled that she passed and was soon hired at a rehabilitation facility where a large number of residents shared Maria's cultural background. Her cultural and linguistic knowledge combined with her CNA training turned out to be an asset in working at this facility, but she also worked well with patients from a wide range of other backgrounds. Although her pay was low and the job could be exhausting, she saved a little each month in a "dream fund." Her dream was to become a physical therapist because of what she observed at the rehabilitation facility. Patients often were admitted directly from the hospital, and after weeks of hard work, they showed enough progress to either return home or move into a less restrictive living arrangement than a skilled nursing facility. Physical and occupational therapists played a key role in helping residents regain their abilities as best as possible. Maria sees herself being a part of that important rehabilitative journey.

The Wide Range of Jobs in Aging

Let's say you are considering working specifically with older adults as a career. What kinds of jobs are there in this field, in addition to the ones already mentioned? The range of options may surprise you. Every year during the month of April, AGHE and the Gerontological Society of America sponsor a **Careers in Aging Week** and encourage campuses throughout the country to help raise awareness of the wide-ranging career opportunities in aging. This event is localized to fit a particular academic community and the surrounding aging community. The box below summarizes the kinds of activities and resources you may find at such events.

Other organizations may host similar events, so we encourage you to attend their job and career fairs to see what kinds of opportunities in the field of aging await you. Even if your future job does not entail working with older adults a majority of your time, it is still possible to apply your knowledge of gerontology to a *portion* of your job. Indeed, we maintain that nearly every job requires some knowledge and skills in interacting with older adults. For example, if you decided to teach at the K–12 level, you will interact with grandparents or even great-grandparents who are the primary caregivers of their grandchildren. Or if you go into law enforcement, you may be in a better position to understand and educate others about crimes that target older people. You can help older adults and their families guard against being the victims of fraudulent businesses that prey on older people, although that may not be what you do full-time. If you go into journalism, you may seek out stories that are of particular interest to elders, or that help the larger population better understand social issues related to aging, especially in light of the aging baby boom population. Just note how many times we have cited news articles about older adults throughout this text.

Career Fair Activities

- Informal "meet and greets" with professionals in the field of aging
- Information booths with pamphlets, brochures, and other materials showcasing the diverse career pathways in aging
- Featured speakers or panel discussions on career opportunities addressing issues faced by older adults
- Symposia, paper, or poster sessions related to aging
- Screening of aging-related films, including mainstream films
- Open houses, receptions, or luncheons so that faculty and students can meet and mingle
- Aging-related games or quizzes to test participants' aging knowledge
- YouTube videos in which students and workers talk about the satisfaction and benefits of working with older adults

No matter where you work, you will encounter active older adults.

The Web site Exploring Careers in Aging (2005) has compiled a list of jobs—more than 100 of them—that involve working with older people and their families. The site separates jobs into 11 categories. Figure 14.1 on p. 397 features some examples from each category. For the full listing of possible jobs, visit the site at http://businessandaging.blogs.com/ecg/101_careers_in_aging/ or search for the terms "Exploring Careers in Aging."

What else can you think of? Take a moment to jot down other jobs that come to mind where knowledge of aging would be helpful. Or maybe you have ideas about how you could create a new job or product, such as the entrepreneurs who have created businesses to help older adults sort through their possessions for a move, or a Web consultant who helps elders set up and update a Web page, blog, or Facebook page. Or recall the emerging opportunities in gerontechnology and universal design discussed in Chapter 12. Workers with sophisticated technical skills will be needed as high-end technological devices are used in the home, workplace, and transportation systems to support active aging. In the following sections, we suggest ways for you to continue this exploration and discovery process.

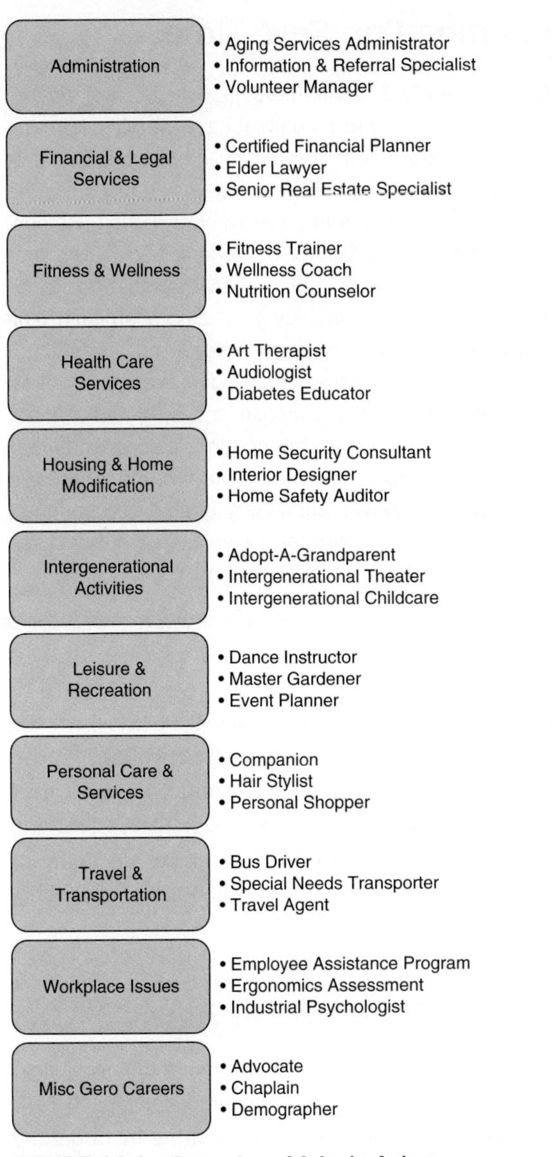

FIGURE 14.1 Examples of Jobs in Aging

Source: Exploring Careers in Aging, 2005, http://businessandaging.blogs.com/ecg/101_careers_in_aging/

Preparing for a Career in Aging

As you are learning in this chapter, there are many ways to prepare for a career in aging, even before taking a certificate program or getting a degree in a field related to aging. You may be at a point in your life when you are seriously looking ahead, wondering how you should spend your working years after college. A large university may have hundreds of degree programs to choose from. A community college may have fewer degree options, but ones that often are practical, are relatively short-term, and can lead to specific jobs with older adults and their families. The important thing to remember is that you can specialize in a field that is clearly focused on working with older adults, such as gerontological social work, geriatric medicine, or geropsychology, or obtaining a degree in gerontology itself. But you can also be employed in other professions or occupations that are not focused on the older adult population, and then concentrate on working with elders within that broader field. For example, someone choosing a career as an exercise physiologist may decide that she wants to work with people 60 years and older. A useful question to ask is, "Are there programs in exercise physiology that provide special training for students interested in working with older people?" A pet therapist may choose to bring pets into adult day health facilities or nursing homes. If so, what programs might help you understand some of the

Benjamin: Future Lawyer and Elder Advocate

Benjamin, a sophomore in college, knows that he would like to work with older adults, but he would like to do this within the parameters of the legal profession. He knows that there are numerous legal issues that are of concern more to older adults than younger ones, and he wants to be the "go-to" person when older adults and their families need help navigating the legal system. He wants to be able to help them with questions relating to estate planning, the use of Medicare and Medicaid, the rights of people living in long-term care facilities, guardianship and conservatorship, advanced care directives, and more. He was pleased to learn that he could specialize in "elder law" as an attorney and that some law schools have special courses, programs, and legal clinics that would help him better serve the older adult population. In fact, the American Bar Association has a Commission on Law and Aging, and his university's law school has a professor who is considered an expert in elder law and who heads an Elder Law Program. Benjamin volunteers for the program now, working under the direction of a law professor and law students, and intends to apply for law school in a couple of years. He feels that he is building a solid foundation for elder law study in the future as well as helping his community by participating in a needed public service.

sensory changes of aging that may affect how elders interact with pets? Or a fitness trainer with a degree in physical education may want to teach older adults to lift weights or lead a "silver" Zumba class and needs to understand normal age-associated physiological changes.

As we discussed earlier, community colleges often offer training for people interested in providing direct care to older adults, whether paid or volunteer. These classes train human service workers, nursing assistants, home care workers, personal care attendants, hospice aides, family caregivers, companions, and others. The MetLife Foundation is a supporter of the community college system as a deliverer of such training. In recent years, the foundation has teamed up with the New York-based Caregiving Project for Older Americans to award grants to community colleges throughout the United States for the development of in-home caregiver training programs. Community colleges are a logical and accessible site for offering classes for paid caregivers, since they provide a range of academic and vocational programs that often lead to some kind of certificate, but not necessarily a formal degree. But they can also be invaluable to unpaid caregivers of family or friends caring for an elder who want more information about resources as well as skills development.

But how do you know that you really want to do a particular kind of job working with elders? The answer is: Do your research! As we noted earlier, you can begin by searching the Web for information related to your career interests. Numerous local, regional, or national professional organizations hold conferences, maintain Web sites and increasingly offer webinars on aging topics, which can be used for information gathering and networking. Learn about volunteer or internship opportunities in your career of interest so you can get firsthand experience observing people at work in your profession. You can do many of these things when you are still in school and considering your career options.

Reflection Break

Consider some ways you might end up working with older adults, either alongside them as coworkers, or as helpers in some capacity: a direct care worker, physical or occupational therapist, physician, nurse, dentist, spiritual counselor, social worker, and so forth. Think about what your next steps should be. How much more education will you need? Where can you get practical experience working with older adults? Who can you talk to for further guidance? What sources will you consult for more information? You can begin by talking with your teacher of the course requiring that you read this book, another faculty member, a knowledgeable relative, someone who already works with elders, an employment counselor, or even older adults themselves to learn how they perceive the needs in the field.

Preparation Can Save Time

Gary is currently a sophomore in college, majoring in General Studies. After completing a service learning experience at a retirement community, he has decided that he wants to get a nursing degree at his university so that he can work with older adults in a health care setting. He consults an advisor at the School of Nursing and learns that to be considered for admission, applicants must complete prerequisite coursework, including specific chemistry, biology, microbiology, and nutrition courses. Applicants must also have earned a minimum grade point average in these courses as well as submit evidence of having had at least 100 hours of health care experience in a paid or volunteer position in one setting for three or more months. There are other requirements as well, and Gary is glad he consulted an advisor early so that he can begin taking his courses prior to applying to the nursing program.

Academic Programs in Aging

Some jobs in the field of aging require a graduate or professional degree. Here are some questions and tips to consider if you want to continue to study aging by obtaining an advanced degree. First, decide what your career goal is. Do you want to become a geriatric nurse or occupational therapist? Or work in a long-term care facility as a recreational therapist or activities director? Or work in a community-based setting as a health educator to promote healthy aging or as an art therapist? Or be an architect or urban planner specializing in universal design to create environments for aging in place?

Perhaps you're not ready to commit to a graduate program yet but are interested in taking a few more courses in gerontology. Many universities offer certificate programs in gerontology that you can complete in the classroom or online. These typically are for students who are interested in the subject or already working in the field but would like to learn more about aging and get a certificate to show that coursework has been completed successfully. Some may allow you the option to take a course or two to test your interest. Most of these can be completed in a year or so. You can study gerontology at the associate's, bachelor's, master's, and doctoral levels, but the length of study will vary depending on the level of specialization you need to attain (AGHE, 2014b).

You may need to look beyond your campus if your college or university does not offer any kind of certificate or degree program in gerontology. If you can identify major organizations that support gerontological education and practice, these will lead you to specific programs. The **John A. Hartford Foundation** is one such organization. Hartford-funded initiatives in medicine, nursing, and social work education and practice can be found throughout the nation. The descriptions of the following programmatic examples contain summaries and excerpts from the John A. Hartford Foundation Web site at www.jhartfound.org. Their site may be able to link you with other relevant organizations and is an excellent resource about trends in gerontology and geriatrics, including the Foundation's Agent Initiative that is focused on practice rather than academic settings.

Workforce Initiatives in Medicine, Nursing, and Social Work One of the Hartford initiatives was created to address the shortage of geriatric faculty members in medical schools. It produced geriatrically knowledgeable scientists, teachers, and clinicians and helped create a higher level of recognition and appreciation of the discipline throughout medical centers, universities, and affiliated clinical service settings. Unfortunately, however, as you learned earlier, the acute shortage of geriatricians still persists.

Hartford-funded Centers of Excellence reached nurses at all educational levels to prepare them to provide high-quality care for older adults in a variety of settings and to improve care through research and in-service training. The foundation maintained that investing in high-quality geriatric nursing can result in better patient recovery, shorter hospital stays, and lower rates of being readmitted to a hospital.

A third workforce initiative targeted social workers. The Hartford Foundation provided support to prepare social work students with geriatric competencies for roles such as care coordination that can ease the transitions between health care settings and locate community resources. Other projects prepared faculty and doctoral students for research and leadership, designed aging-focused practicum settings, and infused gerontology into the classroom curriculum in social work programs throughout the country.

Other national foundations that have supported training, practice, and policy innovations in aging are the Retirement Research Foundation and Atlantic Philanthropies. The organization Grantsmakers in Aging is a good resource to locate foundations in your state or city that support gerontological practice, education, or research and could be sources of future funding if you pursue a career in gerontology (http://www.giaging.org).

Interdisciplinary Teams Interdisciplinary means that specialists from different disciplines or professions such as medicine, nursing, pharmacy, and social work communicate with each other to coordinate their services on behalf of patient care. The Hartford Foundation, among others, has supported interdisciplinary projects in both clinical practice and academic programs. The capacity to work effectively in interprofessional teams is an essential skill, and is even more important under the ACA. Indeed, under the ACA, interdisciplinary teams include direct care workers and families with health care providers. But interdisciplinary collaboration is sometimes difficult to put into practice because of the diversity of disciplinary perspectives and priorities. The term "interdisciplinary" tends to refer to coordination among different types of providers, while "multidisciplinary" recognizes the distinctive but complementary contributions of different fields of practice but is not necessarily a systematic approach. You can see a set of multidisciplinary geriatric competencies developed by the American Geriatrics Society Partnerships for Health in Aging from their Web site, http://www.americangeriatrics.org/.

Gerontological specialists will be needed in all health professions.

Internships and Other Training Opportunities

Internships, whether paid or unpaid, are ways for students to work in a professional setting alongside employees to see what life in the organization is really like. If the internship has a service component to it—for example, helping individuals, families, groups, and communities achieve a better quality of life—the internship might be labeled "service learning." The words "practicum" and "field placement" are also used to describe an internship-like experience. Regardless of what it is called, these training and learning opportunities can be invaluable for students to explore new fields of practice and for the sponsoring organizations that benefit from the students' involvement.

Internships help students learn "on-site," rather than in a classroom or laboratory, and apply their knowledge to real-life situations. Interns get to know the organizational culture, work within the policies, rules, and expectations of the organization, and begin the process of networking and learning to work as a team. An intern working at a hospital, for example, witnesses firsthand how the various hospital staff—physicians, nurses, social workers, therapists, nursing assistants, etc.—coordinate their care on behalf of a patient.

Internships can be as short as a few weeks or as long as a year or more. Sometimes students discover through the internship experience that they do not want to work at a particular site after graduation. This deliberation process should involve the student intern, the site supervisor at the internship site, and the academic advisor at school. For others, an internship can lead to a paid job or other training opportunities.

Although the primary goal in doing an internship is to enhance students' learning about their chosen profession, the National Association of Colleges and Employers (NACE) reports that more than 50 percent of the interns it studied were hired for full-time positions. The 2011 Internship & Co-Op Survey found that an average 39 percent of entry-level hires from the class of 2010 came from organizations' own internship programs and that responding organizations converted nearly 58 percent of their interns into full-time hires. These were internships in general, not just in gerontology. The point is, however, that internships can be an effective entryway to full-time jobs (NACE, 2011).

Your college or university may have an office that publicizes available service learning internships with older adults or their families. If you're already enrolled in a gerontology-related degree program, your department undoubtedly has internship or volunteer information available; indeed, many programs require that students complete an internship.

Applying for an internship can be similar to applying for a job, especially for highly competitive ones. You will likely submit a paper or online application and be invited for an interview (perhaps more than one) and a chance to visit the organization. If offered an internship, you may need to attend orientation training, be issued identification, and begin work like any other new employee. Professionalism and collegiality should serve you well as an intern. Remember, internships are a two-way street. You will observe and learn while doing an internship, but you will also be observed and most likely evaluated on your merits as an intern.

There are also growing numbers of opportunities to interact with older adults that are less time-intensive

Working with Older Veterans

An excellent site for internships is the **U.S. Department of Veterans Affairs**, sometimes referred to as the Veterans Administration or **VA**. It operates a nationwide system of health care services for American veterans that includes hospitals, community-based health care centers, and social services. Because of the scope of patient services and variety of learning opportunities, the VA is considered by many to be an ideal training ground for those interested in working with the veteran population and their families, which includes a sizable older adult segment (e.g., veterans from World War II, the Korean War, and the Vietnam War). Indeed in 2011, they expanded their program of supports for family caregivers of veterans.

The VA trains student interns in a wide variety of areas including medicine, nursing, and social work, to name a few. Interns also serve veterans outside of direct patient care—for example, in health information management, environmental engineering, and public affairs. Interns are supervised by experienced VA professionals called preceptors. Internships generally take place over a period of a year or more, and interns have often been hired by the VA after the internship period has been successfully completed. The VA has 19 Geriatric Research Education and Clinical Centers (GRECCs) throughout the country, which were established in the 1970s to attract scientists and health care providers to geriatric scholarship, education, and practice. These frequently offer stipends to qualified students.

than an internship or service learning. Some academic programs require their students to interact directly with an elder, perhaps through an oral history or research project, as a way to influence students' attitudes toward aging. At the University of New England, medical students specializing in geriatrics live in a skilled nursing facility for two weeks. They are given a "diagnosis" and expected to live as someone with that condition. At Emory University, first-year students in nursing and medicine are linked with a senior mentor living in the community. Students visit their older mentors in their homes and accompany them on a physician visit. And many undergraduate social work degrees structure opportunities for students to interact directly with older adults in one of their required courses. Programs such as these recognize that personal contact is typically the most effective strategy to address students' fears of aging, to understand some of the challenges facing older adults, and to "hook" students on the joys and meaning of working with elders and their families.

Journaling as a Self-Discovery Tool As part of your internship or volunteer experience, you may be required to keep a journal or log of your daily or weekly experiences. Keeping a journal is a good idea, even if not required, especially if this is one of your first times to interact frequently with older people. Journaling can help you process your thoughts, observations, and experiences while they are fresh in your mind—and then reflect on them later. It is also a good way of relieving any stress of an internship as well as recording positive aspects of the experience.

Living Out Your Passion

Karen was raised in a multigenerational household. She lived in a house with a sibling, two parents, and two grandparents. Because Karen's parents were employed full-time, she was often left in the care of her grandparents, to whom she became very close. Both of Karen's grandparents passed away by the time she entered college. Because of her special relationship with her grandparents, Karen was always comfortable around older people and decided she wanted to work with them as part of her career. She explored her options and decided to become a gerontological social worker. As part of her social work education, she was required to complete an internship (usually referred to as a practicum or field placement), and was matched with a social work department in a local hospital. Many of her clients were older adults who had been admitted as patients in the hospital, and much of her work—under the supervision of a field supervisor—involved bringing older adults, family members, and hospital staff together to discuss plans for future care of the clients. She graduated from college and was hired by another hospital, where she spends many hours assisting families who are seeking options for older family members with complex care needs. These families have been grateful for the knowledge and resources that Karen provides them. Karen finds the work satisfying as she knows she is helping older people and their families identify the best care options under often stressful and challenging circumstances. Karen is also a member of professional organizations and community groups, where she advocates for social and institutional changes that benefit older adults.

A Multidisciplinary, Multigenerational Outlook

We applaud you for studying aging and older adulthood by taking this class, reading this book, and visiting Web sites such as those listed in Figure 14.2 on p. 402. We hope that you have gained knowledge, skills, and insights that will serve you well beyond this class. We also hope that this chapter has helped you think about your next steps along your academic journey, perhaps leading to a career in aging if you have been inspired to continue learning about aging in an active manner. Or maybe you will end up working with younger generations, but now have an understanding of the life course and how choices earlier in life affect how we age. We hope that you have acquired a cross-generational and life course perspective that will serve you well in any career as well as in your personal life. In both our professional and personal lives, we all can be an essential part of another person's safety net as well as work to create age-friendly communities.

We began this book by discussing the demographics of aging that underlie everything else discussed in the rest of the chapters: In both the United States and globally, more people are living longer, leading to communities with populations that are older than at any other time in history. In the United States, our older adult

Here is a list of selected Web sites that can help guide and expand your explorations about the field of aging.

Administration on Aging	www.aoa.gov
American Association of Retired Persons (AARP)	www.aarp.org
American Society on Aging (ASA)	www.asaging.org
Association for Gerontology Education in Social Work (AGE-SW)	agesw.org
Association for Gerontology in Higher Education (AGHE)	www.aghe.org
California Council on Gerontology and Geriatrics	www.ccgg.org
AGHE Careers in Aging	www.careersinaging.com
Council on Social Work Education (CSWE)	www.cswe.org
Geriatric Social Work Initiative (GSWI)	www.gswi.org
Gerontological Society of America (GSA)	www.geron.org
Human Resources and Services Administration (HRSA)	www.hrsa.gov
Institute for Geriatric Social Work (IGSW)	www.bu.edu/igsw
MIT Age Lab	agelab.mit.edu
National Association of Social Workers (NASW)	www.naswdc.org
National Association of States United for Aging and Disabilities (NASUAD)	www.nasuad.org
National Association of Area Agencies on Aging (n4a)	www.n4a.org
National Council on the Aging (NCOA)	www.ncoa.org
National Institute on Aging	www.nia.nih.gov
National Association of Professional Geriatric Care Managers	www.caremanager.org

FIGURE 14.2 **List of Handy Web sites about Aging.**

population—currently 13 percent of the total population and growing—is remarkably diverse, consisting of people of different races, ethnicities, immigrant status, abilities, sexual orientation, languages, religions, family structures, educational attainment, socioeconomic status, and so forth. As a result, the need for culturally competent practitioners is imperative. Such practitioners have the knowledge, skills, and personal awareness to effectively interact with diverse elders by ascertaining and building on their

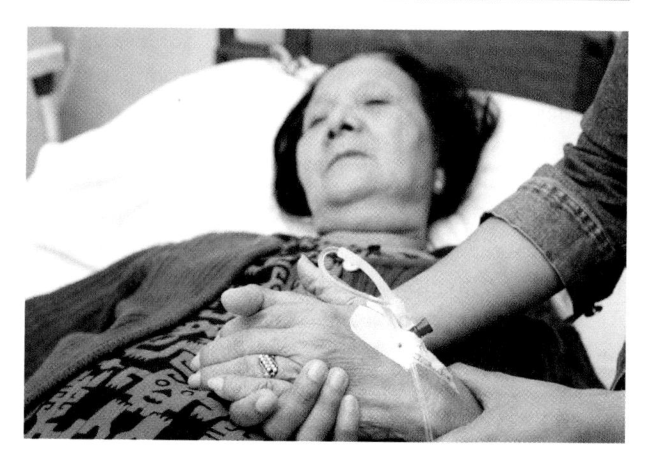

Compassion and sensitivity to people of all ages is vital to a caring society.

specific needs and strengths or assets. Models of cultural competence that are relationship based (e.g., take account of the many dimensions of care influenced by culture, including family interactions) are often more effective than those that are encounter based (e.g., this is what a nurse needs to know about African American patients

Working Toward Solutions, Together

Dr. Linda P. Fried, the dean of Columbia University's Mailman School of Public Health in New York City, has pushed her students, faculty members, and others in the community to think about the right questions and the right solutions to address the needs of an aging world population. In a *New York Times* article, Dr. Fried—a gerontologist and epidemiologist—wants the school to give students the tools to deal with global challenges such as environmental degradation, rising health care costs, and the effects of rapid urbanization along with aging. Enrollment in the school has been climbing. A revised curriculum emphasizes health preservation and disease prevention for every stage of life, an interdisciplinary approach that is required of all students. A renowned gerontological researcher, Dr. Fried's earlier career path included work as a paralegal, social worker, and physical therapist. She later went to medical school in Chicago and worked with veterans on a geriatrics fellowship. Now in her sixties, she earned a black belt in aikido when she was in her thirties. The daughter of an unconventional mother who completed her doctorate in her fifties, Dr. Fried said the most important lesson she learned from her mother was that no human life should be wasted (Pennar, 2012).

The Multidisciplinary Gerontologist: Dr. H. Asuman Kiyak

Students who plan to work with older adults should develop a multidisciplinary mind-set that enables them to welcome the contributions of many different fields of study and areas of expertise. That's what Dr. H. Asuman Kiyak did, and because of it, she helped make the world a better place for current and future generations of older adults and their families. Dr. Kiyak was based in the University of Washington School of Dentistry, where she held the title of professor, but she was not a dentist. She was a psychologist by education, specializing in gerontology, and she used her knowledge to help dental students better understand older adulthood so that they could provide competent care to their older patients. She also taught architecture students about designing homes accessible to people with physical limitations or to those who wanted to age in place. She headed up the University's Certificate Program in Gerontology, often teaching college freshmen, distance education students, and the public about aging. This teaching encompassed not only the psychology of aging, but also more wide-ranging topics, such as issues in long-term care and use of technology to promote active aging. In all her interactions and activities, she was passionate about promoting the well-being of older adults and their families.

Dr. Kiyak's work went beyond the walls of academia. She helped establish a mobile dental clinic that was staffed by dental students and faculty members. Many of their clients were economically disadvantaged and living in underserved communities, but Dr. Kiyak believed they should receive quality oral health care, something that many of them lacked. She had to fight hard to convince funders and providers that these elders deserved quality and accessible dental care.

Dr. Kiyak traveled around the world to present at conferences, not just in dentistry but at multidisciplinary gatherings of gerontologists, such as the Gerontological Society of America. She authored and coauthored a large number of publications spanning decades of research and gave of her time generously as a mentor and adviser. Her coauthored text with Nancy R. Hooyman—*Social Gerontology: A Multidisciplinary Perspective*—reached thousands of students around the world through nine editions. As director of the University of Washington's Institute for Aging, she connected experts across disciplines in the field of gerontology so they knew what each other was doing and could share resources and ideas.

This book would not have been possible without Dr. Kiyak's many years of teaching, research, and service in the field of gerontology. We know they were satisfying ones and that she would want younger generations to consider working with and advocating for older adults, as she did. She demonstrated that one can thrive as a multidisciplinary scholar, advocate, and community builder. Dr. Kiyak was hard at work on this book before she died from cancer in May 2011, but her legacy lives on in her wide-ranging initiatives on behalf of older adults as well as in the relationships she established across cultures, nations, and academic disciplines.

with high blood pressure). To recognize the resilience and diverse assets of elders is to respect and acknowledge their dignity (Parker, 2010–2011).

You have learned how the field of social gerontology addresses the biological, psychological, and social aspects of aging and how these vary both within and across individuals. It is one thing to know that the older adult population is growing; it is another to know how to respond to that growth in a way that enhances the quality of life for older people and the supports available in the communities they live in. As we have discussed throughout the book, some older adults need assistance with activities of daily living due to illness or disability, but most do not. The promotion of mental and physical well-being and the effective management of chronic disease are topics that should concern people of all ages. Individuals, families, and society as a whole benefit when populations age in as healthy a manner as possible. When the risk of disease and illness can be reduced through lifestyle choices, social and health resources can then be directed at those who need them the most in our communities.

Two important themes or "takeaway" points from this book are that caring for older adults is both a multigenerational and multidisciplinary endeavor. It is multigenerational because it requires people of all ages to actively participate in some way—in the way that we think, feel, and behave—with individuals across three, four, or even five generations. A more inclusive, harmonious society begins with a collective will to eliminate social injustice, including ageism and discrimination against elders or ignoring people because of their age. The way individuals perceive older adults will affect the way they interact with them. Social interaction is most meaningful when we view and understand each other as whole persons who happen

Dr. H. Asuman Kiyak.

to be at a certain stage of life and not resort to labels of "old" or "young." Older adulthood should not be viewed as a period of decline, but rather a time of meaning and, for most, continuing purpose and engagement. Of course, some older adults do need various levels of care due to disease or disability. Providing support with compassion and dignity is the cornerstone to building a future that values individuals across the life course, regardless of age or functional ability.

Promoting well-being in old age requires a multidisciplinary perspective because no one discipline can adequately address the complex physiological, psychological, and social changes that occur as we age. Most settings that effectively serve older adults involve multidisciplinary teams where each disciplinary perspective is valued and complementary. As you have learned, there are literally dozens of roles—both paid and unpaid—that one can play as people who care for older adults. Both the postal carrier and the physician can provide an essential service in helping an elder feel safe and secure. A social worker, nurse, and a friendly neighbor can each help an elder in different yet complementary ways.

You will find examples of people in the workplace who are already good role models for adopting a multidisciplinary mind-set when it comes to eldercare. Observe, talk, and learn from them. With Dr. Kiyak, we have introduced you to someone who embodied that way of looking at the field of social gerontology.

As you have seen throughout this text, each of us is a multidimensional being, shaped by life experiences, social identities, and relationships. We can contribute to society in different ways, but we also depend on family, friends, neighbors, and communities—of all ages—to enhance our quality of life, and this relationship of reciprocity across generations will continue throughout and enrich our lives.

Unfortunately, many people still regard aging as a problem and a largely negative experience. This results in part from the prevalence of so-called antiaging commercials, products, and services, as well as the distorted images of older adults often found in popular culture. This fear and disdain of aging can result in a loss of self-esteem as we age and make it difficult to discover the meaning and contentment that make life satisfying. It also drives some people to take unnecessary risks that can jeopardize their health and safety, and to hold negative attitudes about aging that are harmful to their own self-actualization as well as to social relations and social welfare.

A better approach is to learn about the wide range of issues, topics, challenges, opportunities, and concerns related to aging—as you have done by reading this book—and discover for yourself *why aging matters*. Then find positive, healthy ways to prepare for aging and enjoy this natural life process as it unfolds. In her book, *Life Gets Better: The Unexpected Pleasures of Growing Older*, Wendy Lustbader writes about a time in her youth when she regarded older people as being apart from herself, "over there somewhere." Eventually she realized she was really part of a "great continuous flow" that included people of all ages. This realization helped her focus on the positive dimension of growing old, which is the beauty of *growing*, and the heightened awareness and pleasure of living (Lustbader, 2011).

As you consider a career in aging, or a future working and living alongside older adults, we hope you will recognize the vital contributions you can make in creating an environment where people of all ages can thrive, live with dignity, and enjoy support from their peers and across generations—the kind of society we can all look forward to living in as we get older.

summary

The goal of this chapter was to encourage you consider career paths that involve working with older adults. These opportunities will be both plentiful and essential in the years to come. Older adults will be our colleagues, clients, patients, customers, bosses, and associates. Career opportunities are varied and dynamic, as this chapter has illustrated.

Academic preparation, internships, and service learning are ways to access careers in aging. You may also need to pursue education beyond the undergraduate degree if your career goals require it. Professions such as nursing, medicine, dentistry, physical therapy, law, speech pathology and audiology, pharmacy, social work, and so forth can involve years of specialized coursework.

On the other hand, you may want to work in a field that is not typically associated with older people but can be personally fulfilling to you if many of your clients or constituents are older adults. These could include careers in education (e.g., lifelong learning classes), architecture, travel, fitness, recreation, law enforcement, policy-making, or computer technology.

Those who choose to work with older adults, regardless of the specific career path, benefit from having a cross-disciplinary and cross-generational outlook. In fact, the underlying goal of this book has been for you to understand older adulthood from a multidisciplinary and multigenerational perspective. We hope that you see older adulthood as a dynamic, highly variable, and meaningful stage in life—and recognize how aging matters. We also hope we have dispelled any stereotypes you had about older persons. As you have seen throughout the book, some older adults have serious and extensive care needs, but there are also others who are in relatively good health and remain active and socially engaged. Even those who need assistance due to illness, injury, or a disability have many assets to offer society. Regardless of age or ability, we all have the capacity to contribute to another person's well-being.

Social gerontology is an exciting and rapidly changing field. By taking this class and completing this book, you are that much closer to understanding the major concerns of the field and the opportunities awaiting you. We have tried to deliver the key concepts in a friendly and somewhat casual manner at times, but the need to plan and prepare for the so-called graying of society is both serious and urgent. Last, we hope that you see the multiple ways in which age matters for you, your friends and family, and society.

key terms

Association for Gerontology in Higher Education (AGHE), p. 392
Careers in Aging Week, p. 396
Eldercare Workforce Alliance (EWA), p. 394
internship, p. 400
John A. Hartford Foundation, p. 399
U.S. Department of Veterans Affairs (VA), p. 400

review questions

1. What benefits would work in the field of aging or gerontology have for you?
2. If you were to consider working in gerontology, what specifically do you think you might do in this field? What specific job might appeal to you as a career?
3. List some careers in aging that would require an advanced degree (i.e., a degree beyond the bachelor's degree).
4. What are some of the jobs that would enable a person to work with older adults but do not require a college degree?
5. If someone were still on the fence, so to speak, about whether to pursue a career that involved working with older adults, what should he or she do? What resources are available that can provide information to help with the decision-making process?

6. Why did this chapter begin by saying that you will almost certainly be working *alongside* older adults in just about any career that you choose?
7. Name one to three jobs that are not primarily gerontological or geriatric but do involve working with older adults nevertheless.
8. Several key themes of this book have been "diversity," "resilience," and "multigenerational relations." What is your understanding of these concepts now that you have completed reading this book?
9. What is the definition of a multidisciplinary gerontologist? How would a person develop such a mind-set?
10. Based on what you have learned from this chapter, what are your next steps in planning and achieving your long-term career goals?

media resources

Watch

- So Much to Choose From: Phil Zimbardo

View

- Population Age Structure, 2000

references

Association for Gerontology in Higher Education (AGHE). (2014a). *Why study aging and older persons?* Retrieved February 16, 2014, from http://www.aghe.org/500218.

Association for Gerontology in Higher Education (AGHE). (2014b). *How do I become a professional in aging?* Retrieved February 16, 2014, from www.aghe.org/500216.

Bragg, E., & Hansen, J. C. (2010–2011). A revelation of numbers: Will America's eldercare workforce be ready to care for an aging America? *Generations*, 34, 11–19.

GovTrack.us. (2013). *S. 1119—113th Congress: Positive Aging Act of 2013.* Retrieved September 29, 2013, from http://www.govtrack.us/congress/bills/113/s1119

Harahan, M. (2010–2011). A critical look at the looming long-term care workforce crisis. *Generations, 34*, 20–26.

Hooyman, N., & Unutzer J. (2010–2011). A perilous arc of supply and demand. How can America meet the multiplying mental health care needs of an aging populace? *Generations, 34*, 36–42.

Institute of Medicine. (2008). *Retooling for an aging America: Building the healthcare workforce.* Washington, DC: National Academies Press.

Lustbader, W. (2011). *Life gets better: The unexpected pleasures of growing older.* New York: Penguin.

National Association of Colleges and Employers (NACE). (2011). *2011 Internship & Co-op survey.* Bethlehem, Pennsylvania: NACE.

Parker, V. (2010–2011). The importance of cultural competence in caring for and working in a diverse America. *Generations, 34*, 97–102.

Pennar, K. (2012, June 25). Unafraid of aging. *New York Times.* Retrieved January 2013, from http://www.nytimes.com/2012/06/26/science/reframing-views-of-aging.html?pagewanted=all&_r=0.

Pershing, B. (2012, December 19). Mikulski in line to chair powerful appropriations panel. *Washington Post.* Retrieved January 2013, from http://www.washingtonpost.com/local/md-politics/mikulski-in-line-to-chair-powerful-appropriations-panel/2012/12/19/01c8b8da-4a29-11e2-820e-17eef-ac2f939_story.html.

Peterson, L. E., Bazemore, A., Bragg, E., Xierali, I., & Warshaw, G. (2011). Rural–urban distribution of the U.S. geriatrics physician workforce. *Journal of the American Geriatrics Society, 59*, 699–703.

Seavey, D. (2010–2011). Caregivers on the front line: Building a better direct-care workforce. *Generations*, 34, 27–35.

Stone, R., & Barbarotta, L. (2010–2011). Caring for an aging America in the twenty-first century. *Generations, 34*, 5–10.

Glossary

AARP formerly known as the American Association of Retired Persons, a national organization open to all adults age 50 and over, offering a wide range of informational materials, discounted services and products, and a powerful political lobby

accommodative ability capacity of the lens of the eye to change shape from rounded to flat in order to see objects that are closer or farther from the lens; interferes with the ability to see clearly when shifting focus from near to far

Accountable Care Organizations (ACOs) organizations of health care providers that are accountable for the quality, cost and overall care of Medicare beneficiaries and benefit from savings incurred

active adult or lifestyle communities retirement communities that offer a range of activities and amenities, but typically not social and health services

active aging the ability of older adults to do what they want in their home and community

active euthanasia deliberate steps to hasten someone else's death, such as administering a lethal injection; assisted suicide, generally by a physician

active versus dependent life expectancy a way of describing expected length of life, the term *active* denoting a manner of living that is relatively healthy and independent in contrast to being dependent on help from others

activities of daily living (ADLs) summary of an individual's performance in personal care tasks such as bathing, dressing, eating, toileting and walking.

activity theory posits that an older person's self-concept is validated through participation in roles characteristic of middle age and elders who are active are more satisfied and better adjusted than those who are not active

acute (or temporary) conditions short term, such as infections or a cold, which can usually be treated or cured and covered by Medicare

acute illness short-term disease or infection, often more debilitating to older than younger persons

Administration for Community Living (ACL) created in 2012, includes the Administration on Aging, the Administration on Intellectual and Developmental Disabilities and the Center for Disability and Aging Policy in a single agency with the goal of increasing access to community supports and full participation for older Americans and people with disabilities

Administration on Aging (AoA) primary funder of community-based services for older adults; oversees, supports, and advocates for services through the Aging Network; now part of the ACL

adult day care (ADC) a community facility that frail older people living at home can attend several hours each day; those based on a social model focus on structured social and psychotherapeutic activities

adult day health care (ADHC) adult day care with a strong health rehabilitative component, provides several health services and help with medications, in addition to social programs

adult family home (AFH) a private home facility, licensed by the state, in which the owner of the home provides housekeeping, personal care, and some delegated nursing functions for the residents

Adult Protective Services social services provided to older adults or adults with disabilities, typically administered by a state or local government agency charged to investigate complaints of abuse, neglect, or exploitation

advance directives documents such as living wills and durable powers of attorney for health care decisions that outline actions to be taken when an individual is no longer able to do so, often because of irreversible terminal illness

Age Discrimination in Employment Act (ADEA) federal law that protects workers age 40 and over from denial of employment strictly because of age and that eliminated mandatory retirement

age norms open up or close off the roles that people of a given chronological age can play

age stratification theory the societal age structure—or cohorts and the historical time period—affects the experience of aging; cohorts in turn influence patterns of age stratification

age-based entitlement programs government programs only available to people of a certain age; unlike discretionary programs, do not require appropriations from a legislative body; rather, age eligibility triggers receipt of benefits regardless of the program's cost

age-friendly (livable or elder-friendly) communities cities, suburbs, and towns that offer transportation, social and health services, and safe and adaptable housing to help older residents age in place and can benefit all ages

age-related macular degeneration (AMD) loss of vision in the center of the visual field caused by insufficient oxygen reaching the macula

ageism refers to negative stereotypes about old age and may result in discrimination

Aging and Disability Resource Centers (ADRCs) aim to integrate long-term services and supports for both older adults and adults with disabilities into a single coordinated system with one entry point or "no wrong door"

aging in place continuing to live with social supports and services in a private home or apartment in one's neighborhood

Aging Network the system of social services for older adults funded by the Older Americans Act, but increasingly also covering services for people with disabilities

alcoholism four or more drinks in any single day during a typical month; use of alcohol frequently and routinely

Alzheimer's the most common irreversible dementia resulting in severe cognitive decline; 6th most common cause of death; cannot be cured but symptoms managed with medications and behavioral interventions

American Society on Aging (ASA) national association of primarily practitioners interested in gerontology

anthropology of aging the exploration and understanding of aging within and across the diversity of human cultures

anticipatory grief grief for a loved one prior to his or her death, usually occurring during the time that the loved one has a terminal illness that may allow survivors to prepare

anxiety disorder functional psychological disorder often triggered by external stress and accompanied by increased heart rate, fatigue, restlessness and sleep disorders

Area Agencies on Aging (AAA) offices on aging at the regional and local levels that plan and administer services to meet the needs of older adults within that area; established and partially funded through the Older Americans Act

asset mapping involving residents in a process to identify their community's strengths and capacities, including older adults as valuable resources rather than a problem to be solved

assets an individual's savings, home equity, and personal property

assisted living facilities (ALFs) a housing model aimed at elders who need assistance with some activities of Daily Living, but who are not so physically or cognitively impaired as to need 24-hour attention

assisted suicide/physician-assisted suicide (PAS)/physician assistance-in-dying considered active euthanasia when a physician actively aids a person who is dying, typically through the use of drugs

assistive technology a range of electronic and computer technologies that assist people with disabilities to perform as many ADLs as possible, sometimes without help from others

Association for Gerontology in Higher Education (AGHE) the only national membership organization of colleges and other academic groups devoted primarily to gerontological education

atherosclerosis accumulation of fats in the arteries and veins, blocking circulation of the blood

attentional control ability to determine how much attention should be directed at specific stimuli and when to shift our focus to other stimuli

aware home technology systems that support aging in place for persons with dementia by monitoring daily activities such as medication use, mapping trends in ADLs, and assisting elders' communication

baby boomers the cohort or group of people born between 1946 and 1964; currently numbering 79 million people and sometimes referred to as the "senior boom"

bereavement overload an experience of increased frequency of family and friends' deaths and other losses

biculturalism the process of integrating two distinct cultures so that they can meaningfully co-exist

bioethics medical ethics that addresses procedural approaches to questions about death, dying, and medical decision-making

biological aging the physiological changes that reduce the efficiency of organ systems, such as the lungs, heart, and the circulatory system and may affect functioning over time, but not necessarily result in disease or death

birth cohort a group of people born within the same particular time span (for example, 1960s). Also known as cohort

blended families families whose memberships comprise blood and non-blood relationships through divorce or remarriage

brain games computer-based games designed to stimulate brain activity

broadband enables high-speed Internet capability that allows Internet users to watch videos, play games, and engage in other high bandwidth activities online, including telemedicine.

care recipient person receiving paid or unpaid assistance

Careers in Aging Week annual April event on many college campuses that is sponsored by the Association for Gerontology in Higher Education and the Gerontological Society of America to raise awareness of career opportunities in aging

caregiver burden physical, emotional, and financial costs associated with assisting persons with long-term care needs

caregiving the act of assisting people with personal care, household chores, transportation, and other tasks associated with daily living; provided primarily by families without compensation or by direct care workers

caring about the relational aspects of care that involve trust, rapport, compassion, comfort, communication, and a sense of psychological responsibility or nearly constant worry

caring for help with daily personal care tasks that are physically draining, such as bathing, dressing, and eating, involve daily interruptions, and entail intimate contact

cash and counseling programs older adults recieve a monthly cash allowance to hire, supervise, and fire own caregivers or purchase products to allow them to remain at home

cataract clouding of the lens of the eye, reducing sight and sometimes leading to blindness; requires surgical extraction of the lens

cellular aging theory an explanation that aging occurs as cells slow their number of replications, based on the observation that cells grown in controlled laboratory environments are able to replicate only a finite number of times

centenarians people in the population of 100 years or older; see also *super-centenarians*

Centers for Medicare and Medicaid Services (CMS) the federal agency that administers the Medicare and Medicaid programs; prior to 2001, known as the Health Care Financing Administration (HCFA)

cerebrovascular accident (CVA) or stroke occurs when a portion of the brain is completely denied blood, such as through a blood clot

chronic diseases diseases, like heart disease and diabetes, that require long-term medical care and related long-term care services and supports

chronic illness long-term (more than three months), often permanent, and leaving a residual disability that may require long-term management or care rather than cure

chronic obstructive pulmonary diseases (COPDs) result of damaged lung tissue, often due to bronchitis or asthma

chronic sorrow grief that tends to be unending and unpredictable because it is associated with someone still living, not with the deceased and is often experienced by caregivers

chronological aging based on a person's years lived from birth

civic engagement a process in which people actively participate in the life of their communities through individual and collective activities, such as volunteering

Civic Ventures an organization that provides resources for civic engagement and awards to innovators and agencies working for the common good

classic aging pattern the decline observed with aging on some performance scales of intelligence tests versus consistency on verbal scales of the same tests

cognitive-behavioral interventions (CBIs) a form of therapy that uses active, time-limited approaches to change the thinking and behavior that affect depression

cognitive retraining teaching people how to use various techniques to keep their minds active and maintain good memory skills

cohorts groups of people who were born at approximately the same time and therefore share many common life and historical experiences (also known as birth cohort)

cohousing a community of families and/or elders who share some activities and characteristics in a common house, but live independently, in intergenerational or elders-only housing

Community-Based Care Transitions Program Under the Affordable Care Act (ACA), hospitals with high rates of readmission may apply for funds for transitional care coordination with community-based organizations to make transitions smoother and safer. Aim is to reduce risk for rehospitalization, improve quality of care, and decrease Medicare costs

comorbidity simultaneously experiencing multiple health problems, whether acute, chronic or a combination

comparative sociocultural gerontology comparing the experiences of older adults across various cultures; see also *anthropology of aging*

Compassion and Choices the largest and most comprehensive end-of-life organization that offers education, advocacy and legal options

compassionate release releasing nonviolent, older inmates early to improve prisoner health status and reduce health costs in correctional systems

compression of morbidity relatively long periods of healthy, active, high-quality existence, and relatively short periods of illness and dependency in the last few years of life

consumer-directed care under the Medicaid waiver system, older adults can hire personal care attendants, including family members (except for spouses); also includes the concepts of person-centered and participant-directed care

continuing care retirement community (CCRC) a multilevel facility offering a range from independent to congregate living arrangements, including skilled nursing care units

continuity theory central personality characteristics become more pronounced with age, or are retained through life with little change; people age successfully if they maintain their lifelong roles and adaptation techniques

contributory benefits based on employee's mandatory contributions such as to Social Security payroll taxes

coronary heart disease optimum blood flow to the heart is restricted because the cardiac vessels narrow, which may result in intensive care, numerous tests, or extended hospitalization

creativity ability to bring something new and valued into existence

crossover effect elders of color (mostly men) who survive beyond age 75, having longer life expectancies after age 75 than their white counterparts

cross-sectional study research that compares people of different chronological ages at the same measurement period

crystallized intelligence knowledge and abilities one gains through education and experience

culture change new models of nursing home care that attempt to make these facilities more homelike and less institutional and provide residents with greater decision-making autonomy

cumulative disadvantage the process by which structural disparities that are based on age, race, gender, class, or sexuality orientation, experienced by people earlier in life, are intensified in old age because inequities persist across the life course

defined benefit pension plans a specified amount is guaranteed by the company as a lifetime annuity, and employees know what they could count on as retirement income

defined contribution plans such as 401(k) plans, in which the amount of the benefit varies depending on an individual's investment returns and thus carries greater financial risk for the employee

dementia progressive marked decline in cognitive function associated with damage to brain tissue affecting personality and behavior; may be reversible or irreversible type

demographer a person who studies populations and population trends and characteristics

demographic divide dichotomy between the needs of young and old in countries where both age groups need some assistance

demographics the study of populations and their characteristics in a society, e.g., changes in population size due to deaths, births or migrations

demographic trends changes that occur in populations, such as the increase in median age

dependency ratio the number of people age 65 and older to every 100 people of traditional working ages (defined as 18–64)

depression the most common psychiatric disorder in old age, diagnosed if several behavioral and affective symptoms (e.g., sleep and eating disturbances) are present for at least two weeks

developing countries countries with relatively lower material wealth compared with developed nations such as the United States and Japan

diabetes mellitus a disease that impairs the ability of the pancreas to produce insulin, and is characterized by above-normal amounts of sugar in the blood and urine; cannot be cured but can be managed

direct care workers nurse aides, personal assistants, and home care staff who provide hands-on care in both home and long-term care settings

disability an impairment in the ability to complete multiple daily tasks

discretionary funding for programs has to be approved annually by Congress, so amount typically varies each year

disenfranchised grief a loss that is not openly acknowledged, by others, publicly mourned, or socially supported such as with the death of an LGBT partner

disengagement theory older people, because of the inevitable decline with age, become less active with the outer world and increasingly preoccupied with their inner lives, thereby shifting an orderly transfer of power from older to younger people

disuse theory the view that memory fades or is lost because one fails to use the information

diverticulitis a condition in which pouches or sacs (diverticula) in the intestinal wall become inflamed and infected, causing gastrointestinal distress

divided attention tasks involve stimuli in the same sensory mode (e.g., listening to two channels of music simultaneously) or different sensory systems (e.g., listening to spoken words while reading a different set of words)

donut hole prescription costs that a Medicare enrollee must pay 100 percent out of pocket each year, between $2850 and $4550 (in 2014). Amounts below and above this gap are covered partially by Medicare Part D

drug abuse abuse of prescription or over-the counter medications (polypharamcy) or of illicit drugs (heroin, marijuana)

dual eligibles low-income older adults who qualify for both Medicare and Medicaid; Medicaid can be used to help pay for some of the costs not covered by Medicare, such as co-payments

Dying Person's Bill of Rights affirms the dying person's right to dignity, privacy, informed participation, and competent care

dying process likely to consist of feelings of avoidance, confrontation, and accomodation rather than fixed stages; most people fear a painful dying process

economic insecurity living at or below 200 percent of the poverty level, which makes a person at high risk of becoming poor

Eden Alternative a paradigm for nursing home care that encourages active participation by residents and greater staff decision-making

edentulous the absence of natural teeth

ego integrity versus despair the eighth and last stage of psychosocial development in Erikson's model; aging individual achieves wisdom and perspective, or despairs because he or she views one's life as lacking meaning

elder cottages or mother-in-law units a housing option where small units are added to an existing home or as a detached unit on the property

elder mistreatment maltreatment of older adults, including physical, sexual, and psychological abuse, and financial exploitation and neglect

elder neglect deprivation of care necessary to maintain elders' health by those trusted to provide the care (e.g., neglect by others) or by older persons themselves (self-neglect)

Eldercare Workforce Alliance (EWA) a national coalition of professional organizations whose goal is to address the workforce needs in the field of aging and influence federal legislation to expand the geriatric workforce.

eligibility criteria factors that determine whether people can receive benefits from specific programs

empty nest normative for middle-aged parents when adult children leave home for college or employment

encore careers new careers after retirement that may be paid or volunteer

epidermis the outermost layer of skin where the process of cell replacement is slowed with age

erectile dysfunction inability for men to get and sustain an erection; also known as impotence

estrogen a female sex hormone that declines significantly with aging; can be replaced alone (estrogen replacement therapy) or in combination with progesterone, another female sex hormone (also known as **hormone replacement therapy**)

euthanasia the act or practice of killing (active euthanasia) or permitting the death of (passive euthanasia) terminally ill or injured individuals in a relatively painless way; mercy killing

executive function cognitive skills required to organize one's learning function

exergames a wide variety of computer video games to increase people's physical activity, often indoors, while having fun alone or with others.

Experience Corps sponsors school-based programs where older adults work one-on-one with children, create before- and after-school programs, and receive a modest stipend for their service

Family and Medical Leave Act (FMLA) federal legislation passed in 1993 that provides job protection to workers requiring short-term leaves from their jobs for the care of a dependent parent, spouse or child or due to the employee's serious health condition

family caregiving unpaid assistance provided by family members for persons requiring help with ADLs and IADLs

family-centered care an approach to caregivers that views them as clients in need of services and supports to address their own needs and as partners in decision-making

family of choice consists of people who are like family members to someone but may not be formally related to that person.

feminist gerontological theory takes account of how gender-based inequities and the oppression of women across the life course differentially structure men's and women's experiences of aging and disadvantage older women

fictive kin families of choice, not relatives in the formal sense, whose members provide the kind of love and support that caring family members do for each other

filial piety a sense of respectful obedience to elders that has traditionally encouraged care for one's aging family members in Asian cultures

financial abuse a form of mistreatment in which a person's finances are wrongly exploited

"Five Wishes" a living will in 23 languages and in 40 states designed to encourage consideration of broader questions related to health care decisions than those covered in most living wills

flexible housing homes that can be built and remodeled for use throughout a lifetime, such as movable walls

fluid intelligence skills that are biologically determined, independent of experience or learning; require flexibility in thinking

food insecurity the government's official term for hunger; also may include reduced quality, variety or desirability of diet

Foster Grandparents Program volunteer program pairing elders with children with special needs

frailty severe limitations in *ADLs*, such as unintended weight loss, difficulty walking, and chronic exhaustion, which increase the risk of disability

free radical theory a special case of the cross-linkage theory of aging that posits that free radicals (highly reactive molecules) may produce DNA mutations

functional ability the capacity of a given organ to perform its normal function, compared with its function under conditions of illness, disability, and aging, which influences an individuals' ability to perform daily tasks

gatekeepers people in formal (e.g., postal carriers, beauticians) or informal (e.g., friends and neighbors) roles who regularly interact with older adults and can watch for signs indicating a need for assistance

general slowing hypothesis physiological changes that cause slower transmission of information through the nervous system with aging

Generations United a national intergenerational coalition of over 30 organizations, including AARP, the Child Welfare League, and the Children's Defense Fund

generativity the seventh stage of psychosocial development in Erikson's model; caring for and mentoring younger generations, looking toward the future, and not stagnating in the past

geriatrics a specialty within the health professions that is concerned with the prevention or management of diseases that occur as people age

gerontechnology (or **gerotechnology**) a recent field of research and practice aimed at using technology to improve older adults' autonomy

Gerontological Society of America (GSA) an association of researchers, educators, and practitioners interested in gerontology and geriatrics

glaucoma a disease in which there is insufficient drainage or excessive production of aqueous humor, the fluid in the front portion of the eye, and if not treated can lead to blindness

global aging the phenomenon of increases in proportions and numbers of elders in both developed and developing countries

good health more than the mere absence of infirmity, a state of complete physical, mental, and social well-being

Gray Panthers a national organization founded by Maggie Kuhn, which encourages intergenerational alliances around social and environmental issues

graying of the federal budget creation of a wide array of major federal programs and interest groups directed toward older persons in the 1960s and 1970s

"graying of the suburbs" a greater proportion of people who moved into suburban developments in the 1960s and 1970s have remained in these communities after retirement

Green House an expansion of the Eden Alternative that focuses on smaller groups of residents served by a core group of workers who perform multiple tasks in a home-like setting

hardiness how well an individual copes with disease or other stressors. Affected by both genetics and past experiences

hastened death viewed as a more socially acceptable term than euthanasia because it speeds up the inevitable

health care disparities differences in access, quality, and use of health care services, which may result in health disparities

health care power of attorney designates a surrogate decision-maker who has the duty to act according to the patient's known best wishes, when there is no living will and the patient is not mentally competent.

health disparities inequalities in health, well-being, and mortality across the life course, often due to poverty

health homes funded by the Affordable Care Act; similar services to Patient-Centered Medical Home, but with expanded coverage for mental health and substance use services, health promotion, and patient and family support services

health literacy the ability to understand and use health information to make health-related decisions or take action on one's health

health promotion a model in which individuals are largely responsible for and in control of their own health through lifestyle changes, combined with health education and related environmental changes conducive to health

health status the presence or absence of disease, as well as the degree of disability in an individual's level of functioning

healthy life span the number of years in good health and with quality of life

hoarding a type of self-neglect in which the person excessively saves things, often putting themselves or others at risk

home and community-based services (HCBS) residential and community-based long-term services and supports to enable elders to remain in the community

home health care a variety of nursing, rehabilitation, personal care and other therapy services, which are provided to people who are homebound and have difficulty performing ADLs

hormone replacement therapy (HRT) use of estrogen to prevent bone loss in women but used infrequently because of associated health risks

hospice a program of care for dying persons that gives emphasis to the personal dignity of the dying person, reducing pain and sources of anxiety and provides family support when needed

hypertension high blood pressure—a risk factor for heart attack, stroke, and other diseases

hyperthermia body temperatures several degrees above normal for prolonged periods

hypokinesia the degeneration and functional loss of muscle and bone due to physical inactivity

hypotension dizziness and faintness from exertion after a period of inactivity, typically due to low blood pressure

hypothermia body temperatures several degrees below normal for prolonged periods

immunological theory focuses on the deteriorating efficiency of the immune system and resultant loss of ability of the organism to resist pathogens as a cause of age-related changes and chronic diseases

impotence the inability to have and maintain an erection; also known as **erectile dysfunction**

inclusive design the concept and practice of designing physical environments for the widest range of users possible, including designs that promote aging in place and active aging

Independence at Home a model under the Affordable Care Act that funds physicians and nurse practitioners to deliver primary care services in the home to older adults with high-cost multiple chronic illnesses

individual aging process the physiological, psychological, and social aging process in a person, as opposed to population aging, which refers to the aging of an entire population

individual equity person receives benefits such as Social Security based on their earned rights—what they paid as payroll taxes

informal caregiving unpaid assistance provided by family, friends, and neighbors for persons requiring help with ADLs and IADLs

information and communication technologies (ICTs) relates to telecommunication devices or software that either provide electronic access to information or enable communication, or both

informed consent written or oral document that states reasons for treatment, its benefits, risks, and alternatives and is provided to patient to assist with decision-making

instrumental activities of daily living (IADLs) summary of an individual's ability to perform more complex activities such as household and financial management, making a phone call, grocery shopping, meal preparation and taking medications

intelligence the theoretical limit of an individual's performance

internship a way for students to gain practical experience, either paid or unpaid, in a professional setting alongside employees in an organization

intentional communities a group of families or elders with common values (e.g., political, religious, lifestyle) who live relatively independently but share meals, activities, and some expenses

interdependence of generations framework recognition of intergenerational transfers and supports that occur across the life course

interference theory the view that memory fades or is lost because of distractions experienced during learning or interference from similar or new information to the item to be recalled

intergenerational inequity perspective the view that one generation or age group receives benefits that are disproportional to those received by another, or are at the expense of other generations

intergenerational programs services that facilitate the interaction of people across generations, typically young and old

interventions programs, services, counseling, or other systematic strategies to support family caregivers and/or older persons

intimacy at a distance strong emotional ties among family members even though they do not live near each other

intimate partner violence domestic violence between partners/spouses

irreversible dementias have no discernible environmental cause and cannot yet be cured (e.g., Alzheimer's or vascular dementia)

John A. Hartford Foundation the only national foundation focused solely on health and aging that has supported efforts in geriatric medicine, nursing and social work education and practice

kinesthetic system the body system that signals one's position in space

kykyphosis stoop-shouldered or hunched condition caused by collapsed vertebrae as bone mass is lost

leisure any activity characterized by the absence of obligation, which in itself is inherently satisfying

life course perspective understanding older adulthood as part of a continuity of human development across the life span—from birth to old age—and taking into account historical, political, cultural, economic, and other societal circumstances that affect how we age

life expectancy the average length of time persons in a given society and subgroups defined by age, gender, race, and ethnicity are expected to live

lifelong learning pursuing both formal and informal paths to enhancing one's knowledge and understanding about various subjects across the life course

life review a process of introspection, self-reflection, and reminiscence that may include reflecting on themes of loss and often involves reinterpretation of past experiences to achieve a new sense of meaning

life-space the distance a person travels to perform activities over a specified time (e.g., one week, one month)

living will legal document in which an individual's wishes about medical treatment are put in writing should he or she be unable to communicate at the end of life, directing physicians and hospitals to withhold life-sustaining procedures, take all measures to sustain life, or whatever seems appropriate to the person executing the document

longitudinal study research that includes the measurement of the same person or group of people over a specified period of time, typically years

long-term care insurance private insurance designed to cover the costs of institutional and sometimes home-based service for people with chronic illnesses and disabilities

long-term services and supports (LTSS) a range of types of personal assistance to individuals of all ages who, as a result of chronic illness or disability, are limited in their functional ability

male menopause normal changes experienced by men due to declines in testosterone production

master athletes individuals who have continued to participate in competitive, aerobic exercise into the later years

maximum life span the biologically programmed maximum number of years that each species can expect to live

median age The age between two numerically equal groups in a population—one group being older than this age, and the other group being younger than this age.

mediators visual and verbal links between information to be memorized and information that is already in secondary memory

Medicaid a federal and state means-tested program of medical assistance for low-income adults, regardless of age

Medicaid Waiver Program allows states to provide home care services to elders at risk of nursing home placement "outside" of Medicaid regulations; must not cost more than nursing home care

medical alert systems a necklace or bracelet that serves as a communication device, alerting a monitor, emergency personnel, or a designated individual when an elder needs help in an emergency such as a fall

Medicare the social insurance program, part of the Social Security Act of 1965, intended to provide financial protection against the cost of hospital and physician acute care for people age 65 and over

Medicare Advantage includes both parts A and B; comprehensive private insurance coverage

Medicare Part D (Medicare Modernization, Improvement, and Prescription Drug Act) prescription drug reform legislation; older adults pay for a private insurance plan to cover medications; also known as the Medicare Modernization Act

melanin darker skin pigmentation

memory the process of recalling information that was once stored; a part of the brain that retains what has been learned throughout our lives

menopause a gradual cessation of the menstrual cycle, which is related to the loss of ovarian function; considered to have occurred after 12 consecutive months without a menstrual period

mobile health or mHealth the use of mobile communication devices such as smartphones to enhance a person's access to health news, information, and services

mnemonics method of using verbal cues such as riddles or rhymes as aids to memory

modernization theory advances in technology, applied sciences, urbanization, and literacy, which, in this context, are related to a decline in the status of older people

multigenerational family a family with three or more generations alive at the same time; considers the needs of middle generation, not just young and old as with intergenerational

National Council on the Aging (NCOA) national organization of over 2,000 social welfare agencies concerned with aging that provides technical consultation and is involved in federal legislative activities

National Family Caregiver Support Program (NFCSP) requires state and area agencies on aging to provide services to support family caregivers

natural helpers people who assist others because of their concern, interest, and innate understanding

naturally occurring retirement community (NORC) a neighborhood, apartment house, or larger area occupied mostly by older people who have aged in place, but without having been planned specifically for this population

need-based (or means-tested) programs social programs delivered to persons who meet defined criteria of eligibility based on economic need or the ability to pay for benefits

neglect See **elder neglect**

neighborhood and community-building an approach that strengthens a community's self-help and problem-solving capabilities

neurons nerve cells in the brain

nontraditional families family structures that differ from the nuclear family, derived through gay and lesbian partnerships, heterosexual cohabitation, informal adoption, etc.

objective burden reality demands that caregivers face (income loss, job disruption, poor health)

Older Americans Act passed in 1965 to establish a network of social services specifically for age 60 and older people

old-old people who are 75–84 years old

Older Women's League (OWL) a national advocacy organization concerned about issues affecting older women

oldest-old people who are 85 years and older

On Lok a comprehensive program of health and social services provided to very frail older adults, first started in San Francisco and now widely replicated, with the goal of preventing or delaying nursing home placement

Osher Lifelong Learning Institutes (OLLIs) associated with colleges and universities, older participants make decisions about course offerings and may volunteer to teach courses

osteoarthritis gradual degeneration of joints that are subject to physical stress

osteopenia a significant loss of calcium and reduced bone density not associated with increased risk of fractures

osteoporosis a dramatic loss in calcium and bone mass resulting in increased brittleness of the bones and increased risk of fracture, more frequently found in white, small-stature women

oya koko a Japanese concept based on the tradition of filial piety and understood to mean that adult children will take care of their parents when the time comes

palliative care treatment designed to relieve pain provided to persons of all ages with a terminal illness

paranoia a psychiatric disorder characterized by irrational suspiciousness of other people

Parkinson's disease a neurodegenerative disorder that begins as a loss of muscle control and impaired balance and coordination, with tremors in hands and feet

participant-directed care consumers have right and ability to determine how to meet their service needs, including "managing their own risk", even if professionals disagree

passive euthanasia voluntary elective death through the withdrawal of life-sustaining treatments or failure to treat life-threatening conditions

patient-centered medical homes funded by the Affordable Care Act; an interdisciplinary care team coordinates care beyond the physical boundaries of the doctor's office

Patient Protection and Affordable Care Act (ACA) health care reform and insurance passed by Congress in 2010

and currently being implemented to improve the quality of health care and reduce costs

Patient Self-Determination Act federal law requiring that health care facilities inform their patients about their rights to decide how they want to live or die, for example, by providing them information on refusing treatment and on filing advance directives

perceptual speed time required to perceive and react to a stimulus; declines with age

person-centered care individualizing services in skilled nursing facilities to each resident's needs and preferences, such as offering choices in waking, eating, and bathing times; in community settings, older person is at the center of the planning process to meet needs he or she identifies

personality a unique pattern of our innate and learned behaviors, thoughts, and emotions

Pioneer Network a coalition of nursing home staff and long-term care advocates focused on improving quality of care and residents' quality of life by making organizational changes

political economy of aging social class and other structural variables determine older people's position and life satisfaction, with groups in power trying to sustain their own interests by maintaining class inequities

polypharmacy use of multiple medications, or when more drugs are prescribed or taken than is clinically needed

population aging the aging of an entire population, such as the aging of people within a particular country, as opposed to the aging process of an individual

positive aging elders who have maintained their psychological well-being and sense of meaning while coping with multiple challenges throughout life

positivity effect process whereby older adults attend to, learn from, and retain positive information better than neutral or negative stimuli, because it helps them regulate emotional experiences by focusing on positive information

presbycusis age-related hearing loss

primary mental abilities (PMAs) the basic set of intellectual skills, including mathematical reasoning, word fluency, verbal meaning, inductive reasoning, and spatial orientation

primary stressors stress-inducing events that derive directly from an elder's illness, such as memory loss or wandering

privatization changes in Social Security that would divert payroll taxes to private investment accounts

problem solving therapy a type of cognitive-behavioral therapy that teaches patients effective techniques for coping with their concerns, such as related to their depression

productive aging includes both paid and unpaid activity that produces benefits for society, such as caregiving, volunteerism, and contributing informally to family, friends, neighbors, and the community

Program of All-Inclusive Care for the Elderly (PACE) federal demonstration program that replicated On Lok's integrated services to attempt to prevent nursing home placement

prolongevity extending the length of a healthy life but not disrupting fundamental aging processes

psychological aging involves alterations that occur in cognitive abilities (e.g., memory, learning, and intelligence), adaptive capacity, and personality

psychological disorders abnormal changes in personality and behavior that may be caused or triggered by a genetic predisposition, environmental stress, and/or systemic diseases

quality of life the individual's sense of competence, ability to perform activities of daily living, and satisfaction with social interactions in addition to functional health

recall the process of searching through secondary memory in response to a specific external cue

reciprocal exchange sharing resources and assistance among individuals

recognition matching information in secondary memory with the stimulus information

religion an organized formal system of spiritual beliefs, values, and behaviors shared by a community (a denomination), not an individual behavior

religiosity individual's personal experience in the context of organized religion, but does not necessarily require participation in a formal organized setting with others

reminiscence therapy a type of life review in which older adults reflect on both positive and negative life events and process losses

remote patient monitoring collecting patient data such as vital signs from a distance to monitor health status

renal function kidney function, defined by the rate at which blood is filtered through the kidneys

resident-centered care frail elders in long-term care facilities have the right and ability to determine their own needs and how these should be met (sometimes used interchangeably with person-centered care)

resiliency the ability to endure and even thrive under difficult situations, using internal and external resources to turn adversity into a catalyst for growth and emotional well-being

resilient aging older adults who have maintained their optimism and psychological well-being while coping with multiple challenges throughout their lives

respite care short-term relief for caregivers; may be provided in the home or out of the home (e.g., adult day health centers)

Retired and Senior Volunteer Program (RSVP) federally sponsored program that places older adult volunteers in a wide range of service settings

retirement the period of life, usually starting between age 60 and 65, during which an individual stops working in the paid labor force; may be voluntary or involuntary

rheumatoid arthritis a chronic inflammation of the membranes lining joints and tendons, characterized by pain, swelling, bone dislocation, and limited range of motion; can occur at any age

right to die the belief that persons have a right to take their own lives, especially if they experience untreatable pain, often accompanied by the belief that persons have a right to physician assistance in the dying process

Road Scholar a program that offers adventures in learning and travel for adults age 50 and older

robust aging characterized by productive involvement, high physical functioning, and little cognitive impairment or depression

role theory because roles define us and our self-concept and shape our behavior, role loss in old age can negatively affect elders' self-esteem and life satisfaction

sarcopenia atrophy of skeletal muscle mass, generally resulting from a sedentary lifestyle and some chronic diseases

schizophrenia a psychiatric disorder characterized by thought disorders and hallucinations, psychotic behavior, and loss of emotional expression

secondary (long-term) memory permanent memory store; requires processing of new information to be stored and cues to retrieve stored information

secondary stressors do not arise directly from the older person's illness but result when primary stressors affect other areas of the caregiver's life, such as work or friendships; but not secondary in terms of importance.

Section 8 housing subsidy for very-low-income families and individuals, regardless of age

Section 202 the only program specifically for older adults, provides housing for people age 62 and older whose incomes are less than 50 percent of the median income in their areas

selective attention being able to focus on information relevant to a task while ignoring irrelevant information

selective benefits available to recipients on an individually determined need or means basis

self-concept cognitive representation of the self; emerges from interactions with social environment, social roles, and accomplishments

self-efficacy perceived confidence in one's own ability to know how to cope with a stressor and to resolve it

self-esteem feeling about one's identity relative to an "ideal self;" differs from self-concept in being more of an emotional, not cognitive, assessment of self

self-neglect the older adult engages in behavior that threatens their own safety, even if mentally competent

senescence biological aging; that is, the gradual accumulation of irreversible functional losses to which the average person tries to accommodate in some socially acceptable way

Senior Community Service Employment Program (SCSEP) program sponsored by the federal government that provides subsidies for nonprofit groups and businesses to employ older workers

Senior Companion Program a volunteer program in which seniors receive a stipend to assist homebound elders

SeniorHealth a Web site designed for older adults and containing information from the National Institutes of Health

SeniorNet an organization that encourages and helps older adults gain access to computer technologies to enhance their lives and share their knowledge and wisdom

sensor-type games computer-based games that respond to inputs detected by a sensor, such as stepping on a pressure-sensitive device

sensory memory the first step in receiving information through the sense organs and passing it on to primary or secondary memory

sequential design a research method used to study older adults and other groups over a period of time and may come in three types: cohort sequential, time sequential, and cross-sequential

service-enriched housing residential facilities that offer social and health care services in addition to amenities and activities

skilled nursing homes facilities with three or more beds staffed 24 hours per day by health professionals who provide skilled nursing and personal care services to residents who cannot remain in their own homes, typically due to chronic disease, functional disabilities, or significant cognitive impairments

skipped-generation household grandparent-and-grandchild households where the middle or parental generation is absent

smart home a home equipped with technology that promotes safety, telemonitoring, comfort, and other benefits

social adequacy a goal of Social Security that refers to a shared societal obligation to provide a basic standard of living for all who are eligible

social aging an individual's changing roles and relationships with family, friends, and other informal supports, both paid and unpaid productive roles, and within organizations such as religious and political groups

social constructionism aging is defined as a problem by society and our social interactions rather than by biological and physiological changes, or by its subjective meaning

social exchange theory a person's status is defined by the balance between people's contributions to society and the costs of supporting them

social gerontology the multidisciplinary study of the biological, psychological, and social aspects of aging

social networks of choice are mutually helpful social relationships consisting of friends, relatives, and members from the community at large.

social phenomenology a point of view in studying social life that emphasizes the assumptions and meanings of experience rather than the "objective" facts, with a focus on understanding these meanings rather than explaining

social policy government policy designed to address a social problem or issue

Social Security federal program into which workers contribute through a monthly payroll tax on their income and then, typically beginning sometime between ages 62 and 67, receive a monthly check based on the amount they have earned and contributed

social stratification in traditional social systems confers respect and authority to older adults who have control over resources, skills, and knowledge that younger members may find desirable

social support informational, emotional, or instrumental (e.g., help with tasks of daily living) assistance from social networks

socio-emotional selectivity theory (SST) aware of limited time, older adults are more selective about how and with whom they spend their time, and are more likely to pursue emotional satisfaction rather than acquiring information

spatial memory the ability to recall where objects are in relationship to each other in space

spend down to use up assets for personal needs, especially health care, in order to qualify for Medicaid

spirituality believing in one's relationship with a higher power without being religious in the sense of organized religion

spiritual reminiscence a way of telling a life story by emphasizing what gives meaning to life and what has given joy or brought sadness

stage theories of personality development of an individual through various levels, each stage being necessary for adaptation and for psychological adjustment

strengths perspective a way of assessing an individual by focusing on qualities and characteristics that emphasize resilience and effective coping mechanisms

structural lag the inability of social structures (patterns of behavior, attitude, ideas, and policies) to adapt to changes such as aging in population and individual lives

subjective burden the caregiver's experience of caregiver burden; differential appraisal of stress (e.g., worry, anxiety)

successful aging achievement of good physical and functional health and cognitive and emotional well-being in old age, often accompanied by strong social support and productive activity

suicide intentionally killing oneself, with older white men at highest risk for doing so

sun downing a confused state when persons with dementia become fatigued later in the day when natural light levels are lower

super-centenarians older adults who have reached age 110 and beyond

Supplemental Security Income (SSI) federal program to provide a minimal income for low-income older people (and other age groups with disabilities)

support ratio the relationship between the proportion of the population that is employed (defined as "productive" and able to support others) and the proportion that is not in the workforce (viewed as "dependent" or as "requiring support")

sustained attention or vigilance keeping alert to focus on a specific stimulus over time

telehealth transmitting a patient's health status and vital signs via computer or telephone lines directly to a health provider

telemonitoring the monitoring of care recipients from a distance using electronic devices

Third Age stage in life after middle age but before the final stage, and is conceptualized as a time of continued involvement and growth in areas of life beyond employment and family

tip-of-the-tongue states (TOTs) difficulty retrieving names from secondary memory but often spontaneously recalled later

trait characteristics or "typical" attributes that remain relatively stable with age

transitional care coordinated services and supports during the interval between preparing a patient to leave one setting and enter another

undue influence abusive behavior when a person uses role and power to exploit the trust, dependency, and fear of another, often around financial matters

universal design a product, building, or landscape that is accessible to and usable by the broadest range of users of all ages

universal or categorical benefits available as a social right to all persons belonging to a designated group or category, such as age

urinary incontinence diminished ability to control the leakage of urine

U.S. Department of Veterans Affairs (VA) the federal government agency that provides certain benefits, supports, health and social services to U.S. veterans

villages a virtual approach to aging in place in which residents pay an annual fee and receive services and supports, often provided by neighbor volunteers, that allow them to remain in their own homes

viropause male menopause due to testosterone decreases

visual mediators use of visual images to assist recall

vital capacity maximum volume of oxygen intake through the lungs with a single breath

wear and tear theory one of the biological theories of aging; it states that aging occurs because of the system simply wearing out over time

women in the middle women who have competing demands from older parents, partners, children, or employment

working (primary) memory holding newly acquired information in storage; a maximum of 7 ± 2 stimuli before processing into secondary memory or discarding it

Credits

Text Credits

Chapter 1: Page 12: AoA 2012, "A Profile of Older Adults in America: 2011."; Page 15: U.S. Census Bureau, 2010, "The Next Four Decades: The Older Population in the U.S.:2010–2050."; Page 16: U.S. National Center for Health Statistics, 2009.; Page 17: Fries, 1980; 18: U.S. Census Bureau, 2010, "The Next Four Decades: The Older Population in the U.S.: 2010–2050."; Page 20: www.aoa.gov, "Projected Future Growth of the Older Population"; Page 24: www.aoa.gov, "Projections of Future Growth of the Older Population"; Page 26: www.aoa.gov, "A Profile of Older Americans: 2012."; Page 28: AoA, 2012;

Chapter 2: Page 37: Central Intelligence Agency, *World Factbook*, "Life Expectancyat Birth," https://www.cia.gov/library/publications/the-world-factbook/rankorder/2102rank.html. Page 37: World Health Organization, *Active Ageing: A policy framework*. WHO, 2002.; Page 38: Central Intelligence Agency, *World Factbook*, "Field Listing: Median Age," https://www.cia.gov/library/publications/the-world-factbook/fields/print_2177.html.; Page 38: United Nations, 2009.; Page 39: World Population Prospects: The 2004 Revision (2005).; Page 48: Belluck, P. (2010, November 26). In a land of aging, children counter Alzheimer's. *New York Times*, pp. A1, A12.; Page 51: Wilmoth, J. M. (2012). A demographic profile of older immigrants in the U.S. *Public Policy & Aging Report, 22*, 8–11.; Page 53: Shavelson, L. (2008). *Elderly immigrants flow into California*. National Public Radio program and transcript, March 17. Retrieved September 18, 2013, from http://www.npr.org/templates/story/story.php?storyId=88402850.

Chapter 3: Page 63: Sloane, M., Hanna, J. Y Ford, d. (2013, September 3). *'Never, evergive up:' Diana Nyad completes historic Cuba-to-Florida swim.* Retrieved from http://www.cnn.com/2013/09/02/world/americas/diana-nyad-cuba-florida-swim/index.html.; Page 69: Ohayon, M. M., Carskadon, M. A., Guilleminault, C., & Vitiello, M. V. (2004). Meta-analysis of quantitative sleep parameters from childhood to old age in healthy individuals: Developing normative sleep values across the human lifespan. *Sleep, 27*, 1255–1273.; Page 76: Carpenter, S. (2009). Treating illness is one thing. What about a patient with many? *New York Times*. Retrieved from http://www.nytimes.com/2009/03/31/health/31sick.html?emc=eta1&pagewanted=print.; Page 79: Nwankwo, T., Yoon, S. S., Burt, V., & Gu, Q. (2013) *Hypertension among adults in the United States*. Centers for Disease Control and Prevention. Retrieved from http://www.cdc.gov/nchs/data.htm.; Page 79: American Heart Association. (2011). *Women, heart disease and stroke.* Retrieved April 27, 2011, from http://www.americanheart.org.; Page 86: Leland, J. (2008). Once just an aging sign, falls merit complex care. *New York Times*. Retrieved from http://www.nytimes.com/2008/11/08/us/08falls.html?ei=5070&emc=eta1&pagewanted=print.; Page 91: Gable, M. (January/February 2011). Affordable wellness: Creative providers bring wellness programs to affordable senior housing and community services. *LeadingAge Magazine, 1*(1),16–29.

Chapter 4: Page 105: Carlson, M. C., Saczynski, J. S., Rebok, G. W., Seeman, T., Glass, T. A., McGill, S., et al. (2008). Exploring the effects of an "everyday" activity program on executive function and memory in older adults: Experience Corps. *The Gerontologist, 48*, 793–801.; Page 108: Whittle, C., Corrada, M. M., Dick, M., Ziegler, R., Kahle-Wrobleski, K., Paganini-Hill, A., et al. (2007).Neuropsychological data in non-demented oldest-old: The 90+ Study. *Journal of Clinical & Experimental Neuropsychology,29*(3), 290–299.; Page 109: Small, G. (2002). *The memory bible*. New York: Hyperion.; Page 110: Medina, J. (2008). *Brain rules*. Seattle, WA: Pear Press.; Page 115: Vaillant, G. E. (2002). *Aging well.* Boston: Little, Brown. Page 120: Alzheimer's Association, 2013c; Page 122: Knox, R. (2011). *Senior moments: A sign of worse to come*. Retrieved April 11, 2011, from http://www.npr.org/2011/04/11/135243606/sussing-out-senior-moments//.; Page 124: Levine, J. (2004). *Do you remember me? A father, a daughter, and a search for self.* New York: Free Press.; Page 127: Adapted in 2011 from http://www.msnbc.msn.com/id/35519187/ns/health-aging;

Chapter 5: Page 143: Allen, K. E., & Starbuck, J. R. (2009). *I like being old: A guide to making the most of aging*. Retrieved from Iuniverse.com.;

Chapter 6: Page 166: Paul Taylor et al. *The Return of the Multi-generational Household* (Washington, DC: Pew Research Center, March 2010).; Page 167: AARP Public Policy Institute analysis of Current Population Survey Data.; Page 168: Swift, M. (2009, January 24). All in the bigger family. *Seattle Times*, p. A4.; Page 169: Based on Internet releases of data from the 2010 Current Population Survey, Annual Social and Economic Supplement of the U.S. Census Bureau; Page 175: http://www.lambdalegal.org/issues/seniors/; Page 177: Fisher, L. L. (2010). *Sex, romance, and relationships: AARP survey of midlife and older adults*. Washington, DC: AARP. Available at http://assests.aarp.org/rgcenter/general/srr_09.pdf; Page 181: Harmon, A. (2008, November 28). Grandparents stay in touch via webcams. *Seattle Times*. Retrieved September 21, 2013, from http://seattletimes.com/html/nationworld/2008444549_webcam28.html.; Page 184: Eheart, B. K., Hopping, D., Power, M. B., Mitchell, E. T., & Racine, D (2009). *Generations of Hope communities*. White Paper Series. Champaign, IL: Generations of Hope Development Corporation.

Chapter 7: Page 195: Family Caregiver Alliance. (2012a). *Fact sheet: Selected caregiver statistics*. San Francisco, CA: Family Caregiver Alliance.; Page 195: Adapted from the National Center for Gerontological Social Work Education (Gero-Ed) Web site, www.Gero-Ed.org Page 197: Source of Corporate Revenues (2011): CNN Money, "Fortune 500," http://money.cnn.com/magazines/fortune/fortune500/2011/full_list/. Corporate revenues rounded to the nearest billion.

Chapter 8: Page 227: Freedman, M. (2001). Structural lead: Building new institutions for an aging America. In N. Morrow-Howell, J. Hinterlong, & M. Sherraden (Eds.), *Productive aging:*

Concepts and challenges. Baltimore, MD: Johns Hopkins University Press.; Page 229: Sapp, S. (2010). What have religion and spirituality to do with aging? Three approaches. Book reviews. *The Gerontologist, 50*, 271–275.; Page 239: Gross, J. (2008). Its appeal slipping, the senior center steps livelier. *New York Times*. Retrieved September 20, 2013, from http://www.nytimes.com/2008/03/25/us/25cafe.html?pagewanted=print&_r=0.

Chapter 9: Page 261: Dupuis-Blanchard, S. M. (2007). Building a new nest: The experience of women relocating to a seniors-designated apartment building, *Canadian Journal of Nursing Research, 39*(4), 136–153.; Page 275: Sharma, R. L., & Dy, S. M. (2011). Cross-cultural communication and use of the family meeting in palliative care. *American Journal of Hospice and Palliative Medicine, 17*, 212–215, 1–8.;

Chapter 10: Page 287: *Telegraph.* (2009). *Elderly turn to wartime thriftiness during recession, says Age Concern. May 11.* Retrieved February 20, 2011, from http://www.telegraph.co.uk/finance/recession/5303320/Elderly-turn-to-wartime-thriftiness-during-recession-says-Age-Concern.html.; Page 289: Cawthorne, A. (2010). *The not-so golden years: Confronting elderly poverty and improving seniors' economic security.* Washington, DC: Center for American Progress. Retrieved November 5, 2010, from http://www.americanprogress/org/issues/2010/09/not_so_golden_years. Cawthorne, 2010; Uraban Institute, 2009; Page 290: Fleck, C (2012). *Reasons for optimism among older workers.* Washington, DC: AARP. Retrieved September 21, 2013, from http://blog.aarp.org/2012/12/03/reasons-for-optimismamong-older-workers/; Page 293: Social Security Administration. (2013a). *Fast facts & figures about Social Security, 2013.* Washington, DC: Office of Retirement and Disability Policy, Social Security Administration.; Page 294: Bernard, T. S. (2010). *Social Security jitters? Better prepare now.* Retrieved November 5, 2010, from http://www.nytimes.com/2010/07/31/yourmoney/31money.html.; Page 298: Administration on Aging (AoA). (2012). *Profile of olderAmericans: 2011.* Washington, DC: Administration on Aging.; Page 299: Zavis, A. (2010). *For the elderly, poverty doesn't cut it.* Retrieved November 7, 2010, from www.chicagotribue.com/news/local/la-me-elderly-poverty-20101017.story.; Page 300: AARP. (2011). *African Americans hit harder by the recession than whites.* Retrieved February 19, 2011, from http://www.aarp.org/money/budgeting-saving/info-02-2010/economyaa.html.; Page 302: Jaret, P. (2010). *The challenge of having enough to eat intensifiesin these hard economic times.* Retrieved February 12, 2011, from http://www.aarp.org/giving-back/charitable-giving/info-11-2010/hungry_in_america_2010.2.html.;

Chapter 11: Page 311: www.aoa.gov, 2012, A Profile of Older Americans: 2012; Page 312: Bureau of Justice Statistics. (2012). *Criminal victimization in the United States 2010: Statistical tables.* Washington, DC: U.S. Department of Justice.; Page 315: Scharlach, A. (2009). Creating aging-friendly communties. *Generations, 33*(2), 5–11.; Page 317: Susman, T. (2011, June 11). Cross-walks are increasingly deadly for the elderly. *Los Angeles Times*, Retrieved December 3, 2012, from http://www:articles.latimes.com/print.; Page 318: www.partnersincare.org; Page 329: Seattle Times. (2009). Backyard houses in Seattle, pp. B1, B9.; Page 330: Fleck, C. (2008). A growing number of lower and middle-income Americans are finding themselves homeless. *AARP Bulletin.* Retrieved March 30, 2011, from www.aarp.org/home-garden/housing/info.;

Chapter 12: Page 338: Pew Internet & American Life Report. (2011). *Profiles of health information seekers: Caregivers.* Retrieved March 18, 2012, from pewinternet.org/Reports/2011/HealthTopics/Part-2/Caregivers.aspx.; Page 338: Pew Research Center for People & the Press. (2010). *Americans spend more time following the news.* Retrieved April 2011, from pewresearch.org/pubs/1725/where-people-getnews-print-online-readership-cable-news-viewers.; Page 343: Fox, S. (2011). *Health topics.* Pew Research Center Internet & American Life Project and California HealthCare Foundation (CHCF). Retrieved April 2012, from www.pewinternet.org/Reports/2011/HealthTopics.aspx.; Page 343: Mead, S. E., Lamson, N., & Rogers, W. A. (2002). Human factors guidelines for Web site usability: Health-oriented Web sites for older adults. In R.W. Morrell (Ed.), *Older adults, health information, and the World Wide Web* (pp. 89–107). Mahwah, NJ: Lawrence Erlbaum.; Page 348: Binns, C. (2009). Machines that heal. *Popular Science, 275*, 62–63.; Page 353: Van Pelt, J. (2011). Brain fitness games for older adults—Strengthening minds or building false hopes…or both? *Social Work Today* (Web exclusive). Retrieved April 2011, from www.socialworktoday.com/archive/exc_020811.shtml.;

Chapter 13: Page 359: Center on Budget and Policy Priorities. (2013). *Policy basics: Where do your federal tax dollars go?* Washington, DC: Center on Budget and Policy Priorities. Retrieved October 1 2013, from www.chpp.org.; Page 365: Social Security Administration. (2013). *Fast facts 2013.* Washington, DC: Office of Retirement and Disability Policy, Social Security Administration.; Page 366: Social Security Administration. (2013). *Fast facts 2013.* Washington, DC: Office of Retirement and Disability Policy, Social Security Administration.; Page 375: Kaiser Family Foundation. (2013). *Medicaid's role in meeting the long-term care needs of America's seniors.* Washington, DC: Henry J. Kaiser Family Foundation. Retrieved September 28, 2013, from kff.org/medicaid/issuebrief/medicaids-role-in-meeting-the-long-term-careneeds-of-americas-seniors/.; Page 381: Kaiser Family Foundation. (2011a). *Dual eligibles: Medicaid'srole for low income Medicare beneficiaries.* Washington, DC: Henry J. Kaiser Family Foundation. Retrieved from www.kff.org/medicaid/upload/4091-08.pdf.; Page 368: AARP. (2011a). *AARP to members of Congress: Don't cut Medicare, Social Security benefits.* Retrieved October 30, 2011, from www.aarp.org.; 394: Bragg, E., & Hansen, J. C. (2010–2011). A revelation of numbers: Will America's eldercare workforce be ready to care for an aging America? *Generations*, 34, 11–19.

Chapter 14: Page 397: Exploring Careers in Aging, 2005, businessandaging.blogs.com/ecg/101_careers_in_aging/.

Photo Credits

Introduction: Page 1, Chris Steele-Perkins/Magnum Photos; Page 5, GWImages/Shutterstock; Page 8, Thomas M Perkins/Shutterstock;

Chapter 1: Page 10, Rolf Bruderer/Blend Images/Alamy; Page 11, Yuri Arcurs/Shutterstock; Page 16, Katrina Brown/Shutterstock.com; Page 22, David McLain/Aurora Photos; Page 29, val lawless/Shutterstock;

Chapter 2: Page 34, bikeriderlondon/Shutterstock; Page 40, swissmacky/Shutterstock; Page 41, Directphoto.org/Alamy; Page 46, Walter Hodges/Corbis/Glow Images; Page 49, AISPIX by Image Source/Shutterstock; Page 51, ZouZou/Shutterstock;

Chapter 3: Page 60, Martin Schrampf/Imagebroker/Alamy; Page 63, Walter Michot/MCT /Landov; Page 73, Mel Yates/Digital Vision/Getty Images; Page 79, Rob Marmion/Shutterstock; Page 81, Steve Mason/Photodisc/Getty Images; Page 88, Steve Mason/Photodisc/Getty Images; Page 91, Photodisc/Getty Images;

Chapter 4: Page 100, Robert Kneschke/Shutterstock; Page 103, Lisa F. Young/iStockphoto; Page 105, ampyang/Shutterstock; Page 107, Ioannis Ioannou/Shutterstock; Page 110, Rohit Seth/Shutterstock; Page 114, Steve Mason/Photodisc/Getty Images; Page 115, Yuri Arcurs/Shutterstock; Page 119, Sheryl Griffin/iStockphoto; Page 120, EML/Shutterstock; Page 123, Birgitte Magnus/iStockphoto.com;

Chapter 5: Page 138, Halina Yakushevich/Shutterstock; Page 143, Dmitriy Shironosov/Shutterstock; Page 151, Bonnie Schupp/iStockphoto; Page 154, Blend Images/Shutterstock; Page 156, Oscar C. Williams/Shutterstock;

Chapter 6: Page 160, auremar/Shutterstock; Page 164, Monkey Business Images/Shutterstock; Page 165, Blend Images/Shutterstock; Page 167, Steve Mason/Photodisc/Getty Images; Page 170, Monkey Business Images/Shutterstock; Page 172, Maxx Images/Photolibrary/Getty Images; Page 178, Wavebreakmedia ltd/Shutterstock; Page 179, Monkey Business Images/Shutterstock; Page 181, Monkey Business Images/Shutterstock; Page 186, Galina Barskaya/iStockphoto;

Chapter 7: Page 193, baki/Shutterstock; Page 196, Lisa F. Young/iStockphoto; Page 199, Lan shaw/Alamy; Page 204, Ed Kashi/Corbis News Premium/Corbis; Page 209, Supri Suharjoto/Shutterstock; Page 218, Lisa F. Young/Shutterstock;

Chapter 8: Page 226, Blend Images/Alamy; Page 231, Lynne Furrer/Shutterstock; Page 239, Jack Storms; Page 242, Steve Mason/Photodisc/Getty Images; Page 244, Blend Images/Shutterstock; Page 245, YinYang/iStockphoto;

Chapter 9: Page 256, Mark Richards/PhotoEdit; Page 259, Konstantin Sutyagin/Shutterstock; Page 260, Skip Nall/Photodisc/Getty Images; Page 263, LeventeGyori/Shutterstock; Page 267, rj lerich /Shutterstock; Page 268, CHENGYUAN YANG/Shutterstock; Page 270, Ken Tannenbaum/Shutterstock; Page 277, pryzmat/Shutterstock;

Chapter 10: Page 283, Melanie Stetson Freeman/The Christian Science Monitor/Getty Images; Page 286, Yuri Arcurs/Shutterstock; Page 288, Olly/Shutterstock; Page 290, Rob Marmion/Shutterstock; Page 296, Blaj Gabriel/Shutterstock; Page 301, absolut/Shutterstock; Page 302, GeoM/Shutterstock;

Chapter 11: Page 309, Sally and Richard Greenhill/Alamy; Page 311, Vargasandor/Shutterstock; Page 313, Yuri Arcurs/Shutterstock; Page 315, Alvant/Shutterstock; Page 316, Tyler Olson/Shutterstock; Page 321, Steve Mason/Photodisc/Getty Images; Page 322, Flashon Studio/Shutterstock; Page 326, Dennis Sabo/Shutterstock; Page 328, Michelle Gabel/Syracuse Newspapers/The Image Works; Page 331, Galina Barskaya/Shutterstock;

Chapter 12: Page 336, Rob Marmion/Shutterstock; Page 338, Arekmalang/Dreamstime.com; Page 340, Monkey Business Images/Dreamstime.com; Page 346, Nyul/Dreamstime.com; Page 347, Tombaky/Dreamstime.com; Page 352, Paul Maguire/Dreamstime.com;

Chapter 13: Page 357, AP Photo/Haraz N. Ghanbari, File; Page 363, Chrislofoto/Shutterstock; Page 366, alexskopje/Shutterstock; Page 370, Andrew Gentry/iStockphoto; Page 379, Anetta/Shutterstock; Page 381, Rob Marmion/Shutterstock;

Chapter 14: Page 389, Rob Marmion/Shutterstock; Page 393, val lawless/Shutterstock; Page 396, Robert Kneschke/Shutterstock; Page 399, Jeff Banke/Shutterstock; Page 402, ampyang/Shutterstock; Page 404, Katarina Garner, www.jgarnerphoto.com;

Index

D